# CLASSICAL EUROPEAN FURNITURE DESIGN

3 Volumes in 1

# CLASSICAL EUROPEAN FURNITURE DESIGN

## 3 Volumes in 1

Encyclopedia of French Period Furniture Designs
Encyclopedia of Spanish Period Furniture Designs
Encyclopedia of English Period Furniture Designs

José Claret Rubira

GRAMERCY PUBLISHING COMPANY
New York

This omnibus was originally published in separate
volumes under the titles:
*Encyclopedia of French Period Furniture Designs*
© 1983 by Sterling Publishing Co., Inc.
*Encyclopedia of Spanish Period Furniture Designs*
© 1984 by Sterling Publishing Co., Inc.
*Encyclopedia of English Period Furniture Designs*
© 1984 by Sterling Publishing Co., Inc.
All rights reserved.
The material in *Encyclopedia of French Period
Furniture Designs* was originally published in Spain
under the title, "Muebles de Estilo Frances,"
© 1974 by Editorial Gustavo Gili, S.A.
The material in *Encyclopedia of Spanish Period
Furniture Designs* was originally published in Spain
under the title, "Muebles de Estilo Espanol,"
© 1975 by Editorial Gustavo Gili, S.A.
The material in *Encyclopedia of English Period
Furniture Designs* was originally published in Spain
under the title, "Muebles de Estilo Ingles,"
© 1982 by Editorial Gustavo Gili, S.A.

*Encyclopedia of French Period Furniture Designs,*
*Encyclopedia of Spanish Period Furniture Designs,* and
*Encyclopedia of English Period Furniture Designs*
designed by Barbara Busch

*Encyclopedia of Spanish Period Furniture Designs*
and *Encyclopedia of English Period Furniture Designs*
translated by Alice Hobson

This 1989 edition is published by Gramercy Publishing
Company, distributed by Crown Publishers, Inc.,
225 Park Avenue South, New York, New York 10003,
by arrangement with Sterling Publishing Co.

Printed and Bound in the United States of America

Library of Congress Cataloging-in-Publication Data

Claret Rubira, José.
    Classical European furniture design : French, Spanish & English
period furniture design / José Claret Rubira.
        p.     cm.
    Includes index.
    ISBN 0-517-68791-7
    1. Furniture design—France.   2. Furniture design—Spain.
3. Furniture design—England.   4. Furniture—Styles.   I. Title.
NK2548.C477   1989
749.294—dc20                                                      89-7628
                                                                    CIP

ISBN 0-517-68791-7
h g f e d c b a

# CONTENTS

# Volume One
# Encyclopedia of
# French Period
# Furniture
# Designs

# PUBLISHER'S PREFACE

Cabinetmakers, decorators, historians, collectors, artists, stage designers and restorers—all will appreciate this comprehensive source book on French period furniture designs. The more than 3,000 illustrations on the following pages show French furniture from the mid-seventh century to the late nineteenth. Here are examples of almost every important period piece one might wish to build, collect or refer to, with closeup views of some of the more elaborate details. Scattered among the beds, sofas, chairs, cabinets, desks, and wardrobes are interesting footnotes to history: the desk of Louis XV, Marie-Antoinette's jewelry cabinet, the bed of the Empress Josephine, the cradle of Napoleon's son. All of the drawings are based on actual pieces of furniture in the finest museum and private collections.

Furniture-makers and restorers will find this book a treasure house of ideas either to be looked through casually or in search of a specific item or even a finish detail. The index will direct you to all the friezes and key escutcheons as well as wardrobes and armchairs.

Historians and sociologists will find much of interest in the chronological arrangement of the plates in the sense that furniture reflects the culture and life style of its times. On the facing page is the earliest piece shown—the chair of King Dagobert I, who reigned from 629 to 639. This chair is one of the few pieces from the Romanesque period that could be described as truly French. The furniture of the time was imitative of Roman and consisted mostly of tables, tripods and beds—the sort of thing one finds in Pompeii.

During the Gothic and Renaissance periods the furniture became more massive and ornate, and even more elaborate under Louis XIV, Louis XV, and Louis XVI. All this was a reflection of the grandeur of France. Although still elegant and often ornate, the furniture of the post-Revolutionary periods was scaled down and made more comfortable—intended for smaller private apartments.

Whatever the style or the period, however, there is a uniquely French character to the furniture represented. In studying these 1200 years of design, readers will find vast differences, but the furniture is always well made and elegant. It is easy to understand why French furniture makers developed such widespread influence, an influence that is still strong.

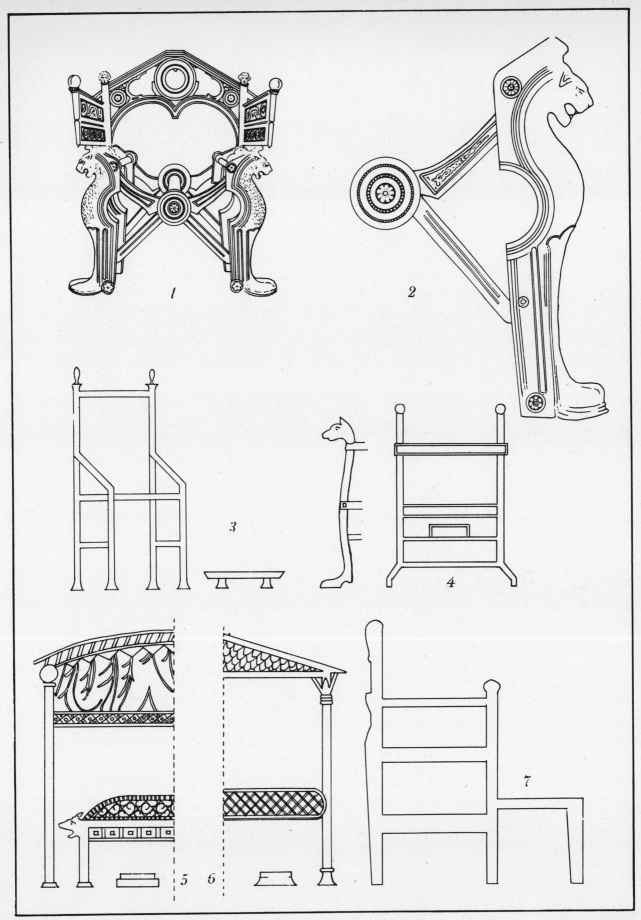

PLATE I                                                                    ROMANESQUE

1. Chair of King Dagobert.    2. Detail.    3. Chair and footstool, as shown in a codex.    4, 5 and 6. Chairs and benches taken from codexes.    7. Chair and footstool, as shown in a stone relief.

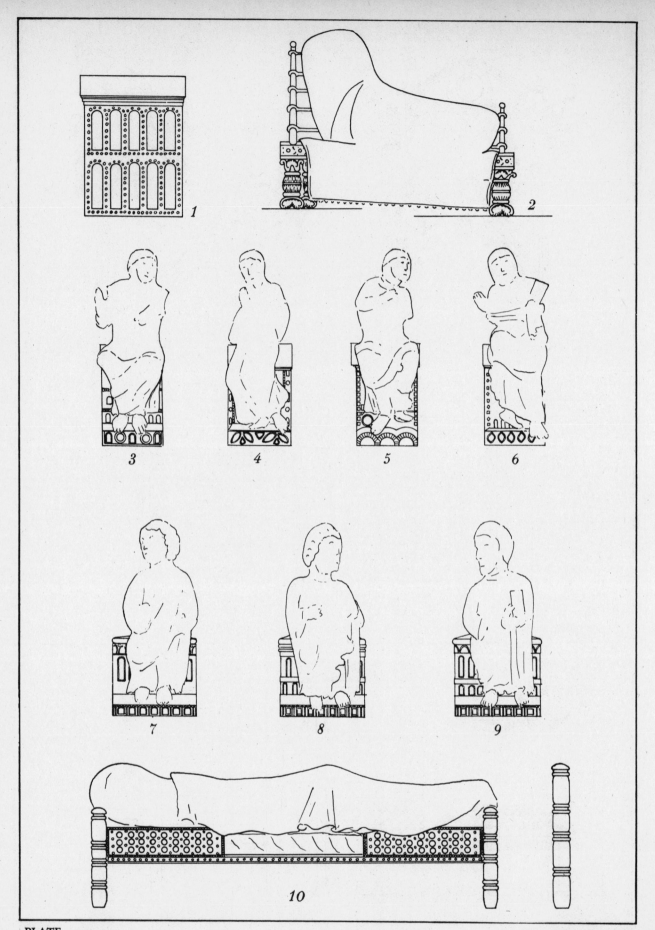

PLATE 2

ROMANESQUE

1. Chair, as shown in a relief.  2. Drawing of a bed, described by Viollet le Duc.  3, 4, 5 and 6. Chairs, as shown in the tympanum of an arch in the church in Carennac.  7, 8 and 9. Chairs, as shown in the sculptures of the porticos of the transept of the cathedral of Bourges.  10. Bed from a stone relief on the lintel of the royal portico at Chartres.

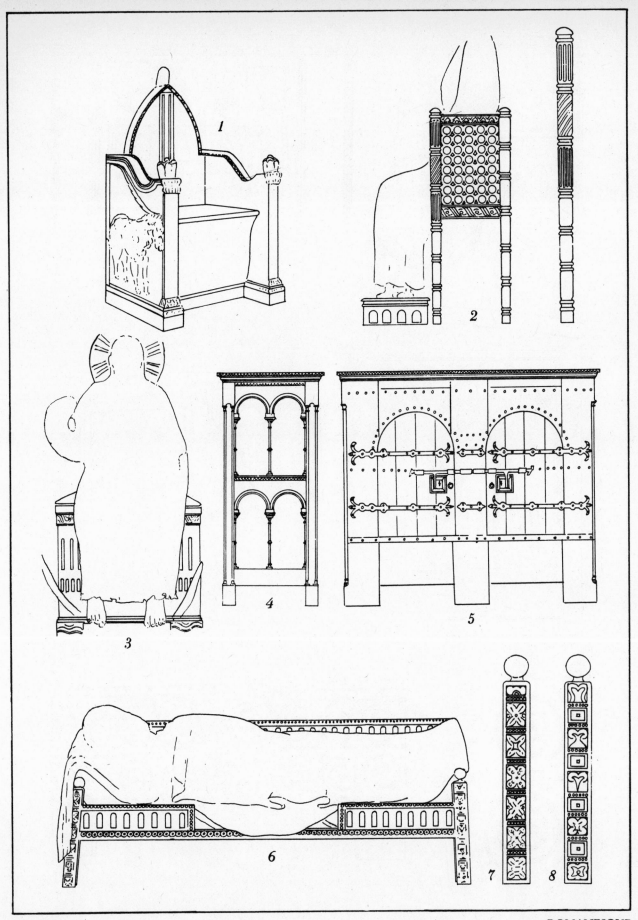

PLATE 3

ROMANESQUE

1. Stone chair in the cathedral of Avignon.   2. Armchair, as shown in the tympanum of the arch of the door of the church of La Charité-sur-Loire.   3. Chair, after a stone sculpture in a portico of the transept of the cathedral of Bourges.   4 and 5. Wardrobe, described by Viollet le Duc.   6. Bed, as shown in a stone relief on a lintel of La Charité-sur-Loire.   7 and 8. Detail of the posts.

PLATE 4                                                   GOTHIC (13th to 15th centuries)
1. Chest from the south of France, 13th century.   2. Oak chest, 14th century.   3, Chest, 15th century.   4, 5 and
6. Details from 1, 2 and 3.

PLATE 5
1. Chest.    2. Post.    3 and 4. Details of the carving of the intermediate upright and tracery.

GOTHIC (15th century)

*John Simon collection, Berlin*

PLATE 6

1. Chest.   2. Detail of the post.   3. Detail of the carving.

GOTHIC (15th century)

*George Hoentschel collection, New York*

PLATE 7                                                              GOTHIC (15th century)
1. Chest.   2. Detail of the corner supports.   3 and 4. Details of the front.

*George Hoentschel collection, New York*

11

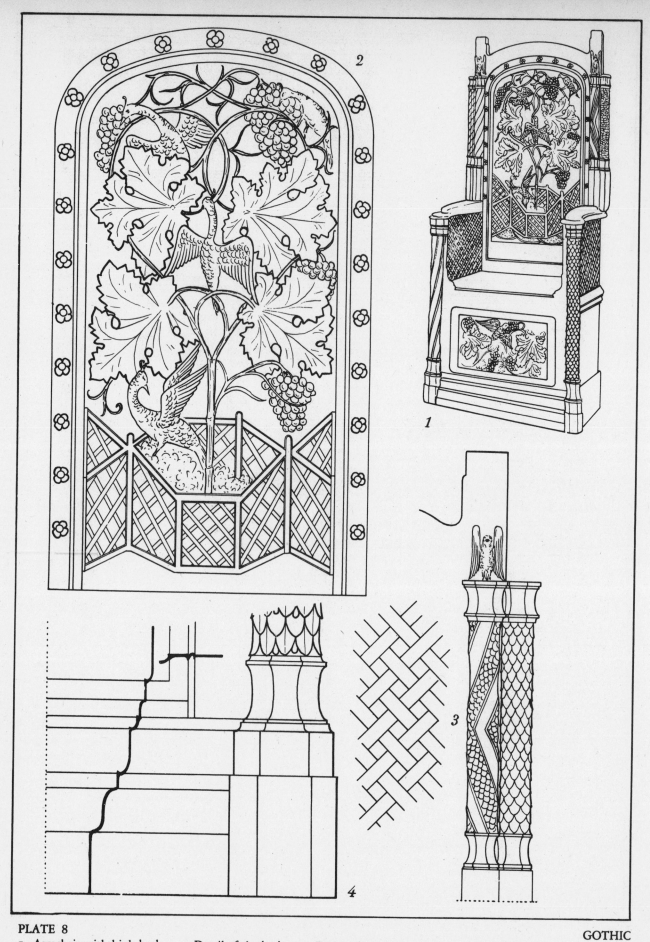

PLATE 8

1. Armchair with high back.  2. Detail of the back.  3. Detail of the back post.  4. Base moulding.

GOTHIC

*Figdor collection, Vienna*

PLATE 9
1. Early chair.   2. Later style chair.   3 and 4. Detail of the legs.   5 and 6. Details of the backs.

*Louvre and private collection*

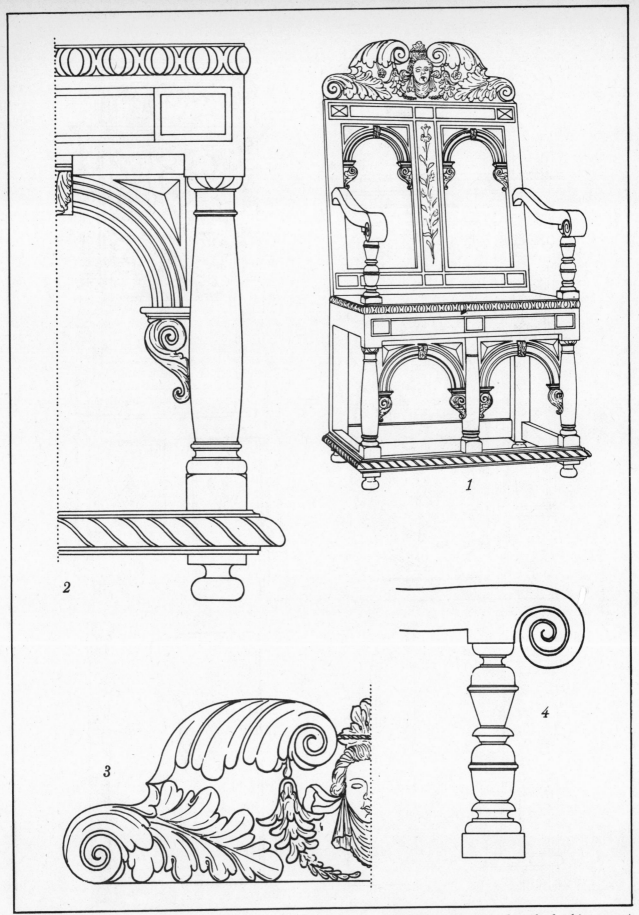

PLATE II                                    RENAISSANCE (second half of 16th century)
1. Armchair.   2. Leg and detail of the front of the seat.   3. Upper crest.   4. Arm and support.

PLATE 12

RENAISSANCE (beginning of 16th century)

1. Walnut armchair with high back. 2. Detail of the back. 3. Detail of the arm. 4. Detail of the leg base. 5. Detail of the front panel. 6. Profile of the panel.

*Museum of Cluny*

PLATE 13
RENAISSANCE (middle of 16th century)

1 and 2. Six-legged walnut chairs, reign of Henry II.   3 and 4. Details of the turned posts.   5. Detail of the seat
edge.   6 and 7. Turned posts of the back.   8. Front legs.

*Museum of Cluny*

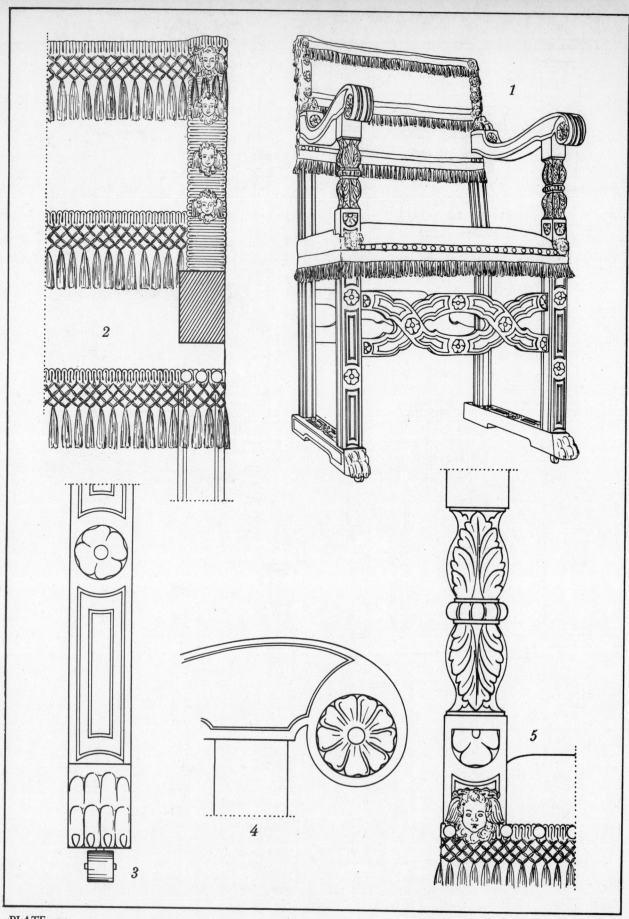

PLATE 14                                                    RENAISSANCE (end of 16th century)
1. Armchair.   2. Back.   3. Detail of the leg.   4. Grip of the arm.   5. Arm support.

*Louvre*

**PLATE 15**

1. Armchair with high back.  2. Detail of the back.  3, 4 and 5. Profiles of mouldings and decorations.

RENAISSANCE (second half of 16th century)

*Museum of Cluny*

PLATE 16                                    RENAISSANCE (second half of 16th century)
1. Armchair with high back.   2. Back.   3. Detail of the lower panel.

*Palace Museum, Berlin*

PLATE 17

RENAISSANCE (second half of 16th century)

1. Armchair.   2. Back.   3. Detail of the leg.   4. Turned arm support.

*Private collection*

PLATE 18                                    RENAISSANCE (first half of the 16th century)

1, 2, 3 and 4. Oak panels from the reign of Francis I.

*Museum of Cluny*

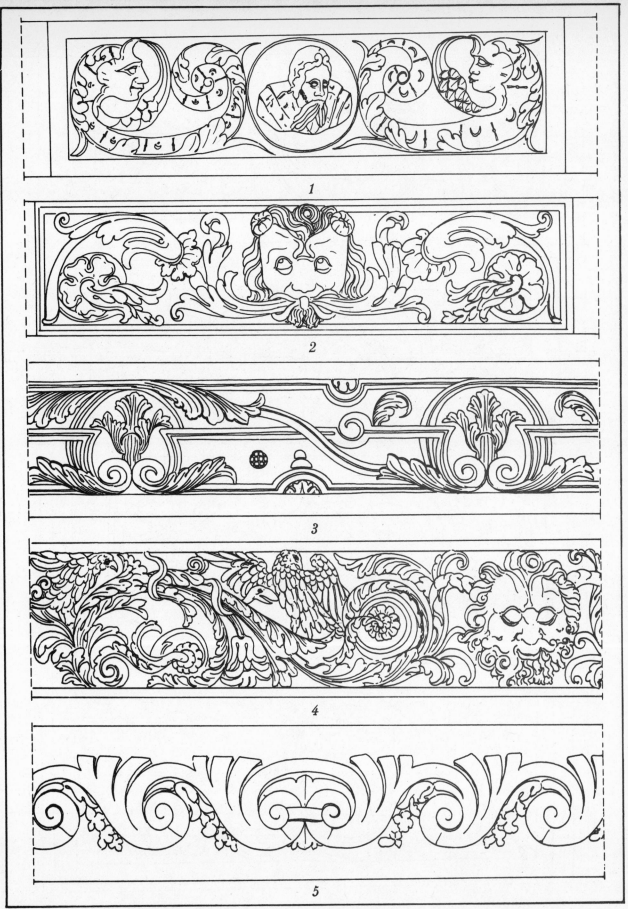

*1*

*2*

*3*

*4*

*5*

**PLATE** 19                                           RENAISSANCE (16th century)

1. Front motif of an early chest of the style.   2. Front motif of a chest of the second half of the 16th century.   3. Border.   4. Oak frieze from the reign of Henry III.   5. Border.

*Museum of Cluny*

PLATE 20                                                   RENAISSANCE (middle of 16th century)
1, 2, 3 and 4. Oak panels, adorned with medallions containing relief figures and arabesques.

*Museum of Cluny*

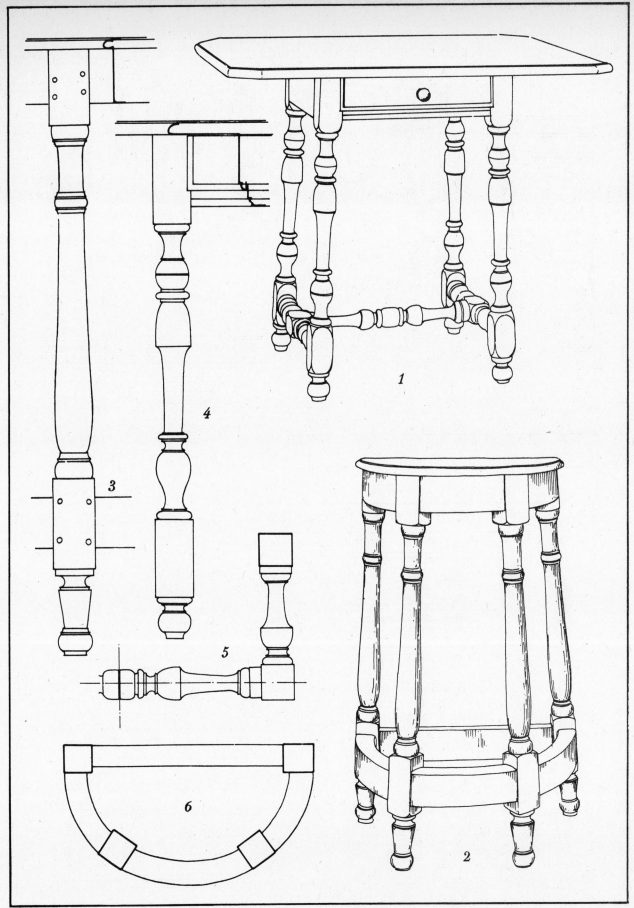

**PLATE 21**  RENAISSANCE (northern and northeastern provinces, Flemish influence)

1. Small table.   2. Four-legged console table.   3 and 4. Legs.   5. Crosspiece.   6. Base of the console.

*Private collection*

PLATE 22

RENAISSANCE (second half of 16th century)

1. Table.   2. Detail of the legs.   3. Side bracket.   4. Side view and hanging turned ornament.

*Private collection*

26

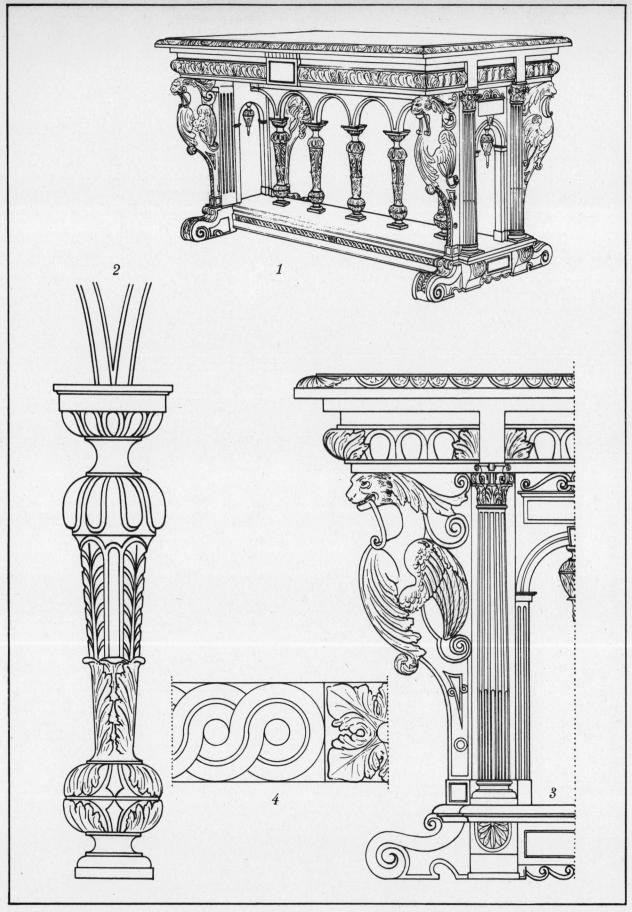

**PLATE 23**                    RENAISSANCE (second half of 16th century)

1. Table.    2. Detail of the turned portion of the archwork.    3. Side support.    4. Adornment of the moulding

*Private collection*

**PLATE 24**

1. Walnut table.  2. Detail of the side face.  3. Detail of a turned piece.

RENAISSANCE (first half of 16th century)

*Museum of Cluny*

28

**PLATE 25**

**RENAISSANCE** (second half of 16th century)

1. Table.    2. Detail of the side post.    3. Moulding.    4. Decoration.    5. Turned portion of the archwork.

*Private collection*

PLATE 26                                    RENAISSANCE (second half of 16th century)
1. Table.    2. Column of the archwork.    3. Details of the side support.    4. Moulding.    5. Inside view of foot.

*Private collection*

**PLATE 27**

1. Walnut table with double-arch support.  2 and 3. Details of the side.  4. Cross section of the support piece between the two arches.

RENAISSANCE (last third of 16th century)

*Museum of Cluny*

31

**PLATE 28**  RENAISSANCE (17th century)

1. Carved walnut table.  2. Detail of the legs.  3. Detail of the tabletop.  4. Connection of the arch.  5. Foot.

*Museum of Cluny*

2

1

3

4

PLATE 29                                                                              RENAISSANCE (Italian influence)
1. Door from the reign of Francis I.    2. Detail of the upper panels and pilasters.    3. Detail of the central panel.    4.
Drawing of the carving that decorates one of the lower panels.

*Museum of Cluny*

33

PLATE 30                                      RENAISSANCE (transition from the Gothic)

1. Early style credenza sideboard from the reign of Louis XII.    2. Detail of the corner pilaster.    3. Top mouldings.    4.
Base mouldings.    5. Detail of the panel sculpture.

*Museum of Cluny*

PLATE 31                                                    RENAISSANCE (first half of 16th century)
1. Sideboard.   2, 3 and 4. Details of the uprights and crosspieces.   5. Leg.   6. Hanging turned ornament.   7. Escutcheon.

*Palace Museum, Berlin*

35

PLATE 32                                          RENAISSANCE (16th century)
1. Walnut credenza sideboard of the Midi.   2. Detail of the post.   3 and 4. Panels.   5. Drawer fronts.

*Museum of Cluny*

36

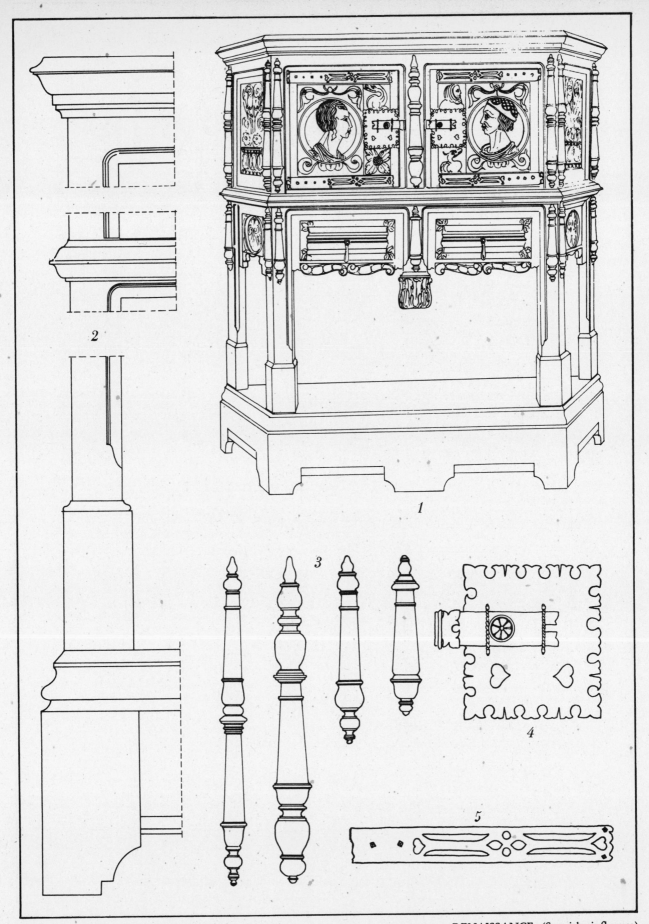

PLATE 33                                              RENAISSANCE (Spanish influence)
1. Credenza sideboard from the Midi.    2. Detail of the uprights.    3. Profiles of the high-relief turned pilasters.    4
and 5. Details of the latches and hinges.

*Museum of Cluny*

PLATE 34

1. Buffet sideboard.    2. Profiles and details of the side pilasters.    3. Detail of the arch.    4. Inside view of the arch.

RENAISSANCE (second half of 16th century)

*Museum of Cluny*

**PLATE** 35

RENAISSANCE (first half of 16th century)

1. Oak credenza sideboard from northern France of the reign of Francis I.    2. Profile and details of the corner pilaster.    3. Central panel.

*Museum of Cluny*

39

PLATE 36                         RENAISSANCE (southeastern school—Burgundy, 16th century)
1. Credenza sideboard.    2. Detail of the post.    3. Detail of the panel.    4. Cross section of the panel.

*Museum of Cluny*

**PLATE 37**
1. Credenza sideboard.   2. Detail of the post.   3. Detail of the panel.   4. Side view of the panel.

RENAISSANCE   (Burgundian school, 16th century)

*Museum of Cluny*

PLATE 38                                          RENAISSANCE (Burgundian school)
1. Walnut credenza sideboard.   2. Detail of the post.   3. Detail of the panel.   4. Profile of the panel.

*Museum of Cluny*

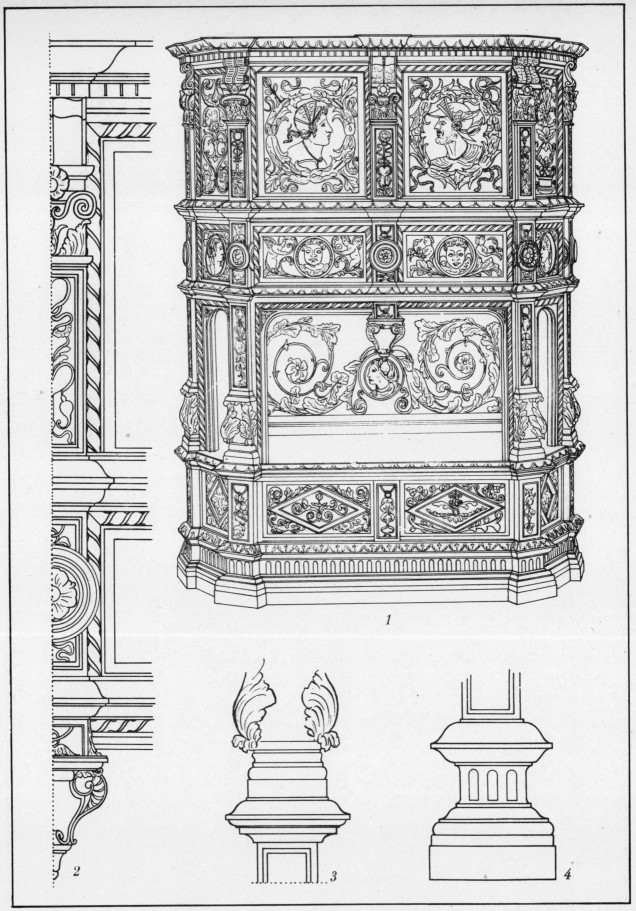

PLATE 39                                RENAISSANCE (first half of 16th century)
1. Sideboard.   2. Detail of the post.   3 and 4. Mouldings of the lower part.

*Spitzer collection, Paris*

PLATE 40                                              RENAISSANCE (first half of 16th century)

1 and 2. Chests (the first from c. 1540).    3. Detail of the central upright.    4. Post.    5. Detail of the mouldings.

*James Simon collection, Berlin and private collection*

**PLATE 41**

1. Walnut wedding chest in the form of a trunk. 2. Profile of the lid. 3 and 4. Detail of the mouldings. 5. Detail of the foot.

RENAISSANCE (school of Tours, 16th century)

*Museum of Cluny*

PLATE 42                                              RENAISSANCE (Flemish origin, 16th century)
1. Coffer.   2. Detail of the post.   3. Detail of the central panel carving.

*Museum of Cluny*

*1*

*2*

*3*　　*4*

**PLATE** 43                                       RENAISSANCE (16th century)
1. Coffer.   2. Detail and side view.   3. Detail of the mouldings that frame the central panel.   4. Cross section of the central panel

*Museum of Cluny*

*1*

*2*

*3*

*4*

PLATE 44                    RENAISSANCE (Italian influence, second half of 16th century)
1. Walnut coffer from the reign of Henry II.   2. Side view.   3. Detail of the pilaster.   4. Motif of small front panel.
*Museum of Cluny*

PLATE 45                                    RENAISSANCE (beginning of 16th century)
1. Chest.   2. Detail of the central panel.   3. Base carving.   4. Upper moulding.

*Private collection*

PLATE 46                     RENAISSANCE (second half of 16th century)
1. Double console.   2. Detail of the post.   3. Detail of the rear pilaster.   4 and 5. Door pulls.

*Private collection*

PLATE 47          RENAISSANCE (influence of the Burgundian school, second half of 16th century)
1. Chest-on-chest wardrobe with four doors.    2 and 3. Details.

*Private collection*

1. Cabinet wardrobe.    2. Detail of the post.    3. Central panel.    4. Cross section of central panel.

*Museum of Cluny*

**PLATE 49**

1. Chest-on-chest wardrobe with four doors from the time of Henry IV.
lower panel. 4 and 5. Upper and lower parts of the corner column.

RENAISSANCE (end of 16th century)
2. Detail of the front post. 3. Detail of the

*Museum of Cluny*

PLATE 50
RENAISSANCE (Flemish school, end of 16th century)

1. Wardrobe.   2, 3 and 4. Side view, details of mouldings.

*Museum of Cluny*

PLATE 51                                          RENAISSANCE (end of 16th century)

1. Chest-on-chest wardrobe with two doors, broken pediment, with inlaid marble, attributed to the Fontainebleau school. 2. Side view and detail of the columns. 3. Upper carving between the columns. 4, 5 and 6. Details of the carvings

*Museum j Clur.y*

55

PLATE 52

RENAISSANCE (end of 16th century)

1. Chest-on-chest wardrobe with two doors, pediment, inlaid marble, attributed to the Fontainebleau school.    2 and 3. Details.

*Museum of Cluny*

**PLATE 53**

RENAISSANCE (middle of 16th century)

1. Inlaid mother-of-pearl chest-on-chest wardrobe with four doors, from the reign of Henry II.  2 and 3. Details.

*Museum of Cluny*

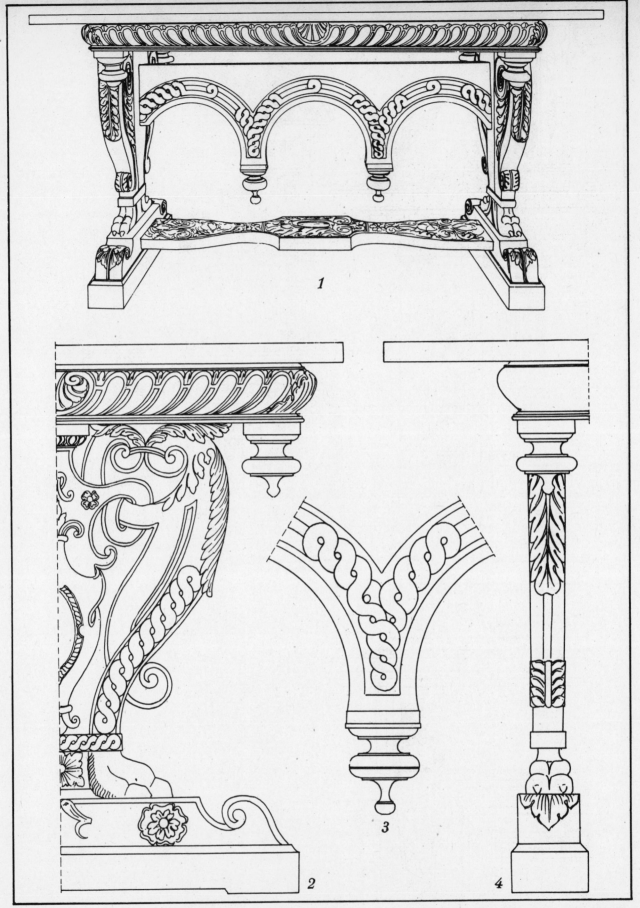

PLATE 54                    RENAISSANCE (late style, 17th century)

1. Walnut table from the reign of Louis XIII.    2. Detail of end.    3. Detail of the arch.    4. Front view of leg.

*Museum of Cluny*

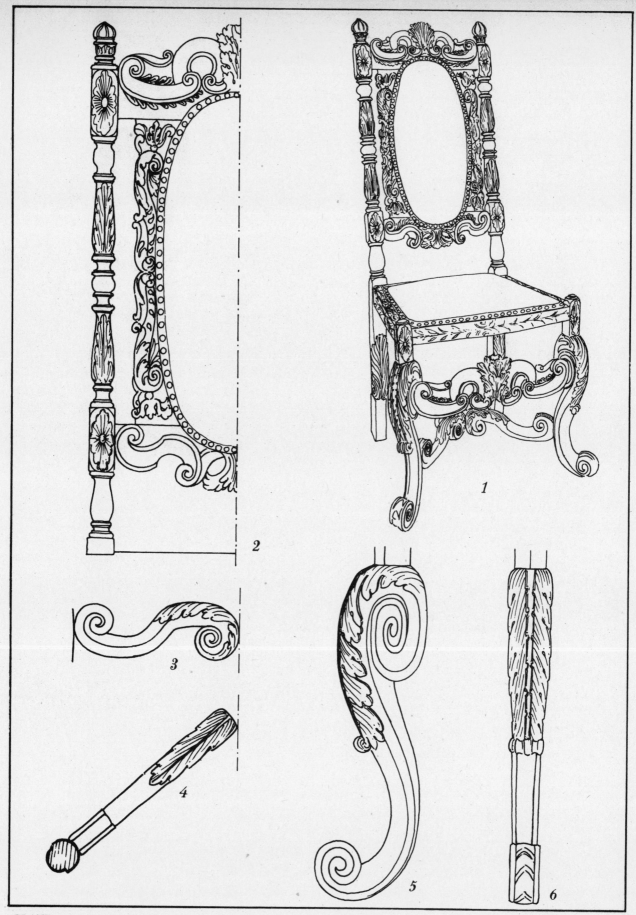

**PLATE 55**

RENAISSANCE (early style)

1. Carved chair from the reign of Louis XII.  2. Detail of the back.  3 and 4. Details of the carved crosspiece that unites the legs.  5 and 6. Front legs.

*Museum of Cluny*

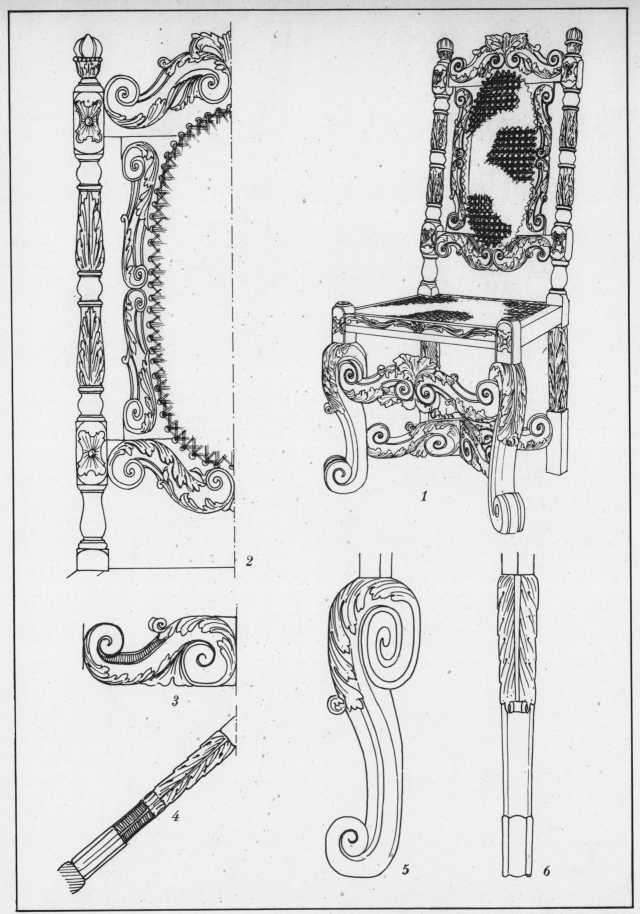

PLATE 56

RENAISSANCE (beginning of 17th century)

1. Carved chair from the reign of Louis XIII.   2. Detail of the back.   3 and 4. Detail of the curved crosspiece that connects the legs.   5 and 6. Front leg.

*Museum of Cluny*

*1*

*2*

*3*

*4*

PLATE 57                                          RENAISSANCE (beginning of 17th century)
1 and 2. Walnut borders from the reign of Louis XIII.   3 and 4. Oak borders from the reign of Louis XIII.

*Museum of Cluny*

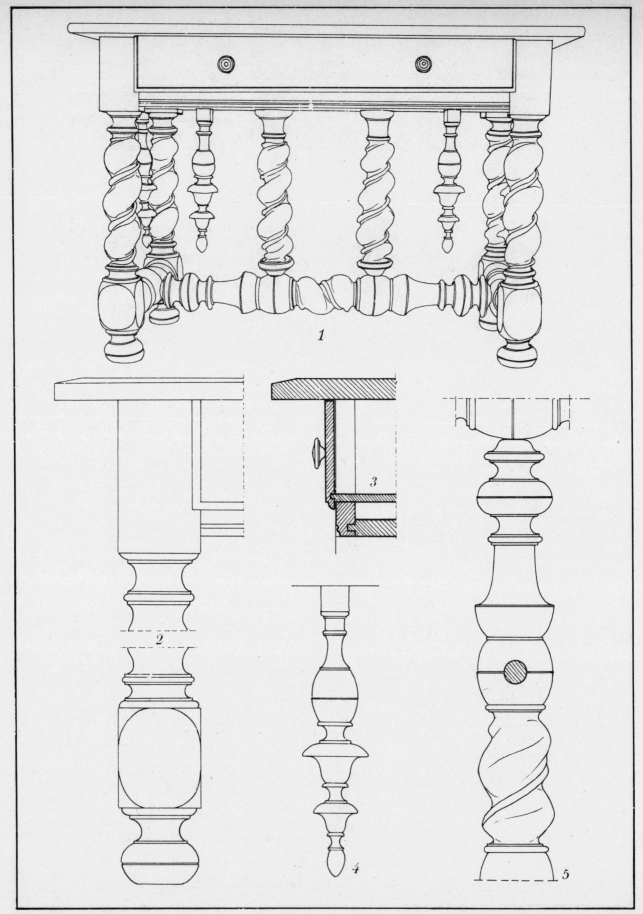

**PLATE 58**                                      RENAISSANCE (beginning of 17th century)

1. Walnut table from the reign of Louis XIII.   2. Detail of the legs.   3. Cross section.   4. Detail of the hanging turned ornament.   5. Crosspiece.

*Museum of Cluny*

**PLATE** 59

RENAISSANCE (beginning of 17th century)

1. Table from the reign of Louis XIII.  2. Detail of the legs.  3. Detail of the turned ornament.  4. Detail of the table.

*Museum of Cluny*

63

**PLATE 60**                    RENAISSANCE (beginning of 17th century)

1. Chest-on-chest wardrobe with four doors and broken pediment from the reign of Louis XIII.    2 and 3. Details of pediment.    4. Details of the upper chest.    5 and 6. Details of the lower chest.

*Museum of Cluny*

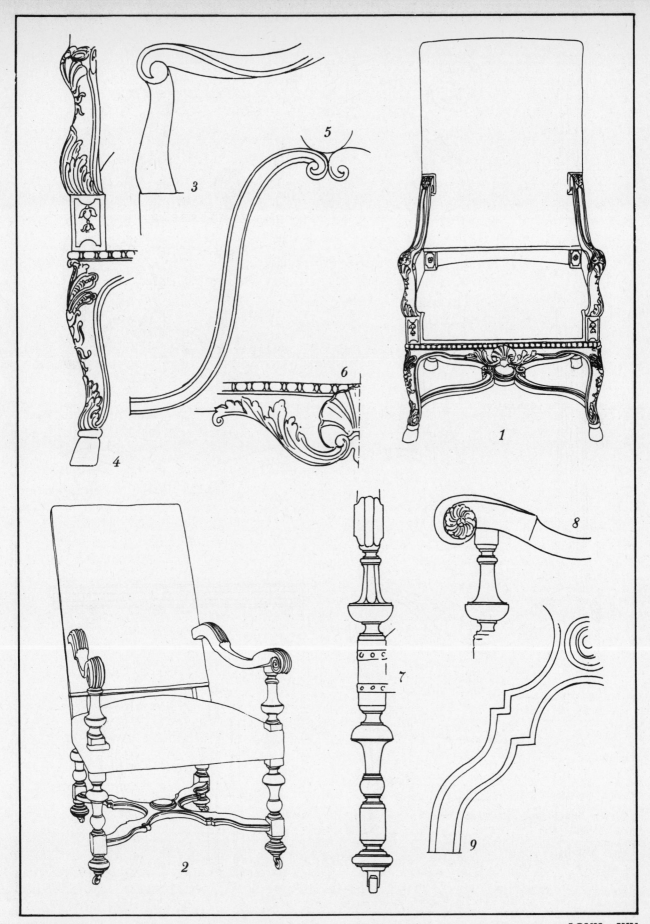

PLATE 61                                                                                                    LOUIS XIV

1. Upholstered armchair, covered with Gobelin tapestry.    2. Armchair, covered with petit point upholstery.    3, 4, 5 and 6. Details of the arm, leg, trim and central motif of the first chair.    7, 8 and 9. Details of the arm, leg and trim of the second chair.

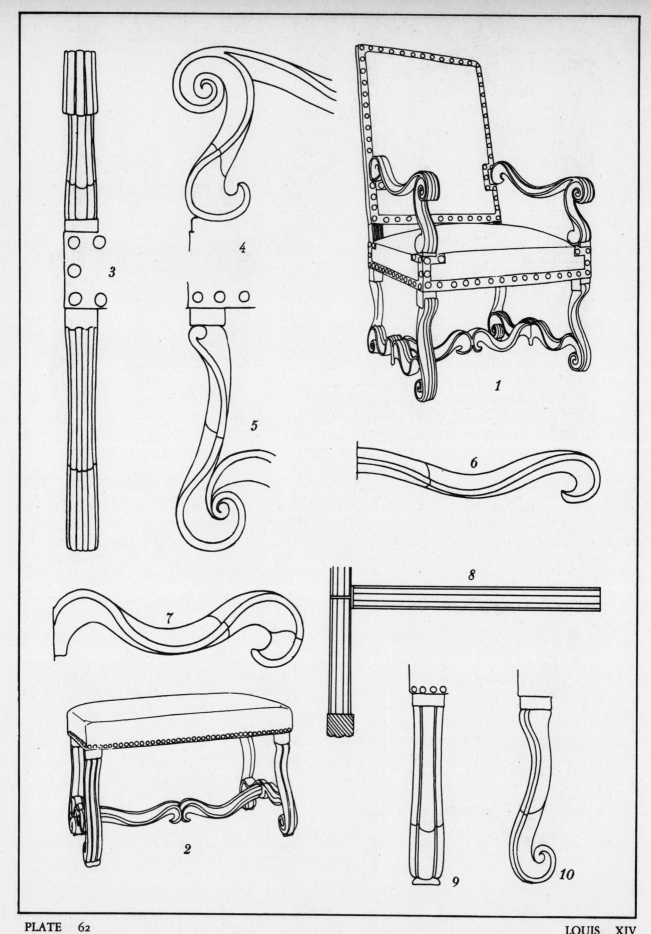

PLATE 62                                                          LOUIS XIV

1. Leather-covered armchair of early style.  2. Stool.  3, 4, 5 and 6. Details of the armchair.  7, 8, 9 and
10. Details of the stool.

*Fontainebleau Palace*

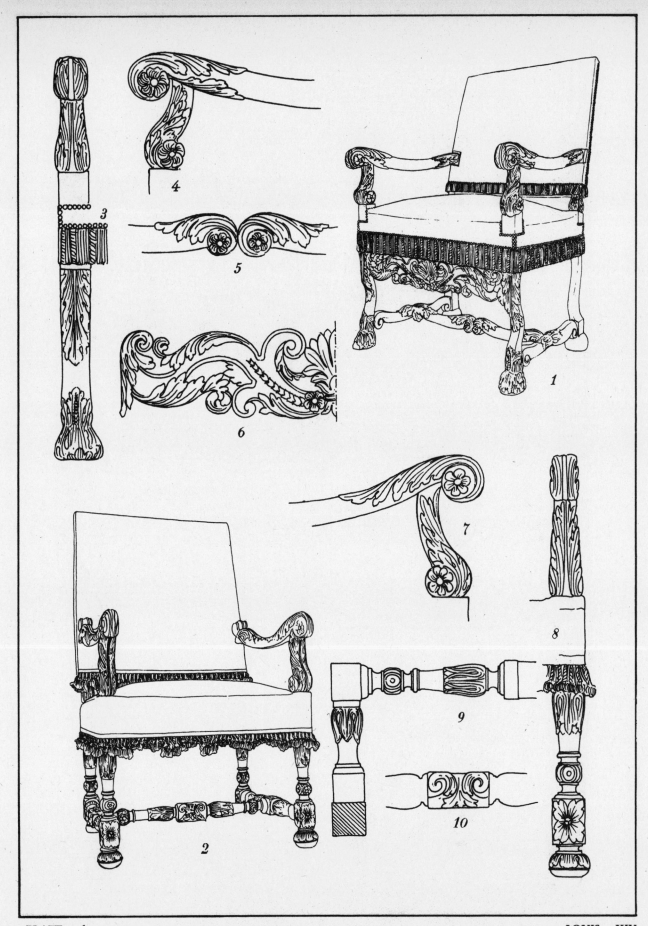

PLATE 63

LOUIS XIV

1. Armchair, covered with floral damask upholstery.  2. Walnut armchair, covered with velvet.  3, 4, 5 and 6. Details of the first chair.  7, 8, 9 and 10. Details of the second chair.

*Fontainebleau Palace and Museum of Decorative Arts, Paris*

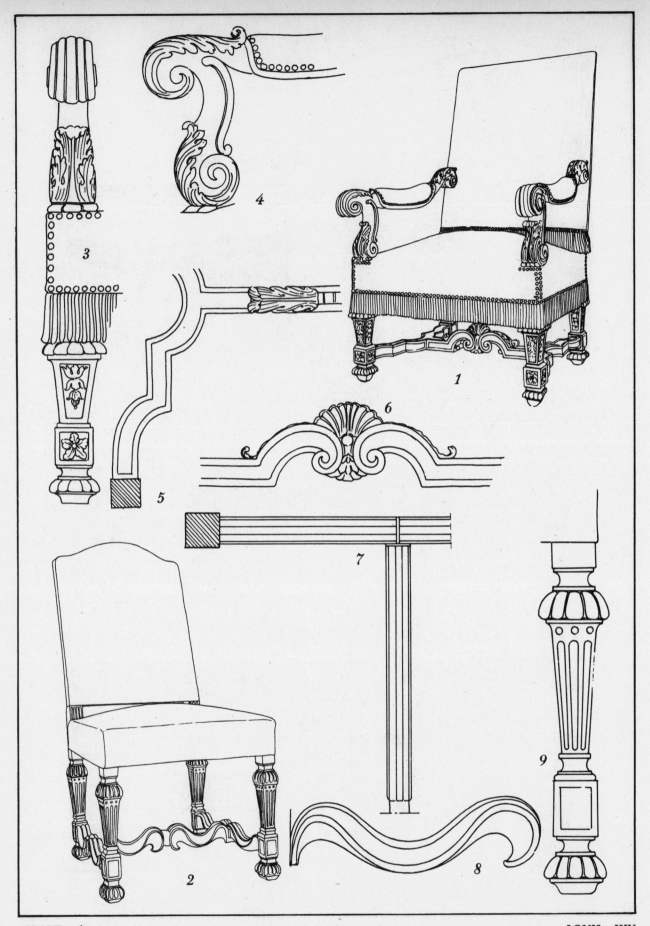

PLATE 64

1. Armchair, with petit point upholstery.   2. Sculptured wooden chair.   3, 4, 5 and 6. Details of the armchair.   7,
8 and 9. Details of the chair.

*Fontainebleau Palace and Museum of Decorative Arts, Paris*

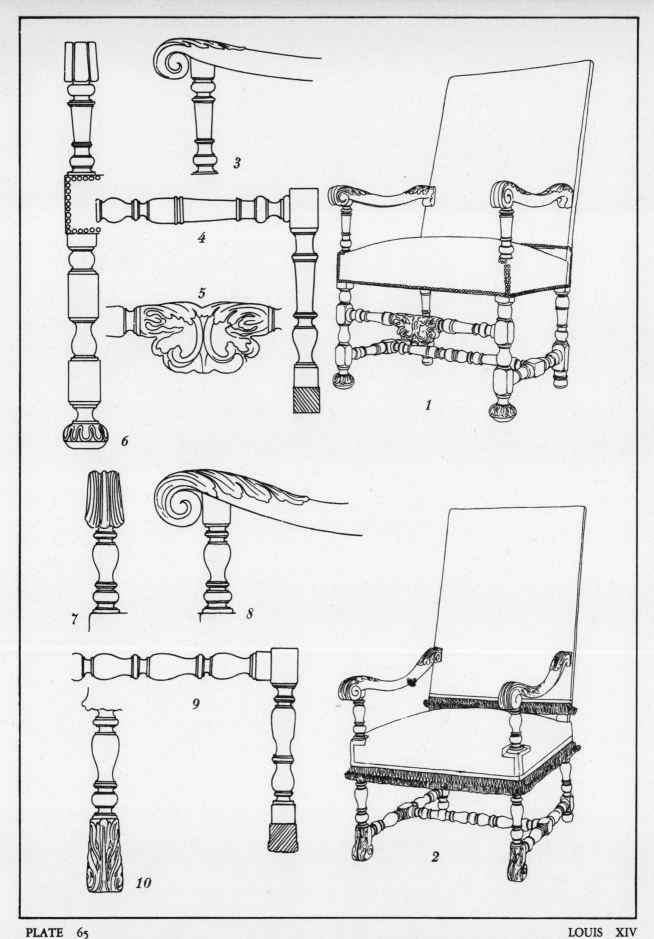

**PLATE** 65                                                            LOUIS XIV

1. Armchair, covered with floral damask upholstery.   2. Armchair, upholstered with petit point.   3, 4, 5 and 6.
Details of the first armchair.   7, 8, 9 and 10. Details of the second armchair.

*Museum of Decorative Arts, Paris and Cinquantenaire, Brussels*

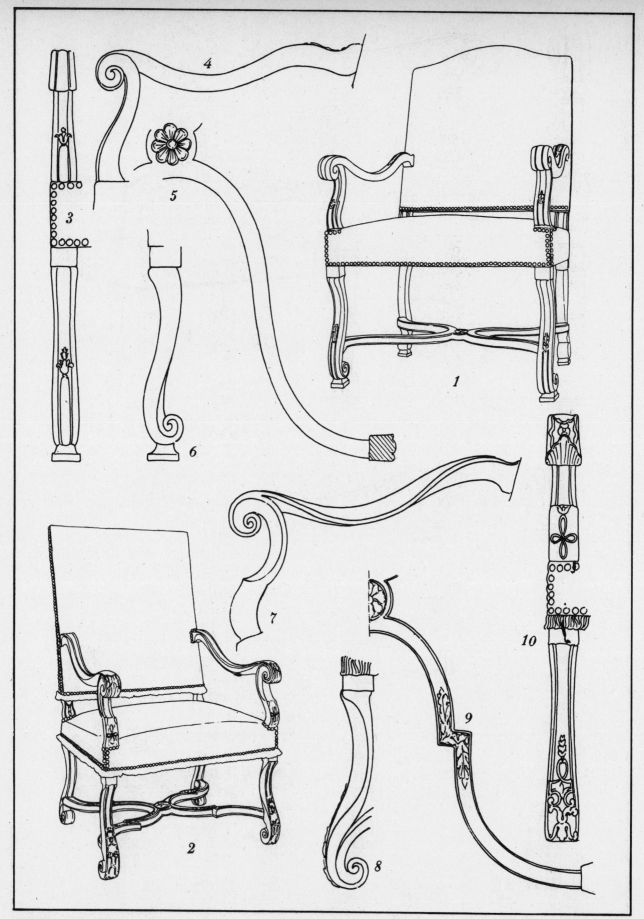

PLATE 66

LOUIS XIV

1 and 2. Armchair, upholstered with tapestry. 3, 4, 5 and 6. Details of the first armchair. 7, 8, 9 and 10. Details of the second armchair.

*Museum of Decorative Arts, Paris and Metropolitan Museum, New York*

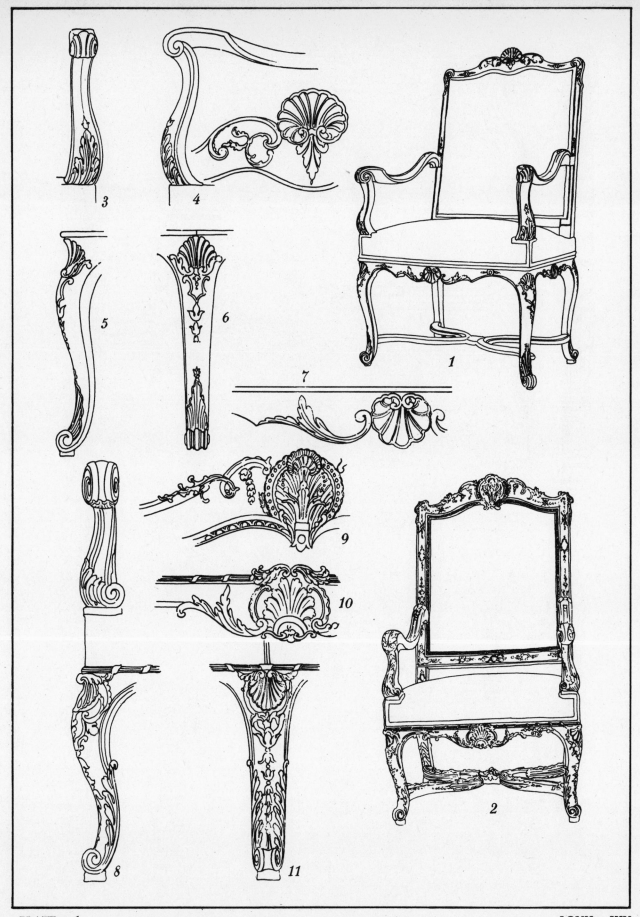

PLATE 67

LOUIS XIV

1. Armchair, upholstered with damask.   2. Armchair, upholstered with velvet.   3, 4, 5, 6 and 7. Details of the first armchair.   8, 9, 10 and 11. Details of the second armchair.

*Museum of Decorative Arts, Paris and the Kann collection*

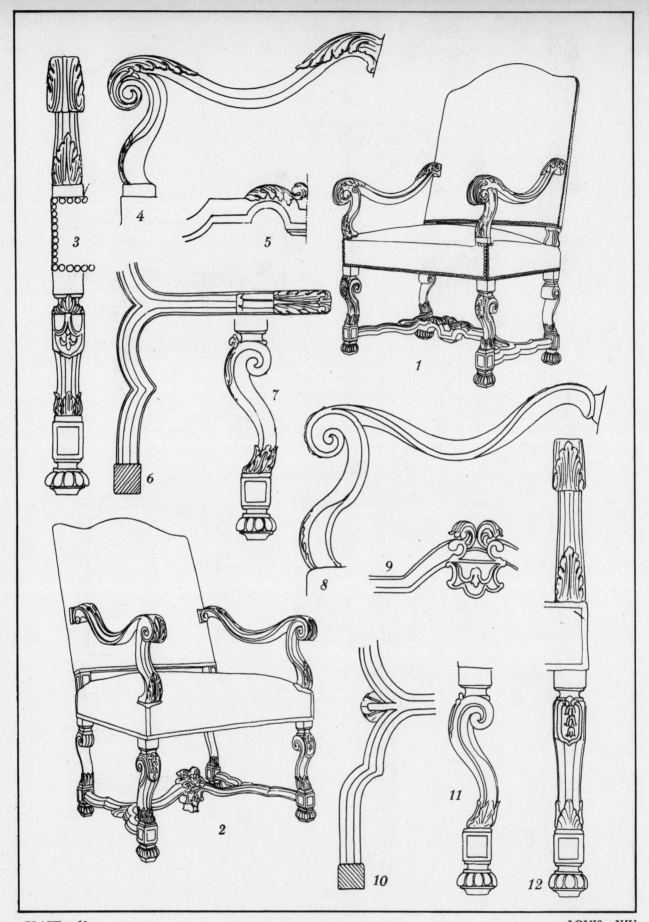

PLATE  68                                                          LOUIS  XIV

1. Armchair, upholstered with damask.  2. Armchair, upholstered with velvet.  3, 4, 5, 6 and 7. Details of the first armchair.  8, 9, 10, 11 and 12. Details of the second armchair.

*Museum of Decorative Arts, Paris and a private collection*

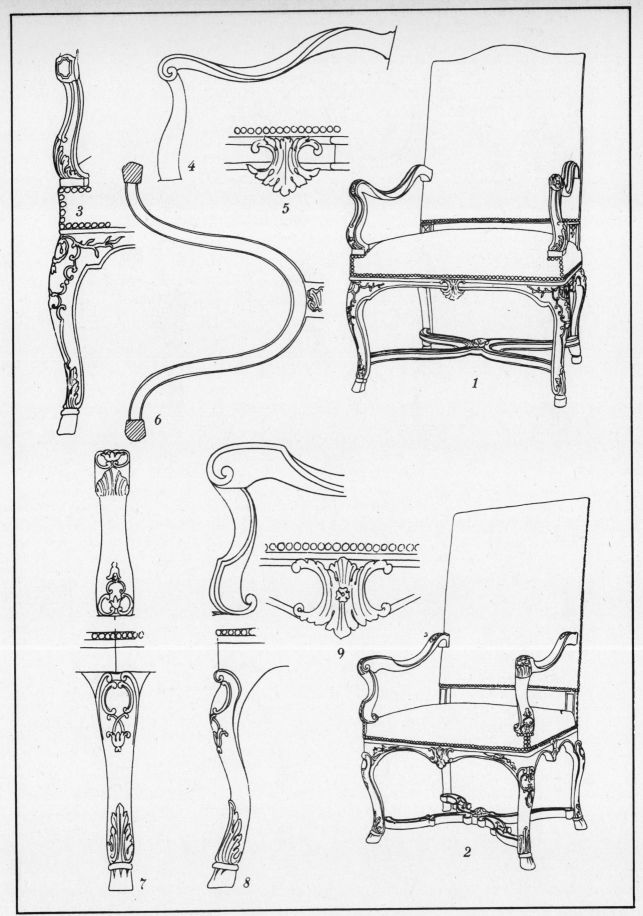

PLATE 69

*1* and *2*. Armchair, upholstered with tapestry. 3, 4, 5 and 6. Details of the first armchair. 7, 8 and 9. Details of the second armchair.

*Museum of Decorative Arts, Paris and Metropolitan Museum, New York*

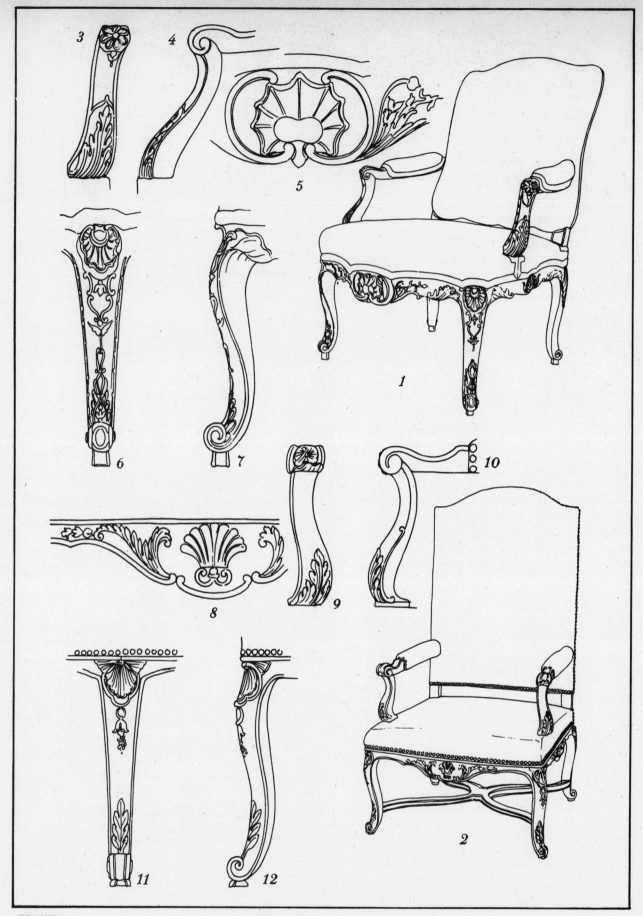

PLATE 70

LOUIS XIV

1. Armchair, upholstered with velvet from Genoa.   2. Armchair, covered with petit point upholstery.   3, 4, 5, 6 and 7. Details of the first armchair.   8, 9, 10, 11 and 12. Details of the second armchair.

*Museum of Decorative Arts, Paris and Bernheimer collection, Munich*

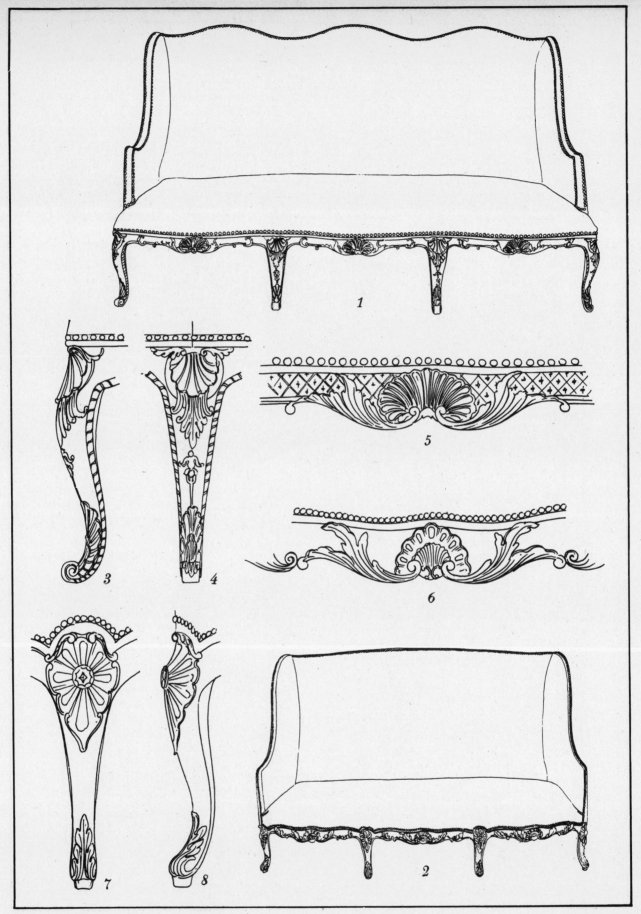

PLATE 71                                                              LOUIS XIV

1 and 2. Wing-back sofas, upholstered with tapestry.    3, 4 and 5. Details of the first sofa.    6, 7 and 8. Details of the second sofa.

*Private collections*

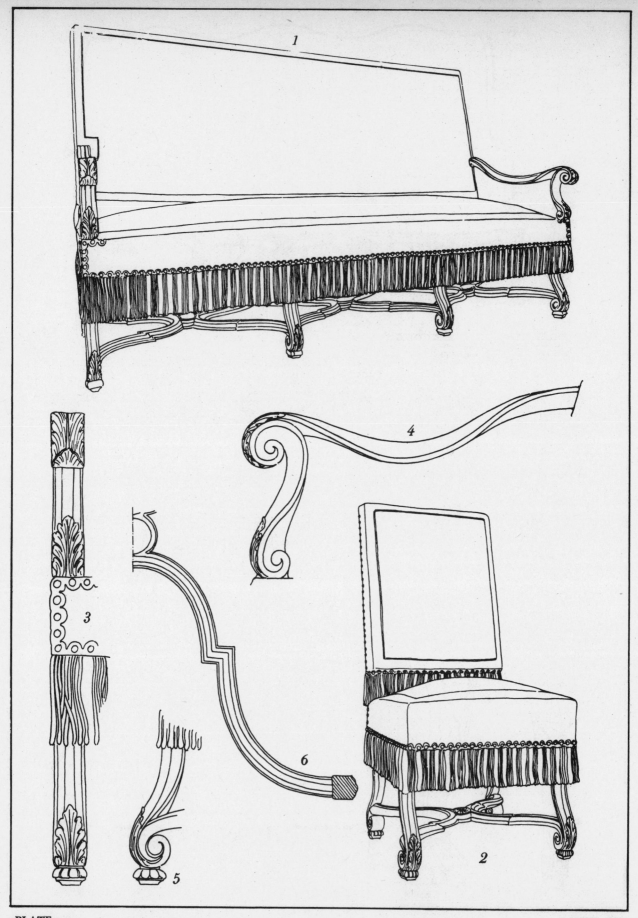

PLATE 72                                                                LOUIS XIV

1. Sofa, covered with floral damask upholstery.   2. Carved wooden chair with floral damask upholstery.   3 and 4.
Details of the sofa.   5 and 6. Details of the chair.

*Fontainebleau Palace*

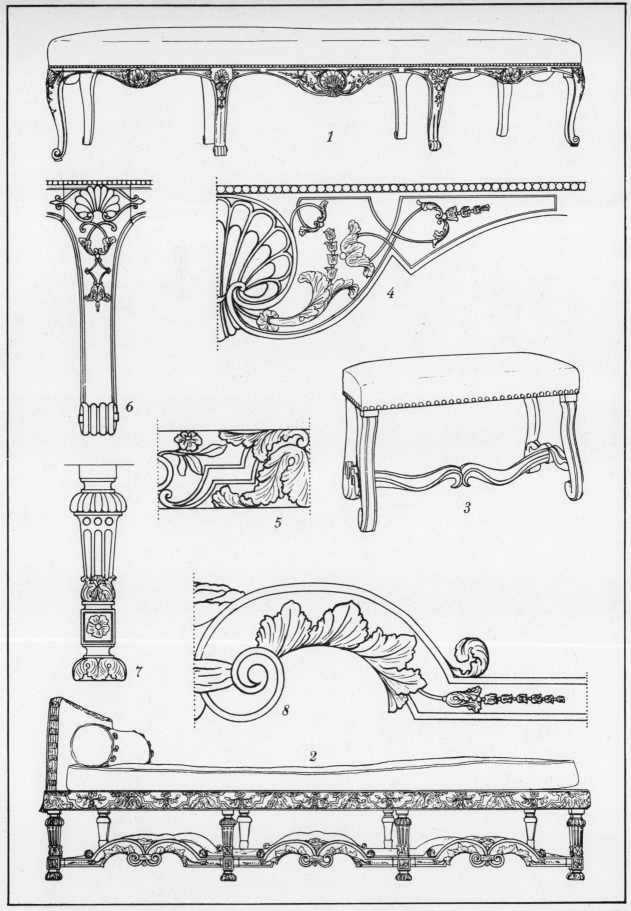

PLATE 73                                                                                                    LOUIS XIV

1. Carved walnut bench (banquette).    2. Chaise longue of gilt carved oak.    3. Stool.    4 and 5. Detail of the aprons.    6
and 7. Detail of the legs.    8. Detail of the rails.

*Museum of Decorative Arts, Paris*

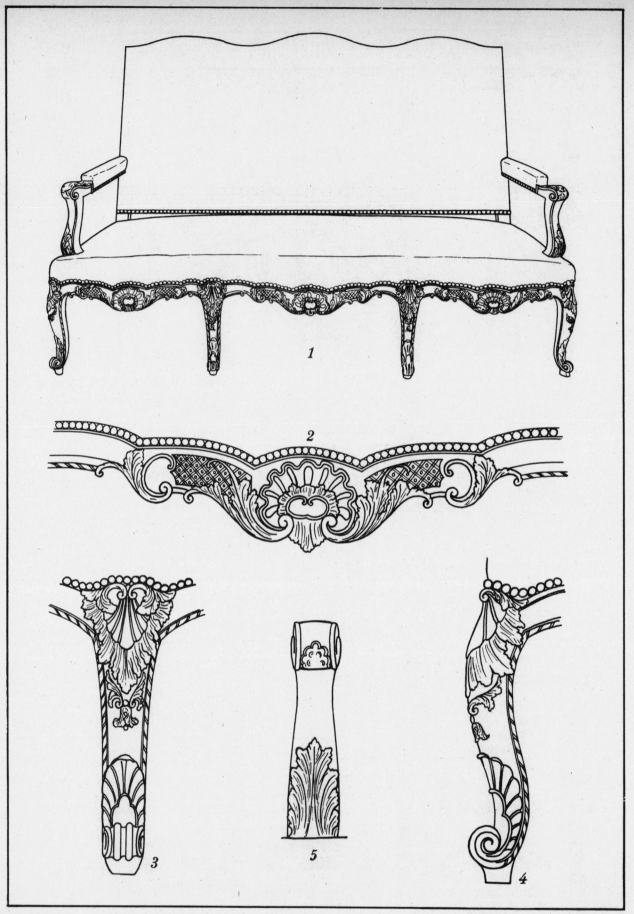

PLATE 74
1. Sofa, upholstered with Gobelin tapestry.  2. Details of the central motif.  3 and 4. Legs.  5. Arm support.

LOUIS XIV

*Lowengard collection, Paris*

**PLATE 75**

1 and 2. Gilt walnut consoles.    3 and 4. Details of the legs.    5 and 6. Details of the fronts of the consoles.

*Lowengard collection, Paris and Metropolitan Museum, New York*

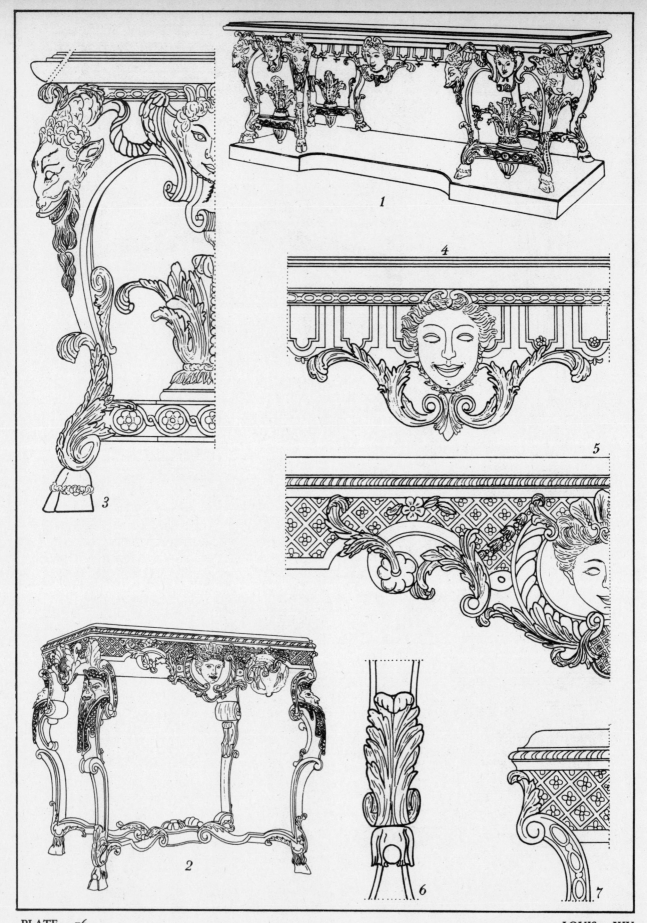

PLATE 76

LOUIS XIV

1. Large natural wood console.    2. Gilt wooden console table.    3. Detail of the legs.    4 and 5. Detail of the central motifs.    6 and 7. Leg and corner of the frieze.

*Bank of France and Museum of Decorative Arts, Paris*

**PLATE** 77

1. Gilt wooden console.    2. Detail of the legs.    3. Middle ornament.    4. Upright crest.

*Bank of France, Paris*

PLATE 78

LOUIS XIV

1. Natural wooden console table.  2. Gilt wooden console table.  3. Leg.  4 and 5. Table front.  6. Leg.

*Bank of France and Museum of Decorative Arts, Paris*

*1*

*2*

*3*  *4*  *5*

**PLATE** 79

LOUIS XIV

1. Gilt wooden console table.  2. Detail of table front.  3. Top-shaped ornament.  4 and 5. Details of the legs.

*Church of Saint-Jacques, Rheims*

PLATE 80                                                                LOUIS XIV

1. Gilt wooden console.   2 and 3. Detail of the leg and table front.   4. Decoration of the crosspieces.

*Museum of Decorative Arts, Paris*

**PLATE 81**

1. **Large gilt wooden console table.**    2. Detail of the leg.    3. Side view of leg decoration.    4. Detail of central motif.

LOUIS XIV

*Louvre*

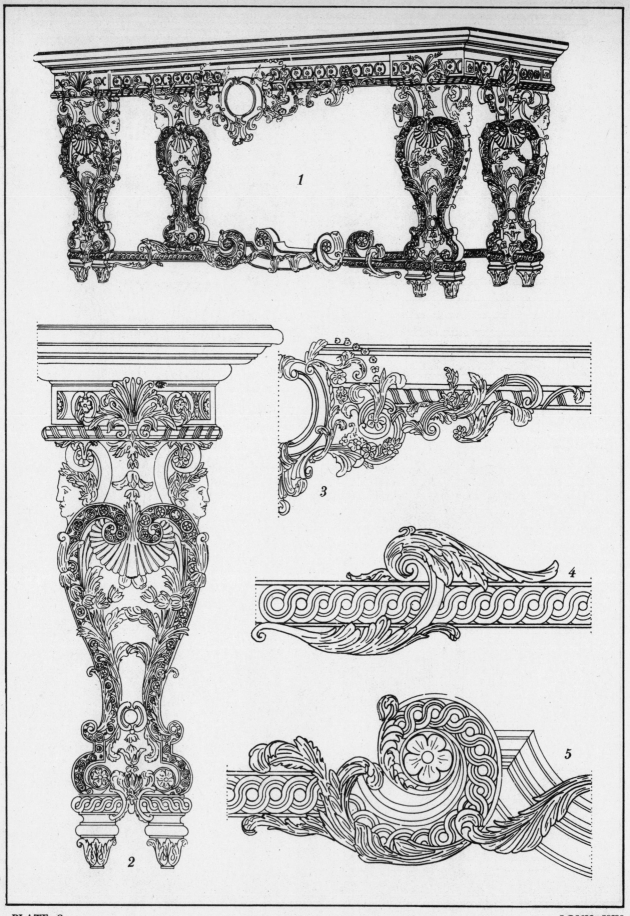

PLATE 82                                                                LOUIS XIV

1. Gilt wooden console.    2. Detail of the legs.    3. Detail of the table front.    4 and 5. Details of the decorations of the crosspiece.

*Louvre*

**PLATE 83**

LOUIS XIV

1. Gilt wooden console.   2. Detail of the legs.   3. Detail of the upper face of the crosspiece.   4. Detail of the table front.

**PLATE 84**  COMPARISON OF THE STYLES OF LOUIS XIV AND LOUIS XV

1. Gilt carved wooden console of Louis XIV style.   2. Gilt carved wooden wall console of early Louis XV style.   3, 4
and 5. Details of the decorations of Louis XIV style.   6, 7 and 8. Details of the decorations of Louis XV style.

*Louvre*

PLATE 85                                        COMPARISON OF THE STYLES OF LOUIS XIV AND THE REGENCY
1. Writing table with ebony and copper marquetry, Louis XIV style.   2. Marble-top sculptured wooden pier table,
Regency style.   3 and 4. Drawer pulls and escutcheons.   5. Details of the table fronts.   6. Detail of the leg.   7.
Moulding.

*Private collection and Castle of Fleury-en-Bière*

PLATE 86    COMPARISON OF THE STYLES OF LOUIS XIV AND LOUIS XV

1. Ebony writing table inlaid with gilt bronze decorations, attributed to A. C. Boulle, Louis XIV style (end of the 17th century).    2. Marquetry writing table with gilt bronze decorations by C. Cressent, Louis XV style (early type).    3 and 4. Details of the legs, each drawing indicating the inlays and bronze work.    5, 6 and 7. Details of the table fronts.

**PLATE 87**                                                 **LOUIS XIV**
1. Marquetry writing desk by A. C. Boulle.    2 and 3. Legs.    4 and 5. Drawer fronts.

*Louvre*

**PLATE 88**                                                                                    LOUIS XIV

1. Marquetry writing table by A. C. Boulle.   2. Detail of the uprights.   3. Escutcheon.   4. Detail of the middle section.

*Wallace collection, London*

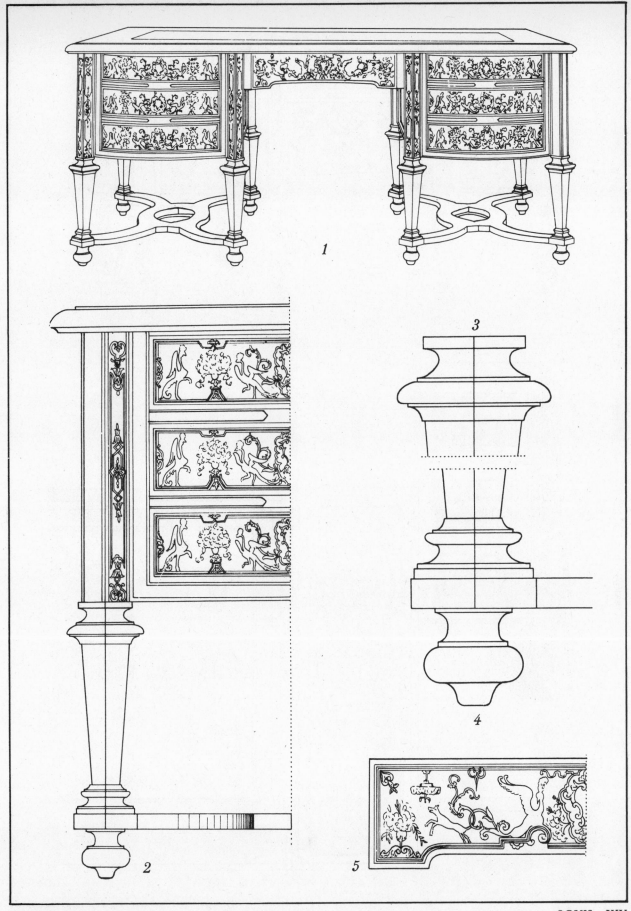

PLATE 89

LOUIS XIV

1. Marquetry writing table by A. C. Boulle.   2. Detail of the upright.   3 and 4. Detail of the leg.   5. Detail of the middle panel.

*Windsor Castle*

*1*

*3*

*2*

PLATE 90                                                                                                          LOUIS   XIV
1. Marquetry writing table by A. C. Boulle.   2. Detail of the upright.   3. Detail of the lower section.

*Munich Museum*

PLATE 91                                                                                    LOUIS XIV
1. Marquetry writing table by A. C. Boulle.   2. Detail of the upright.   3. Leg.   4. Detail of the middle panels.
*Victoria and Albert Museum, London*

PLATE 92

LOUIS XIV

1. Marquetry bureau-type of writing desk by A. C. Boulle.   2. Detail of the post and leg.   3. Detail of the upper face of the crosspiece.   4. Escutcheon.   5. Side view of the leg carving.   6. Detail of middle drawer front.

*Wallace collection, London*

PLATE 93
LOUIS XIV
1. Inlaid ebony commode by A. C. Boulle.    2 and 3. Post and leg.    4 and 5. Outline of the gilt bronze work.

*Louvre*

97

PLATE 94

LOUIS XIV

1. Marquetry commode by A. C. Boulle.   2. Detail of the post.   3. Handle.   4. Upper cross section.   5. Leg.   6. Detail of lower section.

PLATE 95          LOUIS XIV
1. Marquetry commode by A. C. Boulle.    2. Detail of the post.    3. Handle.    4. Leg.    5. Detail of lower section.

*Louvre*

99

PLATE 96                                                                LOUIS XIV
1. Low marquetry wardrobe by A. C. Boulle.   2. Detail of the post.   3. Detail of the middle panel.

*Louvre*

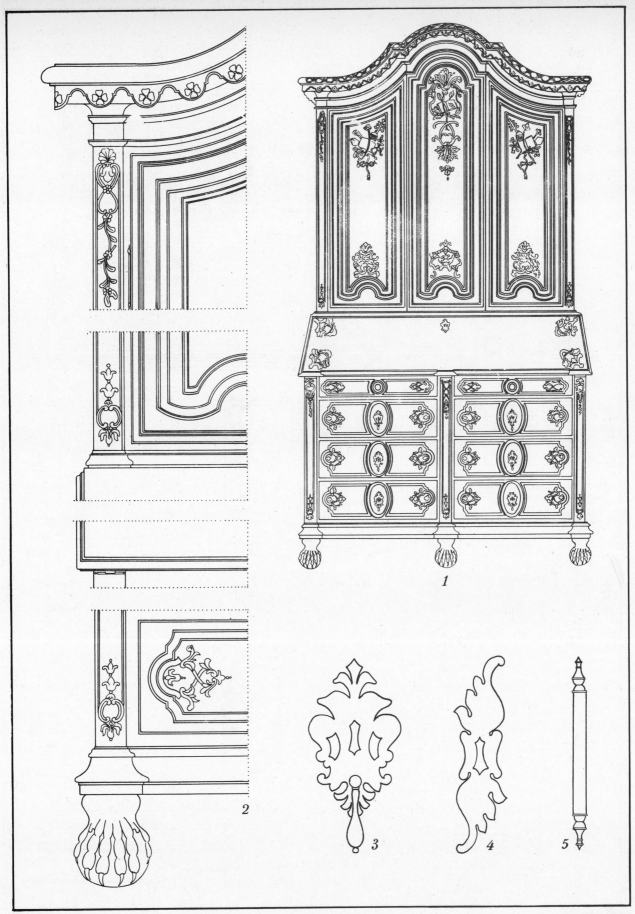

PLATE 97

LOUIS XIV

1. Sculptured wooden wardrobe-shaped commode with drop-leaf writing table.   2. Details.   3 and 4. Escutcheons.   5. Hinge.

*Cinquantenaire, Brussels*

PLATE 98

1. Wardrobe-shaped secretary with colored wooden marquetry.  2, 3 and 4. Details of the uprights.  5. Details of the crest.  6. Pull.  7. Escutcheon.

LOUIS XIV

*Private collection*

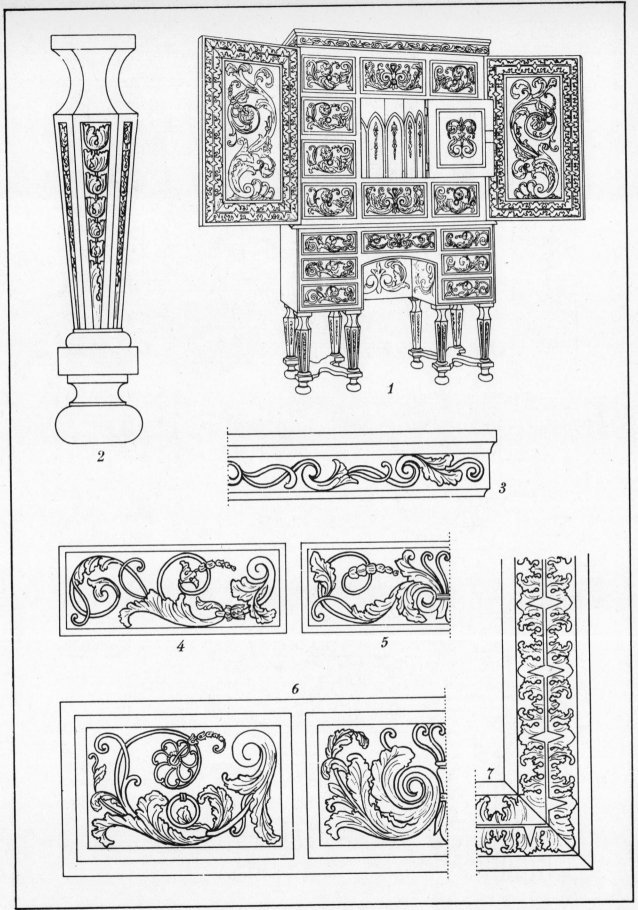

**PLATE** 99

1. Cabinet with copper and shell marquetry.   2. Leg.   3. Drawing of the frieze.   4, 5 and 6. Outlines of the panel designs.   7. Outline of mitred corner.

LOUIS XIV (early type)

*Louvre*

**PLATE** 100

LOUIS XIV (early type)

1. Carved ebony cabinet.　2. Leg.　3. Detail of post.　4. Cross section.　5. Detail of lower section.

*Louvre*

PLATE 101                                                                    LOUIS XIV

1. Chest-on-chest wardrobe of sculpted wood.   2 and 3. Details of the front.   4. Detail of the upper corner of the door.

*Metropolitan Museum, New York*

PLATE 102

LOUIS XIV

1. Wardrobe made of carved wood.   2 and 3. Detail of base and door.   4. Moulding and decorations on panel.

*Metropolitan Museum, New York*

**PLATE 103**

1. Ebony wardrobe with marquetry of copper, shell and blue horn, attributed to A. C. Boulle. 2. Details of the front. 3 and 4. Details of decorations.

*Collection of the Duke of G., Paris*

PLATE 104                                                                LOUIS XIV

1. Ebony wardrobe with marquetry of copper and shell, attributed to A. C. Boulle.   2. Details of the front.   3 and
4. Sketches of decorations and the upper central relief.

*Collection of the Duke of G., Paris*

**PLATE** 105

1. Oversized wardrobe with marquetry by A. C. Boulle.   2. Detail of supports.   3. Bronze design.

LOUIS XIV

*Windsor Castle*

PLATE 106                                                                LOUIS XIV (end of period)

1. Ebony showcase with marquetry of copper over shell.   2 and 3. Details of the bronze decorations.   4 and 5. Profiles of the mouldings.

*Poles collection, Paris*

PLATE 107

1. Bed with tapestry canopy.   2. Detail of the legs.   3. Headboard.   4. Detail of footboard.

LOUIS XIV

*Lowengard collection, Paris*

PLATE 108

1. Clock.  2. Detail.  3. Sketch of face.

*Museum of Decorative Arts, Paris*

**PLATE** 109                                                    LOUIS XIV
1. Clock.    2. Detail.    3. Hands.    4. Detail of lower section.

*Museum of Aix-en-Provence*

**PLATE** 110

1. Clock.   2. Detail.   3. Sketch of bronze ornament.   4. Detail of clockface.

**LOUIS XIV**

*Fontainebleau Palace*

PLATE III

1. Clock on top of a pedestal.    2. Detail of the clock.    3. Detail of upper pedestal.    4. Hands.

*Wallace collection, London*

PLATE 112

1. Clock on top of pedestal.  2. Detail of the clock.  3. Foot of pedestal.  4. Hands.

LOUIS XIV

*Wallace collection, London*

**PLATE** 113

1. Clock.   2. Detail.   3. Hands.

LOUIS XIV

*Museum of Decorative Arts, Paris*

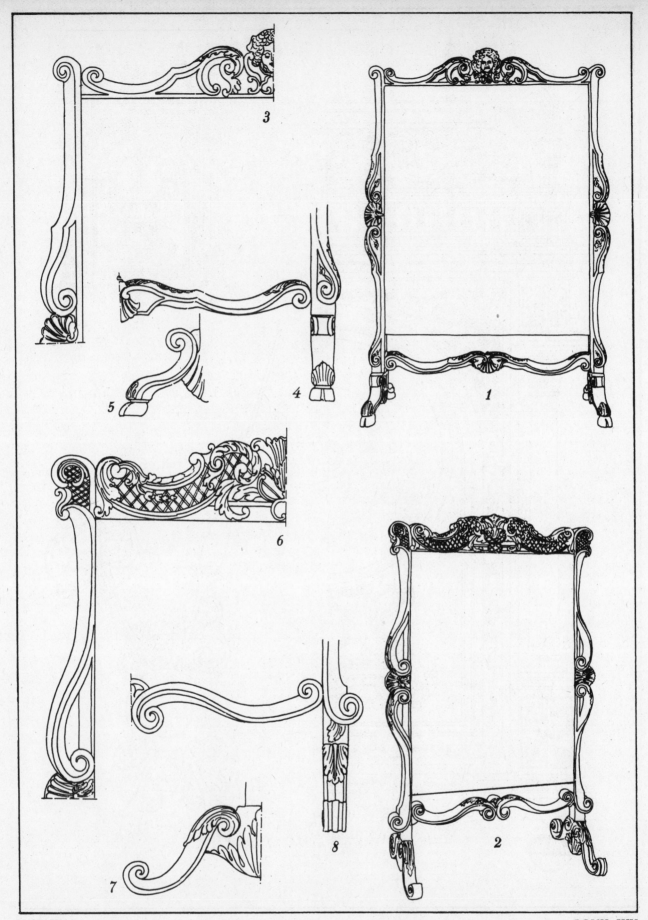

PLATE 114

1 and 2. Fireplace screens with petit point tapestry.   3, 4 and 5. Details of first screen.   6, 7 and 8. Details of second screen.

*Museum of Cluny and Anet Castle*

**PLATE 115**

1 and 2. Gilt wooden fireplace screens with tapestry.    3 and 4. Details of the first and second screens.

LOUIS XIV

*Private collections*

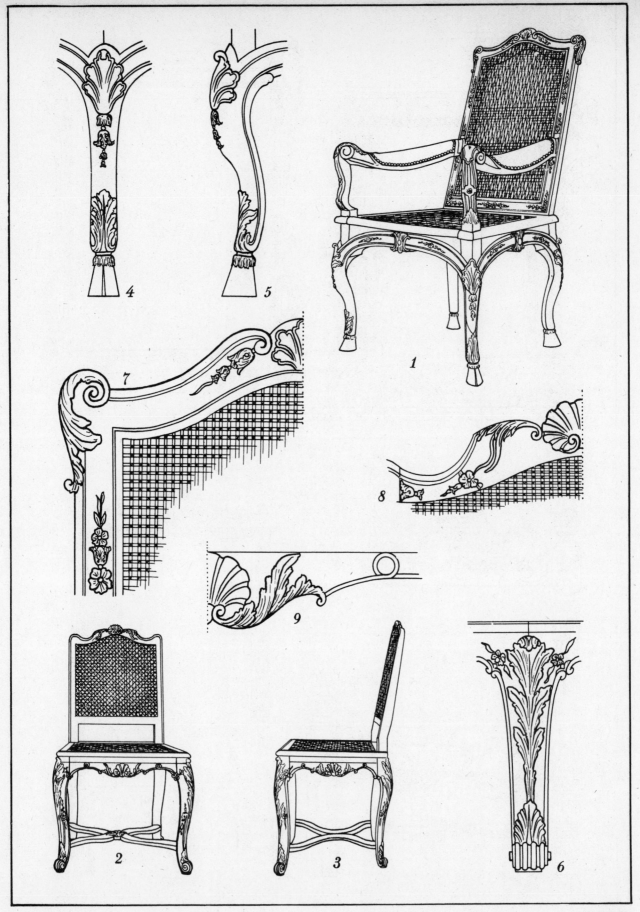

**PLATE 116**                                                   REGENCY

1. Cane armchair.   2 and 3. Cane side chairs.   4, 5 and 6. Legs.   7 and 8. Details of the backs.   9. Detail of the crosspiece of the seat.

*Metropolitan Museum, New York*

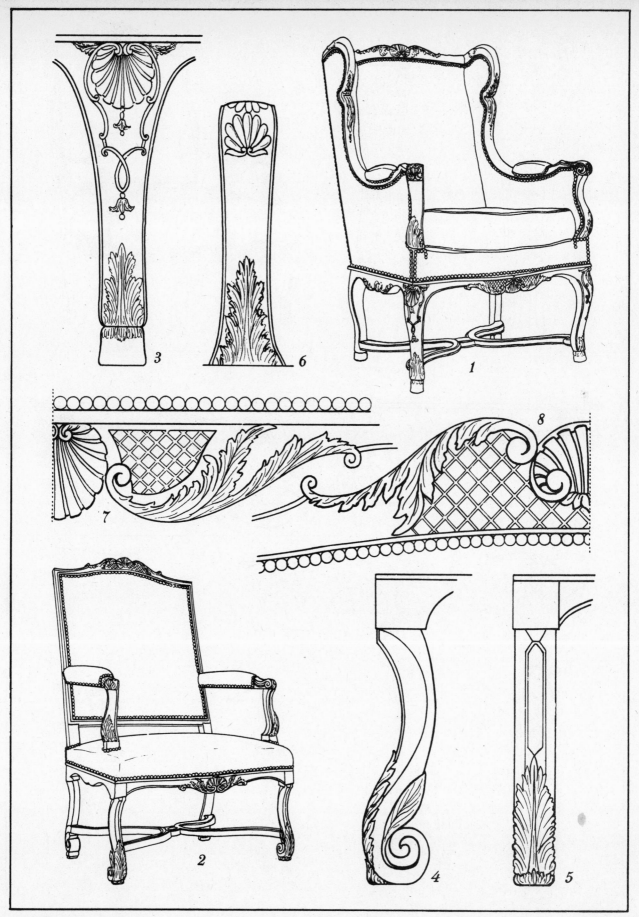

**PLATE 117**

1. "Country" armchair.  2. Armchair.  3, 4 and 5. Legs.  6. Arm support.  7 and 8. Detail of seat and crest of back.

REGENCY

*Museum of Decorative Arts, Paris*

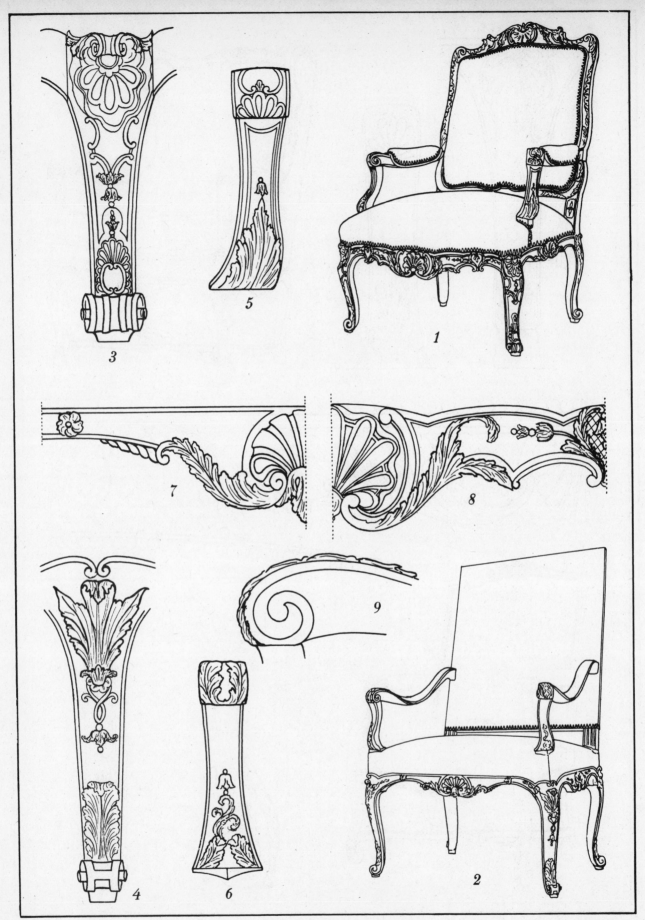

PLATE 118

REGENCY

1 and 2. Armchairs, covered with silk tapestry.   3 and 4. Legs.   5 and 6. Arm supports.   7 and 8. Details of the seat.   9. Front of the arm.

*Museum of Decorative Arts, Paris*

1, 2 and 3. Armchairs, covered with tapestry and velvet with different kinds of backs.   4. Side chair.   5, 6, 7 and 8. Legs.   9, 10 and 11. Fronts of the seats.   12. Corner of the back.

*Metropolitan Museum, New York and private collections*

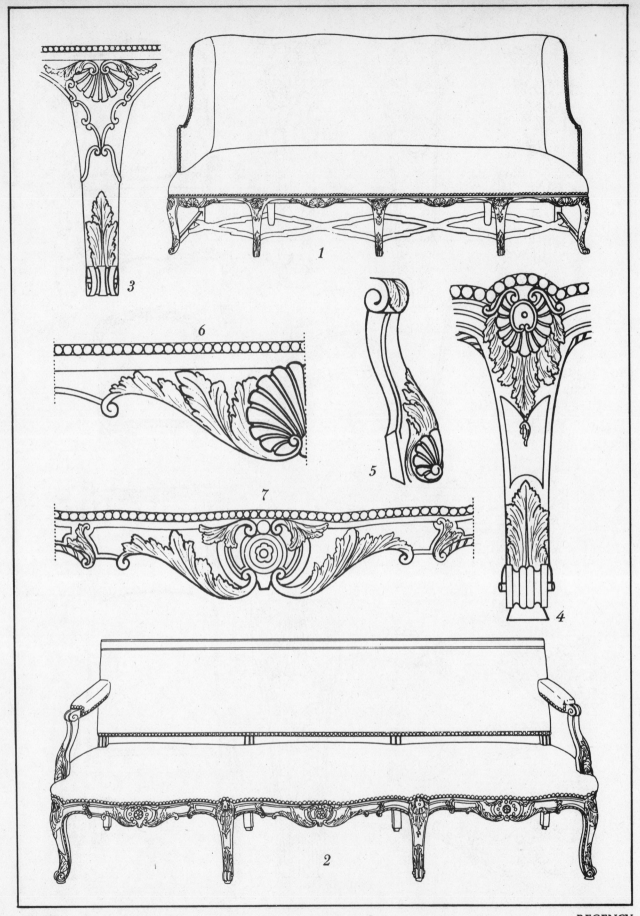

PLATE 120 REGENCY

1 and 2. Sofas, covered with petit point tapestry.  3 and 4. Legs.  5. Arm support.  6 and 7. Details of the decorations on the fronts of the seats.

*Private collections*

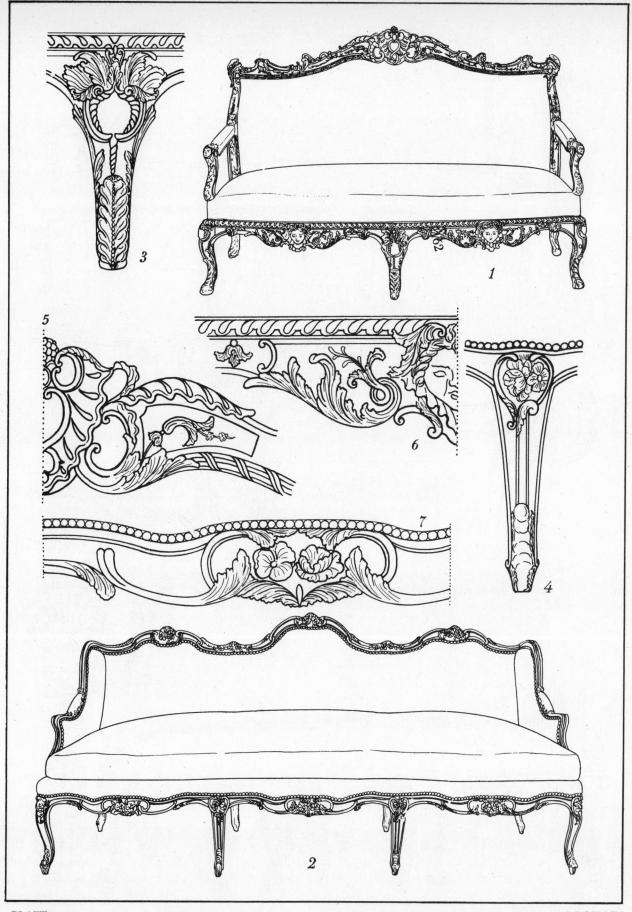

PLATE 121                                                                                                    REGENCY
1 and 2. Sofas, covered with velvet.    3 and 4. Legs.    5. Crest of back.    6 and 7. Detail of the front of the seat.
*Collections of G. Le Breton and Jacques Doucet, Paris*

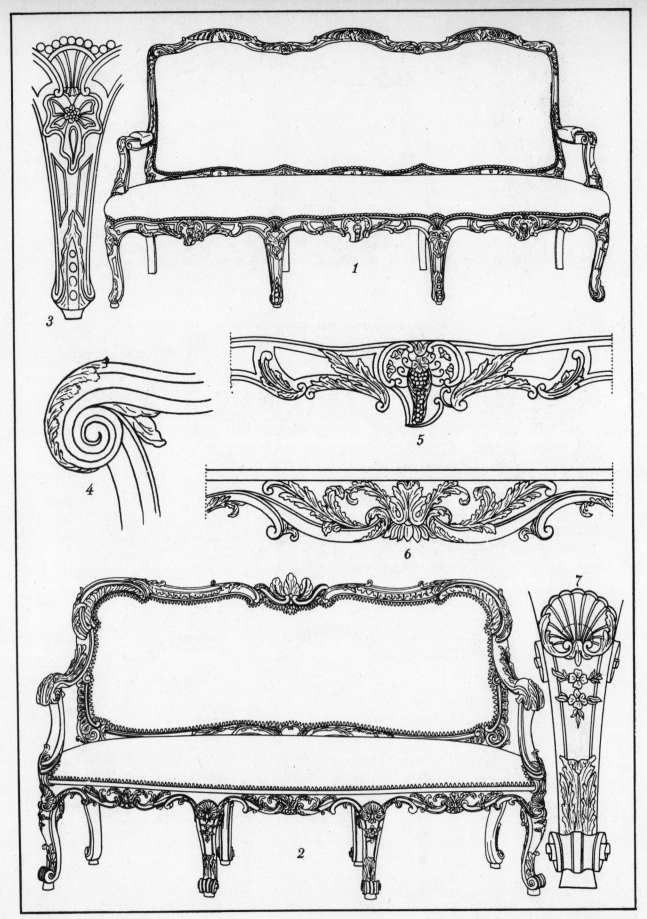

PLATE 122

**REGENCY**

1 and 2. Sofas, covered with tapestry and damask.   3 and 4. Legs and scrolls at end of arm.   5 and 6. Details of fronts of seats.   7. Leg.

*Collections of Charles and Rodolphe Kann, Paris*

PLATE 123

REGENCY

1. Chaise longue of sculpted wood.  2. Cane chaise longue.  3, 4 and 5. Detail of the decorations.  6 and 7. Legs.

*Collections of G. Hoentschel and Jacques Doucet, Paris*

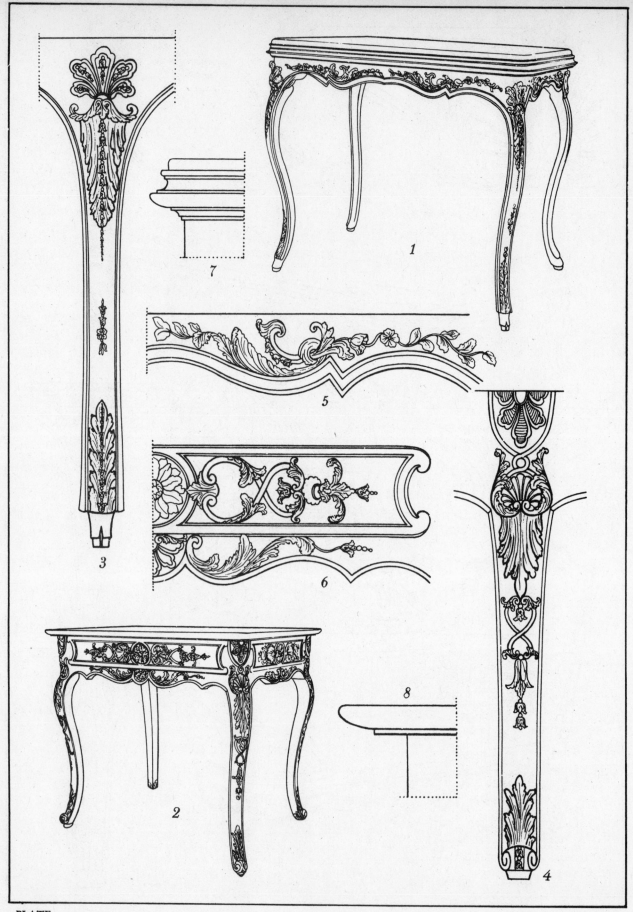

PLATE 124
1 and 2. Tables of carved wood.   3 and 4. Legs.   5 and 6. Details of the front.   7 and 8. Mouldings.

*Museum of Decorative Arts, Paris*

**PLATE 125**                                                                                        **REGENCY**

1. Table of carved wood with mosaic top.   2. Table of carved wood.   3 and 4. Legs.   5 and 6. Mouldings.   7 and 8. Detail of the front.

*Cinquantenaire, Brussels and private collection*

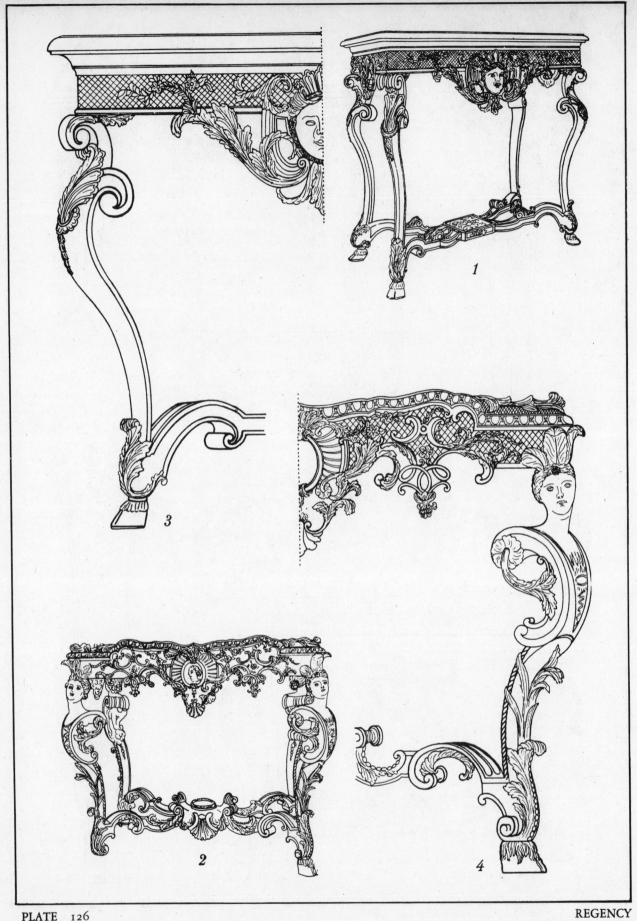

PLATE 126                                                                    REGENCY

1. Small gilt wooden table.    2. Gilt wooden console table.    3 and 4. Detail of first and second tables.

*Lowengard collection, Paris*

PLATE 127

1, 2, 3 and 4. Four wooden console tables. 5, 6, 7 and 8. Details of fronts of tables. 9, 10, 11 and 12. Profiles of the marble mouldings.

*1, 2 and 3 from Aigremont Castle; 4 from Jacques Doucet collection, Paris*

**PLATE** 128                                                                                  REGENCY

1 and 2. Large gilt wooden tables.     3 and 4. Legs.     5 and 6. Detail of table front.     7 and 8. Mouldings.

*Lelong and Rodolphe Kann collections, Paris*

PLATE 129

1, 2 and 3. Gilt wooden console tables. 4, 5 and 6. Fronts of tables. 7, 8 and 9. Profiles of marble mouldings. 10. Leg.

*1 and 2, Metropolitan Museum; 3 from Jacques Doucet collection, Paris*

PLATE 130
REGENCY

1. Smooth writing table with metal marquetry.   2. Carved wooden table with bronze decorations.   3. Table with metal marquetry.   4. Commode with four drawers (partial view).   5. Writing table of Prince Max-Emmanuel (partial view).   6 and 7. Legs.   8. Detail of escutcheon plate and drawer pull on Table 5.   *1. Victoria and Albert Museum, London;*

*2. Elysée Palace, Paris; 3. Private collection; 4. Wallace collection, London; 5. National Museum, Munich*

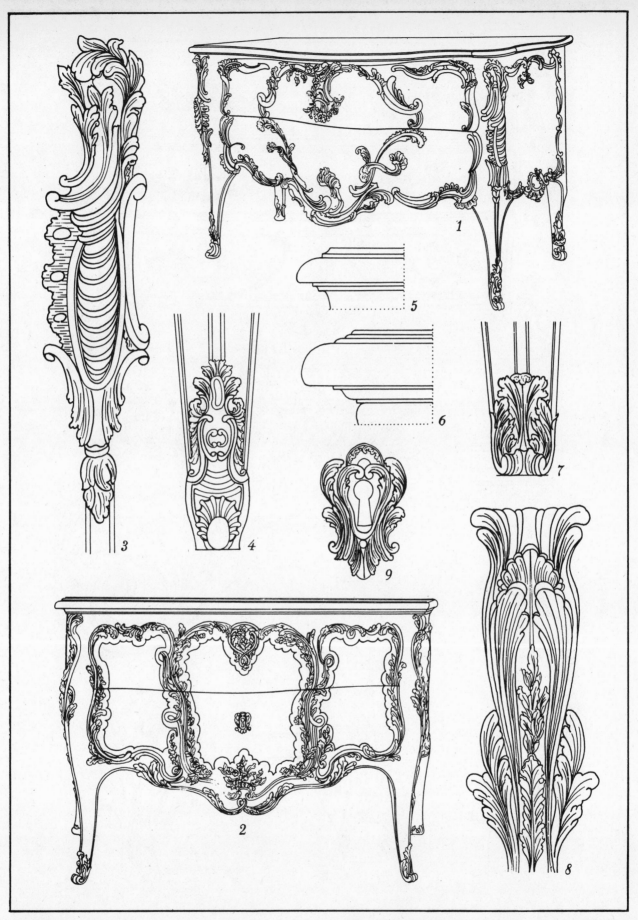

**PLATE 131**                                      REGENCY (end of first half of 17th century)

1. Commode with long legs, contoured apron and two drawers, of gilt lacquer on a black background with Chinese motifs, blond lace in form of drawer pull and carved gilt bronzes.    2. Commode with long arched legs, contoured apron and two drawers.    3 and 4. Bronzes on the uprights.    5 and 6. Profile of the marble tops.    7 and 8. Bronzes on the uprights of the second commode.    9. Escutcheon plate.

*Poles and Dutasta collections*

PLATE 132

REGENCY

1. Big-bellied "tomb-shaped" commode made of Brazilian rosewood, with short legs and three drawers. "Pebble" motifs, heads known as "espagnolettes," other carved gilt bronzes and inlaid marble top. 2. Detail of an upright with an "espagnolette." 3. Leg. 4. Drawer pull and escutcheon plate. 5. Escutcheon plate. 6. Bottom decoration.

*Carnavalet Museum, Paris*

**PLATE** 133

1. Short-legged commode, with ten drawers and panels of old Japanese lacquer in the form of mountainous landscapes in gilt relief on a black background, framed with thin copper rods, with bronzes and marble at the top. 2. Profile of the marble top. 3. Leg. 4. Lower middle design. 5. Design at top of upright. 6 and 7. Escutcheon plate and drawer pull.

*Ganay collection, Paris*

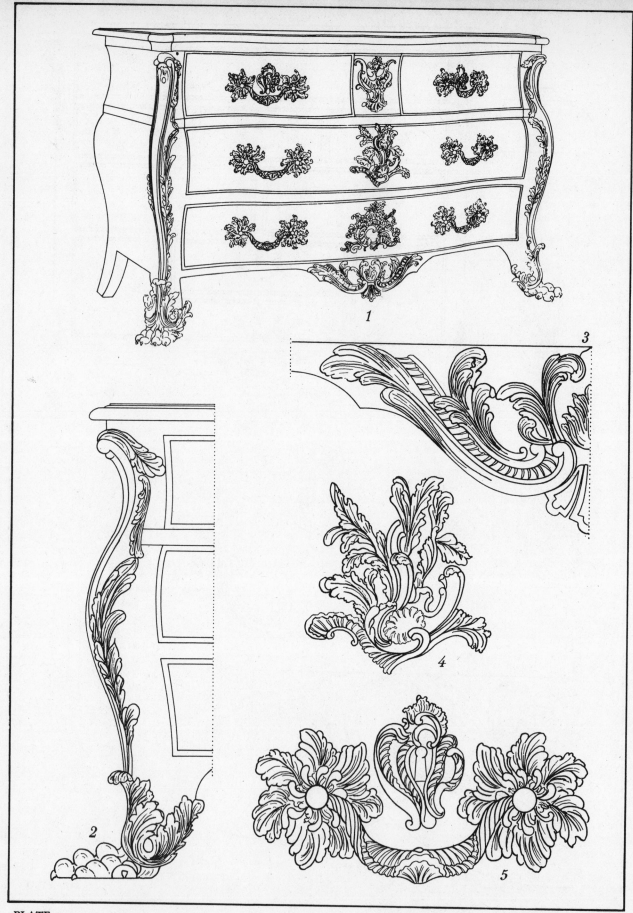

**PLATE 134**                                    REGENCY (end of first half of 17th century)

1. Big-bellied "tomb-shaped" commode with short legs and three drawers, with marquetry of violet, satined Brazilian rosewood. "Pebble" motifs, gilt, carved bronzes and a marble top.    2. Detail of the upright.    3. Lower middle motif.    4. "Pebble" design.    5. Escutcheon plate and drawer pull.

**PLATE** 135

1. Console table with metal marquetry.    2. Detail of the leg.    3. Decoration and handle.    4. Bronze design.

*Grand Trianon, Versailles*

PLATE 136

REGENCY

1. Commode, with two drawers and long curved legs, with marquetry.   2. Commode, with front made of two pieces of wood and long curved legs of wood veneer. Both commodes have carved gilt bronzes and marble tops.   3 and 4. Details of the bronzes on uprights and legs.   5 and 6. Lower middle motifs.   7. Escutcheon plate.

*Darthy collection, Paris*

PLATE 137

REGENCY

1. Wood-veneer commode with short legs, three drawers, carved gilt bronzes and marble top. 2 and 3. Detail of the bronzes on uprights and legs. 4 and 5. Bronzes in panel corners and lower middle decoration. 6. Drawer pull and escutcheon pull.

*Parent collection, Paris*

PLATE 138

REGENCY

1. Commode with four drawers.    2. Profile of upper moulding.    3. Corner of drawers.    4 and 5. Escutcheon plate and drawer pull.    6. Leg.    7. Central lower detail.

*Ansbach Castle collection*

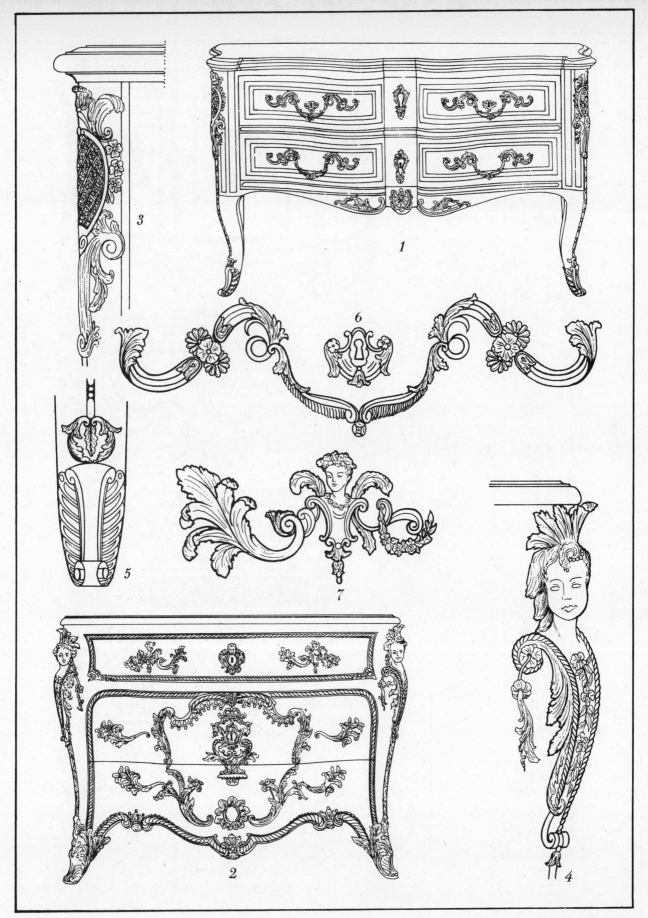

PLATE 139

REGENCY

1 and 2. Commodes with marquetry. 3 and 4. Detail of uprights and corner decorations. 5. Leg. 6. Drawer pull and escutcheon plate. 7. Drawer pull.

*F. Leuy and Kraemer collections, Paris*

PLATE 140

1. Sideboard with two doors.　2. Detail of upright.　3. Detail of central lower bronze.　4. Escutcheon plate.　5. Sketch of the frieze.　6. Corner of door panel.　7. Middle detail.　8. Marble moulding.

*Versailles Palace*

PLATE 141

REGENCY

1 and 2. Carved wooden sideboards.   3 and 4. Detail of fronts.   5 and 6. Details of upper mouldings.

*Cinquantenaire, Brussels and Choquières Museum, Lieja*

PLATE 142

1. Carved wooden chest-on-chest.  2, 3 and 4. Details of upper chest.  5. Details of lower chest.

*Bernheimer collection, Munich*

**PLATE 143**                                                       REGENCY (influence of Netherlands, 17th century)

1. Chest-on-chest; upper chest has two doors and lower one has three. Numerous scenes in marquetry of a variety of colored woods; crowned with turned gable. 2 and 3. Details of uprights. 4. Crest of gable. 5. Escutcheon plate. 6. Hinge.

*Private collection*

PLATE 144

1. Carved wooden wardrobe.    2 and 3. Details of door.

REGENCY

*Victoria and Albert Museum, London*

**PLATE 145**                                                              REGENCY

1. Carved wooden wardrobe.    2. Detail of upper middle section.    3, 4 and 5. Details of the doors and uprights.

*Cinquantenaire, Brussels*

PLATE 146                                                             REGENCY
1. Carved wooden chest-on-chest.   2 and 3. Details of same.

*Museum of Decorative Arts, Paris*

**PLATE** 147                                                             **REGENCY**

1. Carved wooden wardrobe.    2. Detail of doors and upright.    3. Detail of gable.

*Victoria and Albert Museum, London*

**PLATE 148**

1. Large wardrobe of satined rosewood, gilt carved bronzes, attributed to Charles Cressent.   2. Profile of the upright.   3. Detail of bronze decoration.

*Poles collection*

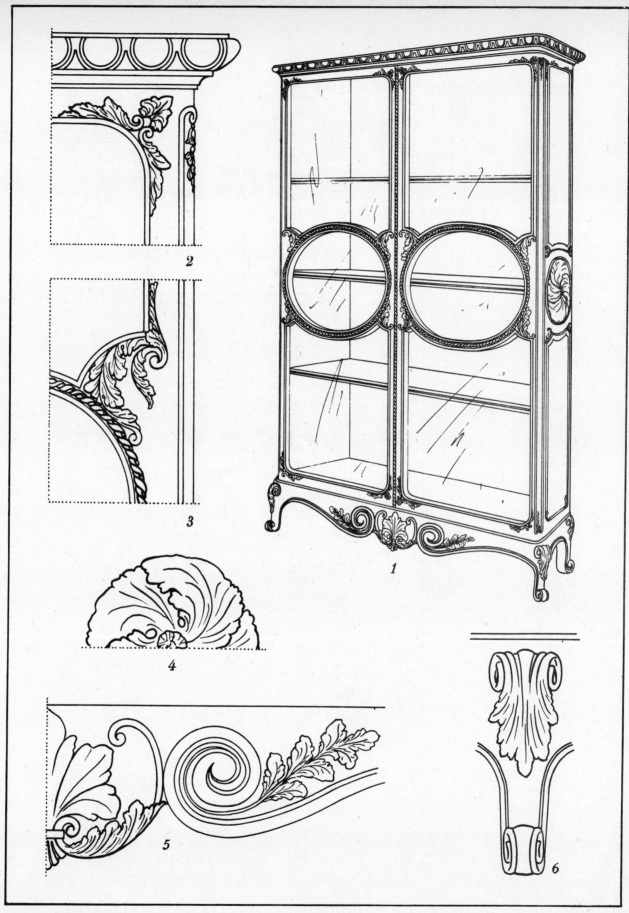

PLATE 149                                                                                    REGENCY

1. Wooden showcase carved in two pieces.   2 and 3. Details of doors and uprights.   4 and 5. Side and lower crosspiece
motifs.   6. Leg.

*Private collection*

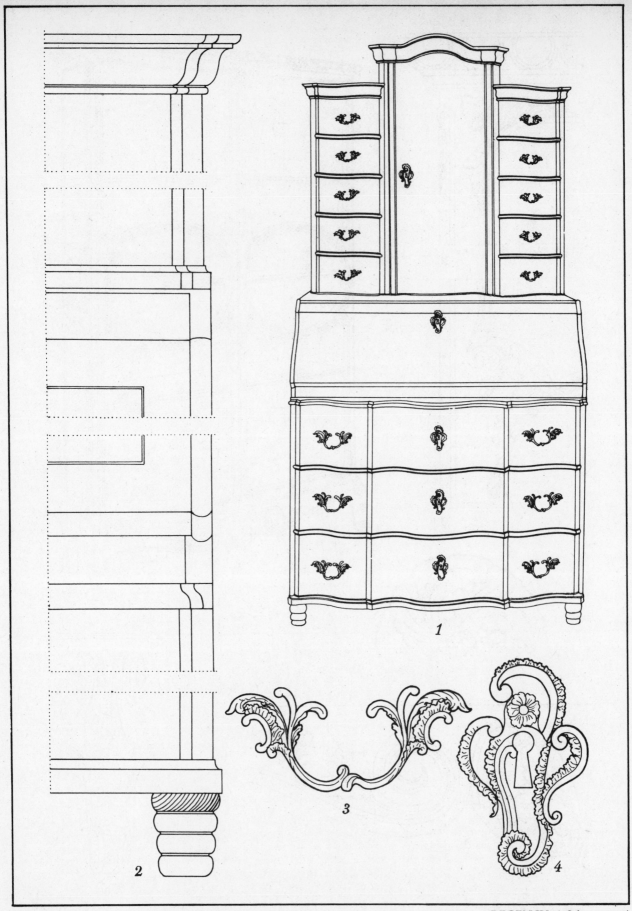

PLATE 150 REGENCY (18th century)
1. Wood-veneer secretary.   2. Details of upright.   3 and 4. Drawer pull and escutcheon plate.

*Private collection*

**PLATE 151**

1. Carved wooden chest-on-chest.    2 and 3. Escutcheon plates.    4 and 5. Details of upper chest.    6 and 7. Details of lower chest.

REGENCY

*Cinquantenaire, Brussels*

PLATE 152                                                               REGENCY
1. Oak clock.    2. Details of the crest and mouldings.    3. Detail of socle and mouldings.    4. Sketch of hands.

*Cinquantenaire, Brussels*

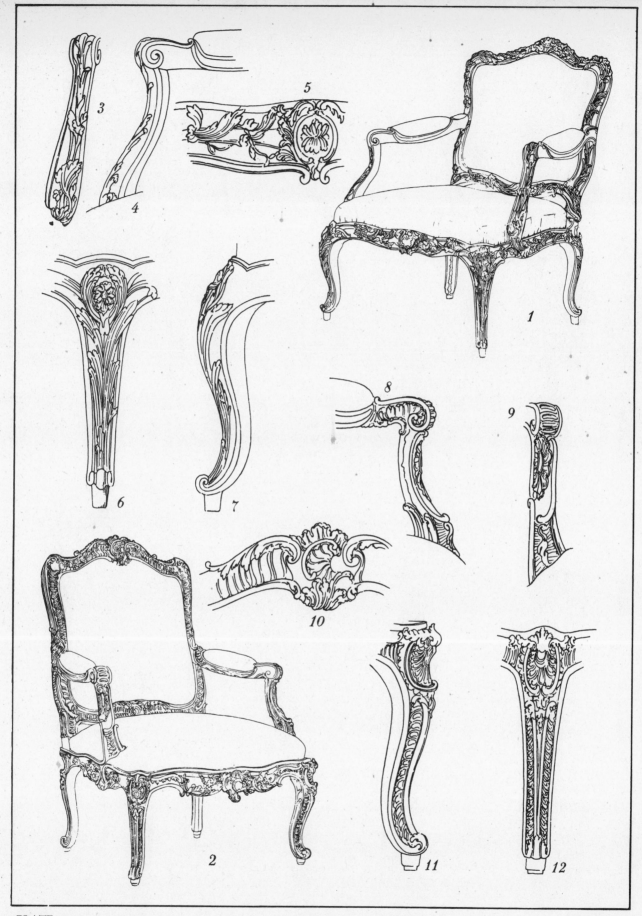

PLATE 153                                                                                                    LOUIS XV

1 and 2. Carved wooden armchairs. The upper one is painted with colors, and the lower one is covered with velvet from
Genoa.   3, 4, 5, 6 and 7. Details of the first chair.   8, 9, 10, 11 and 12. Details of the second chair.

*Louvre*

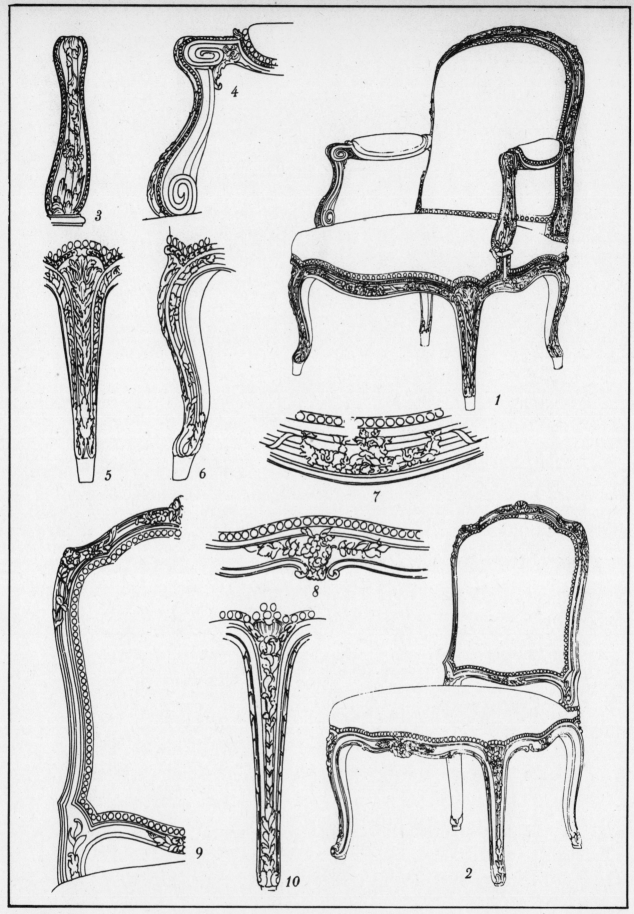

PLATE 154                                                                   LOUIS XV

1 and 2. Armchair and chair of gilt carved wood, upholstered with tapestries.   3, 4, 5 and 6. Details of arm supports
and legs.    7 and 8. Details of moulding.    9. Chair back.    10. Leg.

*Louvre*

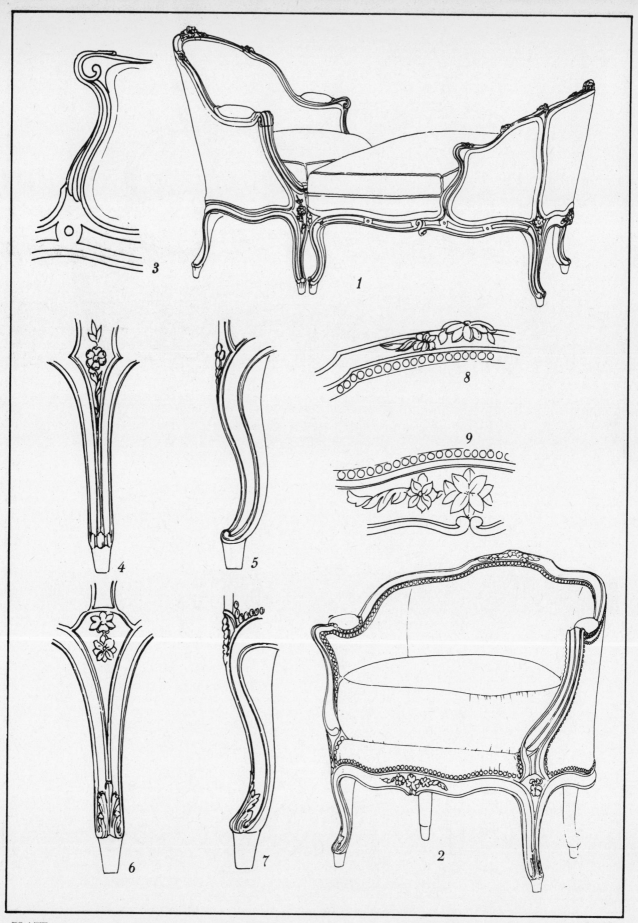

PLATE 155　　　　　　　　　　　　　　　　　　　　LOUIS XV (towards the end of the period)

1. Gilt carved wooden chaise longue.　2. "Marchioness" armchair of painted and gilt carved wood.　3, 4 and 5. Details of the arm, back and legs of the chaise longue.　6, 7, 8 and 9. Details of the legs and back of the armchair.

*Louvre*

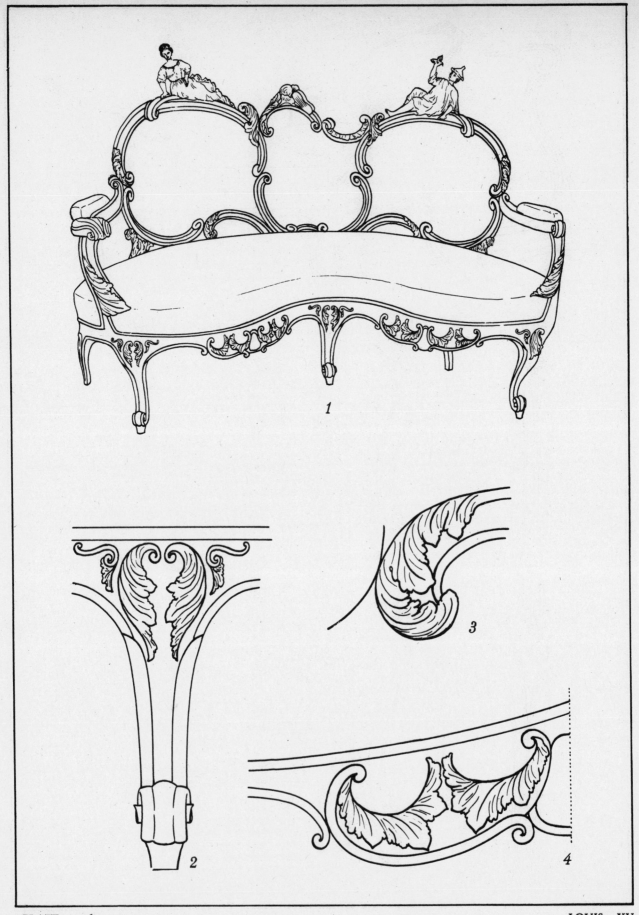

PLATE 156
1. Sofa, showing influence of Far East.   2. Detail of leg.   3 and 4. Decorations.

LOUIS XV

*Chantilly Castle*

PLATE 157

LOUIS XV (towards end of period)

1. Daybed, also known as a bedroom sofa.   2. Uprights.   3. Leg.   4. Details of middle crest of back.

*Private collection*

PLATE 158

LOUIS XV (end of period)

1 and 2. Small sewing tables. Upper one has removable box.    3 and 4. Uprights.    5 and 6. Escutcheon plates.    7. Section of upright.    8. Leg.

*Private collection*

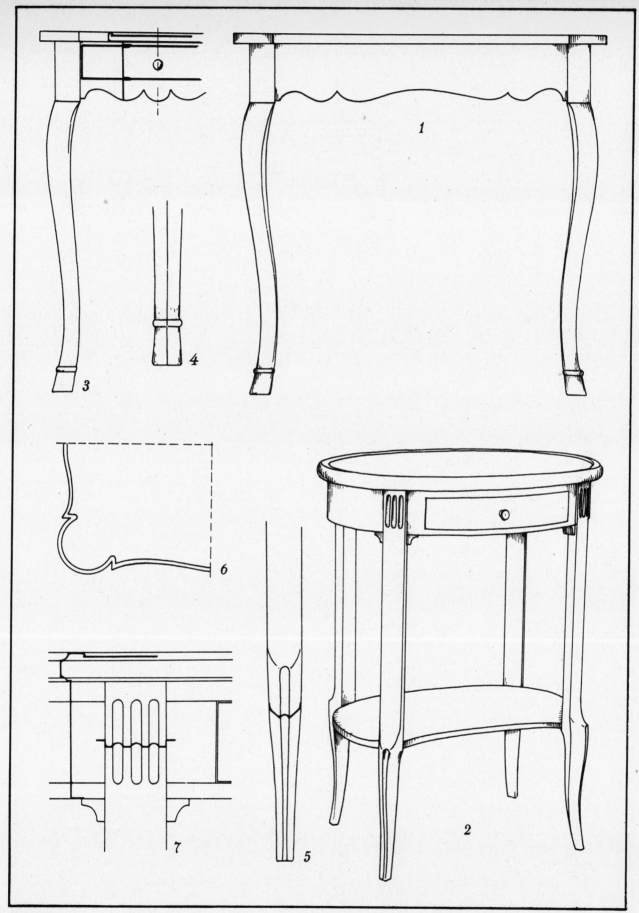

**PLATE 159**                                          LOUIS XV (beginning of Louis XVI. Simple treatment.)
1. Small table.   2. Small oval table.   3, 4 and 5. Details of leg.   6. Silhouette of tabletop.   7. Detail of upright.

*Private collection*

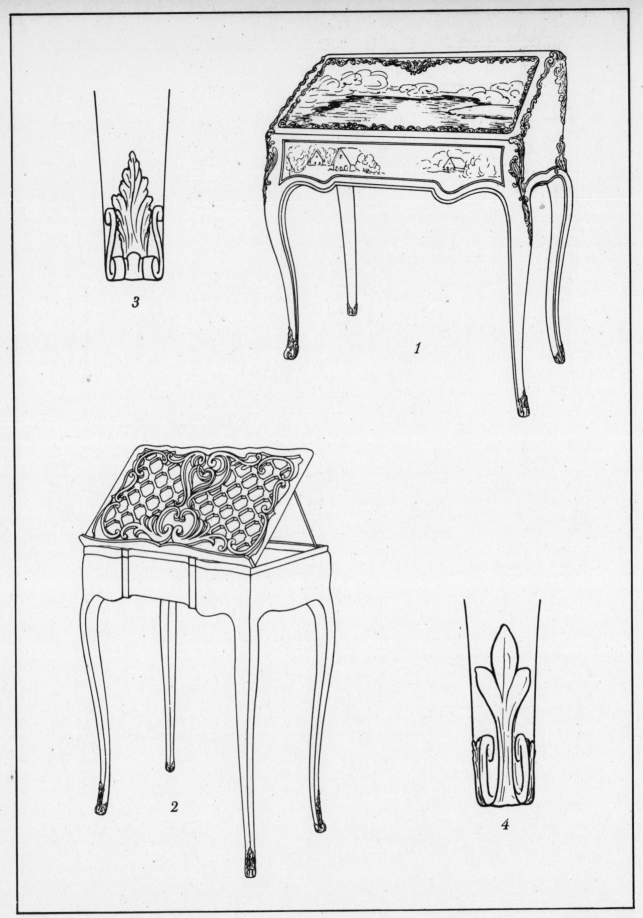

PLATE 160
1 and 2. Ladies' desks.  3 and 4. Legs.

LOUIS XV

*Private collection*

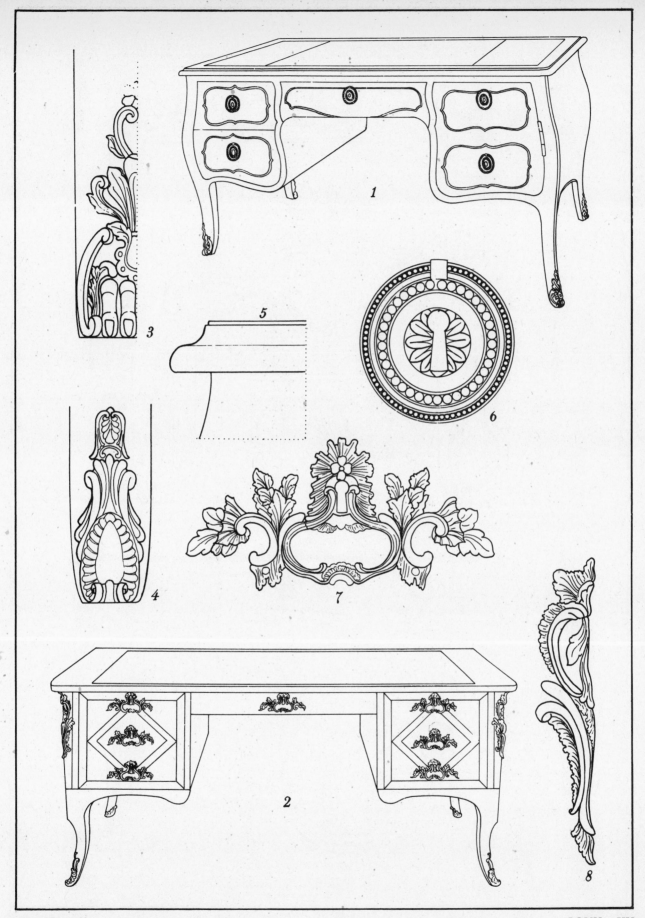

PLATE 161

LOUIS XV

1 and 2. Large writing tables. 3 and 4. Legs. 5. Profile of top. 6. Detail of escutcheon plate. 7. Drawer
pull. 8. Corner decoration.

*Mobilier National de France*

PLATE 162

1 and 2. Writing tables. 3 and 4. Legs. 5 and 6. Drawer pulls. 7. Moulding.

LOUIS XV

*Private collections*

**PLATE 163**

LOUIS XV

1 and 2. Writing tables.   3 and 4. Escutcheon plates on first writing table.   5. Details of upright.   6. Leg.   7.
Upper moulding.   8. Escutcheon plate.

*Private collection and Dutasta collection, Paris*

**PLATE** 164

1. Writing table with three drawers.  2. Tulipwood writing table.  3. Panel moulding.  4. Escutcheon plate.  5 and 6. Profiles.

PLATE 165                                                LOUIS XV
1 and 2. Desk with paper case and writing table.    3 and 4. Drawer pulls.    5. Detail of desk.    6. Leg of writing
table.

*Private collection and Nogent Abbey, Aisne*

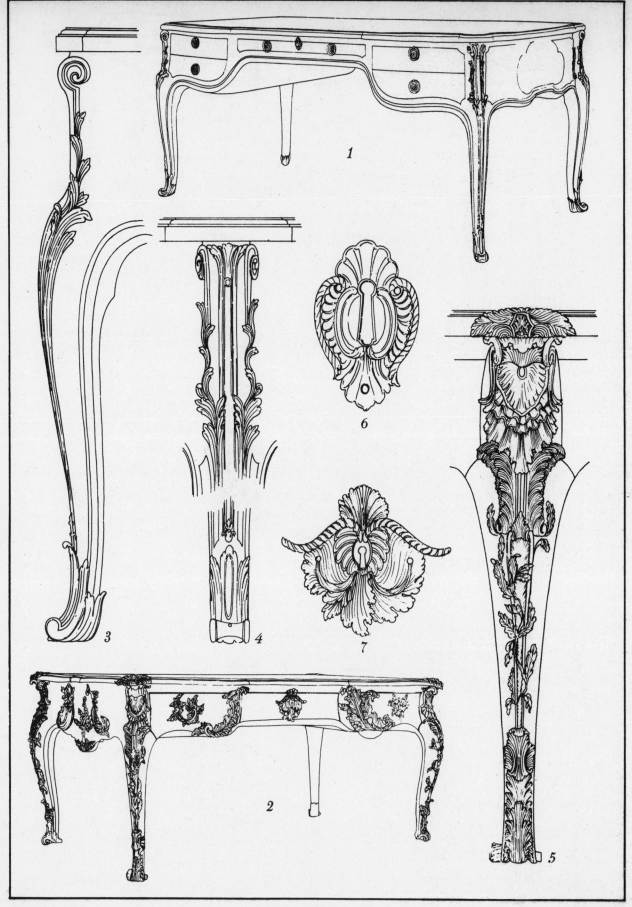

PLATE 166                                                            LOUIS XV

1 and 2. Rosewood writing tables with marquetry and bronze decorations.    3, 4 and 5. Legs.    6 and 7. Escutcheon plates.

*Louvre*

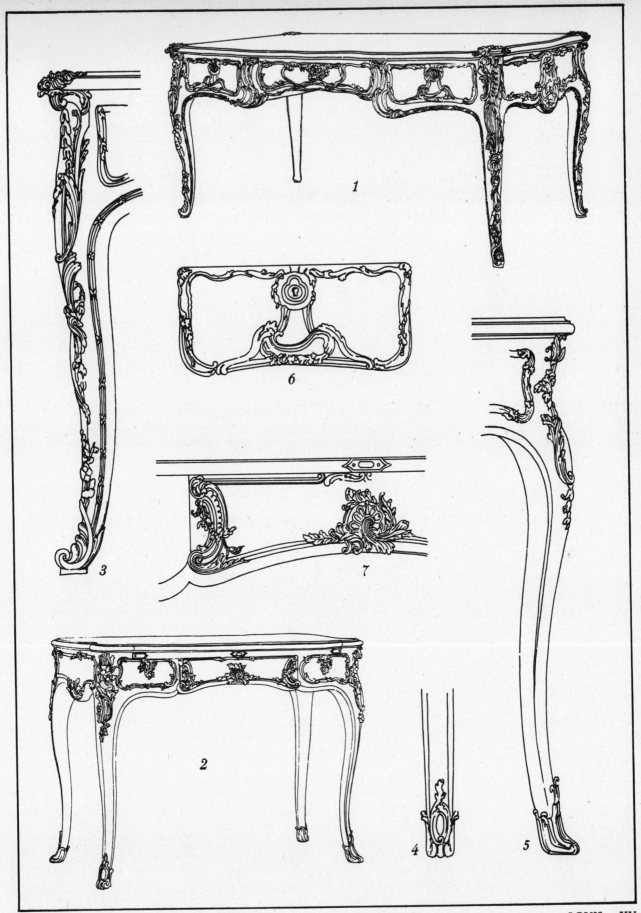

**PLATE** 167

1. Chinese black lacquer desk with gilt bronze.   2. Lady's desk with marquetry and gilt bronze.   3, 4 and 5. Detail of the legs.   6 and 7. Details of drawer fronts.

*Louvre*

**PLATE 168**

1 Desk of King Louis XV. Marquetry by J. F. Oeben and J. H. Riesener. Bronzes by Duplessis, Winant and Hervieux (1760–1769). 2, 3, 4 and 5. Details of legs, upright and drawer fronts.

*Louvre*

**PLATE 169**

LOUIS XV

1. Low commode with a "tomb-shaped" desk on top, with marquetry in a "pebble" frame.   2. Low wood-veneer wardrobe with two doors and a drawer on top.   3 and 4. Bronzes on the uprights and legs.   5 and 6. Lower middle appliqué and escutcheon plate.

*Private collection*

PLATE 170

LOUIS XV

1. Louis XV style commode by Ceffieri.   2. Commode in the grand Regency period by Charles Cressent.   3 and 4. Details of the legs.

*South-Kensington Museum, London and Richard Wallace collection, London*

PLATE 171

1 and 2. Commodes with marquetry decorated with gilt bronzes. The second commode by Charles Cressent. 3 and 4. Legs. 5 and 6. Detail of drawer fronts.

*Louvre*

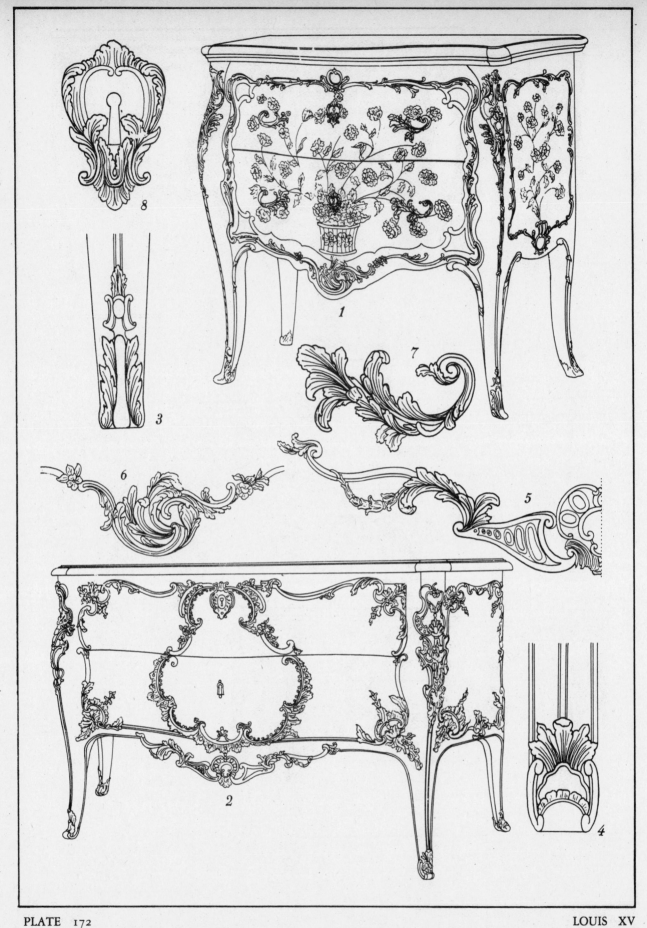

PLATE 172 LOUIS XV

1. Commode with two drawers and marquetry with flower design, forming panels framed by bronzes.   2. Commode with two drawers with antique lacquers by Coromandel. Both commodes have bronzes.   3 and 4. Details of the legs.   5 and 6. Bronze appliqués on the apron.   7 and 8. Details of drawer pull and escutcheon plate.

PLATE 173

1. Wood-veneer commode with two drawers and bordered by decorative lines.  2. Commode with two drawers and marquetry in flower designs.  3, 4, 5 and 6. Details of uprights and legs.  7, 8 and 9. Drawer pulls and escutcheon plate.

*Hodgkins collection and private collection*

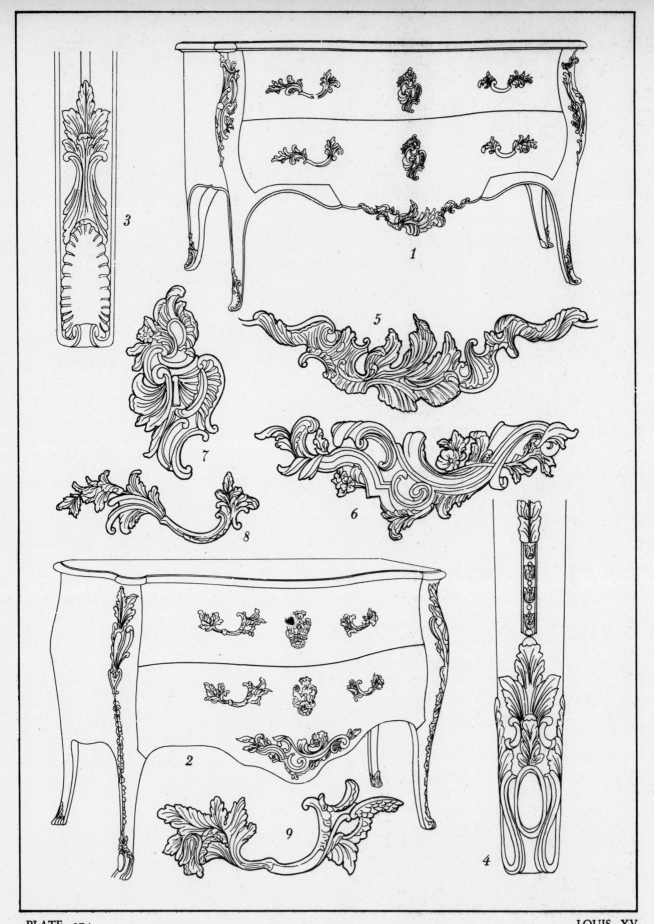

PLATE 174

1 and 2. Commodes with two drawers. The lower drawer of the first commode has a middle apron. The marquetry, in floral and leaf design, is in stark contrast. The second commode has gilt carved bronzes.   3 and 4. Details of the legs.   5 and 6. Sketches of the aprons.   7, 8 and 9. Escutcheon plate and drawer pulls.

*Private collections*

PLATE 175                                                                LOUIS XV

1 and 2. Commodes with curved profiles, with two drawers and marquetry in floral design and gilt carved bronzes. 3. Bronze on the upright. 4 and 5. Bronze appliqués on the apron. 6 and 7. Escutcheon plate and drawer pull. 8. Detail of the leg.

*Private collections*

PLATE 176

LOUIS XV

1. "Harant" style commode with curved profile, long legs and marquetry in quadrille shape, surrounding a medallion. 2.
Commode similar in shape to the first one, with marquetry in flower designs. Both commodes have carved gilt bronzes. 3
and 4. Bronze motifs on uprights. 5. Drawer pull.

*Poles collection*

**PLATE** 177

1 and 2. Commodes with curved shape and long legs, with lacquer and carved gilt bronzes.   3, 4, 5 and 6. Details of uprights.   7 and 8. Drawer pull and escutcheon plate.

*Private collections*

PLATE 178                                                          LOUIS XV

1. Commode with two drawers, marquetry of flowers and leaves. The lower apron is part of the lower drawer.    2. Wood-
veneer commode from the mid-18th century, framed with colored decorative lines. Both commodes have carved gilt
bronzes.    3. Detail of the upright.    4 and 5. Escutcheon plate.

*Private collection and Dutasta collection*

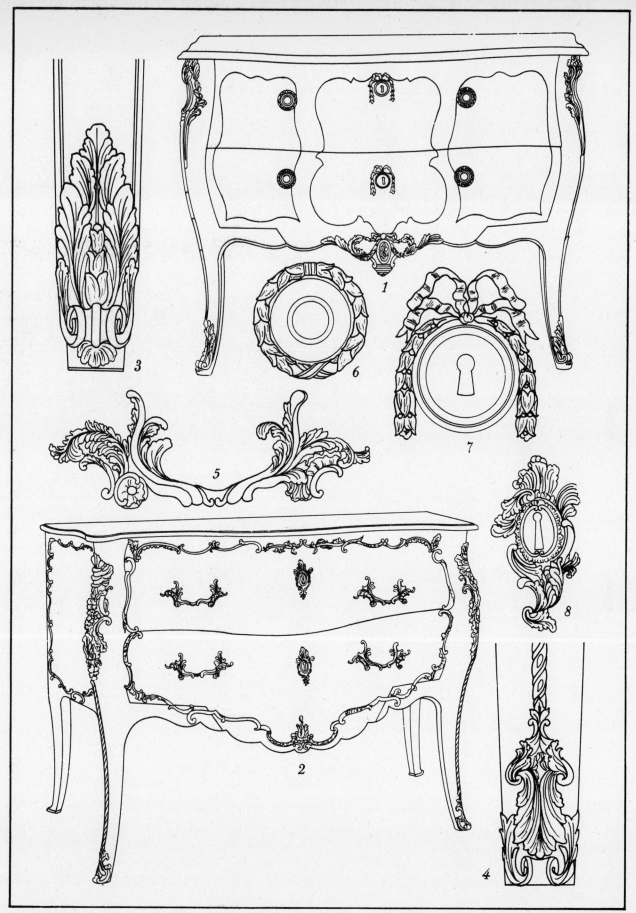

**PLATE** 179           LOUIS XV (third quarter of the 18th century)
1. Commode from the end of the style, with two drawers, the lower one with an apron.    2. Commode with two drawers, the lower one with an apron. Both commodes have marquetry of flowers and leaves and gilt carved bronzes.    3 and 4. Details of legs.    5, 6, 7 and 8. Escutcheon plates and drawer pull.

      *Private collection and Altona-Colonna collection*

**PLATE 180**　　　　　　　　　　　　　　　　LOUIS XV (second half of 18th century)

1. Wood-veneer commode from end of period, with console legs, four doors and three drawers at top.　2. Large commode in shape of low wardrobe, console legs, with two drawers.　3 and 4. Legs.　5 and 6. Detail of the middle bronze appliqués.　7 and 8. Escutcheon plates.

　　　　　　　　　　　*Collection from Fleury-en-Bière Castle*

PLATE 181

LOUIS XV (towards end of period)

1. Small commode with two drawers and marquetry in form of superimposed dados.    2. Small commode with two drawers with marquetry in the corners and frieze of intertwining lines.    3, 4 and 5. Bronzes on uprights and legs.    6 and 7. Details of the lower middle bronze appliqués.    8 and 9. Escutcheon plate and drawer pull.

PLATE 182 LOUIS XV (late period)

1 and 2. Small commodes with long console legs and two drawers. Upper commode has marquetry and lower one has wood-veneer central panels.  3, 4 and 5. Bronze appliqués on uprights and legs.  6, 7 and 8. Escutcheon plates and drawer pulls.

*Private collection and Darthy collection*

**PLATE 183**

LOUIS XV (towards end of period)

1. Commode with three wood-veneer drawers. 2. Commode with two drawers and multi-colored marquetry in diamond shapes. 3 and 4. Details of bronze appliqués. 5. Detail of leg. 6. Detail of top of upright. 7, 8, 9 and 10. Drawer pulls and escutcheon plate.

*Beuret and Ganay collection*

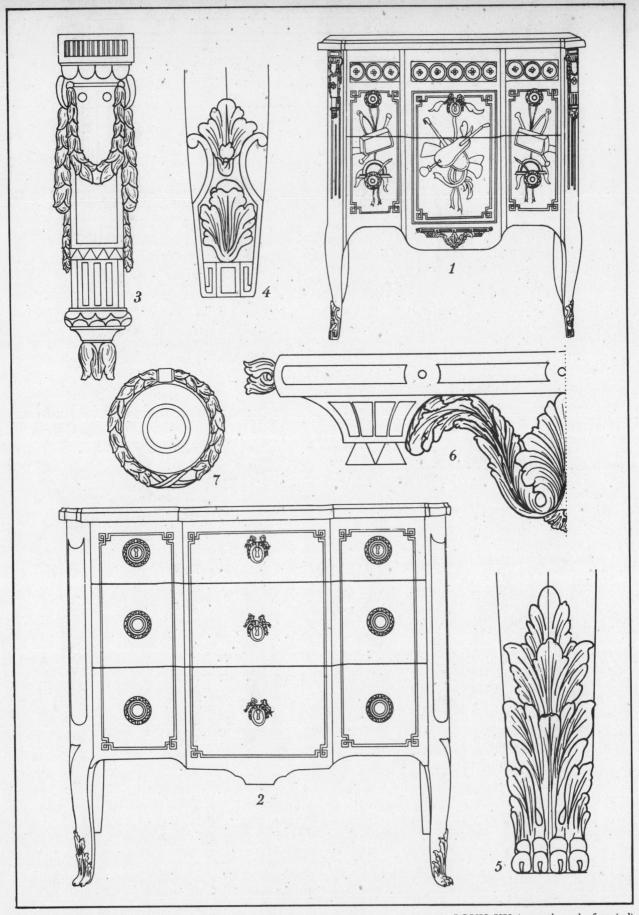

**PLATE 184**  LOUIS XV (towards end of period)

1. Small commode with two drawers with marquetry.  2. Wood-veneer commode with three drawers.  3, 4 and 5.
Detail of bronzes on uprights and legs.  6. Middle lower bronze.  7. Drawer pull.

*Private collections*

PLATE 185

1. Wood-veneer commode with three drawers.  2. Commode with two drawers, decorated with squares of marquetry.  3, 4 and 5. Bronzes on legs and upright.  6 and 7. Details of the middle appliqués.  8 and 9. Drawer pull and escutcheon plate.

PLATE 186

1. Small console table with trapezoidal base, with two drawers in front of two side doors.   2. Small Louis XVI style commode.   3 and 4. Bronze on the upright.   5 and 6. Drawer pull and escutcheon plate.

*Bardac collection and private collection*

PLATE 187

LOUIS XV

1. Sideboard.   2. Wardrobe with two doors and marquetry.   3. Detail of bronze on sideboard.   4 and 5. Door handle and bronze escutcheon plate on wardrobe.   6. Detail of the mouldings and leg.

*Louvre and private collection*

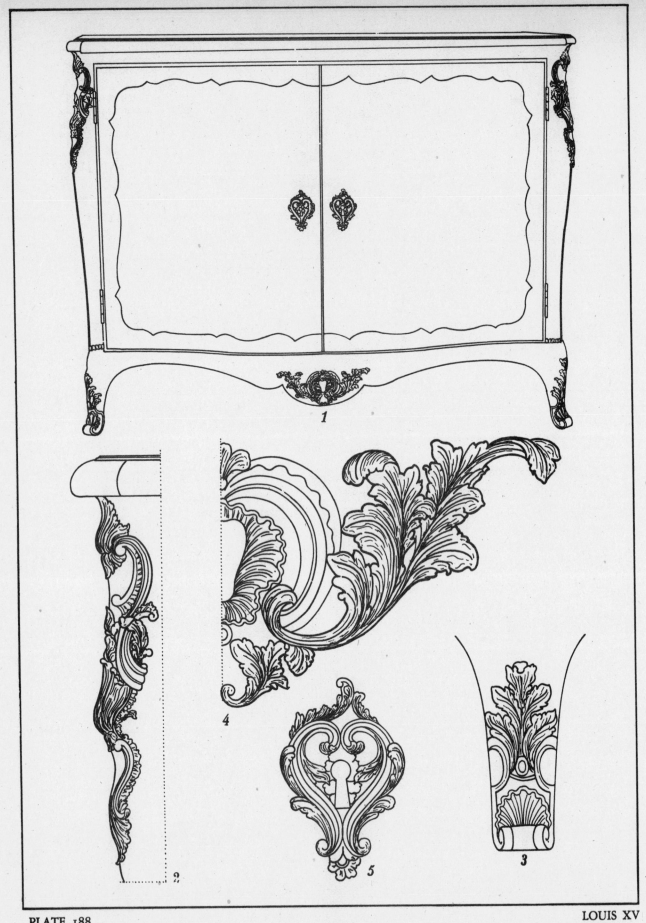

**PLATE 188**

LOUIS XV

1. Entredeux, a console placed between two windows or openings. 2 and 3. Details of bronzes on upright and leg. 4 and 5. Central bronze decoration and escutcheon plate.

*Private collection*

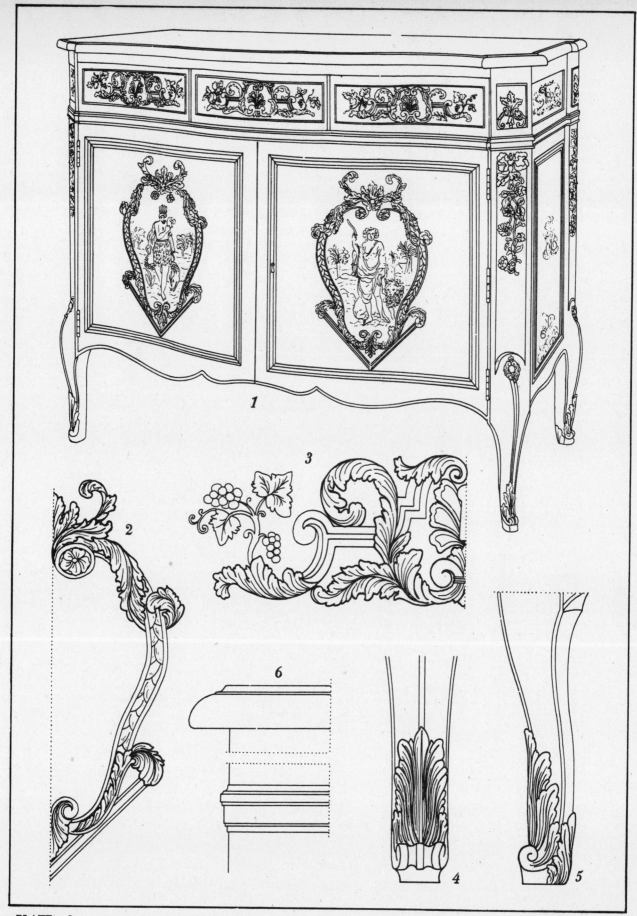

PLATE 189                                               LOUIS XV (towards end of period)
1. Wood-veneer entredeux with three drawers and bronze decorations  2. Detail of middle bronze.  3. Sketch of the
bronze frieze.  4 and 5. Leg.  6. Mouldings.

*Poles collection*

PLATE 190

LOUIS XV (towards end of period)

1 and 2. Secretary and sideboard ("high support"). 3, 4 and 5. Details of the uprights and legs. 6 and 7. Escutcheon plate and door handle.

*Louvre*

1. Wood-veneer wardrobe.   2. Library cabinet.   3, 4 and 5. Details of bronze from wardrobe.   6 and 7. Bronze door handle and decoration.

*Dutasta and Poles collection, Paris*

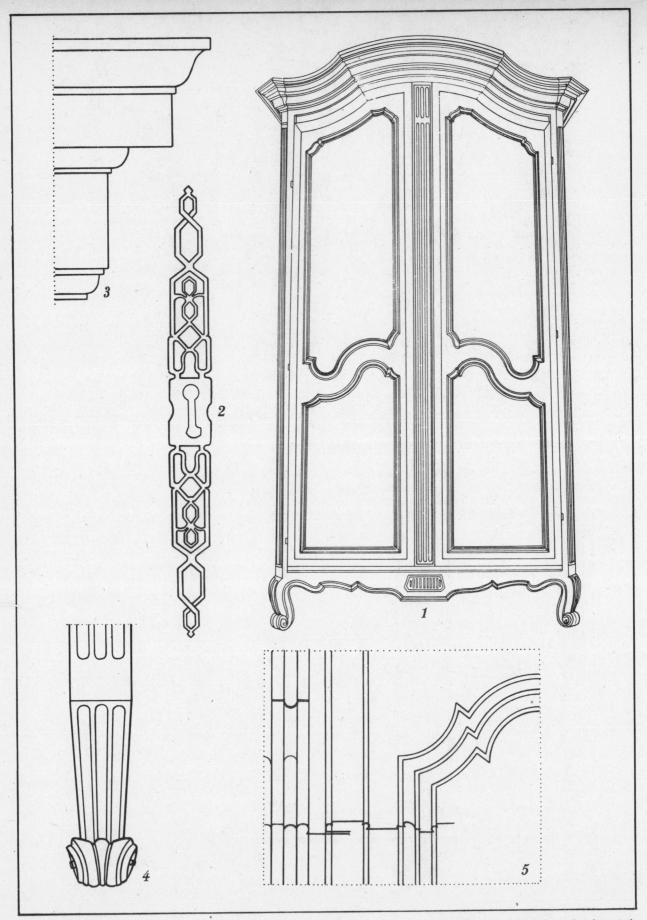

PLATE 192

LOUIS XV (towards end of period)

1. Large mahogany wardrobe from the southwest of France. Fluting on uprights, the sloping corners and the sharpness of cornice mouldings and in the style of Louis XVI.   2. Detail of escutcheon plate.   3. Cornice.   4. Leg.   5. Mouldings.

*Private collection*

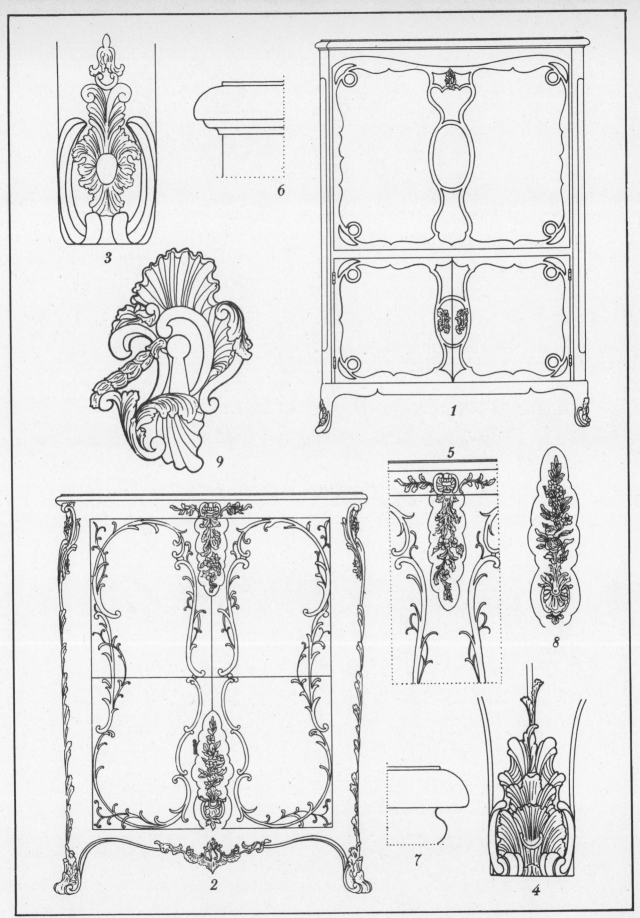

PLATE 193

LOUIS XV (towards end of period)

1 and 2. Secretaries: the decorative lines are of marquetry, the rest, covered with bronze. 3, 4 and 5. Details of legs and upright. 6 and 7. Profiles of tops. 8. Bronze design. 9. Escutcheon plate.

*Private collections*

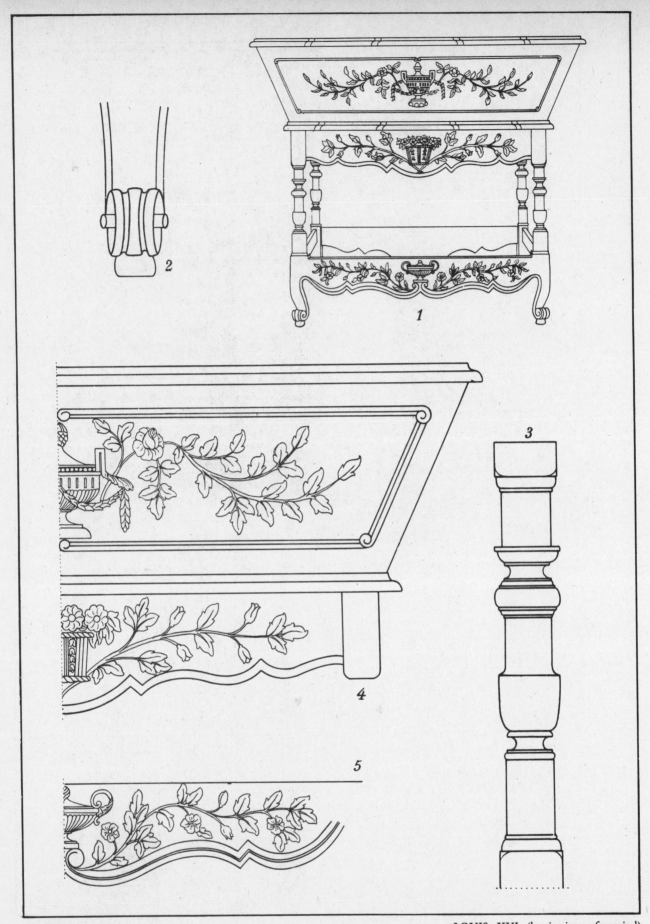

PLATE 194                                                                    LOUIS XVI (beginning of period)
1. Walnut trough from Arles, the shape is in the style of Louis XV, and the motifs in Louis XVI.   2. Leg.   3. Turned
post.   4 and 5. Details of the work.

*Private collection*

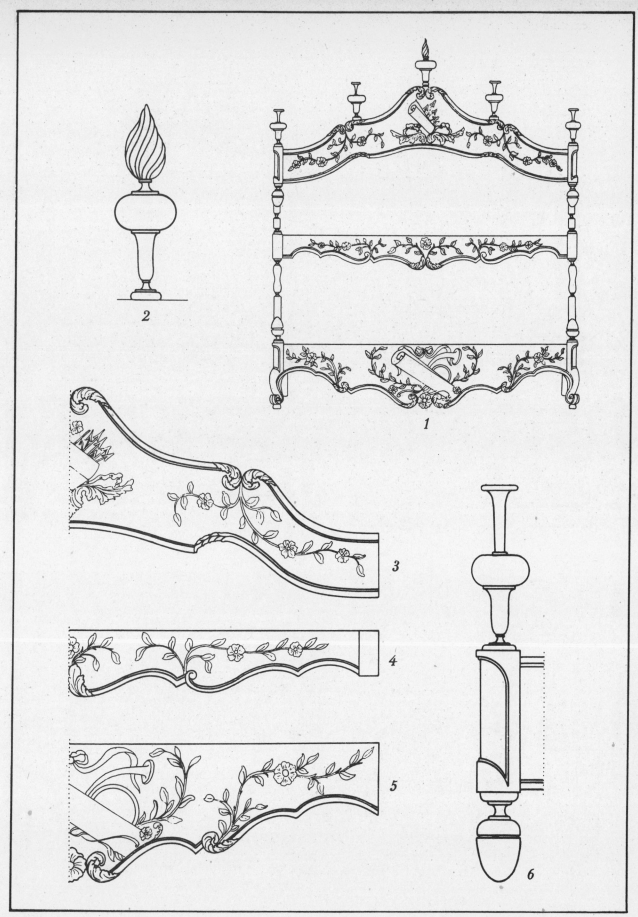

PLATE 195                                                                    LOUIS XVI (beginning of period)

1. Walnut bookcase from Arles. Shape is Louis XV and motifs are Louis XVI.   2. Finial.   3, 4 and 5. Details of the
front.   6. Turned post.

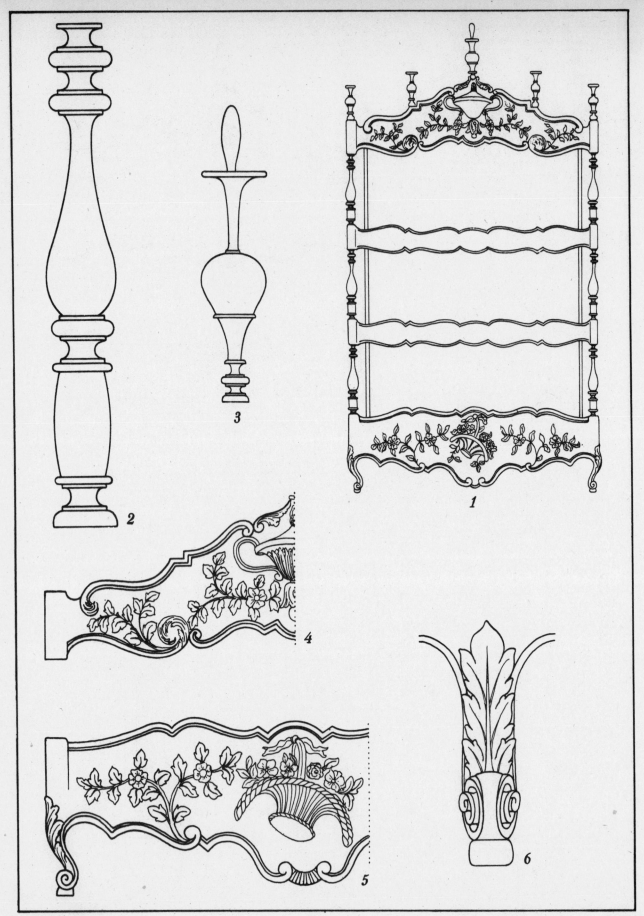

PLATE 196                                              LOUIS XVI (beginning of period)

1. Walnut bookcase from Provence. Shape is Louis XV and motifs are Louis XVI.    2 and 3. Finial and turned posts.    4
and 5. Crest and front.    6. Leg.

*Private collection*

PLATE 197 LOUIS XVI (beginning of period)

1. Small rosewood wardrobe, wood grain on bias, contoured with decorative line. Shape is Louis XVI style.   2. Another bias rosewood wardrobe with repetitive panels.   3, 4 and 5. Detail of the bronzes.   6 and 7. Escutcheon plates.

*Private collections*

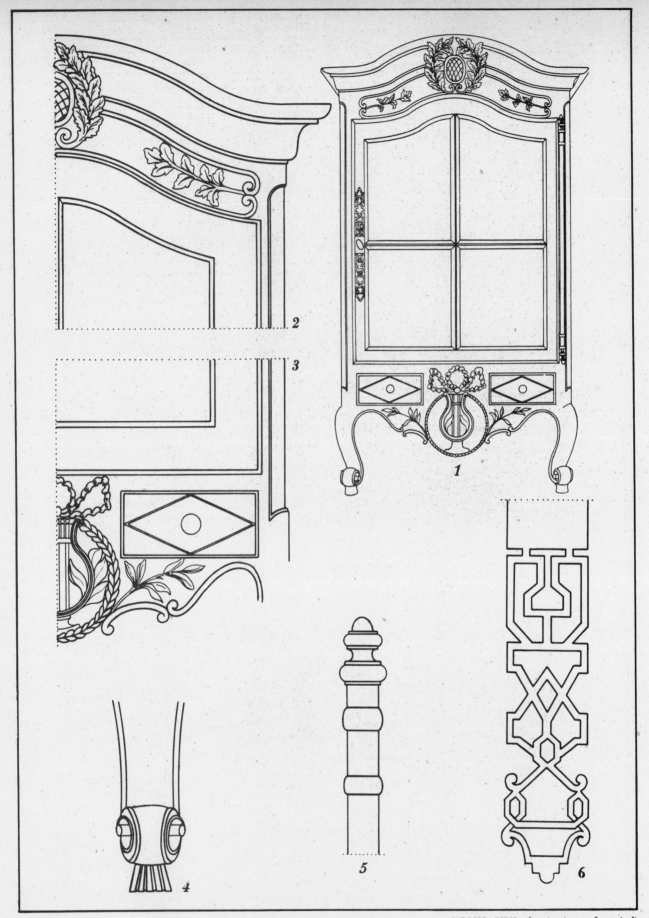

PLATE 198

LOUIS XVI (beginning of period)

1. Small walnut showcase from Provence. Shape is Louis XV and motifs are Louis XVI.   2 and 3. Upper and lower details.   4. Leg.   5. Turned post of upright.   6. Escutcheon plate decoration.

*Private collection*

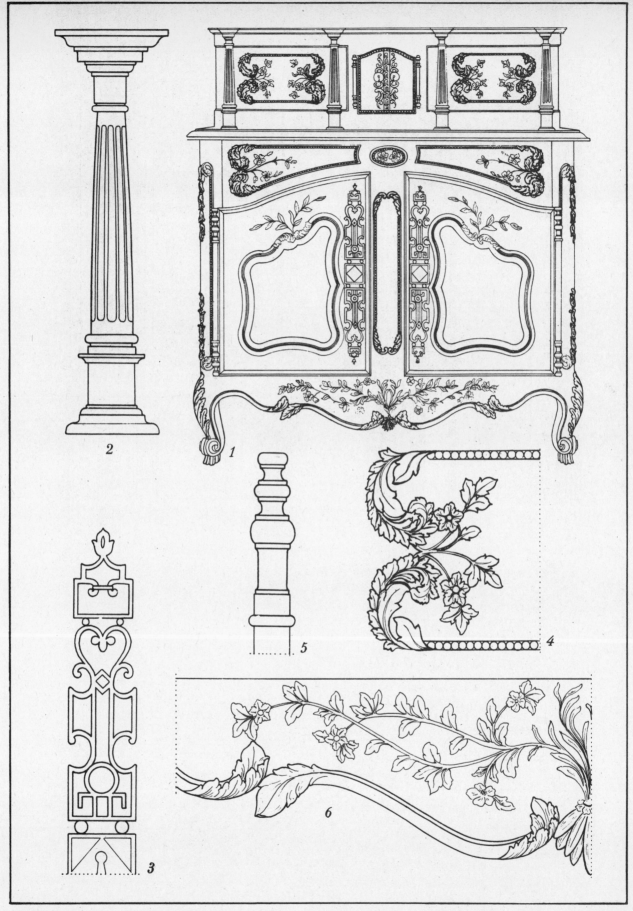

**PLATE 199**                                   LOUIS XVI (beginning of period)

1. Walnut sideboard from Arles. Shape is Louis XV and motifs are Louis XVI.   2. Detail of pilaster.   3. Escutcheon plate.   4. Relief at top.   5. Turned post for the position of the hinges.   6. Detail of bottom.

*Private collection*

**PLATE 200**

1. Large semicircular wardrobe from la Gironde. The shape of the panels, the lower crosspiece and the feet are in the style of Louis XV, the motifs are Louis XVI. 2. Escutcheon plate. 3. Cornice. 4. Detail of bottom.

*Private collection*

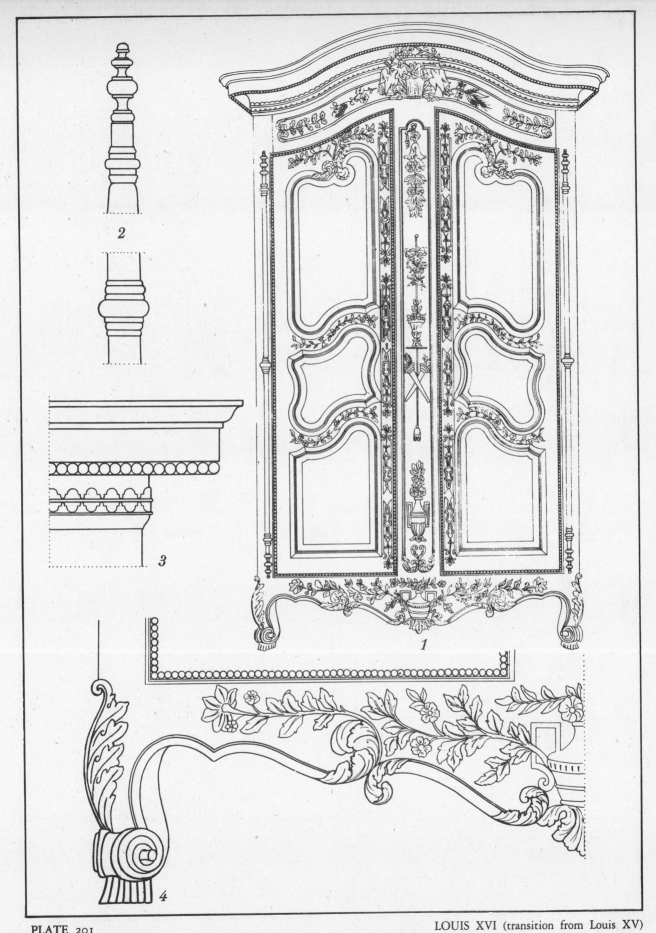

**PLATE 201**

LOUIS XVI (transition from Louis XV)

1. Walnut Provençal wardrobe. The structural lines and the lines of panels are in the style of Louis XV, the decorative motifs in that of Louis XVI.   2. Details of the upright.   3. Cornice.   4. Leg and lower detail.

*Private collection*

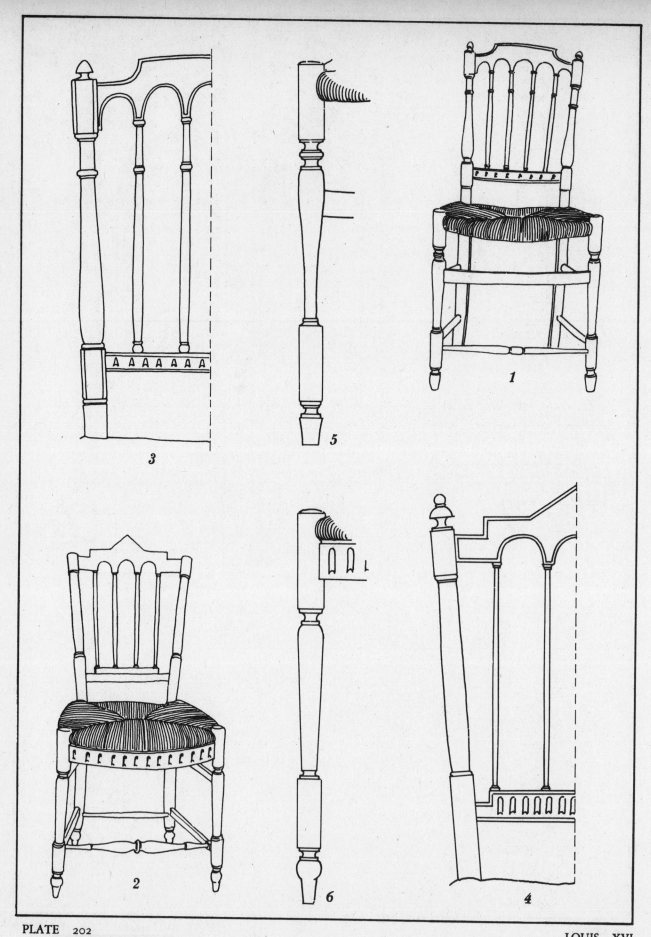

PLATE 202

1 and 2. Chairs with reed seats and backs of thin columns.   3 and 4. Backs.   5 and 6. Legs.

LOUIS   XVI

*Private collection*

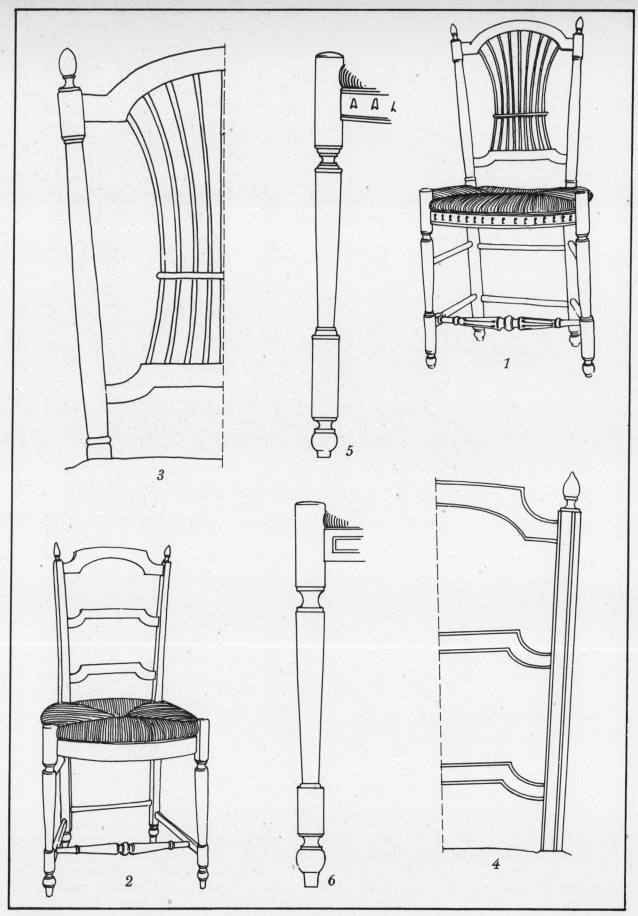

PLATE 203                                                              LOUIS XVI

1 and 2. Chairs with reed seats and fan-shaped backs with horizontal crosspieces curved at the ends.    3 and 4. Backs.    5 and 6. Legs.

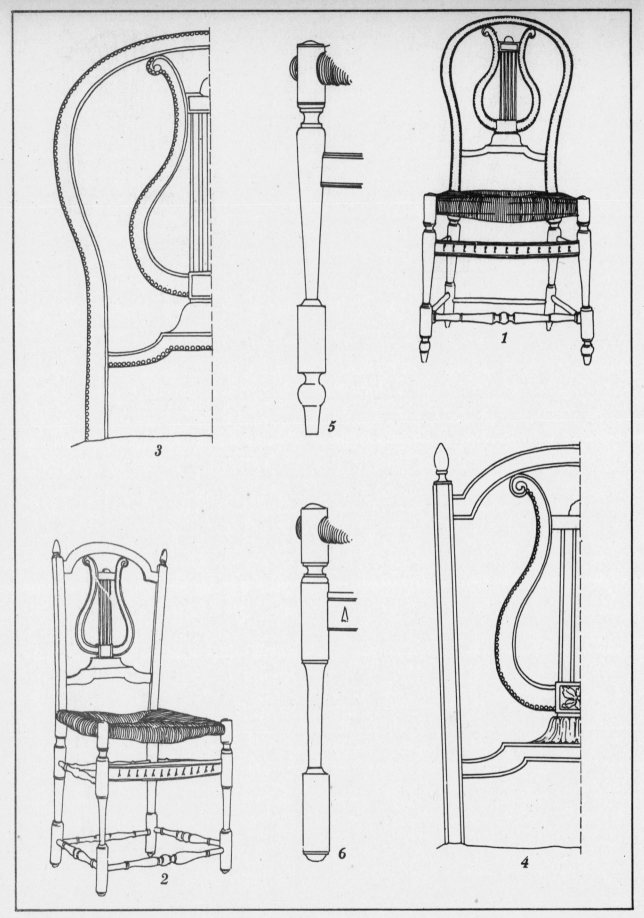

PLATE 204

LOUIS XVI

1 and 2. Chairs with reed seats and lyre motifs. The first chair has a "globe-shaped" back. 3 and 4. Backs. 5 and 6. Legs.

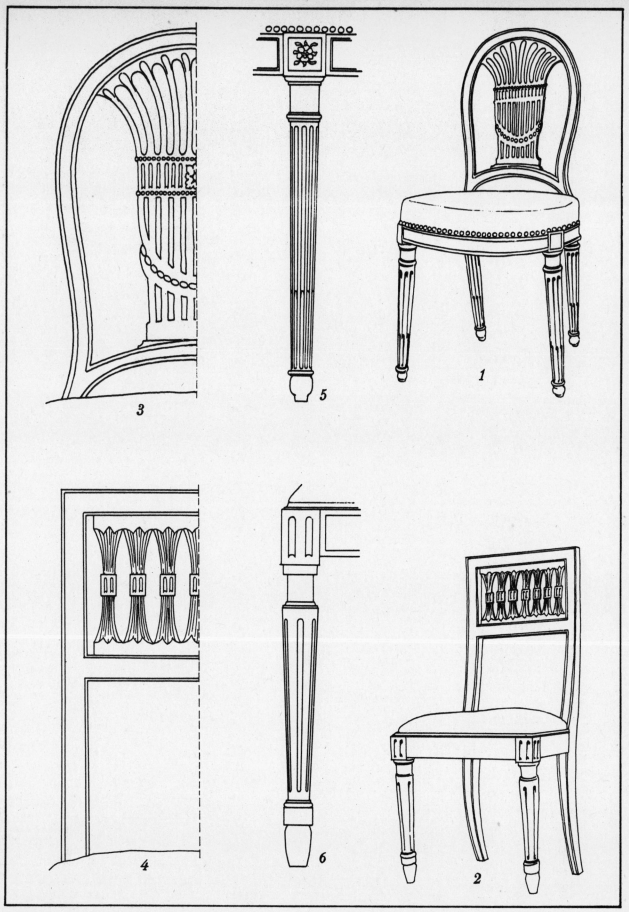

PLATE 205                                                                                              LOUIS XVI

1 and 2. Dining-room chairs. Back of second chair is in form of basket.    3 and 4. Backs.    5 and 6. Legs.

*Private collection*

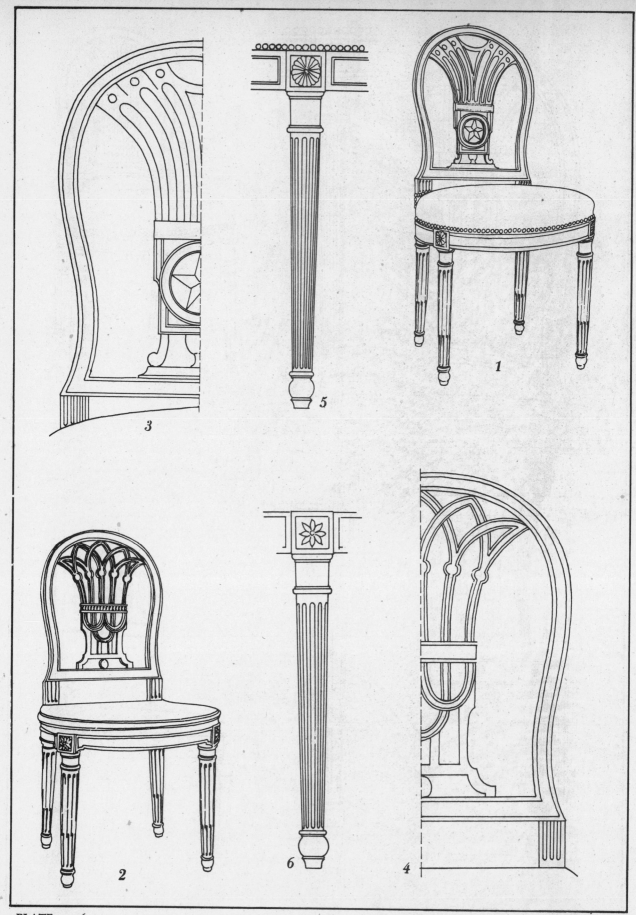

PLATE 206

LOUIS XVI

1 and 2. Dining-room chairs whose backs have central design in shape of fans or baskets.  3 and 4. Backs.  5 and
6. Legs.

*Private collection*

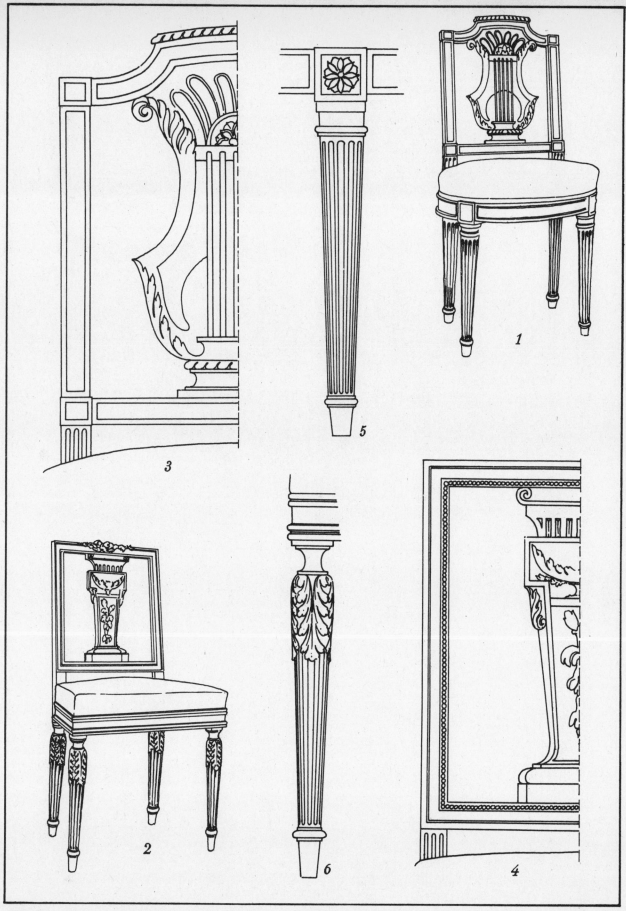

PLATE 207

LOUIS XVI

1 and 2. Gilt wooden chairs with lyre- and baluster-shaped backs.   3 and 4. Detail of the backs.   5 and 6. Legs.

*Private collection*

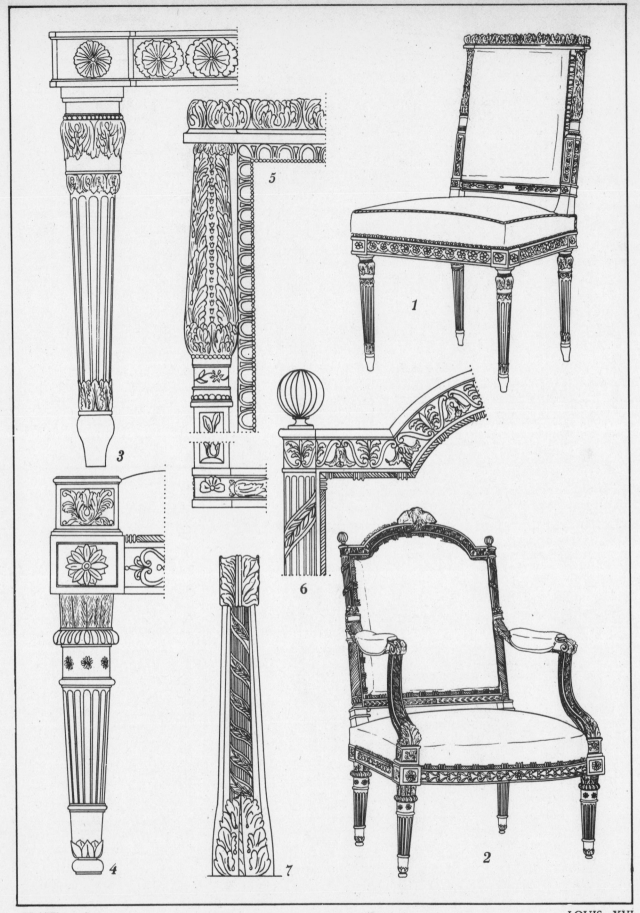

PLATE 208 LOUIS XVI

1 and 2. Gilt carved wooden chair and armchair. Chair is covered with Beauvais tapestry and armchair with silk.  3 and 4. Detail of legs.  5 and 6. Details of uprights of backs.  7. Detail of arm of armchair.

*Louvre*

**PLATE** 209

1 and 2. Carved wooden chair and armchair, both covered with silk. Chair is painted by Dupain and armchair is gilt (Haure, Sene and Vallois).    3 and 4. Detail of legs.    5 and 6. Detail of backs.    7. End of arm.

*Louvre*

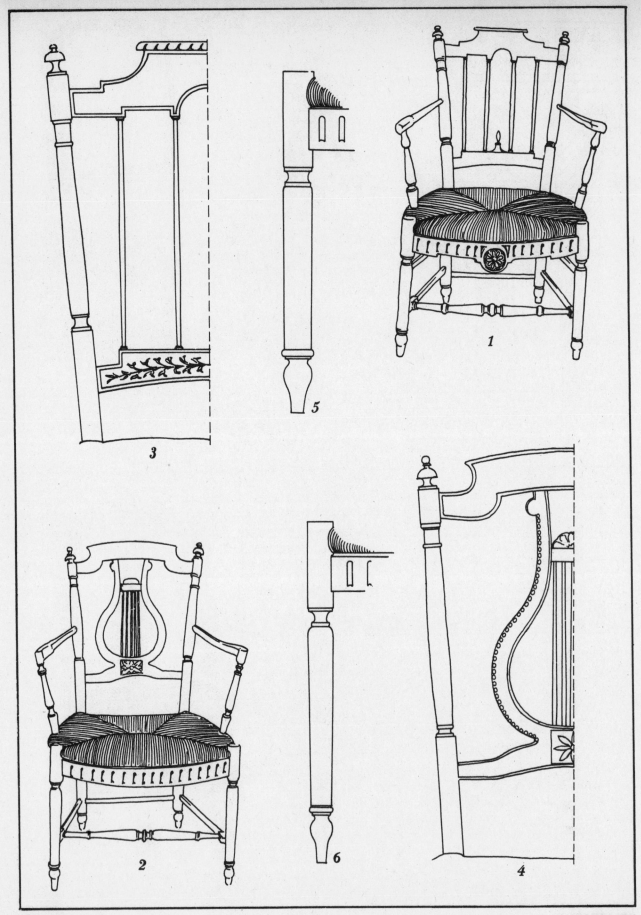

PLATE 210

LOUIS XVI

1 and 2. Armchairs with reed seats and backs with thin columns and lyre motif.   3 and 4. Backs.   5 and 6. Legs.

*Private collection*

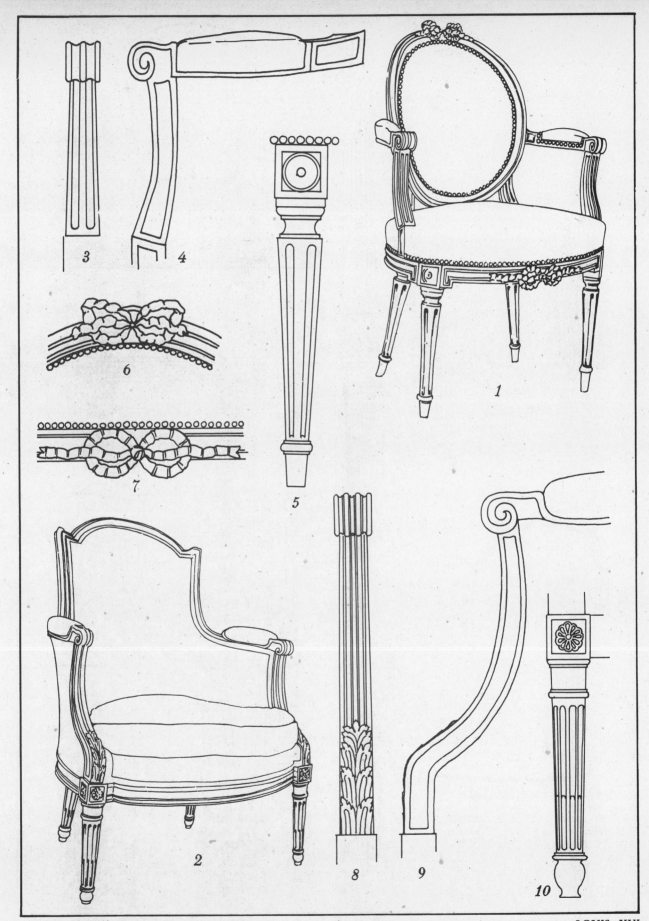

**PLATE 211**

1 and 2. "Carriage" armchair and wingchair.   3, 4 and 5. Details of arm and leg.   6 and 7. Sketches of decorations.   8, 9 and 10. Arm and leg of second chair.

*Private collections*

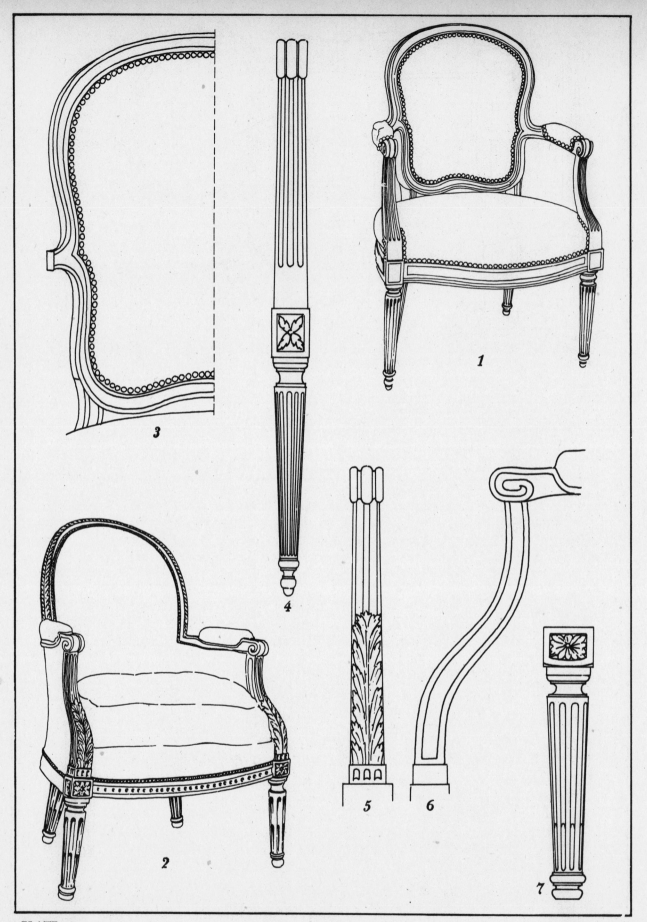

PLATE 212

1 and 2. "Carriage" armchair and wingchair. The first one has a "violin" back. The second is of painted wood.  3 and
4. Back and front upright of first chair.  5, 6 and 7. Details of arm and leg of second chair.

*Private collection*

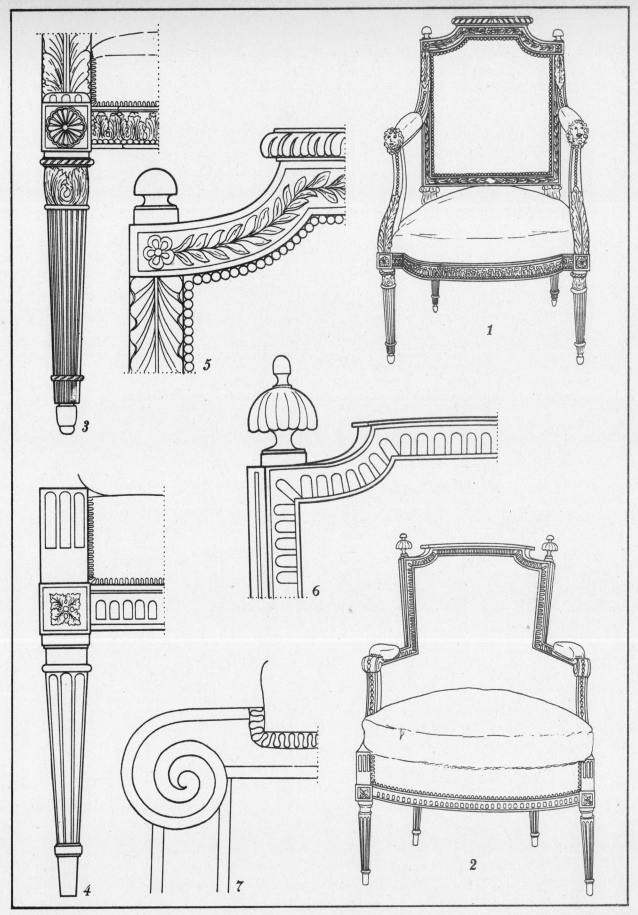

**PLATE** 213

1 and 2. Armchairs, the second one of painted wood.   3 and 4. Legs.   5 and 6. Backs.   7. Arm.

LOUIS XVI

*Private collections*

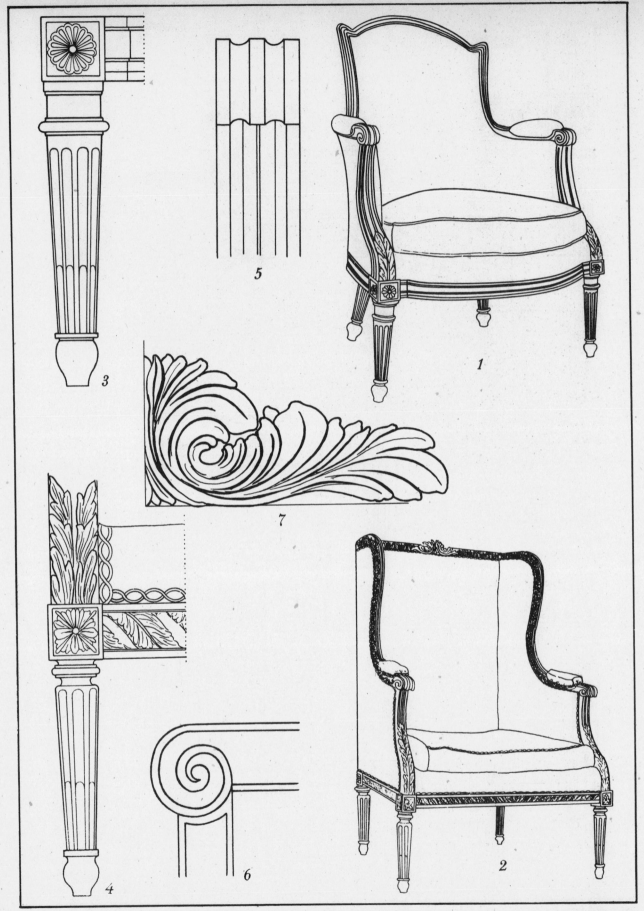

PLATE 214          LOUIS XVI

1 and 2. Walnut wing chairs with velvet from Utrecht. The second one, "confessional" style, has raised back and painted wood.    3 and 4. Legs.    5 and 6. Detail of arm.    7. Detail of crest on back.

*Private collections*

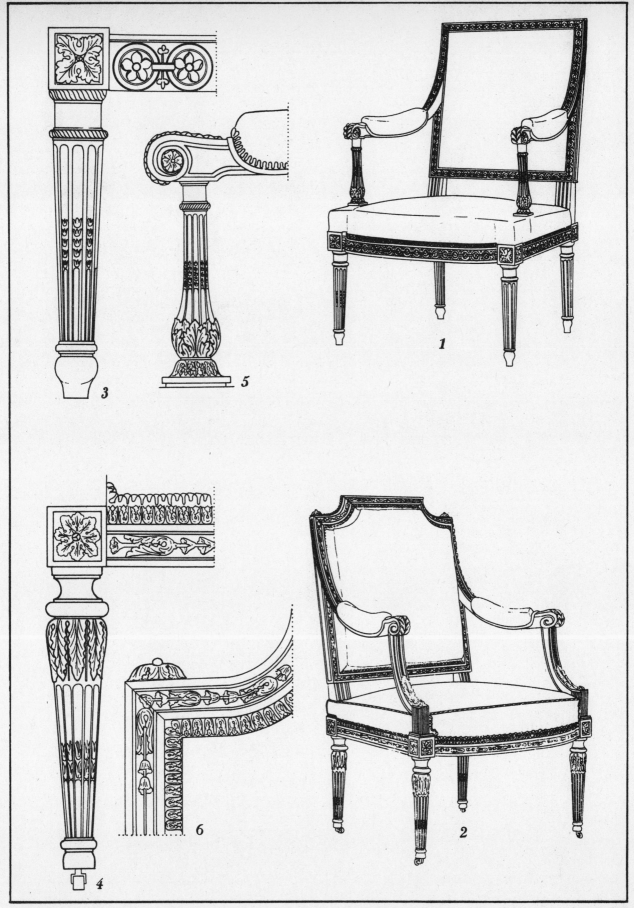

**PLATE 215**                                                                                    LOUIS XVI

1 and 2. Carved wooden armchairs by G. Jacob. The upper one is painted and covered in silk. The lower one is gilt and covered with Beauvais tapestry.   3 and 4. Legs.   5. Arm support.   6. Back moulding.

*Louvre*

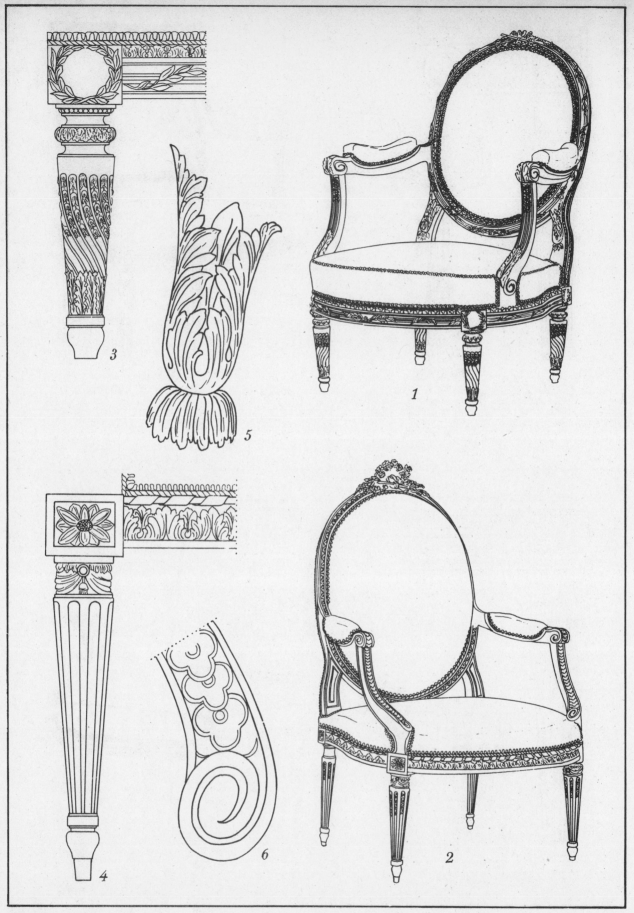

PLATE 216                                                              LOUIS XVI

1 and 2. Carved wooden armchairs by J. Nadal L'Aine and Ph. Poirie (around 1760), covered with Beauvais tapestry. The lower chair is gilt.   3 and 4. Detail of legs.   5 and 6. Details of arm support and back.

*Louvre*

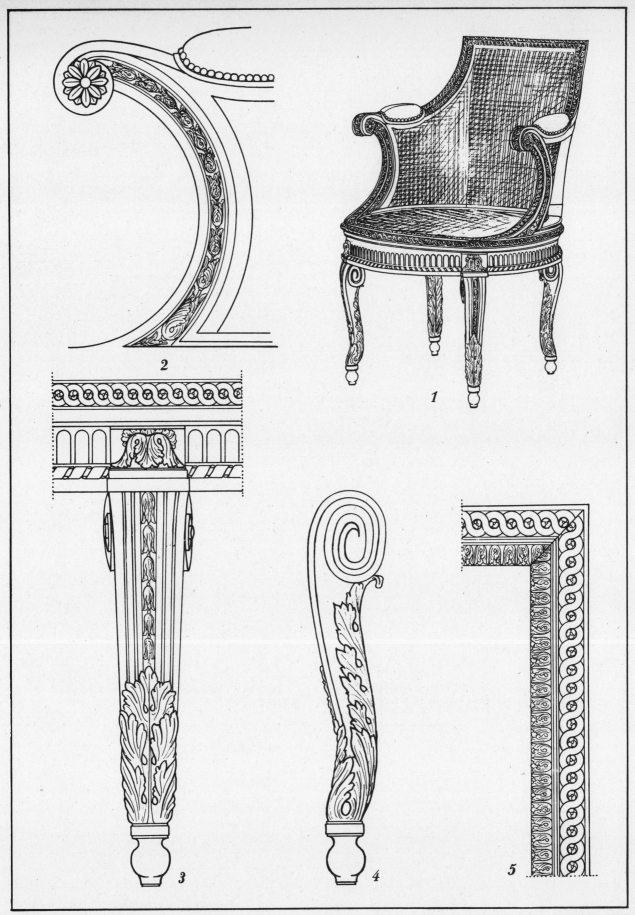

**PLATE 217**

1. Desk chair made of gilt carved wood and cane, by G. Jacob. 2. Detail of arm support. 3 and 4. Front and side views of leg. 5. Detail of moulding.

*Louvre*

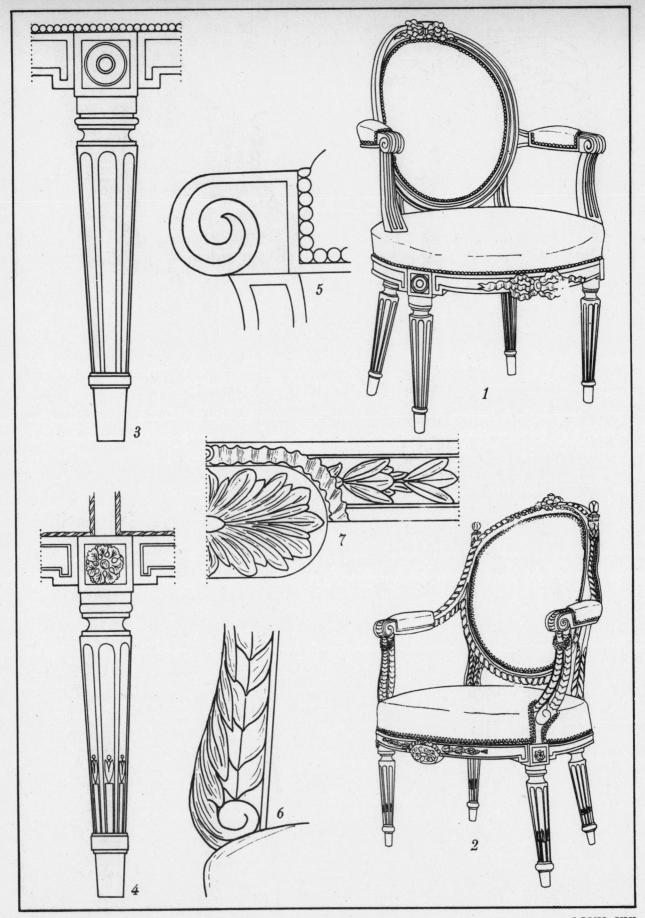

PLATE 218

LOUIS XVI

1 and 2. "Carriage" armchairs with medallion backs. The first chair is of walnut, the second of gilt wood.   3 and 4. Legs.   5 and 6. Arm support.   7. Decoration.

*Private collections*

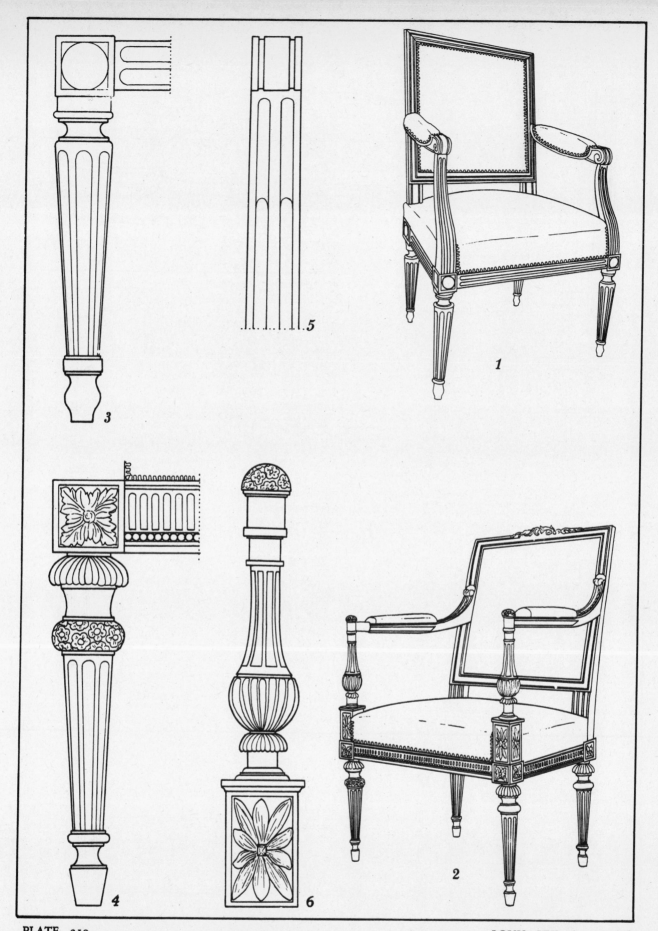

**PLATE 219**                                                          LOUIS XVI (late period)

1 and 2. Armchairs with square backs. The first chair is of walnut, the second of gilt wood.   3 and 4. Legs.   5. Arm support.   6. Arm support in the form of baluster.

*Private collection*

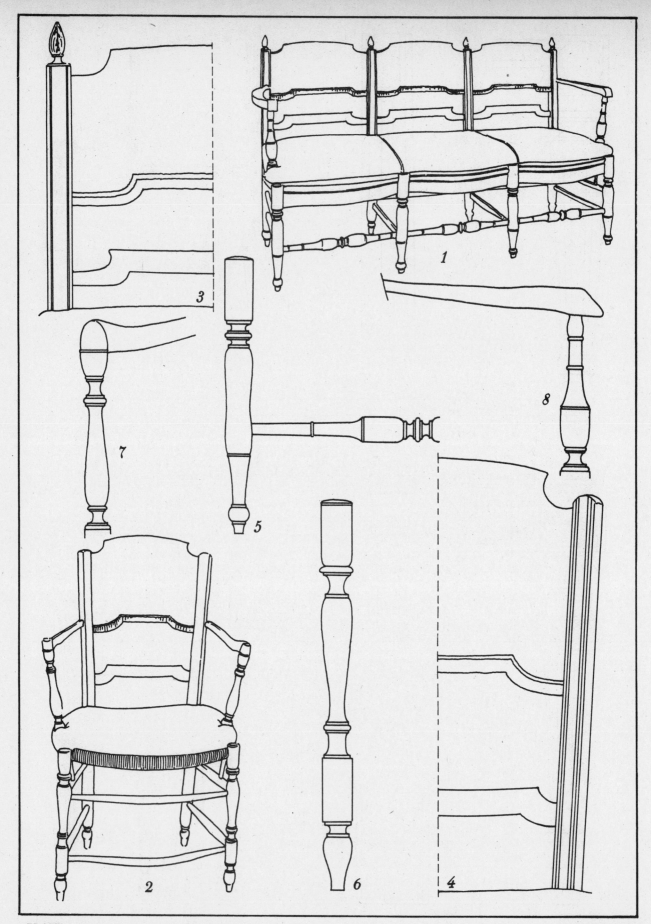

**PLATE** 220                                                       LOUIS XVI

1 and 2. Provençal sofa and armchair with straw seat, covered with cushions.   3 and 4. Backs.   5 and 6. Legs.   7 and 8. Arm supports.

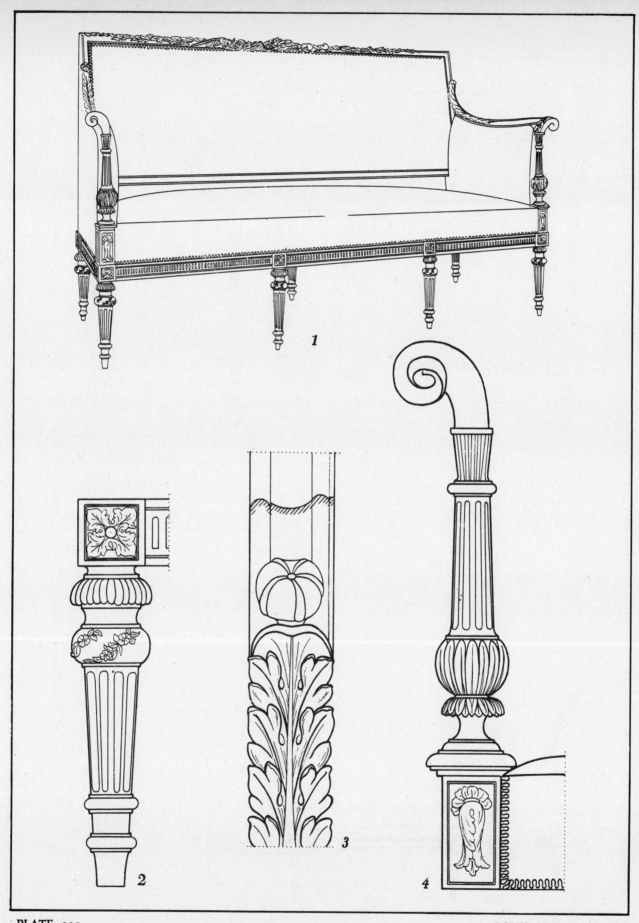

PLATE 221                                                    LOUIS XVI (late period)

1. Sofa.   2. Leg.   3. Detail of arm.   4. Detail of end of arm support.

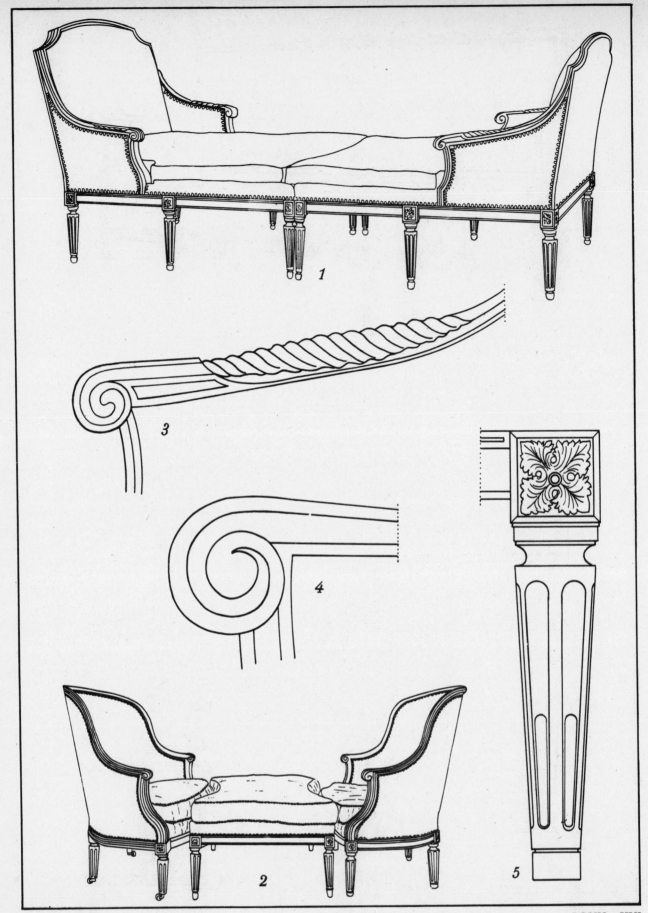

PLATE 222

1 and 2. Chaise longues: sectional furniture for reclining. The first one has two identical sections, the second one has three sections.   3 and 4. Detail of the arms.   5. Leg.

*Private collections*

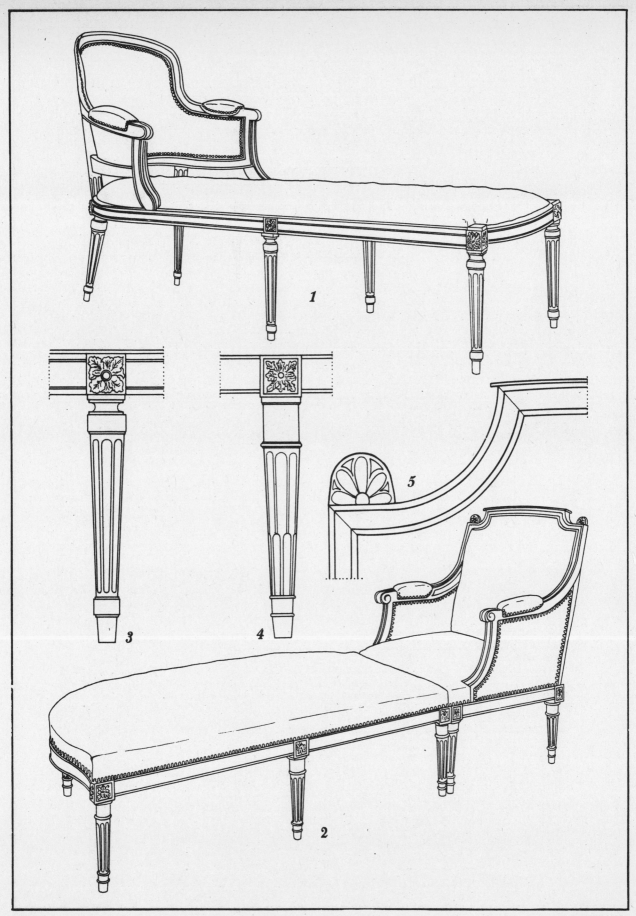

PLATE 223            LOUIS XVI

1 and 2. Chaise longues. The first one is called a "gondola," the second one has two sections.   3 and 4. Legs.   5. Back.

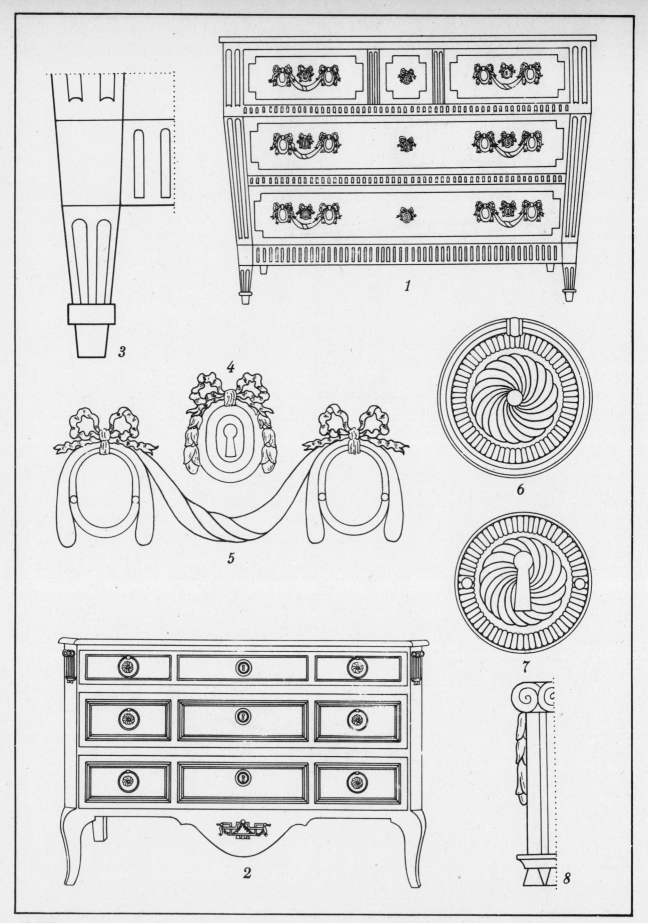

PLATE 224

LOUIS XVI (transition from Louis XV period)

1 and 2. Commodes. The first one, rustic style (from the southwest of France), is of walnut, the second one is of Brazilian rosewood and lemon. 3. Leg. 4, 5, 6 and 7. Escutcheon plates and drawer pulls. 8. Detail of decoration on upright.

PLATE 225

LOUIS XVI (early period)

1, 2 and 3. Commodes with diverse characteristics within the style. The first one has some characteristics of Louis XV style; the second has escutcheon plates showing foreign influence; the third has curved legs, a transition from Louis XV. 4, 5, 6, 7 and 8. Escutcheon plates and drawer pulls.

*Private collections*

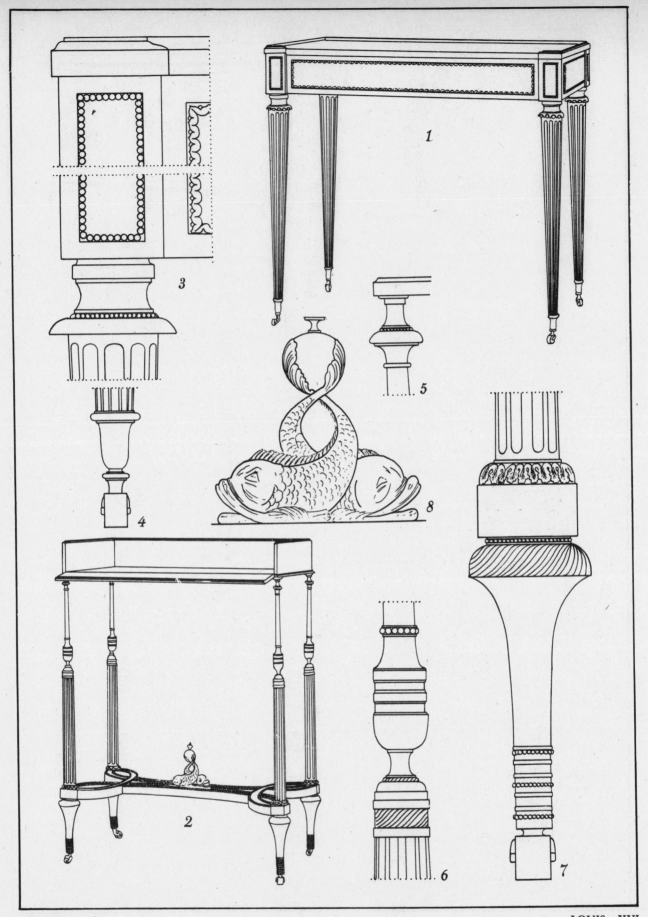

PLATE 226 LOUIS XVI

1. Mahogany lady's desk.   2. Mahogany sewing desk. The two gilt bronzes are by J. H. Riesener.   3 and 4. Leg and foot.   5, 6 and 7. Details of leg.   8. Bronze dolphins.

*Louvre*

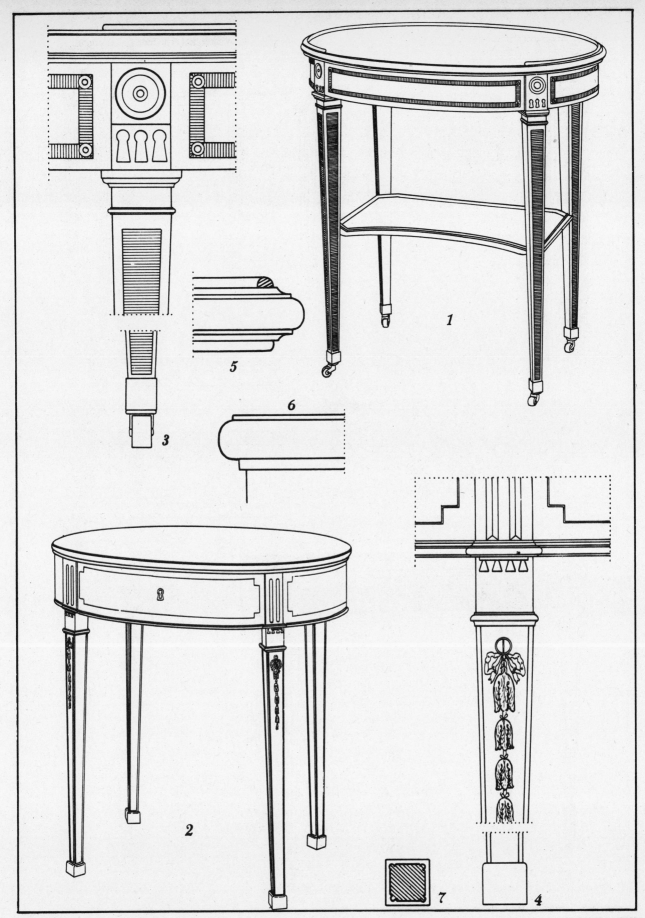

PLATE 227                                    LOUIS XVI

1 and 2. Oval pedestal tables with some bronze decorations and marquetry. 3 and 4. Details of legs. 5 and 6. Upper mouldings. 7. Leg section.

*Versailles Palace*

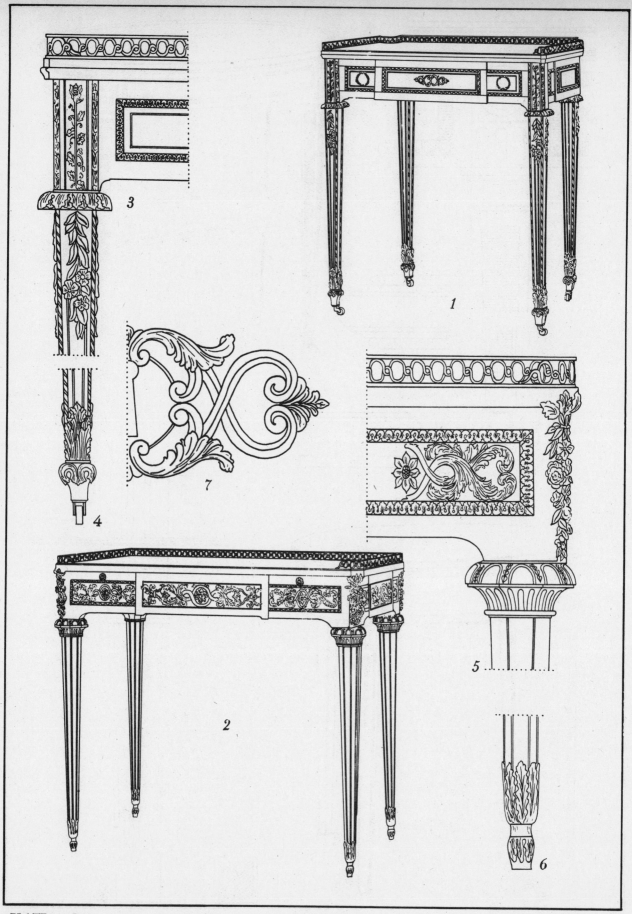

PLATE 228
1 and 2. Riesener ladies' desks with marquetry and gilt bronzes. 3, 4, 5 and 6. Details of uprights and legs. 7. Escutcheon plate.

*Louvre*

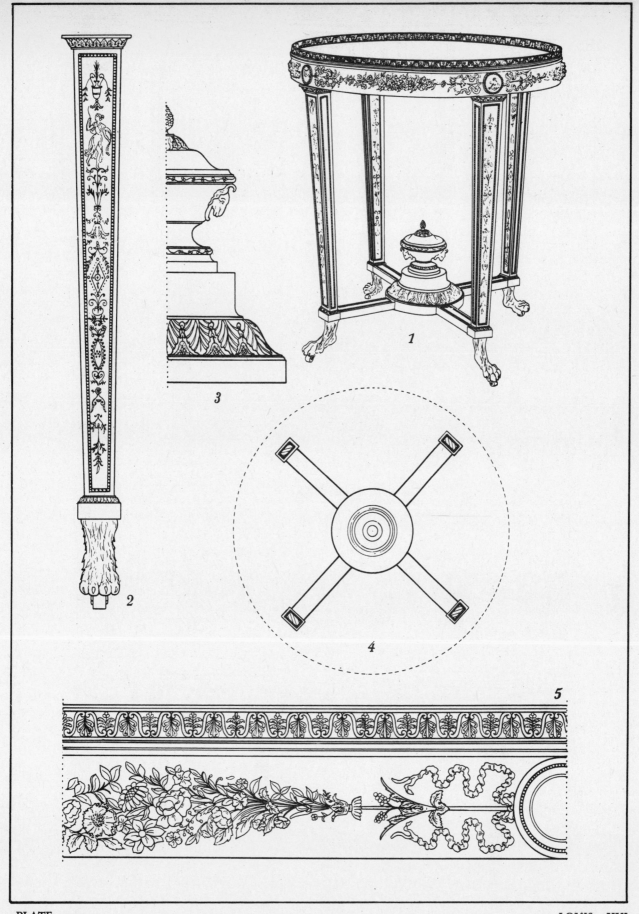

PLATE 229                                                                                    LOUIS XVI

1. Oval mahogany pedestal table, decorated with bronzes and uprights with delicate paintings in cameos; glass bottom with marble top. Used by Queen Marie Antoinette. 2. Detail of legs. 3. Central urn. 4. Position of the base. 5. Detail of decoration and upper edge.

*Petit Trianon*

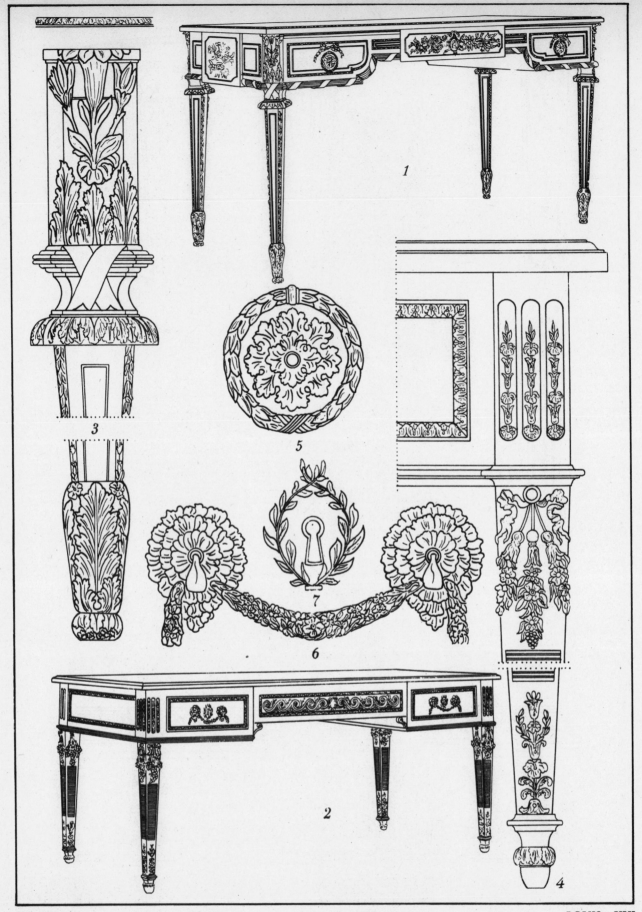

**PLATE 230**

LOUIS XVI

1 and 2. Desks with gilt bronzes. The upper one has marquetry and the lower one is of mahogany.   3 and 4. Details of the uprights and legs.   5 and 6. Drawer pulls.   7. Escutcheon plate.

*Louvre*

PLATE 231

LOUIS XVI

1. Rolltop desk, Louis XVI transition style.    2. Louis XV transition style desk.    3, 4 and 5. Details of bronzes.    6 and 7. Sketch of the panel that trims the upper part.    8. Upright and moulding on leg.

*Fleury-en-Bière Castle and private collection*

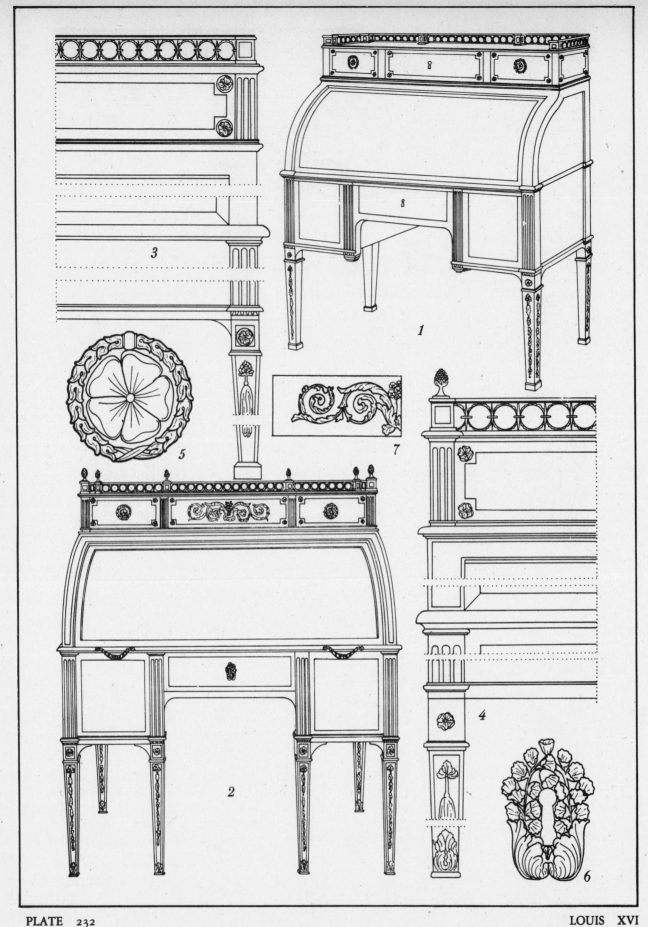

PLATE 232

1 and 2. Rolltop desks with marquetry and gilt bronzes (by David Roentgen). 3 and 4. Details of uprights and legs. 5, 6 and 7. Drawer pull, escutcheon plate and decoration.

*Poles and Arnold Seligmann collections*

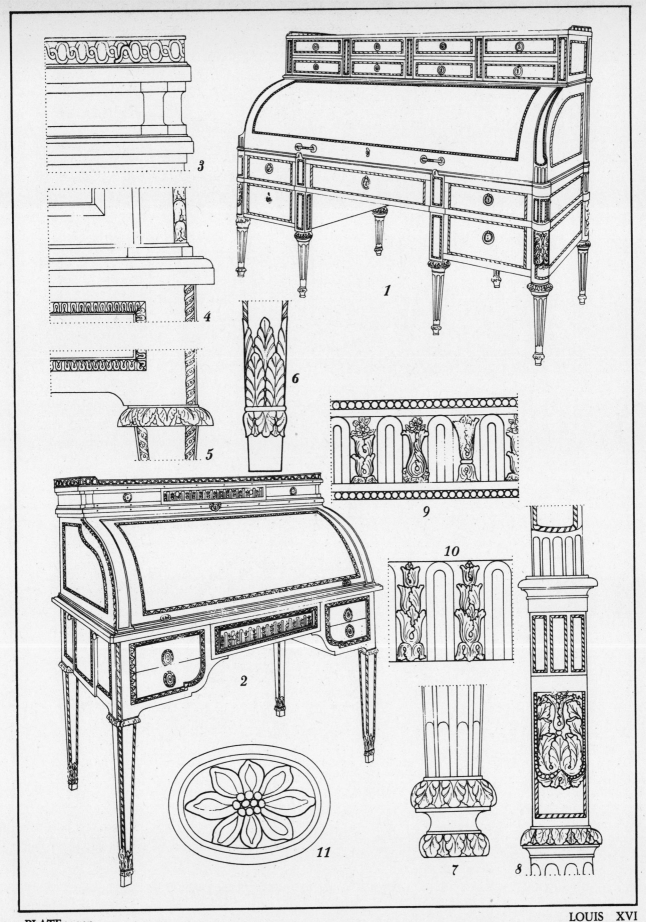

**PLATE 233**

LOUIS XVI

1 and 2. Mahogany desks with carved gilt bronzes. The second desk is by J. H. Riesener. 3, 4, 5 and 6. Details of the upright and leg of the second desk. 7 and 8. Upright and leg of the first desk. 9 and 10. Details of the decoration on middle front drawers. 11. Knob.

*Private collection and Poles collection*

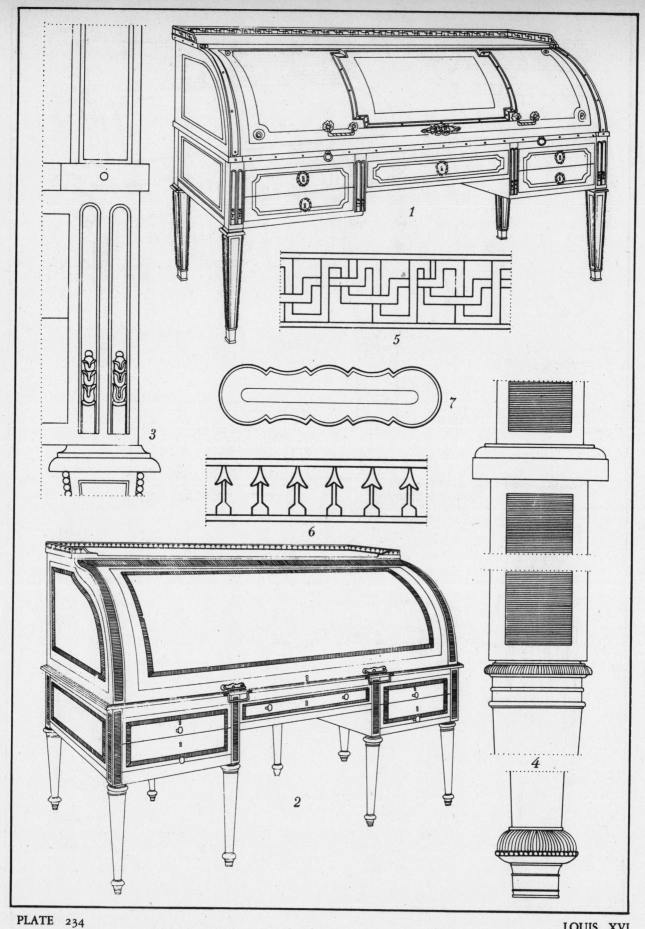

PLATE 234

LOUIS XVI

1 and 2. Desks, the first one in marquetry, the second one in mahogany.   3 and 4. Details of uprights.   5 and 6. Sketches of the trim that skirts the upper edge.   7. Handle.

*Private collection and Ministry of Foreign Affairs, Paris*

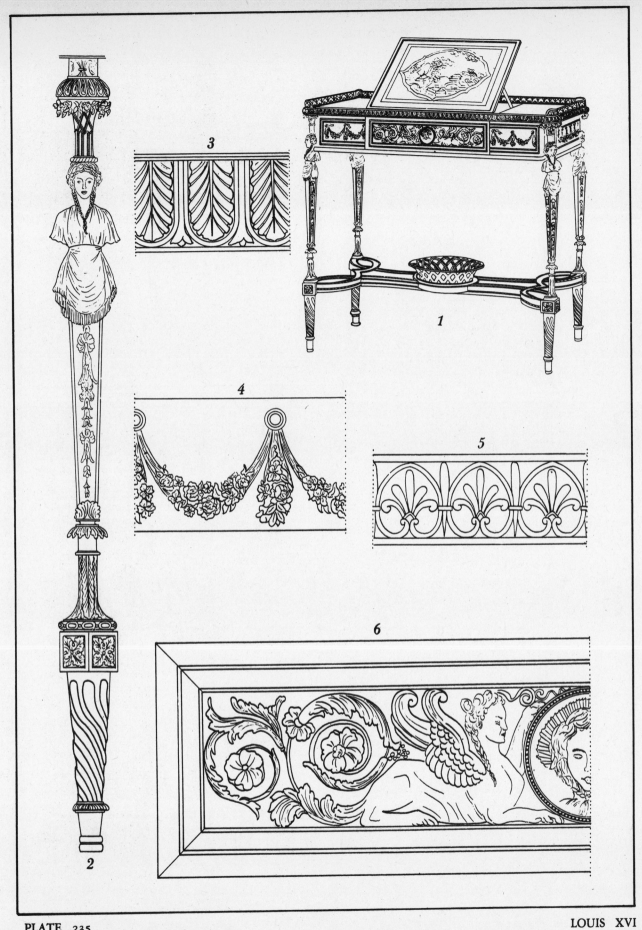

PLATE 235

**PLATE 235**
1. Ebony lady's desk, black Japanese lacquer with gilt bronzes.   2. Detail of leg.   3. Sketch of moulding at top.   4, 5 and 6. Details of the bronzes.

LOUIS XVI

*Louvre*

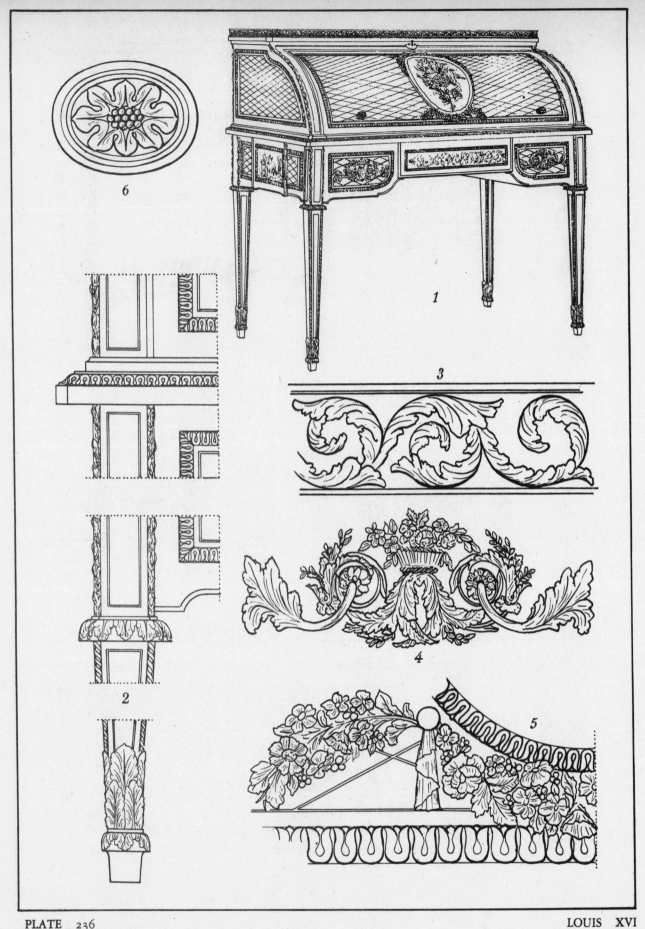

PLATE 236                                                                                     LOUIS XVI

1. Lady's desk of marquetry (by J. H. Riesener, 1784).   2. Uprights.   3, 4 and 5. Details of the moulding, very
elaborate escutcheon plate and central motif.   5. Knob.

*Louvre*

PLATE 237                                                                                    LOUIS XVI

1. Mahogany lady's desk in shape of commode, with gilt bronzes.    2 and 3. Detail of bronze on upright.    4. Upper
moulding.    5. Detail of lower decoration.    6. Frieze decoration.    7 and 8. Escutcheon plate and decoration.

*Louvre*

PLATE 238                                                                                    LOUIS XVI

1. Ebony lady's desk with gilt bronzes.   2. Detail of upright.   3. Moulding on panel.   4. Detail of the frieze and mouldings.

*Louvre*

**PLATE** 239

LOUIS XVI

1. Mahogany desk adorned with gilt bronzes by E. Lavasseur.   2. Detail of upright.   3. Bronze motif.   4. Moulding on panel.   5. Upright and trim at top.

*Louvre*

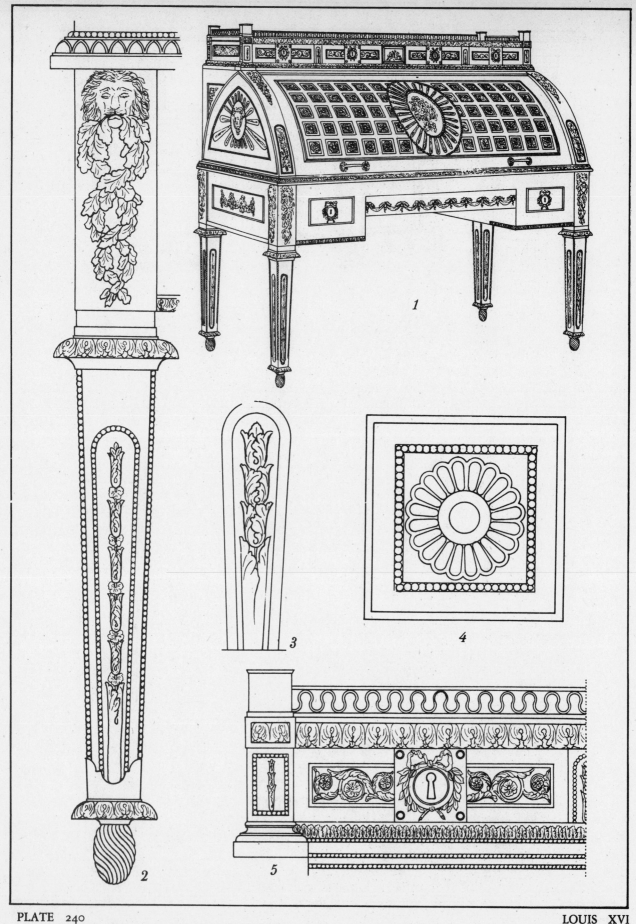

PLATE 240

LOUIS XVI

1. Desk of marquetry with gilt bronzes (by Roentgen, 1785).  2. Detail of leg.  3 an 4. Detail of bronzes.  5. Detail of upper body and the trim that skirts the top.

*Louvre*

PLATE 241                                                          LOUIS XVI

1. Desk with marquetry of rosewood and lemonwood. Carved gilt bronzes. Marble top with trim.   2 and 3. Top of upright.   4. Lower detail of upright and foot.   5. Frieze decoration.   6. Escutcheon plate.

*Museum of Decorative Arts, Paris*

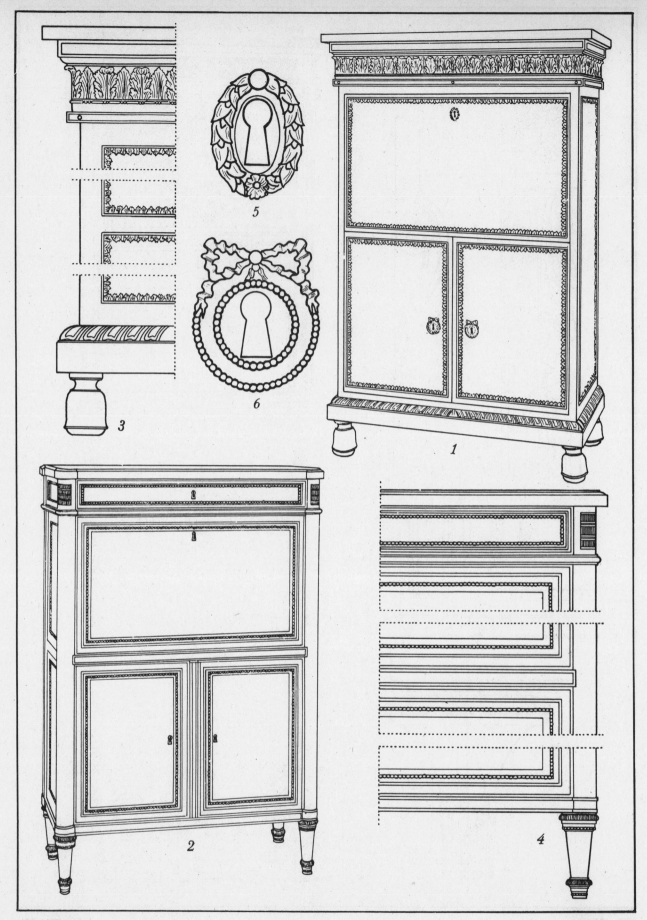

PLATE 242

1 and 2. Desks of mahogany and of lemonwood and amaranth, respectively. The first desk has carved gilt bronzes; the second desk has gilt bronze and a marble top.  3 and 4. Details of uprights and legs.  5 and 6. Escutcheon plates.

*Versailles Palace*

**PLATE 243**                                                    LOUIS XVI (second half of 18th century)

1. Small secretary of marquetry.    2. Detail of upright.    3 and 4. Moulding and sketch of frieze marquetry.

*Private collection*

PLATE 244

1. Secretary with marquetry of colored woods and gilt bronzes.   2. Corner cabinet with marquetry.   3 and 4. Escutcheon
plate and detail of frieze from secretary.   5. Detail of upright.   6. Sketch of frieze.   7. Escutcheon plate.

*Private collections*

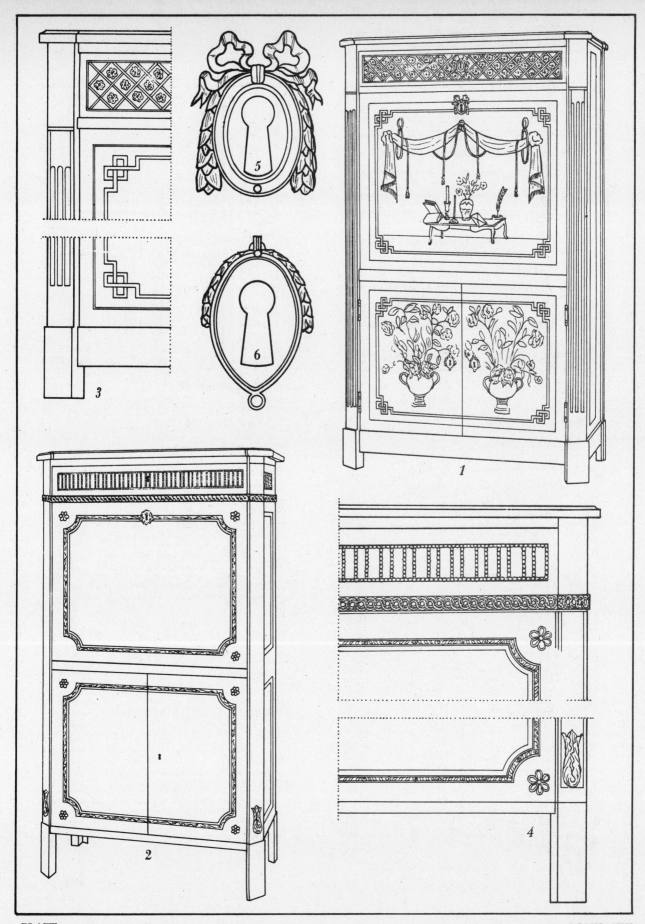

**PLATE 245**                                                                                    LOUIS XVI

1 and 2. Small desks. The first one has decorations in marquetry of violet wood, rosewood and lemonwood, with decorative lines of boxwood and amaranth. The second desk is of satined rosewood and violet wood.    3 and 4. Detail of upright.    5 and 6. Escutcheon plates.

**PLATE 246**

1 and 2. Mahogany desks. The first one has a trim that skirts the top. The second desk has gilt bronzes, carved bronzes and a slab of marble.   3 and 4. Details of desks.

LOUIS XVI

*Versailles Palace and Mobilier National de France*

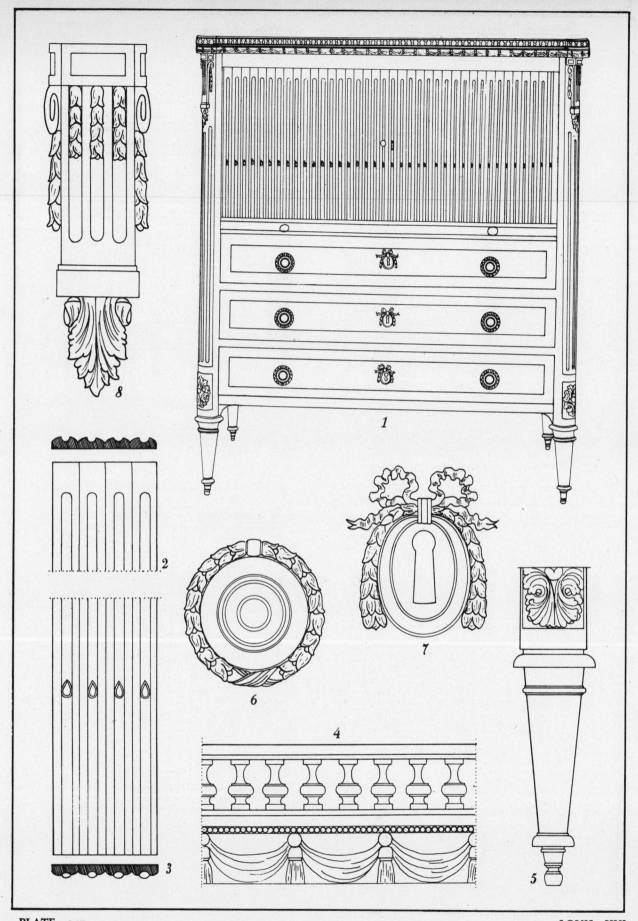

PLATE 247

LOUIS XVI

1. Mahogany desk commode with bronzes.   2 and 3. Reliefs on upper middle panel.   4. Detail of trim at top.   5. Leg.   6, 7 and 8. Drawer pull, escutcheon plate and bronze decoration.

*Private collection*

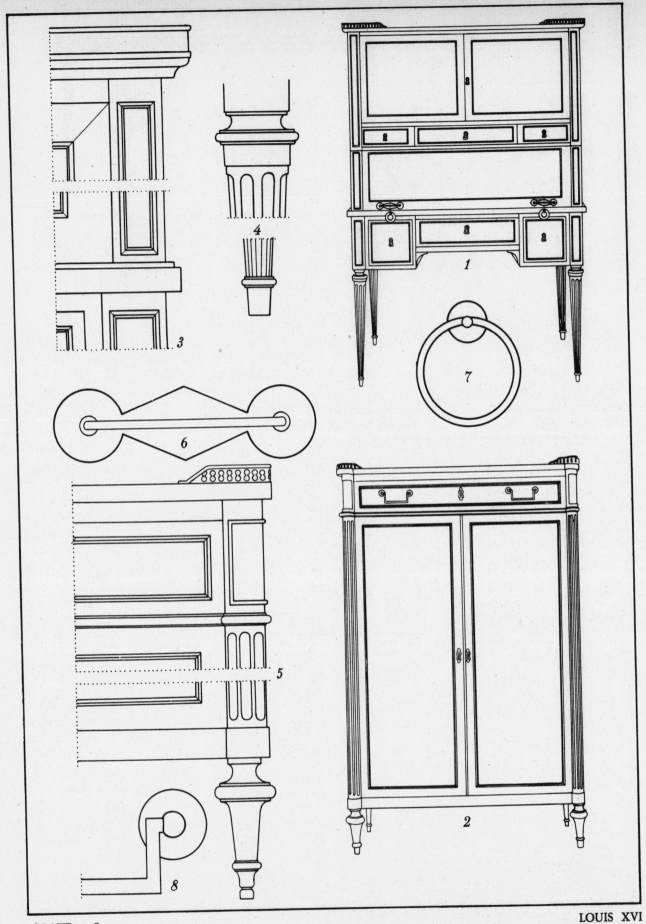

**PLATE 248**
1. Cylindrical mahogany "bonheur-du-jour" (desk with paper cabinet), with decorative lines of copper and trim skirting the top.   2. Mahogany and copper showcase.   3, 4 and 5. Details of uprights and legs.   6, 7 and 8. Drawer pulls.

*Private collection*

PLATE 249

1 and 2. Secretaries with marquetry of colored woods.    3. Apron of second secretary.    4, 5 and 6. Escutcheon plate.

LOUIS XVI

*Private collections*

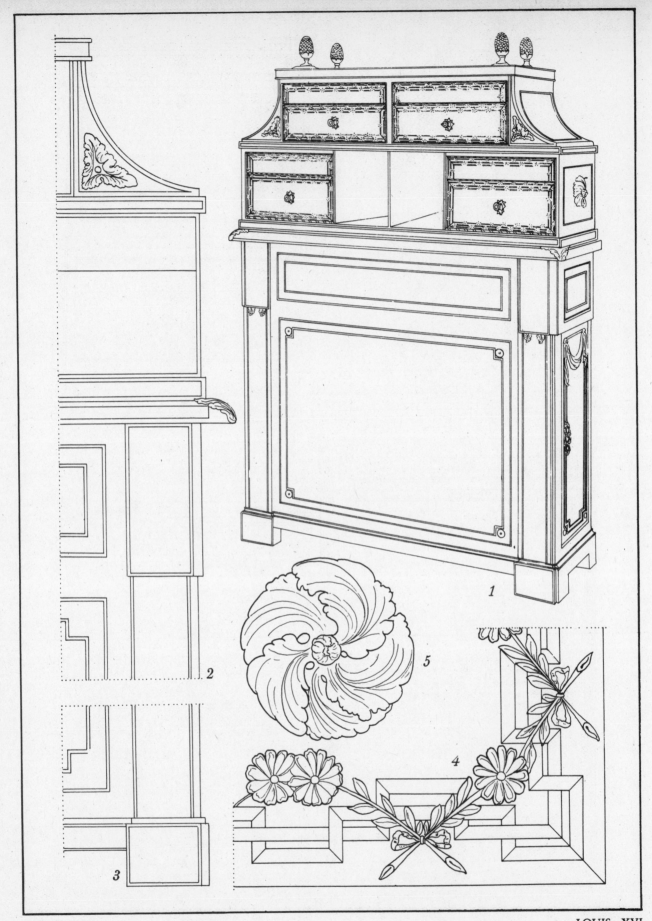

PLATE 250
1. Office paper cabinet of black wood with decorative lines of copper and bronze decorations.   2 and 3. Details of uprights.   4. Detail of drawer decorations.   5. Rosette.

*Private collection*

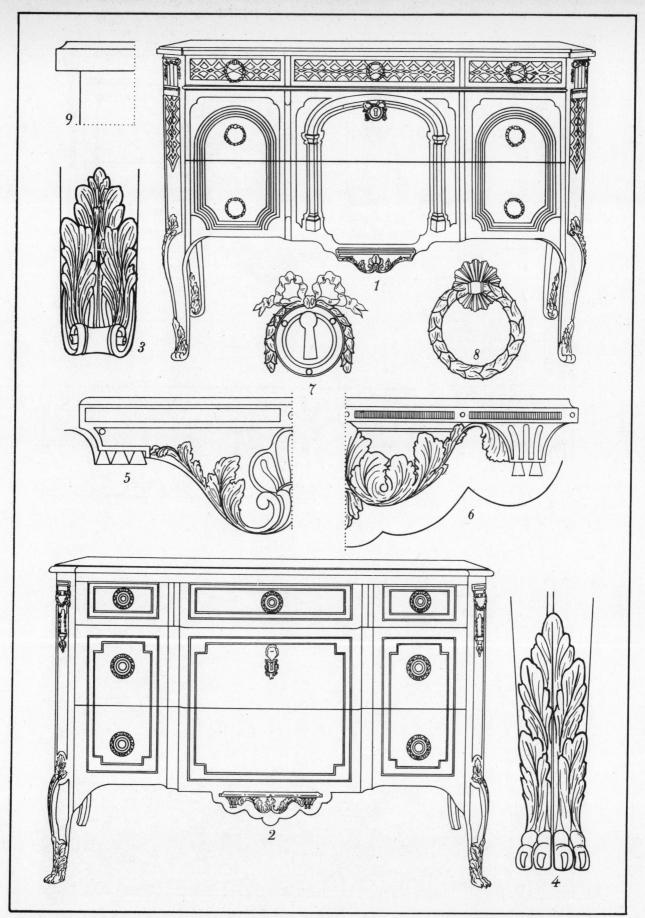

**PLATE 251**                                    LOUIS XVI (transition from Louis XV)

1. Commode with five drawers. The pilaster arches, mouldings, friezes and decorations are in bronze.   2. Commode with five drawers with marquetry of different colored woods.   3 and 4. Legs.   5 and 6. Central decorations.   7 and 8. Escutcheon plate and drawer pull.   9. Profile of marble top.

*Private collections*

PLATE 252
LOUIS XVI (transition from Louis XV)

1. Commode with five drawers, with marquetry of amaranth, maple and other woods, carved gilt bronzes, white marble top.   2 and 3. Details of upright and leg.   4, 5 and 6. Detail of the decorations.   7. Corner rosettes.

*Mobilier National de France*

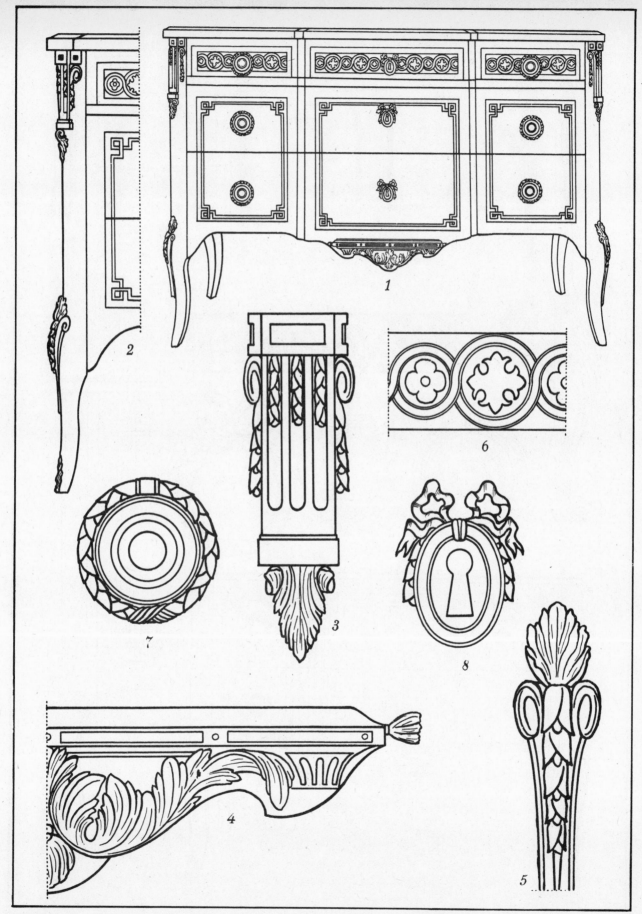

PLATE 253

LOUIS XVI (transition from Louis XV)

1. Commode with three drawers, with marquetry of rosewood, plane tree and lemonwood, gilt carved bronzes and a marble top. 2. Detail of upright and leg. 3, 4 and 5. Details of the decorations. 6. Detail of marquetry border. 7 and 8. Drawer pull and escutcheon plate.

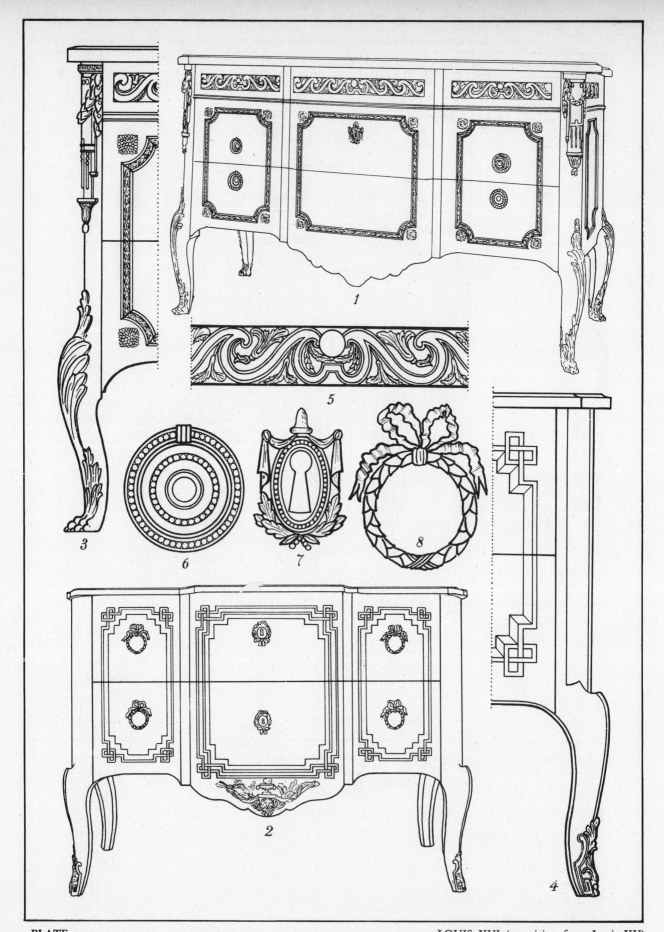

PLATE 254                                    LOUIS XVI (transition from Louis XV)

1 and 2. Commodes with gilt carved bronze decorations and marble tops. The first commode has five drawers and marquetry of rosewood and amaranth. The second one has two drawers and marquetry of rosewood and lemonwood. 3 and 4. Details of uprights. 5. Detail of frieze. 6, 7 and 8. Drawer pulls and escutcheon plate.

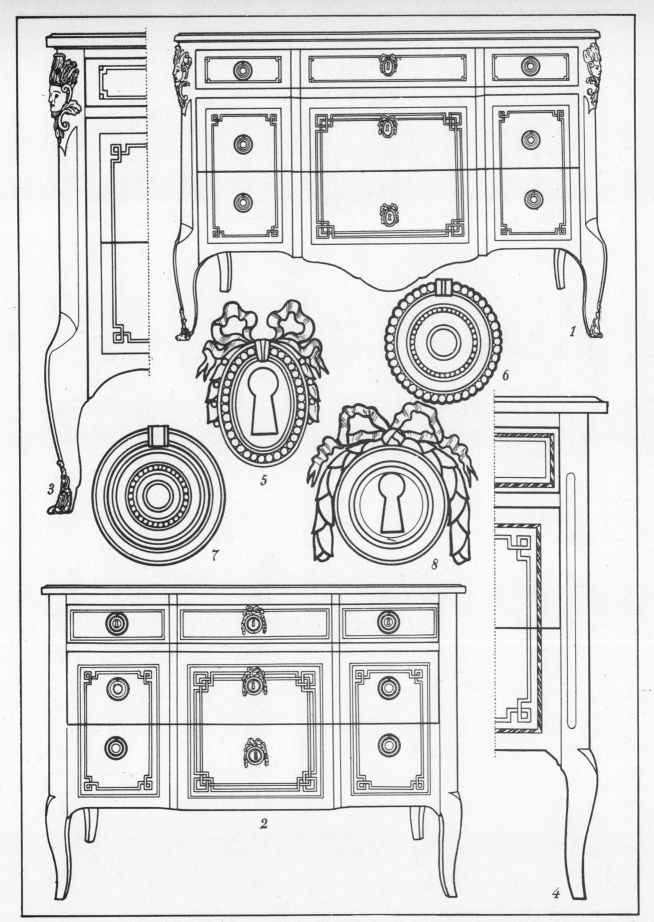

**PLATE 255**                                              LOUIS XVI (transition from Louis XV)

1 and 2. Commodes with marble tops. The first one has three drawers, marquetry of rosewood, amaranth and other woods, and carved bronzes. The second one has marquetry of violet wood, rosewood and amaranth.   3 and 4. Details of uprights and legs.   5, 6, 7 and 8. Drawer pulls and escutcheon plates.

*Mobilier National de France*

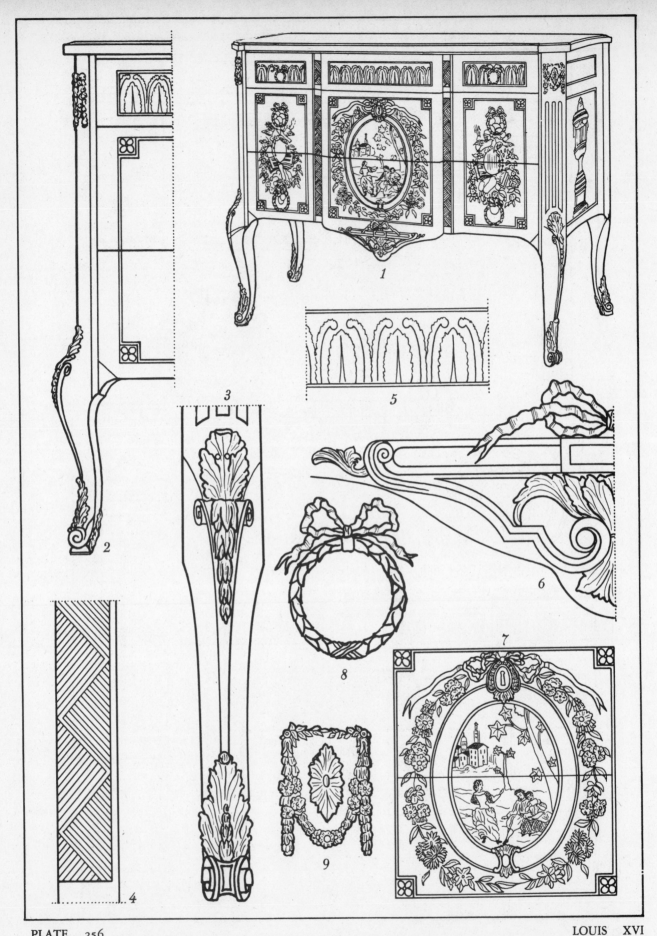

PLATE 256

LOUIS XVI

1. Commode with five drawers and marquetry of rosewood, amaranth and lemonwood with gilt bronze decorations and a marble top. 2. Detail of leg and upright. 3. Front view of leg. 4. Alternation of different woods. 5. Sketch of upper marquetry. 6. Sketch of lower part. 7. Sketch of central marquetry. 8 and 9. Drawer pull and decoration.

PLATE 257

1. Commode with five drawers and marquetry of amaranth, lemonwood and maple, gilt carved bronzes (influence of Louis XV style on legs), and marble top.   2 and 3. Details of upright and legs.   4, 5, 6 and 7. Details of decorations.   8. Drawer pull.

PLATE 258                                                                                    LOUIS XVI

1. Commode with two drawers and marquetry of lemonwood and amaranth.   2. Commode with three drawers and marquetry of walnut, Brazilian rosewood and with decorative lines of boxwood.   3 and 4. Details of uprights and legs.   5, 6 and 7. Drawer pulls and escutcheon plate.

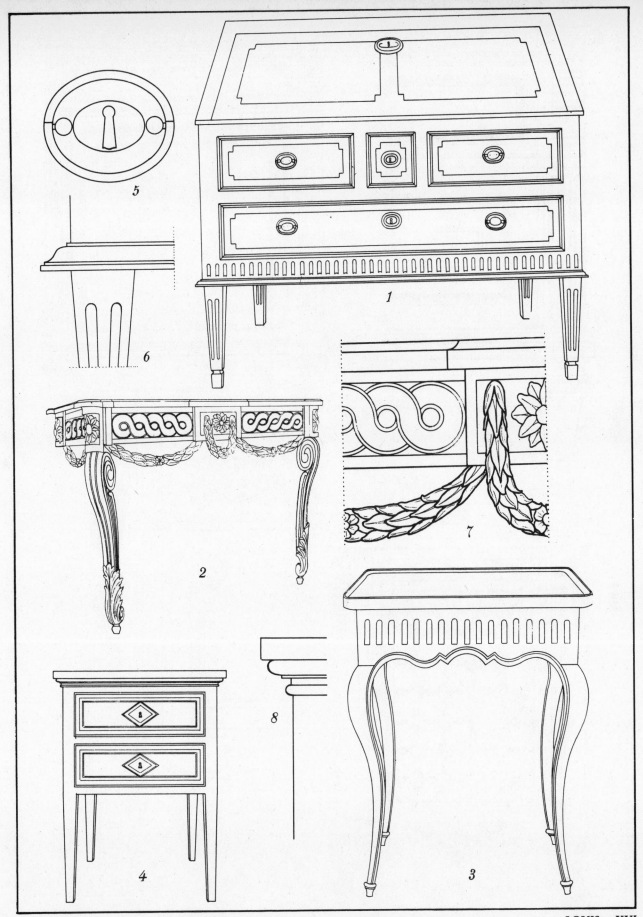

PLATE 259

LOUIS XVI

1. Desk commode in the early style.   2. Very ornate console table.   3. Small table in the early style.   4. Chiffonier.   5 and 6. Escutcheon plate and detail of moulding.   7. Detail of frieze decoration on console table.   8. Moulding.

*Private collections*

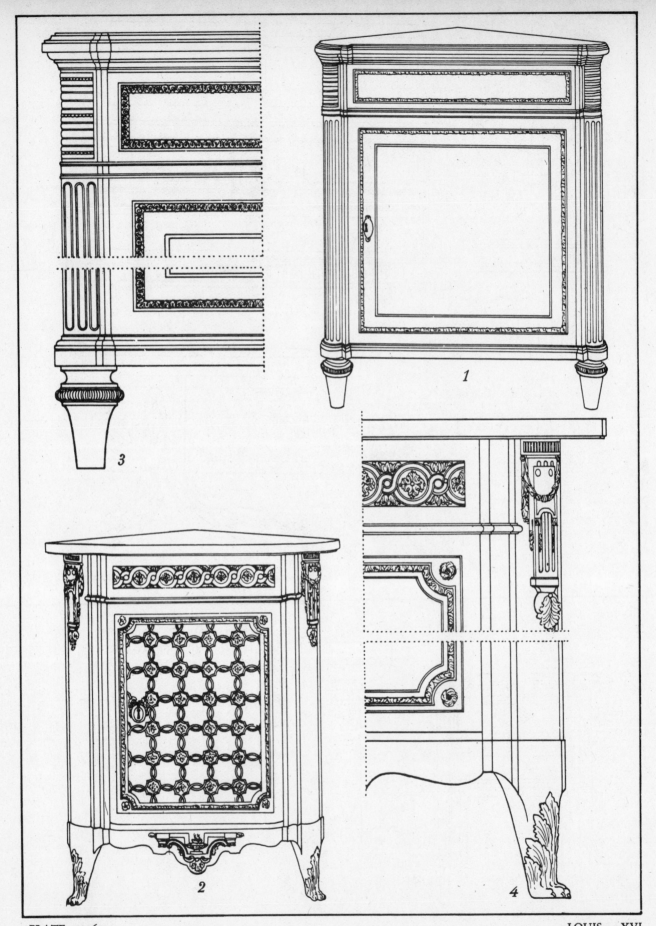

PLATE 260

1 and 2. Mahogany corner cabinets. The first one has mouldings of gilt bronze and white marble. The second cabinet has marquetry of rosewood and amaranth with decorative lines of boxwood and ebony, and gilt carved bronzes. 3 and 4. Details of uprights and legs.

*Champs-Élysée Palace*

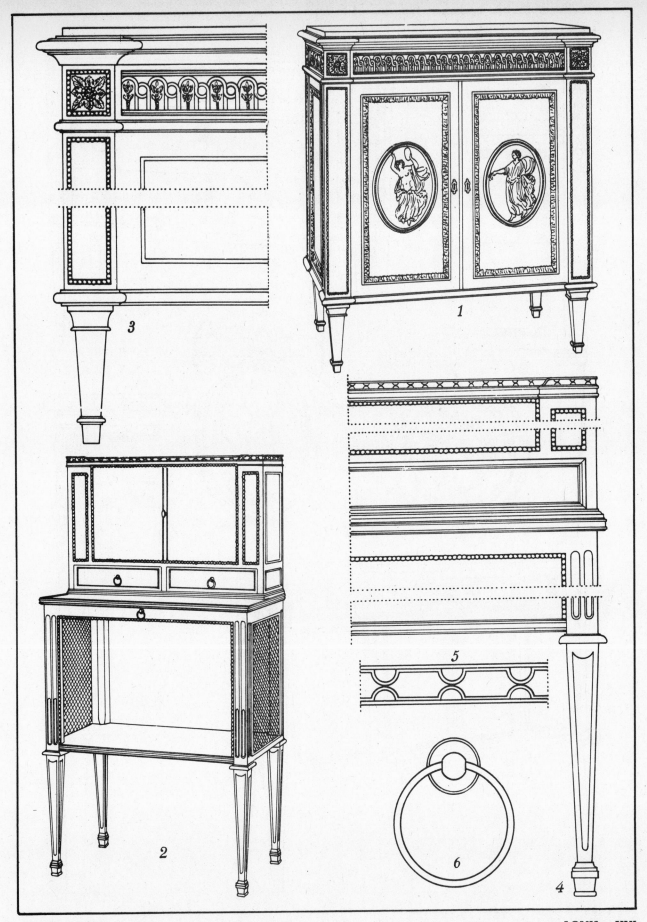

PLATE 261                                                          LOUIS XVI

1. Small mahogany commode with medallions of Sèvres porcelain, gilt carved bronzes and marble top.  2. Small mahogany desk—paper cabinet with moulding and trim of gilt bronze.  3 and 4. Details of uprights and legs.  5. Sketch of bronze trim skirting top.  6. Drawer pull.

PLATE 262
LOUIS XVI
1 and 2. Commodes of three and five drawers, satined wood and mahogany, respectively. Both have gilt carved bronzes and marble tops. 3 and 4. Details of uprights. 5 and 6. Drawer pull and escutcheon plate.

*Versailles Palace*

PLATE 263

**PLATE** 263             LOUIS XVI

1 and 2. Mahogany commodes with five drawers, gilt carved bronzes and marble tops. The second one has trim skirting the top.     3 and 4. Details of uprights and legs.     5, 6 and 7. Drawer pull and escutcheon plates.

*Mobilier National de France and Champs-Élysée Palace*

PLATE 264

1. Mahogany commode with nine drawers.   2. Mahogany commode with swinging doors, with three drawers at the top.
Both numbers one and two have gilt bronze mouldings and marble tops.   3 and 4. Details of uprights and legs.   5 and
6. Escutcheon plate and drawer pull.

**PLATE 265**

1 and 2. Small commodes with marquetry of rosewood and amaranth, decorative lines of boxwood and marble tops. The first commode has two drawers and curved doors. The second one has five drawers.   3 and 4. Details of uprights and legs.   5, 6 and 7. Escutcheon plates and drawer pull.

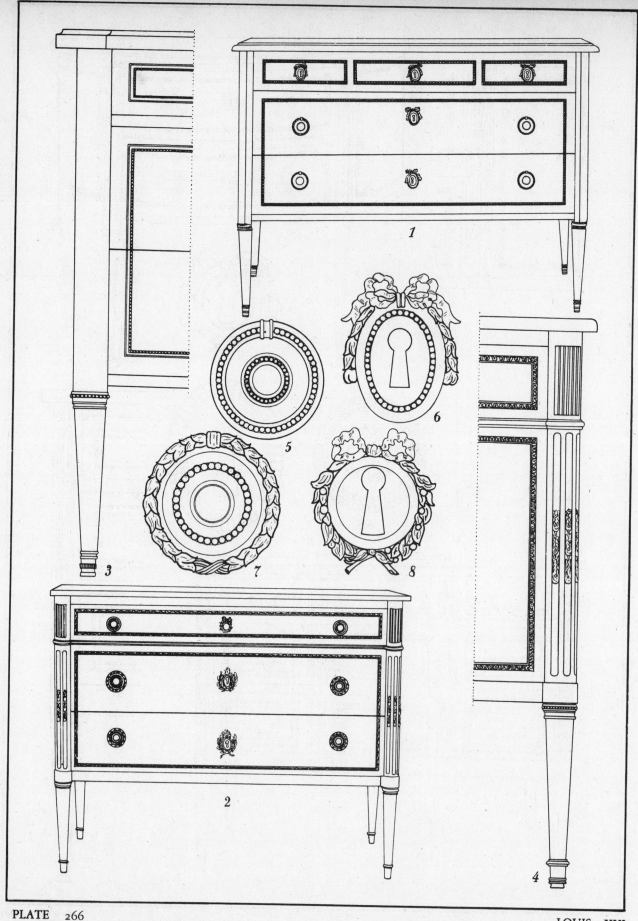

**PLATE 266**

LOUIS XVI

1 and 2. Commodes with straight lines and five drawers. The upper one has wood veneer; the lower one is of moulded mahogany.   3 and 4. Details of uprights and legs.   5, 6, 7 and 8. Drawer pulls and escutcheon plates.

*Private collection*

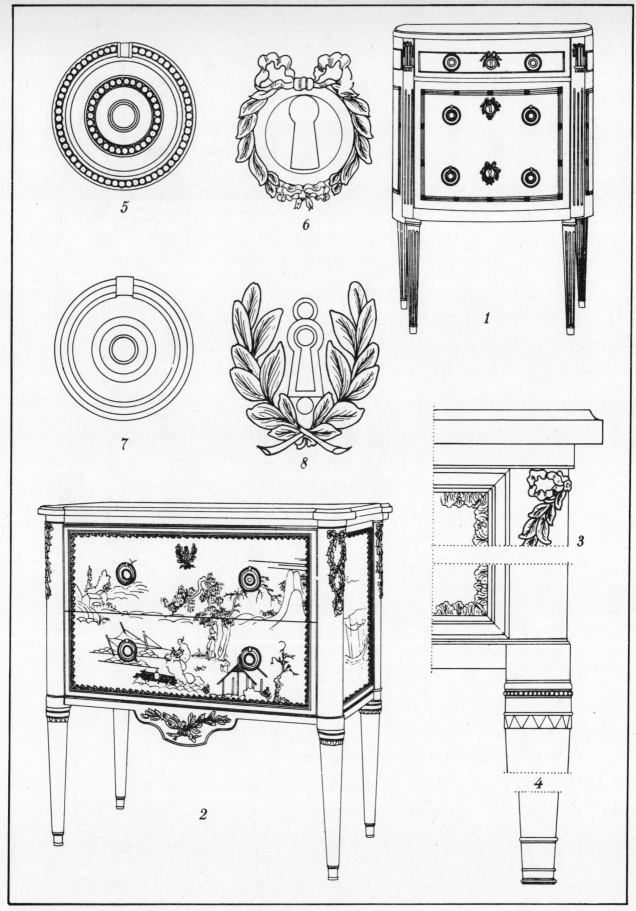

PLATE 267

1 and 2. Small commodes. The first one has three drawers and is of wood veneer. The second one has two drawers and
is of black lacquer and gold.    3 and 4. Details of the uprights.    5, 6, 7 and 8. Drawer pulls and escutcheon plates.

*Private collections*

PLATE 268

1 and 2. Circular commodes with long legs, two drawers in front and swinging doors on the sides, with two kinds of wood. The decorations, drawer pulls and escutcheon plates are of carved copper on the upper commode, of bronze on the lower commode.   3, 4, 5 and 6. Escutcheon plates and drawer pulls.   7 and 8. Details of leg.

PLATE 269

1 and 2. Mahogany commodes with three drawers, gilt bronze mouldings and marble tops. The second one has pieces of carved bronze.   3 and 4. Details of uprights and legs.   5 and 6. Drawer pull and escutcheon plate.

*Versailles Palace*

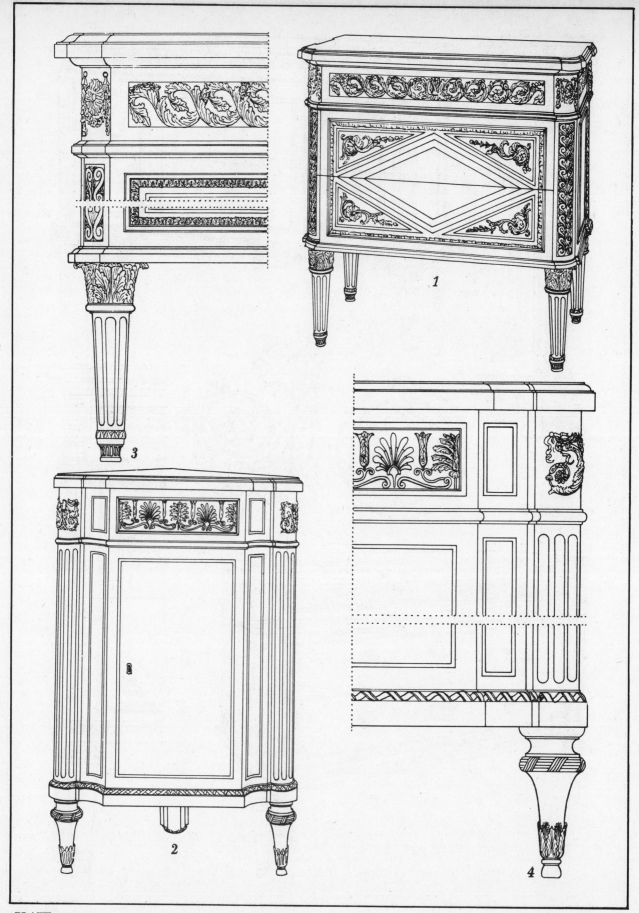

PLATE 270

1. Small commode with three drawers and marquetry of amaranth, holly, rosewood, lemonwood and sycamore.   2. Mahogany corner commode. Both commodes have carved gilt bronzes and marble tops.   3 and 4. Details of uprights and legs.

PLATE 271

LOUIS XVI

1. Commode with four drawers, Chinese lacquer over a black base, carved gilt bronze mounts. 2. Commode with nine drawers, red marquetry, carved gilt bronze mounts, white marble top. 3 and 4. Details of posts and legs. 5, 6, 7 and 8. Drawer pulls and escutcheons.

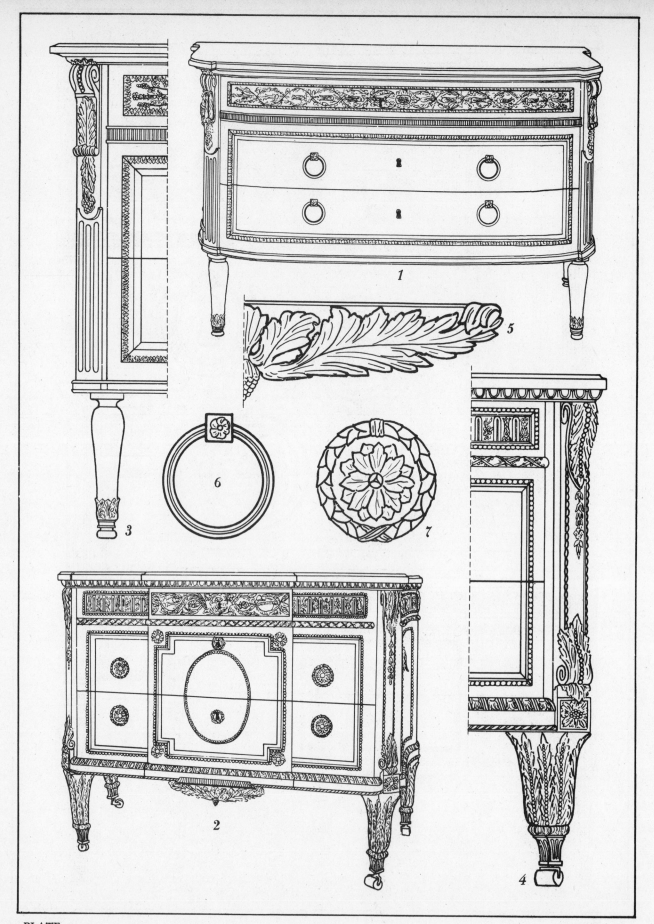

PLATE 272

1 and 2. Commodes with three and five drawers, and marquetry of rosewood, amaranth and other woods. The lower one is of amaranth and stained banana wood and has carved gilt bronzes. The first commode has a turquoise blue marble top. 3 and 4. Details of uprights and legs. 5. Decorations. 6 and 7. Drawer pulls.

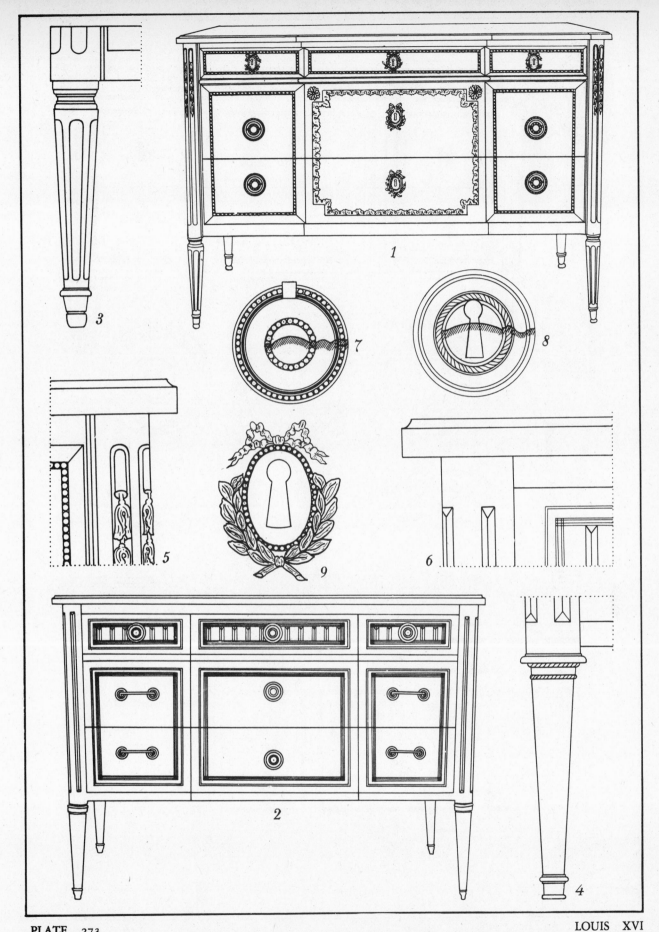

**PLATE** 273

1 and 2. Commodes with five drawers. The upper one has mahogany veneer, the lower one is of rosewood. 3 and 4. **Legs.** 5 and 6. Profiles of marble tops. 7, 8 and 9. Drawer pull and escutcheon plates.

*Private collection and Ministry of War, Paris*

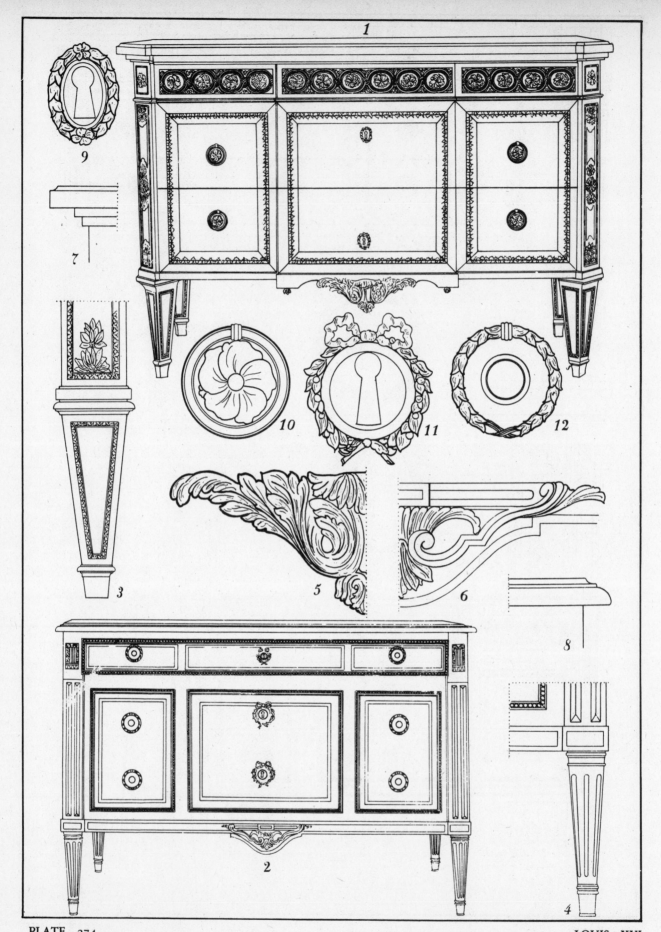

PLATE 274                                                    LOUIS XVI

1 and 2. Straight-line commodes with five drawers. The upper one has satined wood and amaranth veneer. The lower one has marquetry on uprights and wood veneer. 3 and 4. Legs. 5 and 6. Details of lower middle decorations. 7 and 8. Profiles of marble tops. 9, 10, 11 and 12. Drawer pulls and escutcheon plates.

*Poles collection and private collection*

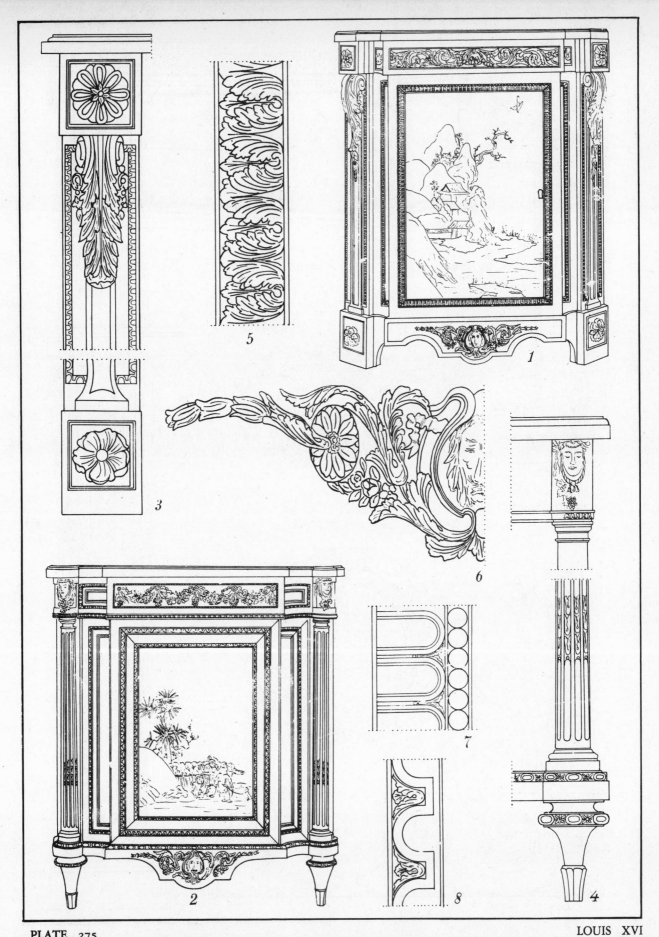

PLATE 275

1 and 2. Corner commodes of ebony, black Japanese lacquer, gilt bronzes and marble tops (M. Carlin, 1782). 3 and
4. Details of uprights and legs. 5 and 6. Details of moulding and central motif from lower apron. 7 and 8. Details
of mouldings.

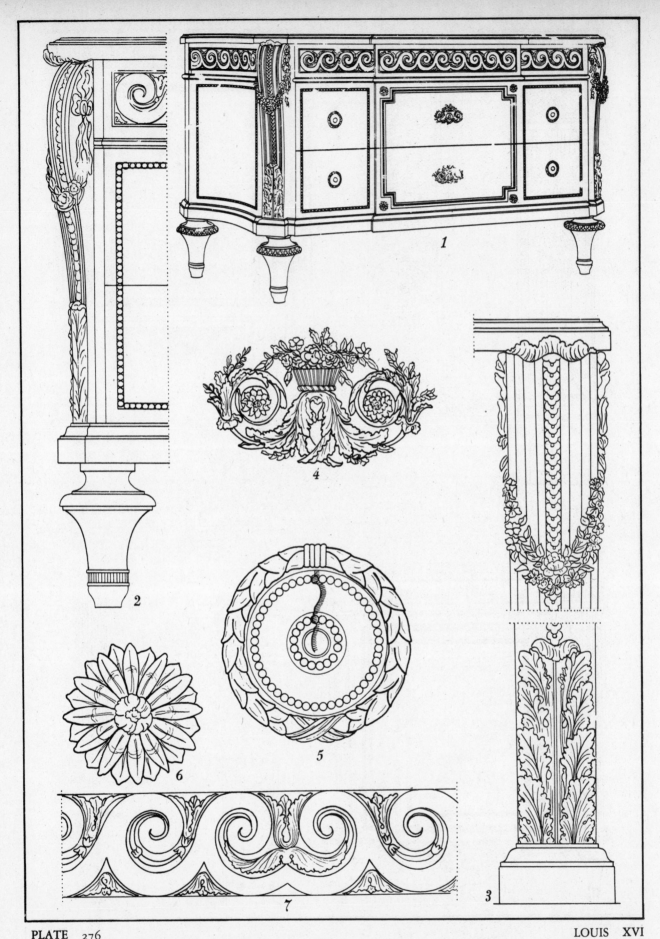

PLATE 276                                                                    LOUIS XVI

1. Mahogany commode with gilt bronzes and marble top (Riesener, 1786).   2. Detail of upright and leg.   3. Front of upright.   4. Escutcheon plate.   5. Drawer pull.   6. Rosette.   7. Detail of frieze decoration.

*Louvre*

**PLATE** 277

1. Commode with marble top (Riesener, 1782).  2. Detail of upright and leg.  3. Detail of bronze decorations of frieze.  4. Escutcheon plate and trim on central decoration.  5. Bronze design, middle lower apron.  6. Drawer pull.

*Louvre*

PLATE 278

LOUIS XVI

1. Light mahogany and amaranth commode with hinged doors, carved gilt bronzes. There are two drawers at top, and three inside. White marble top.   2 and 3. Details of upright and leg.   4, 5 and 6. Sketches of the decorations.

*Fontainebleau Palace*

PLATE 279
LOUIS XVI
1. Mahogany commode with gilt bronzes attributed to Gouthieri (G. Benaman, 1786). 2. Detail of upright and leg. 3. Rosette on curved panels. 4 and 5. Mouldings.

*Louvre*

PLATE 280

LOUIS XVI

1. Cabinet of inlaid ebony, decorated with gilt bronzes.   2. Detail of leg.   3 and 4. Details of the bronzes.   5. Border moulding.

*Louvre*

PLATE 281

LOUIS XVI

1. Small office wardrobe with marquetry of copper on shell. 2. Detail of front. 3. Central detail. 4. Detail of bottom.

*Private collection*

PLATE 282                                                    LOUIS XVI
1. Marie-Antoinette's mahogany jewelry cabinet, with gilt carved bronzes, paintings and cameos.   2. Detail of upright
and leg.   3. Detail of central design.

*Versailles Palace*

*1*

*4*      *5*      *6*

*2*      *3*

**PLATE** 283                                                    LOUIS XVI

1. Dining-room sideboard.   2 and 3. Upper and lower details of upright.   4, 5 and 6. Drawer pull, escutcheon plate and rosette.

*Dutasta collection*

1

2

3

4

5

PLATE 284

1. Mahogany-paneled cabinet (J. H. Riesener).   2. Detail of upright and leg.   3, 4 and 5. Decorations.

*Poles collection*

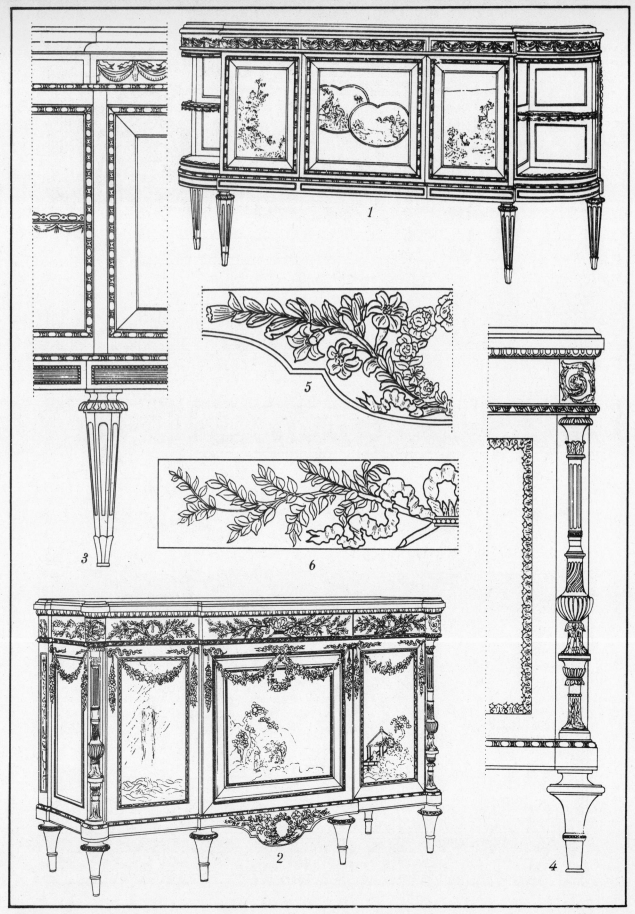

PLATE 285

1 and 2. Dining-room sideboard, of black Japanese lacquer, with gilt bronzes (M. Carlin).   3 and 4. Detail of uprights
and legs.   5 and 6. Sketches of the bronzes.

LOUIS XVI

*Louvre*

PLATE 286 LOUIS XVI

1. Mahogany dining-room sideboard, with gilt bronzes and Sèvres porcelains (G. Beneman, 1787). 2. Detail of the graceful design on the front. 3 and 4. Foot and border moulding.

*Louvre*

PLATE 287                                                                    LOUIS XVI
1. Dining-room sideboard of mahogany and ebony, with gilt bronzes (Hauri and G. Beneman, 1786–1787).   2. Detail
of upright.   3. Detail of foot.   4 and 5. Mouldings.

*Louvre*

PLATE 288                                                          LOUIS XVI

1. Brazilian rosewood sideboard with gilt bronzes and painting on glass.   2. Detail of upright.   3. Detail of frieze decoration.   4 and 5. Bronzes on the legs.   6. Detail of panel moulding.

*Louvre*

PLATE 289

LOUIS XVI

1 and 2. Mahogany sideboards with gilt bronzes.   3 and 4. Details of uprights and legs.   5 and 6. Sketch of moulding, bordering central panel of frieze.

*Louvre*

PLATE 290

LOUIS XVI

1. Corner console table of ebony and black Japanese lacquer, with gilt bronzes and marble top (M. Carlin, 1785). 2. Detail of corner post. 3. Detail of frieze. 4. Sketch of lower bronze decoration.

*Louvre*

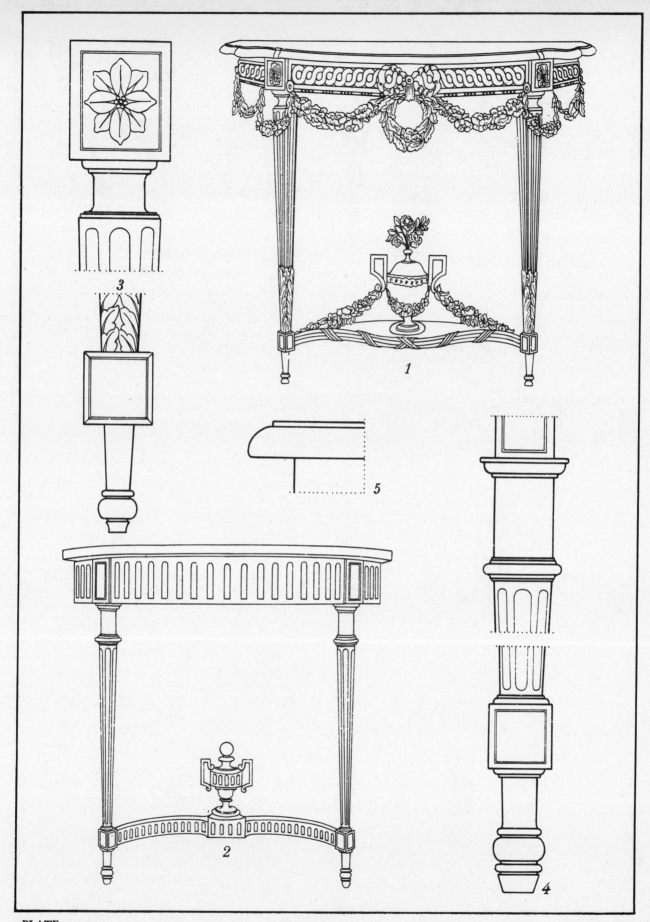

PLATE 291

1 and 2. Two-legged console tables of painted wood and walnut.   3 and 4. Legs.   5. Profile of top.

LOUIS   XVI

*Private collections*

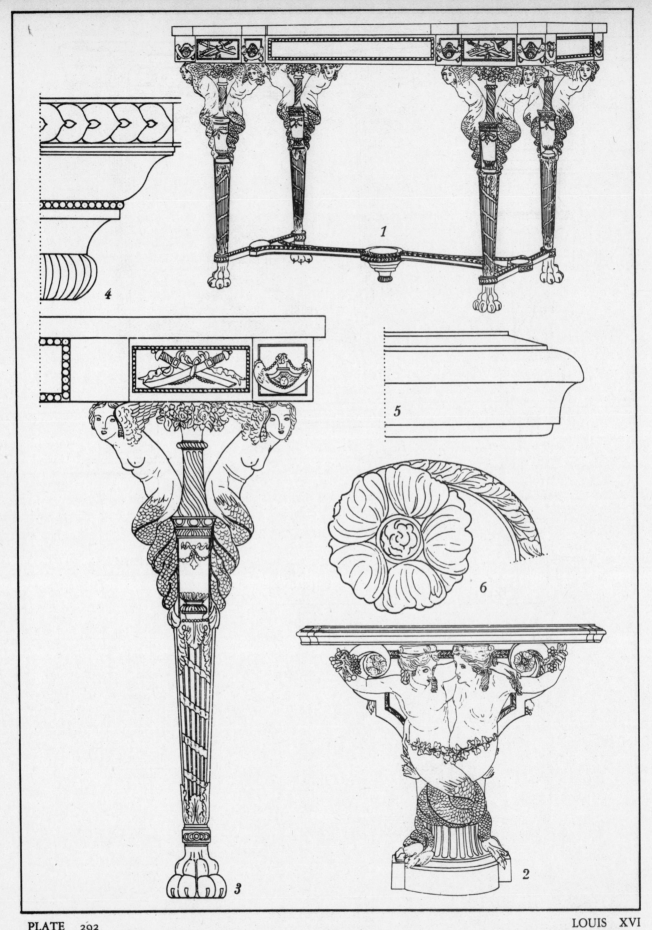

PLATE 292

LOUIS XVI

1 and 2. Carved wooden console tables (J. Jacob).   3. Detail of leg.   4. Detail of middle foot of lower crosspiece.   5. Moulding at top of console table.   6. Detail of large flower at top.

*Louvre*

PLATE 293

LOUIS XVI

1. Console table of gilt carved wood.  2. Detail of foot.  3. Detail of frieze carving.  4. Profile of frieze.  5. Detail of piece joining the legs.

*Louvre*

PLATE 294                                                                    LOUIS XVI (end of style)

1. Mahogany commode, decorated with Wedgewood plaques and gilt bronzes. 2. Mahogany commode, decorated with gilt bronzes. 3 and 4. Details of uprights and legs. 5 and 6. Escutcheon plate and drawer pull.

*Louvre*

PLATE 295                                        LOUIS XVI (towards end of style)

1. "Bonheur-du-jour," document case of ebony black Chinese lacquer and gilt bronzes (B. Molitor).    2. Detail of uprights and legs.    3. Upright sculpture.

*Louvre*

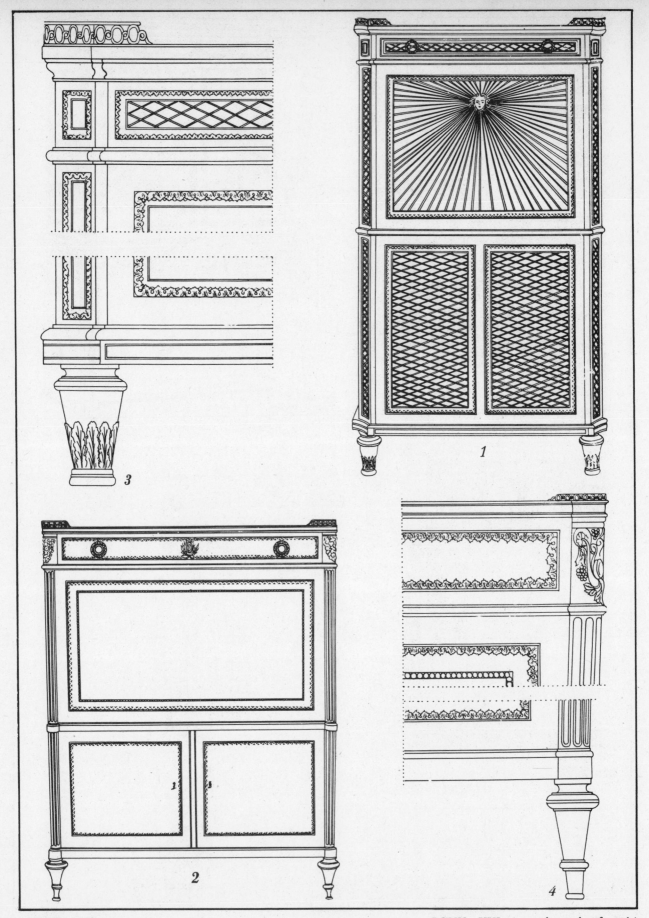

PLATE 296                                                    LOUIS XVI (towards end of style)

1. Marquetry secretary.   2. Mahogany secretary. Both secretaries have bronzes and copper trim skirting the top.   3 and 4. Details of uprights.

*Poles collection and private collection*

PLATE 297

LOUIS XVI

1. Carved wooden bed in the Renaissance tradition.    2. Post.    3. Cornice.    4. Top of the headboard.

*Private collection*

301

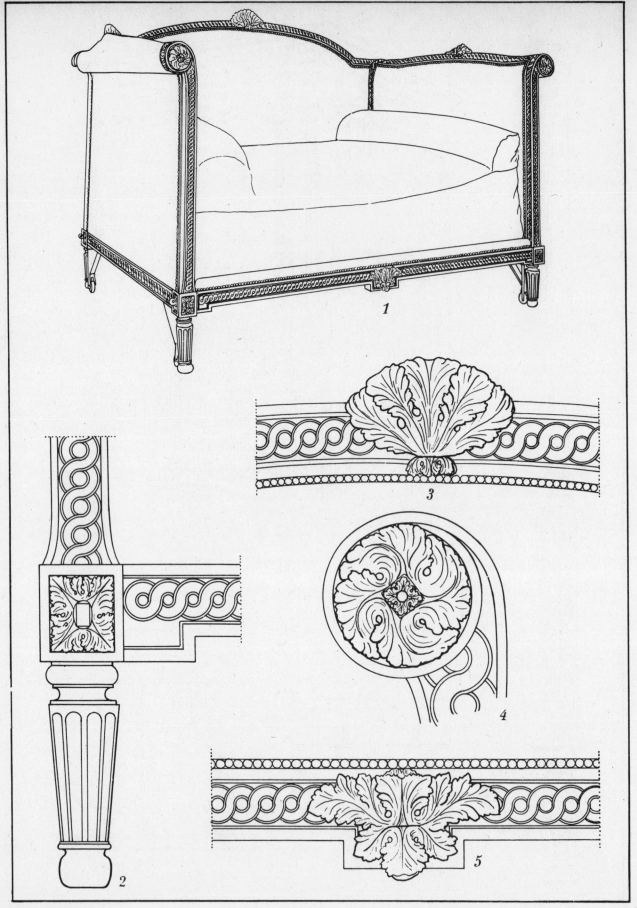

PLATE 298                                                    LOUIS XVI
1. Gilt carved wooden bed, upholstered in velvet.   2. Detail of leg.   3, 4 and 5. Details of carved motifs.

*Louvre*

PLATE 299
1. Bed.   2. Upright   3 and 4. Moulding decorations.

LOUIS XVI

*Louvre*

PLATE 300

1. Gilt carved wooden bed, upholstered in silk.  2. Detail of upright.  3. Detail of crest of headboard.

LOUIS XVI

*Louvre*

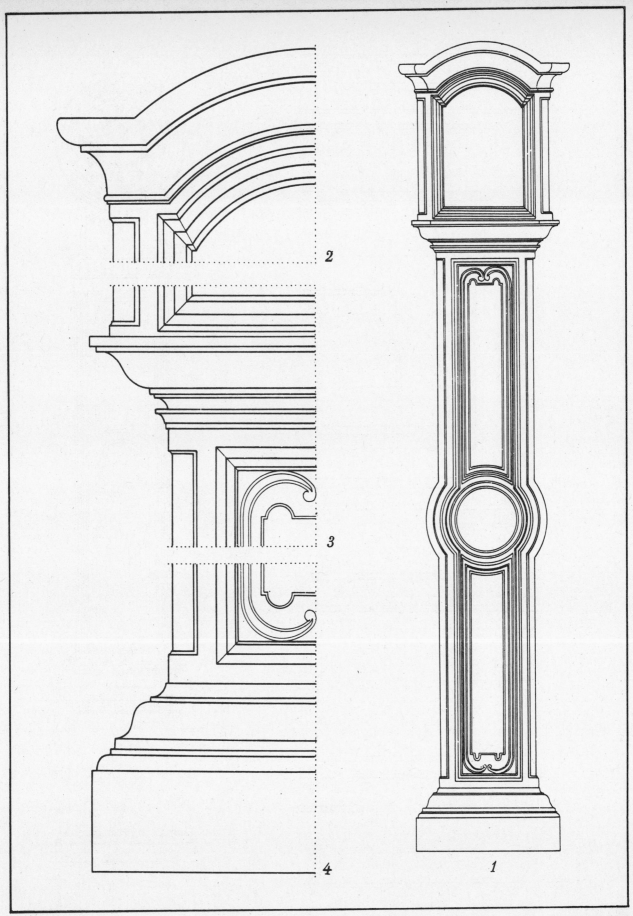

PLATE 301

1. Oak clock cabinet.   2, 3 and 4. Details of front.

LOUIS XVI

*Private collection*

PLATE 302

1. Oak clock cabinet.    2. Details of the cabinet.

LOUIS XVI

*Private collection*

**PLATE** 303

1. Clock cabinet with marquetry and gilt bronzes (M. Carlin and Gouthiere).   2. Detail.   3. Leg.   4. Hands.

*Louvre*

PLATE 304

LOUIS XVI

1. Mahogany barometer with gilt bronzes (M. Carlin).   2. Detail of top.   3. Detail of bottom.   4 and 5. Hands.

*Louvre*

308

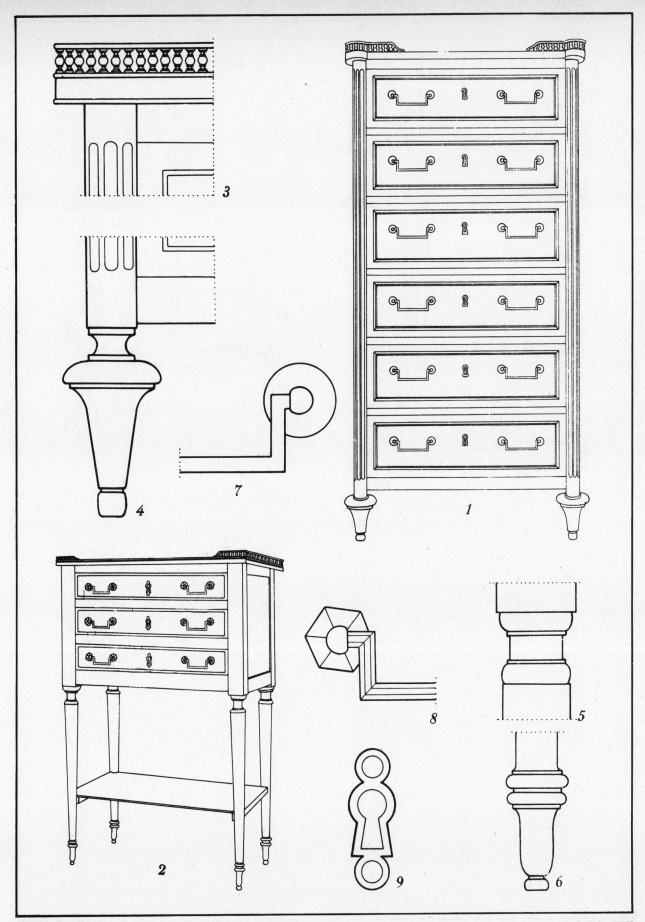

PLATE 305

LOUIS XVI

1 and 2. Mahogany and copper chiffoniers.  3, 4, 5 and 6. Details of uprights.  7, 8 and 9. Drawer pulls and escutcheon plate.

*Private collections*

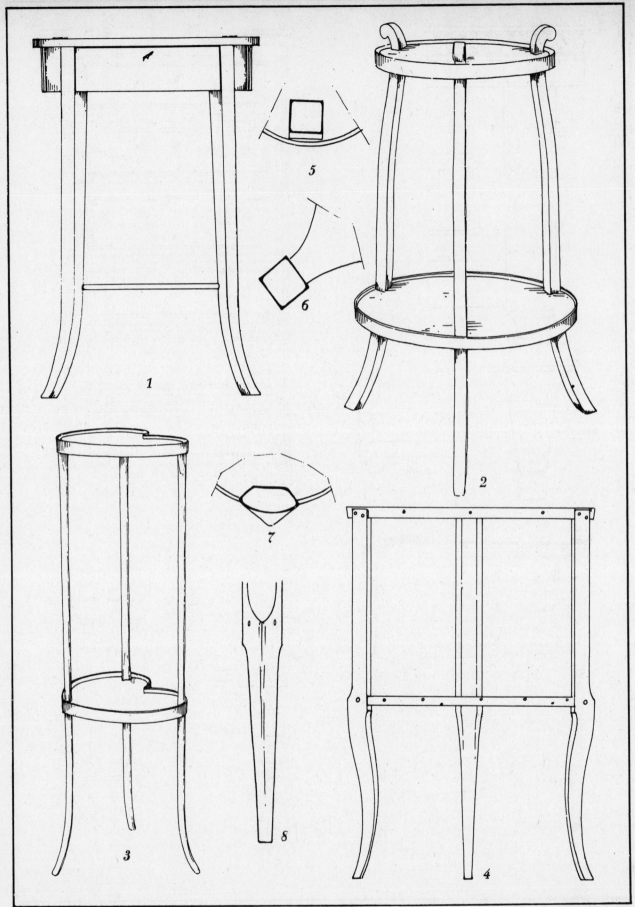

PLATE 306

Simple furniture with some elements of the style: 1. Small worktable. 2. Small stand. 3. Small table with heart-shaped shelves. 4. Small table with shelf. 5, 6 and 7. Leg sections. 8. Leg.

*Private collections*

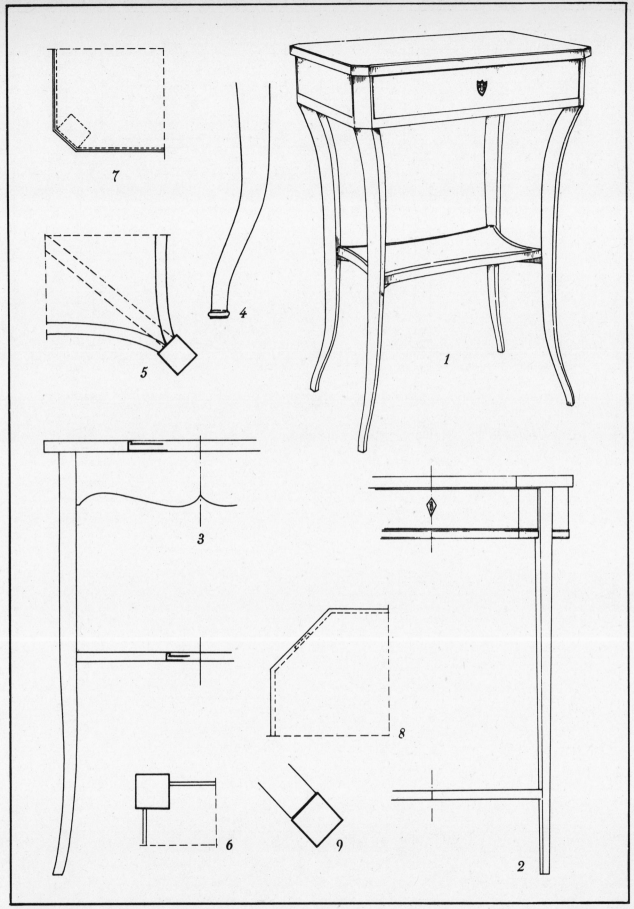

PLATE 307

LOUIS XVI

1 and 2. Small worktables.  3. Small table.  4. Leg.  5 and 6. Shape of lower shelves.  7 and 8. Shape of table corners.  9. Placement of the leg on the diagonal.

*Private collections*

PLATE 308                                                LOUIS XVI

1 and 2. Small worktables.   3. Side view (these tables are pushed up against the wall).   4. Leg.   5. Cross section of the leg.   6. Detail of turned leg.

*Private collections*

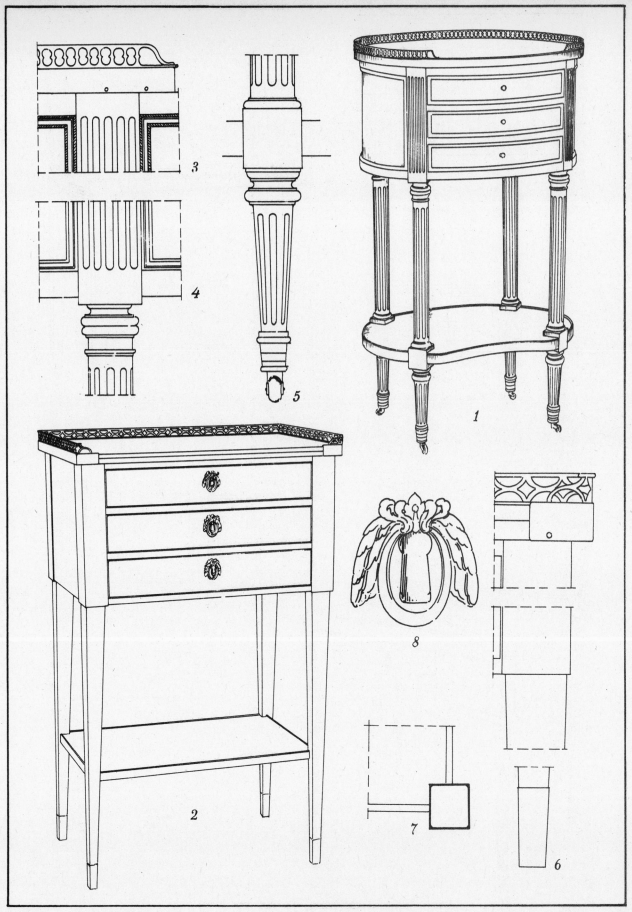

PLATE 309
LOUIS XVI
1 and 2. Small sewing tables.   3, 4 and 5. Details of leg.   6 and 7. Leg of second table.   8. Escutcheon plate.
*Private collections*

313

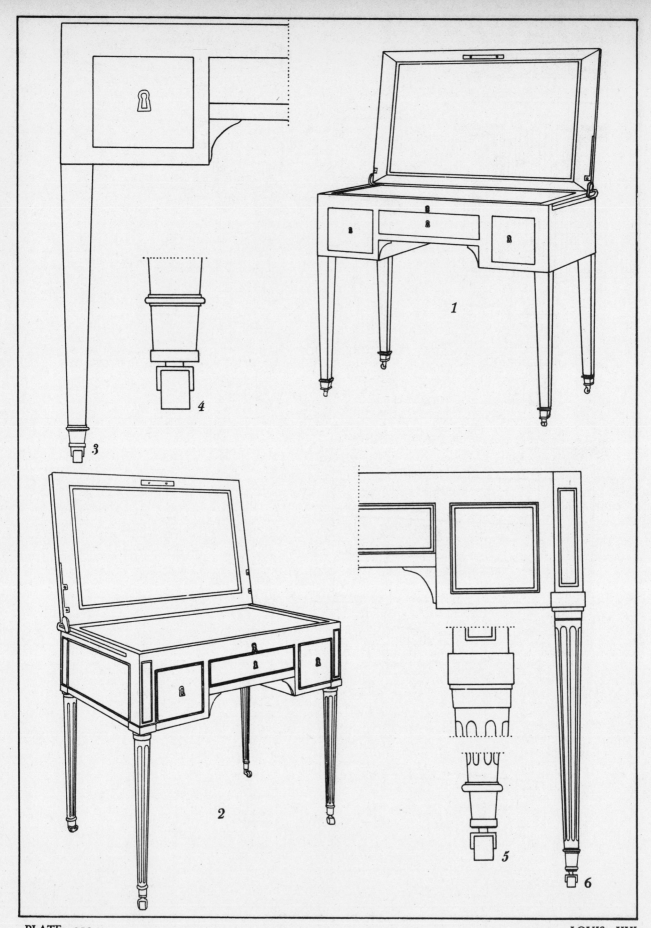

PLATE 310                                                                 LOUIS XVI

1 and 2. Mahogany vanities with mirrors in movable frames. The second has panels outlined with gilt bronze decorative lines.   3, 4, 5 and 6. Details of uprights and legs.

*Fontainebleau Palace*

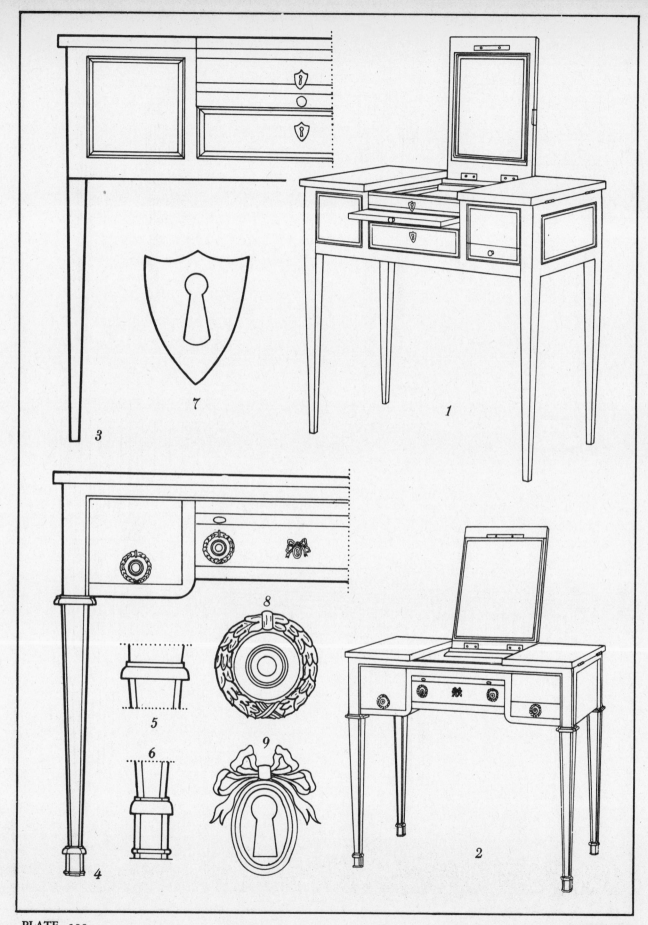

PLATE 311

LOUIS XVI

1. Vanity with marquetry and decorative lines of rosewood.   2. Mahogany vanity with bronzes.   3 and 4. Details of uprights and legs.   5 and 6. Details of moulding.   7, 8 and 9. Escutcheon plates and drawer pull.

*Museum of Decorative Arts, Paris*

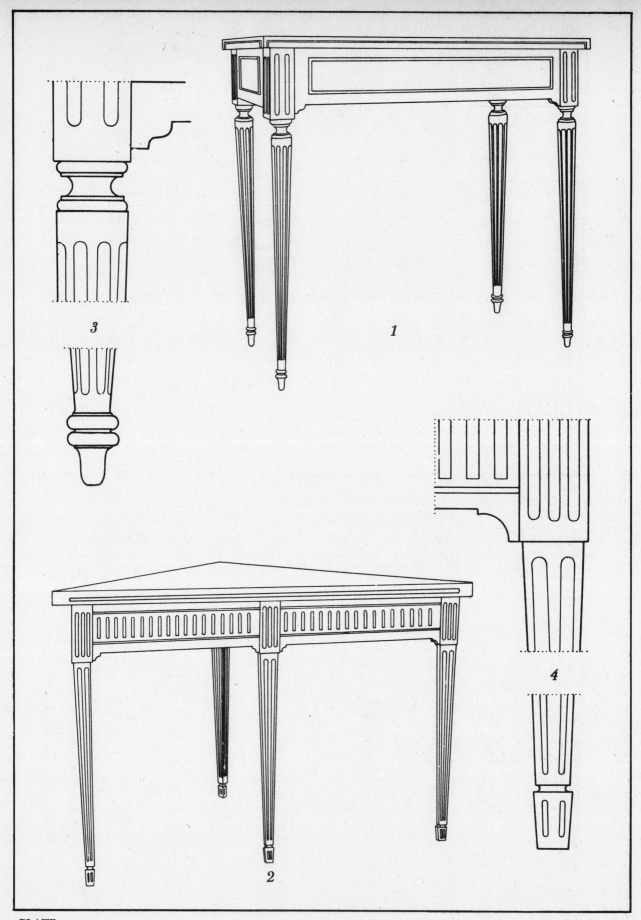

**PLATE** 312

1. Game table.   2. Triangular plant table.   3 and 4. Details of legs.

*Private collection*

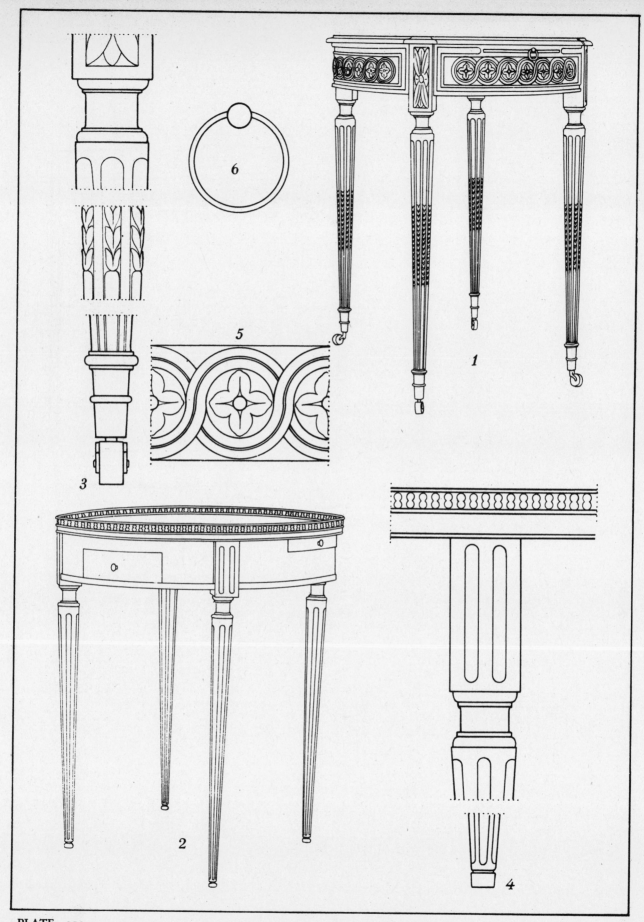

PLATE 313

LOUIS XVI

1 and 2. Small game tables. The first table is of marble and gilt wood. The second one is of mahogany, copper and marble. 3 and 4. Legs. 5. Decoration. 6. Drawer pull.

*Private collections*

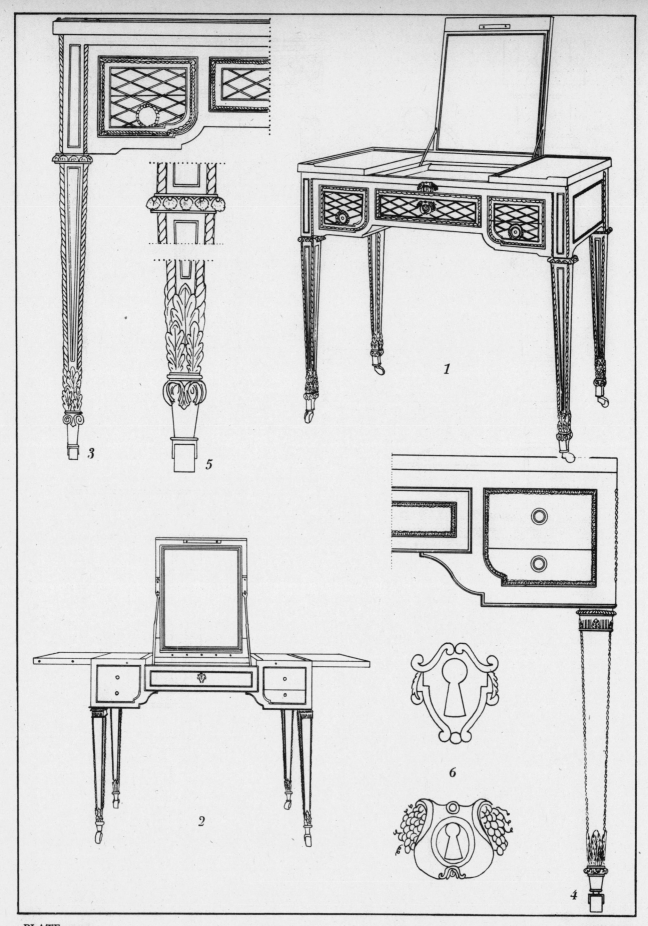

PLATE 314

1 and 2. Mahogany vanities, with ornamented lines. The first one is outlined in gilt bronze, the second in marquetry.   3 and 4. Details of uprights and legs.   5. Detail of leg.   6. Escutcheon plates.

*Mobilier National de France and Petit Trianon*

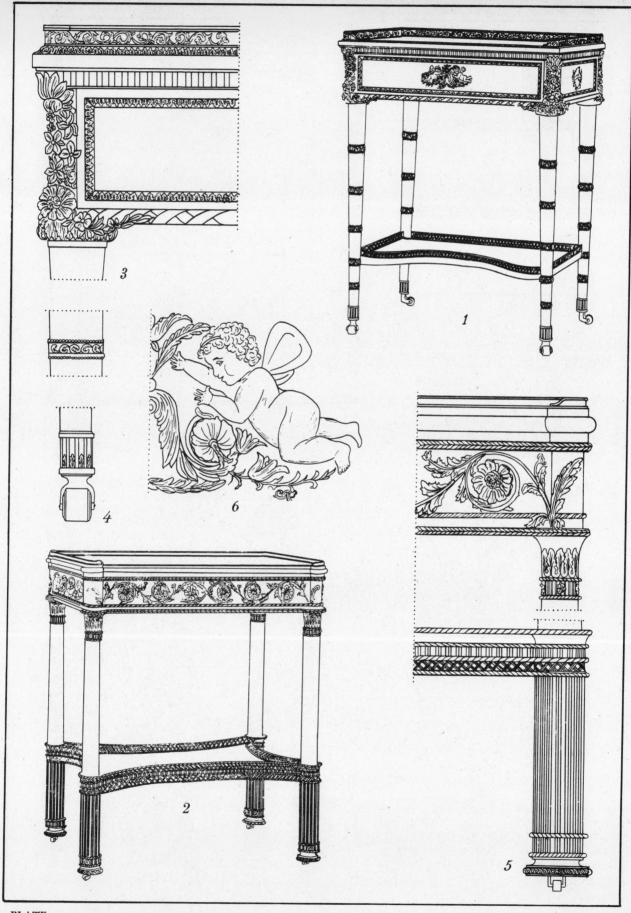

PLATE 315

LOUIS XVI

1 and 2. Worktable and lady's desk, both of mahogany and decorated with gilt bronzes. 3, 4 and 5. Details of uprights. 6. Sketch of escutcheon plate.

*Louvre*

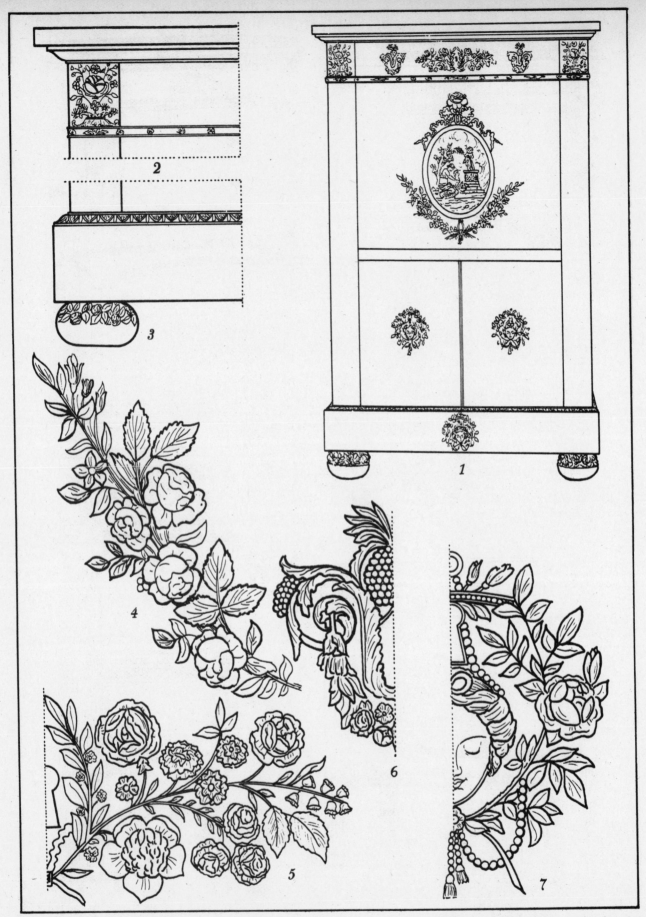

PLATE 316                                                    LOUIS XVI (end of style)
1. Mahogany and ebony desk with carved gilt bronzes and a turquoise blue marble top.   2 and 3. Detail of top of upright and foot.   4, 5, 6 and 7. Bronze decorations.

*Fontainebleau Palace*

PLATE 317

1, 2 and 3. Small framed mirrors with finials of cut and very ornately carved wood.   4 and 5. Details of frames.

*Private collections*

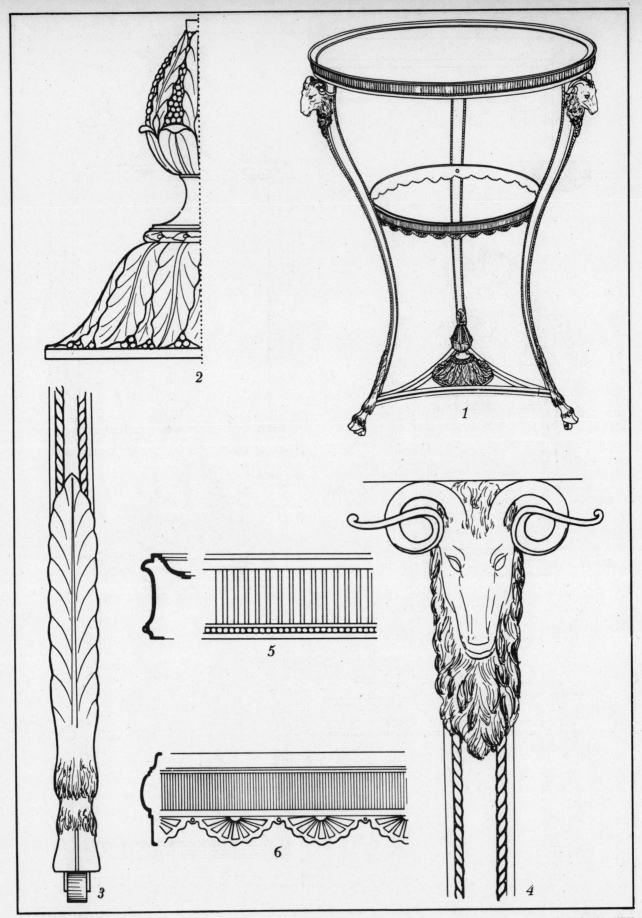

PLATE 318                                                    LOUIS XVI

1. Bronze pedestal table.   2. Detail of central finial.   3 and 4. Details of legs.   5 and 6. Mouldings.

*Champs-Élysée Palace*

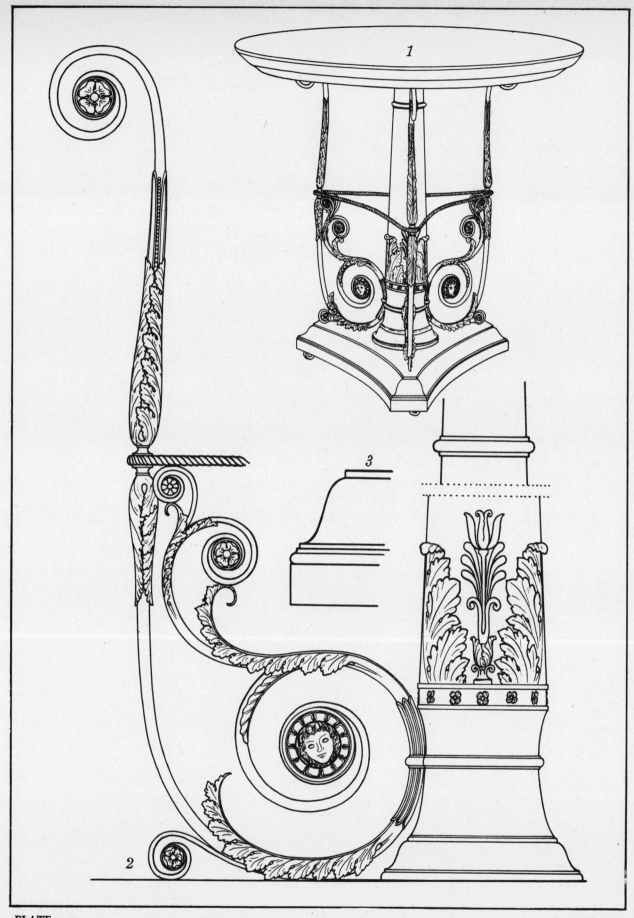

PLATE 319

LOUIS XVI

1. Small circular pedestal table of mahogany with a marble top and bronze decorations.　2. Detail of wooden middle support and bronze side supports.　3. Lower moulding.

*Versailles Palace*

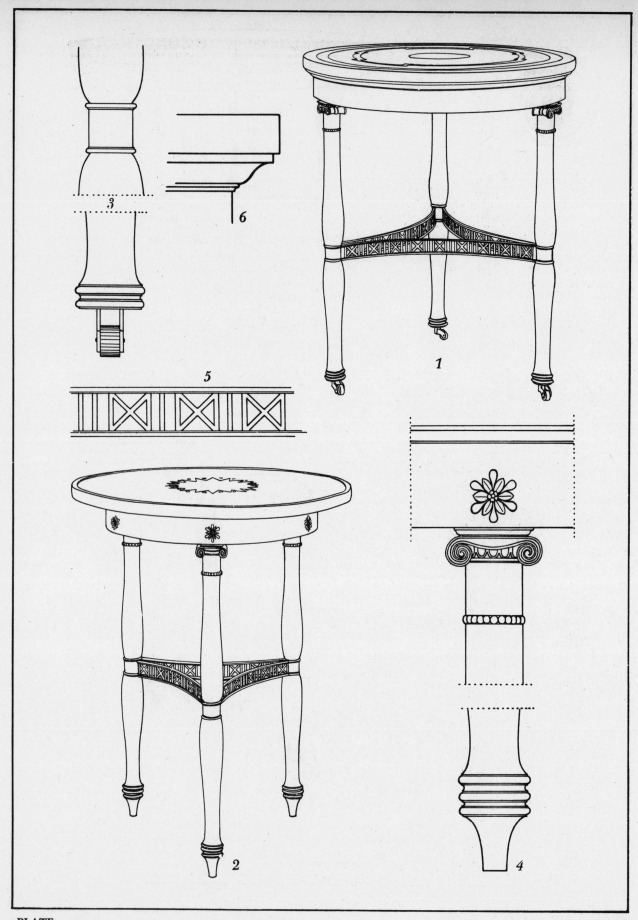

PLATE 320

LOUIS XVI

1 and 2. Small mahogany pedestal tables, with marble tops, bronze decorations and bronze festoons between the legs.   3 and 4. Legs.   5. Detail of festoon.   6. Profile of the moulding.

*Malmaison Castle and Fontainebleau Palace*

PLATE 321                                                                                      LOUIS XVI

1 and 2. Round mahogany pedestal tables with bronzes.   3 and 4. Details of legs.   5. Detail of upper trim and
decorations.   6. Profile of same.

*Versailles Palace and Petit Trianon*

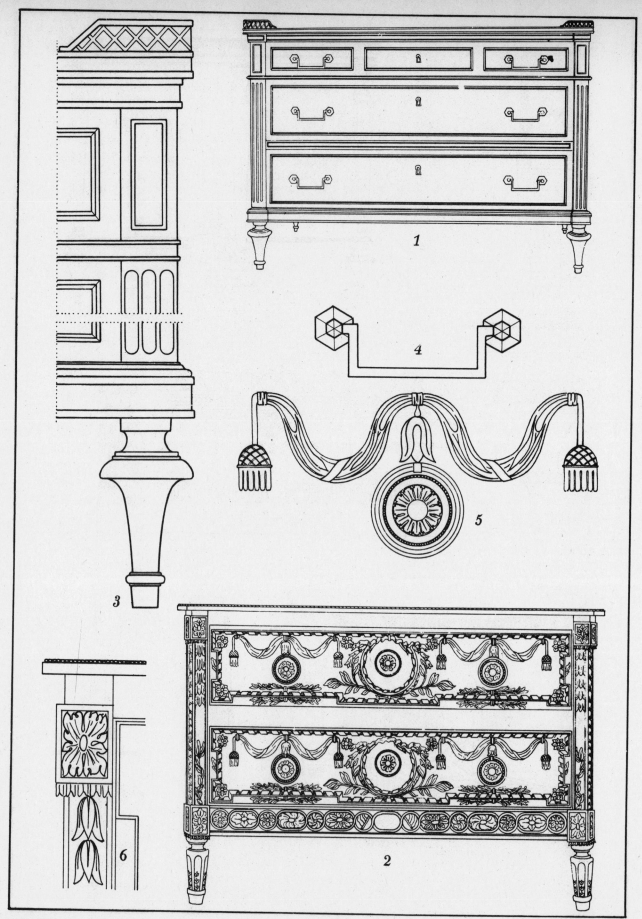

PLATE 322                                                                LOUIS XVI

1 and 2. Commodes: The first one is characterized by severe lines; the second one, from the region of Provence, by revolutionary emblems.   3. Detail of upright.   4 and 5. Drawer pulls.   6. Detail of upright.

*Private collections*

**PLATE 323**                                           LOUIS XVI (transition to Directoire)

1. Wardrobe with two doors (the escutcheon plate is in the style of Louis XV).   2 and 3. Details of escutcheon plate and hinge.   4 and 5. Cornice and base of leg.

*Private collection*

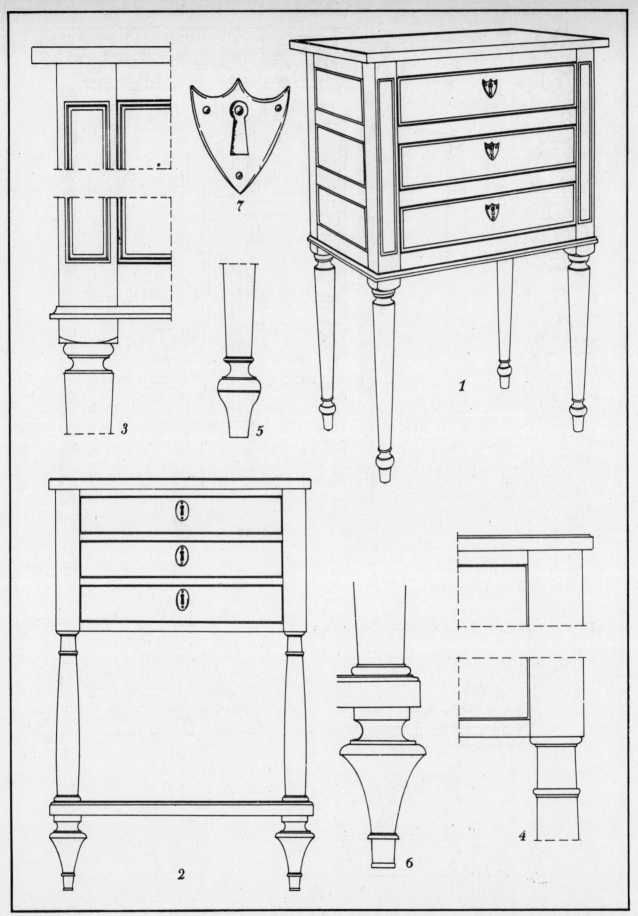

PLATE 324          END OF LOUIS XVI AND BEGINNING OF DIRECTOIRE (simplified style)
1. Small commode with three drawers.   2. Small sewing table.   3 and 4. Details of uprights.   5 and 6. Legs.   7. Escutcheon plate.

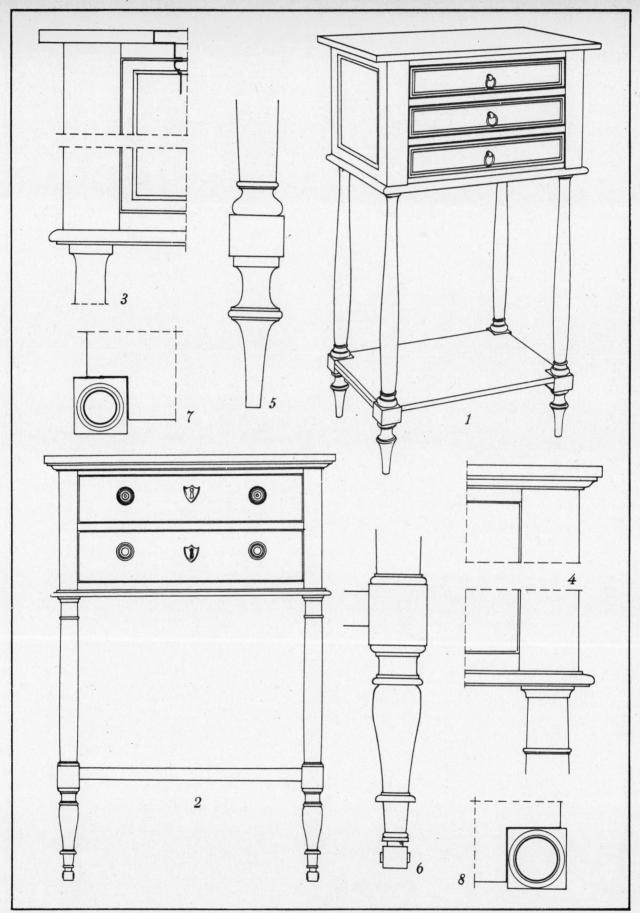

**PLATE 325**     END OF LOUIS XVI AND BEGINNING OF DIRECTOIRE

1 and 2. Small sewing tables with two and three drawers.   3 and 4. Uprights.   5 and 6. Legs.   7 and 8. Cross section of uprights.

**PLATE 326**                                      END OF LOUIS XVI AND DIRECTOIRE

1 and 2. Small pedestal tables.    3 and 4. Supports.    5 and 6. Turned posts.    7 and 8. Balusters on lower shelf.

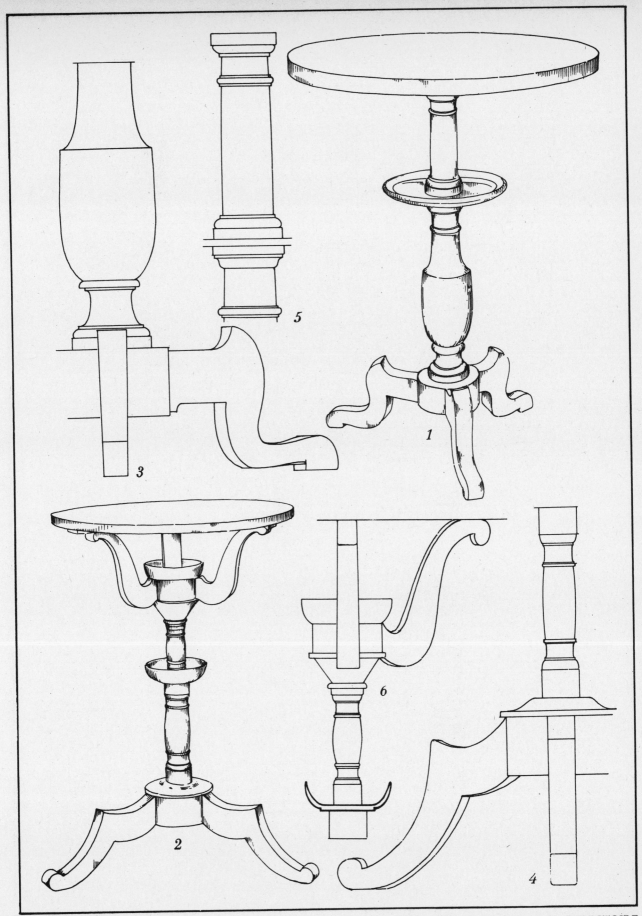

PLATE 327                                                    END OF LOUIS XVI AND DIRECTOIRE
1 and 2. Small pedestal tables.    3 and 4. Supports.    5 and 6. Turned central posts.

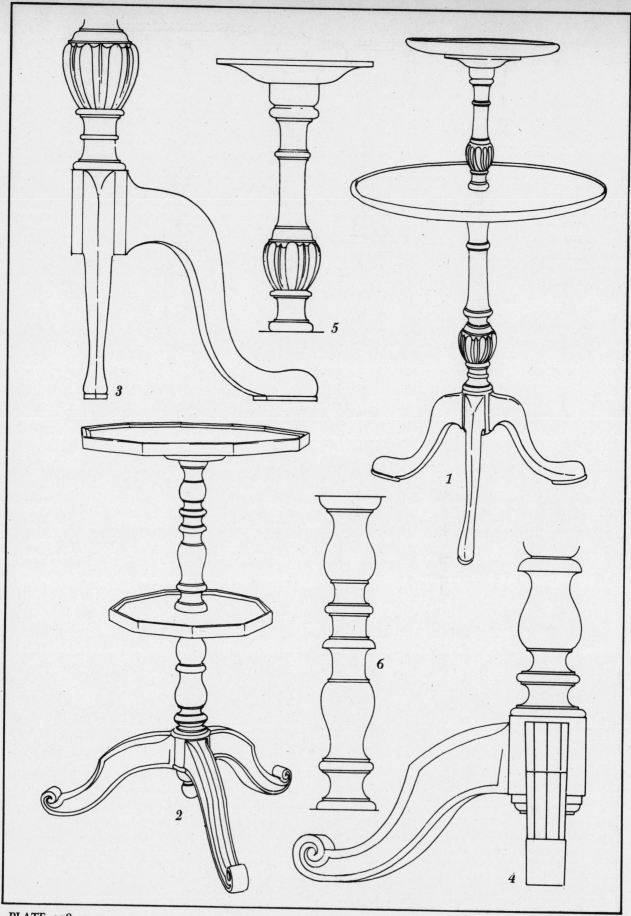

PLATE 328

1 and 2. Small pedestal tables.    3 and 4. Supports.    5 and 6. Turned central posts.

END OF LOUIS XVI AND DIRECTOIRE

**PLATE 329**

1 and 2. Small pedestal tables called "servantes" (servant girls) with three shelves.   3 and 4. Details of supports.   5 and 6. Turned central posts.

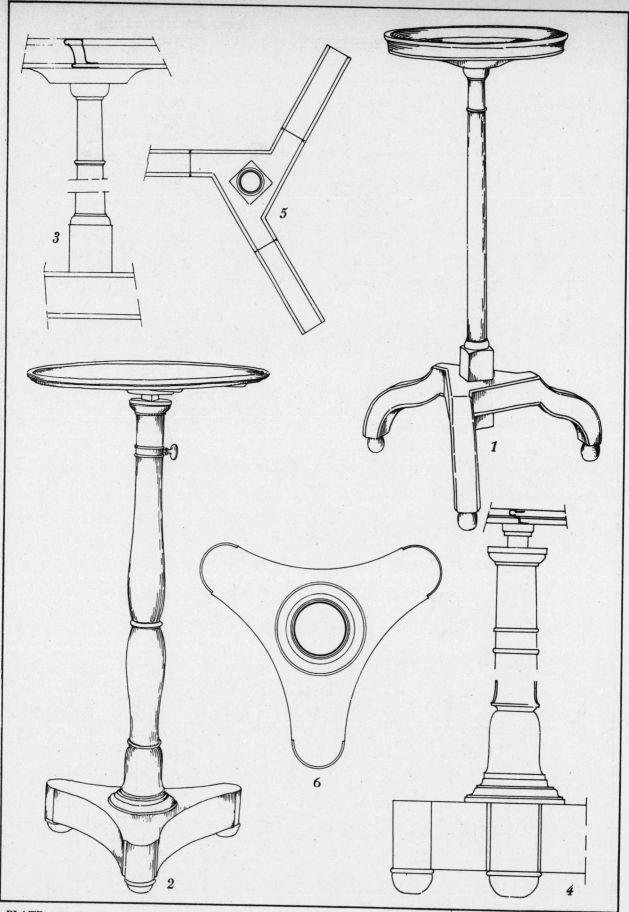

PLATE 330

1 and 2. Small pedestal tables.    3 and 4. Details of the supports.    5 and 6. Base of pedestals.

END OF LOUIS XVI AND DIRECTOIRE

334

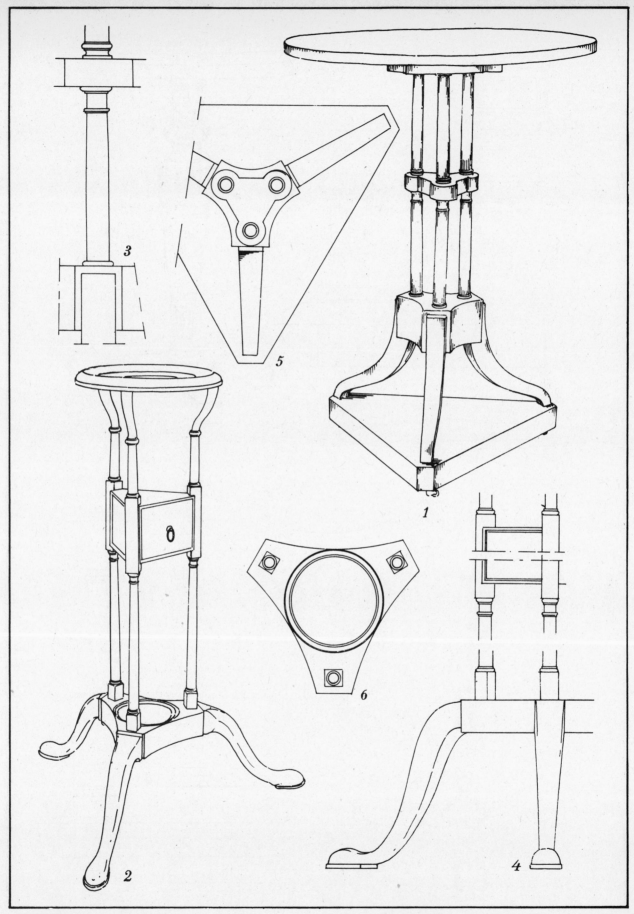

PLATE 331
END OF LOUIS XVI AND DIRECTOIRE
1 and 2. Small pedestal side tables.    3 and 4. Supports.    5 and 6. Base of pedestals.

335

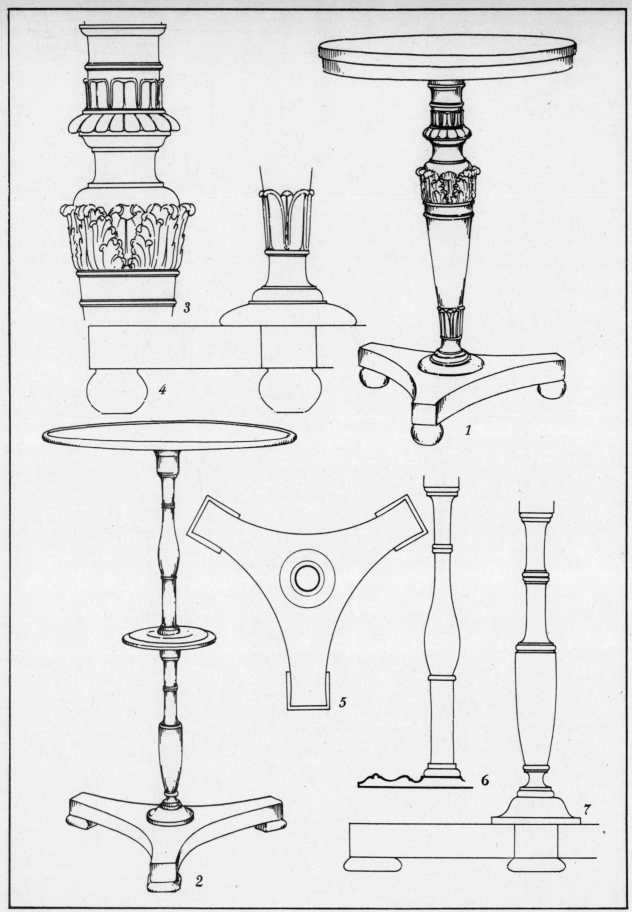

PLATE 332            END OF LOUIS XVI AND DIRECTOIRE

1 and 2. Small pedestal tables.    3 and 4. Details of the support.    5. Base.    6 and 7. Turned posts of second table.

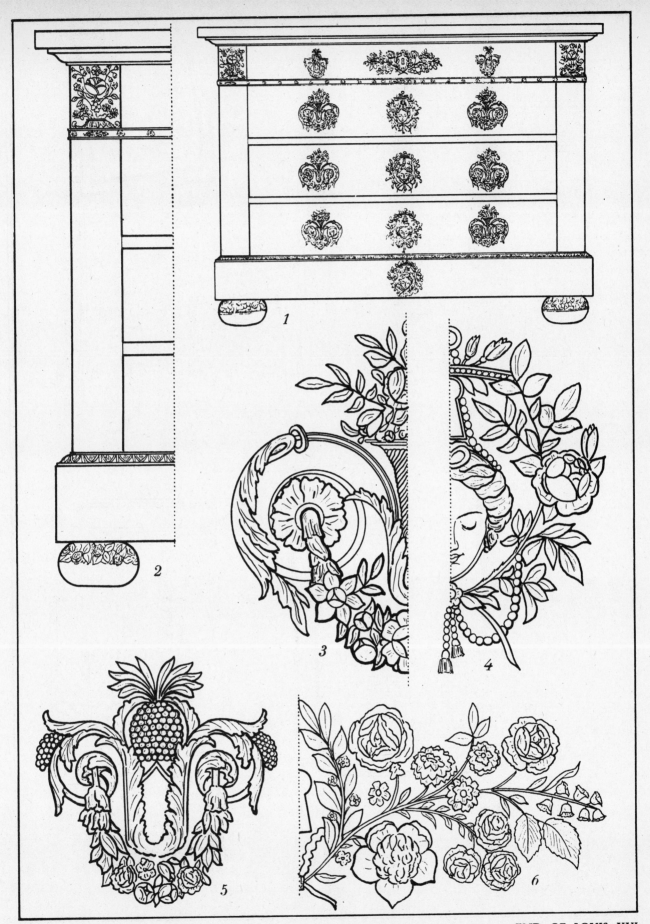

PLATE 333

END OF LOUIS XVI

1. Mahogany and ebony commode with four drawers, carved gilt bronzes and turquoise blue marble.   2. Details of upright and leg.   3 and 4. Decorative drawer pulls.   5 and 6. Very elaborate large escutcheon plates.

*Fontainebleau Palace*

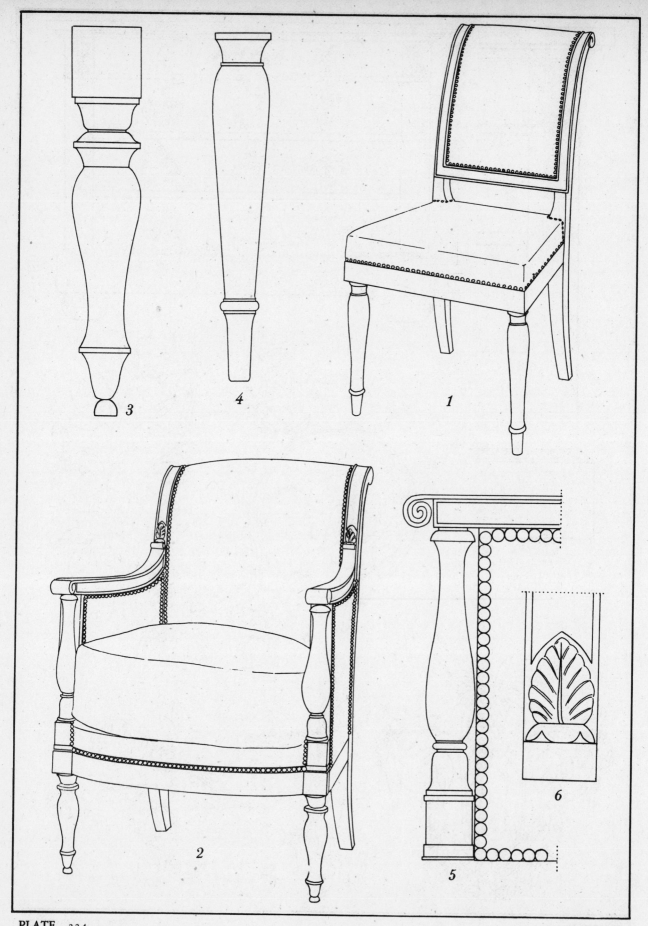

PLATE 334

1. Mahogany chair with rolled back. Back and seat are covered with cloth and horsehair. 2. Mahogany wing chair. Back is covered in silk. 3 and 4. Turned legs. 5. Arm support. 6. Detail of carving on upright.

*Malmaison Castle and Compiègne Palace*

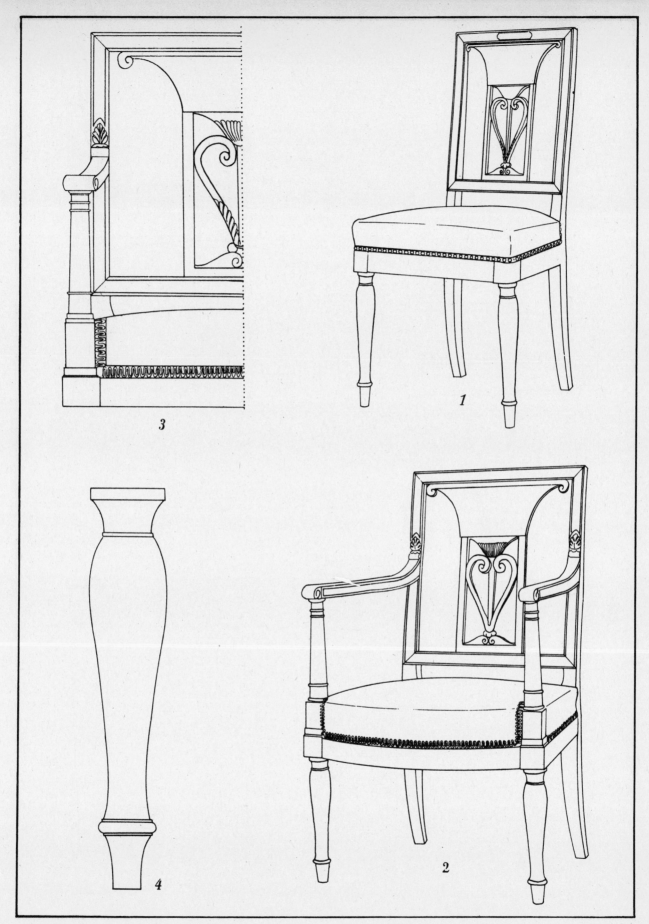

**PLATE** 335

**DIRECTOIRE**

1 and 2. Mahogany chair and armchair with openwork backs. Seat of first one is covered with leather, of second one with velvet.   3. Detail of straight back.   4. Leg.

*Malmaison Castle and Mobilier National de France*

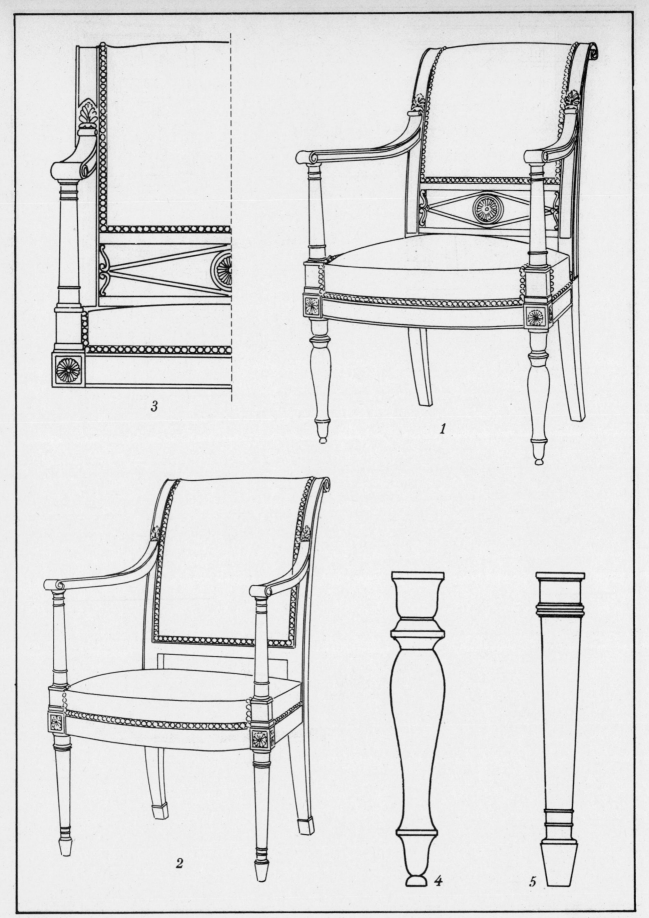

PLATE 336                                                                                  DIRECTOIRE

1 and 2. Mahogany armchairs covered in silk and leather, respectively.   3. Detail of back.   4 and 5. Turned legs in baluster and conical shapes which define this style.

*Compiègne Palace*

PLATE 337

DIRECTOIRE

1. Small mahogany chair with rolled openwork back and silk seat.  2. Mahogany chair with rolled openwork back and low seat, to go next to the fireplace.  3. Leg.  4. Scroll of rolled back.  5. Detail of back.  6. Rosette on rear upright.

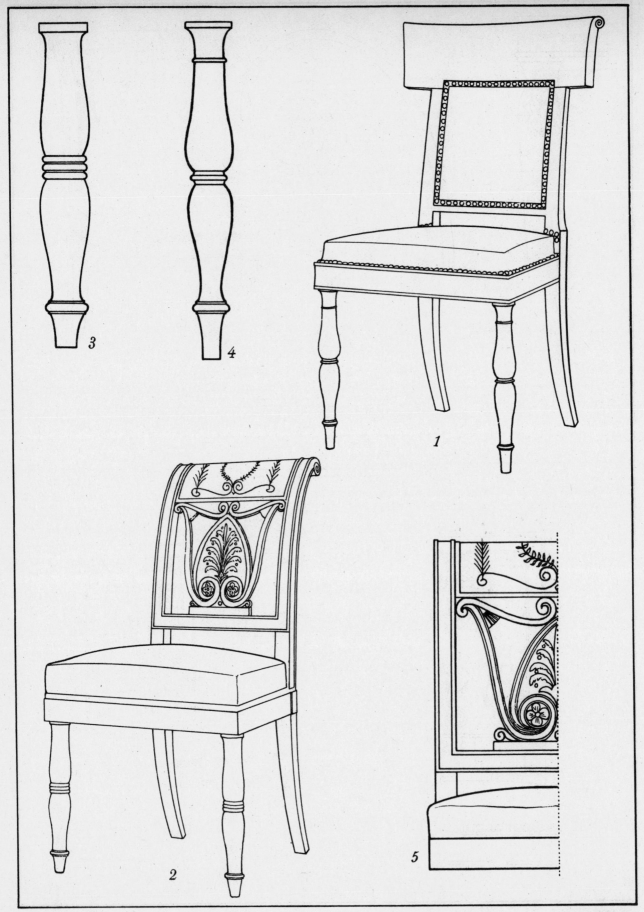

PLATE 338

1 and 2. Mahogany chairs. The first chair has a cylindrical back; the second one has a rolled back.   3 and 4. Legs.   5. Back.

*Fontainebleau Palace*

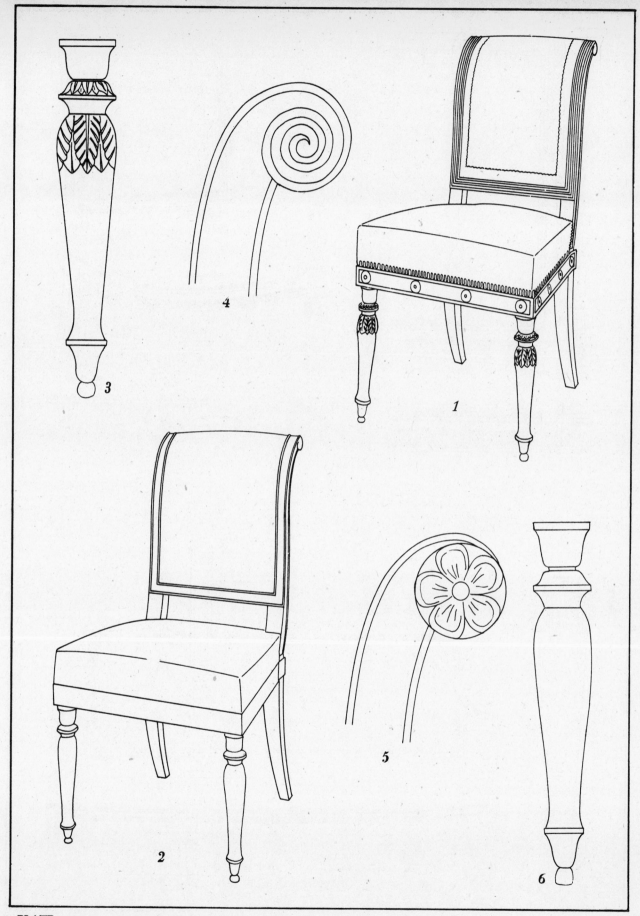

**PLATE** 339

1 and 2. Chairs with rolled backs and turned legs.   3 and 4. Leg and scroll on back of first chair.   5 and 6. Leg and scroll of second chair.

DIRECTOIRE

*Malmaison Castle*

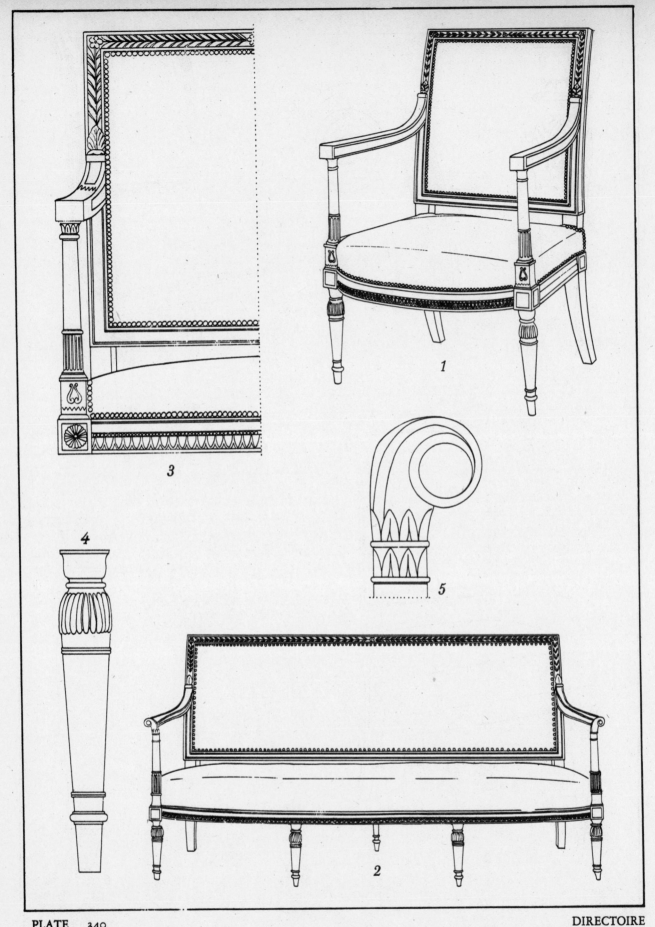

PLATE 340

DIRECTOIRE

1 and 2. Carved wooden armchair and sofa, painted grey and covered with Beauvais tapestry. 3. Back. 4. Leg. 5. Scroll at end of arm.

*Fontainebleau Palace*

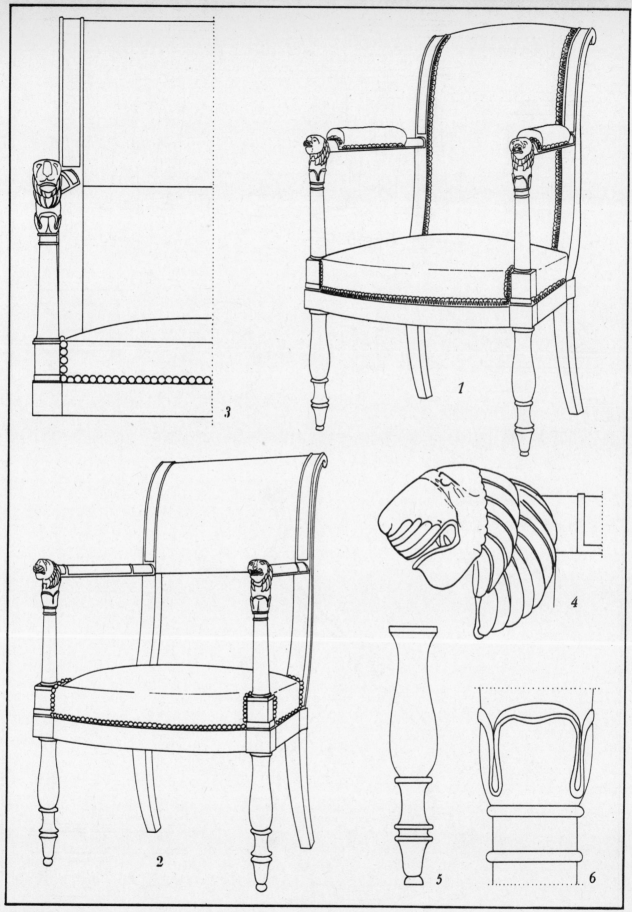

PLATE 341                                                                  DIRECTOIRE

1 and 2. Mahogany armchairs with rolled backs, arms ending in lions' heads and covered in silk and velvet.   3. Back.   4. End of arm.   5. Turned leg.   6. Detail of arm support.

*Mobilier National de France*

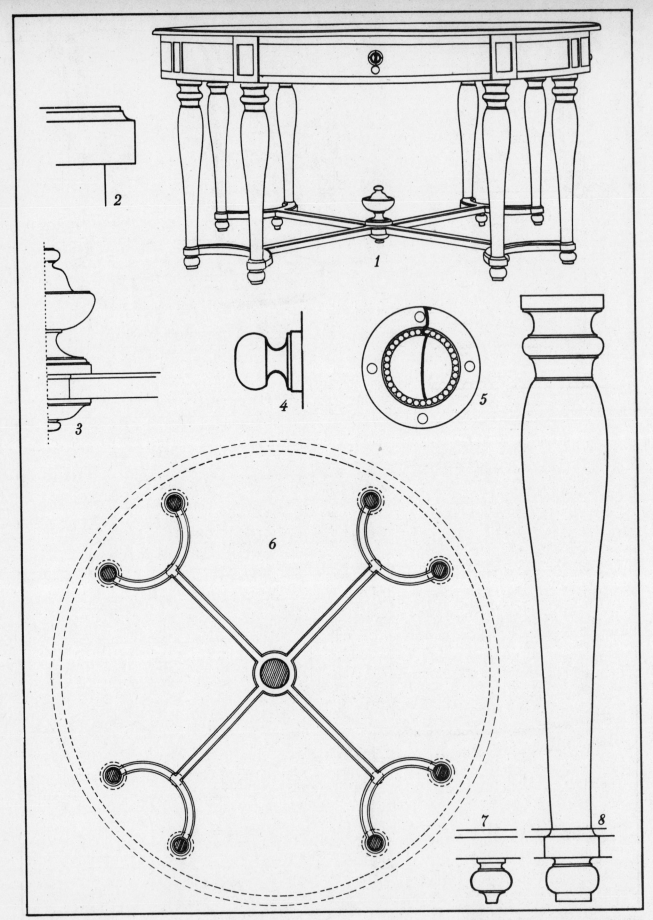

**PLATE 342**                                   DIRECTOIRE (beginning of style)

1. Round table of blackened beechwood with eight turned legs.  2. Upper moulding.  3. Central finial.  4 and 5. Drawer pull and escutcheon plate on drawer.  6. Base.  7 and 8. Leg and details of feet.

*National Archive (Spain)*

**PLATE** 343

1 and 2. Console tables of Brazilian rosewood and pear. 3 and 4. Details of uprights. 5, 6 and 7. Drawer pulls and escutcheon plate.

*Private collection*

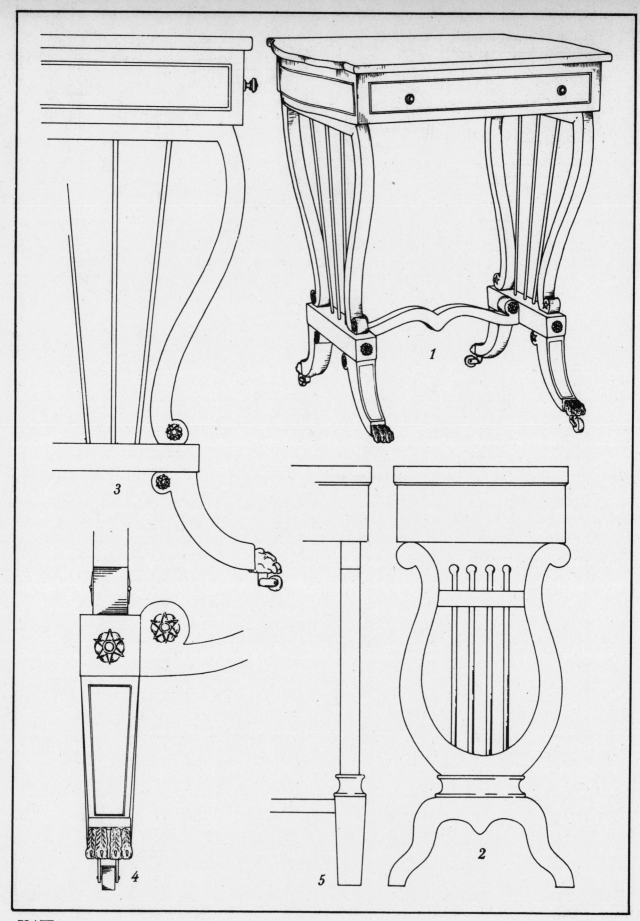

PLATE 344

1 and 2. Small worktables.   3. Side view.   4 and 5. Legs.

DIRECTOIRE

*Private collection*

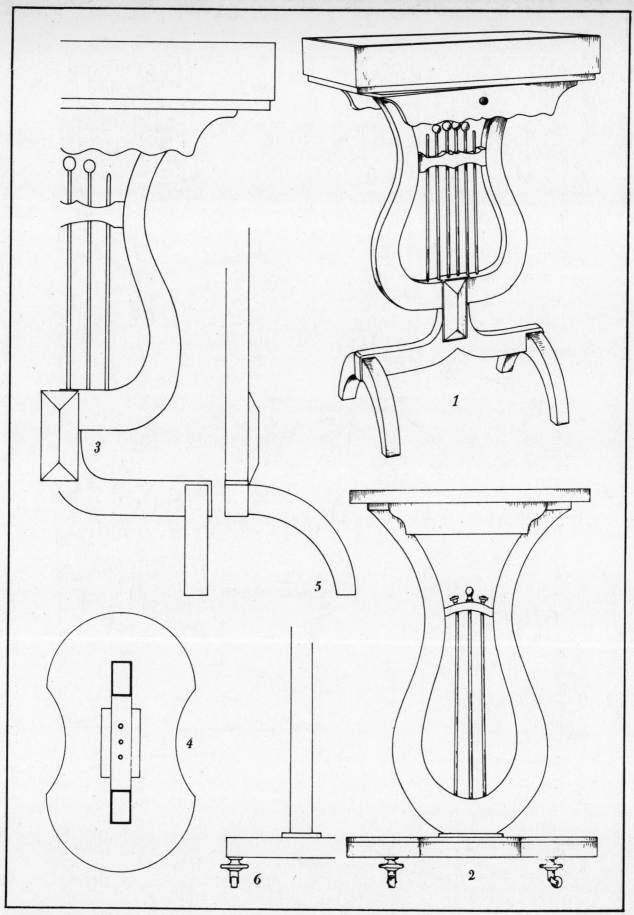

PLATE 345

1 and 2. Small knitting tables called "knitters."   3. Detail.   4. Shape of lower bracket.   5 and 6. Legs.

DIRECTOIRE

*Private collection*

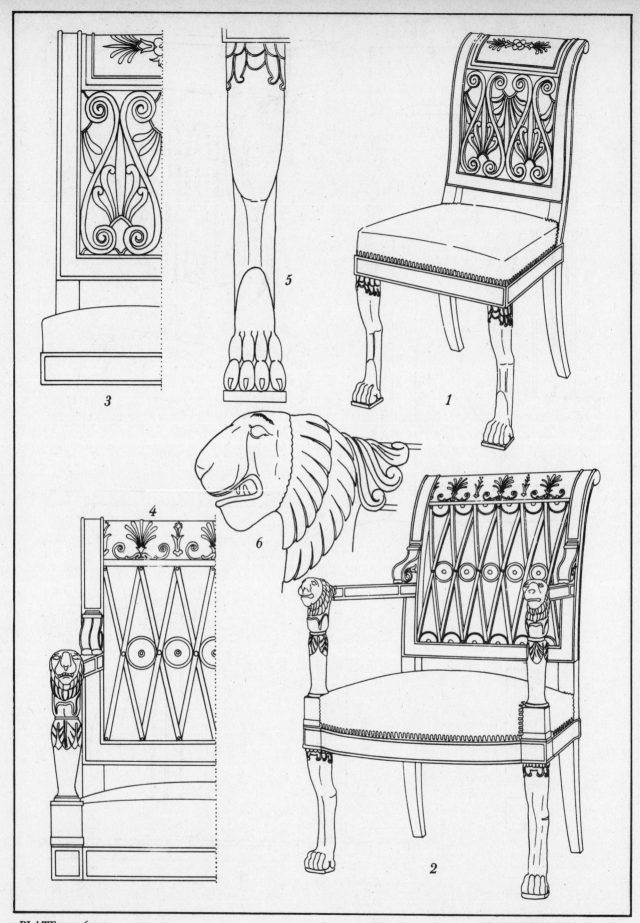

PLATE 346

DIRECTOIRE (Consulate)

1. Mahogany chair with rolled openwork back and clawed feet.   2. Mahogany armchair with arms ending in lion's head and rolled openwork back.   3 and 4. Backs.   5. Legs.   6. Arm end.

*Malmaison Castle and Mobilier National de France*

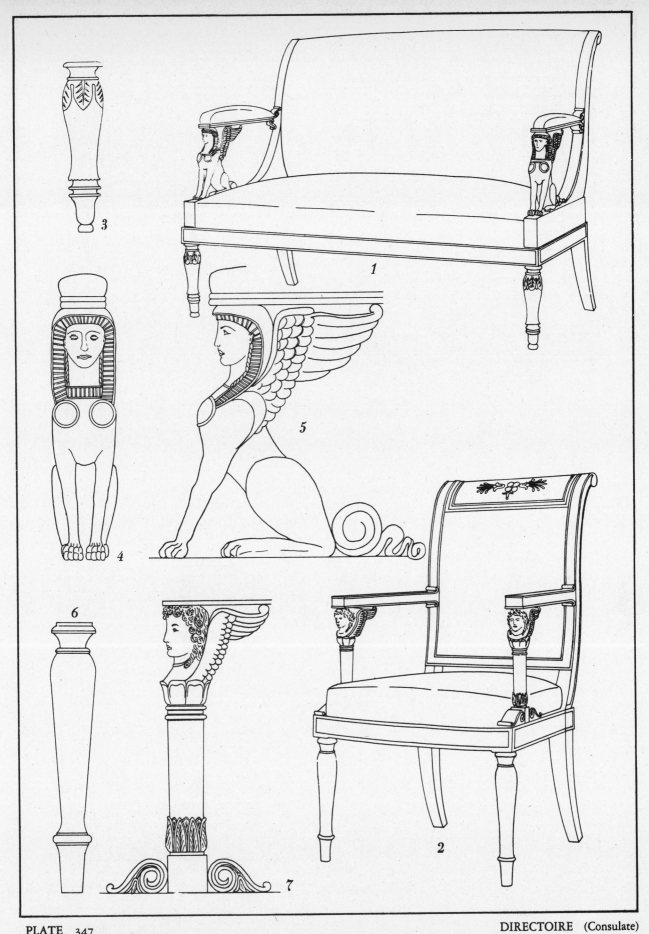

PLATE 347                                                          DIRECTOIRE (Consulate)

1 and 2. Sofa and armchair with rolled backs and arm supports in the shape of winged chimeras and women's heads.   3,
4 and 5. Leg and arm support from sofa.   6 and 7. Leg and arm support from armchair.

*Mobilier National de France*

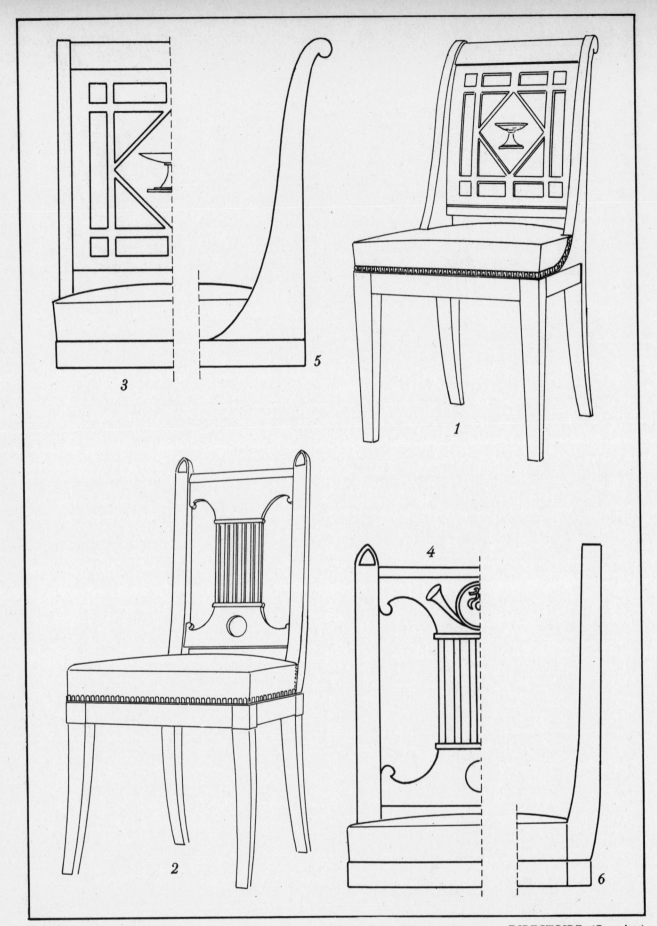

PLATE 348                                                                                                        DIRECTOIRE (Consulate)

1 and 2. Mahogany armchairs with openwork backs and square legs, the rear ones slightly curved. The first chair has a rolled back, the second chair, a straight one.    3 and 4. Backs.    5 and 6. Profile of backs.

*Mobilier National de France and Fontainebleau Palace*

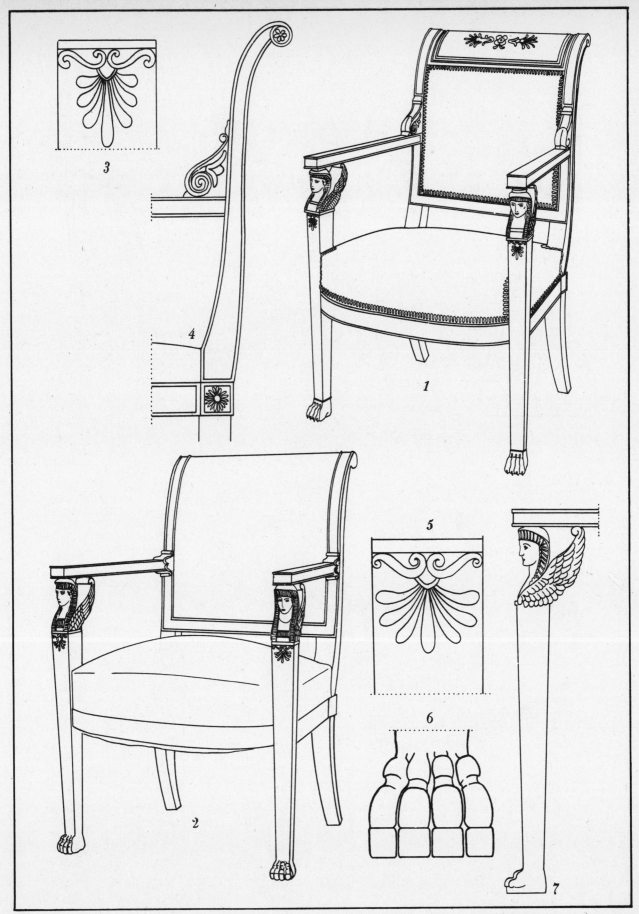

PLATE 349

DIRECTOIRE (Consulate)

1 and 2. Mahogany armchairs, the arms supported by Egyptian heads. 3 and 4. Decoration and back. 5, 6 and 7. Decoration on leg and clawed foot.

*Malmaison Castle and Mobilier National de France*

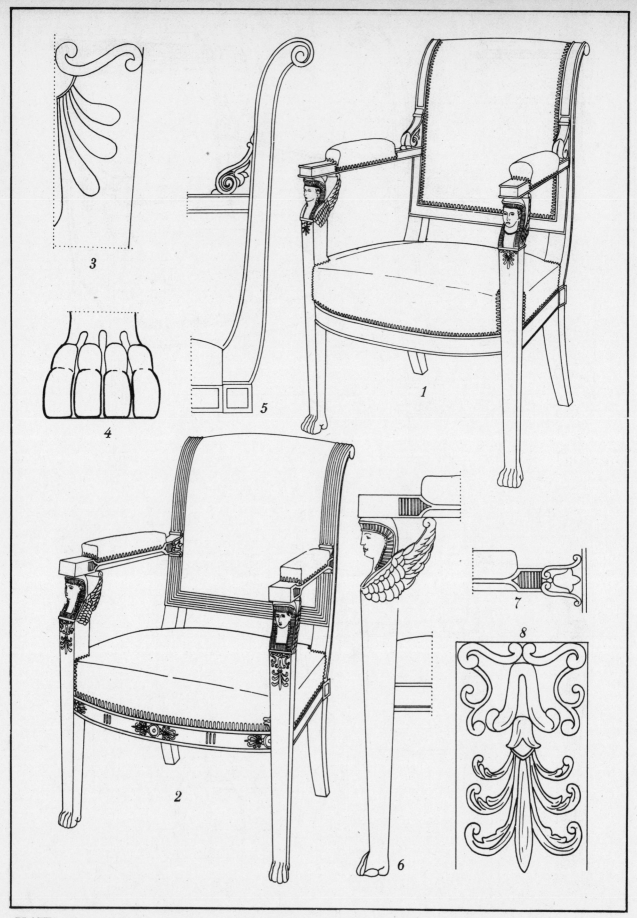

**PLATE** 350                                                                                           DIRECTOIRE (Consulate)

1 and 2. Gilt carved wooden armchair, arms supported by Egyptian heads, and rolled backs.   3, 4 and 5. Details of leg ornamentation and back of first chair.   6, 7 and 8. Decorative legs and connection of arms to back.

*Malmaison Castle*

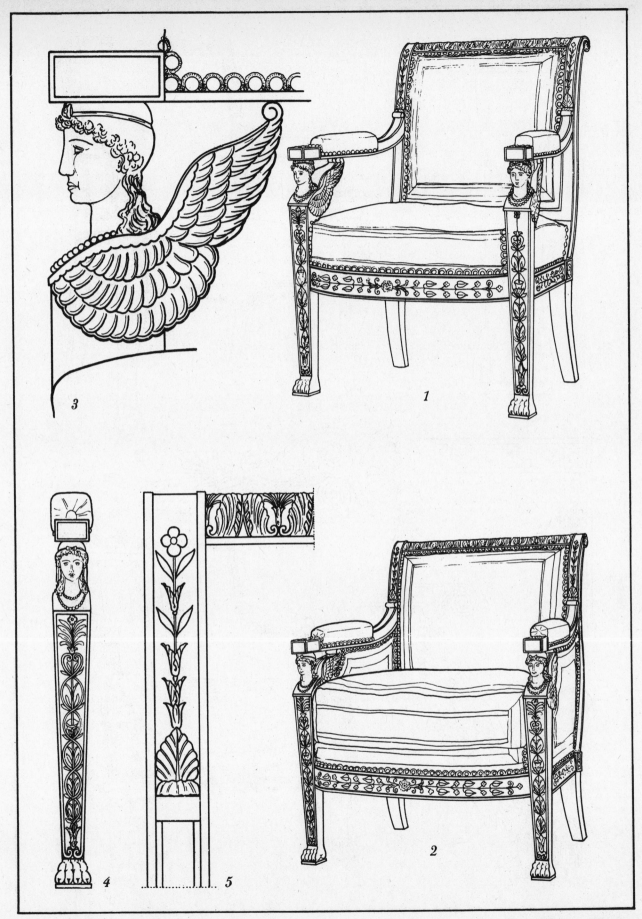

**PLATE 351**                                                    DIRECTOIRE (Consulate)

1 and 2. Armchairs with rolled backs and arms supported by winged Egyptian heads. The second one is a wing chair. 3.
Detail of arm support.   4. Leg.   5. Back upright.

*Mobilier National de France*

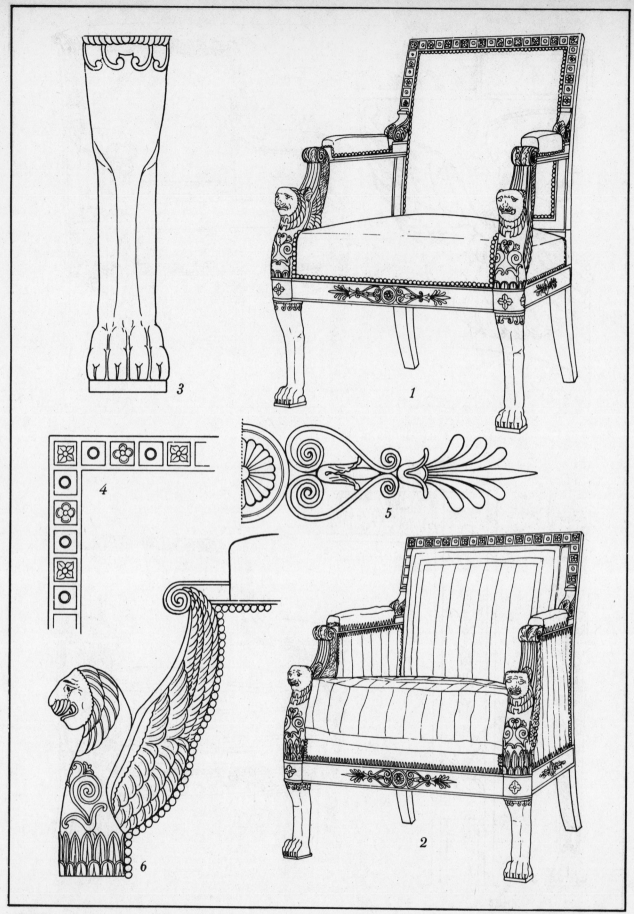

PLATE 352                                                    DIRECTOIRE (Consulate)
1 and 2. Armchairs with straight backs and arms supported by carved winged leopards' heads. The second one is a wing
chair.   3. Leg.   4 and 5. Decorations.   6. Detail of arm support.

*Mobilier National de France*

PLATE 353                                          DIRECTOIRE (end of Consulate)
1 and 2. Daybeds of gilt carved wood.   3. Side support.   4. Detail of support.   5. Carved design.   6. Clawed foot.

*Mobilier National de France*

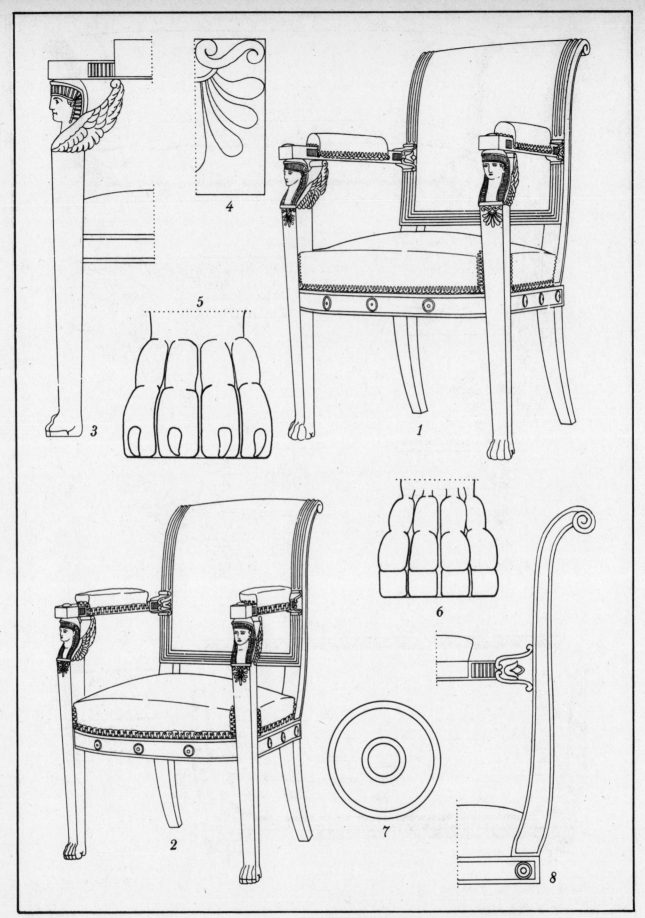

PLATE 354                        DIRECTOIRE (end of Consulate and beginning of Empire)

1 and 2. Gilt carved wooden armchairs with rolled backs and arms supported by Egyptian heads.   3, 4 and 5. Details of leg, decoration and clawed foot of first chair.   6, 7 and 8. Details of back, foot and decorative disk.

*Fontainebleau Palace and Mobilier National de France*

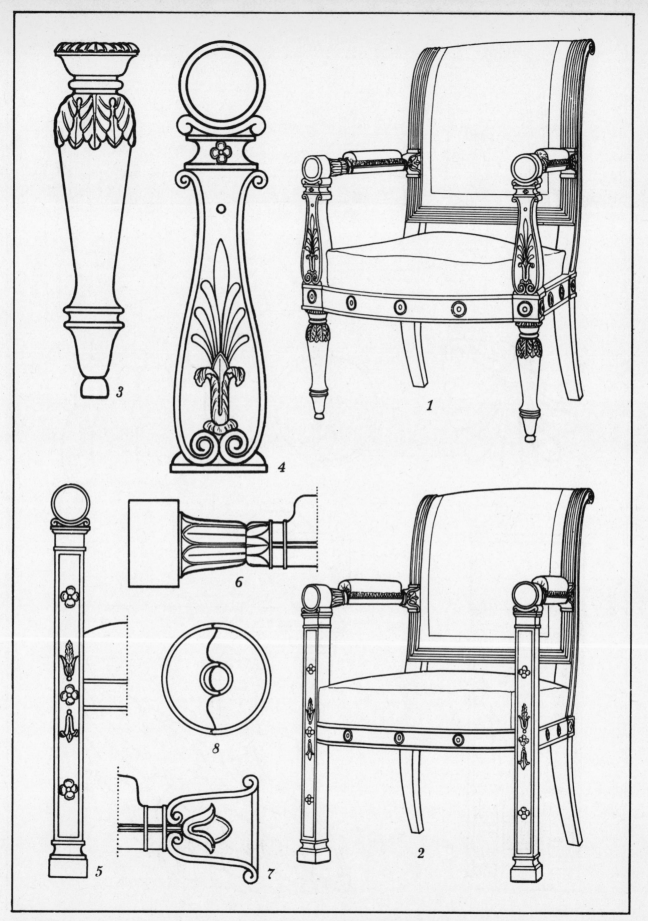

**PLATE 355**                                        DIRECTOIRE (end of Consulate and beginning of Empire)
1 and 2. Gilt carved wooden armchairs with rolled backs.    3 and 4. Leg and arm support.    5. Leg and support.    6
and 7. Details of connections of arm with support and with back.    8. Decorative disk.

*Mobilier National de France and Fontainebleau Palace*

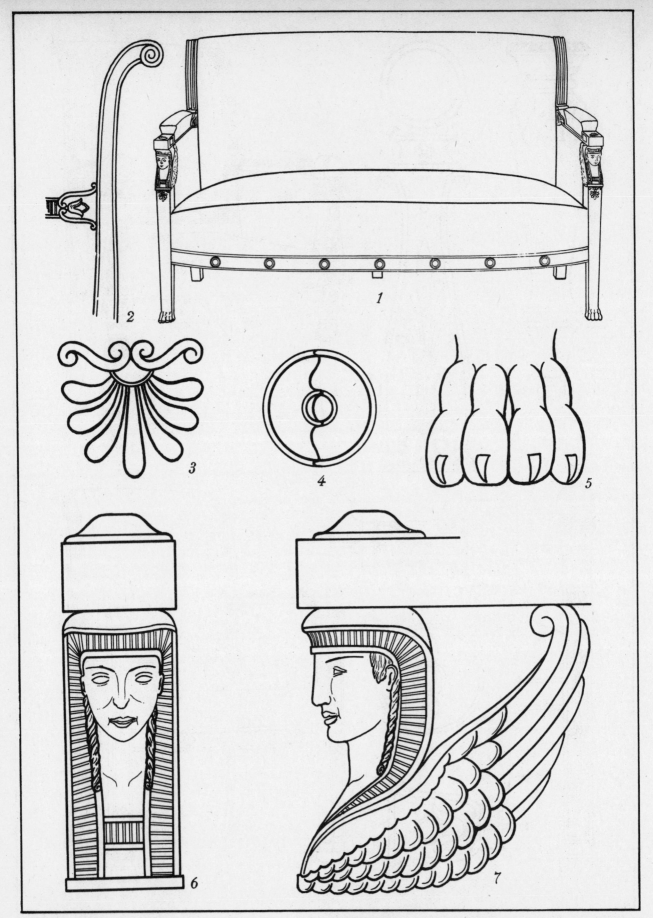

**PLATE 356**                    DIRECTOIRE (end of Consulate and beginning of Empire)

1. Gilt carved wooden sofa with rolled back, arm supports end in Egyptian heads.   2. Back.   3, 4 and 5. Decoration, disk and clawed foot.   6 and 7. Details of Egyptian woman's head.

*Mobilier National de France*

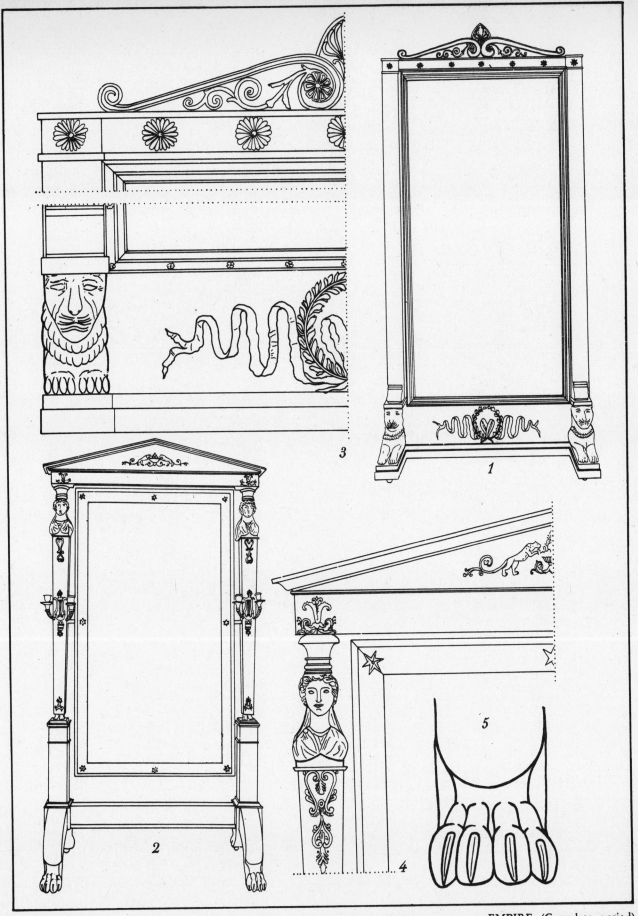

**PLATE 357**                                                    EMPIRE (Consulate period)

1 and 2. Portable mahogany mirrors with bronzes.   3 and 4. Details of uprights.   5. Clawed foot.

*Mobilier National de France and Fontainebleau Palace*

**PLATE 358**                                              EMPIRE (Consulate period)

1 and 2. Portable mahogany mirrors with bronzes.    3, 4 and 5. Details of uprights of first mirror.    6. Support.    7. Rosette.    8. Decoration.

*Mobilier National de France*

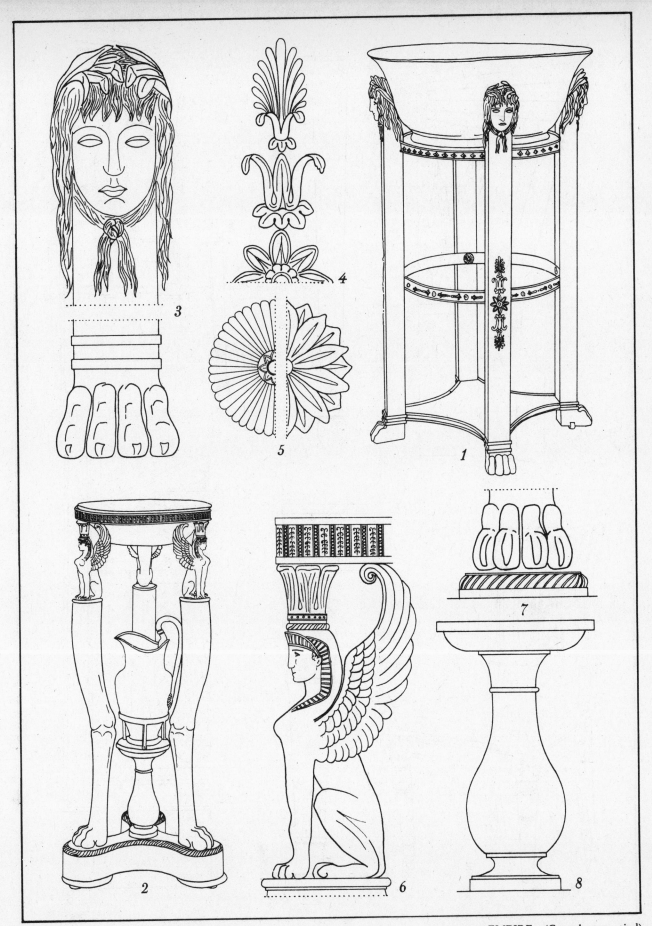

**PLATE 359**          EMPIRE (Consulate period)

1 and 2. "Athenian" mahogany washstands with gilt bronzes, with decorated basins of Sèvres porcelains. 3. Upright and clawed foot. 4 and 5. Details of decorations and rosettes. 6. Detail of upright. 7. Claws. 8. Turned support for pitcher.

*Malmaison Castle*

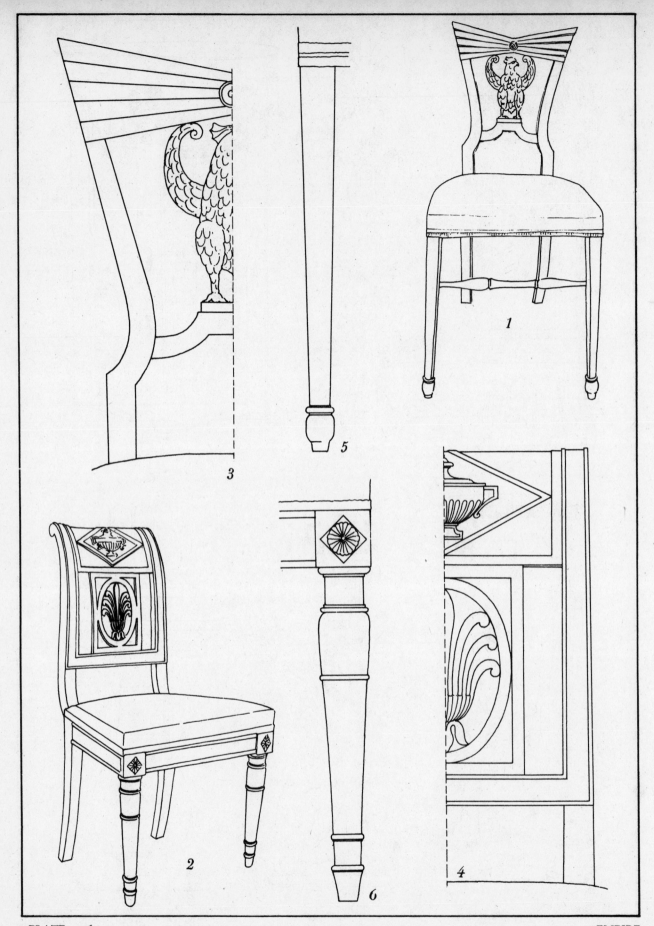

PLATE 360                                                                                    EMPIRE

1. Mahogany chair from time of Revolution.   2. Chair with rolled back.   3 and 4. Details of backs.   5 and 6.
Legs.

*Private collections*

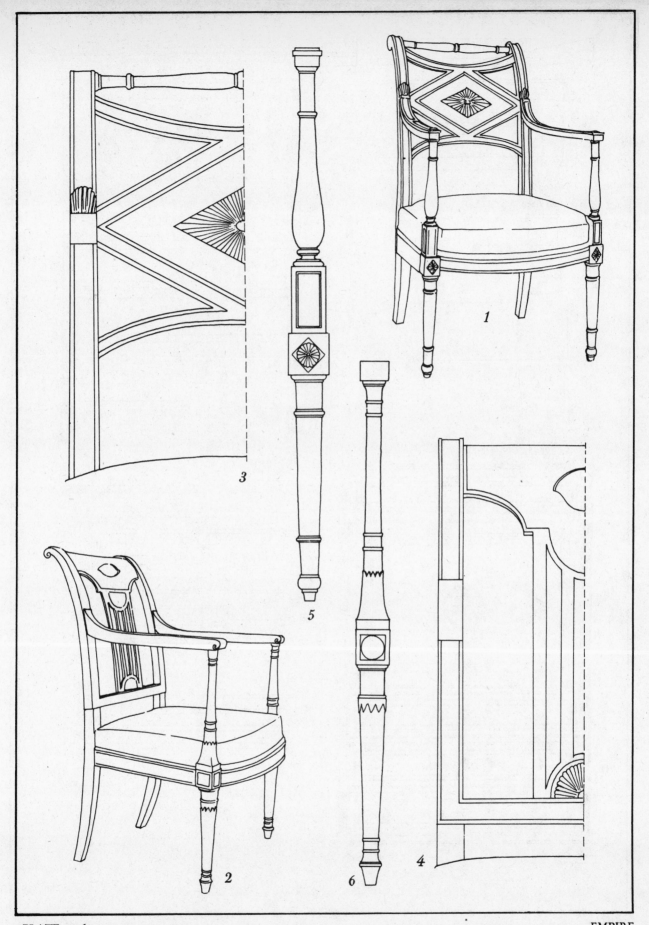

PLATE 361
EMPIRE
1 and 2. Painted wooden armchairs with openwork backs, which curve backwards at top.   3 and 4. Details of backs.   5
and 6. Legs and arm supports.

*Private collections*

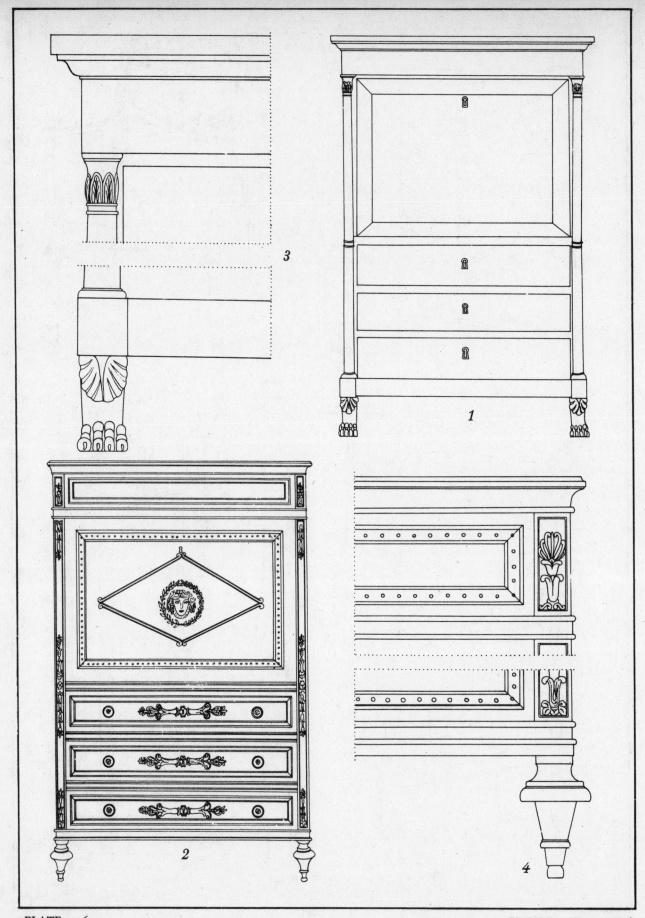

PLATE 362

EMPIRE (First period)

1 and 2. Wardrobes of mahogany, and mahogany and lemonwood, respectively, with carved gilt bronzes. The second one is by Georges Jacob (around 1795). 3 and 4. Details of uprights and legs.

*Mobilier National de France and private collection*

PLATE 363

EMPIRE (beginning)

1. Mahogany commode with straight lines, three drawers and clawed feet. 2. Mahogany commode with short baluster-shaped legs and uprights decorated with palm leaves in Consulate style. 3. Marble moulding. 4, 5 and 6. Rosette, escutcheon plate and bronze drawer pull. 7. Detail of upright. 8 and 9. Copper drawer pull and bronze escutcheon plate.

*Private collections, Paris and elsewhere*

PLATE 364

EMPIRE

1. Straight-line commode on crosspiece ending in clawed feet. 2. Mahogany commode with three drawers, like the previous one, with uprights in the shape of small columns. 3 and 4. Details of uprights. 5 and 6. Escutcheon plate and central decoration of bronze frieze.

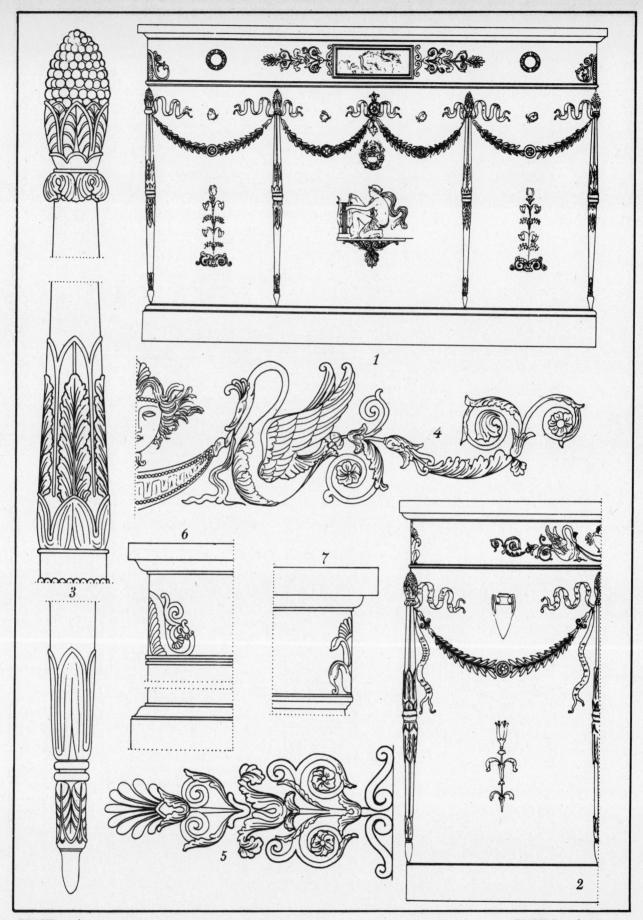

PLATE 365

EMPIRE (beginning)

1. Entredeux console, placed between two windows, with two unequal hinged doors and one drawer. 2. Partial view of another entredeux. 3. Detail of thyrsus. 4 and 5. Detail of friezes. 6 and 7. Profiles.

*Ministry of Foreign Affairs and Bardac collection*

PLATE 366

EMPIRE

1. Painted wooden bed with rolled back, from the early period. 2. Chaise longue with unequal ends. 3. Mahogany secretary, with inlaid copper, from the early period. 4. Upright and leg of bed. 5. Upper detail of secretary. 6. Detail of upright and leg of secretary.

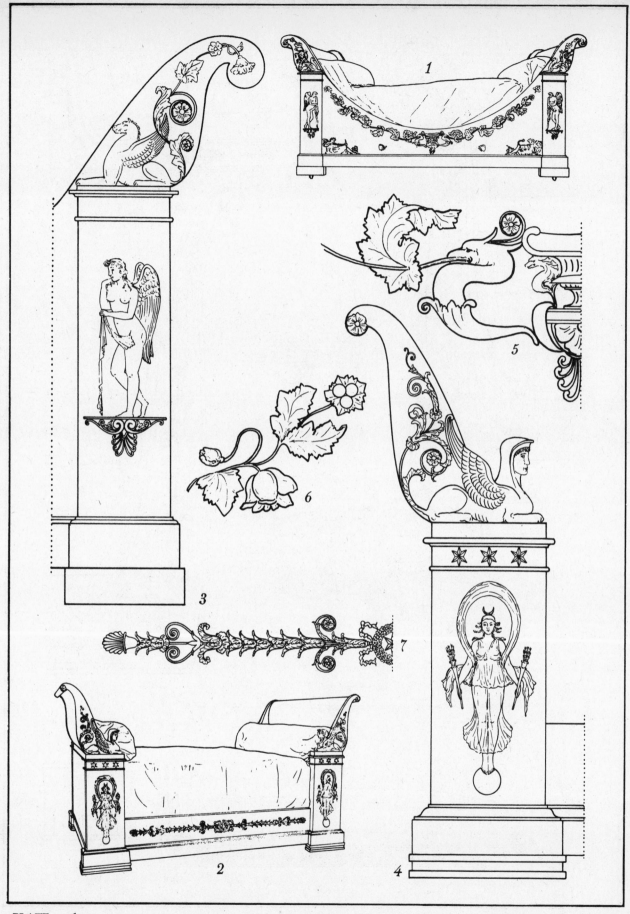

PLATE 367

1 and 2. Beds.   3 and 4. Details of uprights.   5, 6 and 7. Sketches of the decorations.

EMPIRE   (around 1800)

*Museum of Decorative Arts, Paris*

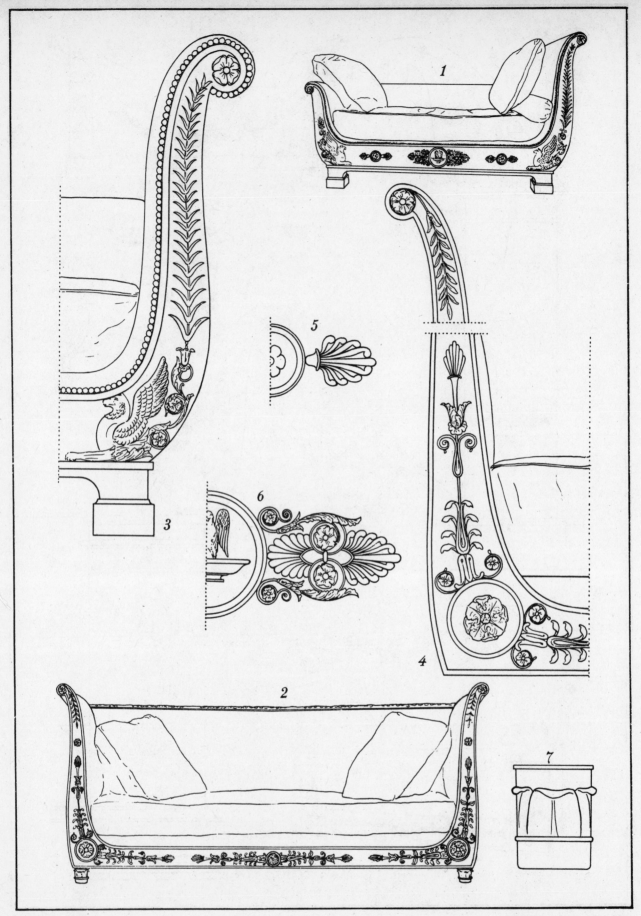

PLATE 368                                                                    EMPIRE (around 1800)

1 and 2. Sofas or daybeds.    3 and 4. Details of uprights.    5, 6 and 7. Sketches of decorations and foot.

*Museum of Decorative Arts, Paris*

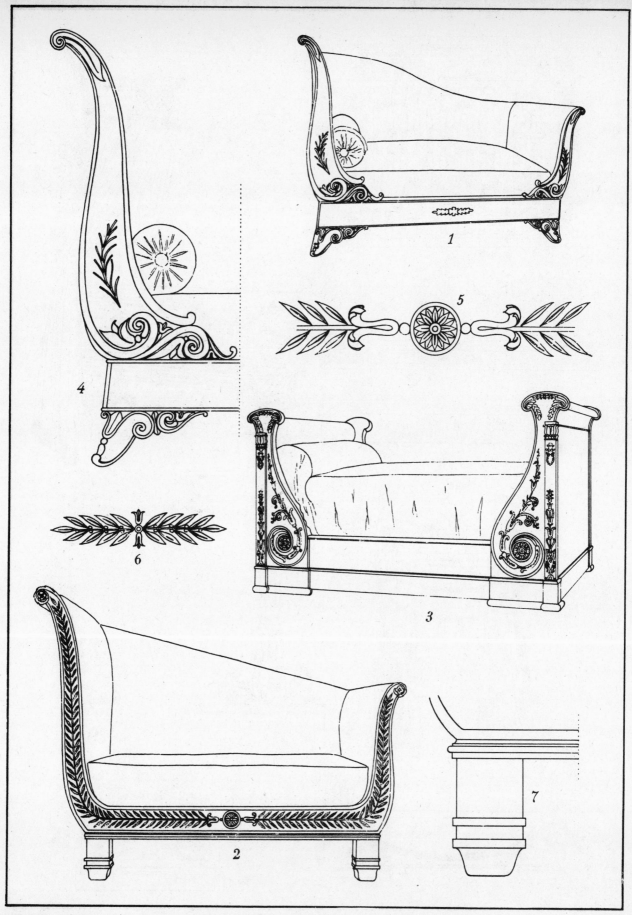

PLATE 369

1 and 2. Daybeds.   3. Napoleon's bed.   4. Detail of upright.   5 and 6. Details of decorations.   7. Leg.

*Private collection, Compiègne Castle and Grand Trianon*

PLATE 370            EMPIRE

1. Cradle of the King of Rome.    2. Bed designed by Percier and Fontaine.    3. Detail of cradle.    4 and 5. Front and bottom of base.    6. Detail of column.    7. Detail of upright.

*Fontainebleau Palace and album of Percier and Fontaine*

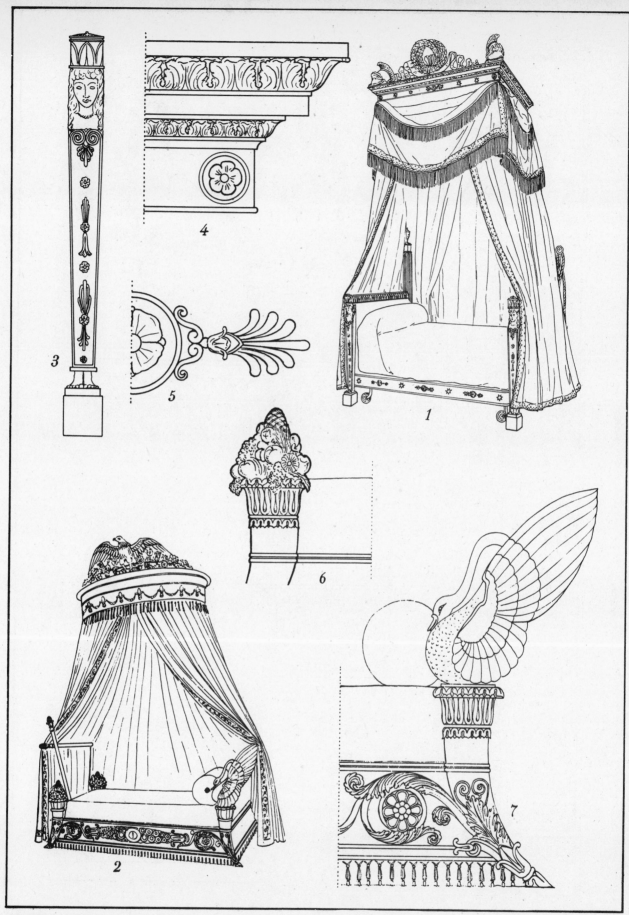

PLATE 371

EMPIRE (around 1800)

1 and 2. Elegant beds (the second one belonged to the Empress Josephine). 3 Detail of upright. 4. Cornice. 5. Decoration. 6 and 7. Details of corner supports.

*Fontainebleau Palace and Malmaison Castle*

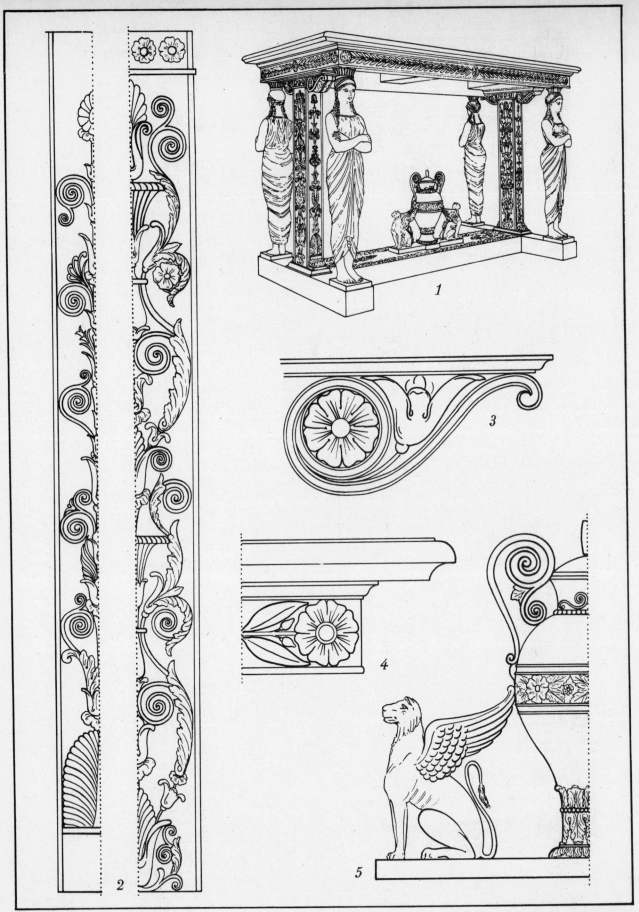

PLATE 372

1. Elegant table.   2. Details of uprights.   3. Brace.   4. Profile of moulding.   5. Detail of decorative vase at bottom.

EMPIRE (around 1800)

*Grand Trianon*

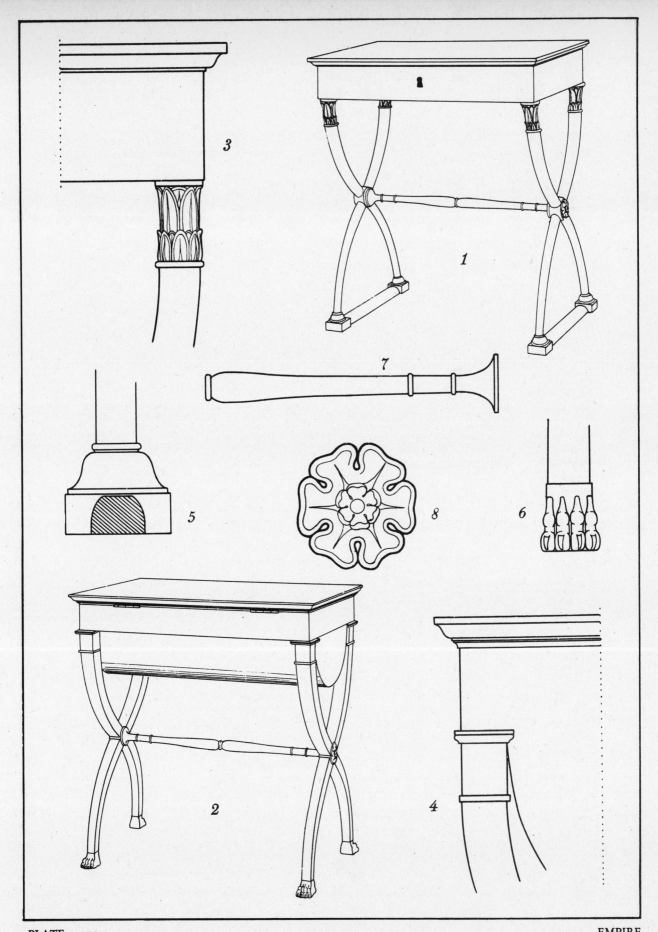

PLATE 373

EMPIRE

1 and 2. Small mahogany worktables with legs in X, carved gilt bronze decorations.   3 and 4. Details of top of legs.   5 and 6. Lower part of legs.   7. Profile of turned crosspiece.   8. Button trim.

*Grand Trianon and Petit Trianon*

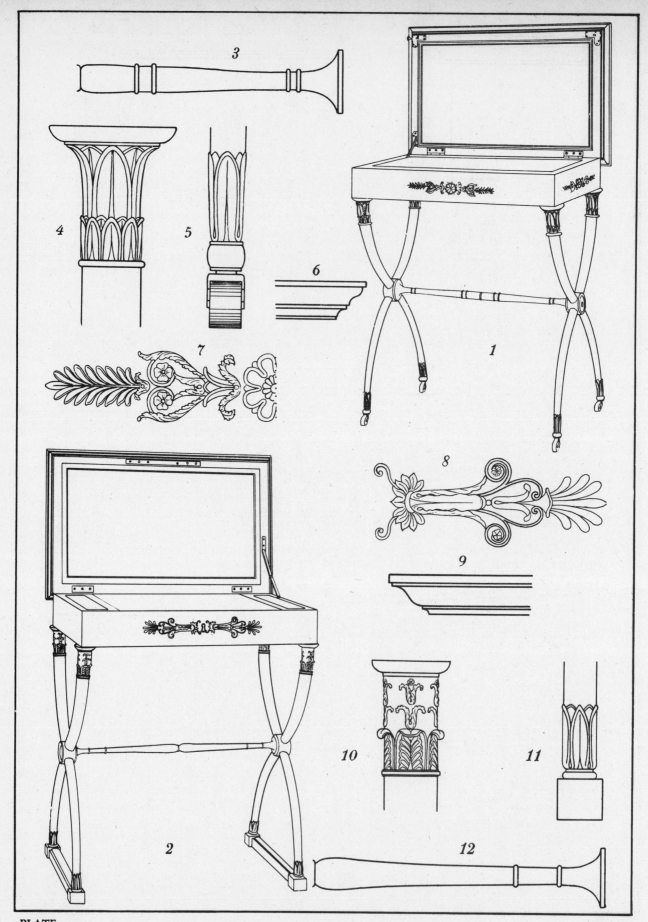

PLATE 374

1 and 2. Small mahogany worktables with legs in X, with gilt bronze decorations.   3, 4, 5, 6 and 7. Details of upper table.   8, 9, 10, 11 and 12. Details of lower table.

*Fontainebleau Palace and Malmaison Castle*

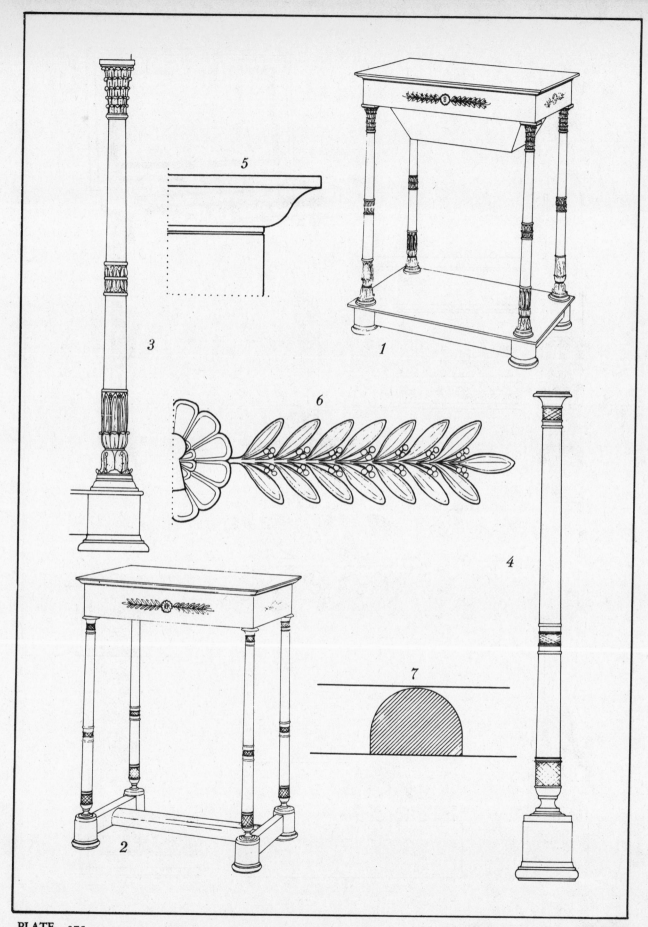

PLATE 375                                                                                    EMPIRE

1 and 2. Small mahogany worktables with turned uprights and bronzes, used by the Empress Josephine and Marie-Louise.  3 and 4. Details of uprights.  5. Upper moulding.  6. Sketch of bronze escutcheon plate.  7. Cross section of lower crosspiece.

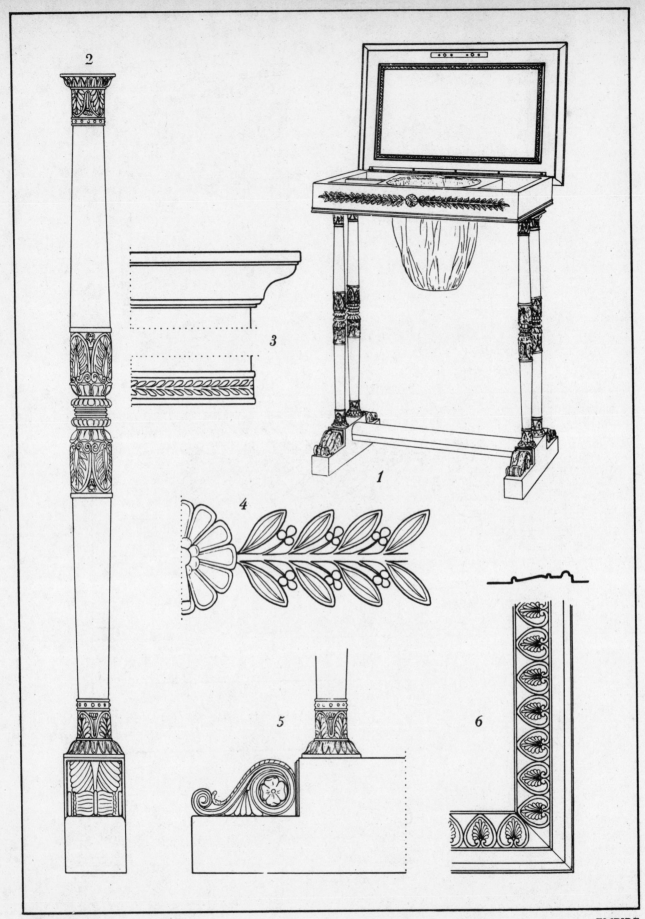

PLATE 376
EMPIRE

1. Small mahogany worktable, decorated with bronzes, which belonged to Empress Josephine.   2. Detail of column.   3. Moulding on lid and front of table.   4. Escutcheon plate.   5. Detail of foot.   6. Moulding on inside of lid.

*Malmaison Castle*

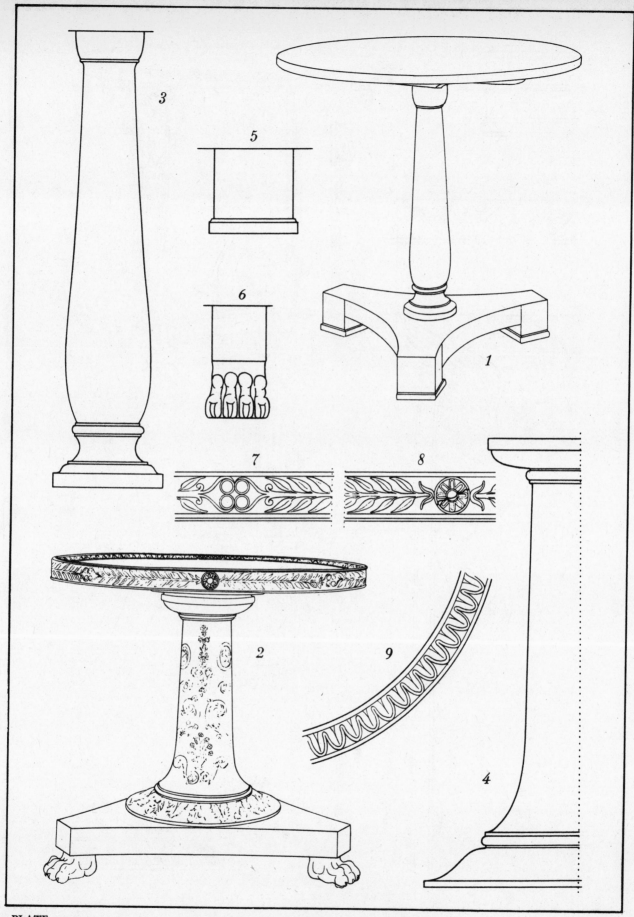

PLATE 377

*3*

*5*

*6*

*7*

*8*

*1*

*2*

*9*

*4*

EMPIRE

1 and 2. Round pedestal tables. The first table is of mahogany, the second one of Sèvres porcelain, decorated with gilt bronzes. 3 and 4. Supports. 5 and 6. Feet. 7, 8 and 9. Border decorations.

*Fontainebleau Palace*

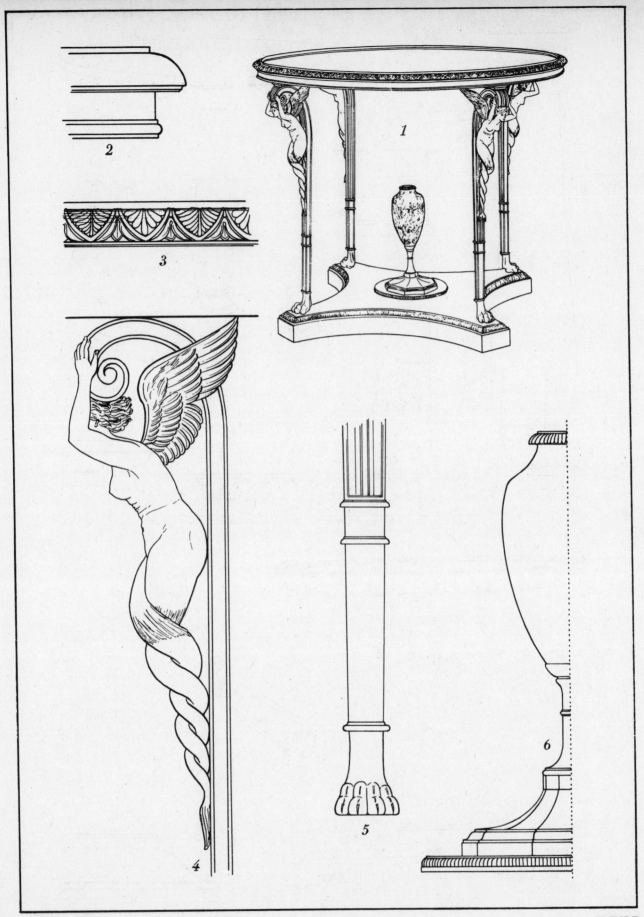

PLATE 378

EMPIRE

1. Small pedestal table made of yew, with bronzes.  2 and 3. Upper moulding.  4. Figure of a siren in black bronze.  5. Clawed foot.  6. Detail of vase.

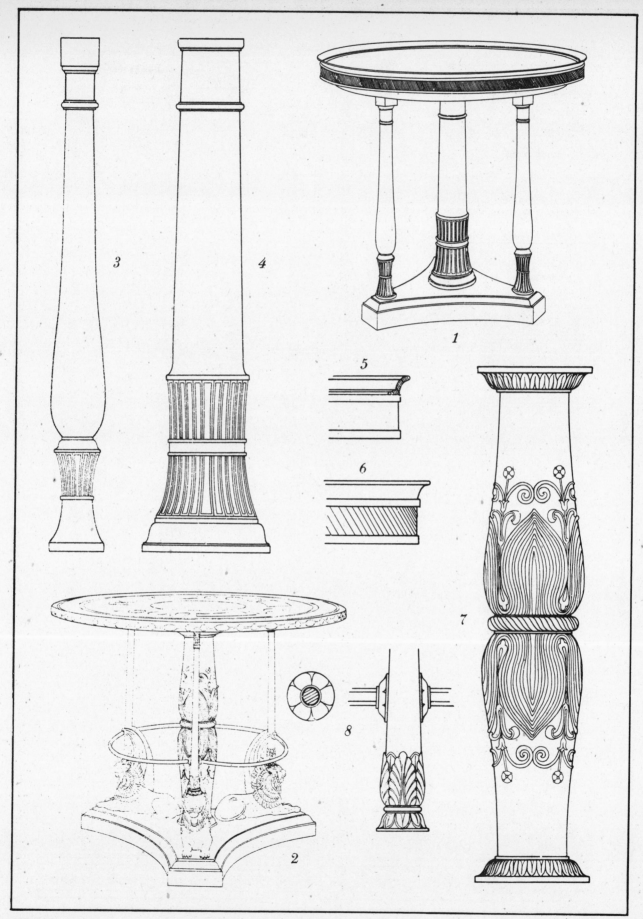

PLATE 379

EMPIRE

1 and 2. Round mahogany pedestal tables. The first one has a top of red porphyry, the second one of marble. 3 and 4. Detail of leg and central column. 5 and 6. Detail of moulding porphyry top. 7. Middle column of gilt carved wood. 8. Detail of bottom of copper uprights resting on winged lions.

*Malmaison Castle and Grand Trianon*

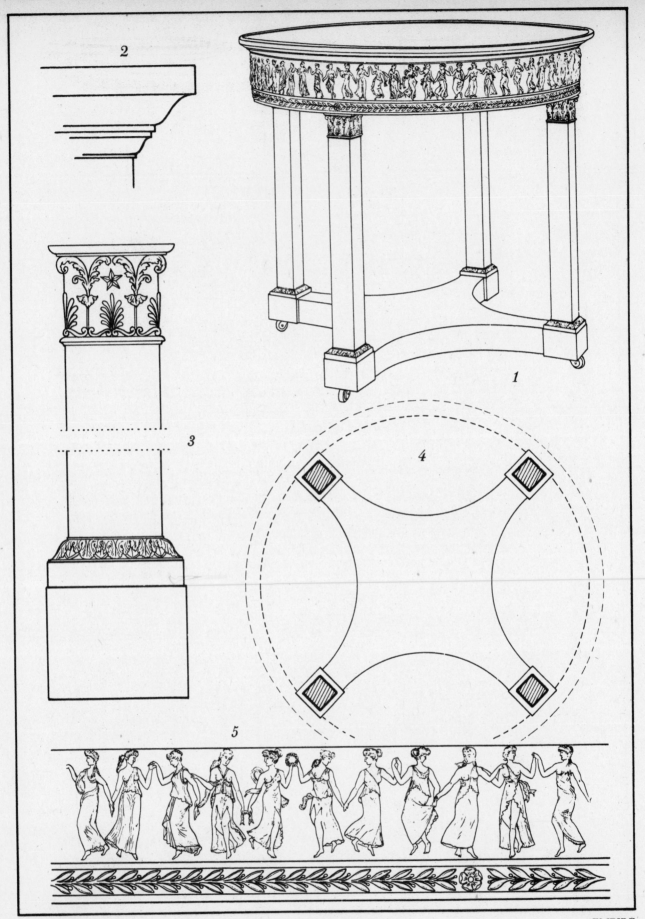

PLATE 380

EMPIRE

1. Mahogany pedestal table, decorated with bronzes and with a marble top.  2. Marble moulding.  3. Detail of legs.  4. Bottom of table.  5. Detail of frieze.

*Grand Trianon*

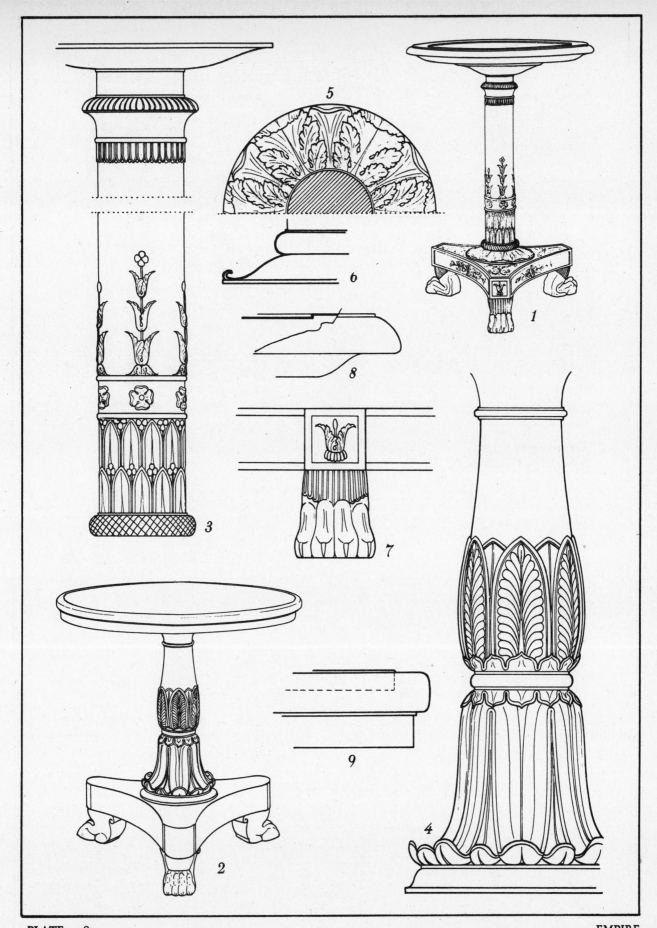

PLATE 381                                                                    EMPIRE

1 and 2. Small round pedestal tables with tops of marble and mosaic, respectively.   3 and 4. Detail of columns.   5
and 6. Front and cross section of base.   7. Detail of carved wood foot.   8 and 9. Mouldings around top.

*Ministry of War and Grand Trianon*

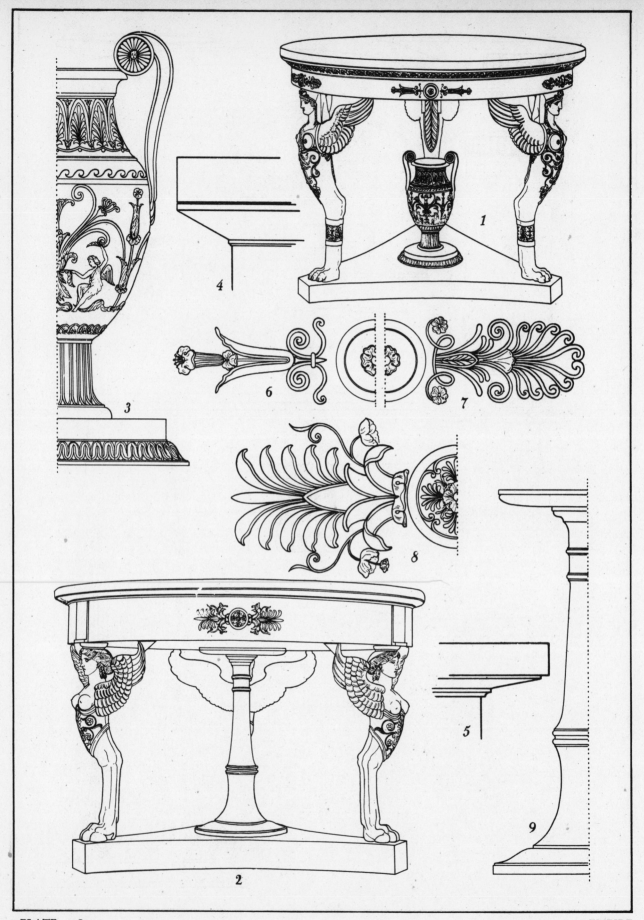

PLATE 382

EMPIRE

1 and 2. Mahogany pedestal tables decorated with bronzes and with legs in shape of winged figures (upper one, Egyptian).   3. Detail of vase.   4 and 5. Upper moulding and cross section of marble.   6, 7 and 8. Details of bronzes.   9. Middle support.

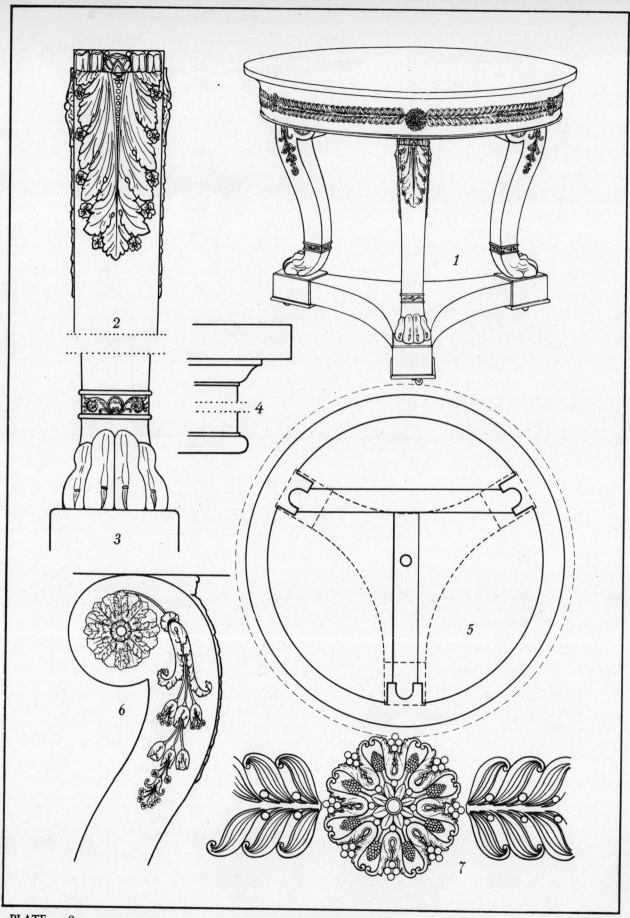

PLATE 383

EMPIRE

1. Round mahogany pedestal table with bronze decorations and clawed feet. 2 and 3. Details of legs. 4. Mouldings. 5. Base. 6. Side view of leg. 7. Bronze decoration.

*Compiègne Palace*

PLATE 384

1. Round pedestal table.   2. Detail of leg.   3. Sketch of decoration on top.   4. Frieze outlined by lower interlace.   5. Central part of interlace.

EMPIRE

*Grand Trianon*

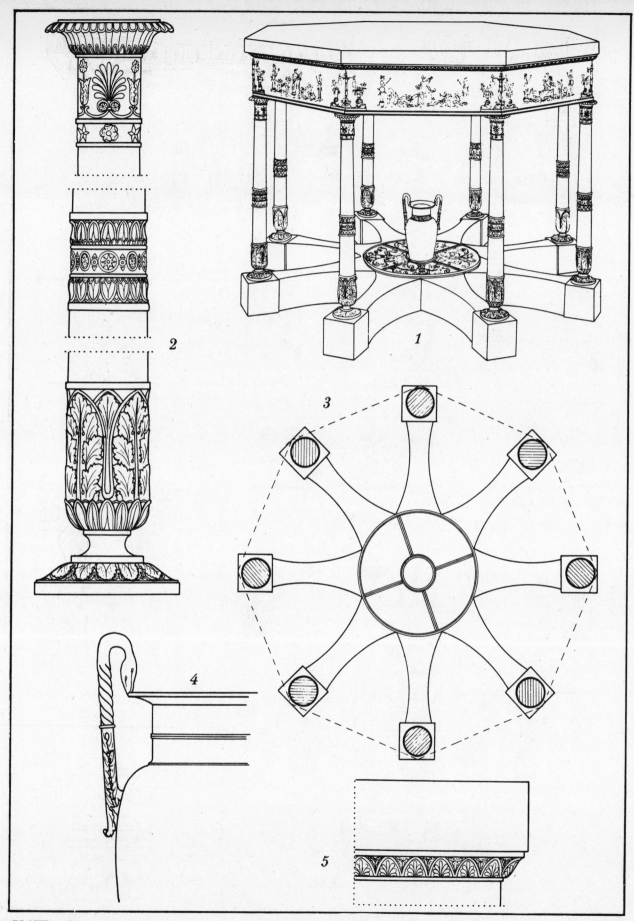

PLATE 385                                                           EMPIRE

1. Octagonal mahogany table with bronze decorations and marble top supported by eight columns. 2. Detail of column. 3. Base of table. 4. Detail of vase in middle. 5. Upper moulding.

*Malmaison Castle*

PLATE 386                                                                                                    EMPIRE

1. Oval elm-root table, legs are decorated with gilt carved sphinxes.   2. Round top with top of colored varnished steel.   3, 4 and 5. Details of sphinx, bronze border and decoration on upright.   6, 7 and 8. Details of vase, leg and decoration.

*Fontainebleau Palace*

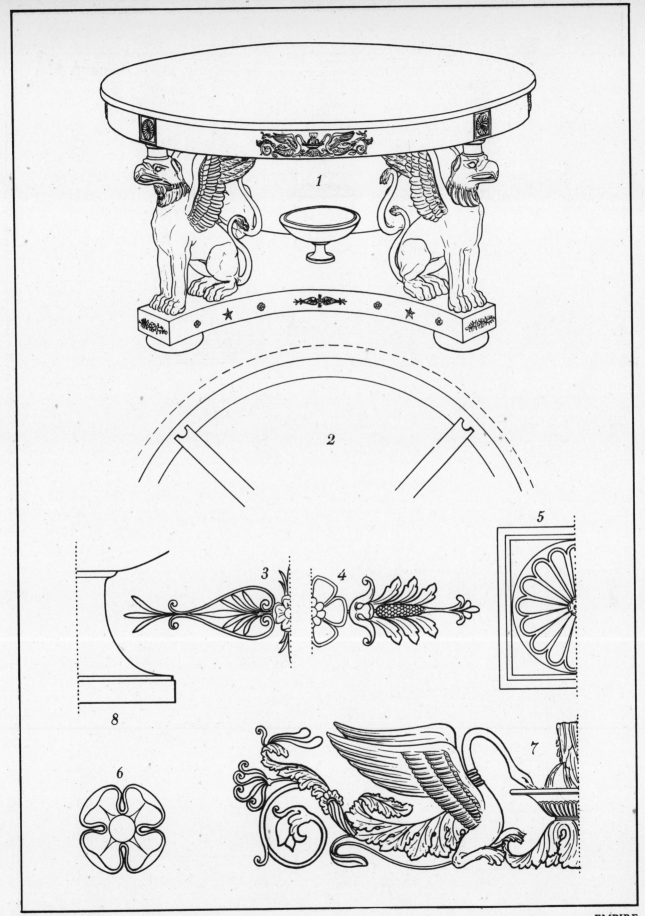

**PLATE 387**

1. Round mahogany table, supported by winged sphinxes and decorated with gilt bronzes. 2. Table frame. 3, 4, 5, 6 and 7. Details of bronzes. 8. Detail of chalice in middle.

EMPIRE

*Compiègne Palace*

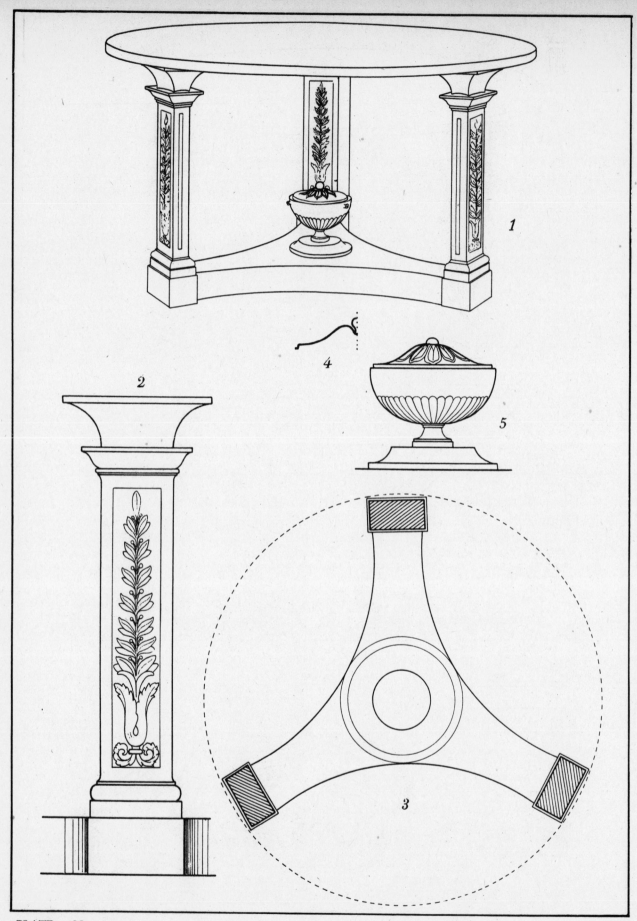

PLATE 388

1. Round three-legged table with marquetry.   2. Detail of leg.   3. Placement of legs.   4 and 5. Detail of urn in middle.

EMPIRE

*Grand Trianon*

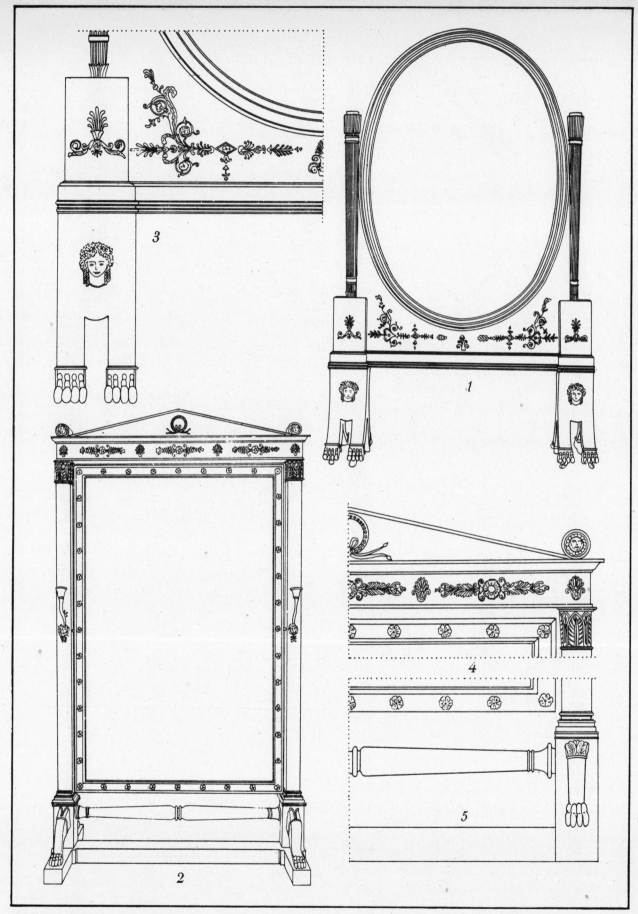

PLATE 389

PLATE 389                                                           EMPIRE (first period)

1 and 2. Portable mahogany mirrors with bronzes (the first one belonged to Empress Josephine).   3, 4 and 5. Details
of upright and frame.

*Mobilier National de France and Fontainebleau Palace*

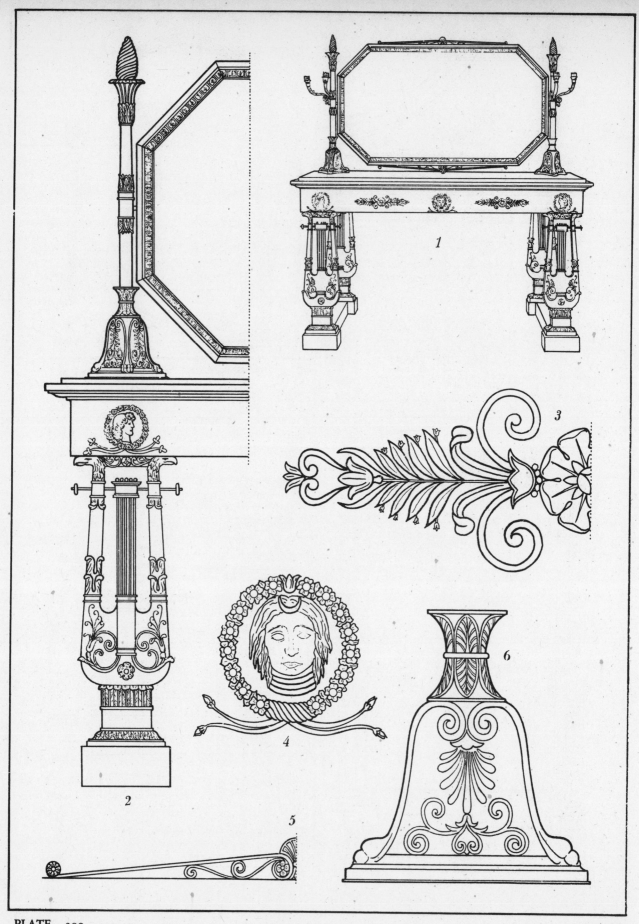

PLATE 390

1. Mahogany dressing table, which belonged to Empress Josephine, decorated with carved gilt bronzes; the legs are in the shape of a lyre.   2. Detail of upright.   3, 4 and 5. Details of bronzes.   6. Detail of base.

*Mobilier National de France*

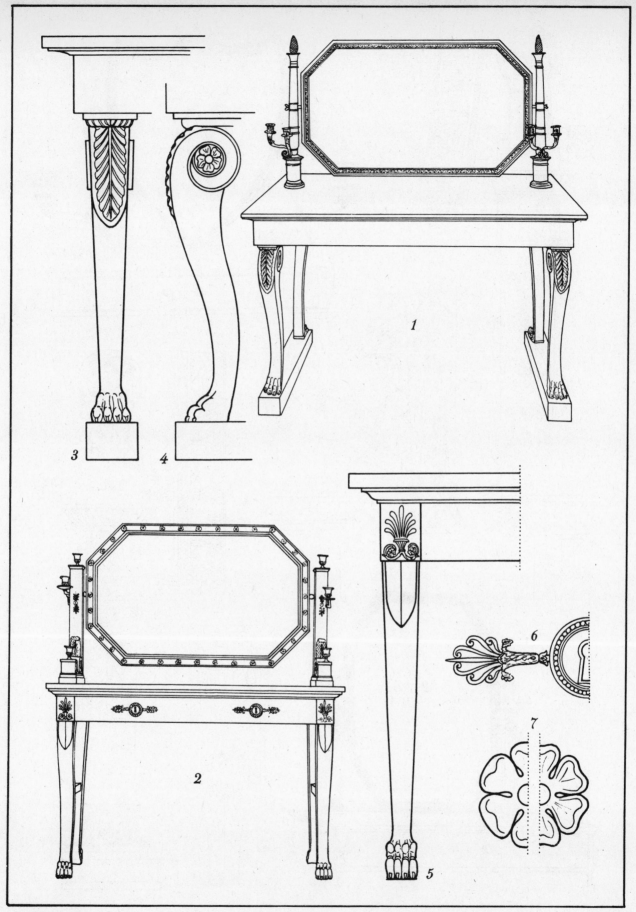

PLATE 391

EMPIRE

1 and 2. Mahogany dressing tables, decorated with carved gilt bronze. 3, 4 and 5. Details of legs. 6 and 7. Details of escutcheon plate and rosette.

*Fontainebleau and Compiègne Palaces*

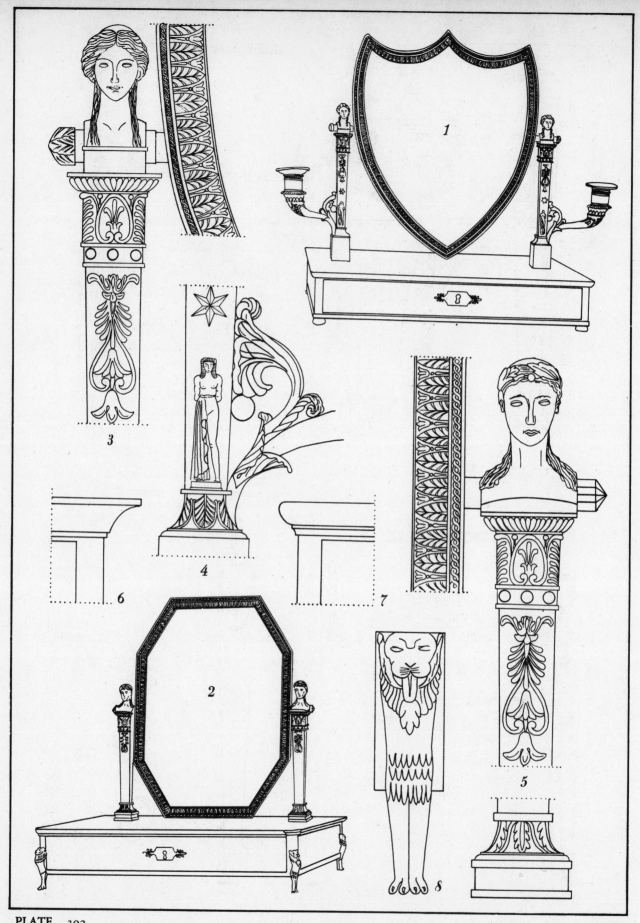

PLATE 392

1 and 2. Small mahogany dressing tables, decorated with bronzes.   3, 4 and 5. Details of mirror supports.   6 and
7. Mouldings.   8. Leg.

EMPIRE

*Malmaison Castle and Fontainebleau Palace*

**PLATE** 393

1 and 2. Portable mahogany mirrors decorated with gilt copper and bronze.   3, 4, 5 and 6. Details of uprights and clawed foot.   7 and 8. Details of frame.

*Museum of Decorative Arts, Paris and Fontainebleau Palace*

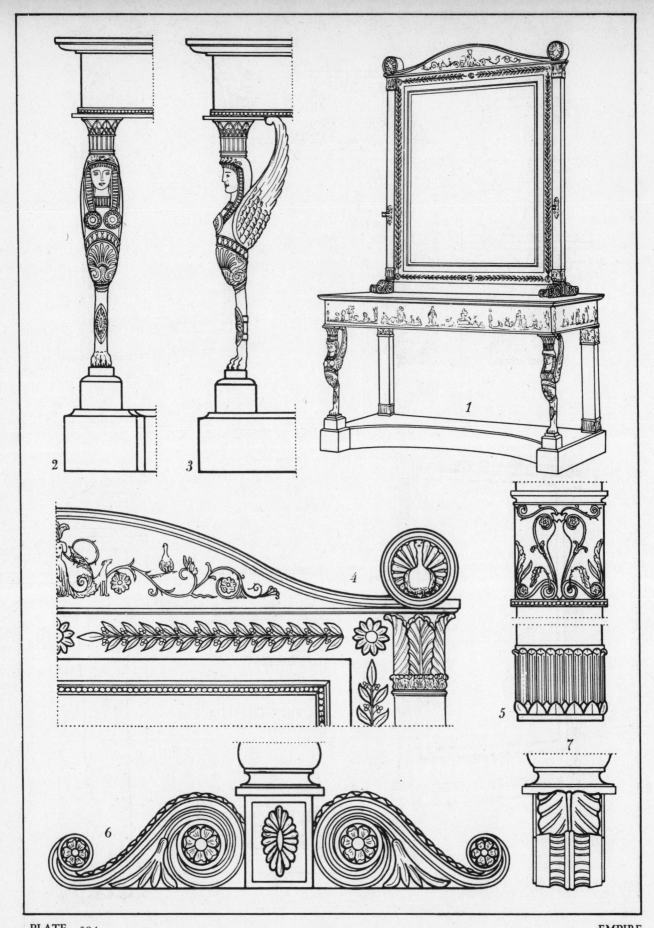

## PLATE 394

1. Large ash dressing table decorated with carved gilt bronzes.   2 and 3. Details of legs.   4. Upper crest.   5. Detail of rear pilaster.   6 and 7. Base of mirror frame.

**EMPIRE**

*Fontainebleau Palace*

**PLATE** 395

1. Elm-root dressing table, decorated with carved gilt bronzes.    2. Mahogany dressing table with clawed feet. The mirror supports are square and end in women's heads of gilt bronze.    3 and 4. Details of uprights and legs.    5 and 6. Decorations.    7. Drawer pull.

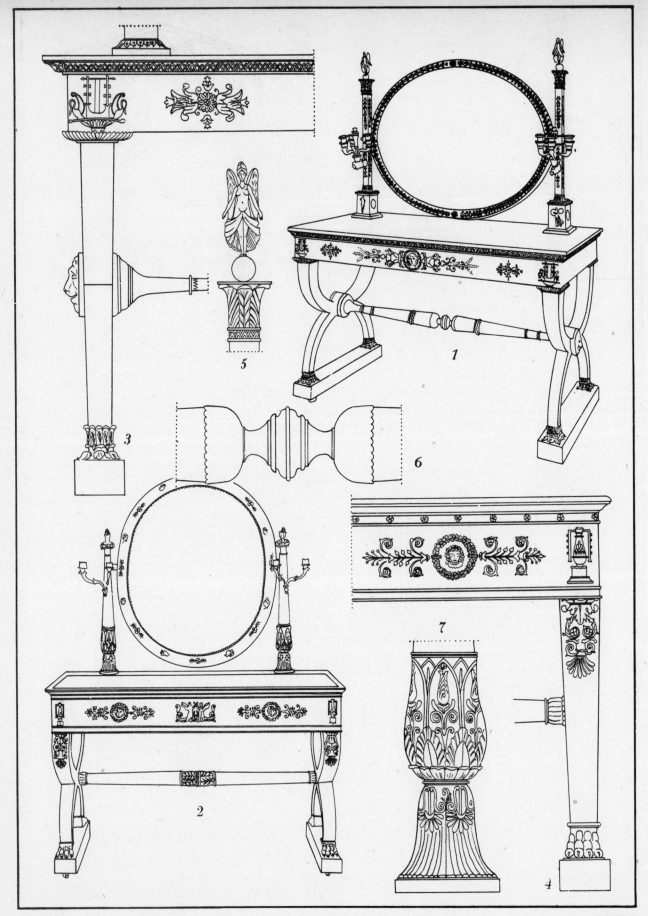

PLATE 396

EMPIRE

1 and 2. Mahogany dressing tables, adorned with carved gilt bronzes and decorative legs.    3 and 4. Details of uprights and legs.    5. Finial.    6. Turned lower crosspiece.    7. Base of mirror support.

*Fontainebleau Palace and Malmaison Castle*

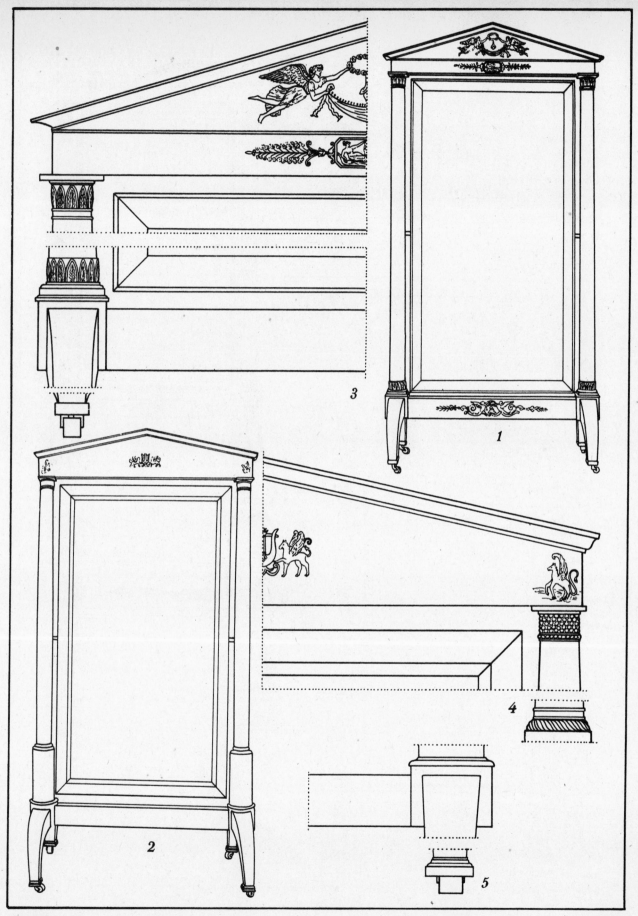

**PLATE** 397

1 and 2. Portable mahogany mirrors with bronzes.    3, 4 and 5. Details of uprights and frames or mirrors.

*Mobilier National de France and Ministry of War*

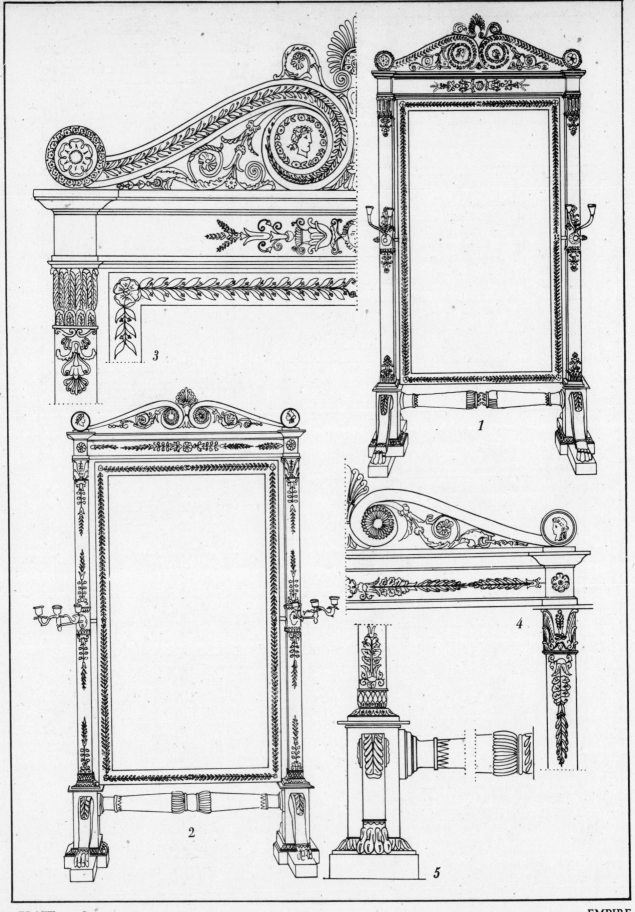

PLATE 398

1 and 2. Portable mahogany mirrors with bronzes.   3, 4 and 5. Details of uprights, frames and support.

*Fontainebleau and Compiègne Palaces*

EMPIRE

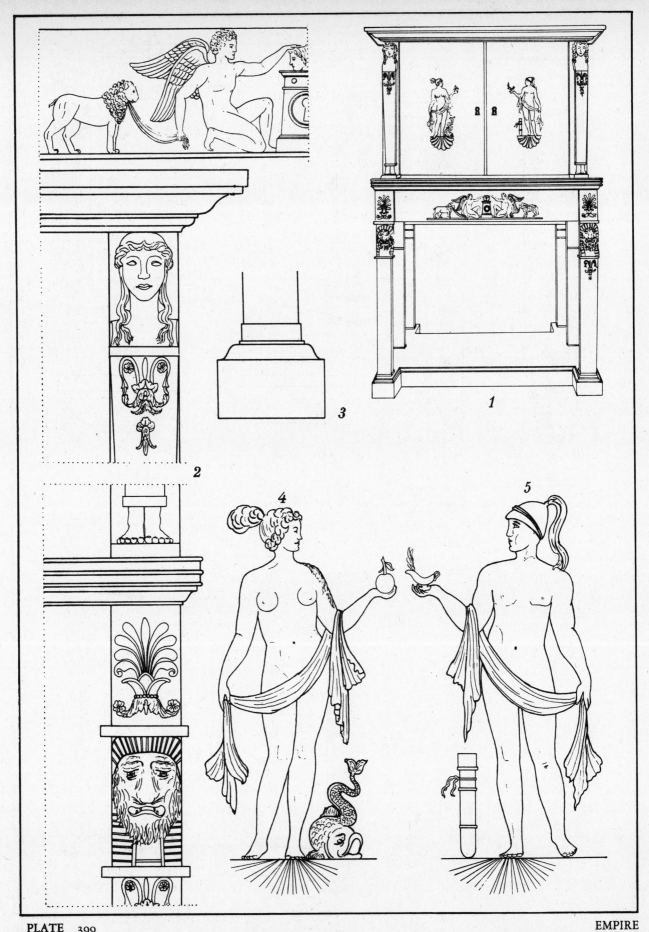

**PLATE** 399

EMPIRE

1. Mahogany "bonheur-du-jour" paper cabinet, with gilt bronze decorations.   2. Detail of uprights.   3. Base.   4 and
5. Central figures.

*Private collection*

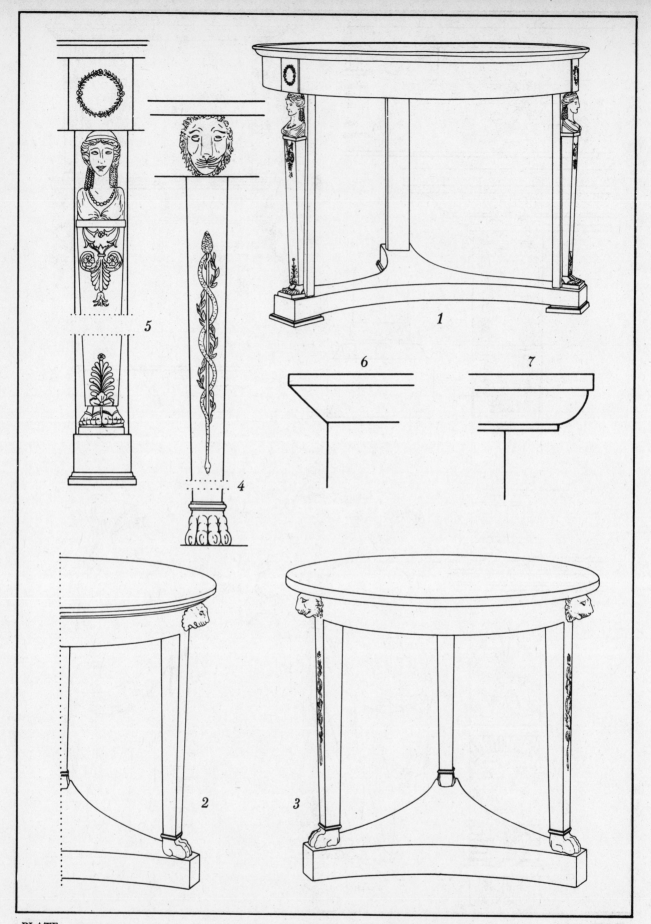

PLATE 400                                                                                                    EMPIRE

1, 2 and 3. Round mahogany pedestal tables with three legs, carved gilt bronzes, marble tops and decorated with sphinx's heads and lions' claws.    4 and 5. Details of legs.    6 and 7. Marble moulding.

*Museum of Decorative Arts, Paris and Compiègne and Fontainebleau Palaces*

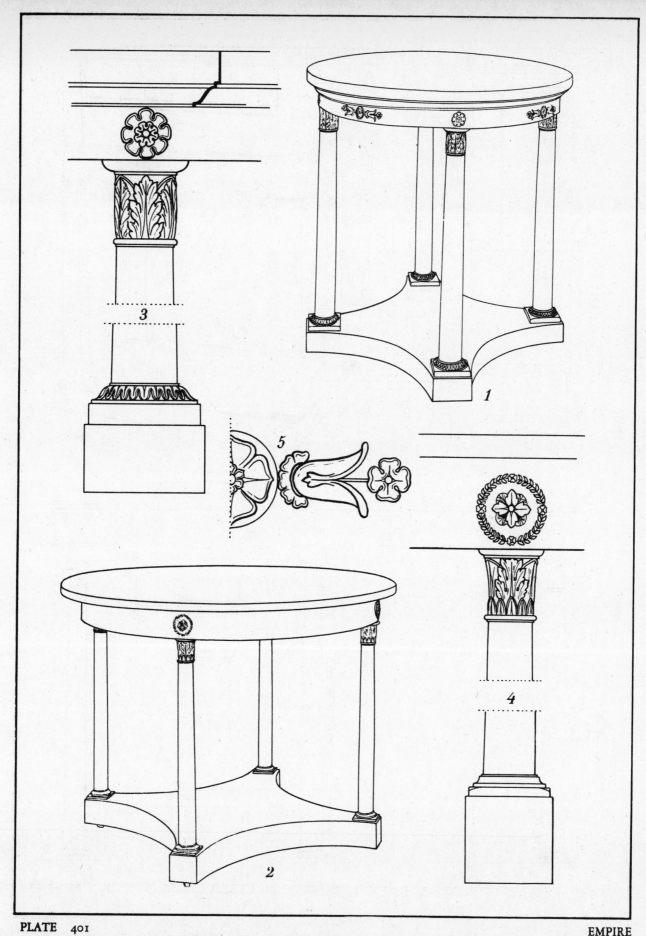

PLATE 401

EMPIRE

1 and 2. Small round pedestal tables supported by four columns, with bronze decorations and white marble tops. 3 and 4. Details of columns. 5. Sketch of bronze decoration.

*Grand Trianon and Fontainebleau Palace*

PLATE 402

EMPIRE

1 and 2. Small worktables.    3 and 4. Details of uprights.    5. Foot.    6. Small column.

*Private collections*

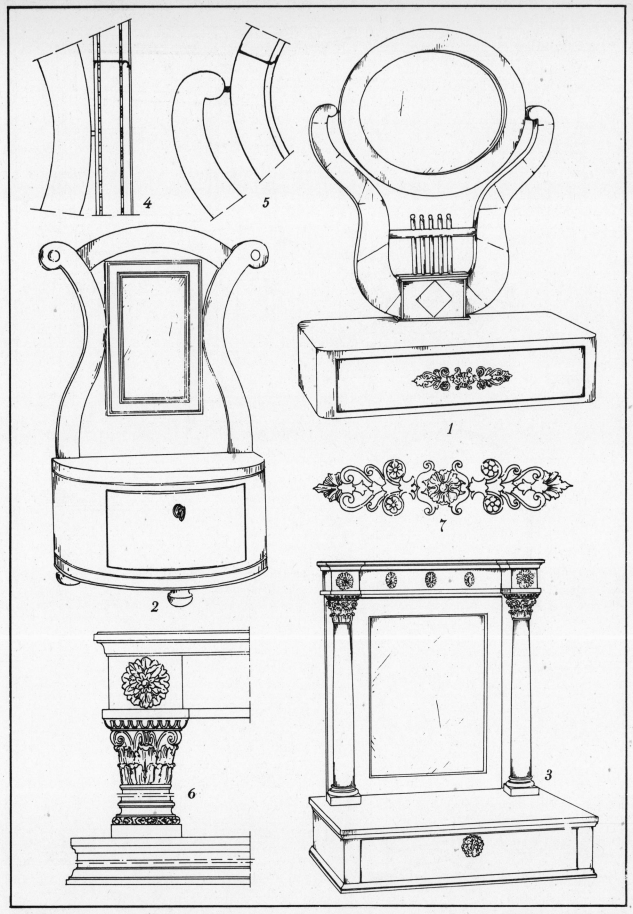

PLATE 403

EMPIRE (Restoration)

1, 2 and 3. Small mirrors for dressing tables.   4, 5 and 6. Details of same.   7. Bronze decoration.

*Private collections*

PLATE 404                                                    EMPIRE (Restoration)
1 and 2. Elm-root and mahogany dressing tables with bronze decorations.  3 and 4. Uprights and legs.  5 and 6.
Escutcheon plate decorations.

*Grand Trianon and Malmaison Castle*

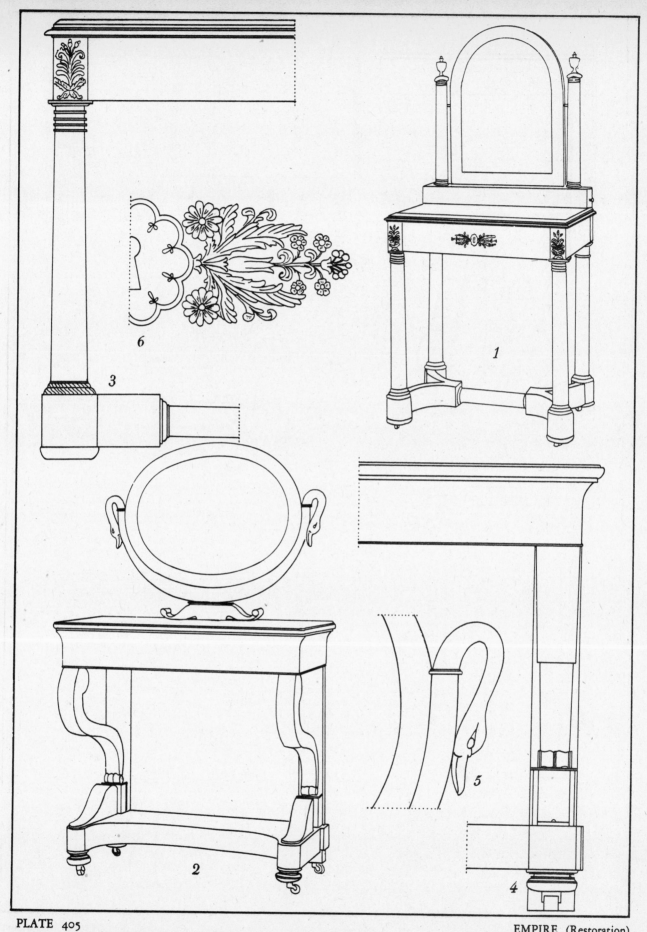

PLATE 405

EMPIRE (Restoration)

1 and 2. Mahogany dressing tables. The first one has bronze decorations; the second one has an oval mirror. 3 and 4. Uprights and legs. 5. Swan's head. 6. Detail of escutcheon plate.

*Ministry of Justice and Mobilier National de France*

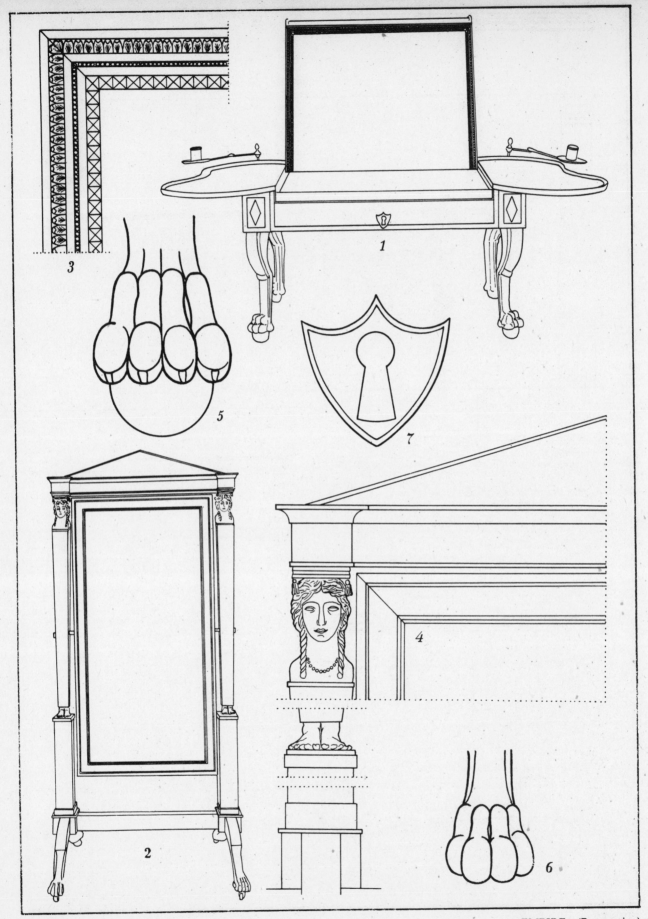

PLATE 406

EMPIRE (Restoration)

1. Small portable dressing table or bed tray of mahogany and maple with inlaid ebony and tin on the claws. 2. Portable mahogany mirror with gilt bronze decorations. 3 and 4. Details of frame. 5 and 6. Claws. 7. Escutcheon plate.

*Malmaison Castle and Fontainebleau Palace*

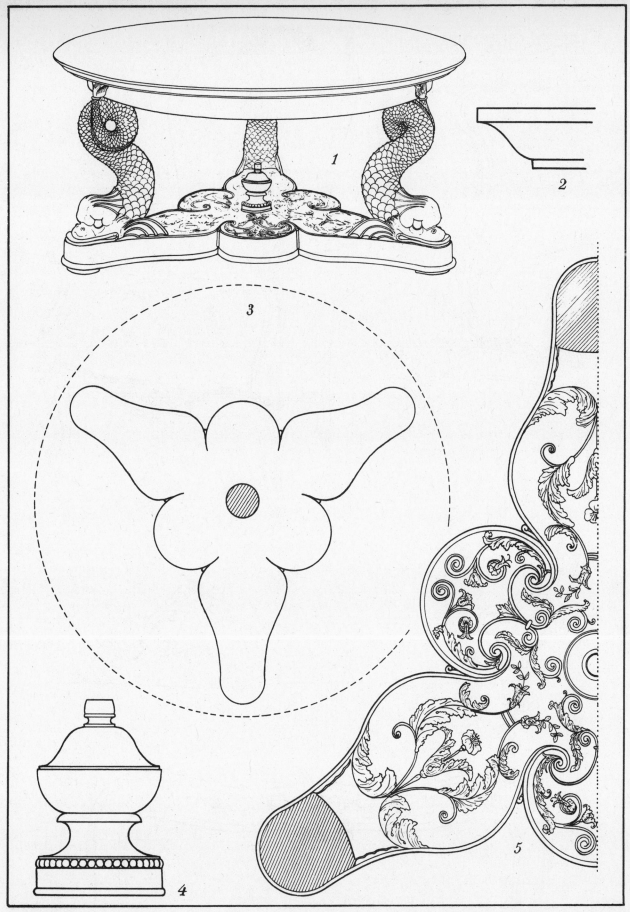

PLATE 407

**EMPIRE** (Restoration)

1. Round table with fine marquetry, supported by three dolphins.   2. Upper moulding.   3. Bottom.   4. Central finial.   5. Detail of marquetry.

*In a diplomatic building*

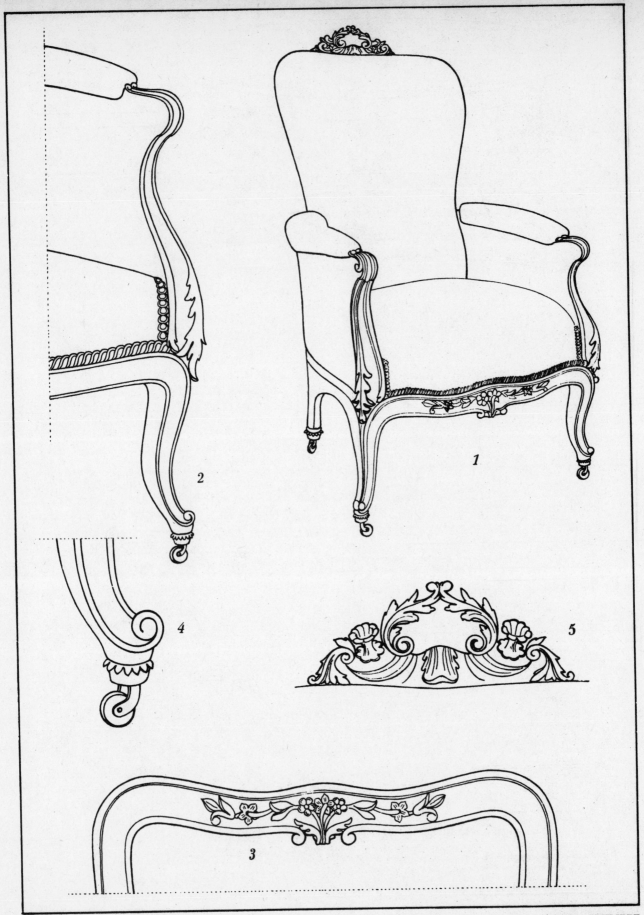

**PLATE 408**                                                                                          LOUIS PHILIPPE

1. Armchair.    2. Detail of arm and leg.    3. Sketch of middle lower carving.    4. Detail of foot.    5. Upper crest of back.

*Fontainebleau Palace*

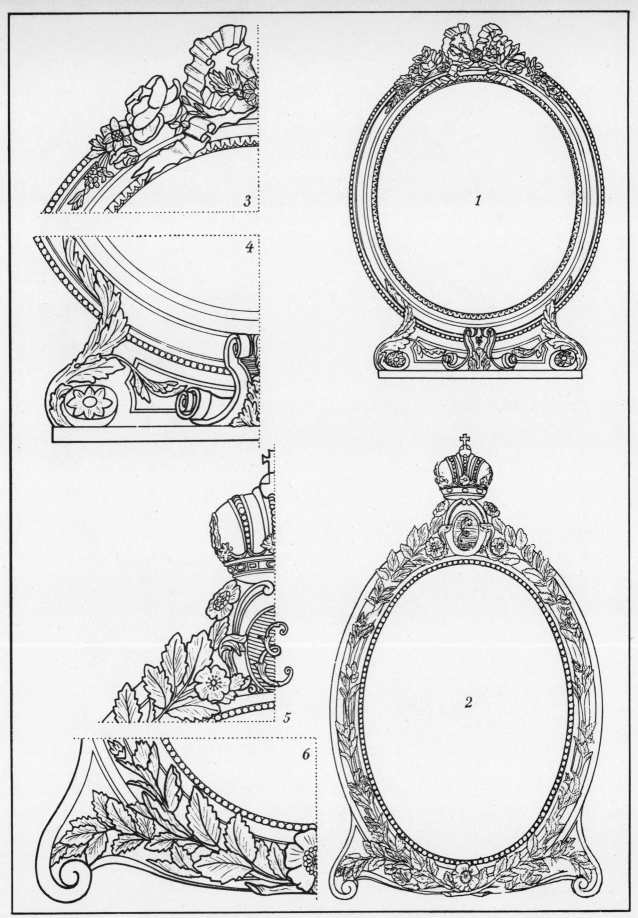

PLATE 409
SECOND EMPIRE

1. Medallion mirror of gilt carved wood. 2. Dressing-table mirror of gilt carved wood, belonging to Empress Eugénie. 3, 4, 5 and 6. Details.

*Mobilier National de France*

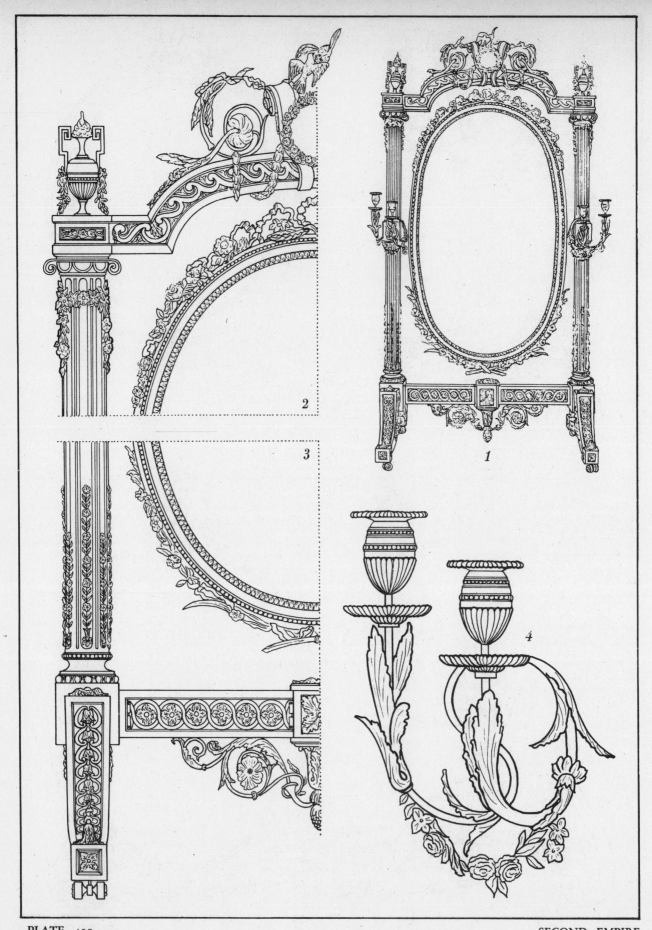

PLATE 410                                                                 SECOND EMPIRE

1. Portable mahogany mirror with bronzes, which belonged to Empress Eugénie.   2 and 3. Details of upright, frame and support.   4. Candelabra.

*Mobilier National de France*

PLATE 411                                                    SECOND EMPIRE
1. Small dressing-table mirror of carved gilt bronze which belonged to Empress Eugénie.   2 and 3. Details.

*Compiègne Palace*

# INDEX

# Volume Two
# Encyclopedia of Spanish Period Furniture Designs

# PUBLISHER'S PREFACE

Lovers of fine furniture, cabinetmakers, decorators, restorers, artists, stage designers—indeed, all who take pleasure in things of beauty will find something of value in this comprehensive source book on Spanish period furniture.

The illustrations on the following pages show Spanish furnishings from the Gothic period through the nineteenth century, offering a treasure house of ideas and details, in which can be found representatives of virtually every important period piece. The rich fabric of Spanish history embraced many cultural influences and they are all lavishly displayed here. Not only the furniture of palaces is to be seen, but also that of peasants. There are folk designs and motifs rarely found in books of this kind. The Moorish influence is seen in numerous pieces: in carved Mudejar benches and chests, in elaborate braziers and candle holders, in the exquisite tracery of wrought-iron.

The religious nature of the Spanish was another influence affecting the furniture. Stage designers and historians will delight in the church stalls and "confessional" armchairs. Some of the carvings that can be seen in the "church furniture" also influenced the carving of the home furnishings.

Spain also paid homage through its furnishings to other nations. Here are beds of Portuguese style, chairs of French influence and desks that might have been designed by Chippendale. But always there is an Hispanic flavor and charm.

All the magnificent massive pieces that most of us think of when we discuss Spanish furniture are shown, but there are many, many surprises—pieces of extreme delicacy and sometimes whimsy. The multiplicity of cultural influences combined to create a wealth of design that is unsurpassed in its variety.

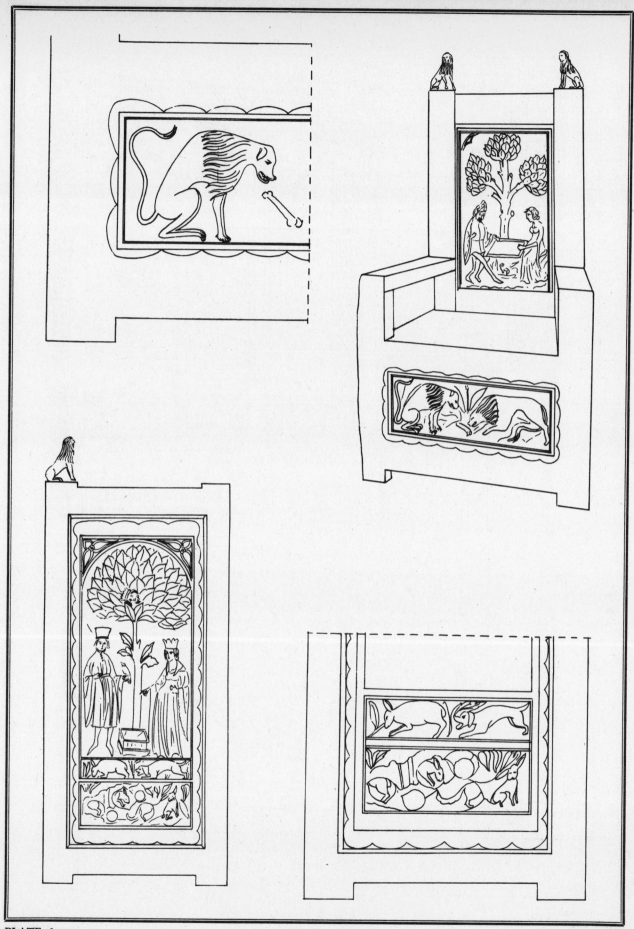

PLATE 1

"Box" armchair, carved on both sides, from Alfabia (Majorca).

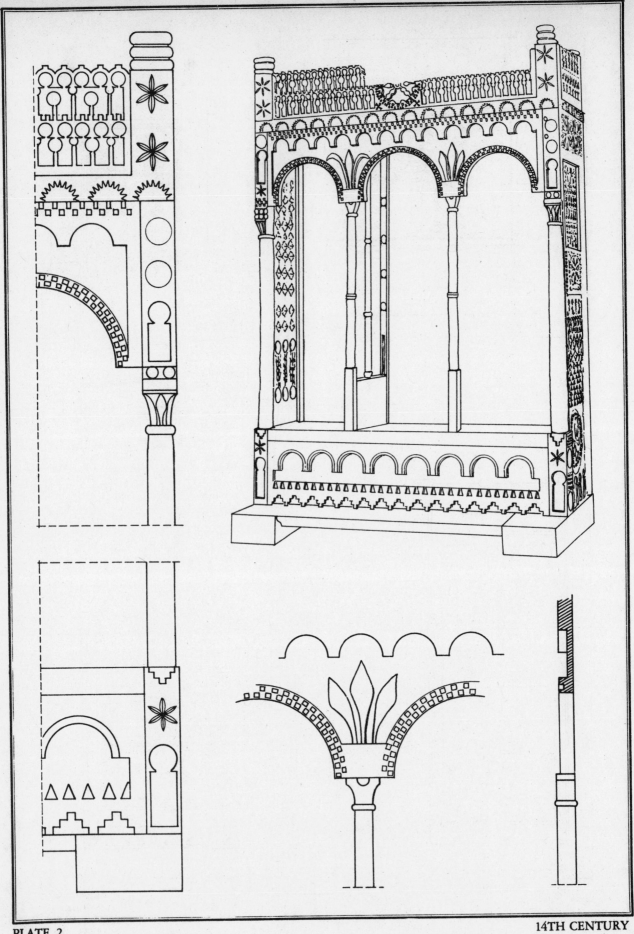

**PLATE 2**
Mudejar bench from church of Tahull.

*Museum of Art of Catalonia, Barcelona*

PLATE 3
LATE 14TH OR EARLY 15TH CENTURY

Faldistorium of King Martin I of Aragon, "The Humane" (1395–1410), which serves as a shrine for the monstrance in the Corpus Christi processions.

*Treasury of the Cathedral, Barcelona*

PLATE 4

Small chest with carved decoration in the shape of "cloister windows."

LATE 14TH OR EARLY 15TH CENTURY

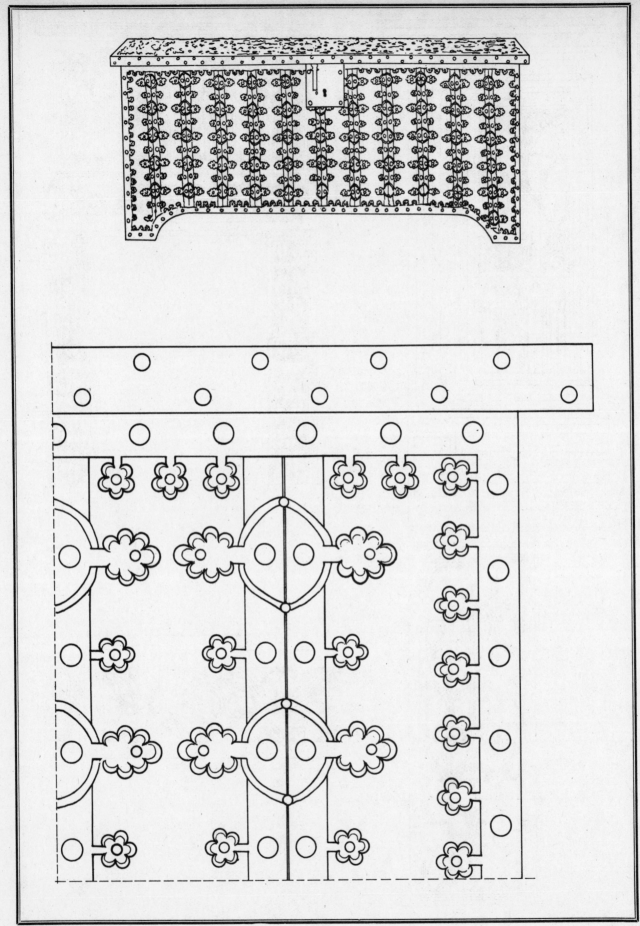

PLATE 6

Chest with wrought-iron trimming.

**PLATE 8**
Small carved chest with Gothic tracery.

15TH CENTURY

*Valencia Don Juan Institute, Madrid*

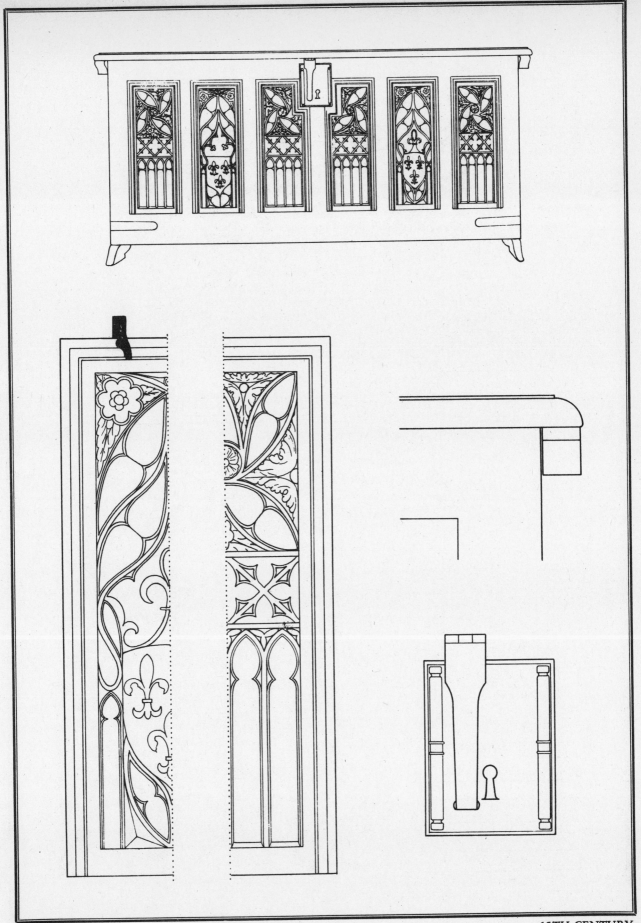

**PLATE 9**
Large carved chest with Gothic tracery.

*National Archeological Museum, Madrid*

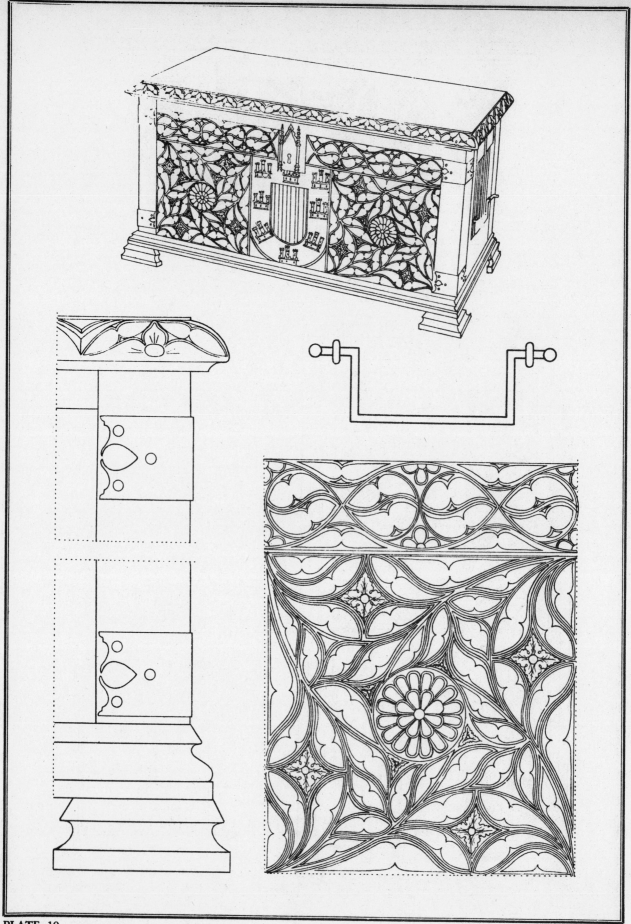

**PLATE 10**
Large carved chest with Gothic tracery and heraldic motif.

**15TH CENTURY**

*Valencia Don Juan Institute, Madrid*

**PLATE 11**
Large carved chest with Gothic tracery.

*Lazaro Galdiano Museum, Madrid*

**PLATE 12**
Small gothic chest with carved decoration.

LATE 15TH CENTURY

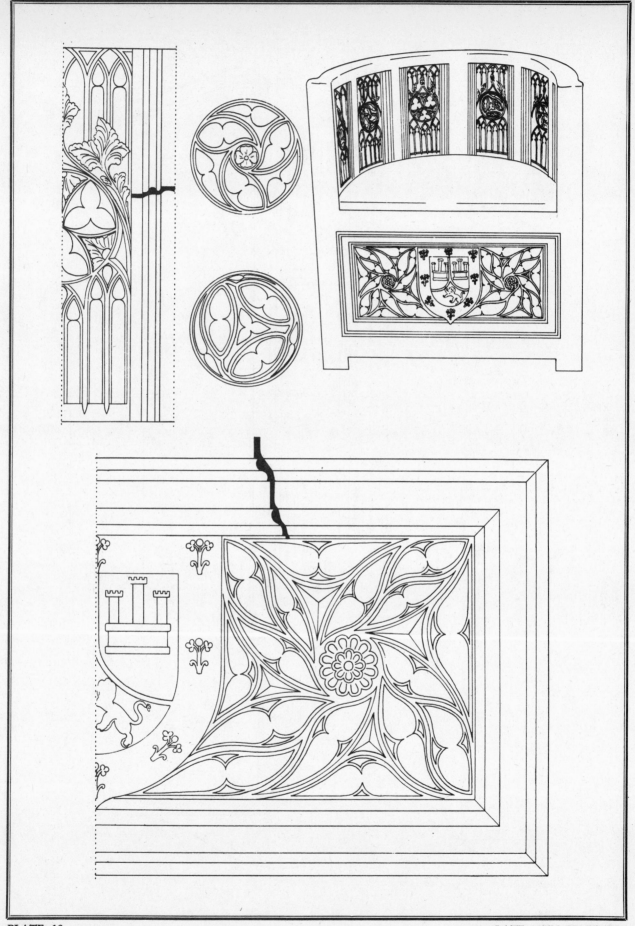

PLATE 13

LATE 15TH CENTURY

"Box" armchair with semicircular base and coat of arms of the Enríquez family, Castilian admirals.

*National Archeological Museum, Madrid*

PLATE 14
Gothic wardrobe with "parchment" design.

**PLATE 15**
Wardrobe with Mudejar decoration of joined wood.

*National Archeological Museum, Madrid*

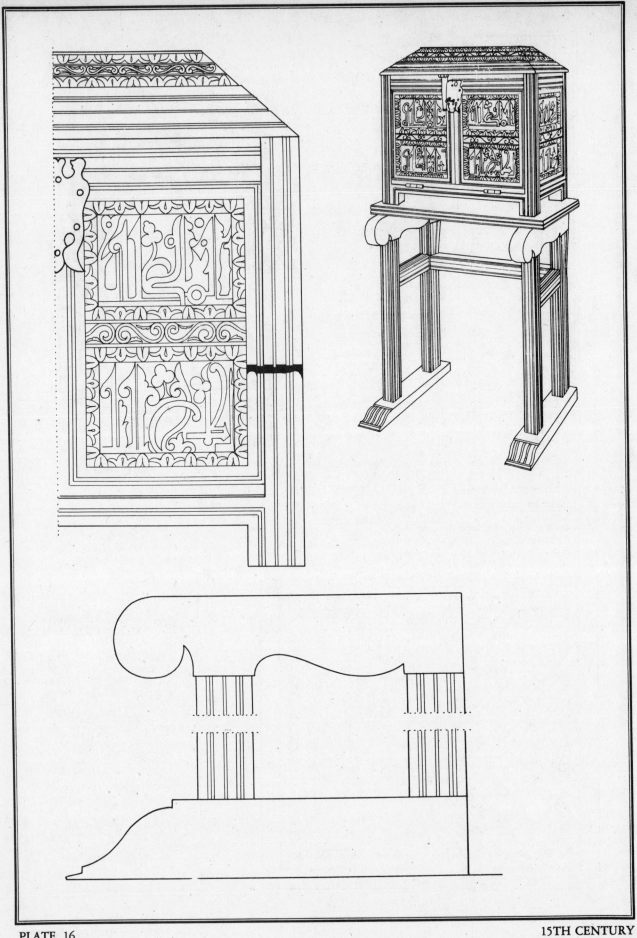

**PLATE 16**
Mudejar writing desk.

*Tavera Hospital, Toledo*

**PLATE 17**
Mudejar wardrobe.

LATE 15TH OR EARLY 16TH CENTURY

*Museum of Art of Catalonia, Barcelona*

**PLATE 18**
Desk decorated with Gothic-Renaissance motifs.

16TH CENTURY

*Private collection, Madrid*

22

**PLATE 19**
Desk of cypress wood decorated with fine Gothic carving.

16TH CENTURY

*National Archeological Museum, Madrid*

**PLATE 20**
Mudejar chest with bone inlays.

*Lazaro Galdiano Museum, Madrid*

**PLATE 21**
Small chest, with bone inlays, from Granada.

16TH CENTURY

*National Archeological Museum, Madrid*

**PLATE 22**
Small Mudejar chest with bone inlays.

16TH CENTURY

26

**PLATE 23**
Small Mudejar chest with bone inlays.

16TH CENTURY

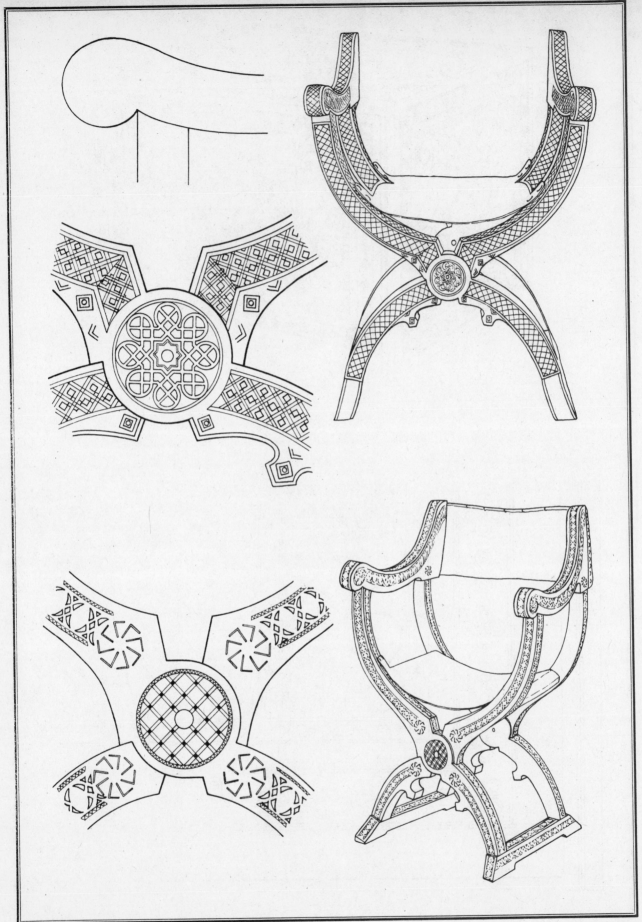

PLATE 24
Mudejar "sidesaddle" or scissors armchairs with bone inlays.

16TH CENTURY

*National Archeological Museum, Madrid*

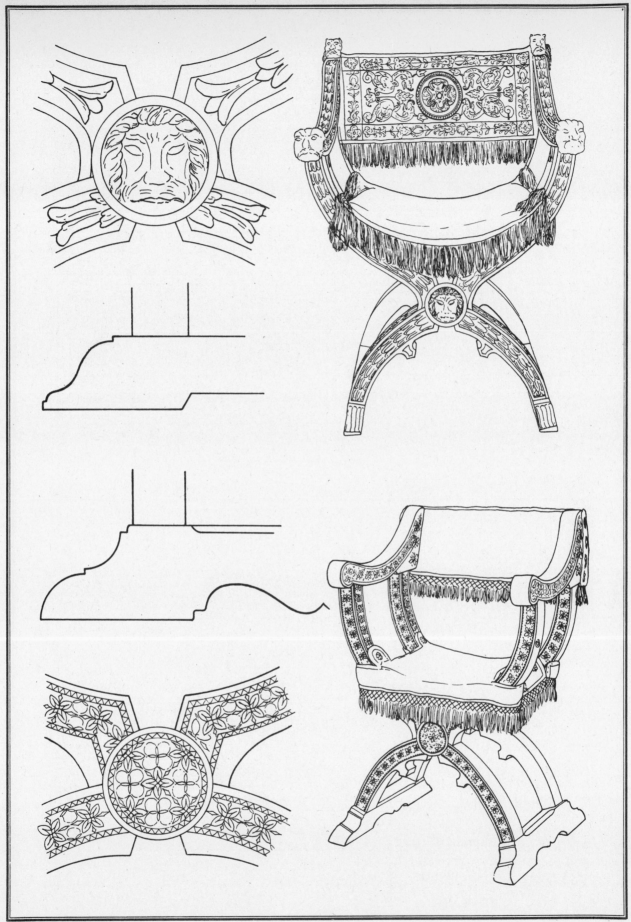

PLATE 25

"Sidesaddle" or scissors armchairs with Renaissance (upper chair) and Mudejar (lower chair) decoration.

*Valencia Don Juan Institute, Madrid*

PLATE 26
Writing desk with Mudejar marquetry.

*National Archeological Museum, Madrid*

PLATE 27
Desk top with Mudejar marquetry.

*National Archeological Museum, Madrid*

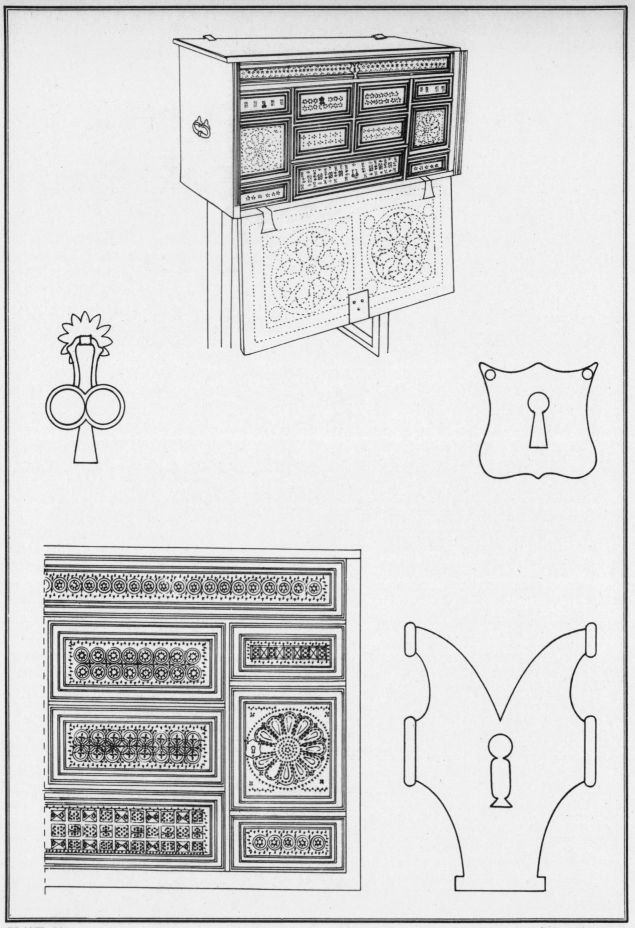

**PLATE 28**
16TH CENTURY
Fancy inlaid gilt secretary with Mudejar marquetry.

*National Archeological Museum, Madrid*

32

**PLATE 29**
Small chest with Mudejar marquetry from Granada.

*National Archeological Museum, Madrid*

**PLATE 30**
Mudejar marquetry on front of drawers of fancy inlaid gilt secretary.

**PLATE 31**
Renaissance fancy inlaid gilt secretary with "bridge" base. Mudejar-style marquetry on front of drawers.

16TH CENTURY

*Lazaro Galdiano Museum, Madrid*

**PLATE 32**
Seat with Renaissance decoration, reminiscent of Gothic style.

**PLATE 33**
Church stall with plateresque carvings.

MID-16TH CENTURY

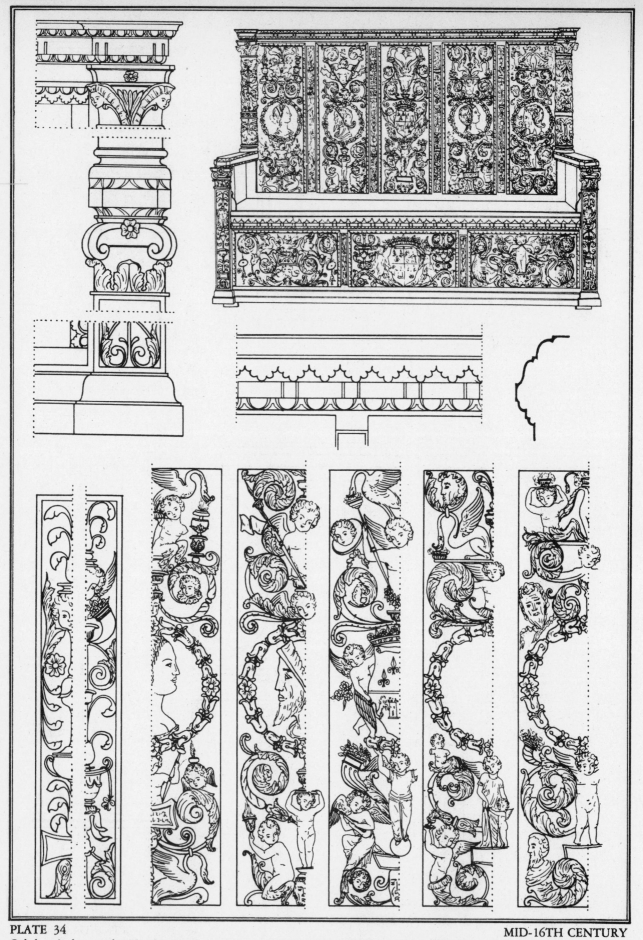

PLATE 34
Oak bench decorated with plateresque carvings with coat of arms of Dukes of Medinaceli.

*Collection of Dukes of Medinaceli, Madrid*

**PLATE 35**
Bench decorated with plateresque carvings.

MID-16TH CENTURY

*Museum of Decorative Arts, Madrid*

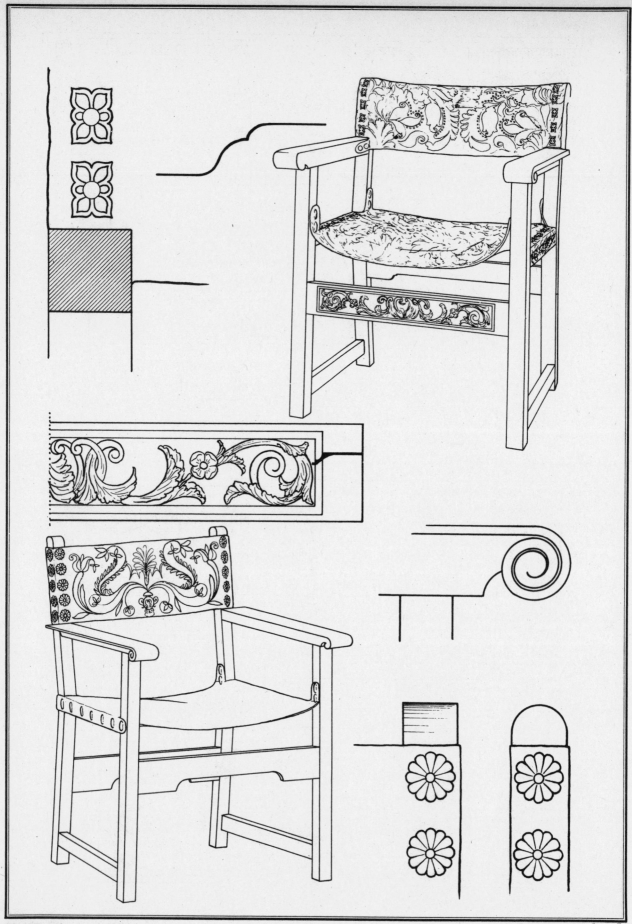

**PLATE 36**
Friars' armchairs trimmed with multicolored embossed leather.

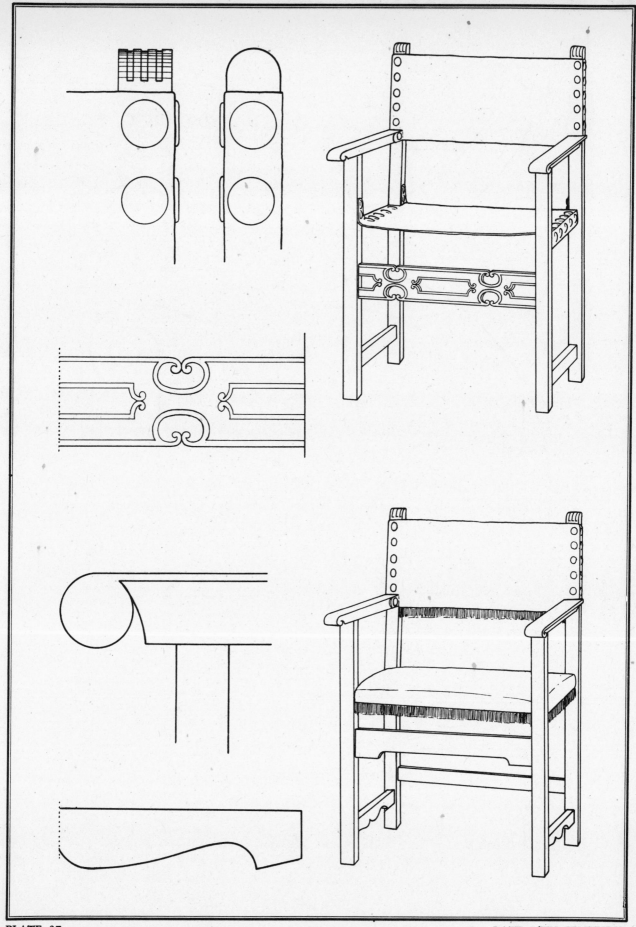

PLATE 37

Friars' armchairs trimmed with leather (upper chair) and cloth (lower chair).

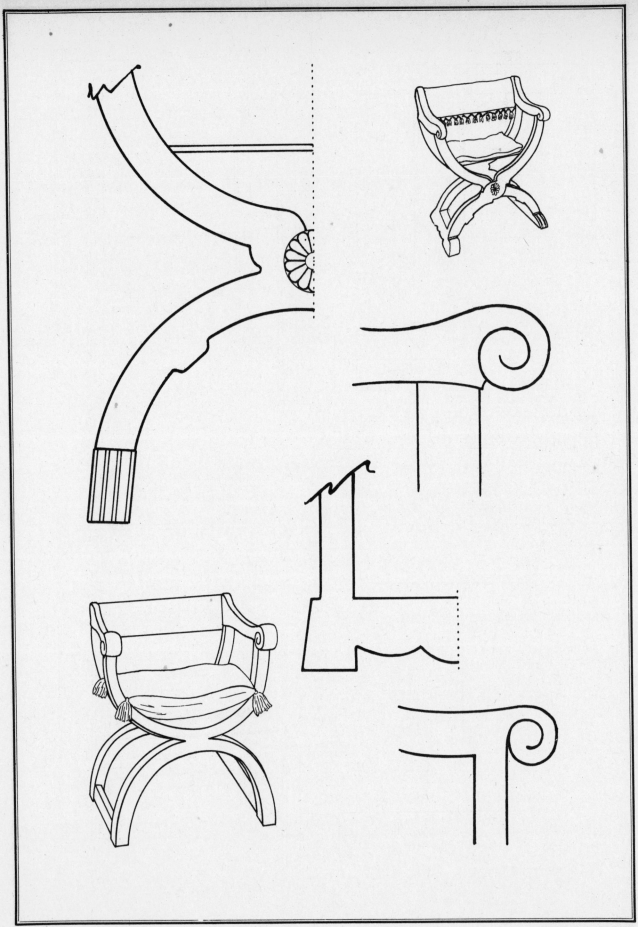

PLATE 38
"Sidesaddle" or scissors chairs.

*Casa de las Duenas, Seville*

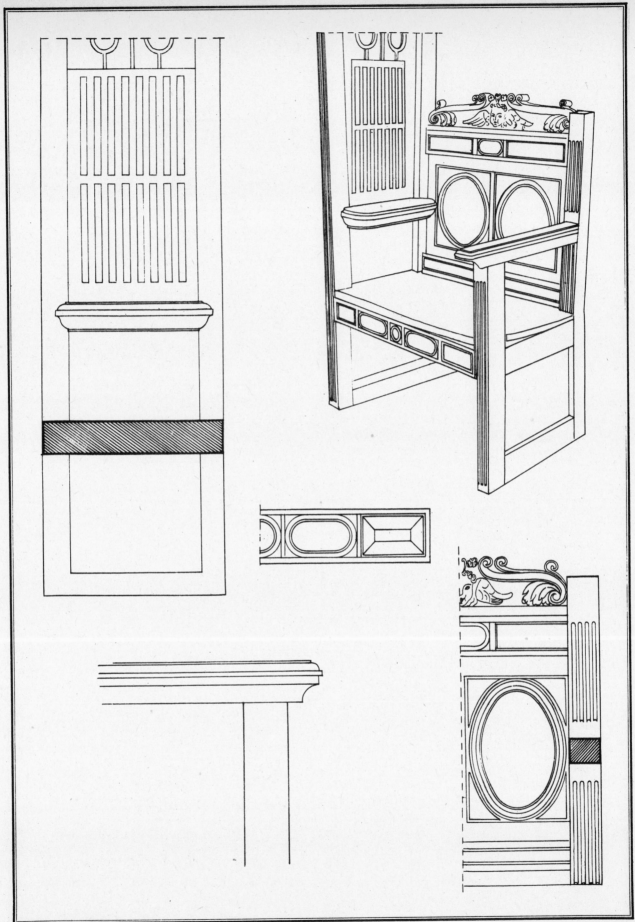

PLATE 39
Armchair-confessional decorated with Renaissance motifs.

LATE 16TH CENTURY

*Museum of Decorative Arts, Madrid*

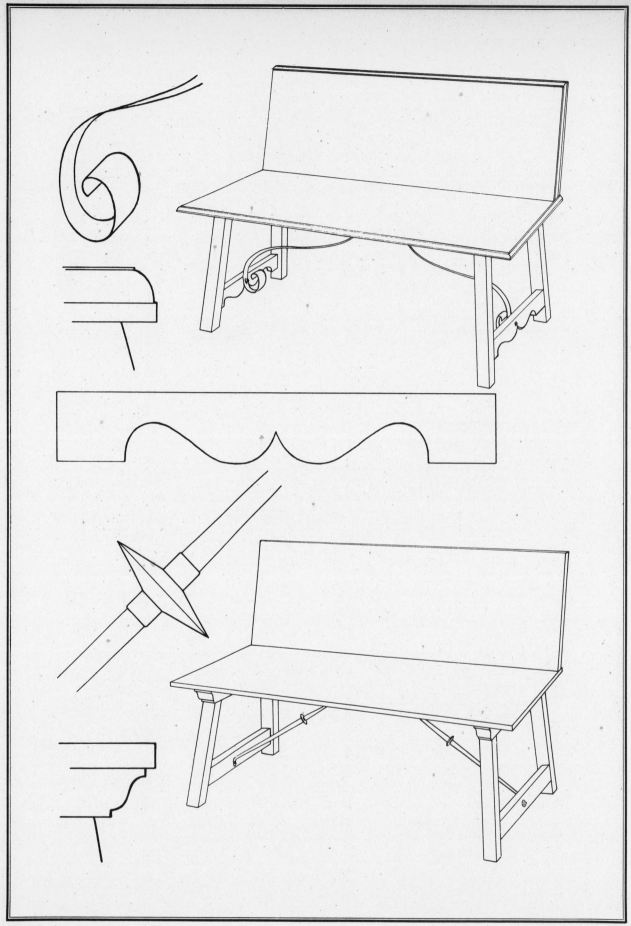

PLATE 40
Benches with wrought-iron ligatures.

16TH CENTURY

*Paradors of Merida and Oropesa*

44

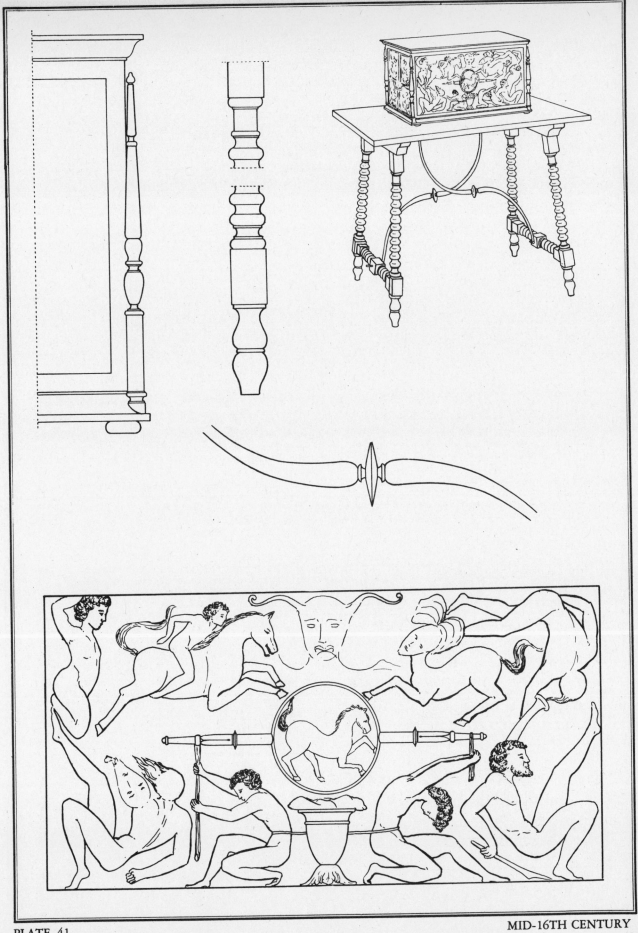

PLATE 41
Chest decorated with Renaissance motifs.

*Valencia Don Juan Institute, Madrid*

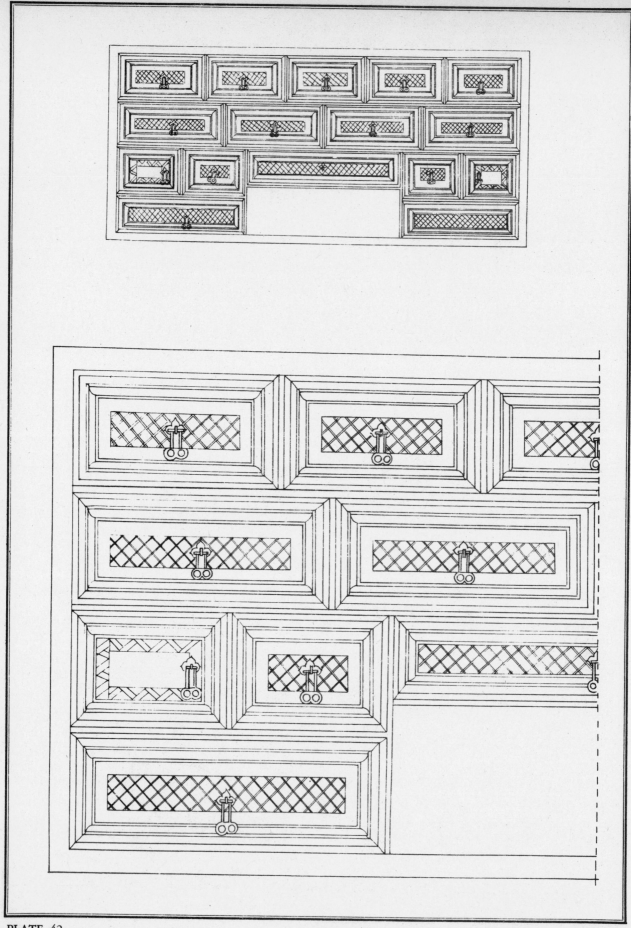

**PLATE 42**
Fancy inlaid gilt secretary decorated with mouldings and fine Gothic-style carvings.

MID-16TH CENTURY

*Museum of Decorative Arts, Madrid*

**PLATE 43**
Desk with "bridge" base and drawers decorated with plateresque carvings.

*Private collection*

PLATE 44
Desk decorated with Renaissance marquetry, on "bridge" base.

SECOND HALF OF 16TH CENTURY

*Museum of Art of Catalonia, Barcelona*

**PLATE 45**
SECOND HALF OF 16TH CENTURY

Fancy inlaid gilt secretary with Renaissance marquetry on "bridge" base.

*Lazaro Galdiano Museum, Madrid*

49

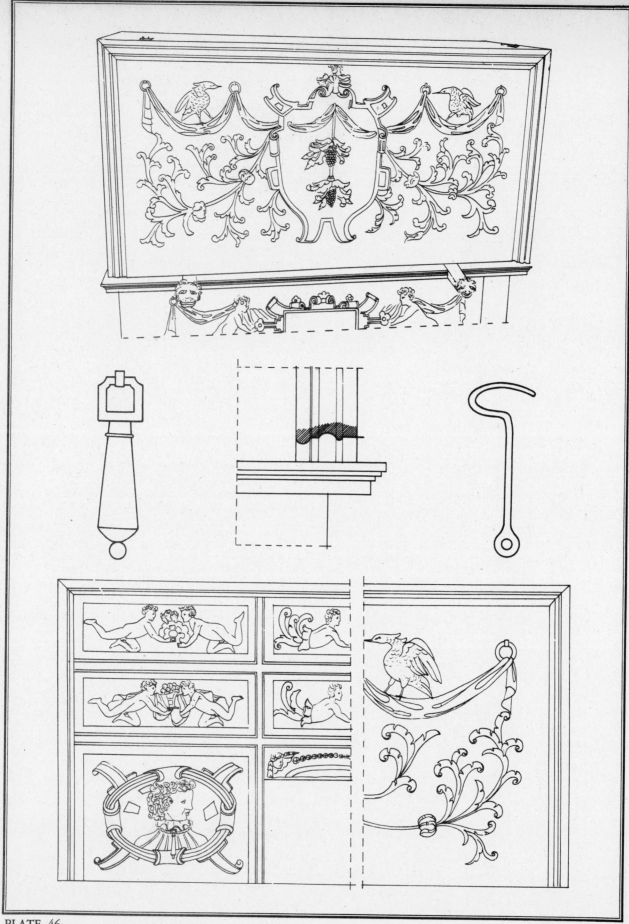

PLATE 46
Desk decorated with Renaissance motifs.

**16TH CENTURY**

*National Archeological Museum, Madrid*

PLATE 47
Desk decorated with Renaissance marquetry.

*Museum of Decorative Arts, Madrid*

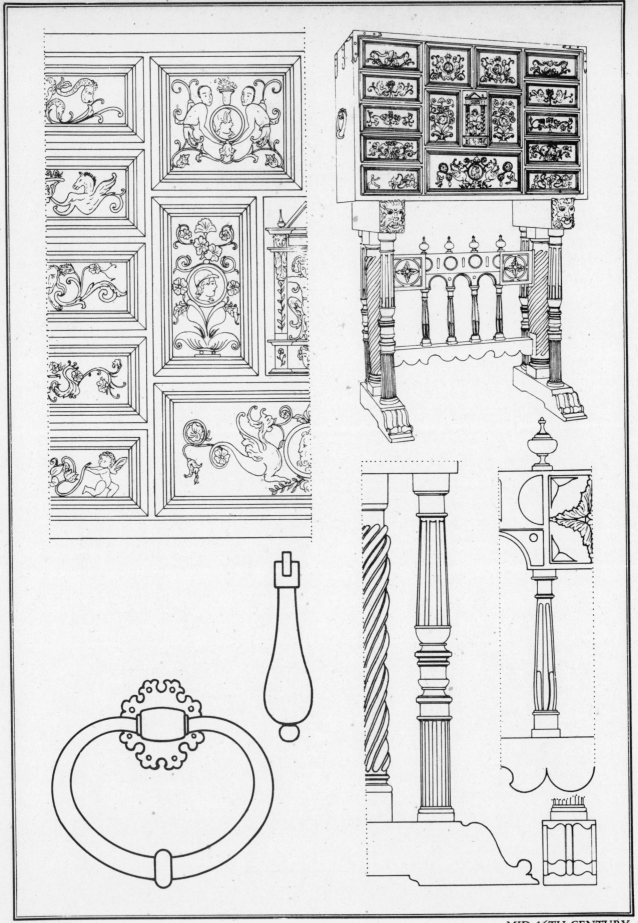

PLATE 48
Fancy inlaid gilt secretary of walnut, decorated with plateresque carvings on a "bridge" base.

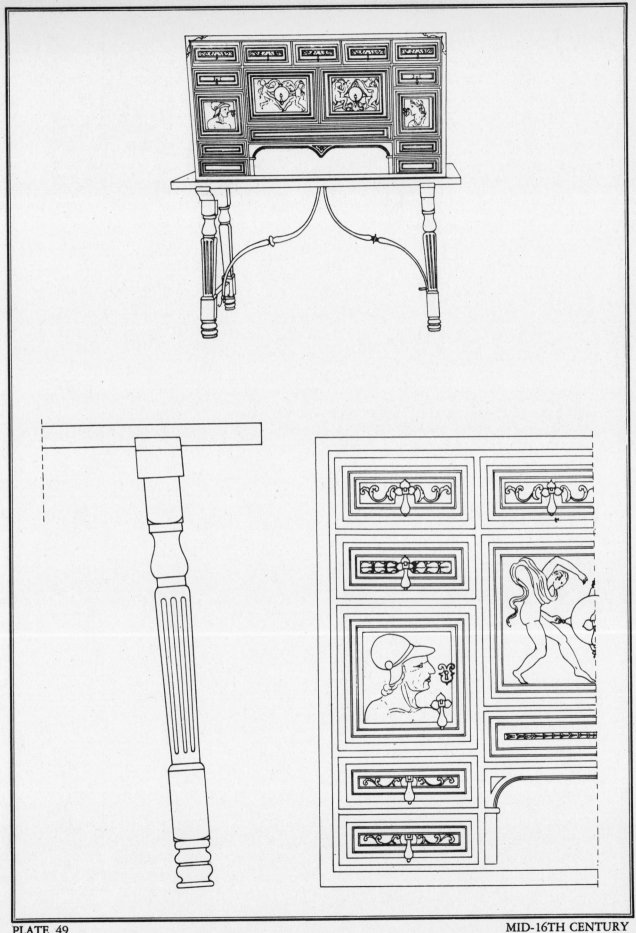

**PLATE 49**
Fancy inlaid gilt secretary decorated with Renaissance carvings.

MID-16TH CENTURY

*Museum of Decorative Arts, Madrid*

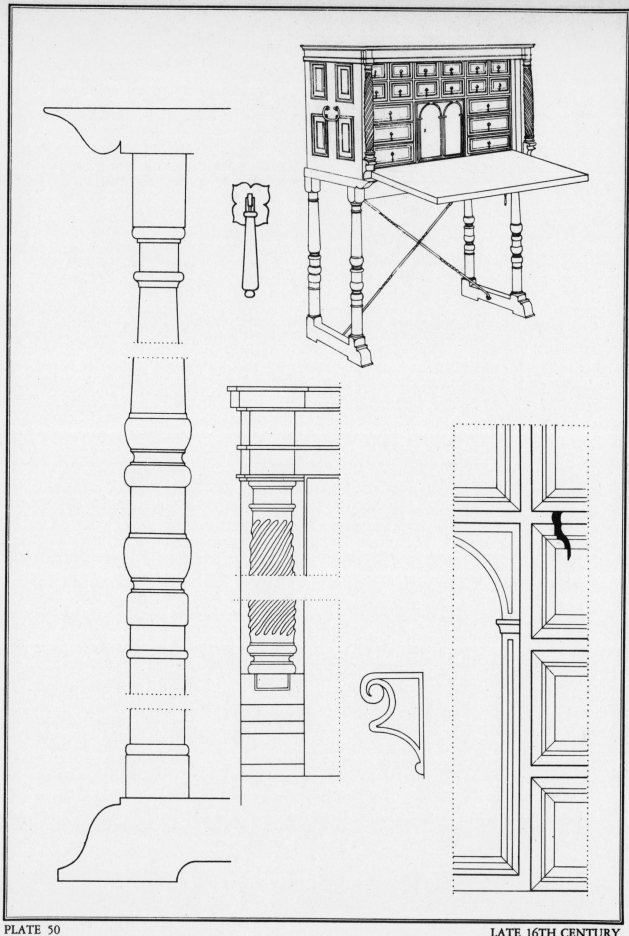

PLATE 50
Desk with Renaissance architectonic motifs.

*Tavera Hospital, Toledo*

**PLATE 51**
Large chests decorated with floral and geometric motifs.

*Upper chest: Riudabell Castle*

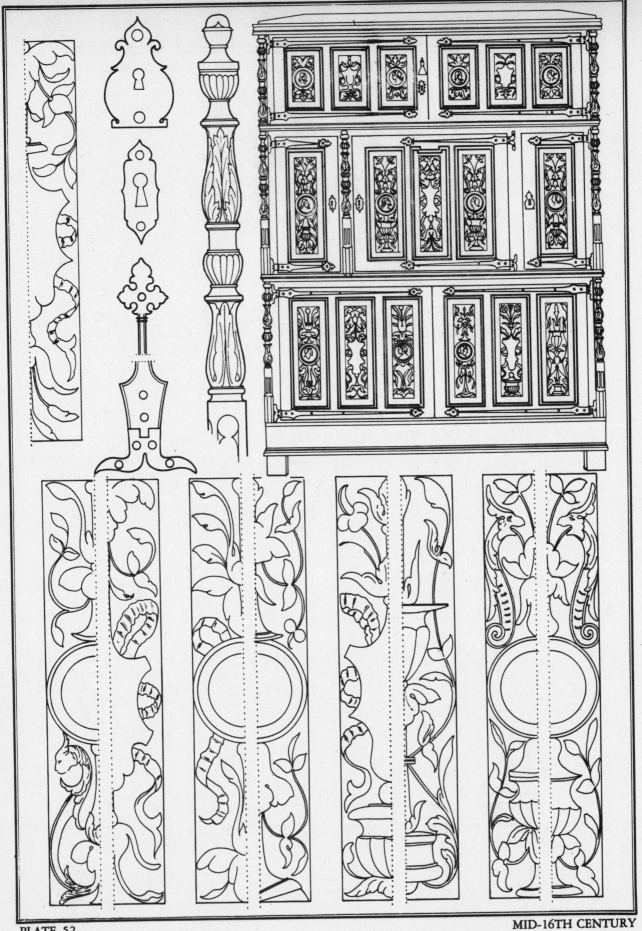

PLATE 52
Wardrobe decorated with plateresque carvings.

MID-16TH CENTURY

*Paredes de Nava Parochial Church, Palencia*

PLATE 53
Wardrobe decorated with plateresque carvings.

MID-16TH CENTURY

*National Archeological Museum, Madrid*

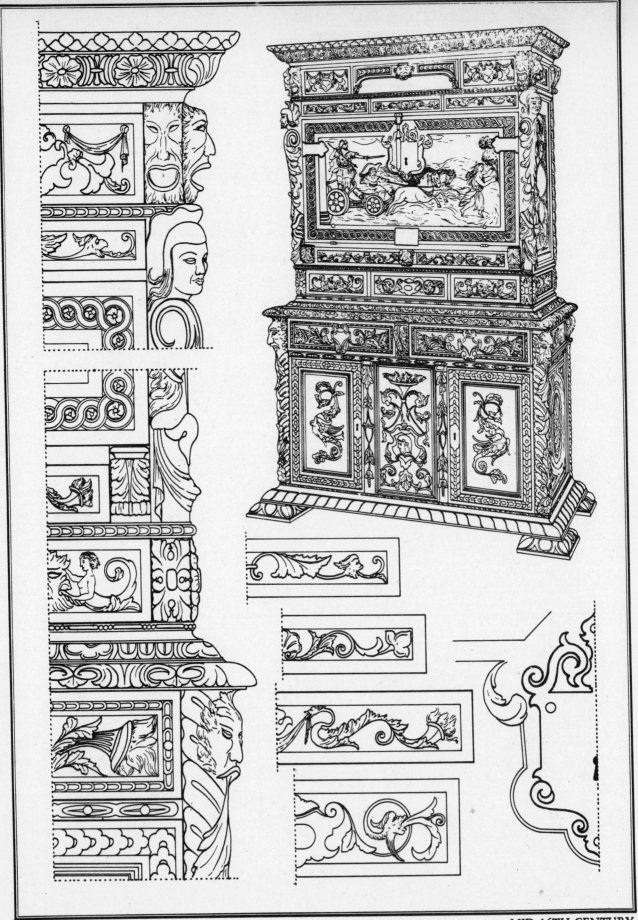

PLATE 54
Chest-on-chest decorated with Renaissance carvings.

MID-16TH CENTURY

*Private collection*

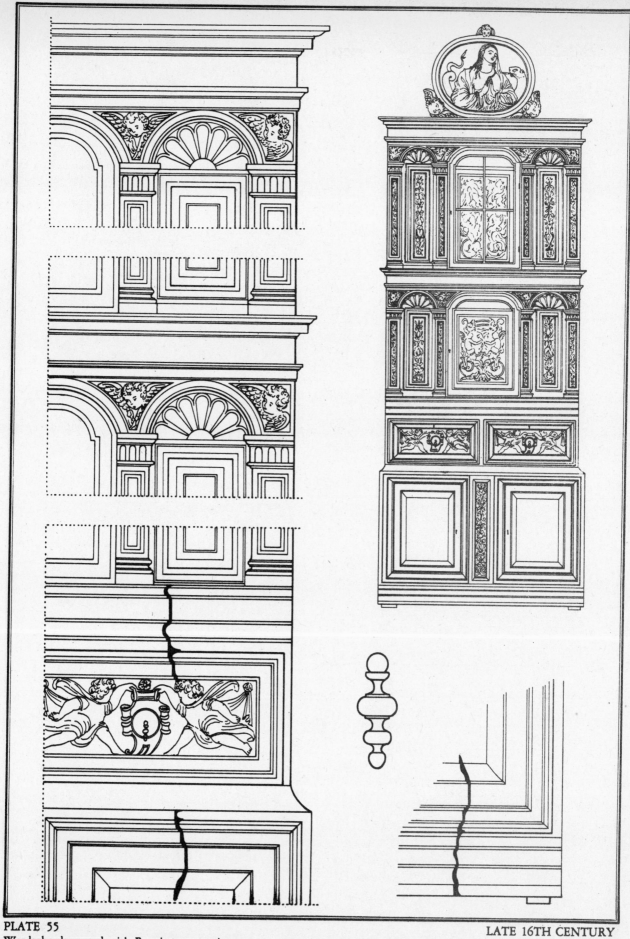

**PLATE 55**
Wardrobe decorated with Renaissance carvings.

*Private collection*

PLATE 56
Chest-on-chest decorated with Renaissance carvings.

PLATE 57
Chest-on-chest decorated with Renaissance carvings and Gothic-style "parchments."

MID-16TH CENTURY

PLATE 58

**MID-16TH CENTURY**

Chest-on-chest decorated with Renaissance carvings and Gothic-style "parchments."

PLATE 59
Desk decorated with Renaissance carvings.

MID-16TH CENTURY

PLATE 60

MID-16TH CENTURY

Italian-style desk decorated with Renaissance carvings.

PLATE 61

Italian-style desk decorated with Renaissance carvings.

PLATE 62
Italian-style chest-on-chest decorated with Renaissance carvings.

*Museum of Art of Catalonia, Barcelona*

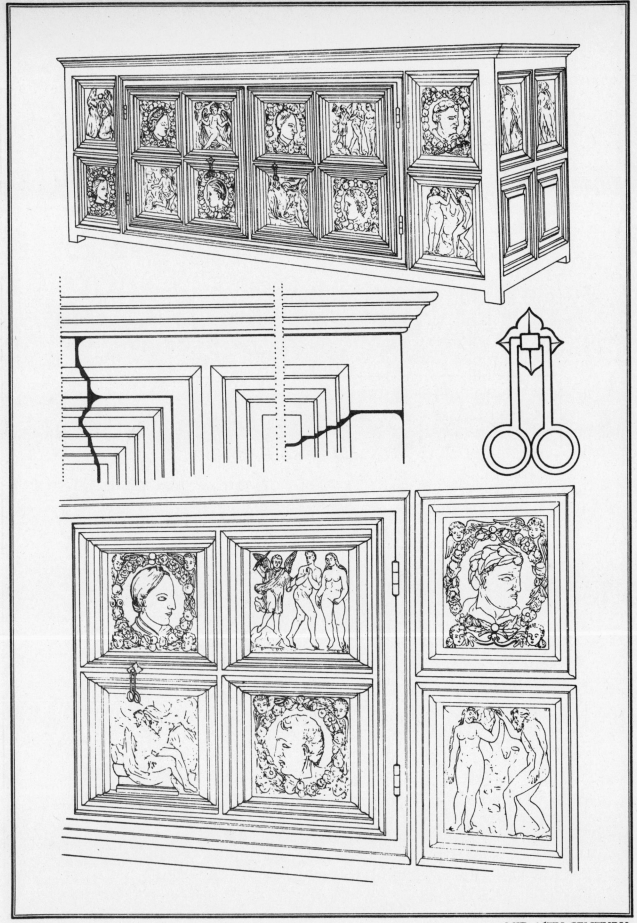

PLATE 63
Large wardrobe-chest decorated with plateresque carvings.

MID-16TH CENTURY

*Chapel of the Constable, Cathedral of Burgos*

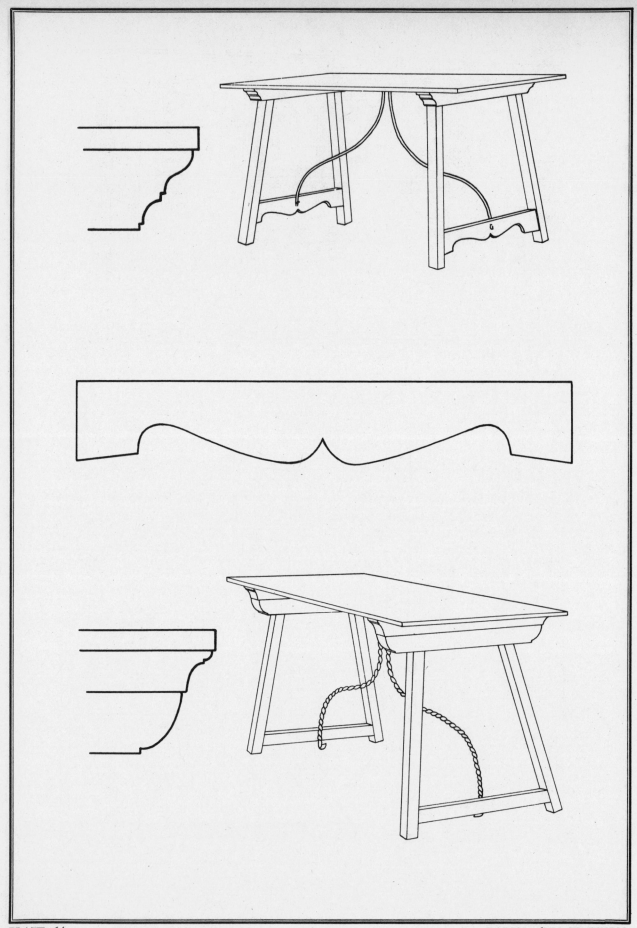

PLATE 64

Writing desks with pyramidal construction and ligatures of wrought iron.

**PLATE 65**
Chest-on-chest decorated with Renaissance carvings.

SECOND HALF OF 16TH CENTURY

*Lazaro Galdiano Museum, Madrid*

**PLATE 66**
Heads of wrought-iron nails.

*Lazaro Galdiano Museum, Madrid*

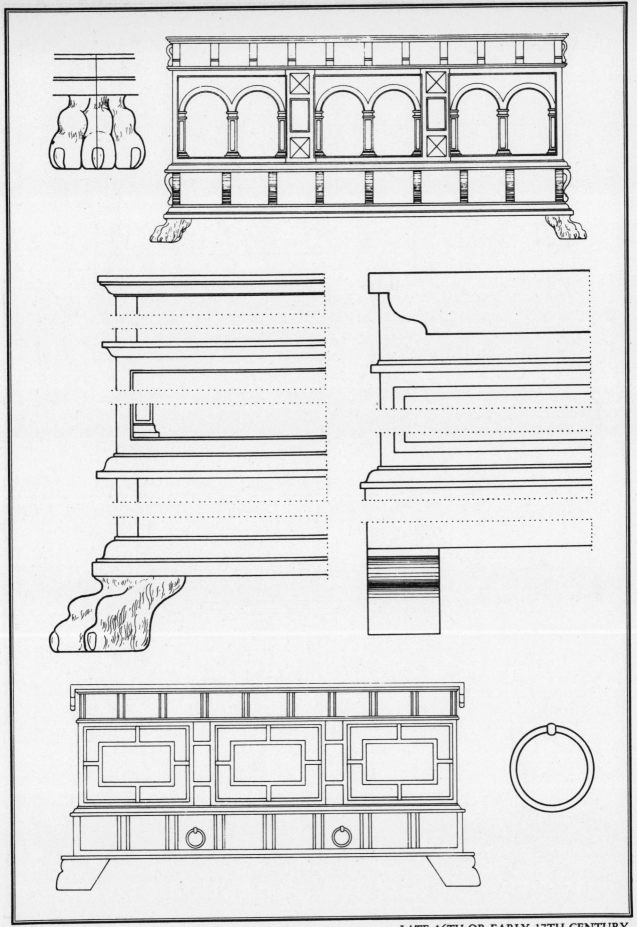

**PLATE 67**
Large chests of Renaissance design.

LATE 16TH OR EARLY 17TH CENTURY

*Riudabell Castle*

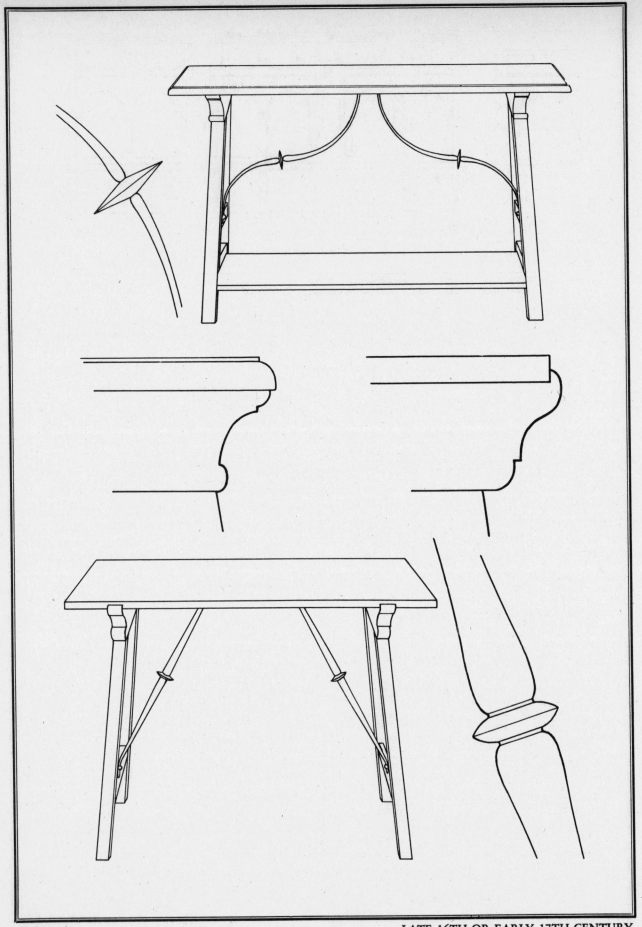

PLATE 68

LATE 16TH OR EARLY 17TH CENTURY

Writing desks with pyramidal construction and ligatures of wrought iron.

*Museum of Bilbao and Parador of Santillano, Santander*

**PLATE 69**
Carved panels with plateresque motifs.

*From the doors of the Alcazar of Toledo, which were destroyed in 1936*

73

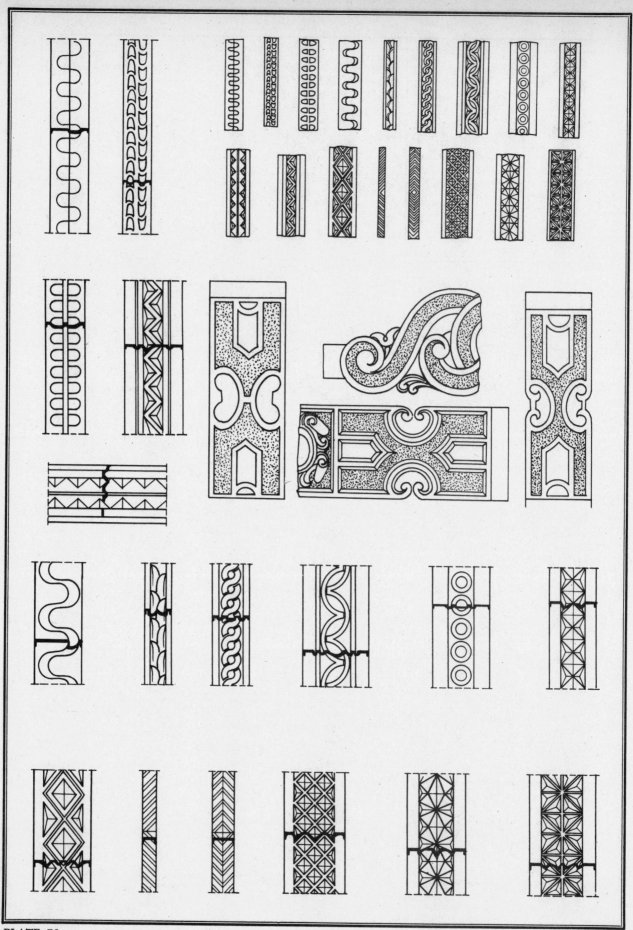

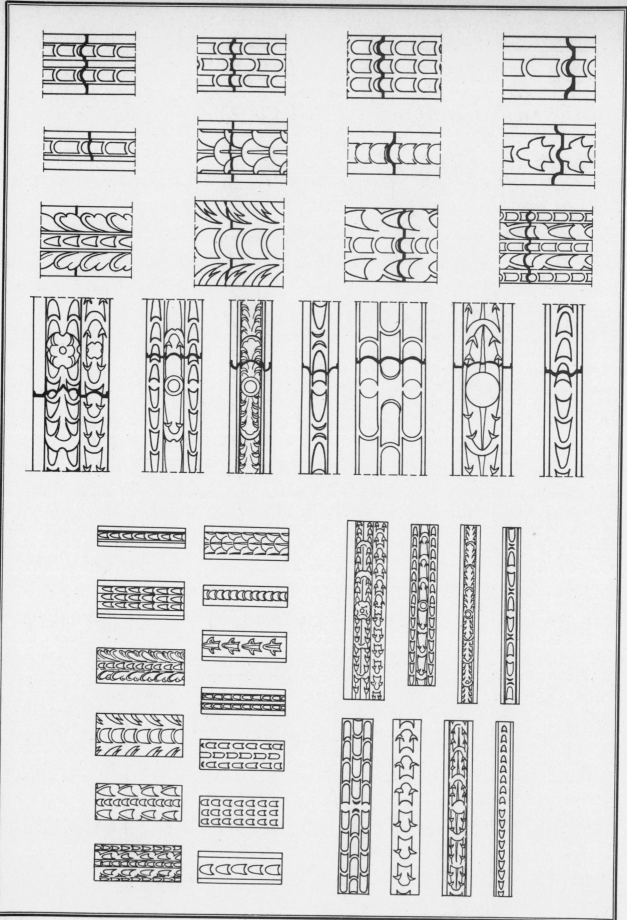

PLATE 72
Decorations of 16th and 17th centuries.

LATE 16TH OR EARLY 17TH CENTURY

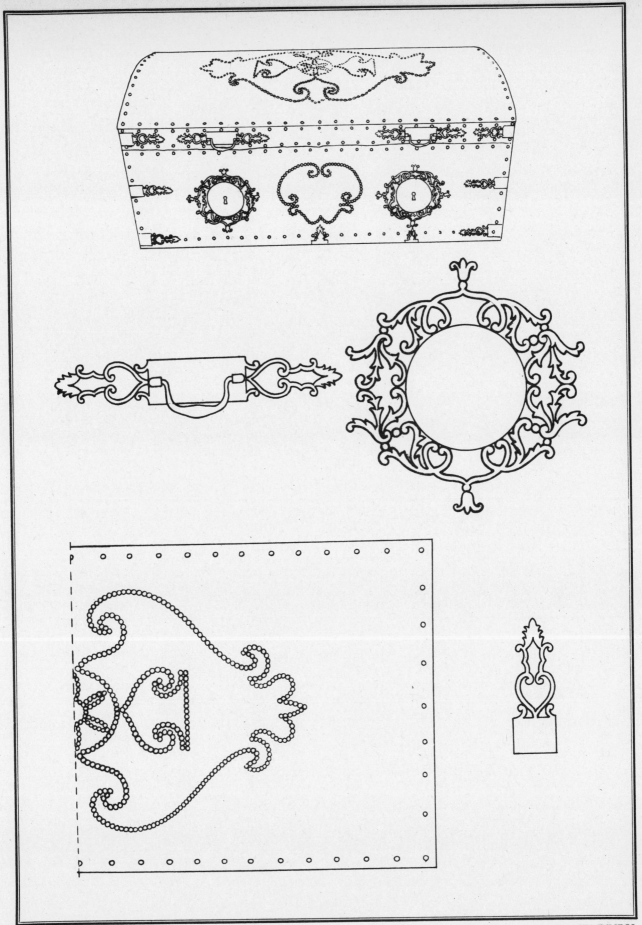

PLATE 73

17TH CENTURY

Leather chest decorated with metal nails and gilt ironwork.

*Museum of Decorative Arts, Madrid*

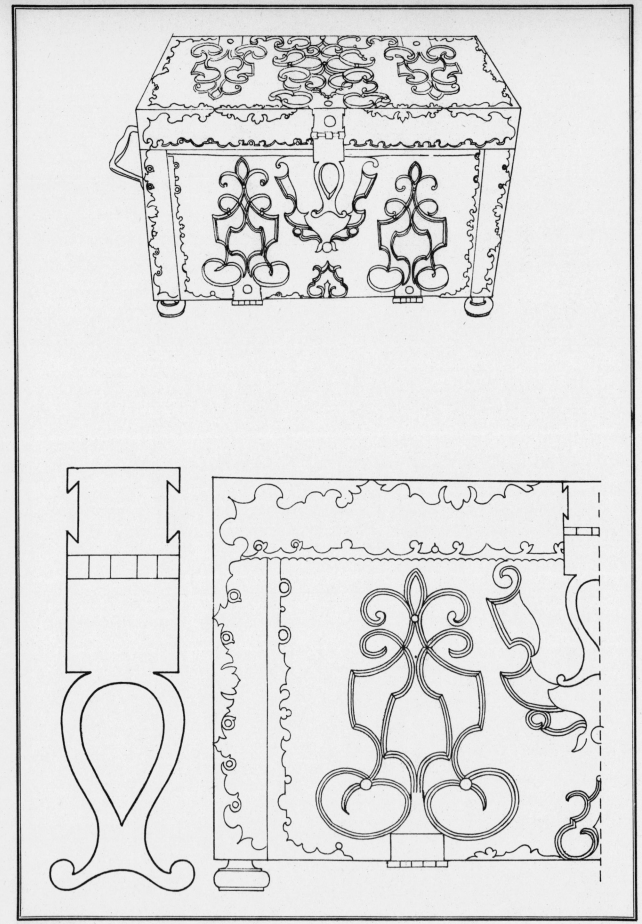

**PLATE 74**
Small chest decorated with gilt ironwork.

*National Archeological Museum, Madrid*

**PLATE 75**
Small wooden chest with carved decoration.

*Museum of Decorative Arts, Madrid*

**PLATE 76**
Wooden chest decorated with baroque carvings.

*March collection, Palma de Mallorca*

**PLATE 77**
Wardrobes with panelled doors.

*Gustavo Gili Collection, Santillana del Mar*

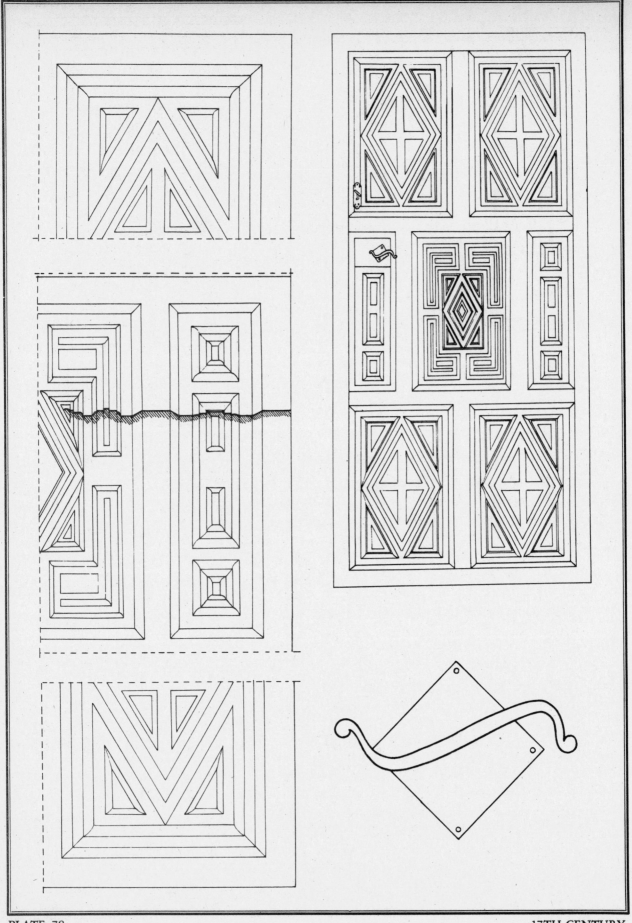

**PLATE 78**
Door decorated with geometric motifs.

*Arciprestal de Santa Maria, Castellon*

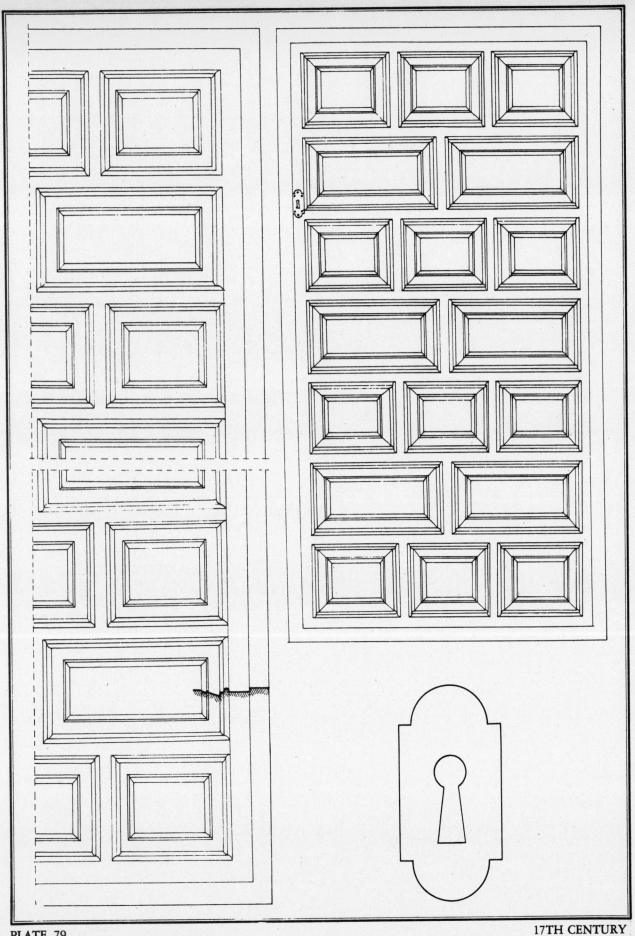

**PLATE 79**
Panelled door.

17TH CENTURY

*Private collection*

PLATE 80
Panelled door.

*Private collection*

**PLATE 81**
Wardrobe decorated with carvings and turned balusters.

*Museum of Decorative Arts, Madrid*

PLATE 82
Wardrobe decorated with zigzag moulding.

17TH CENTURY

*Tavera Hospital, Toledo*

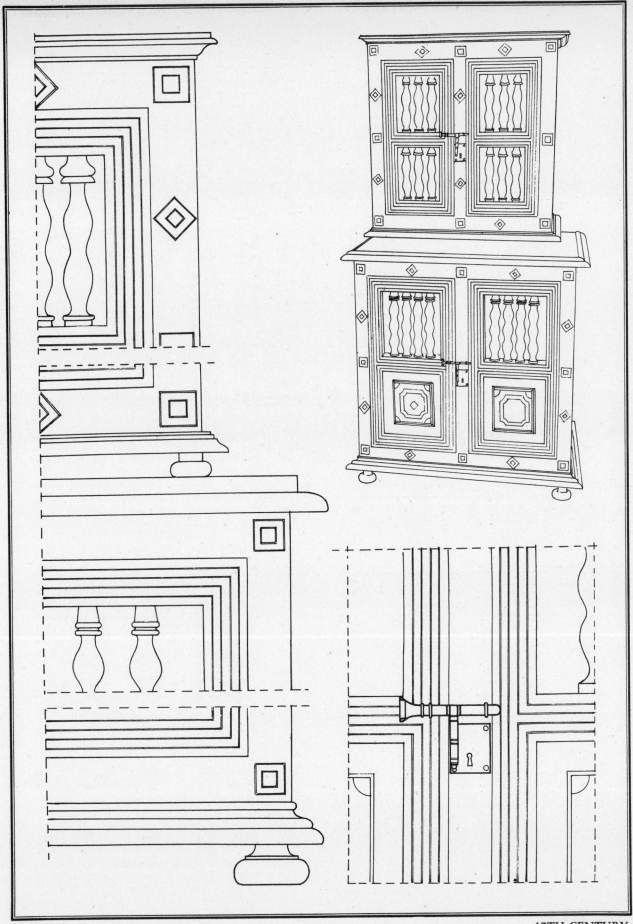

**PLATE 83**
Wardrobe with turned balusters on doors.

17TH CENTURY

*Museum of Decorative Arts, Madrid*

PLATE 84
Low wardrobe decorated with mouldings.

17TH CENTURY

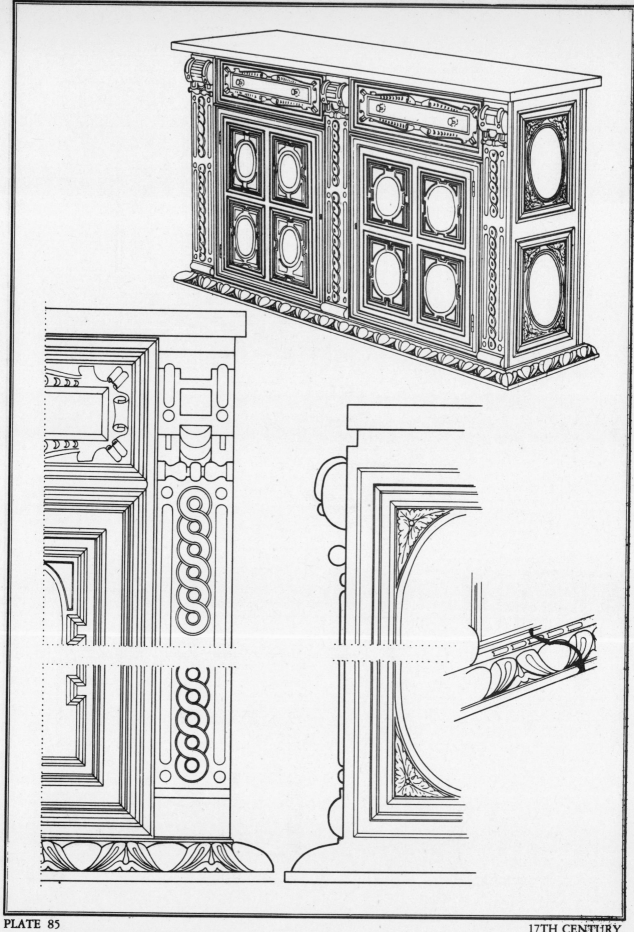

**PLATE 85**
Low wardrobe decorated with baroque carvings.

17TH CENTURY

**PLATE 86**
Low wardrobe decorated with baroque carvings and twisted columns.

*Museum of Painting, Seville*

**PLATE 87**
Wardrobe with latticework and turned balusters.

*Private collection*

**PLATE 88**
Low wardrobe decorated with mouldings and baroque carvings.

PLATE 89
Wardrobe completely decorated with baroque carvings.

**PLATE 90**
Low wardrobe with decoration showing Central European influence.

**17TH CENTURY**

**PLATE 91**
Chest-on-chest decorated with baroque carvings and turned balusters.

17TH CENTURY

*Private collection*

**PLATE 92**
Chest-on-chest decorated with baroque carvings and turned balusters.

*Private collection*

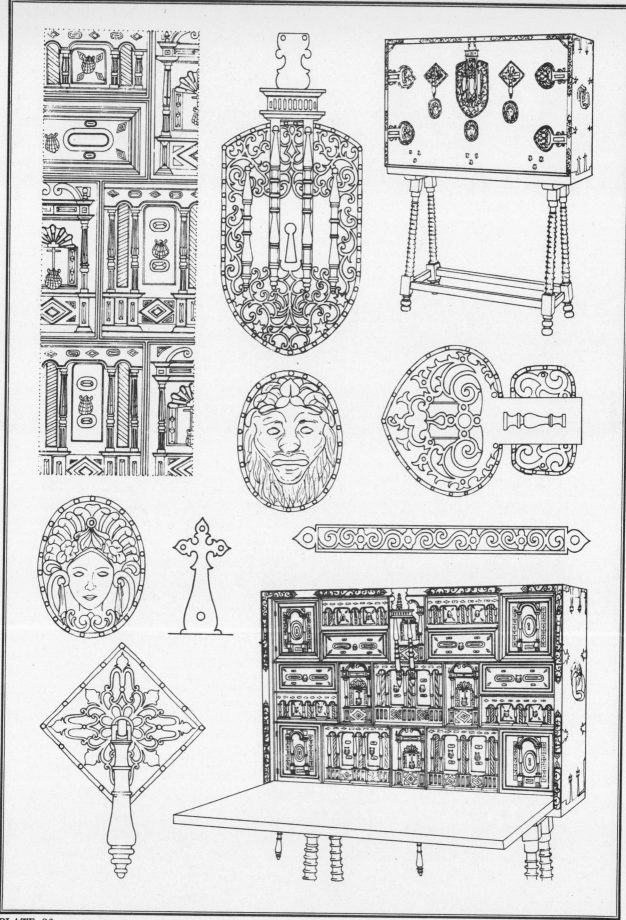

PLATE 93

FIRST HALF OF 17TH CENTURY

Desk decorated with pieces of multicolored and gilt bone. Top with fine gilt ironwork. Writing table with turned legs.

*Tavera Hospital, Toledo*

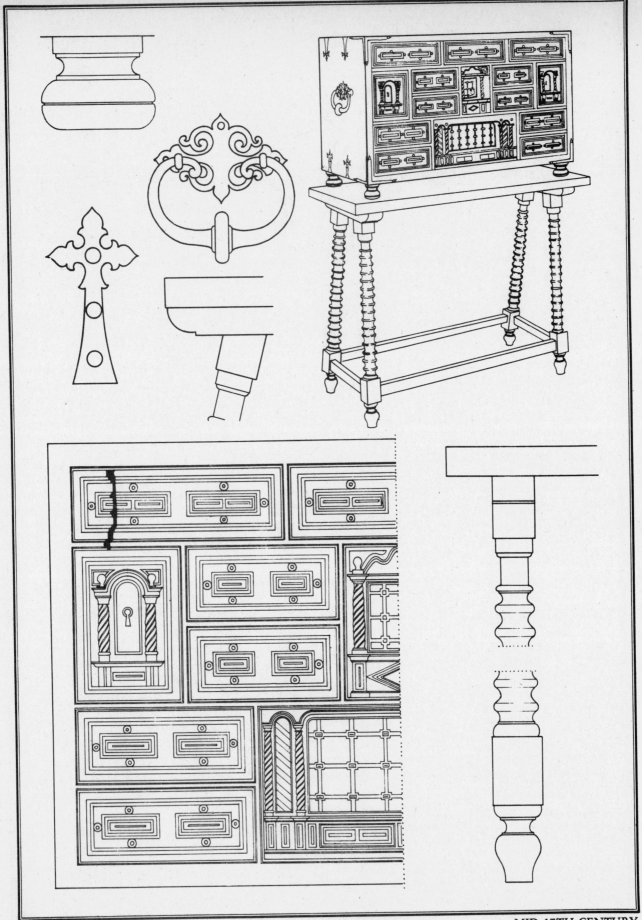

**PLATE 94**
Fancy inlaid gilt secretary decorated with mouldings and small turned posts.

MID-17TH CENTURY

*Tavera Hospital, Toledo*

PLATE 95
Desk on top of chest of drawers with gilt hardware.

FIRST HALF OF 17TH CENTURY

*Cervantes' house, Valladolid*

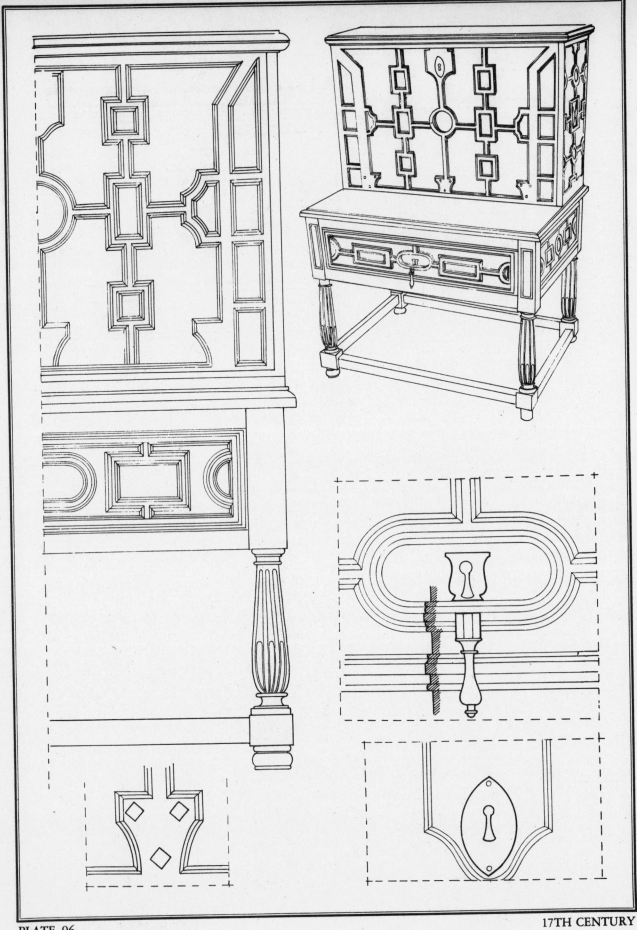

PLATE 96
Desk decorated with mouldings.

**17TH CENTURY**

*National Archeological Museum, Madrid*

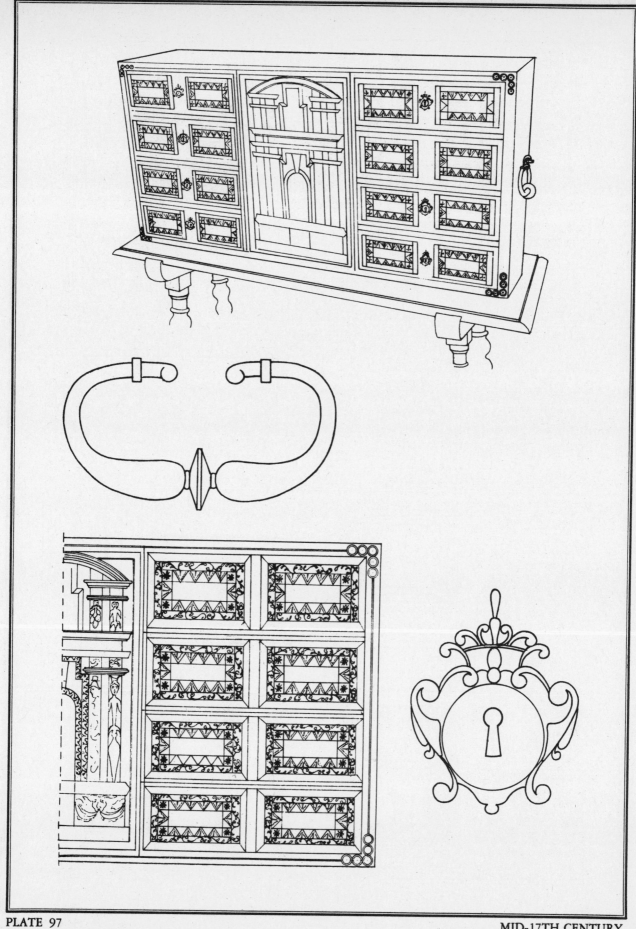

**PLATE 97**
Fancy gilt secretary decorated with inlaid bone.

MID-17TH CENTURY

*National Archeological Museum, Madrid*

**PLATE 98**
Fancy inlaid gilt secretary decorated with bone plaques with ornamental engraving.

MID-17TH CENTURY

*Lazaro Galdiano Museum, Madrid*

**PLATE 99**
Small wooden chest decorated with burned engravings.

MID-17TH CENTURY

*Tavera Hospital, Toledo*

PLATE 100
Small desk decorated with bone marquetry.

MID-17TH CENTURY

*Tavera Hospital, Toledo*

PLATE 101

MID-17TH CENTURY

Fancy inlaid gilt secretary decorated with engraved plaques of bone, on pedestal in form of inverted truncated rectangular pyramids.

PLATE 102
Desk on base of twisted columns.

SECOND HALF OF 17TH CENTURY

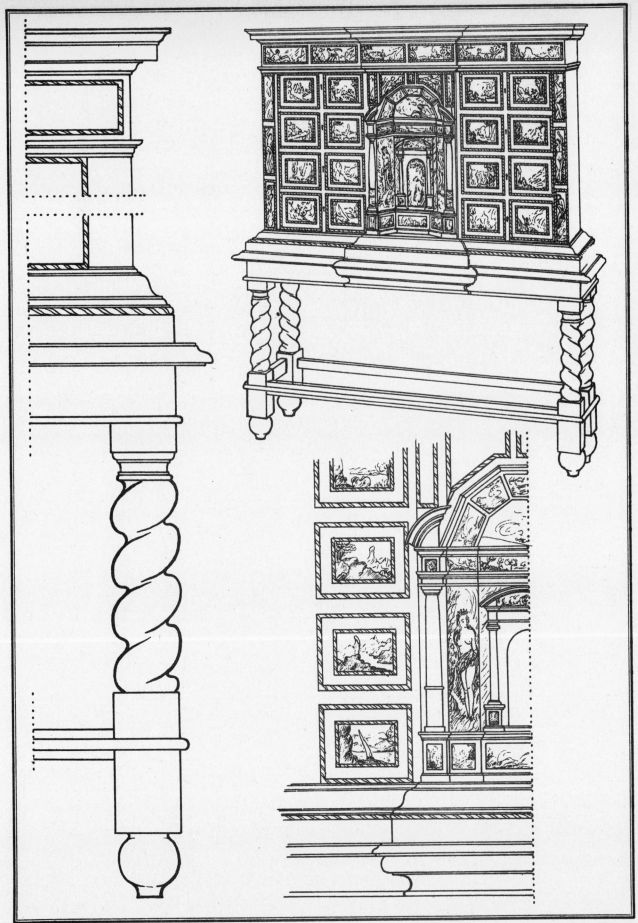

**PLATE 103**
Fancy inlaid gilt secretary decorated with painted mirrors, on a base of twisted columns.

PLATE 104

SECOND HALF OF 17TH CENTURY

Fancy inlaid gilt secretary decorated with tortoiseshell plaques and gilt metal locks and decorative lines.

*Private collection*

**PLATE 105**

SECOND HALF OF 17TH CENTURY

Fancy inlaid gilt secretary covered with tortoiseshell, with openwork cornice and gilt metal lines and decorations.

*Private collection*

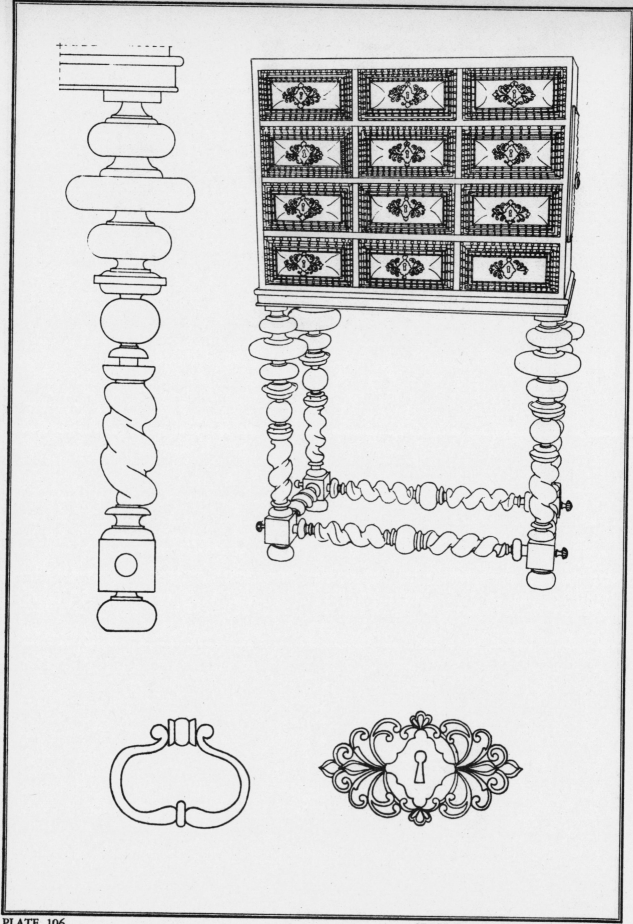

**PLATE 106**

SECOND HALF OF 17TH CENTURY

Portuguese-style counter. Drawers decorated with rippled ebony mouldings. Base of twisted columns.

*Museum of Decorative Arts, Madrid*

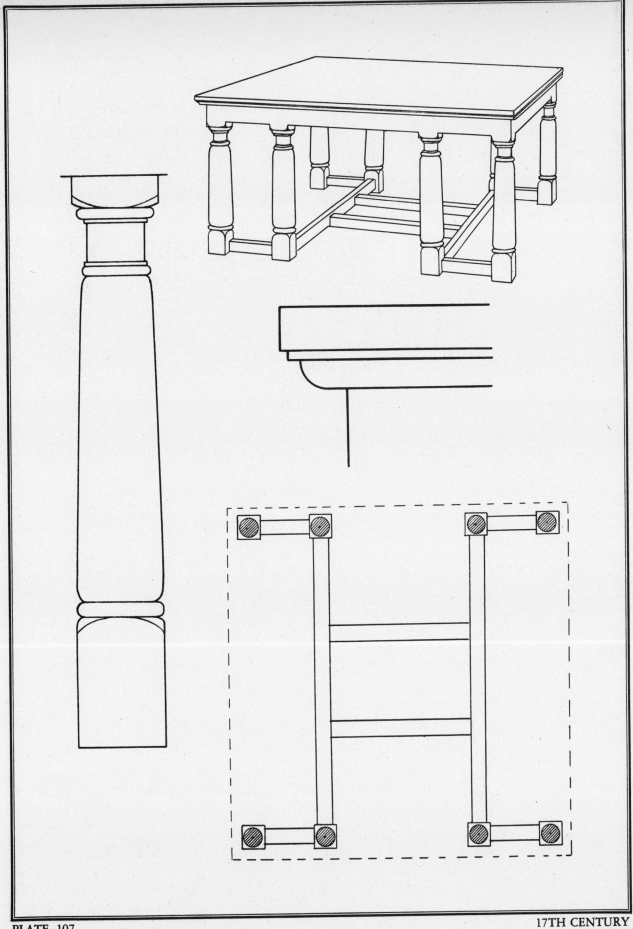

**PLATE 107**
Table with eight legs joined by wooden beams.

*Riudabell Castle*

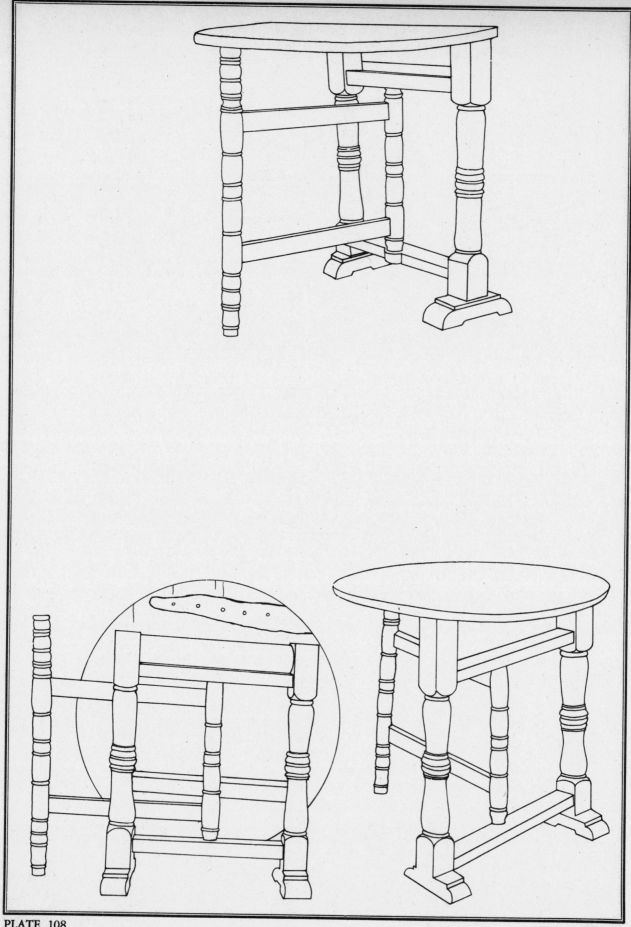

**PLATE 108**
Folding table with turned legs.

*Gustavo Gili collection, Santillana del Mar*

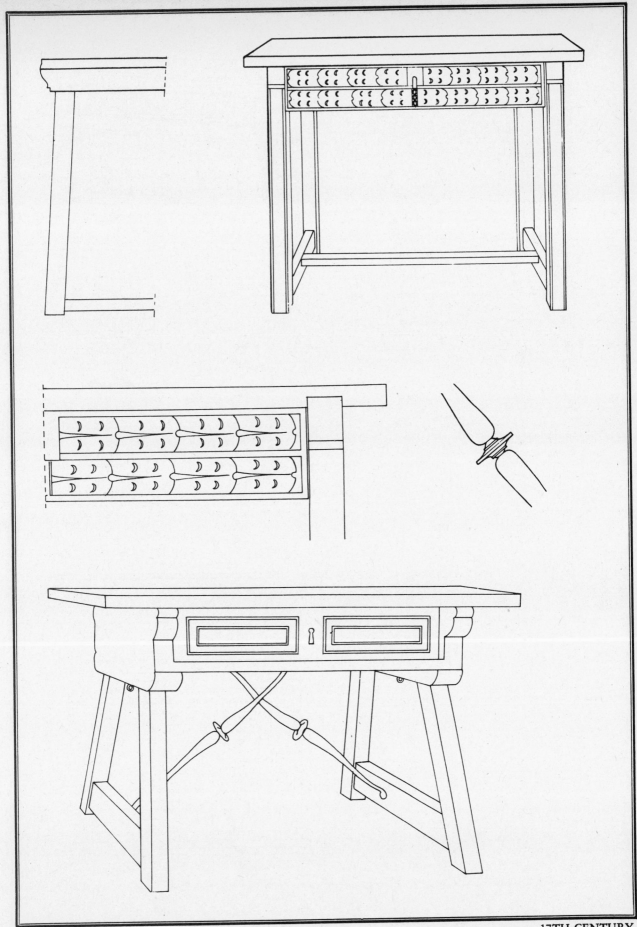

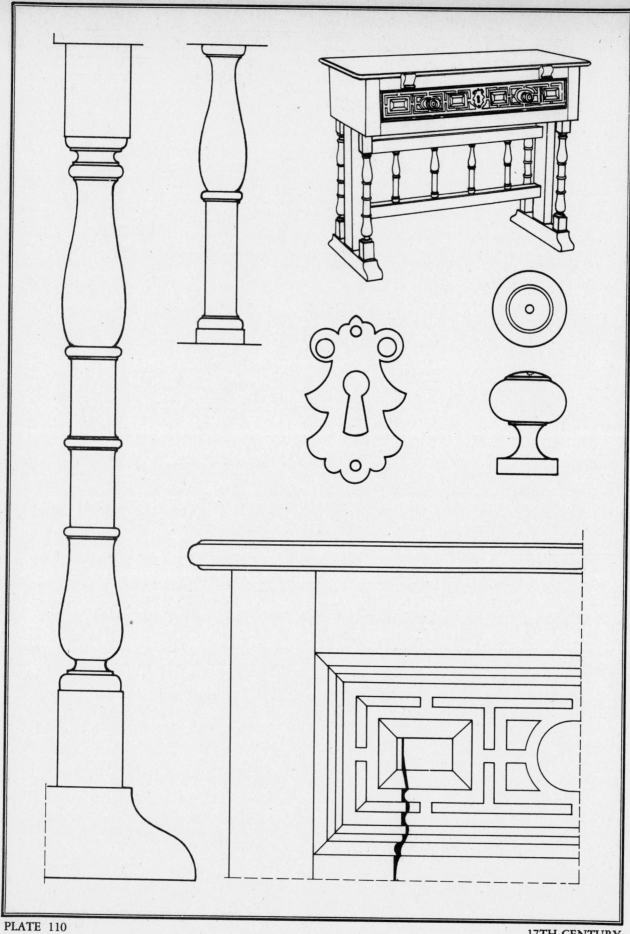

**PLATE 110**
Table with carved drawer fronts and a "bridge" base.

**17TH CENTURY**

*Museum of Decorative Arts, Madrid*

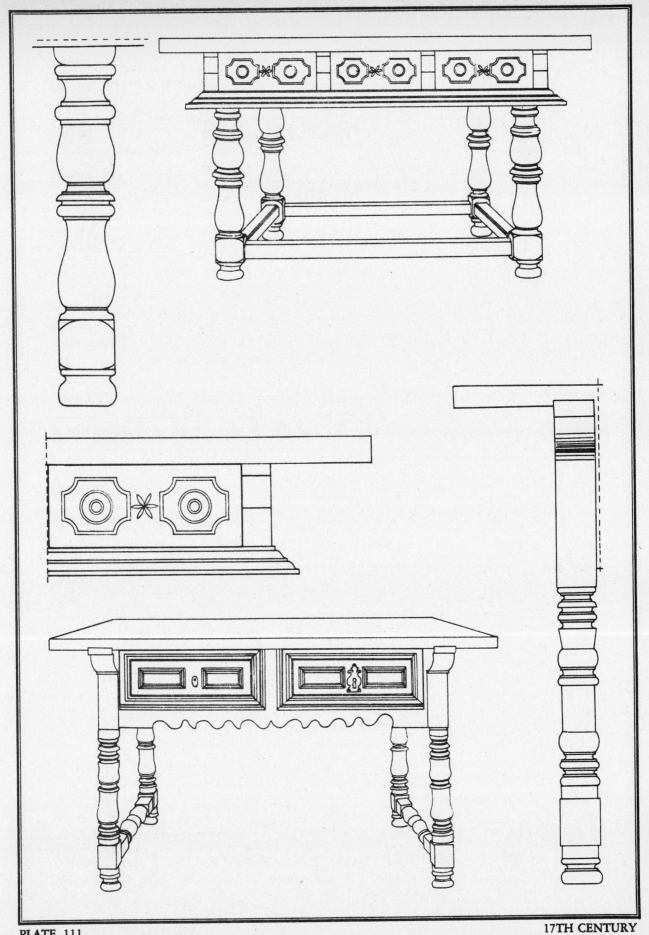

Tables with turned legs and drawers decorated with mouldings.

*Municipal Museum, Romantic Museum and Fundaciones Vega Inclán, Madrid*

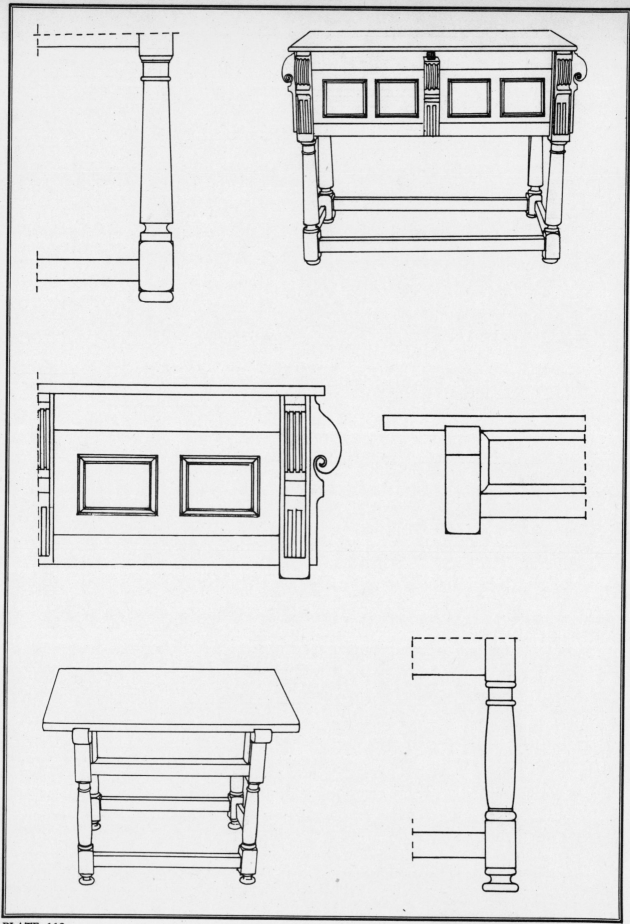

PLATE 112
Portable table.

FIRST HALF OF 17TH CENTURY

*Museum of Decorative Arts, Madrid*

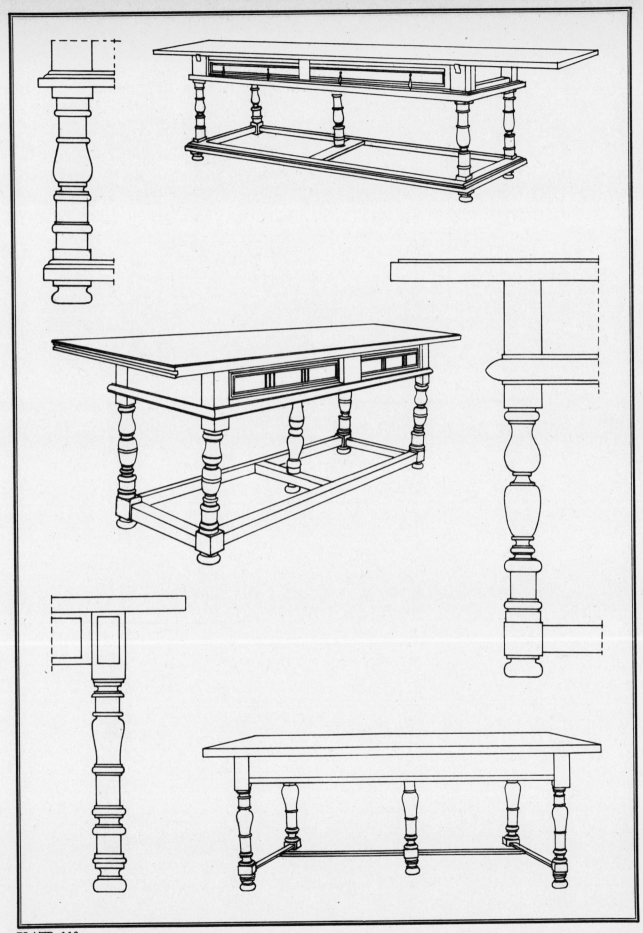

**PLATE 113**
Table-counter with turned legs.

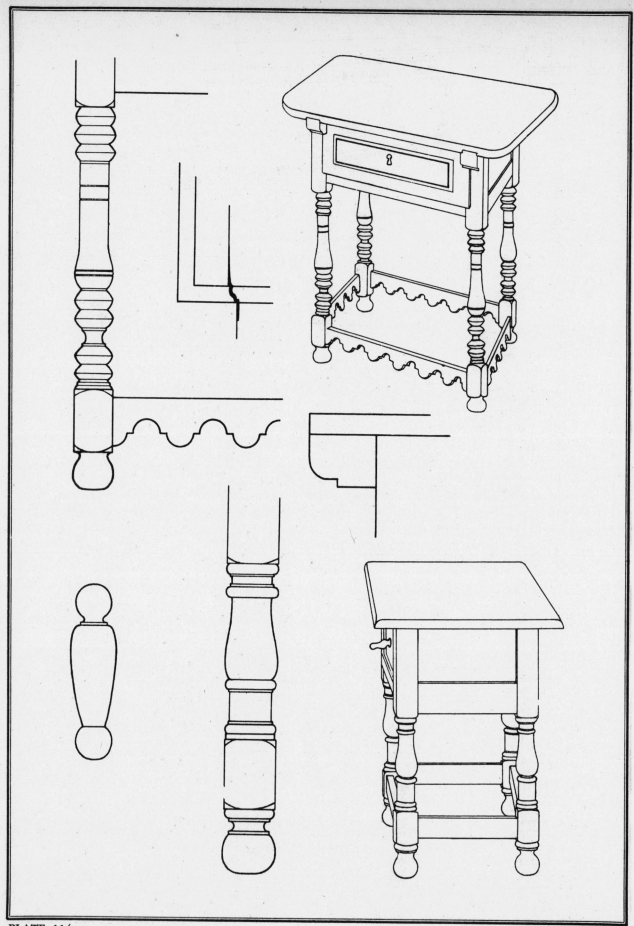

PLATE 114
Small portable tables with turned legs.

*Lope de Vega's house, Madrid, and private collection, Granada*

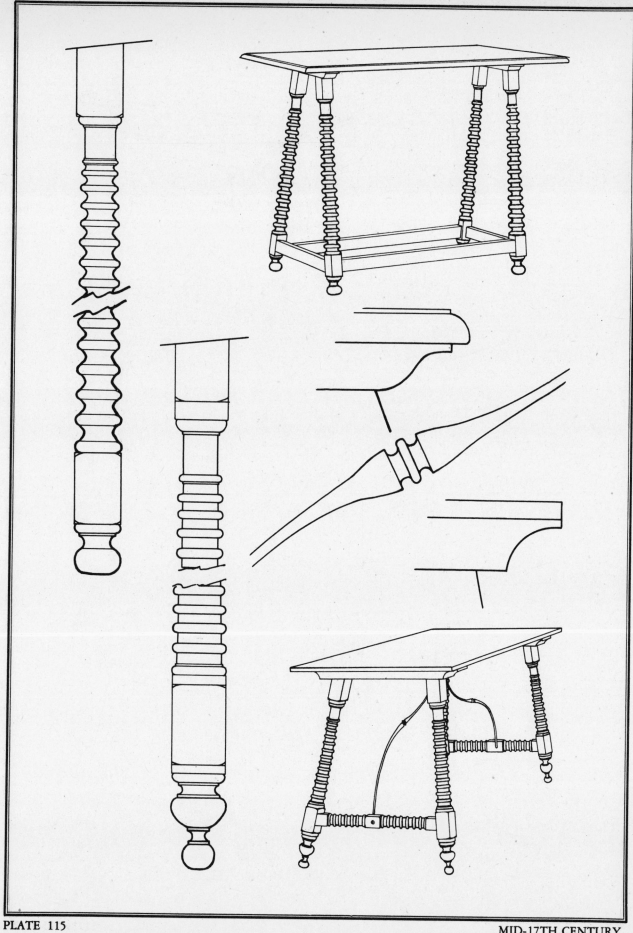

PLATE 115
Pyramid-base writing tables with turned legs.

MID-17TH CENTURY

*Museum of Bilbao and Casa Dameto, Palma de Mallorca*

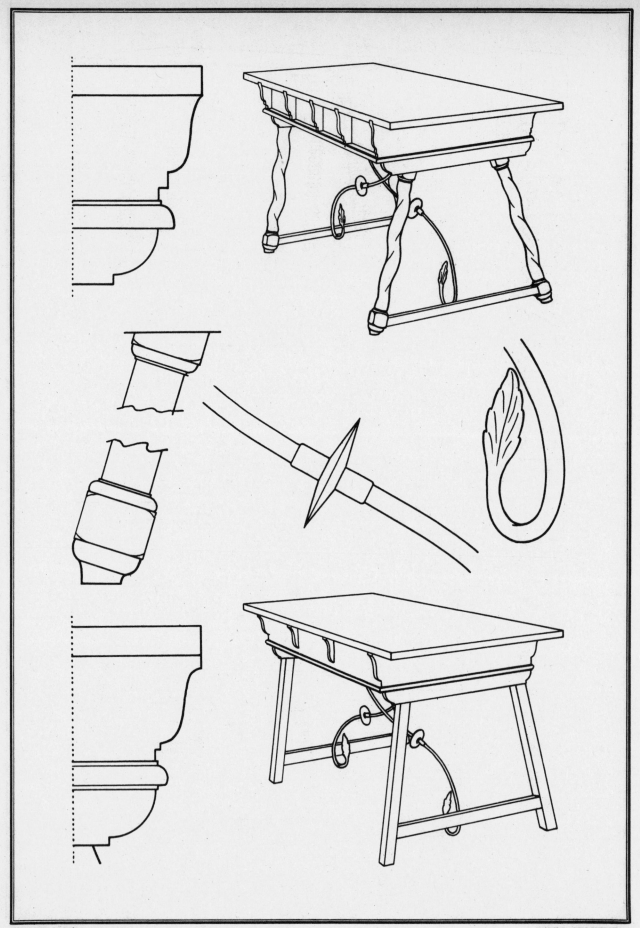

**PLATE 116**
Pyramid-base writing tables with wrought-iron ligatures.

**17TH CENTURY**

*Parador of Santillana del Mar*

120

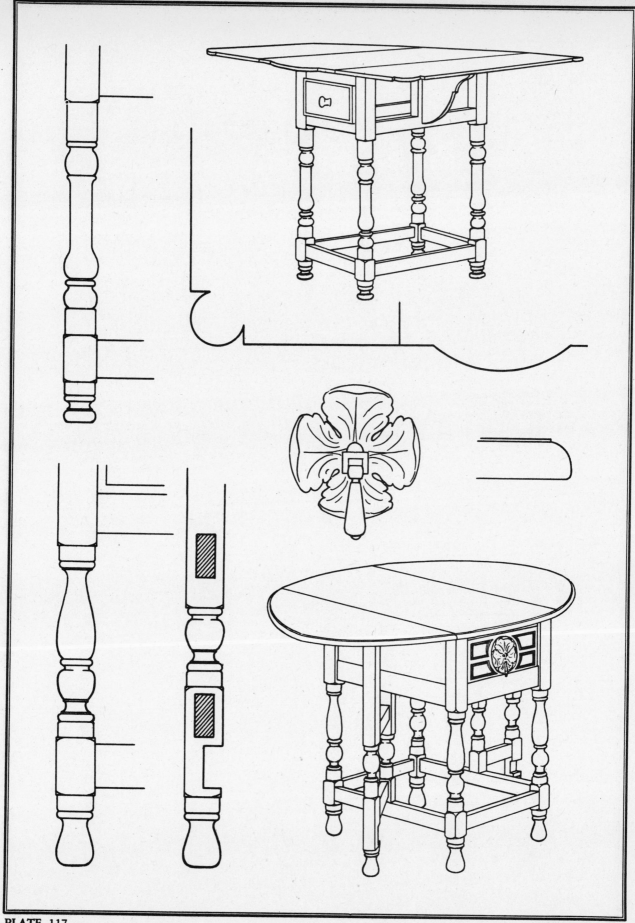

**PLATE 117**
Folding tables with turned legs.

17TH CENTURY

*Parador of Gredos, Avila and Parador of Ubeda, Jaen*

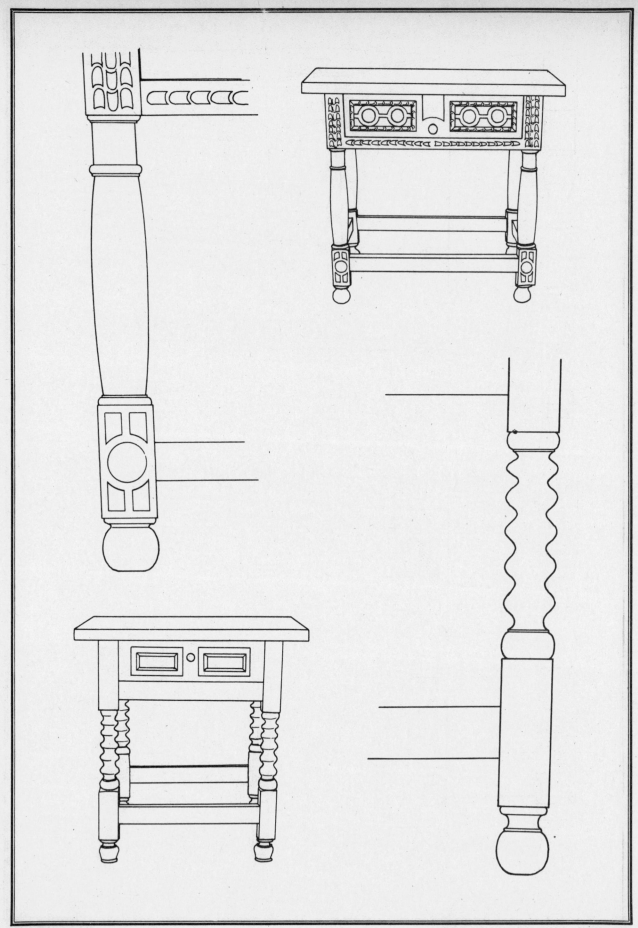

PLATE 118
Small portable table decorated with carved tracery.

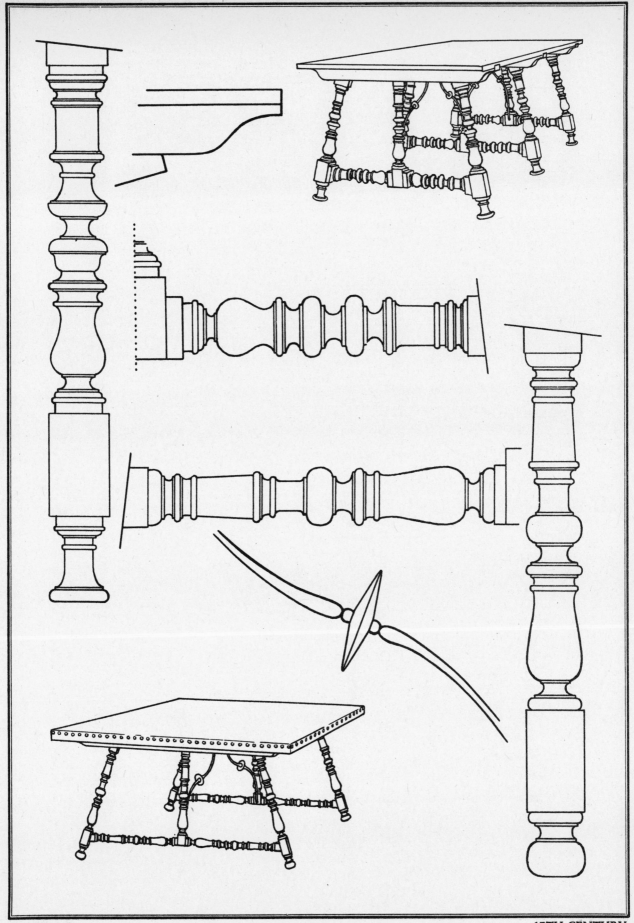

PLATE 119                                                        17TH CENTURY
Small portable tables with turned legs and wrought-iron ligatures.

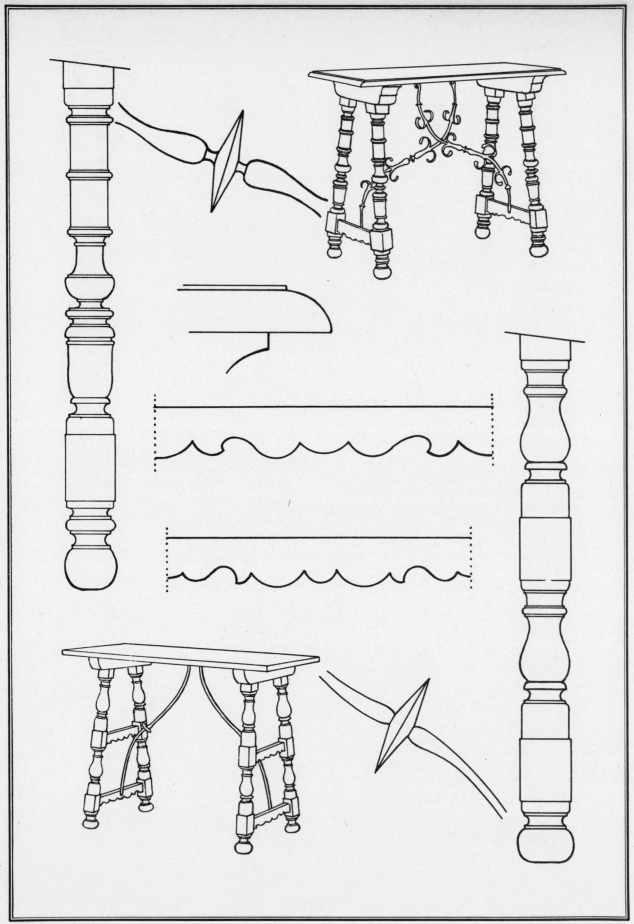

Small writing tables with turned legs and wrought-iron ligatures.

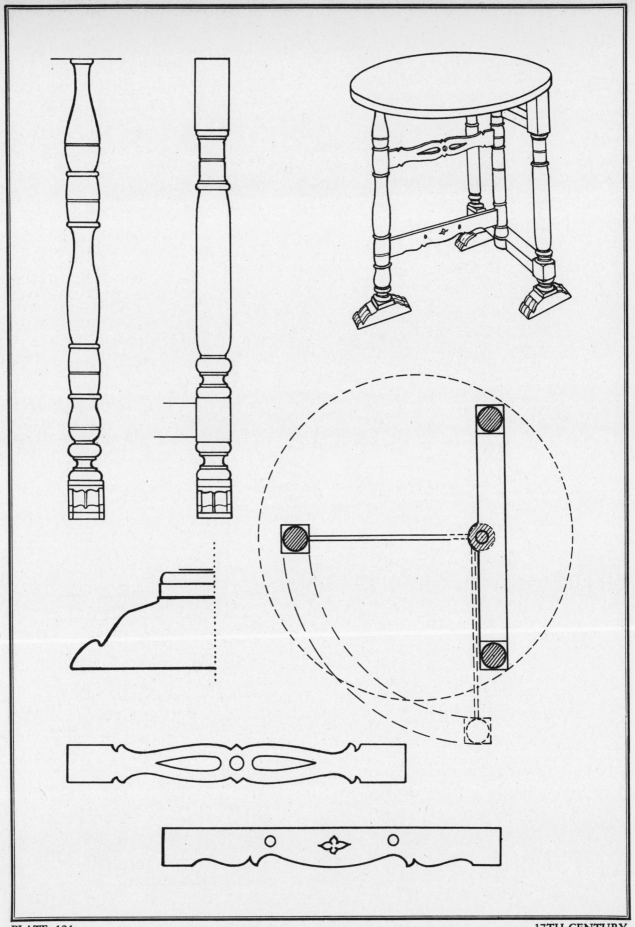

PLATE 121                                                17TH CENTURY
Small folding table with a round top and turned legs.

**PLATE 122**
Table decorated with carvings of folk art.

PLATE 123
Table with turned wooden legs and crosspieces; drawer fronts decorated with folk art carvings.

**PLATE 124**
Tables with legs decorated with wavy or spiral stria.

**PLATE 125**
Table with turned legs and carved decoration on the front.

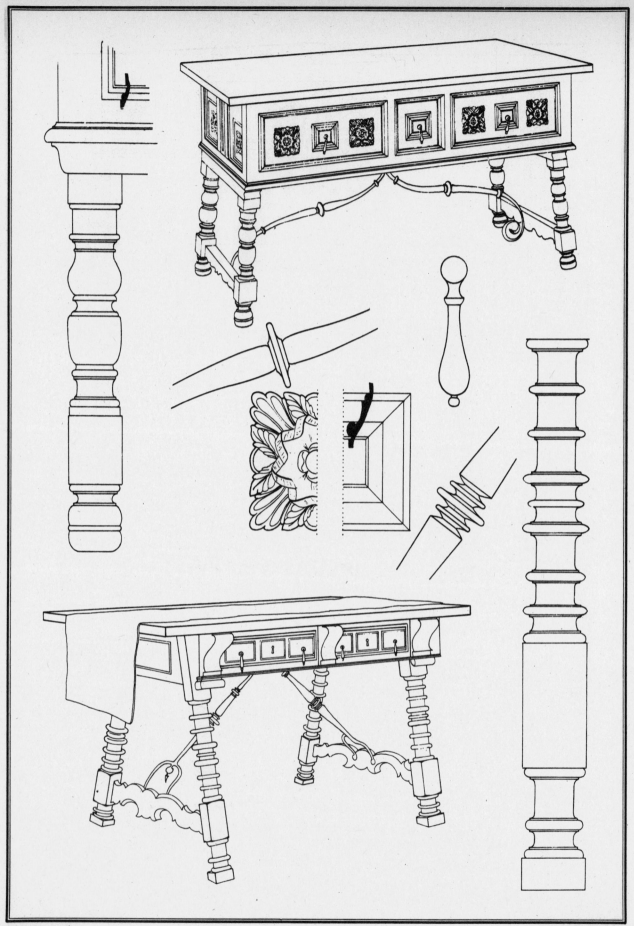

**PLATE 126**
Tables with turned legs in form of pyramid with wrought-iron crosspieces.

**17TH CENTURY**

*Tavera Hospital, Toledo*

**PLATE** 127
Tables with turned legs and decorative baroque carvings on front.

*Museum of Decorative Arts, Madrid*

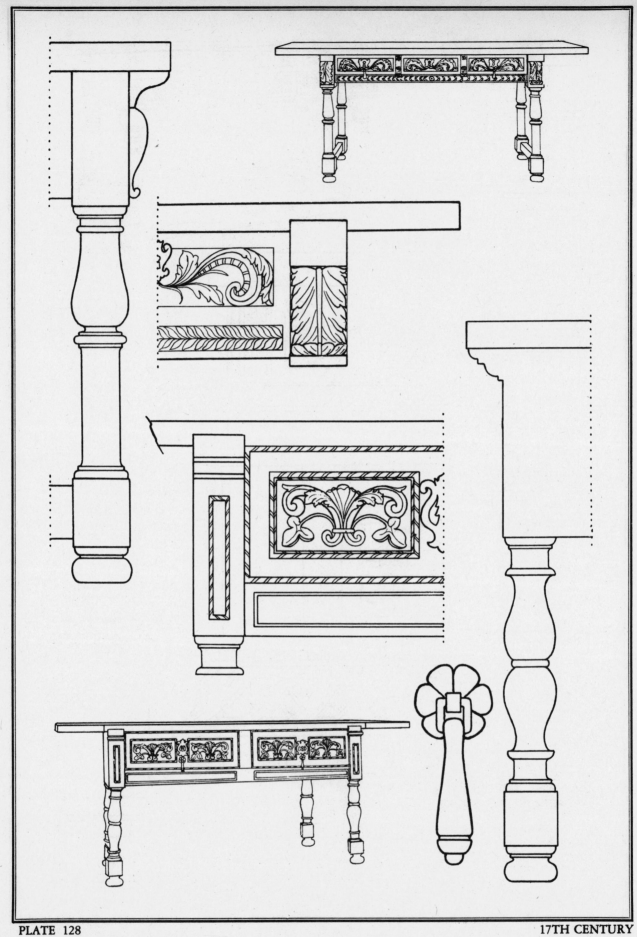

**PLATE 128**

**17TH CENTURY**

Tables with turned legs and decorative baroque carvings on front.

*Museum of Decorative Arts, Madrid*

**PLATE 129**

Tables with turned legs and decorative baroque carvings on front.

*Museum of Decorative Arts, Madrid*

PLATE 130                                                              17TH CENTURY
Small tables with turned legs and decorative baroque carvings on the front.

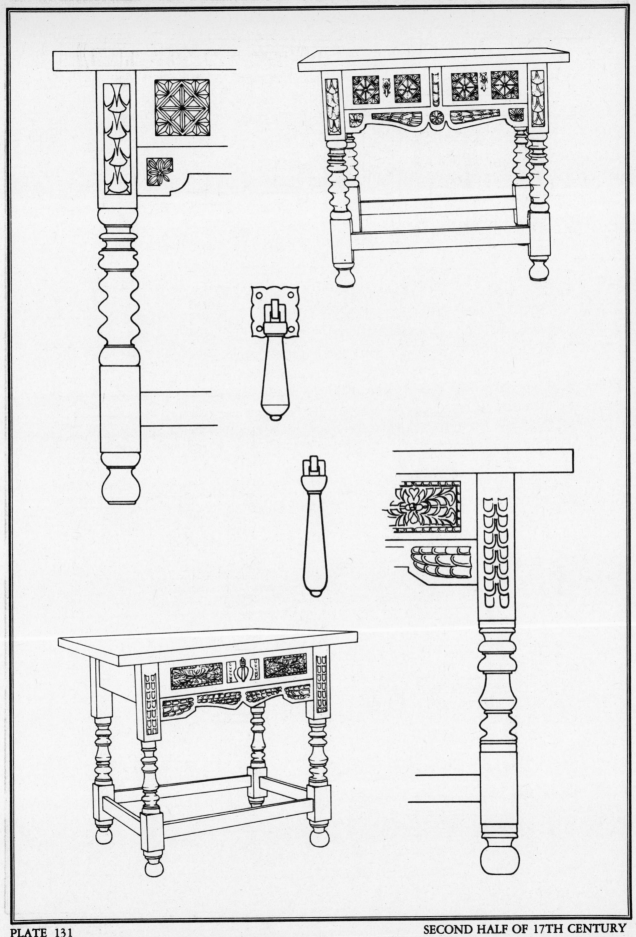

PLATE 131
Small tables with decorative carvings in folk motifs.

SECOND HALF OF 17TH CENTURY

*Private collection*

135

**PLATE 132**
Small tables with decorative carvings in folk motifs.

*Private collection*

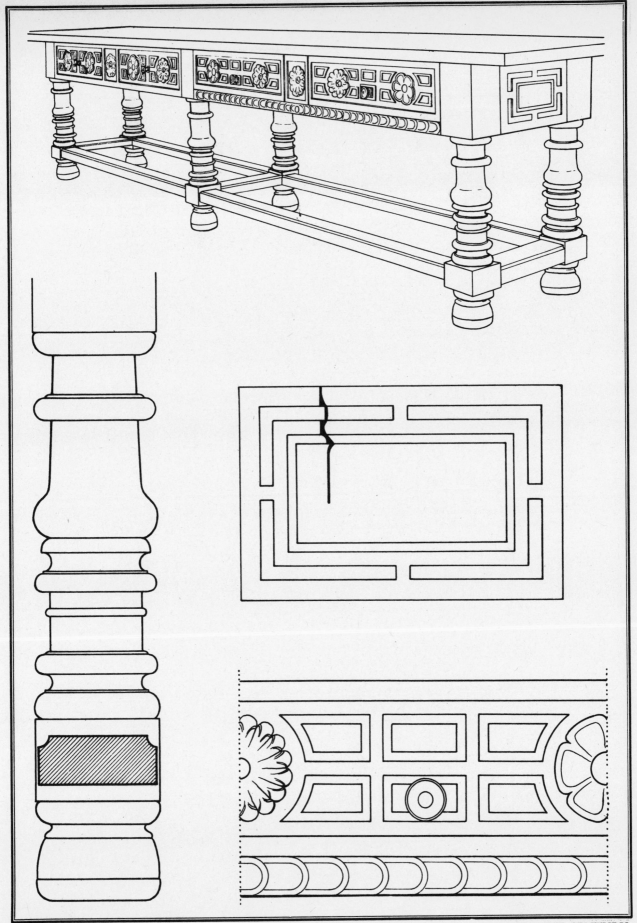

**PLATE 133**
Table-counter decorated with baroque carvings on the front.

MID-17TH CENTURY

*Private collection*

**PLATE 134**
Table decorated with baroque carvings.

*Museum of Decorative Arts, Madrid*

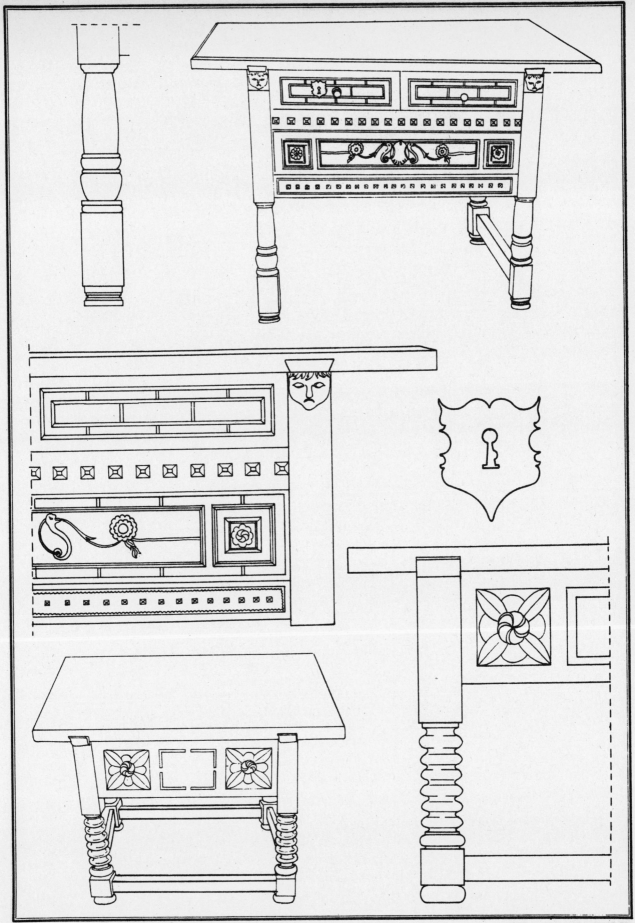

**PLATE 135**
Tables with drawers decorated with moulding and carvings.

*Museum of Decorative Arts, Madrid*

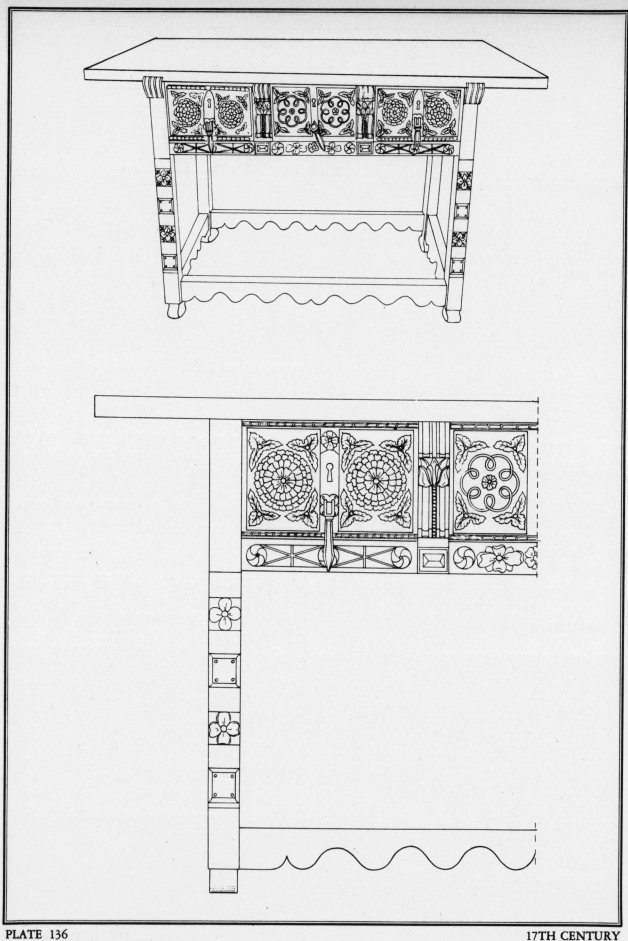

**PLATE 136**
Table decorated with folk carvings.

*Museum of Decorative Arts, Madrid*

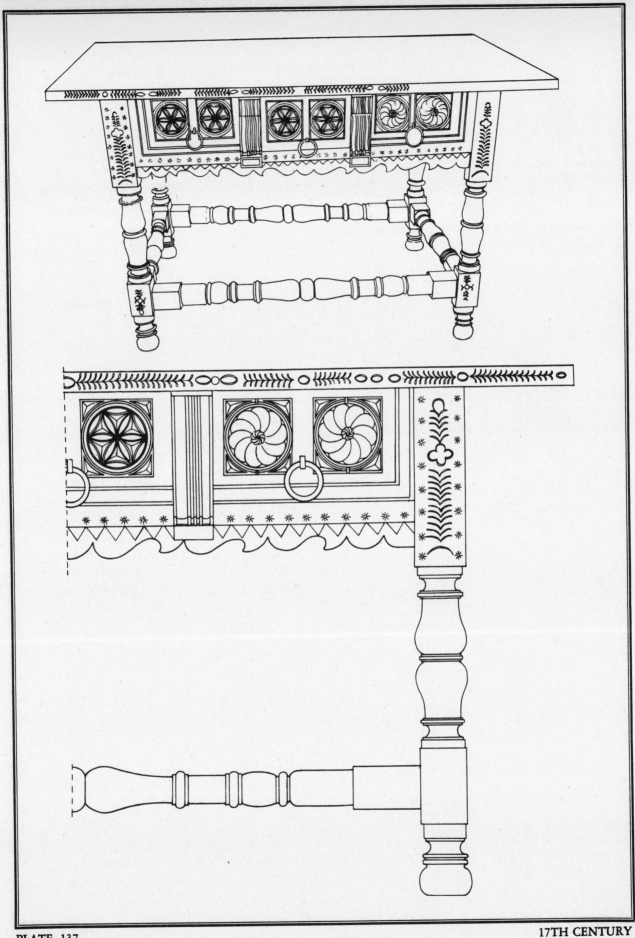

**PLATE 137**
Table decorated with folk carvings.

*Museum of Decorative Arts, Madrid*

**PLATE 138**
Tables decorated with folk carvings.

**17TH CENTURY**

*Museum of Decorative Arts, Madrid*

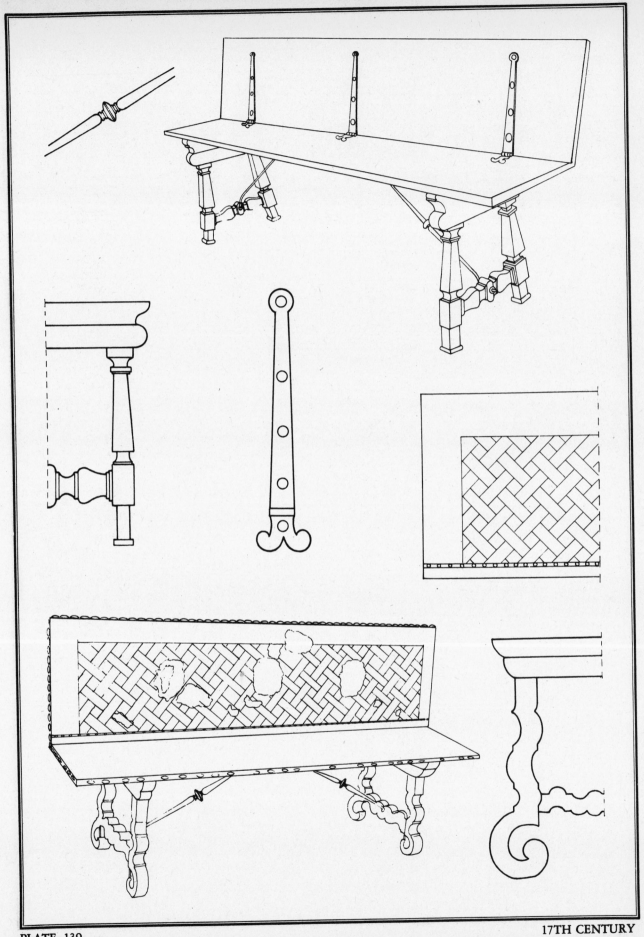

**PLATE 139**
Bench with wrought-iron hinges and crosspieces. Bench with a braided leather back, cut legs and wrought-iron crosspieces.
*Museum of Decorative Arts and National Archeological Museum, Madrid*

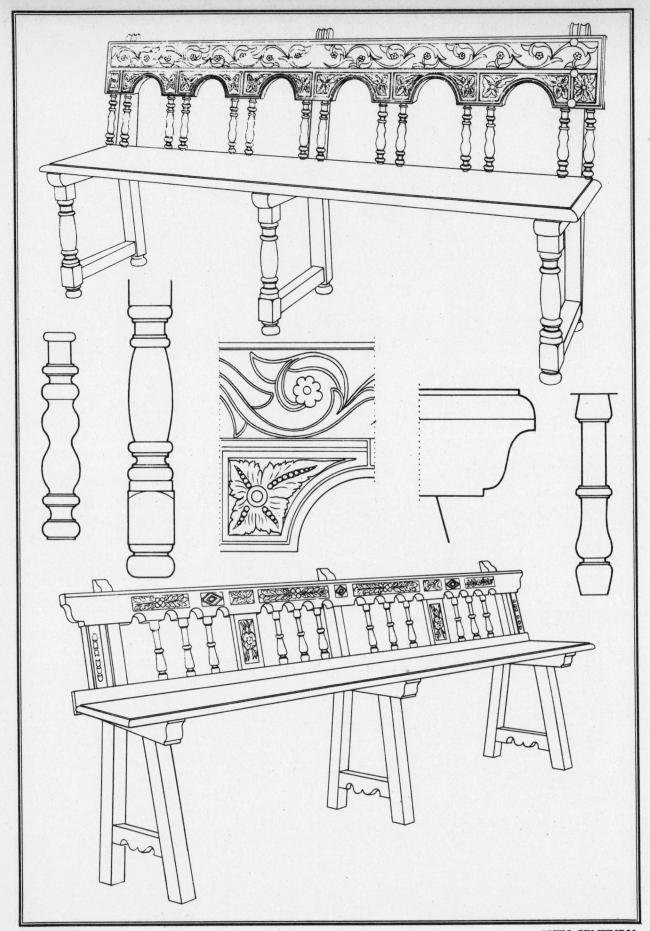

PLATE 140
Bench with "bridge" back and turned legs. Bench with "bridge" back.

**17TH CENTURY**

*Private collection and Parador of Gredos, Avila*

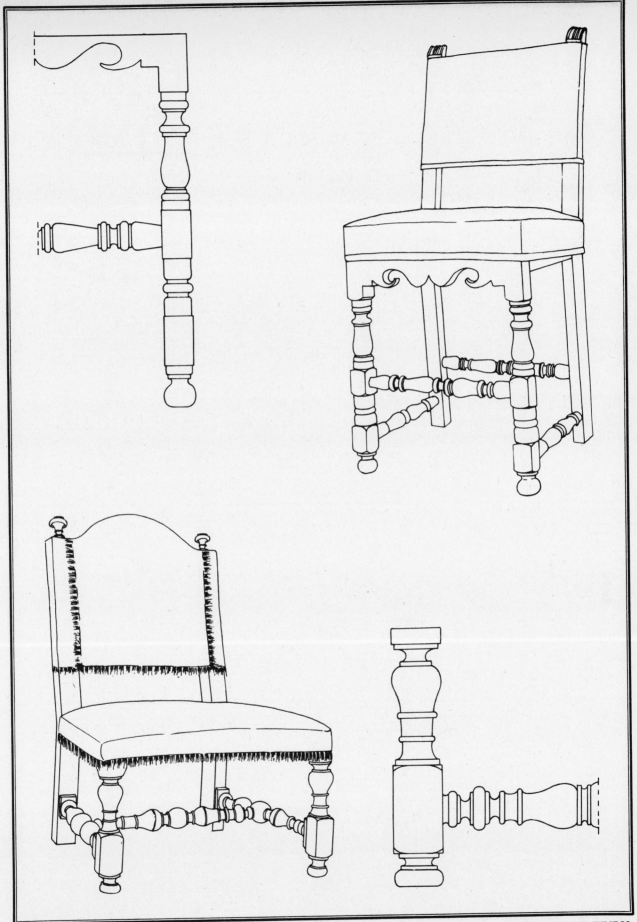

**PLATE 141**
Cloth-trimmed chairs with turned legs.

*Gustavo Gili collection, Santillana del Mar*

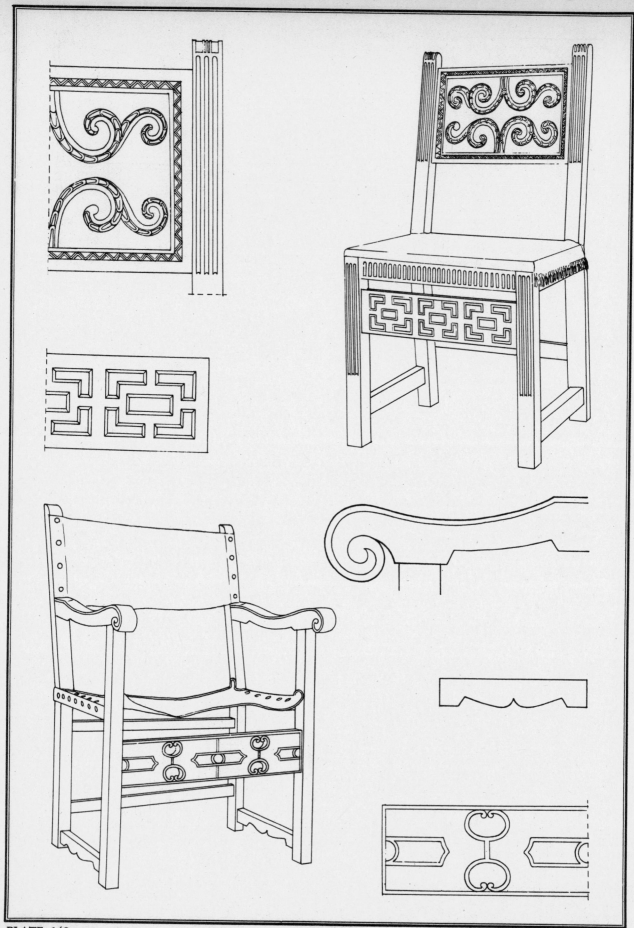

PLATE 142

Cloth-trimmed chair decorated with geometric motifs on front. Friar's armchair trimmed with leather and gilt metal nails.

*Gustavo Gili collection, Santillana del Mar*

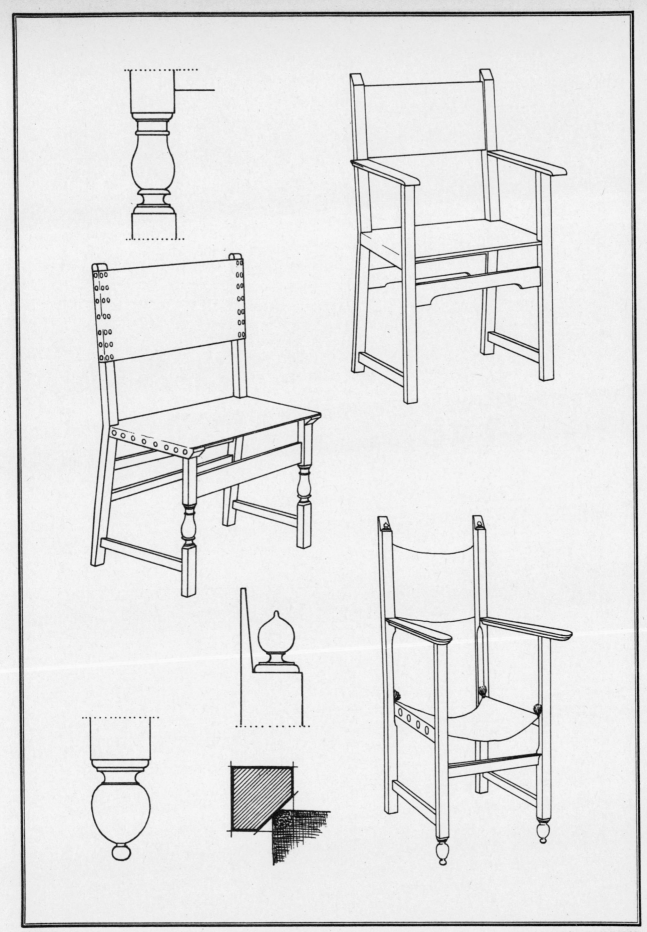

**PLATE 143**
Friars' armchairs and chair trimmed with leather and gilt metal nails.

17TH CENTURY

147

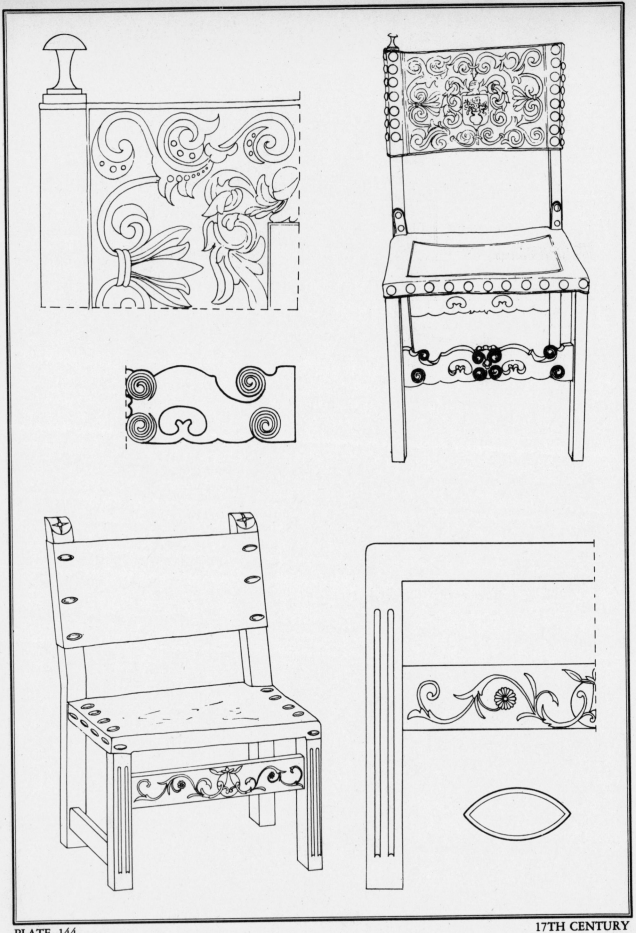

PLATE 144

Chair with multicolored, embossed leather back. Chair trimmed with leather and gilt metal nails.

*Museum of Decorative Arts, Madrid*

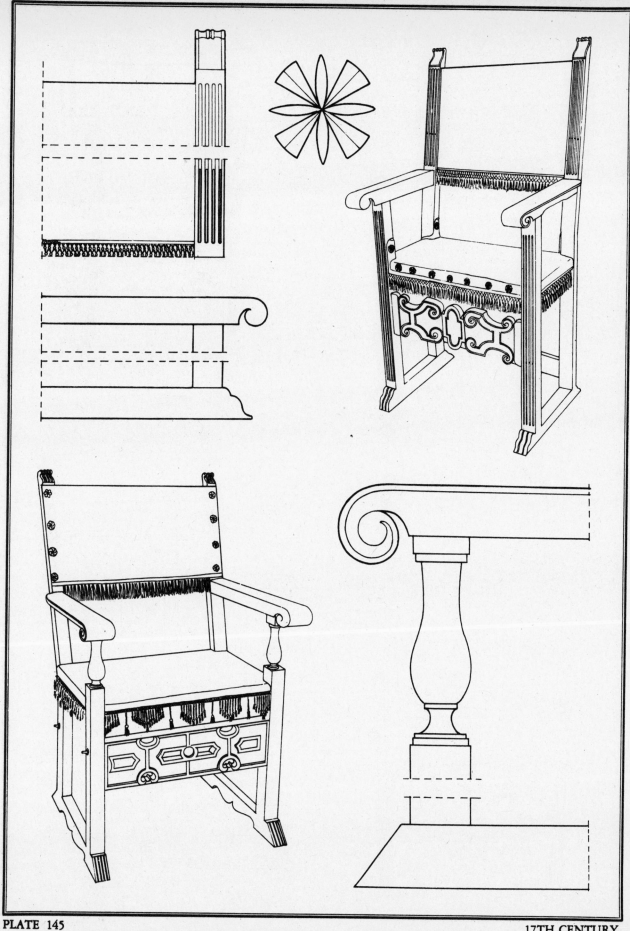

**PLATE 145**
Friars' armchairs trimmed with cloth and openwork fronts.

**17TH CENTURY**

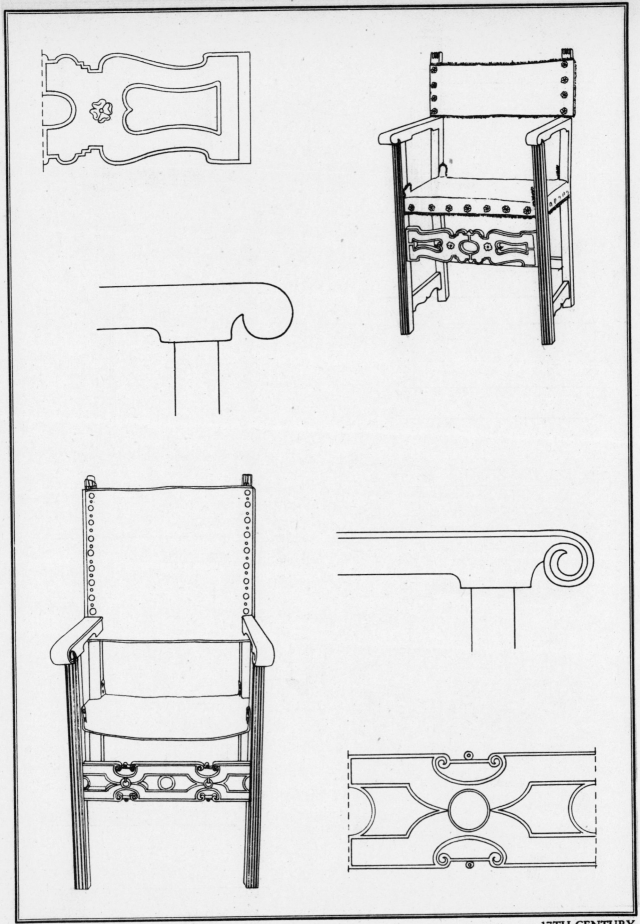

PLATE 146
Friars' armchairs with openwork front, trimmed with leather and gilt nails.

*Museum of Decorative Arts, Madrid*

**PLATE 147**

17TH CENTURY

Friars' armchairs. The lower one has carved brackets supporting the arms, round finials and ornate gilt metal nails, and is from El Greco's house in Toledo.

*Upper chair: Parador of Gredos, Avila*

151

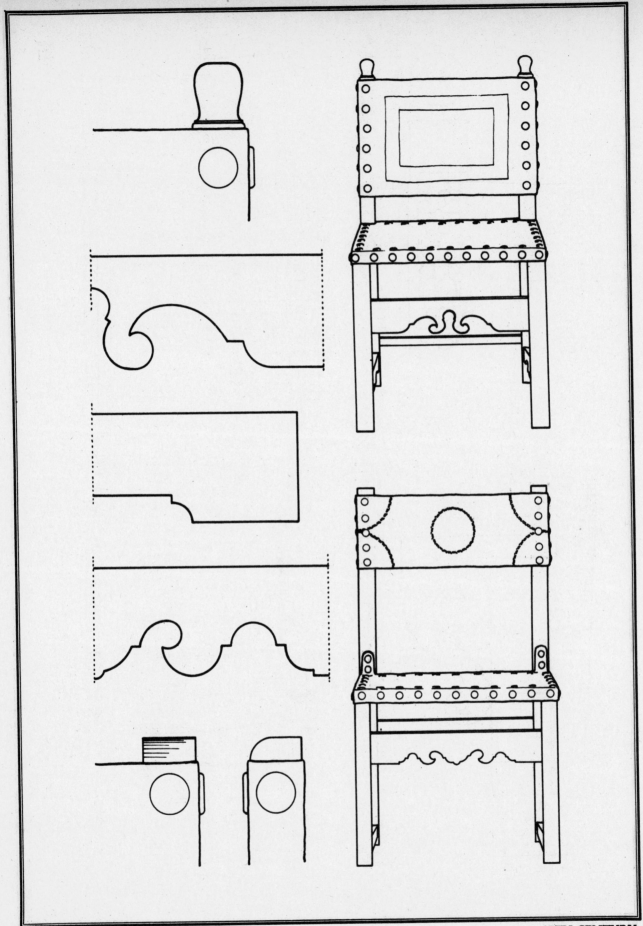

**PLATE 148**
Chairs trimmed with leather with cut-wooden crosspieces and gilt metal nails.

**PLATE 149**
Chair and armchair trimmed with cloth, with gilt metal nails and decorated with baroque carvings.

**17TH CENTURY**

*Private collection*

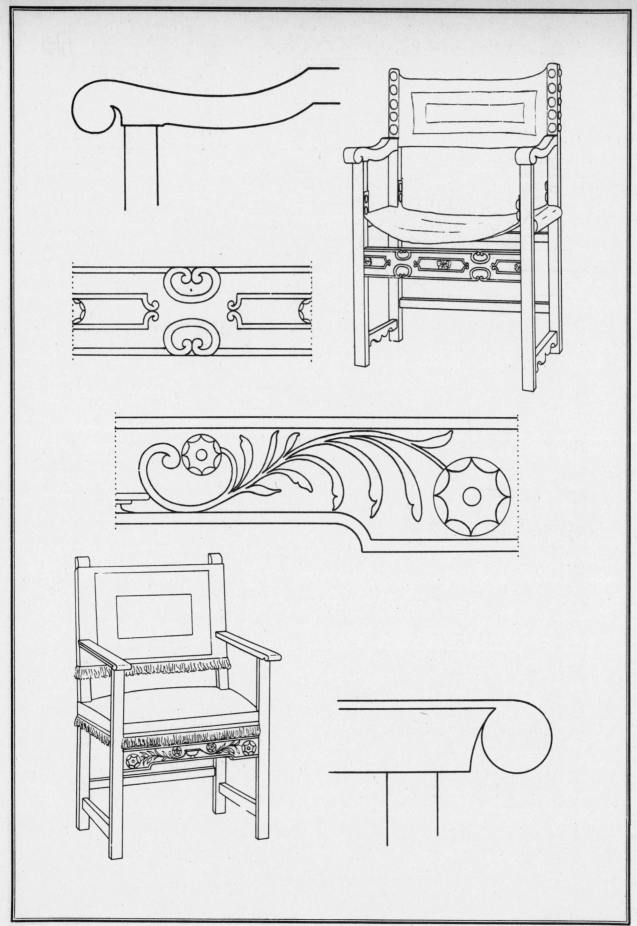

Friars' armchairs. The upper one is trimmed with leather and has an openwork crosspiece; the lower one is trimmed with cloth and has a carved crosspiece.

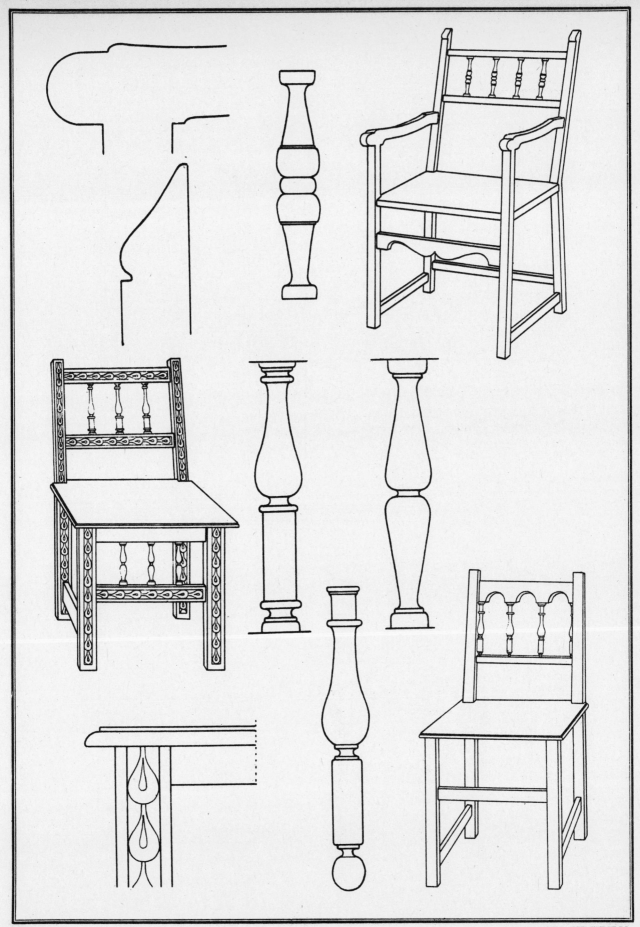

**PLATE 151**
Chairs and armchair in folk style with backs of turned balusters.

PLATE 152
Cloth-trimmed armchairs with "table" arms and carved openwork crosspieces.

**17TH CENTURY**

*Riudabell Castle*

**PLATE 153**

High-backed chairs of Central European style trimmed with engraved leather, turned legs and openwork crosspieces.

*Lower chair: Museum of Decorative Arts, Madrid*

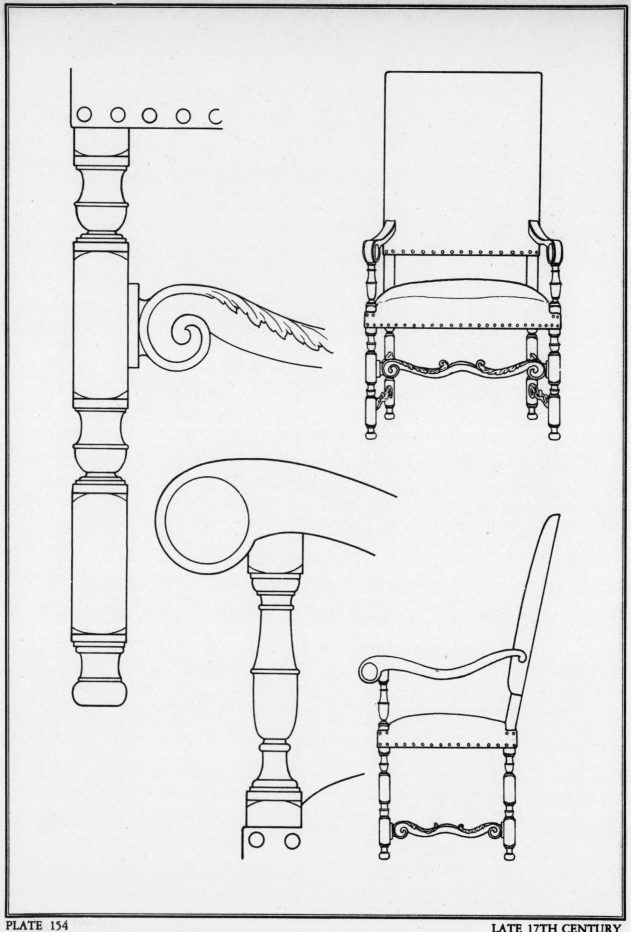

PLATE 154
High-backed armchair of Central European style, trimmed with cloth, and with turned legs.

*Babra Arroyos collection*

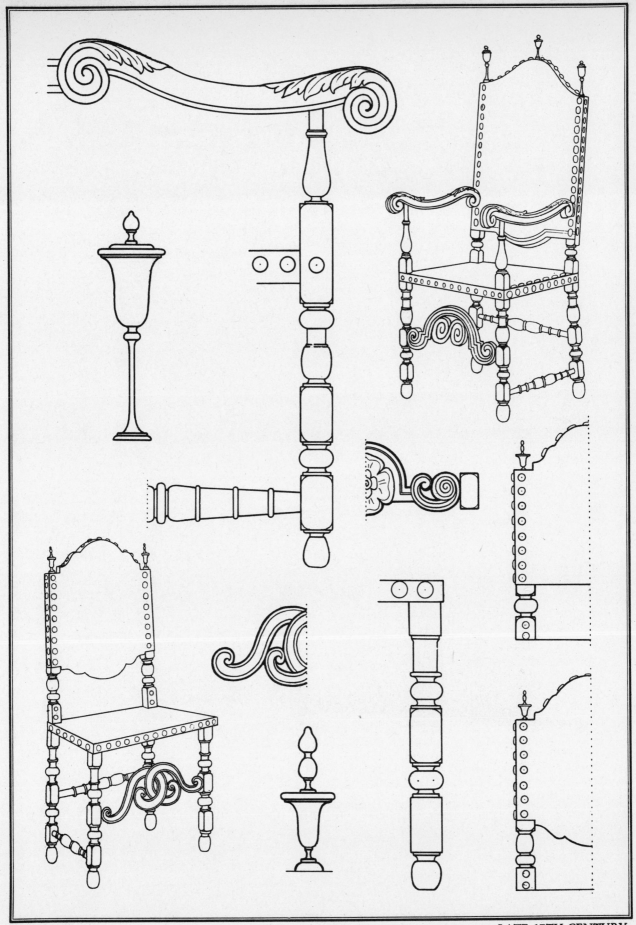

**PLATE 155**

High-backed chair and armchair of Central European style, trimmed with cloth, and with openwork crosspieces.

LATE 17TH CENTURY

*Palace of the Counts of Perelada, Palma de Mallorca*

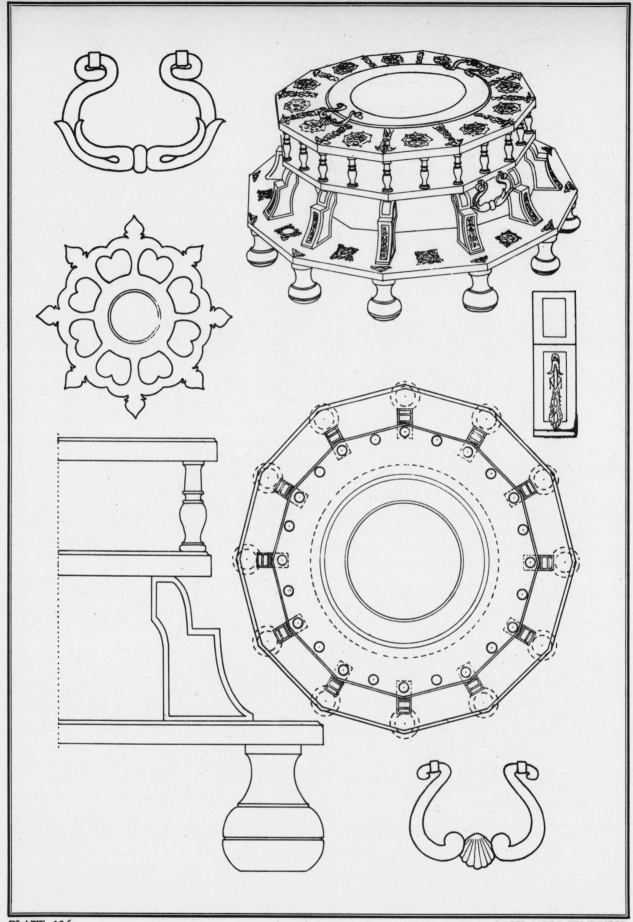

PLATE 156

Three-piece brazier decorated with carvings and copper nails.

LATE 17TH CENTURY

*Tavera Hospital, Toledo*

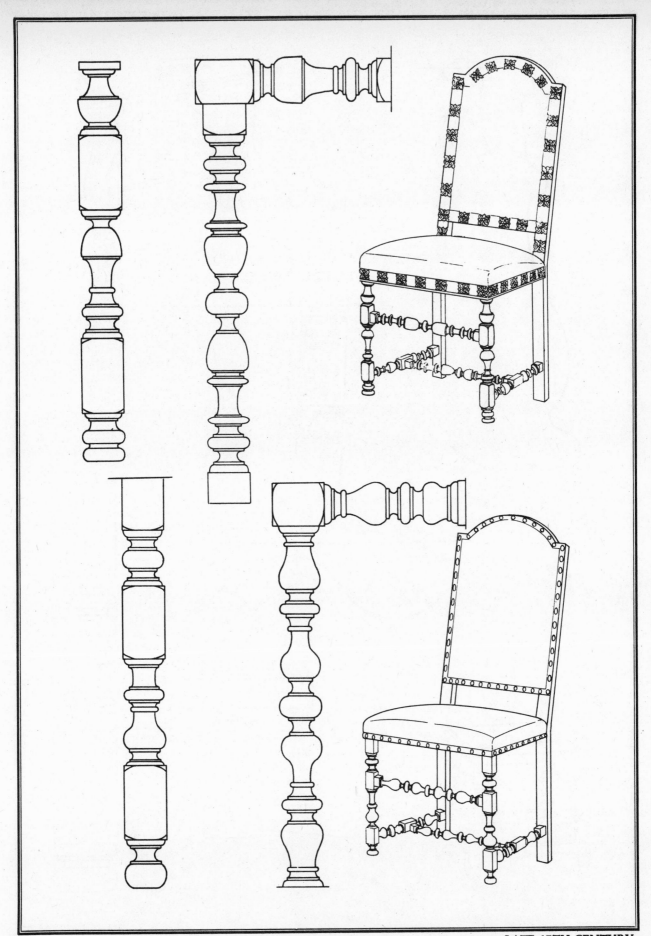

**PLATE 157**

Central European style of chairs with high backs, turned legs, and trimmed with cloth and gilt metal nails.

*House of the Marquis of Campofranco and Casa Olaya, Palma de Mallorca*

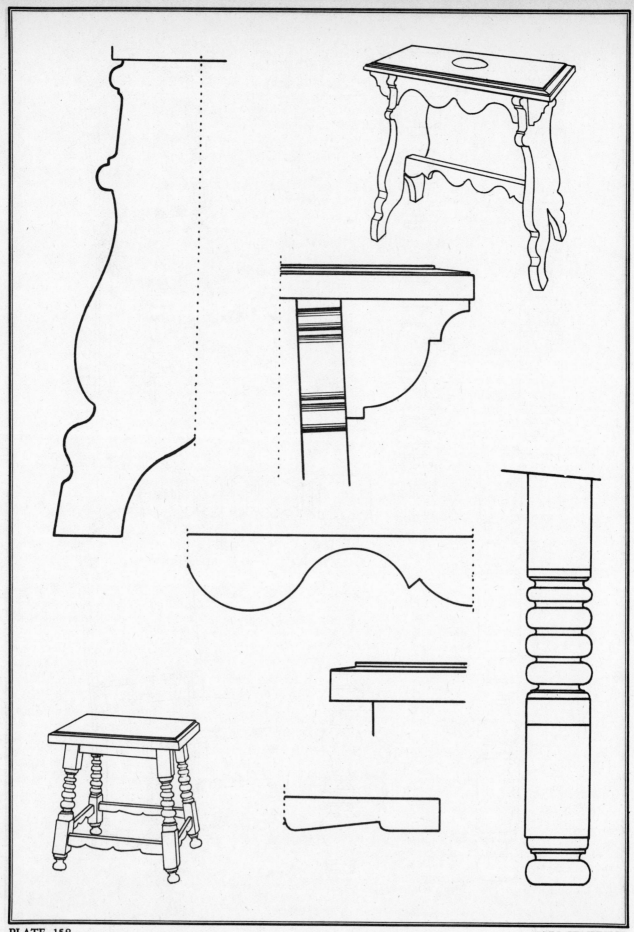

**PLATE 158**
Wooden benches with cut or turned legs.

17TH CENTURY

162

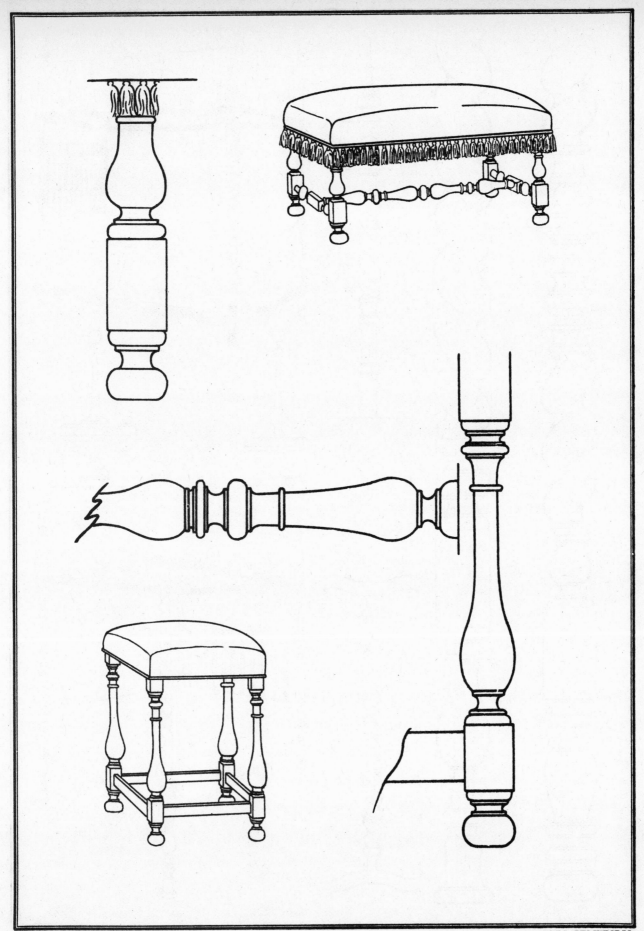

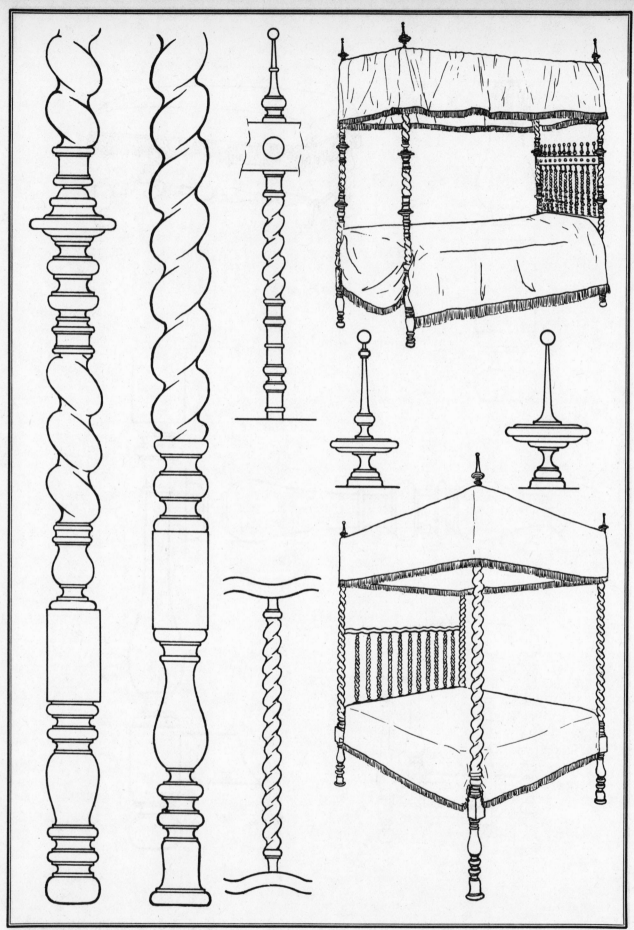

**PLATE 160**
Beds with canopies and valances. Turned posts and balusters in form of twisted columns.

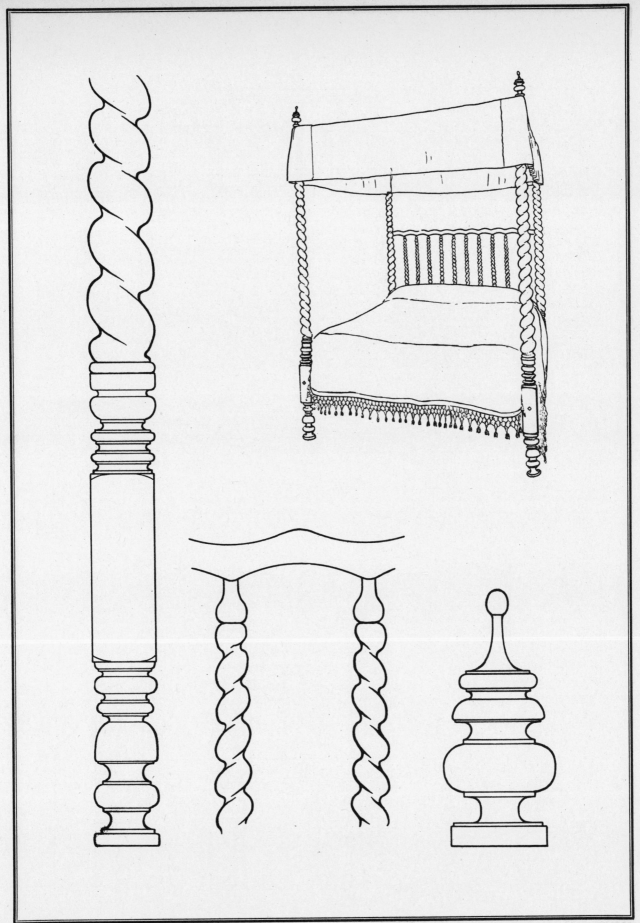

**PLATE 161**
Bed with canopy and valance. Turned posts and balusters in form of twisted columns.

**LATE 17TH CENTURY**

*Barcelona*

**PLATE 162**
Turned and carved wooden bed.

LATE 17TH CENTURY

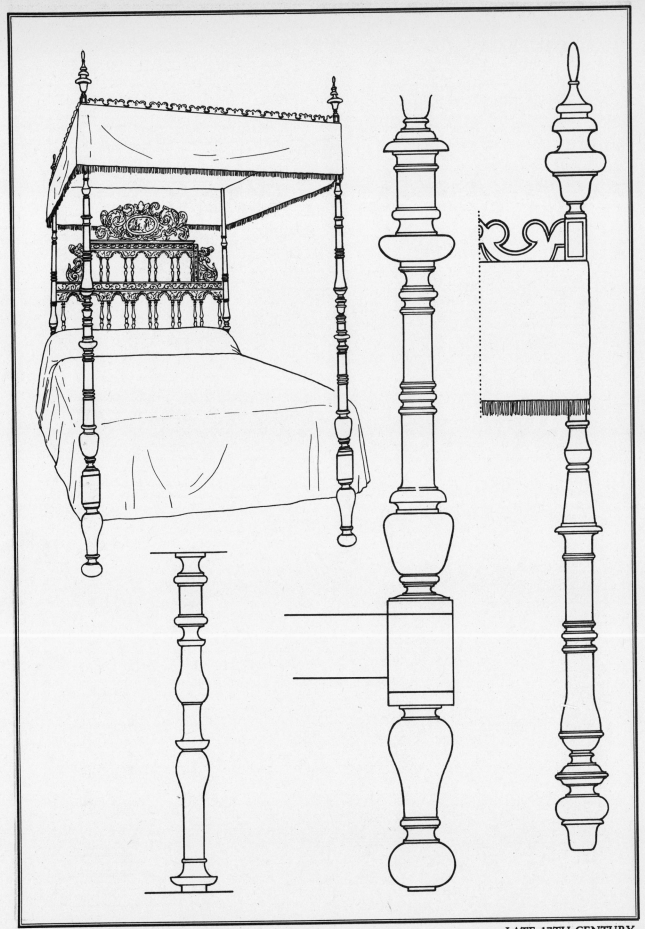

**PLATE 163**

Portuguese-style bed of foreign woods, with gilt metal decorations. Posts and balusters of back were worked on a lathe.

*Mrs. Anton Matheus collection*

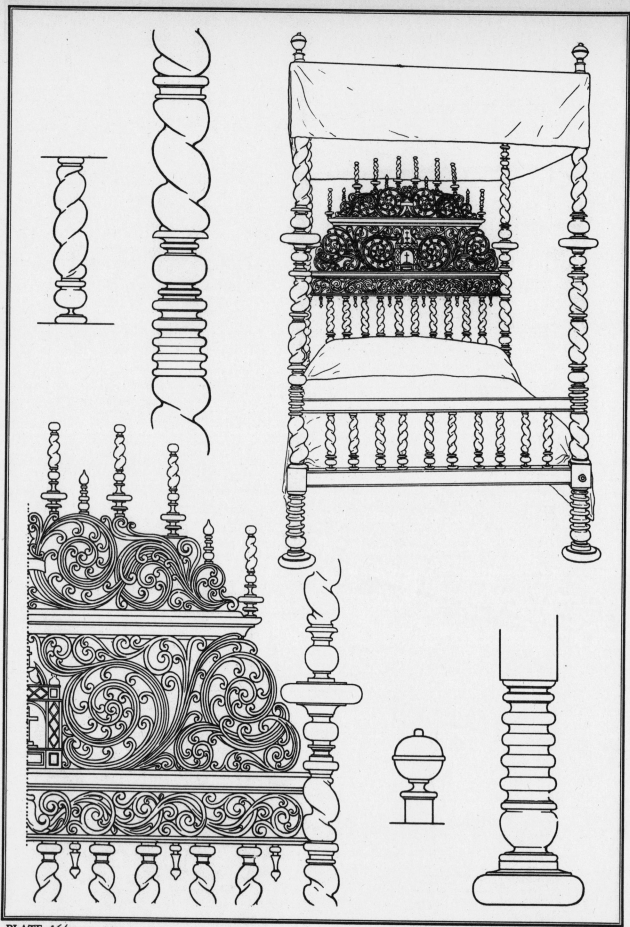

**PLATE 164**

Portuguese bed. Turned posts and balusters in form of twisted columns. Gilt metal decorations.

*Richard Blanco collection, Santiago de Compostela*

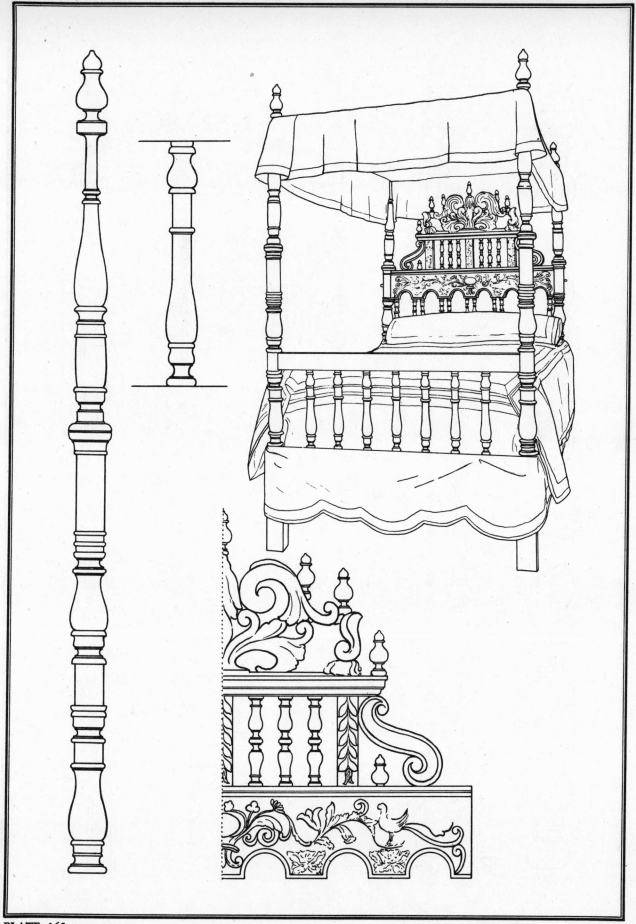

PLATE 165 LATE 17TH CENTURY

Portuguese-style bed. Posts, headboard and footboard of turned wood. Gilt metal decorations.

*Beancharro collection, Pontevedra*

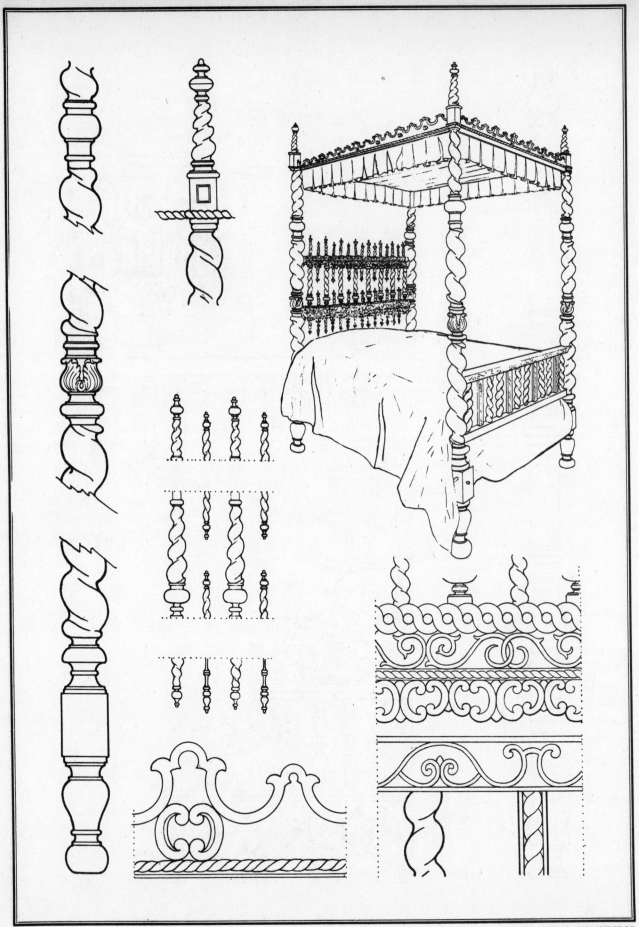

PLATE 166
LATE 17TH CENTURY

Portuguese bed with canopy and valance. Posts and balusters in form of twisted columns. Gilt metal decorations.

*Canet de Mar, Barcelona*

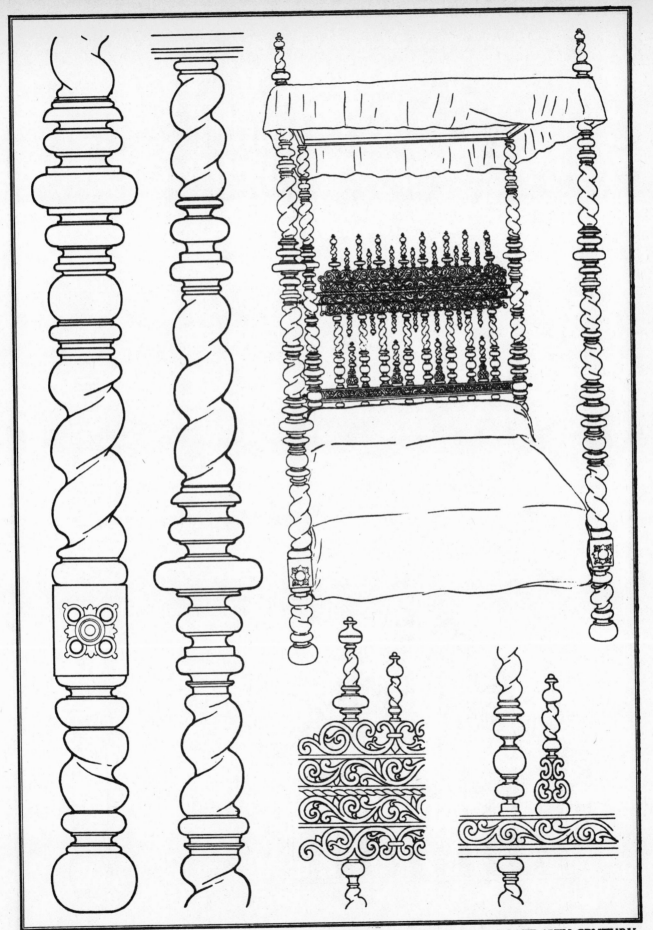

PLATE 167

LATE 17TH CENTURY

Portuguese bed with canopy and valance. Posts and balusters are in the form of twisted columns. Gilt metal decorations.

*Solsona, Lerida*

**PLATE 168**
Portuguese bed of ebony with gilt metal decorations.

**LATE 17TH CENTURY**

*Museum of Decorative Arts, Madrid*

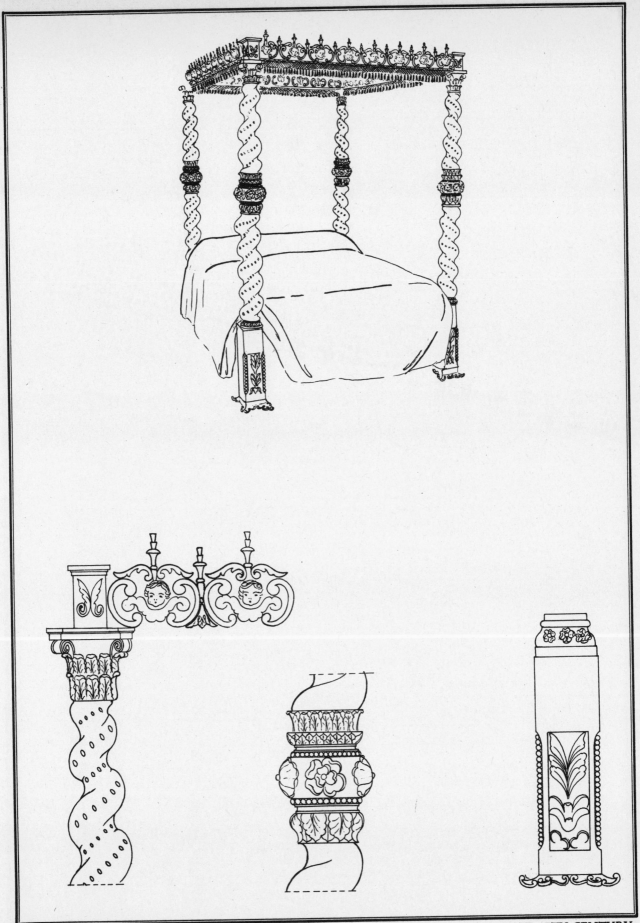

PLATE 169

LATE 17TH CENTURY

Portuguese bed of ebony with twisted posts. Openwork cornice and gilt metal decorations.

*Museum of Decorative Arts, Madrid*

**PLATE 170**
Braziers with decorative copper nails and engraved copper handles.

*National Archeological Museum, Madrid*

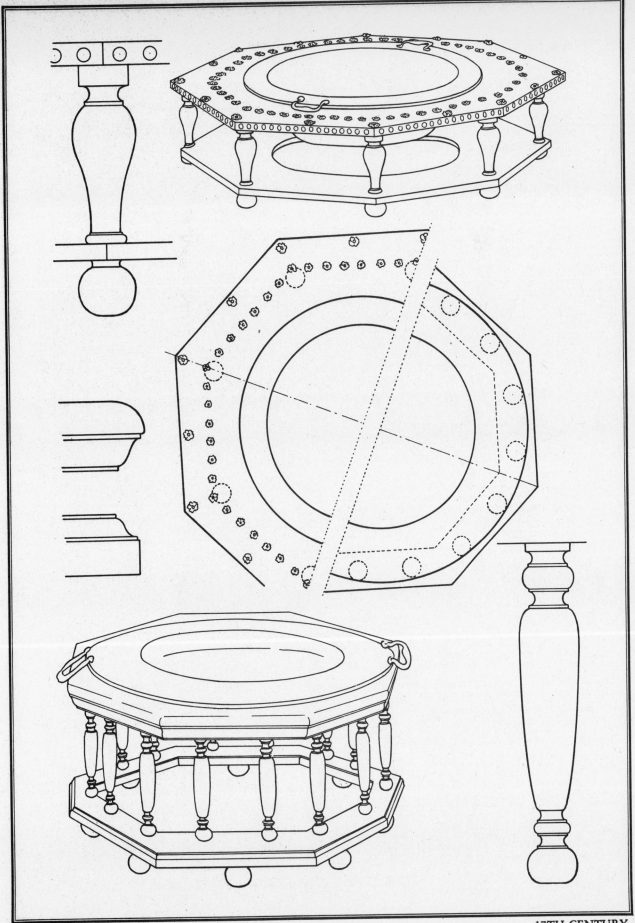

**PLATE 171**
Braziers supported by balusters and decorated with copper nails.

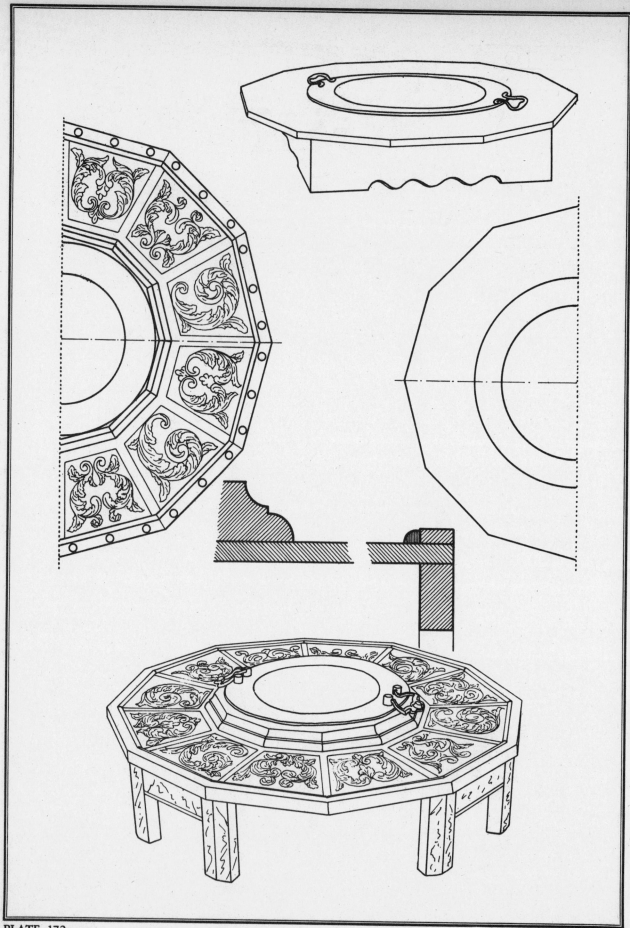

PLATE 172
Braziers. The lower one is decorated with baroque pictures.

**17TH CENTURY**

*Tavera Hospital, Toledo*

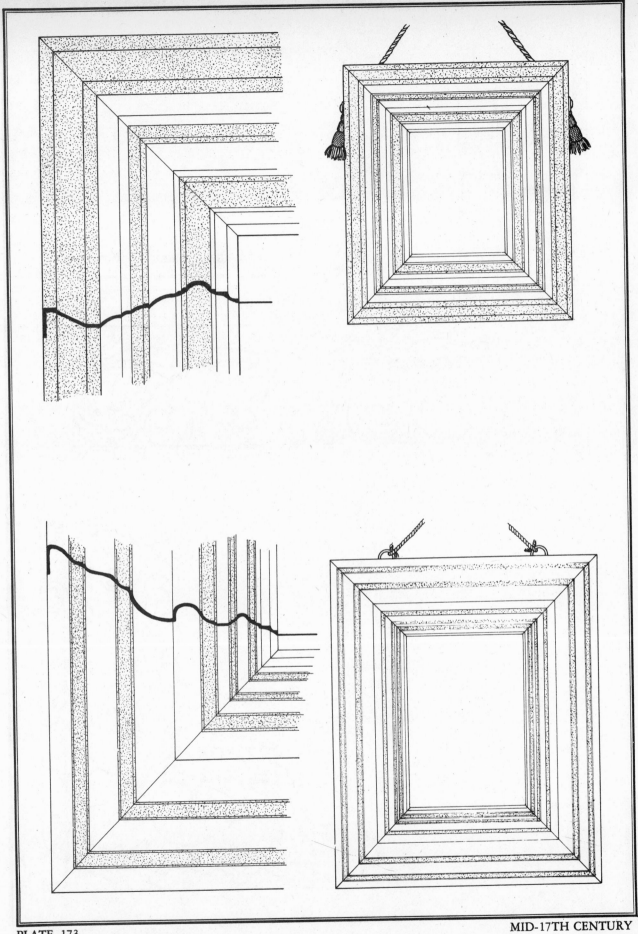

**PLATE 173**
Mirror frames of ebony moulding.

*Lope de Vega's house, Madrid*

PLATE 174
Picture frames decorated with baroque carvings in corners and centers.

SECOND HALF OF 17TH CENTURY

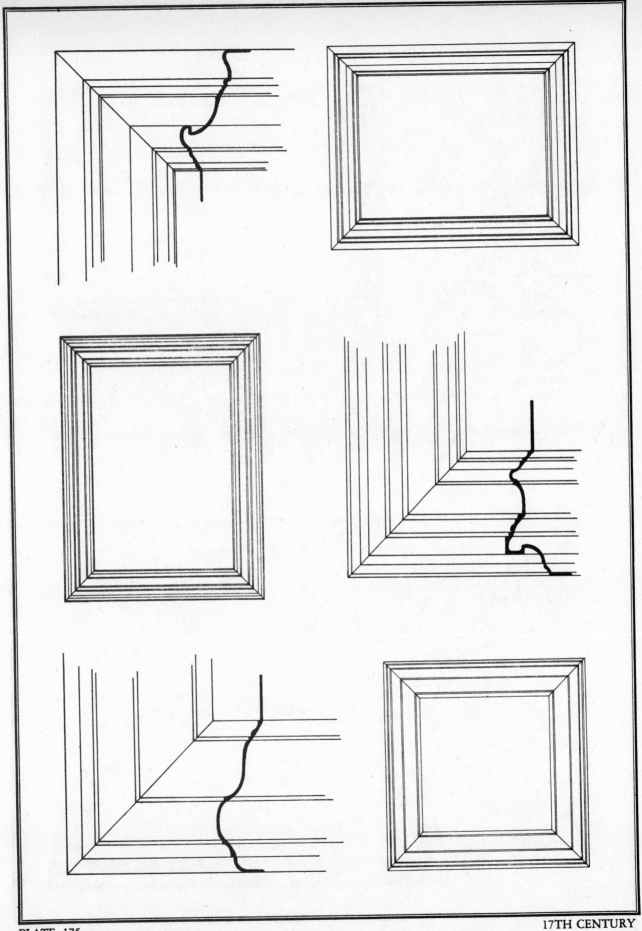

PLATE 175
Picture or mirror frames of moulded wood painted black.
*Museum of Paintings, Bilbao; Romantic Museum and Fundaciones Vega Inclán, Madrid and Parador of Merida, Badajoz*

PLATE 176
Picture frames decorated with baroque carvings.

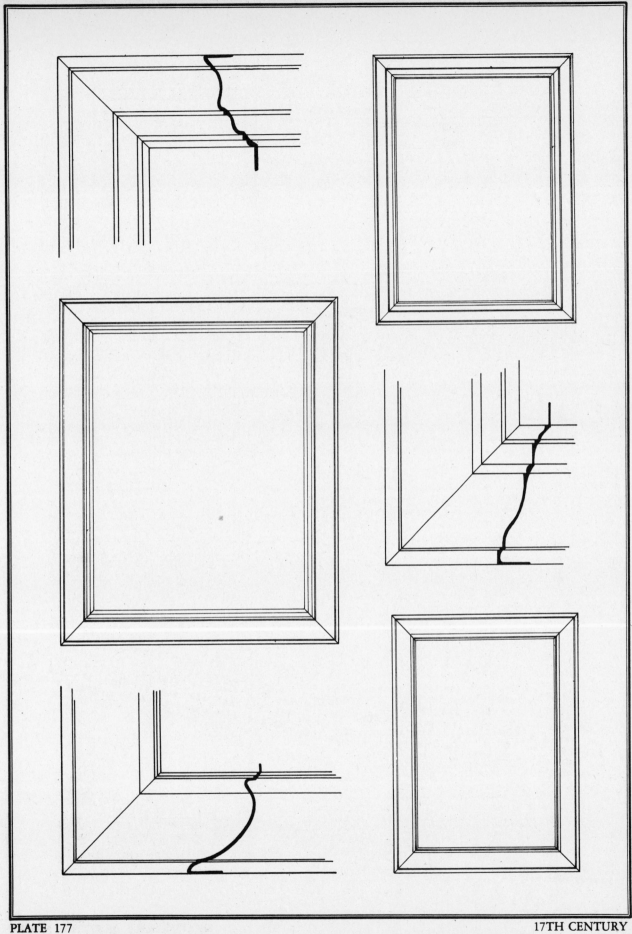

PLATE 177

Frames of moulded wood painted black.

*Romantic Museum, Fundaciones Vega Inclán and Lope de Vega's house, Madrid and Museum of Painting, Seville*

PLATE 178
Frames with baroque decoration.

**SECOND HALF OF 17TH CENTURY**

*Casa Dameto, Palma de Mallorca; Museum of Painting, Seville and Museum of Painting, Bilbao*

**PLATE 179**
Brass candle holders.

SECOND HALF OF 17TH CENTURY

*Lope de Vega's house, Madrid*

**PLATE 180**
Large Mudejar-style chest.

*Grases collection, Barcelona*

**PLATE 181**
Large folk-style chest.

*Museum of Decorative Arts, Madrid*

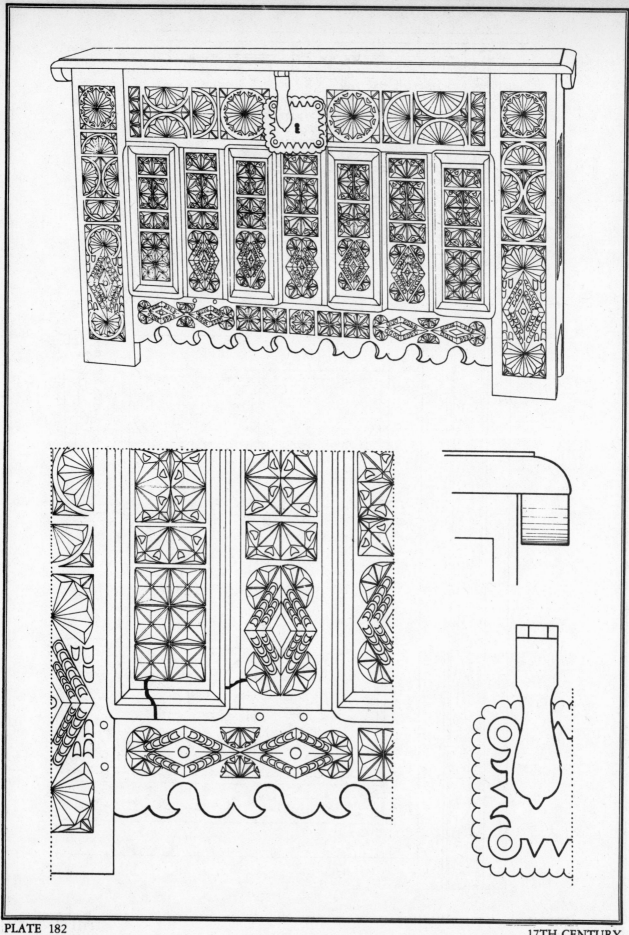

**PLATE 182**
Large Mudejar-style chest.

*Gazolaz Parochial Church, Navarre*

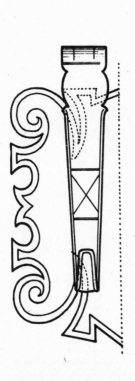

**PLATE 183**
Large folk-style chest.

17TH CENTURY

*Marquis de la Torre collection, Palma de Mallorca*

**PLATE 184**
Chest in folk design.

17TH CENTURY

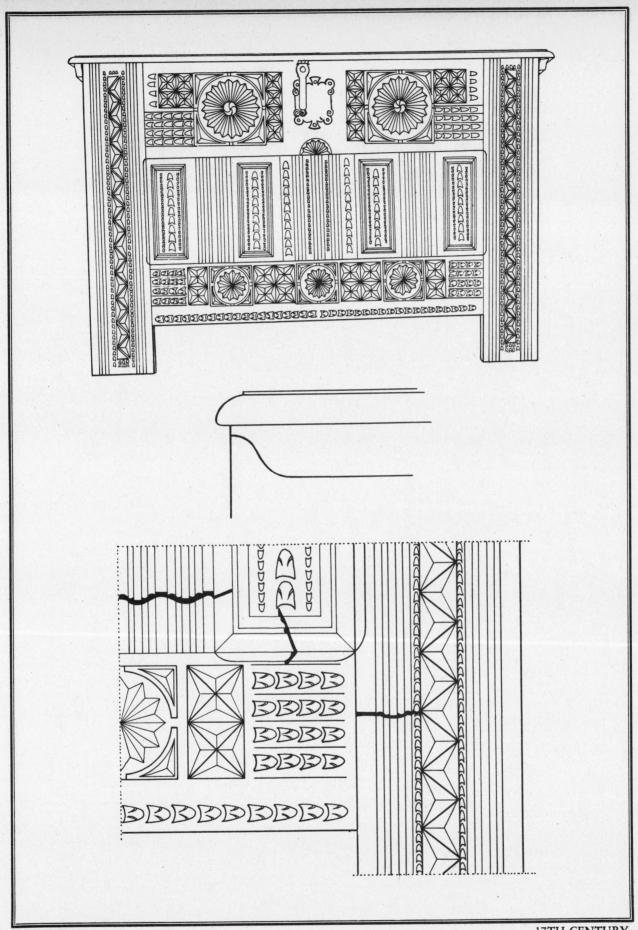

PLATE 185
Large folk-style chest.

17TH CENTURY

189

PLATE 186
Large chest.

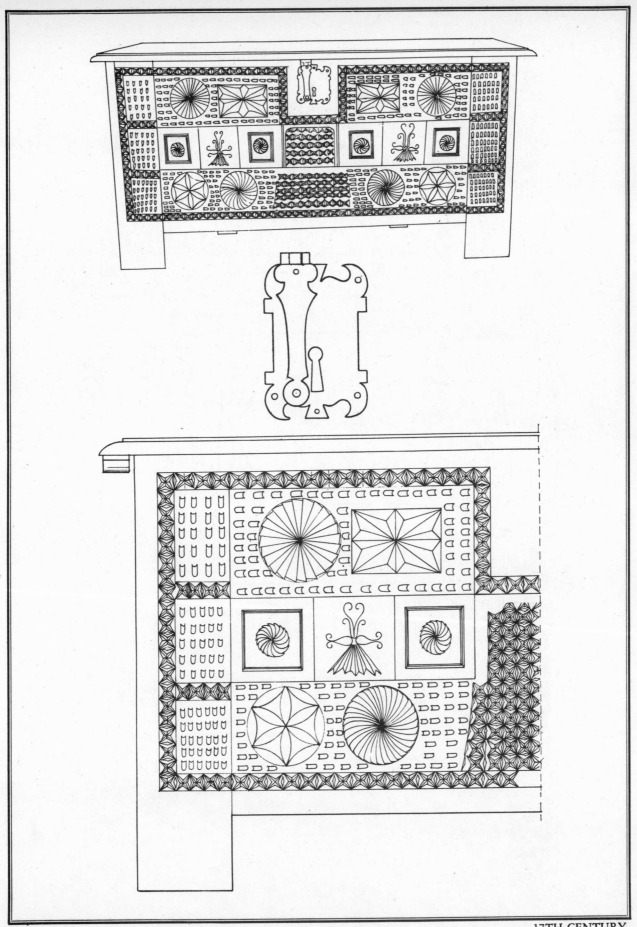

**PLATE 188**
Large chests.

**PLATE 189**
Folk-style chest.

*Museum of Decorative Arts, Madrid*

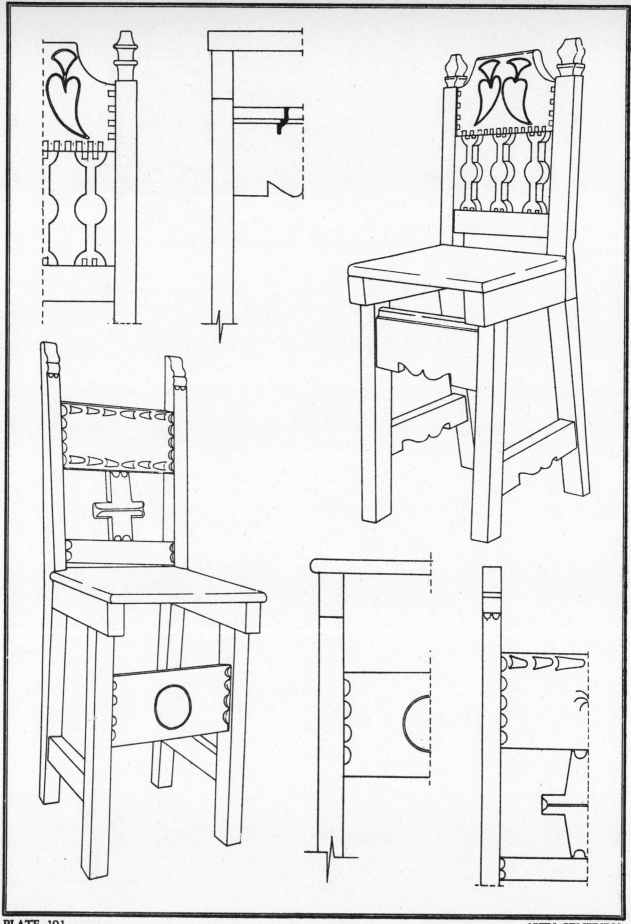

**PLATE 191**
Chairs of folk design.

*Gustavo Gili collection, Santillana del Mar*

**PLATE 192**
Folk-style chest.

*Museum of Decorative Arts, Madrid*

**PLATE 193**
Folk-style chest.

*Museum of Decorative Arts, Madrid*

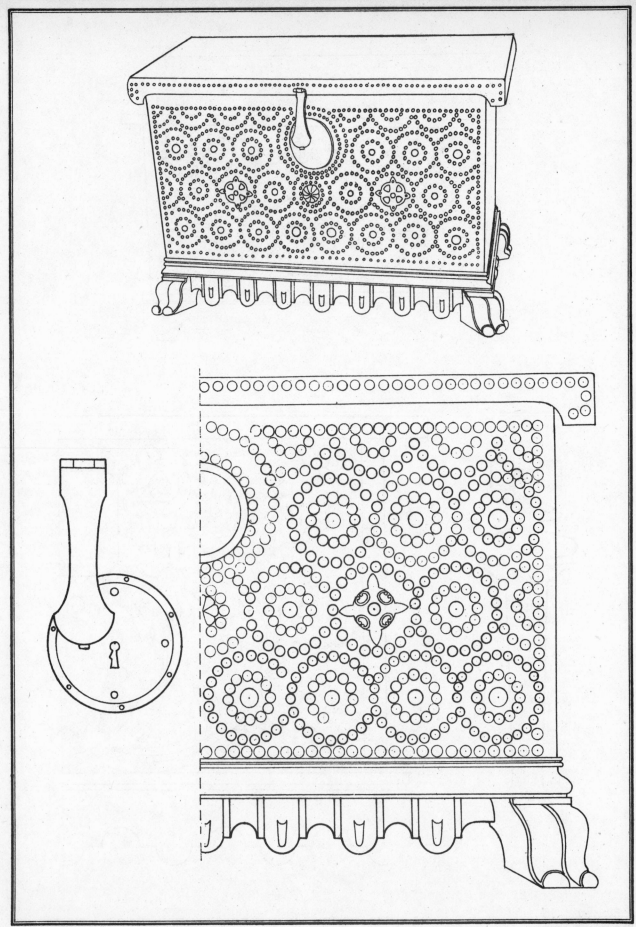

**PLATE 194**
Chest covered with leather and decorative nails.

*Museum of Decorative Arts, Madrid*

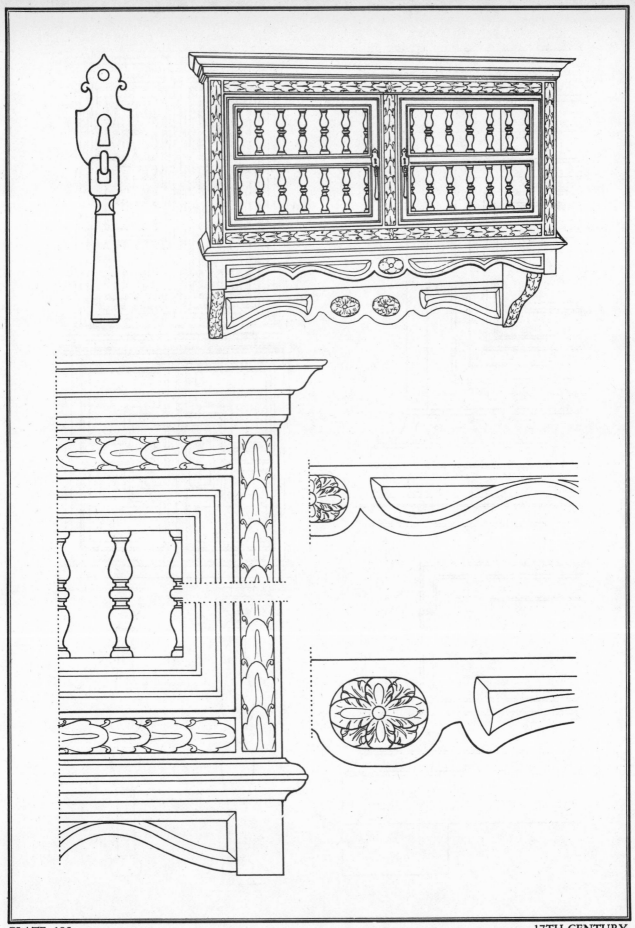

PLATE 195
Folk-style cupboard.

**PLATE 196**
Chest-on-chest.

**17TH CENTURY**

*El Greco's house, Toledo*

200

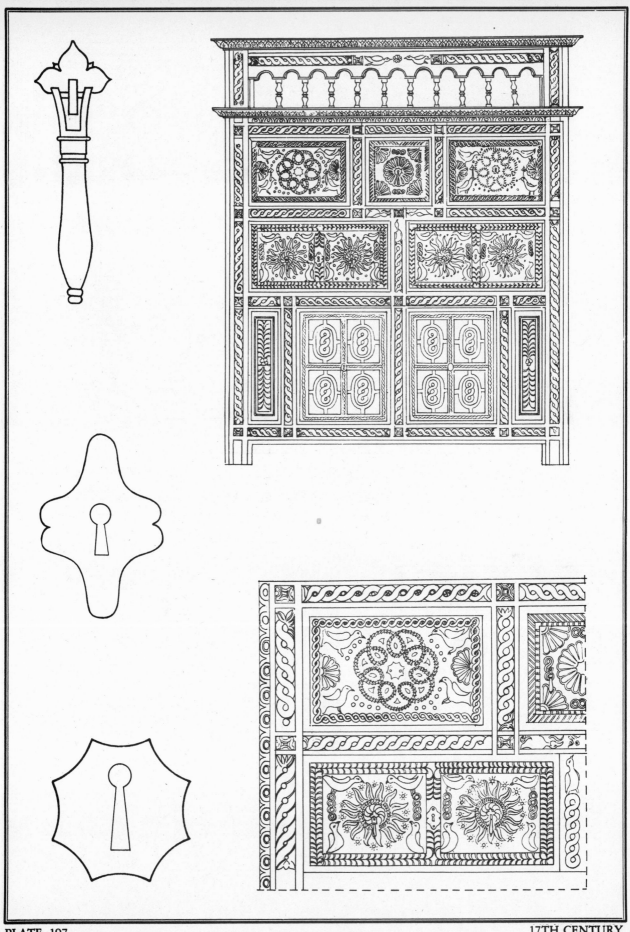

**PLATE 197**
Carved wardrobe of folk design.

*Museum of Decorative Arts, Madrid*

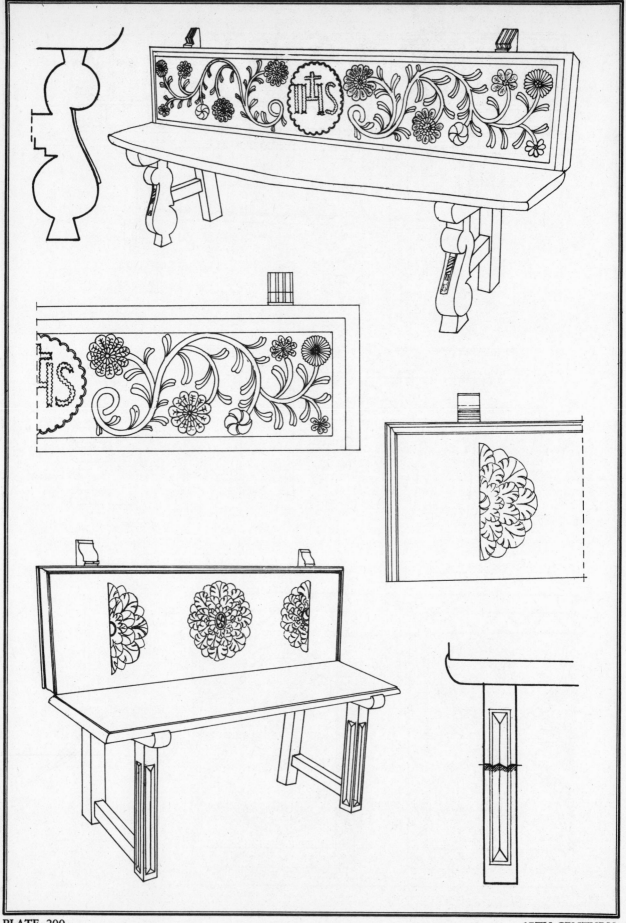

**PLATE 200**
Folk-style benches with decorative carvings.

*Museum of Decorative Arts, Madrid*

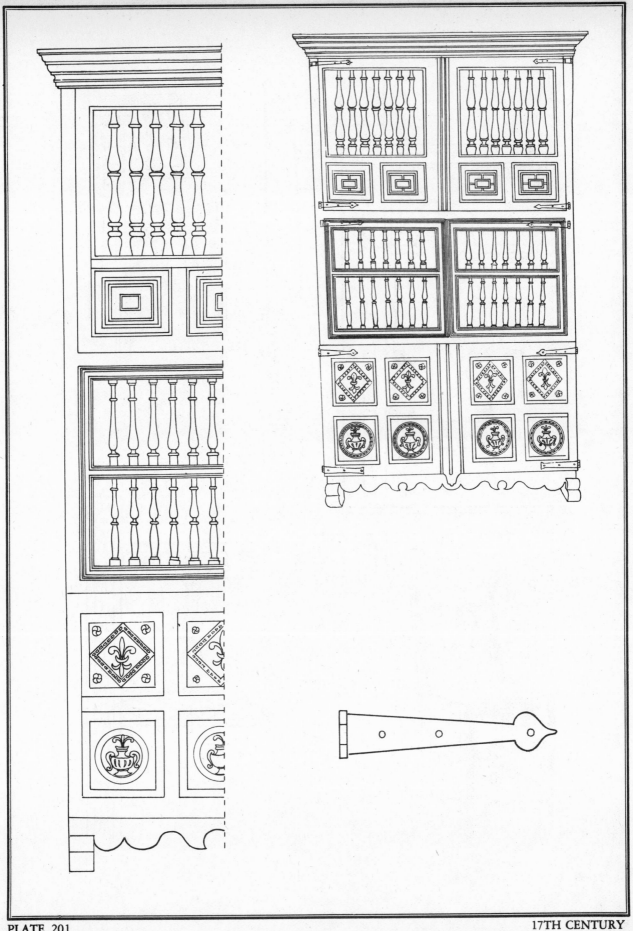

**PLATE 201**
Folk-style wardrobe.

*Museum of Decorative Arts, Madrid*

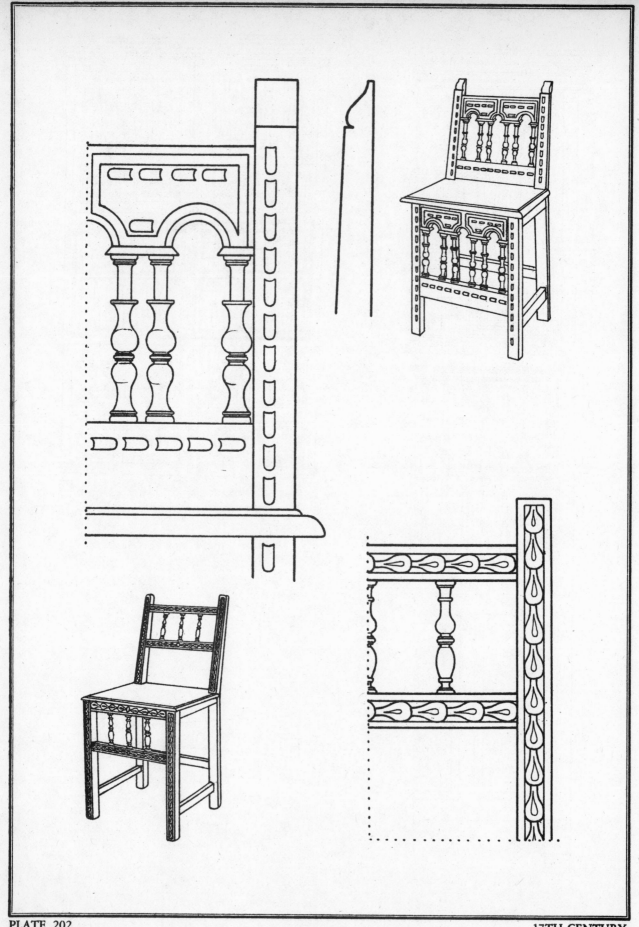

**PLATE 202**
Folk-style chairs.

**17TH CENTURY**

206

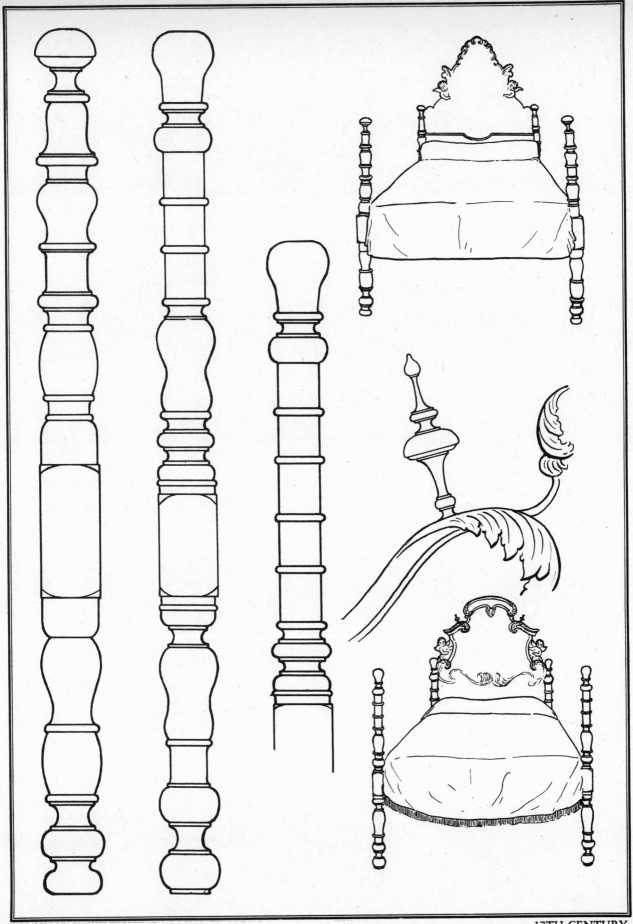

PLATE 203
Beds of folk design.

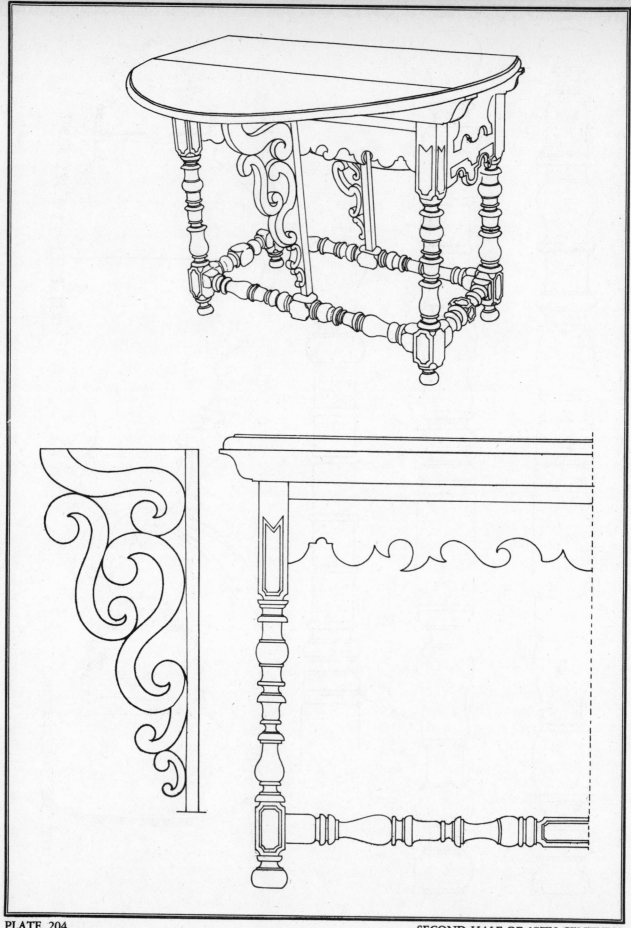

PLATE 204
Table with folding leaves.

SECOND HALF OF 17TH CENTURY

*Museum of Decorative Arts, Madrid*

208

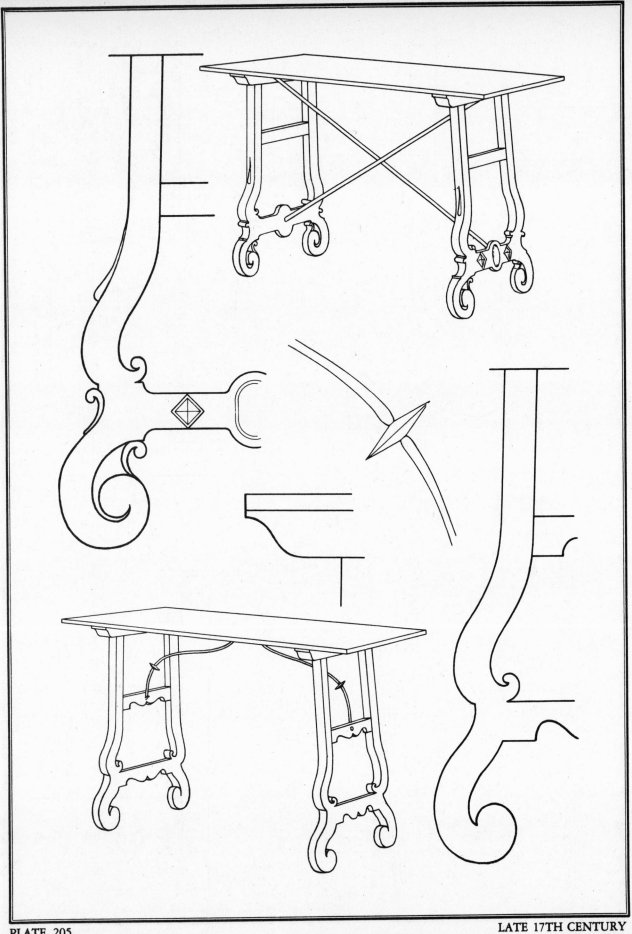

**PLATE 205**
Two tables.

*Museum of Pontevedra and the Parador of Santillana del Mar*

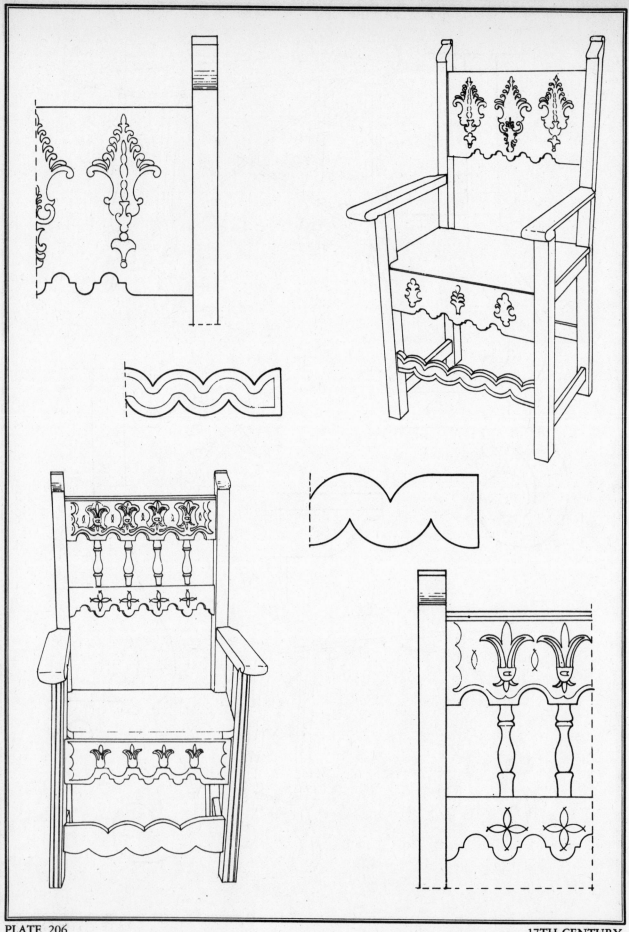

**PLATE 206**
Folk-style armchairs.

*Museum of Decorative Arts, Madrid*

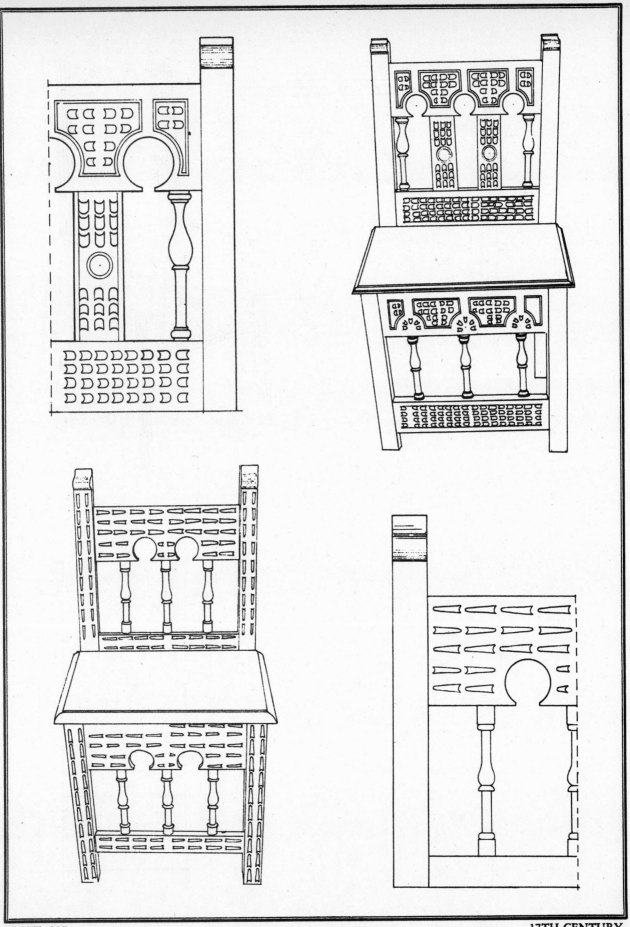

**PLATE 207**
Folk-style chairs.

*Museum of Decorative Arts, Madrid*

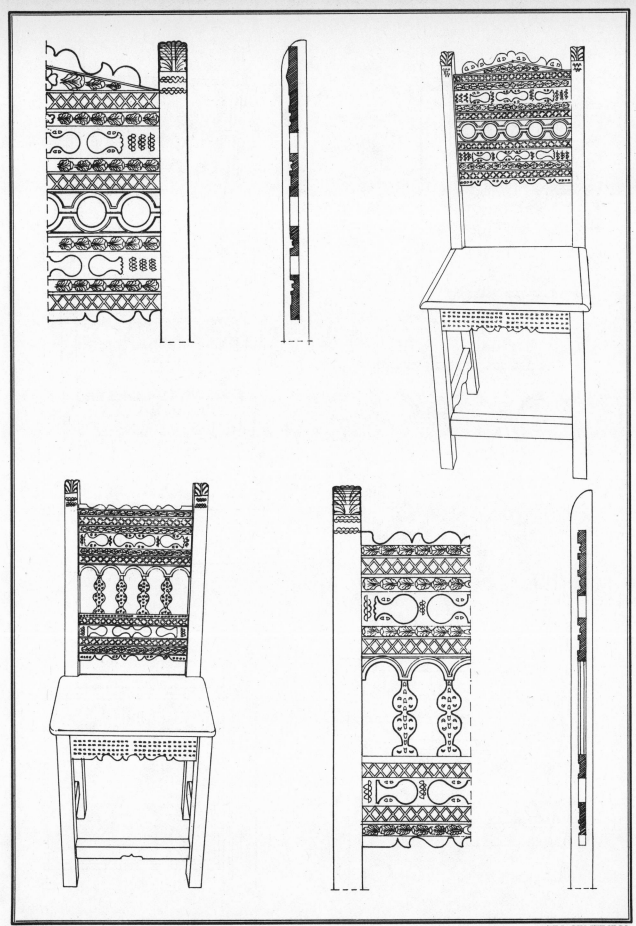

PLATE 211
Folk-style chairs.

17TH CENTURY

215

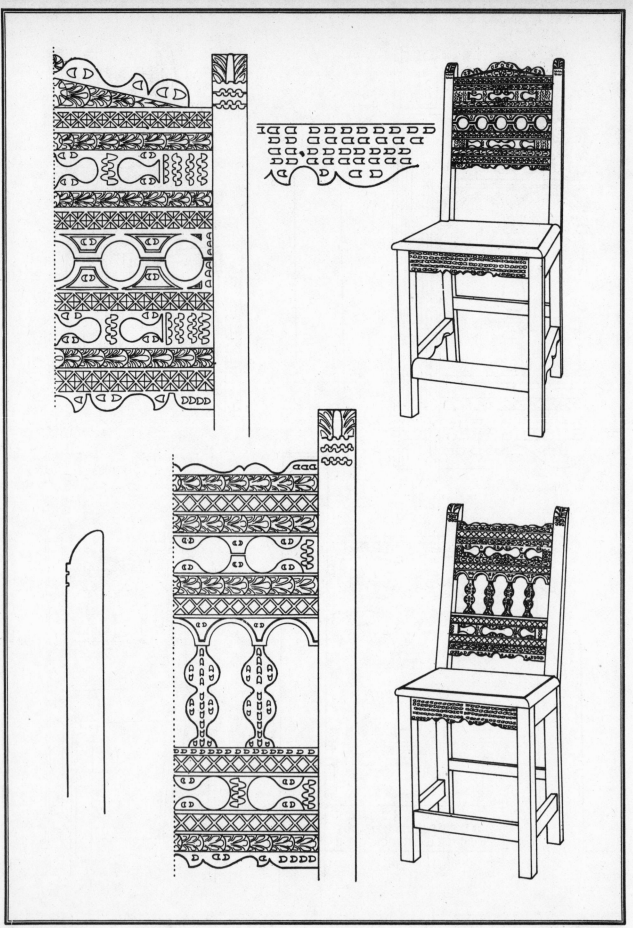

PLATE 212
Folk-style chairs.

17TH CENTURY

216

**PLATE 213**
Folk-style chairs.

17TH CENTURY

217

PLATE 214
Folk-style chairs.

17TH CENTURY

218

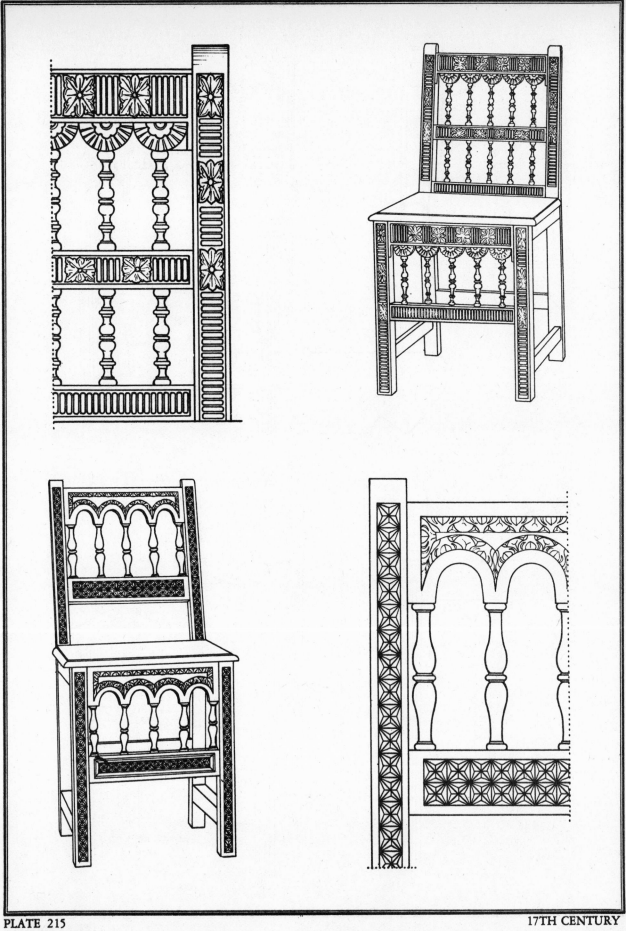

**PLATE 215**
Folk-style chairs.

17TH CENTURY

219

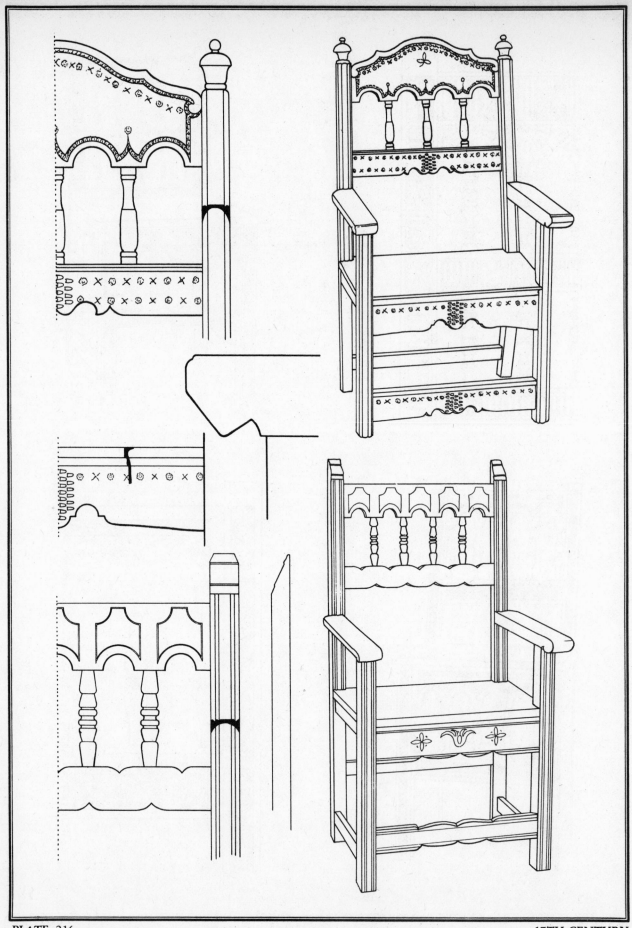

PLATE 216
Folk-style chairs.

17TH CENTURY

*Tavera Hospital, Toledo*

220

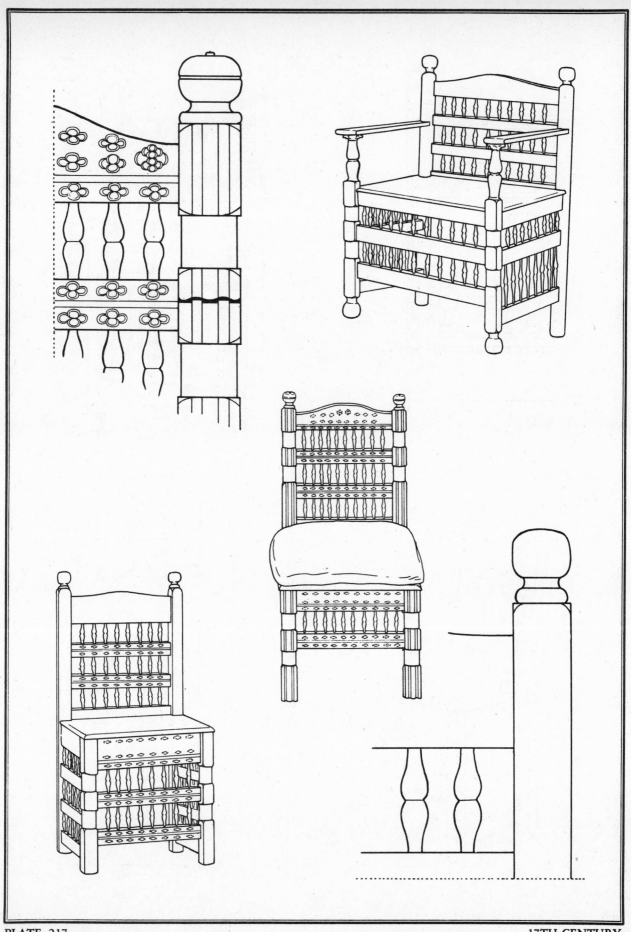

**PLATE 217**
Folk-style chairs.

**17TH CENTURY**

221

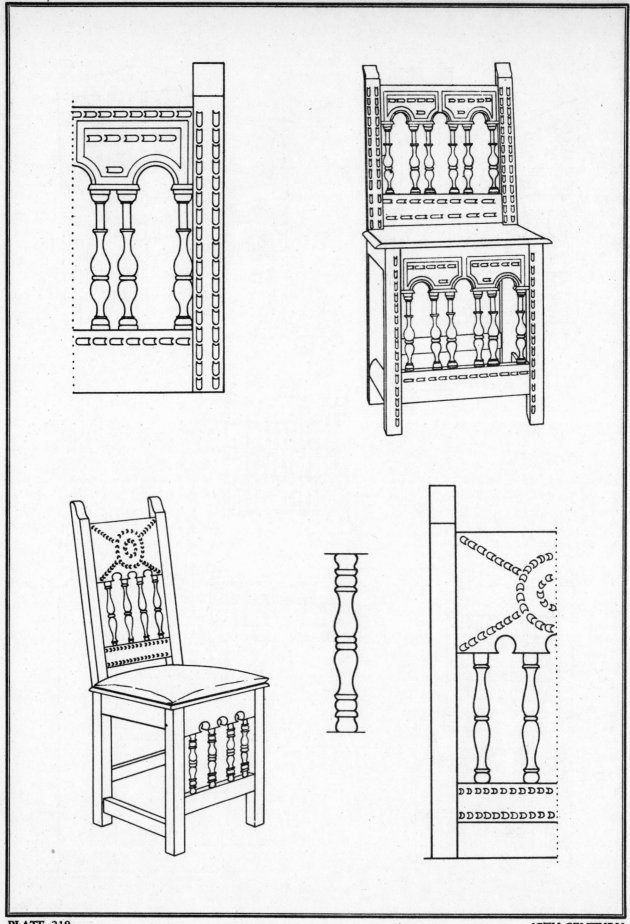

**PLATE 218**
Folk-style chairs.

*National Museum of Decorative Arts and Hostería del Estudiante, Alcalá de Henares*

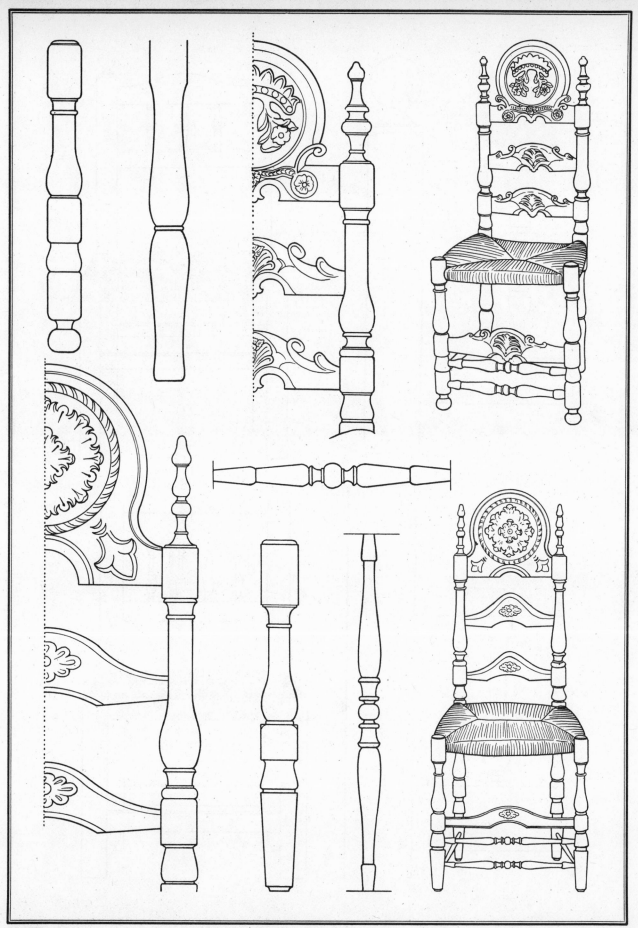

**PLATE 219**
Chairs of folk design.

*Francisco Fábregas collection*

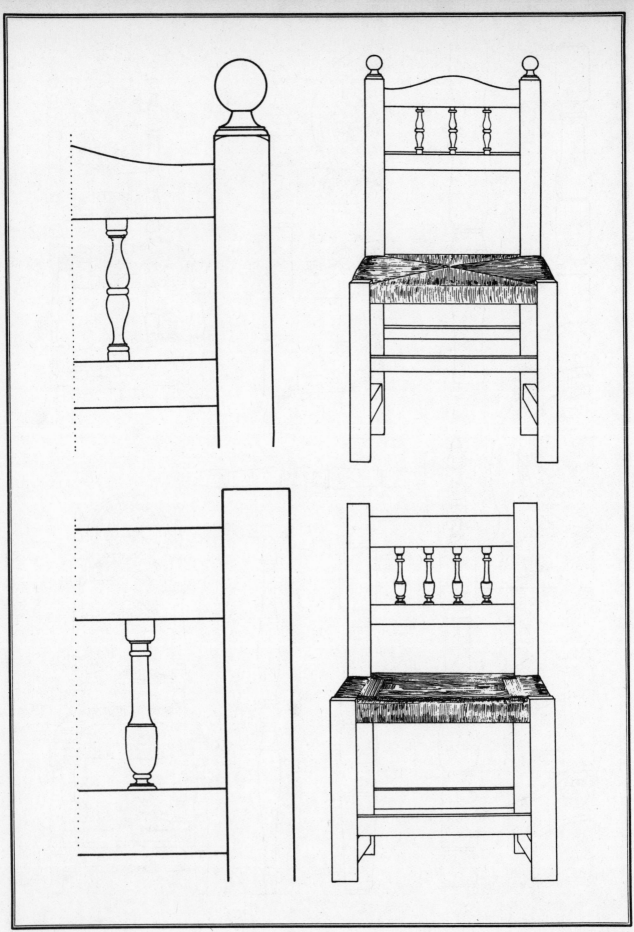

**PLATE 220**
Two chairs of folk design.

*Hostería del Estudiante, Alcalá de Henares*

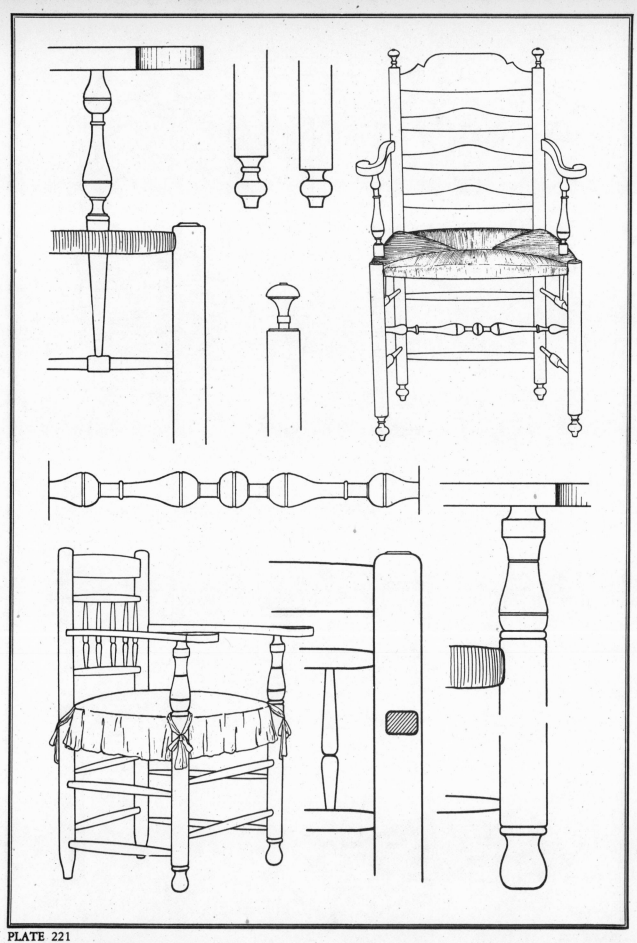

**PLATE 221**
Two armchairs of folk design.

*Laguardia, Alava and Manor house in Santander*

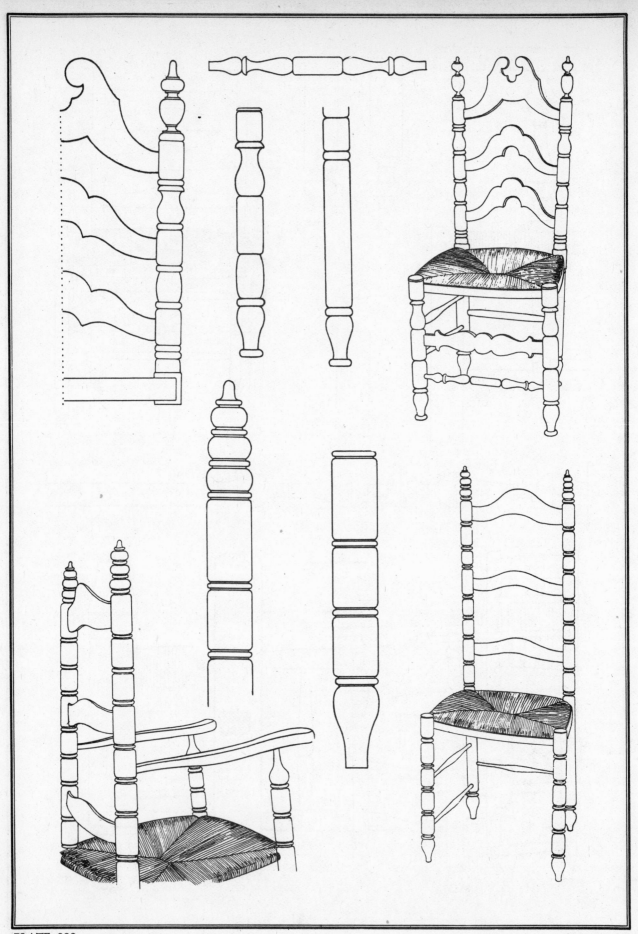

**PLATE 222**
Two chairs of folk design.

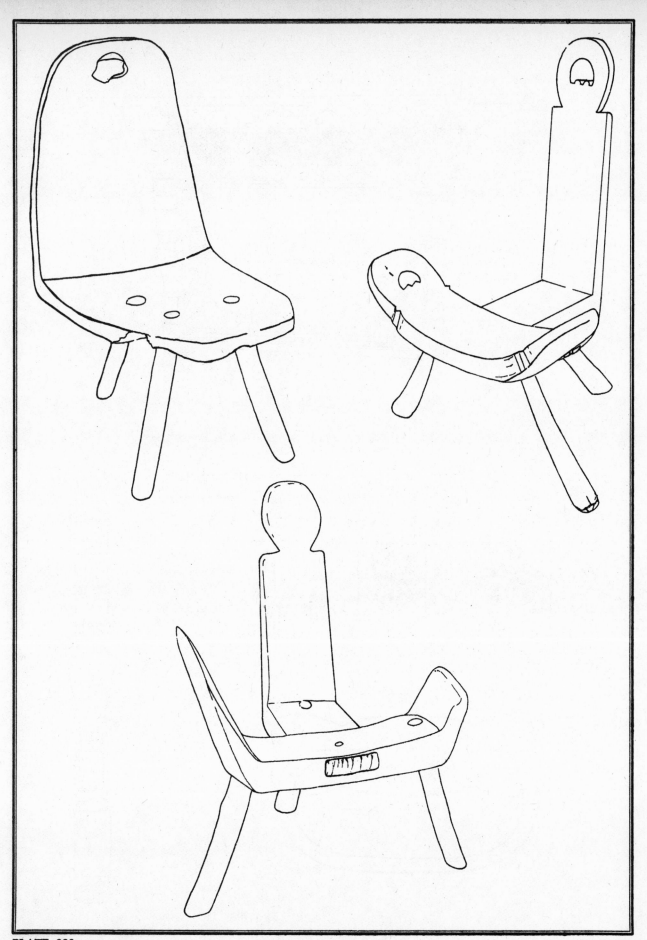

**PLATE 223**
Rustic three-legged chairs.

**PLATE 224**
Folk-style table.

*Museum of Decorative Arts, Madrid*

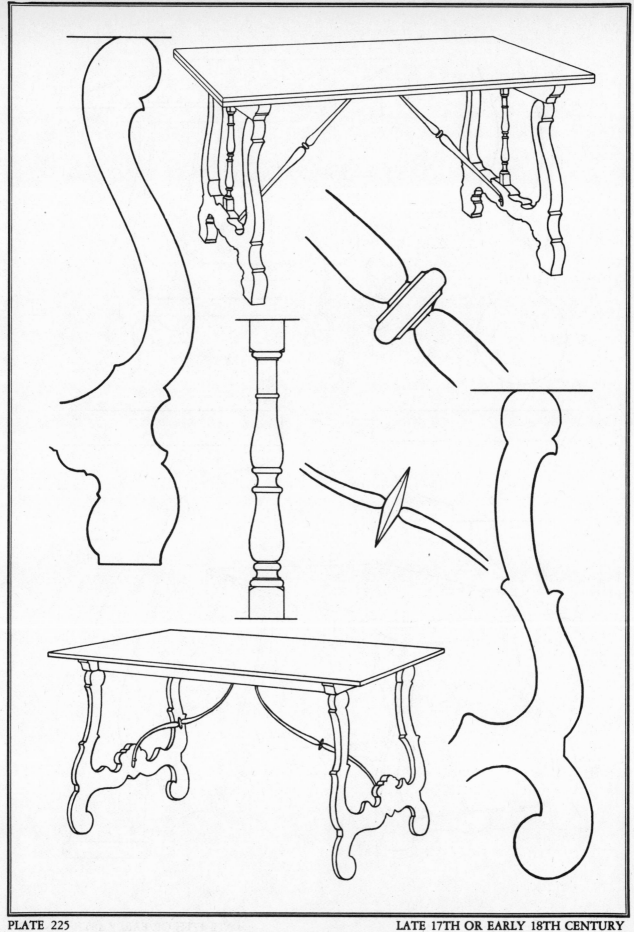

PLATE 225
LATE 17TH OR EARLY 18TH CENTURY
Tables with legs cut from wood and with wrought-iron ligatures.

*Parador of Gredos, Avila and Parador of Ubeda, Jaen.*

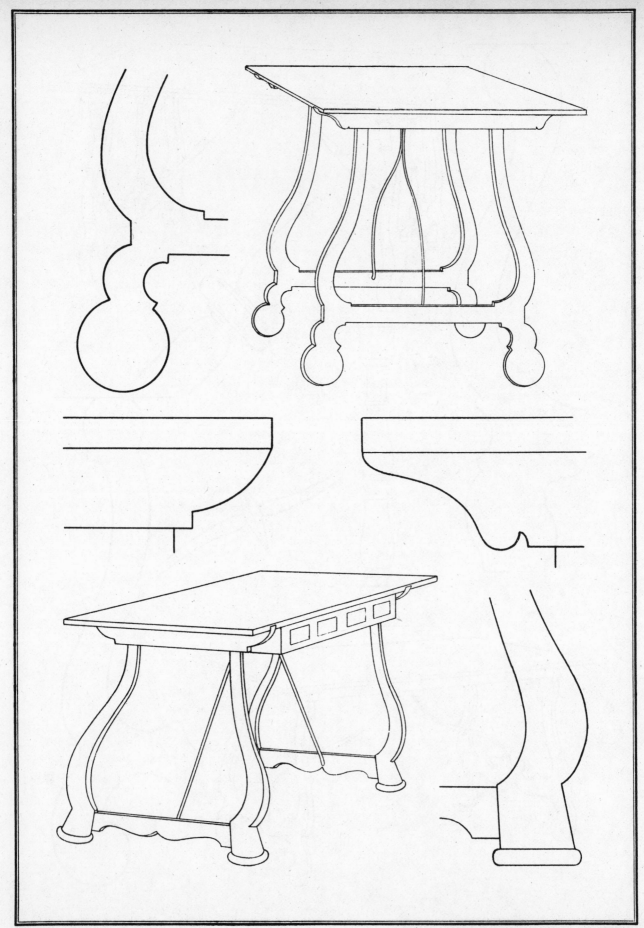

**PLATE 226**
Tables with legs cut from wood and with wrought-iron ligatures.

LATE 17TH OR EARLY 18TH CENTURY

*Quinta de Raixa, Palma de Mallorca*

230

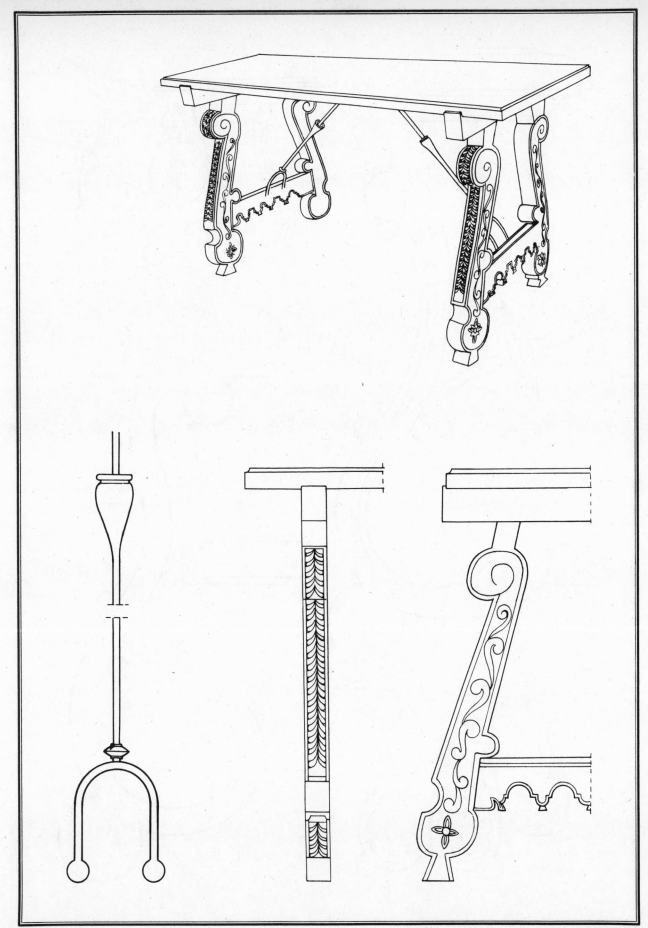

PLATE 227
Table with cut and carved wooden legs and wrought-iron ligatures.

LATE 17TH OR EARLY 18TH CENTURY

*Museum of Decorative Arts, Madrid*

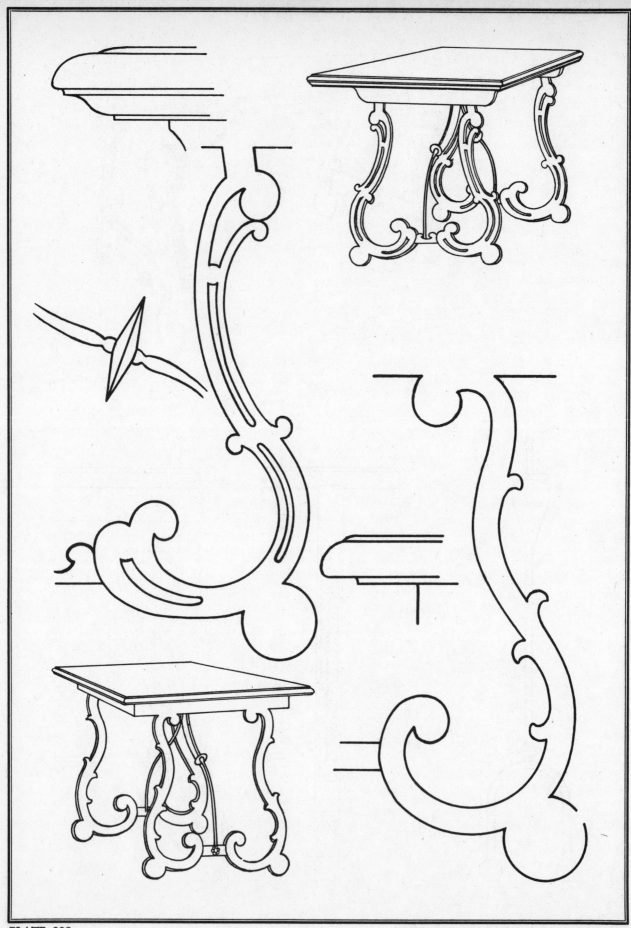

**PLATE 228**
Small tables with cut wooden legs and wrought-iron ligatures.

**LATE 17TH OR EARLY 18TH CENTURY**

*Weisberger collection, Madrid*

232

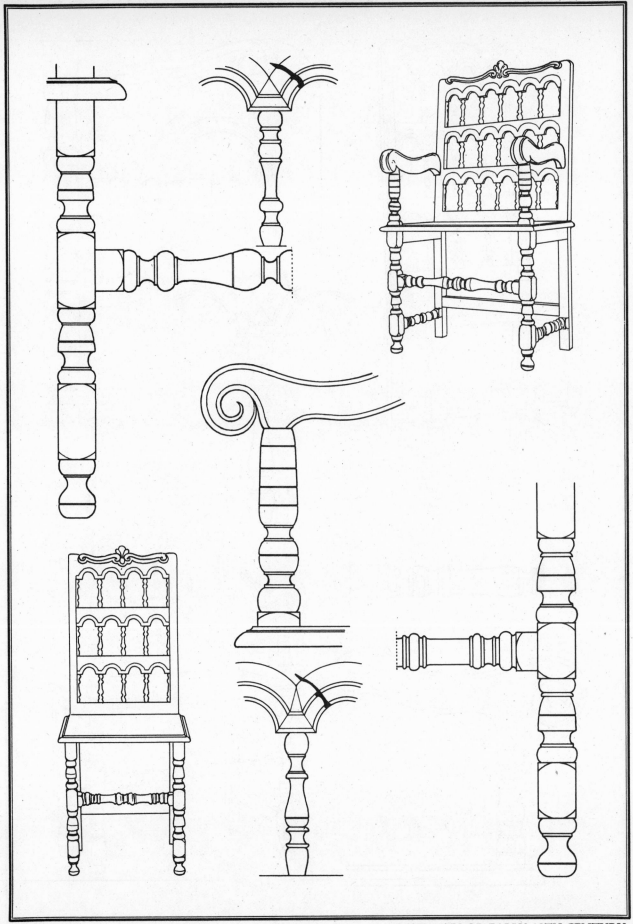

**PLATE 229**
Chair and armchair with "bridge" backs and turned wooden legs.

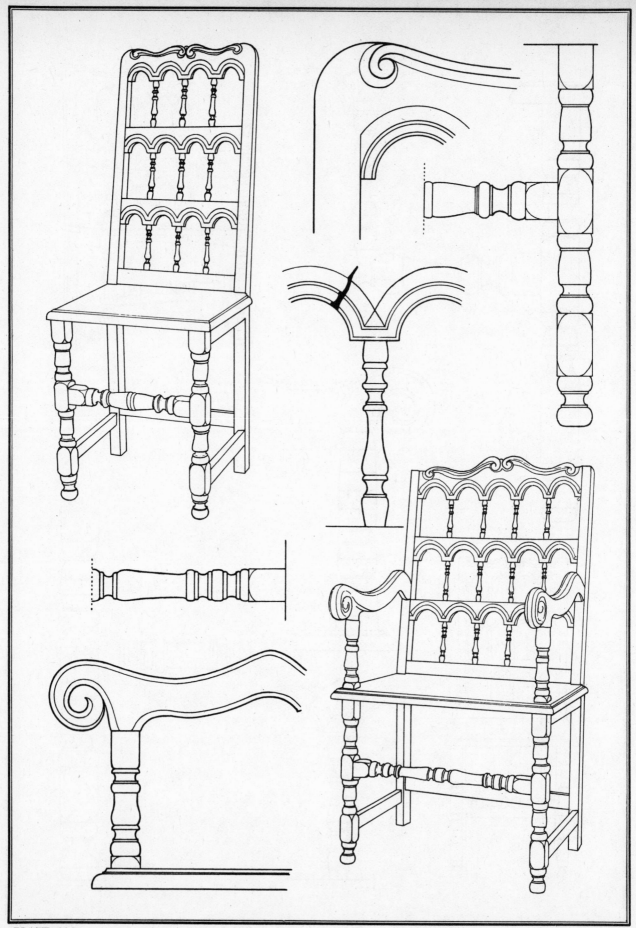

**PLATE 230**
Chair and armchair with "bridge" backs and turned legs.

LATE 17TH OR EARLY 18TH CENTURY

*From a manor house in Huesca province*

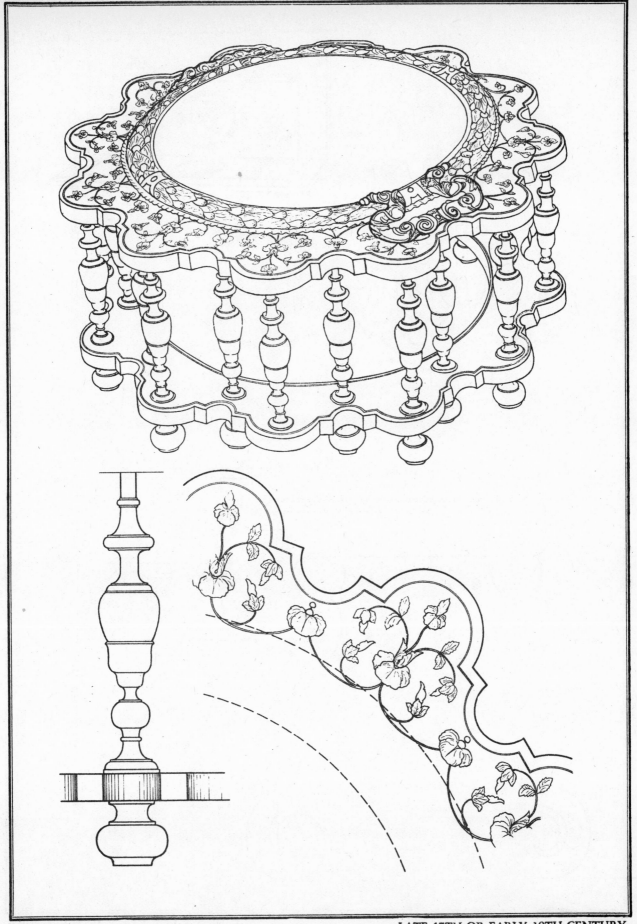

**PLATE 231**
Brazier supported by balusters and decorated with engraved vegetable motifs.

LATE 17TH OR EARLY 18TH CENTURY

*Marqués de la Cenia collection, Palma de Mallorca*

235

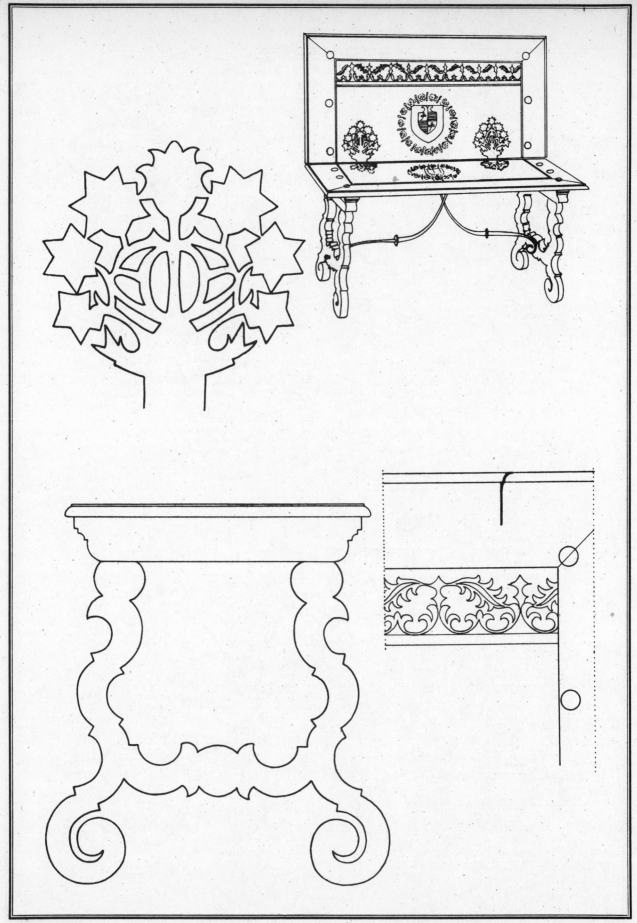

**PLATE 232**

Bench with wrought-iron hinges and crosspieces and cut legs. Marquetry decoration.

*Valencia Don Juan Institute, Madrid*

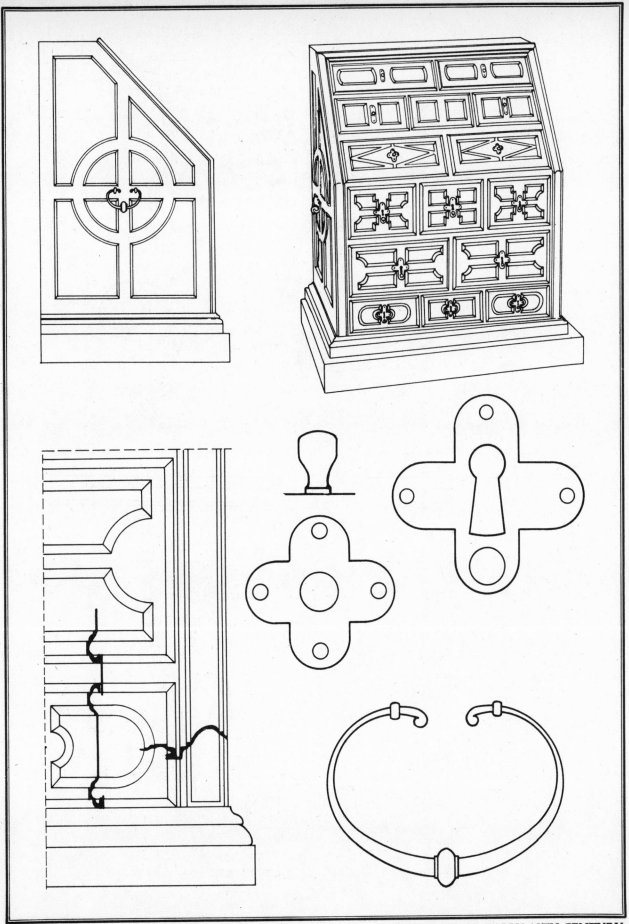

PLATE 233
Commode decorated with mouldings.

LATE 17TH OR EARLY 18TH CENTURY

*Museum of Decorative Arts, Madrid*

237

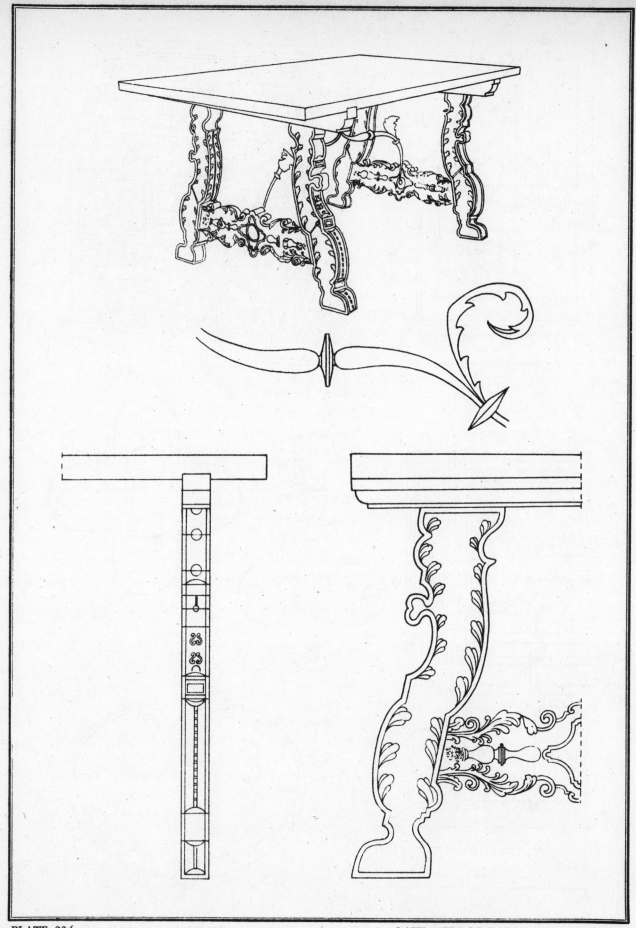

PLATE 234

LATE 17TH OR EARLY 18TH CENTURY

Carved table with legs of cut wood and with wrought-iron "bobèche" crosspieces.

*Museum of Decorative Arts, Madrid*

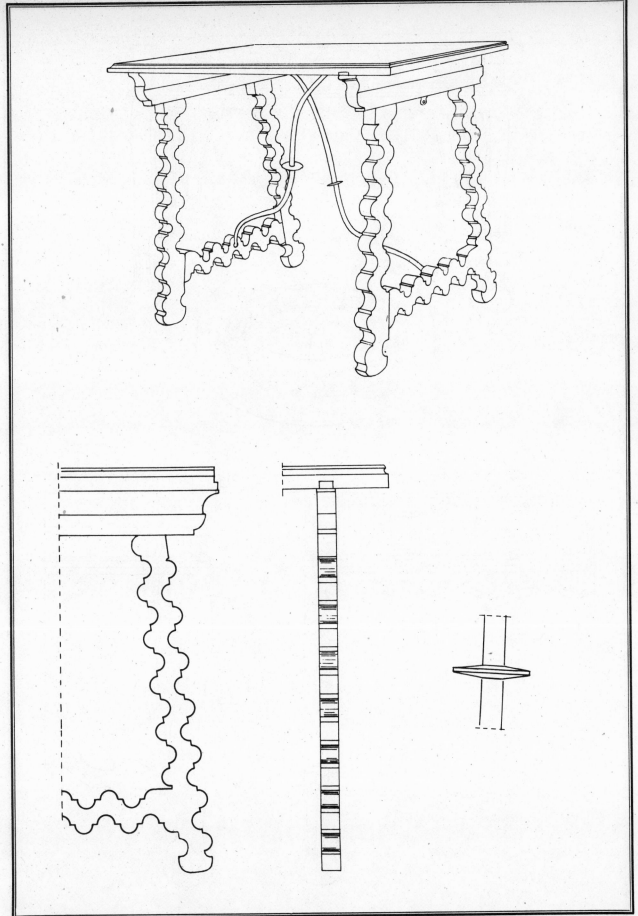

**PLATE 235**

LATE 17TH OR EARLY 18TH CENTURY

Table with wooden legs cut in a wavy pattern and with wrought-iron crosspieces.

*Romantic Museum and Fundaciones Vega Inclán, Madrid*

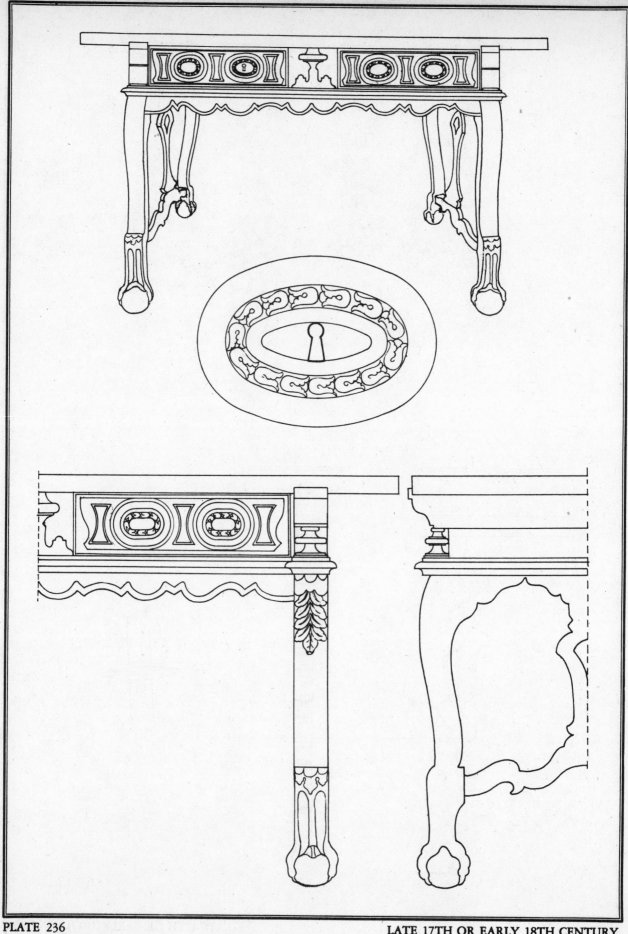

PLATE 236
Renaissance-style table.

LATE 17TH OR EARLY 18TH CENTURY

*Museum of Decorative Arts, Madrid*

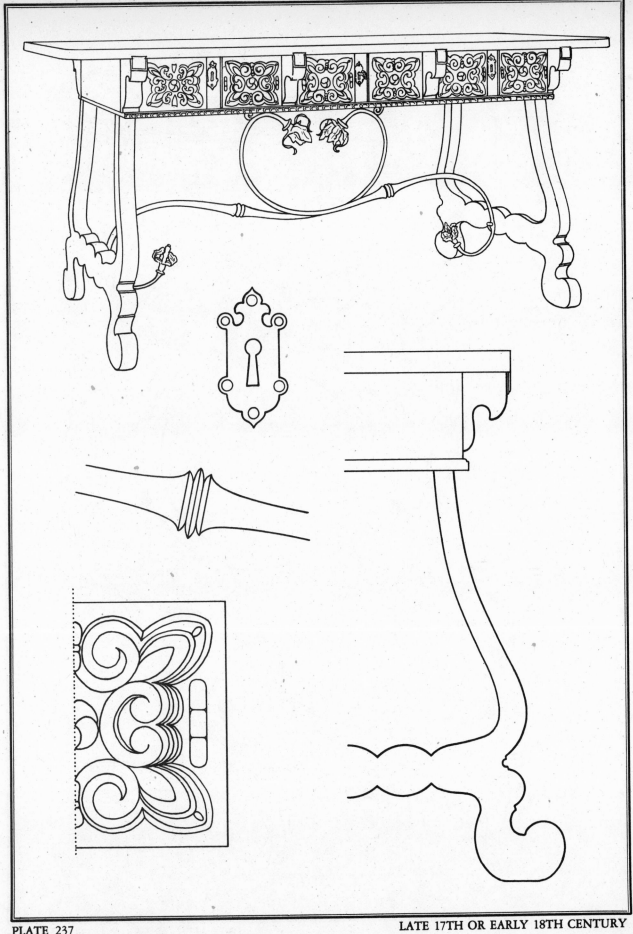

PLATE 237
Table.

LATE 17TH OR EARLY 18TH CENTURY

*Private collection*

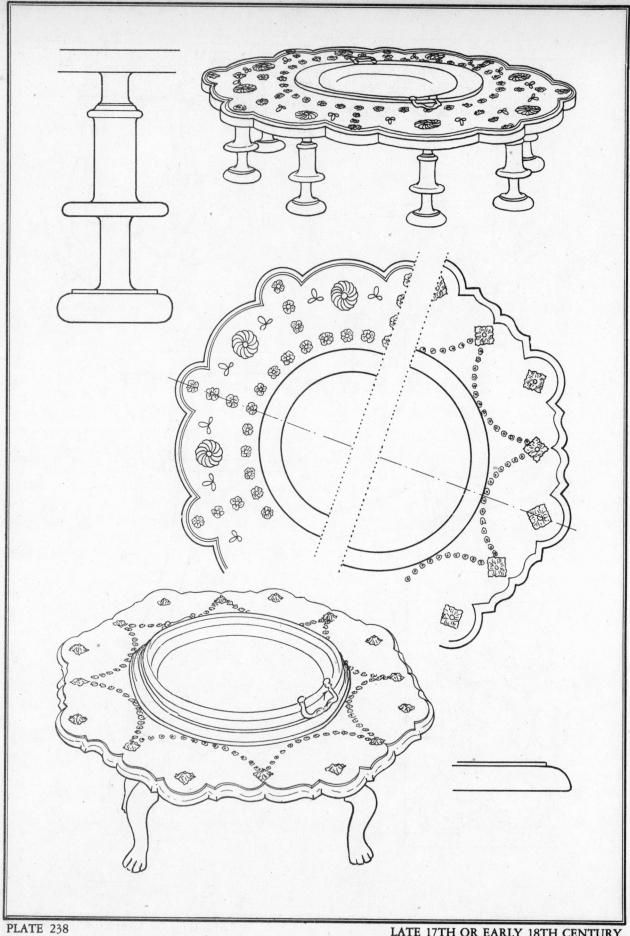

PLATE 238
Braziers.

LATE 17TH OR EARLY 18TH CENTURY

242

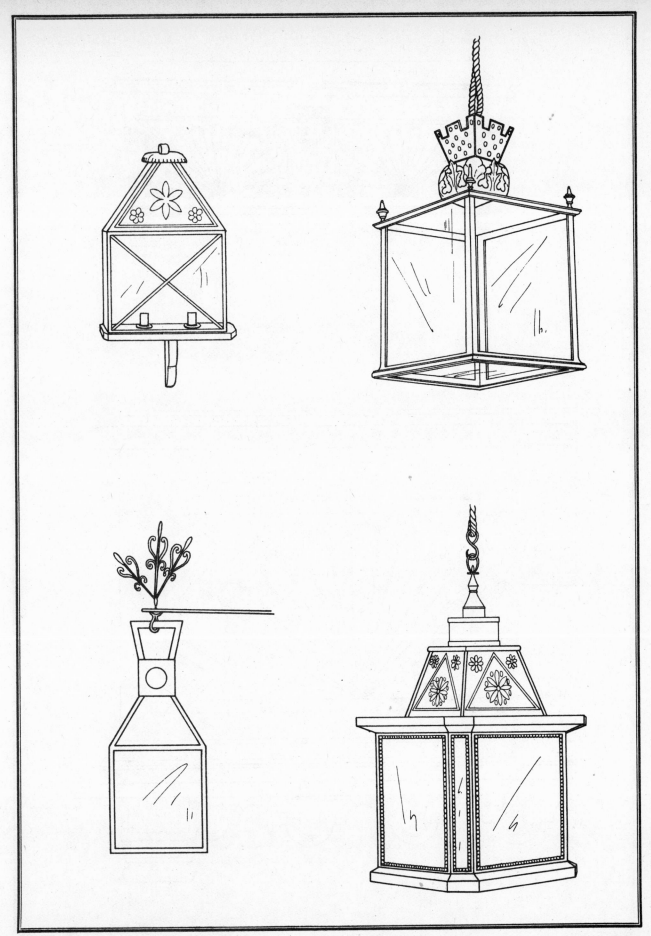

**PLATE 239**
Four lanterns of folk design.

*Parador of Toledo and Inns in Alcalá de Henares and Gredos*

PLATE 240
Chest of folk design.

LATE 17TH OR EARLY 18TH CENTURY

*Museum of Decorative Arts, Madrid*

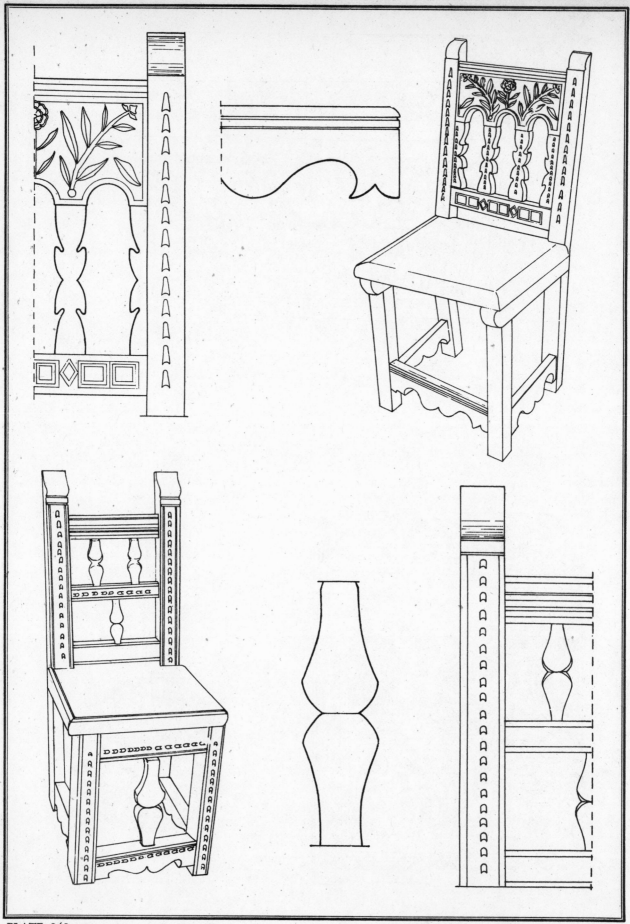

**PLATE 242**
Chairs of folk design.

*Museum of Decorative Arts, Madrid*

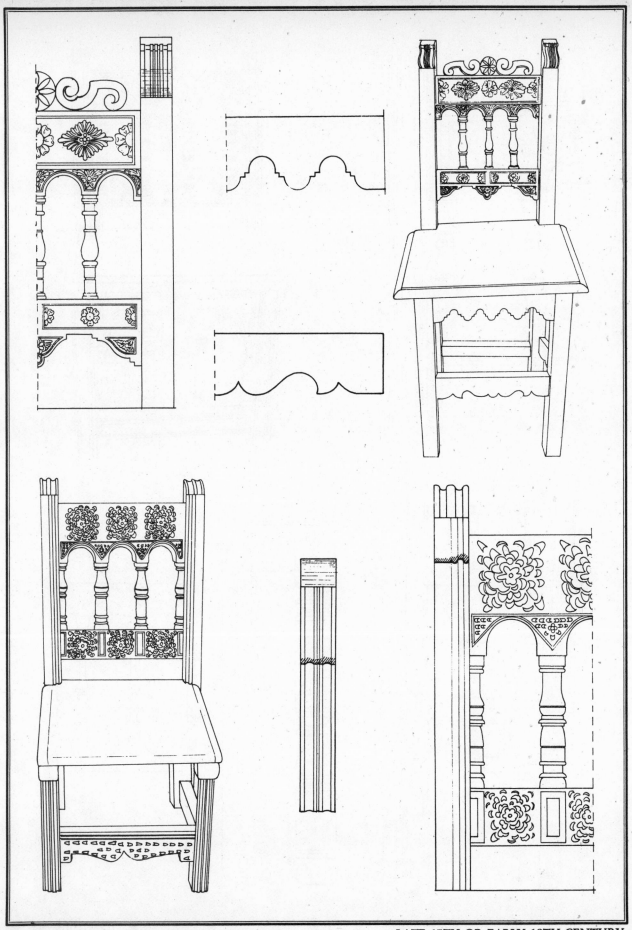

PLATE 243
Chairs of folk design.

LATE 17TH OR EARLY 18TH CENTURY

*Museum of Decorative Arts, Madrid*

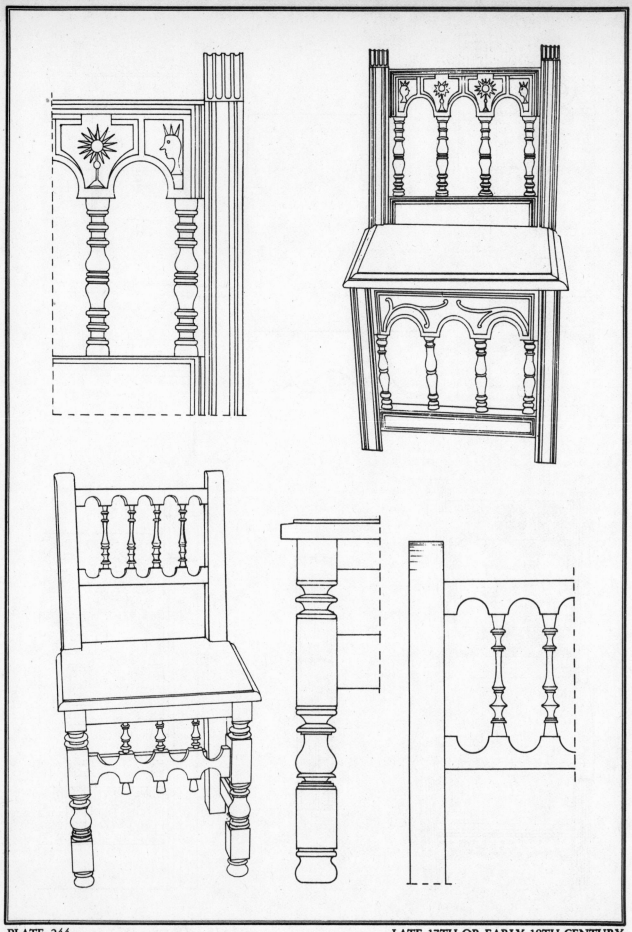

**PLATE 244**
Chairs of folk design.

*Museum of Decorative Arts, Madrid*

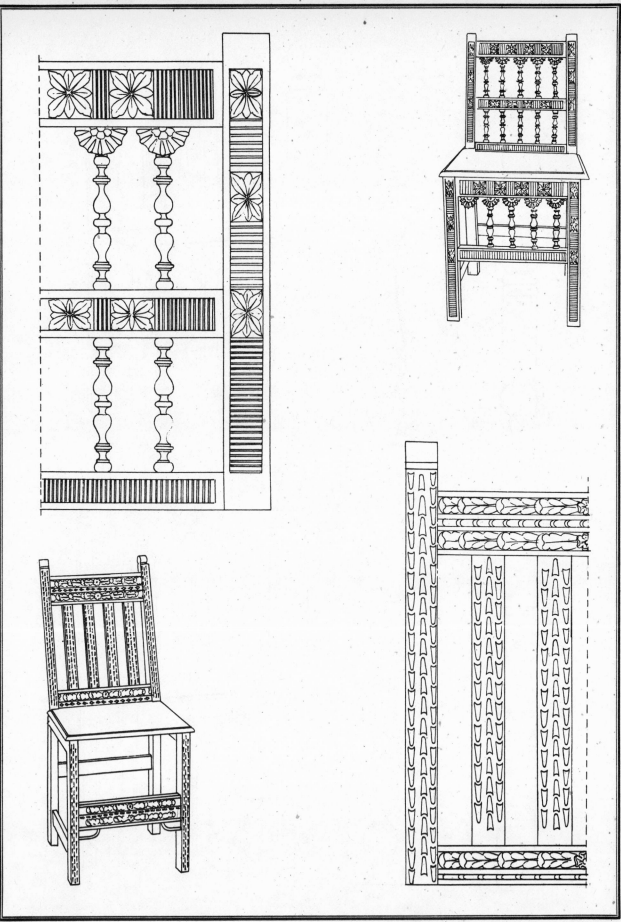

**PLATE 245**
Chairs of folk design.

LATE 17TH OR EARLY 18TH CENTURY

*Upper chair: Museum of Decorative Arts, Madrid*

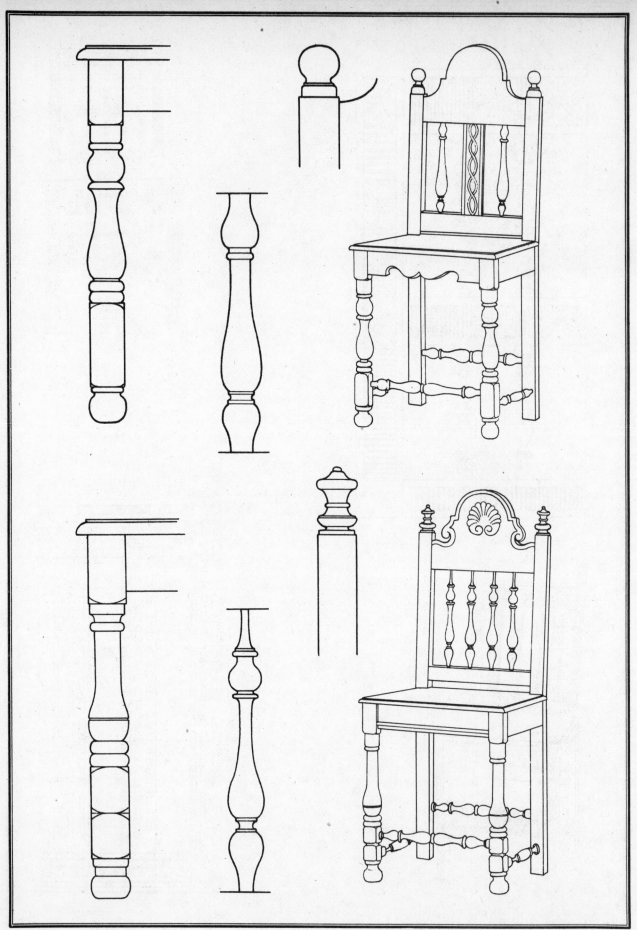

**PLATE 246**
Chairs of folk design.

*Paradors of Santillana del Mar and Santander*

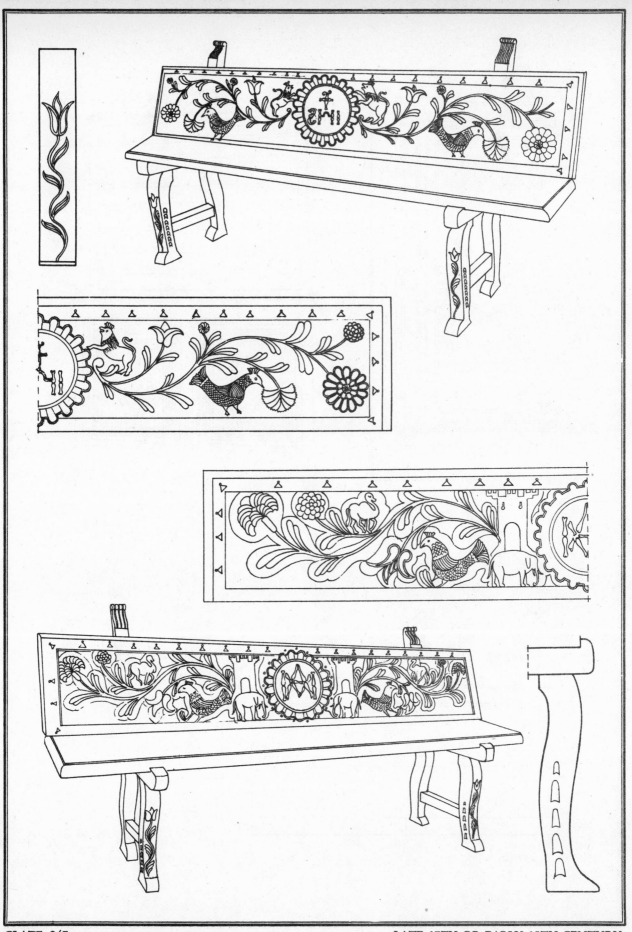

**PLATE 247**
Folk-style benches with decorative carvings.

LATE 17TH OR EARLY 18TH CENTURY

*Museum of Decorative Arts and Romantic Museum, Madrid*

PLATE 248
Buffet of folk design.

LATE 17TH OR EARLY 18TH CENTURY

*Tavera Hospital, Toledo*

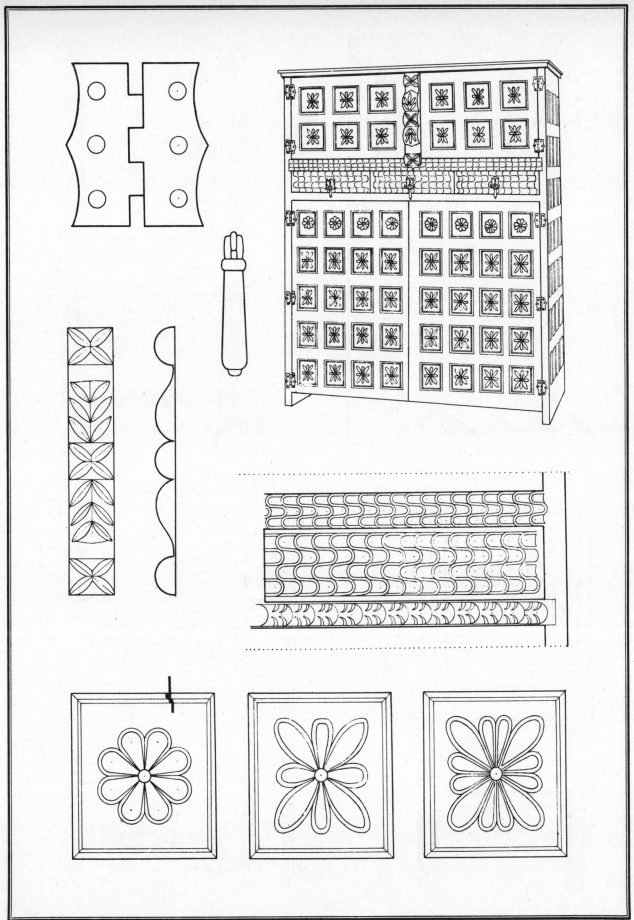

**PLATE 249**
Wardrobe of folk design in two pieces.

*Tavera Hospital, Toledo*

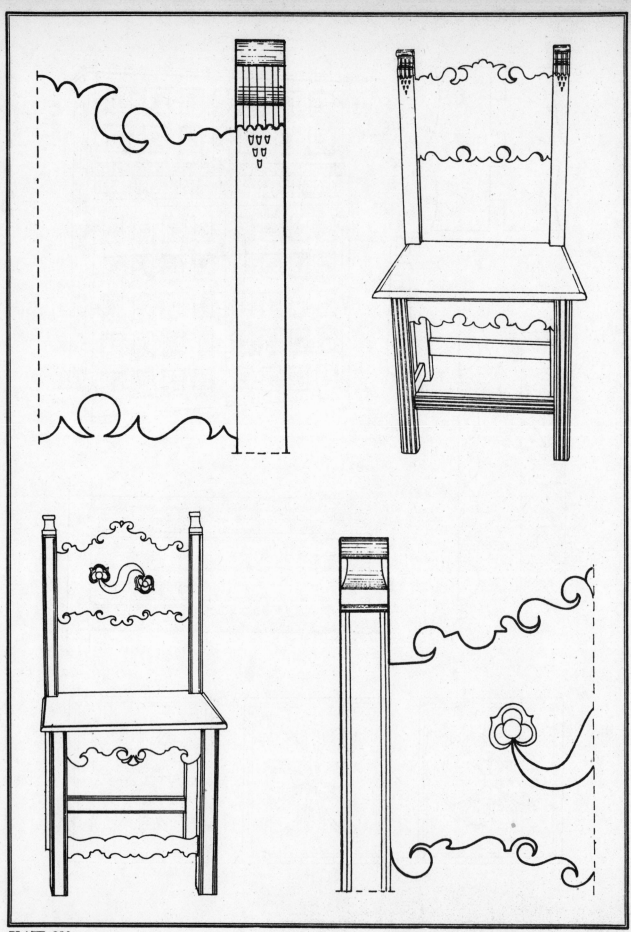

PLATE 250
Two chairs of folk design.

LATE 17TH OR EARLY 18TH CENTURY

*Museum of Decorative Arts, Madrid*

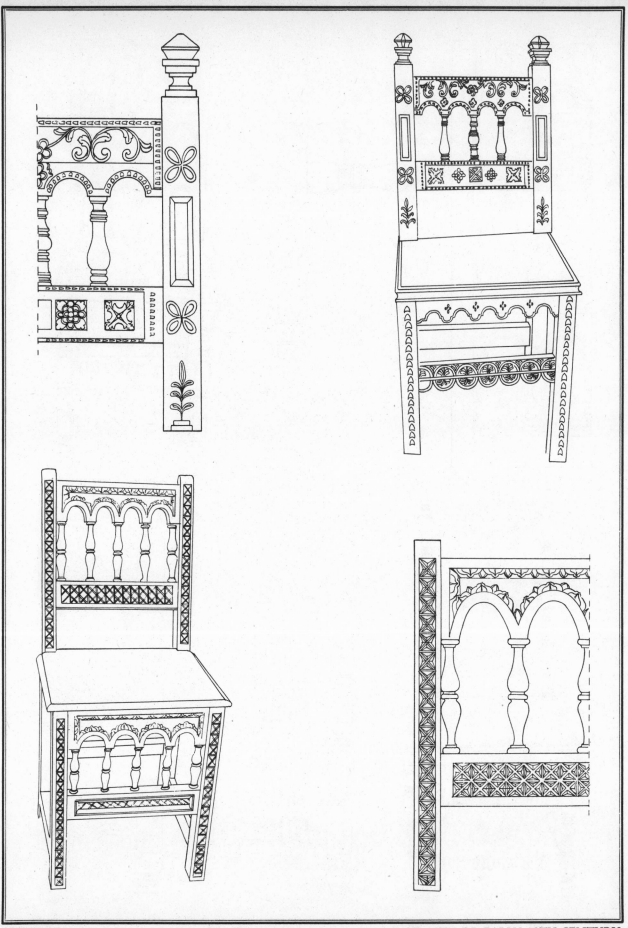

**PLATE 251**
Chairs of folk design.

*National Archeological Museum and Museum of Decorative Arts, Madrid*

**PLATE 252**
Chairs of folk design.

LATE 17TH OR EARLY 18TH CENTURY

*Museum of Decorative Arts, Madrid*

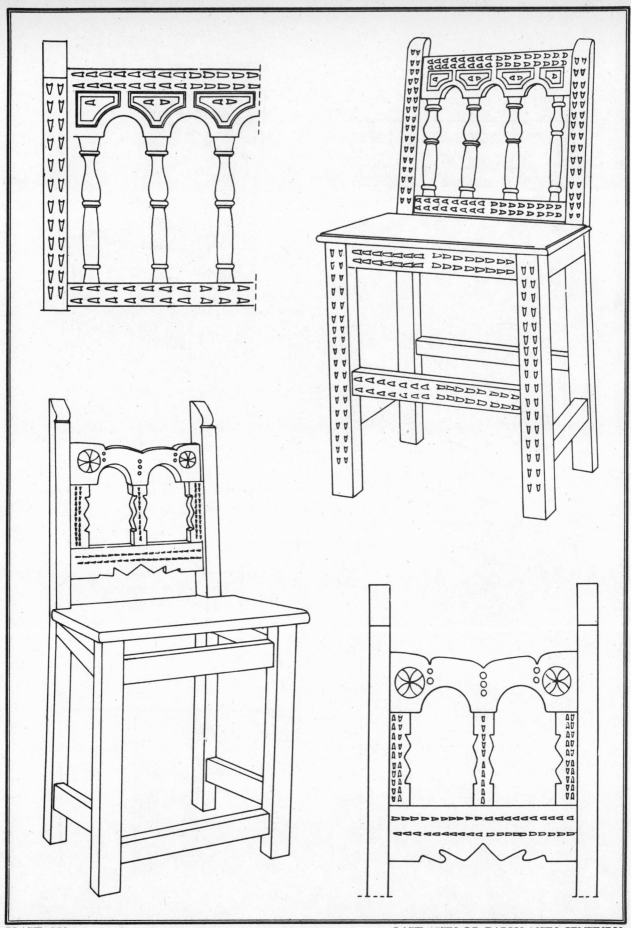

**PLATE 253**
Chairs of folk design.

LATE 17TH OR EARLY 18TH CENTURY

*Gustavo Gili collection, Santillana del Mar*

257

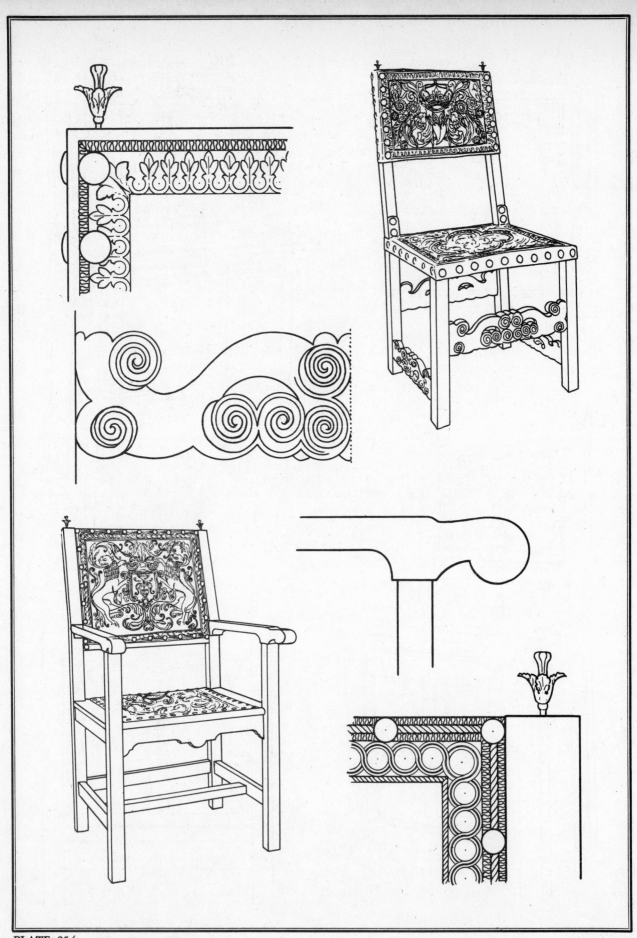

**PLATE 254**
Chair and armchair of folk design.

*Beancharro collection, Pontevedra*

**PLATE 255**
Folk-style armchairs.

*Museum of Decorative Arts, Madrid*

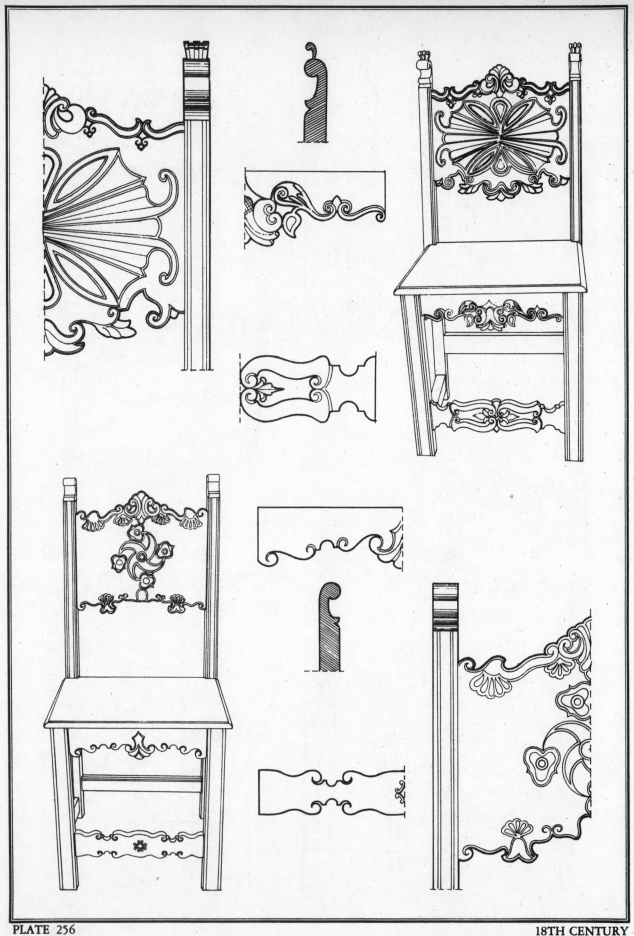

PLATE 256
Folk-style chairs.

**18TH CENTURY**

*Museum of Decorative Arts, Madrid*

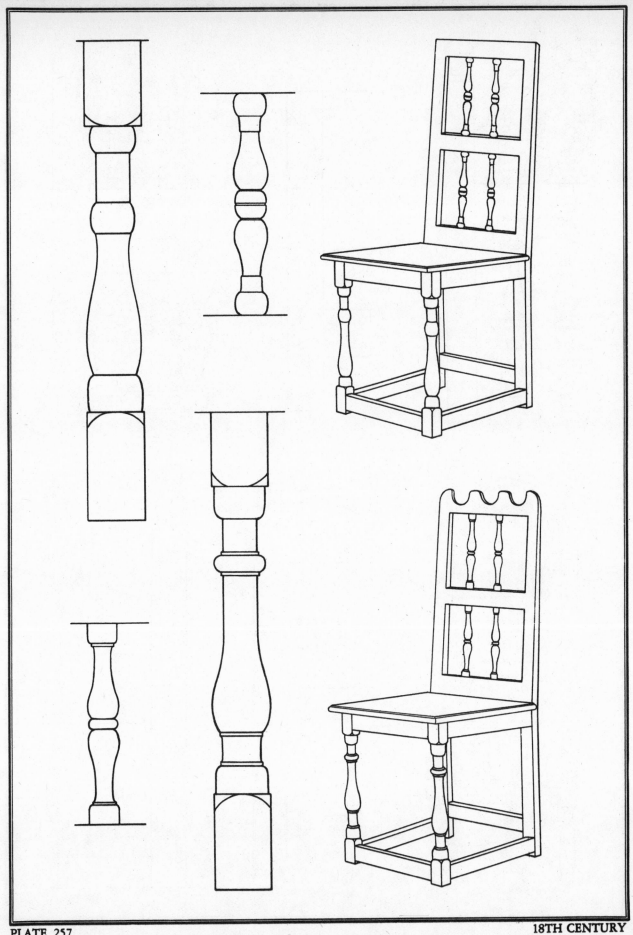

PLATE 257
Folk-style chairs.

18TH CENTURY

*Parador of Gredos, Avila*

261

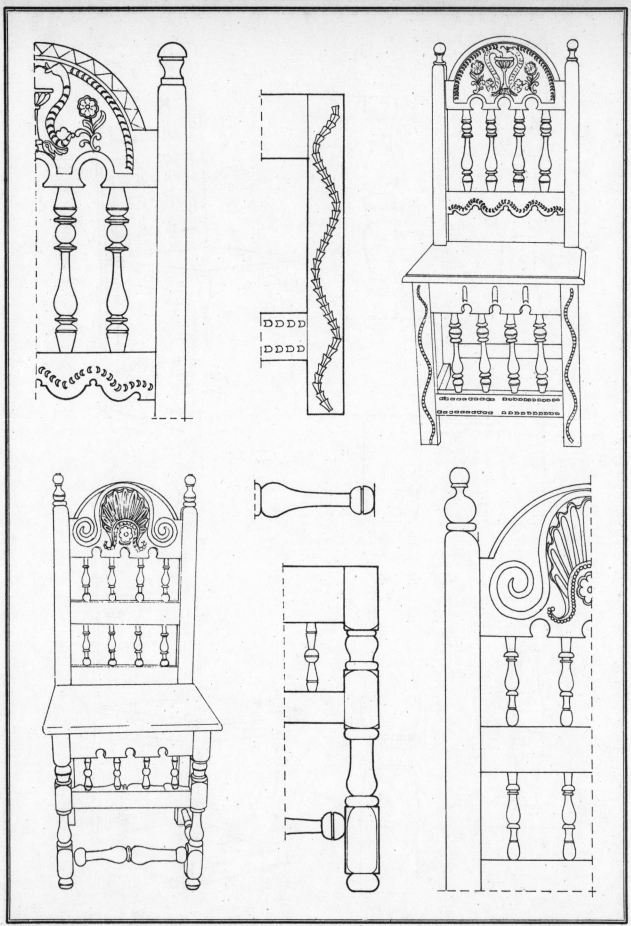

**PLATE 258**
Folk-style chairs.

**18TH CENTURY**

*Museum of Decorative Arts, Madrid*

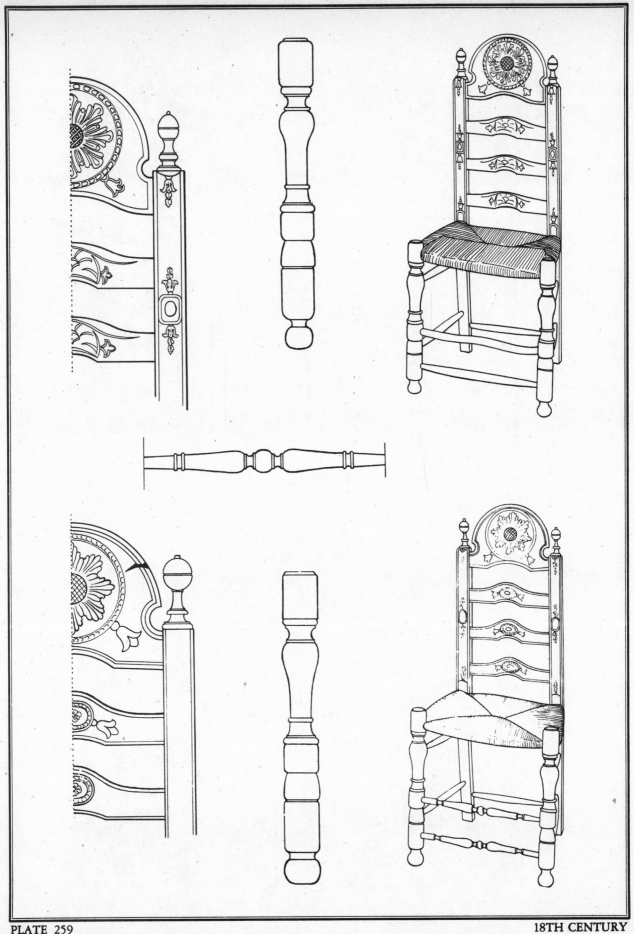

PLATE 259
Chairs.

18TH CENTURY

*Museum of Decorative Arts, Madrid*

263

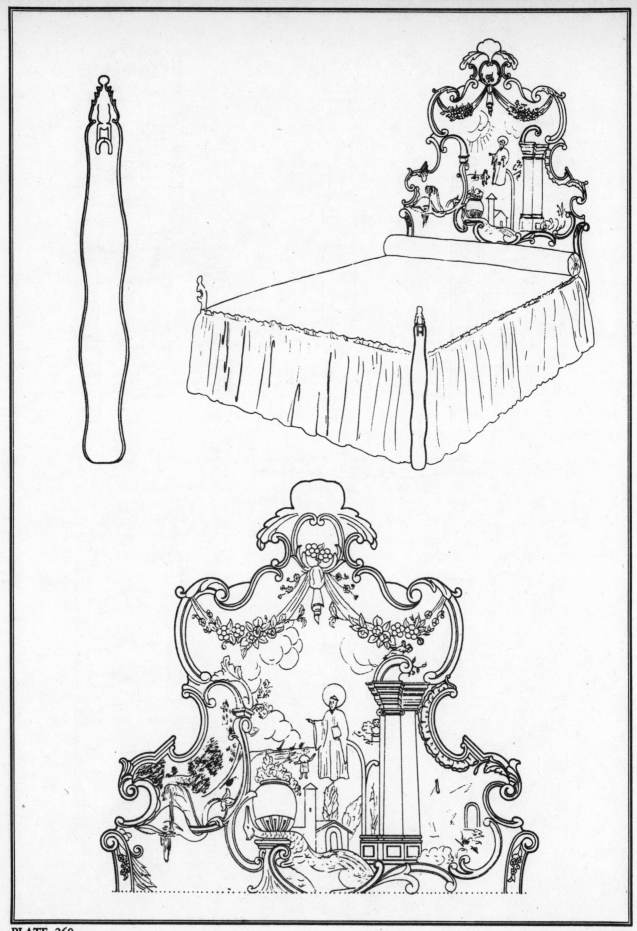

**PLATE 260**
Catalonian bed with painted headboard.

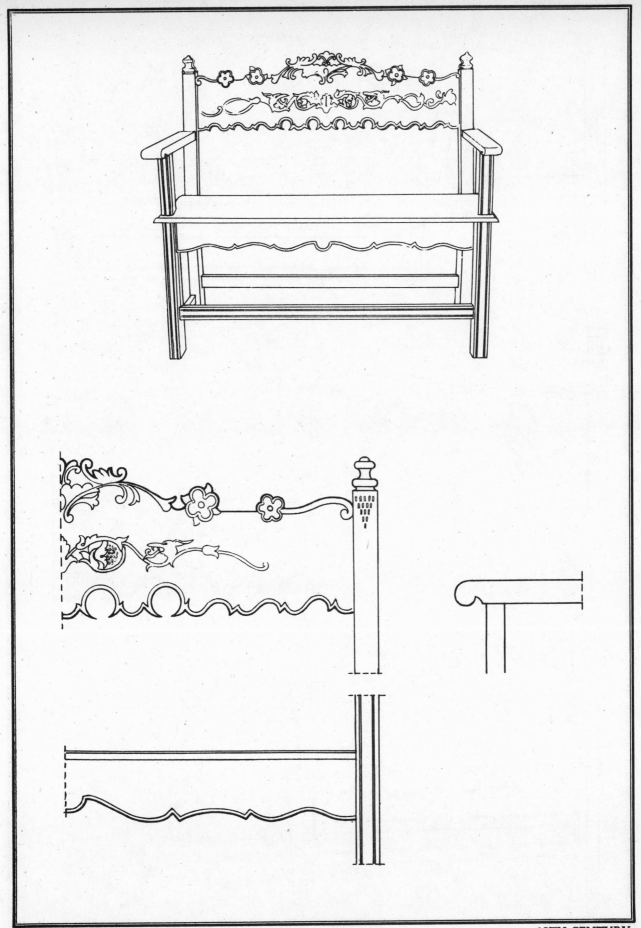

PLATE 261
Folk-style bench with carved back.

*Romantic Museum, Madrid*

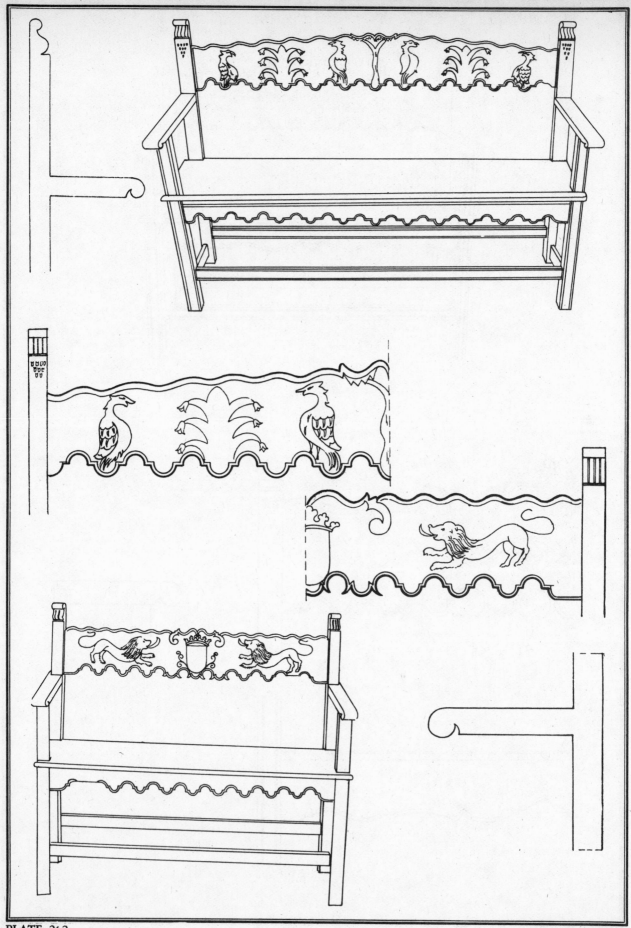

**PLATE 262**
Folk-style benches with carved backs.

*Romantic Museum, Madrid*

266

**PLATE 263**
Two sofas of baroque design.

*Parador of San Francisco, Granada and Museum of Painting, Seville*

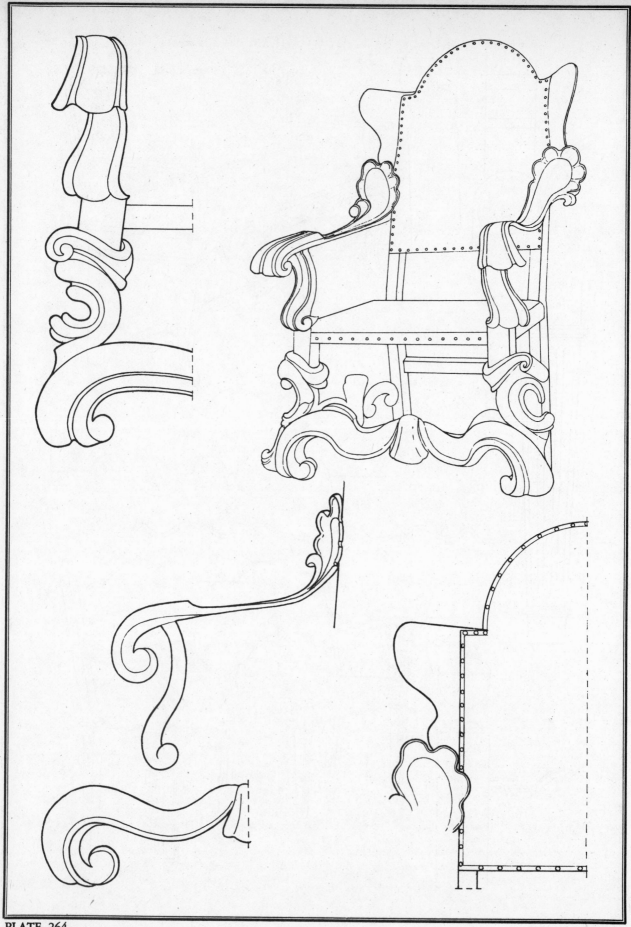

PLATE 264
Baroque armchair of Padre Alvarez de Sotomayor.

*Private collection*

**PLATE 265**
Folk-style bench.

*Municipal Museum, Madrid*

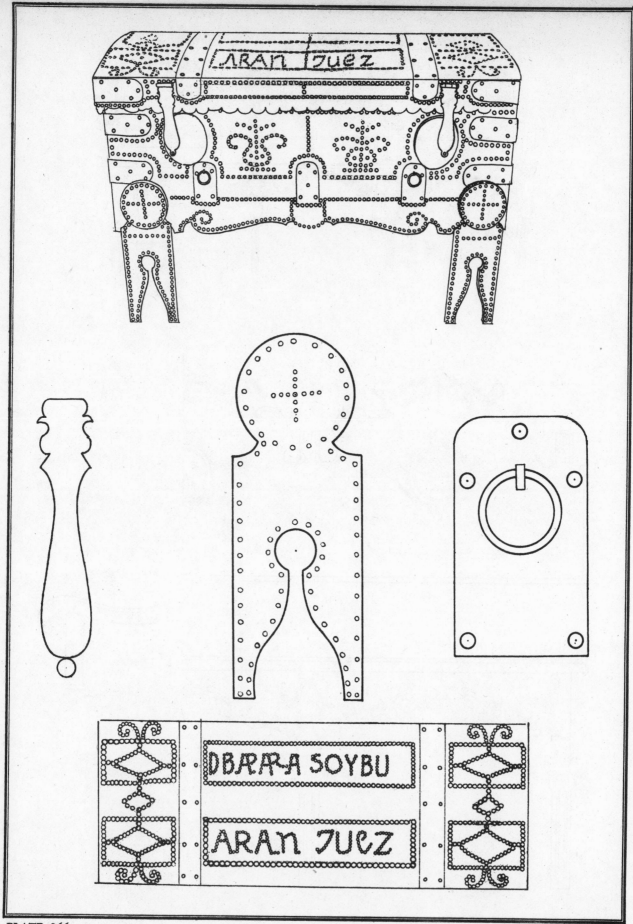

**PLATE 266**
Large leather chest with decorative nails.

18TH CENTURY

*Museum of Decorative Arts, Madrid*

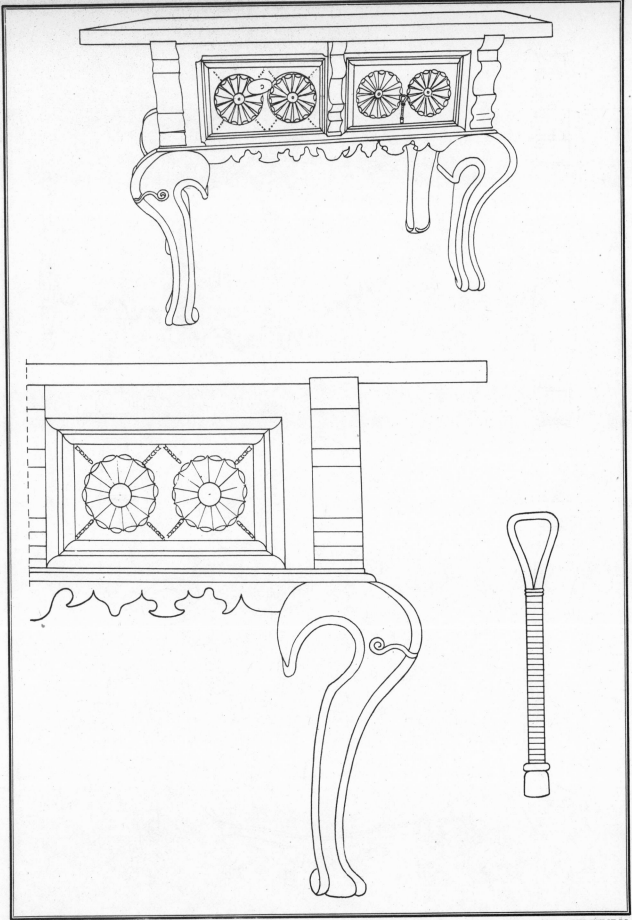

PLATE 267
Folk-style table.

*Museum of Decorative Arts, Madrid*

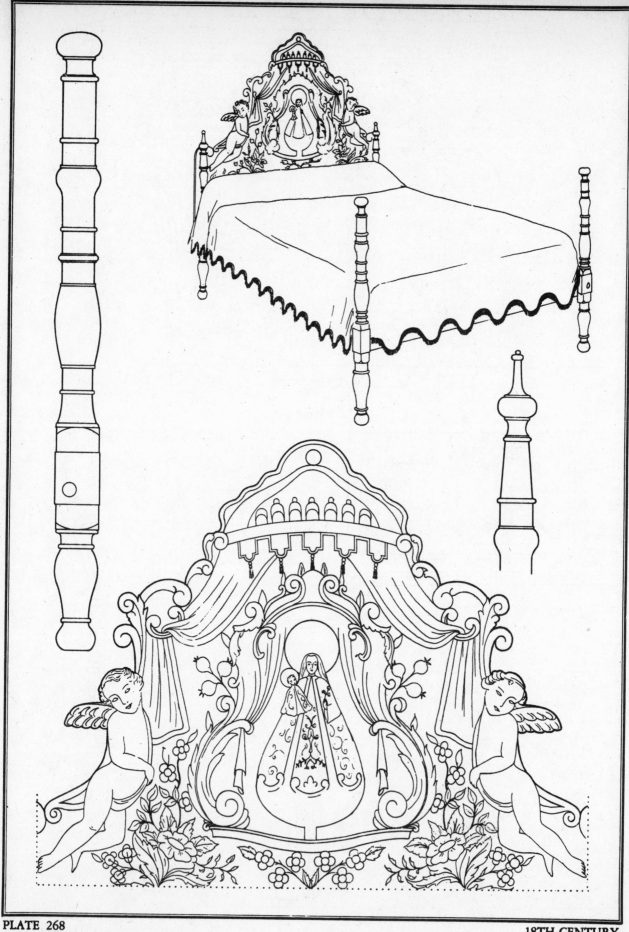

**PLATE 268**
Catalonian bed with painted headboard.

**PLATE 269**
Catalonian baroque-style bed.

PLATE 270
Braziers.

18TH CENTURY

274

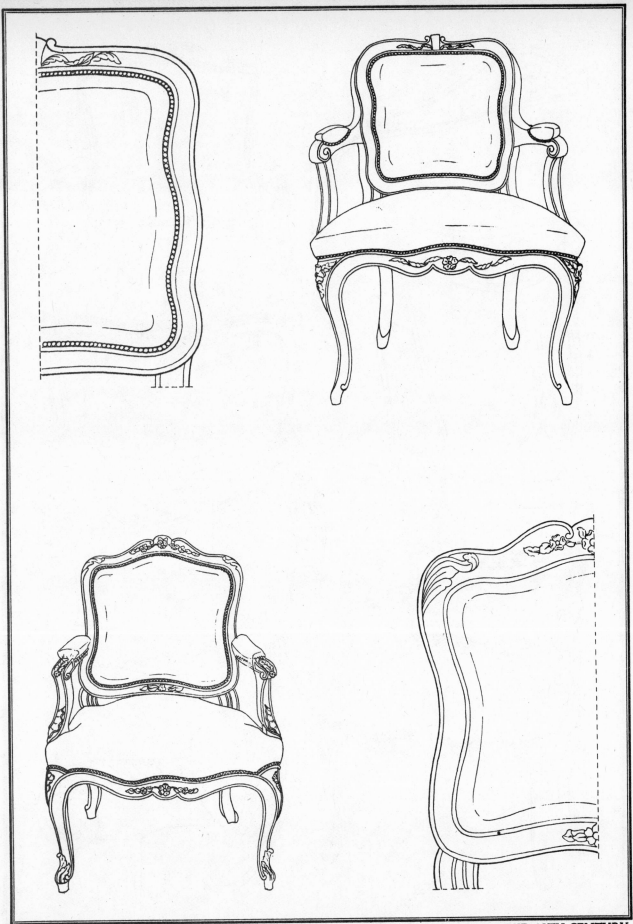

PLATE 271
Louis XV armchairs.

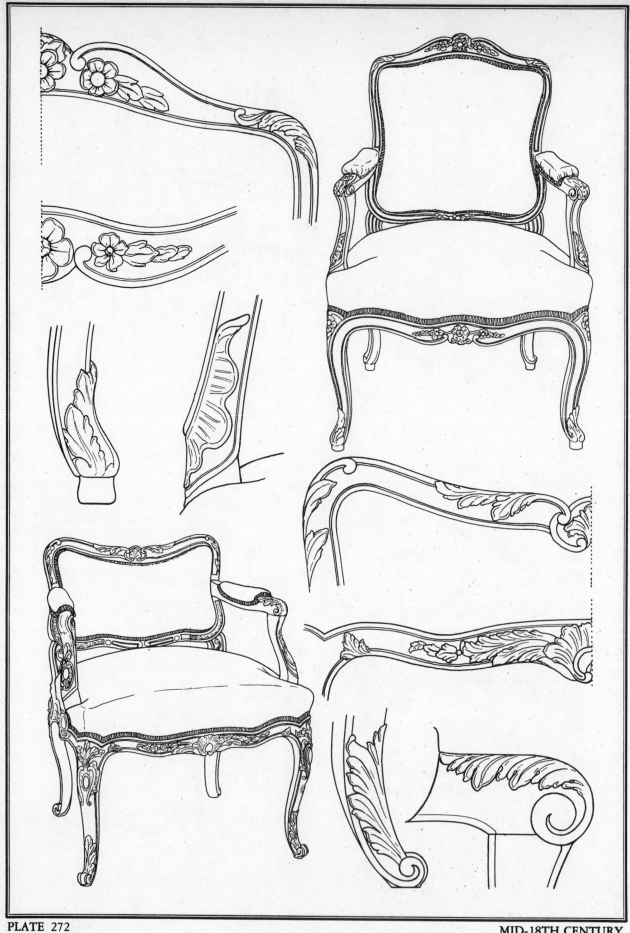

PLATE 272
Louis XV armchairs.

**MID-18TH CENTURY**

*Royal Palace, Madrid*

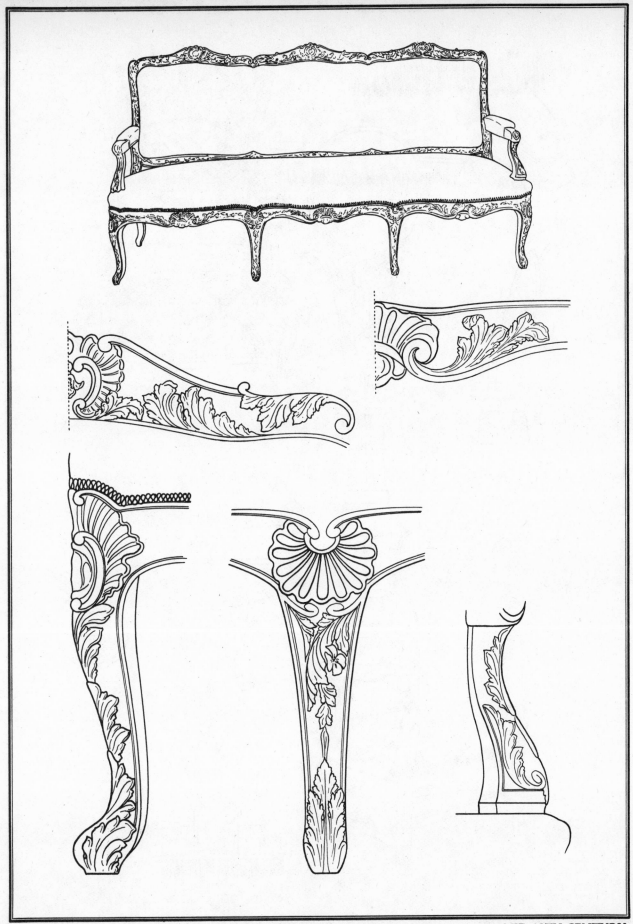

**PLATE 273**
Louis XV sofa.

*Royal Palace, Madrid*

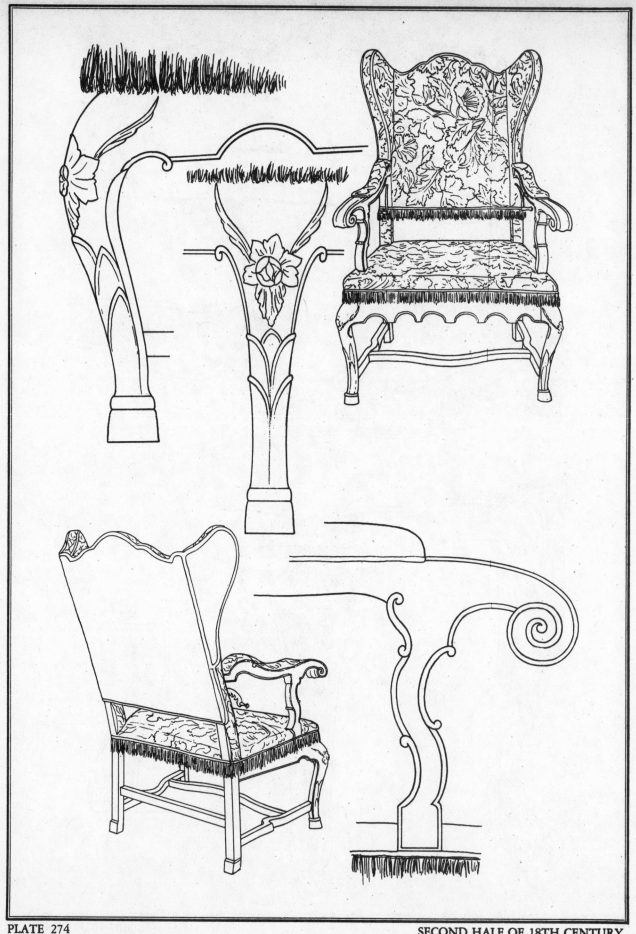

PLATE 274
Winged armchair, "Voltaire" style.

SECOND HALF OF 18TH CENTURY

PLATE 275 FIRST HALF OF 18TH CENTURY
Baroque armchair and footstool, to hold a statue of the Virgin Mary. Louis XV armchair.

*Museum of Decorative Arts, Madrid*

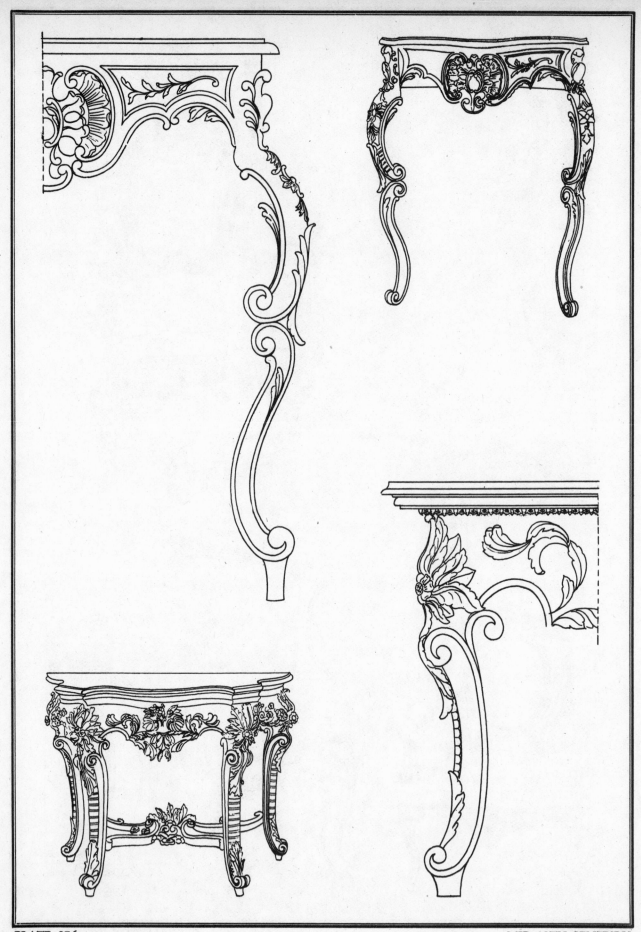

**PLATE 277**
Baroque consoles inspired by the lines of the Louis XV style.

*Municipal Museum, Madrid*

**PLATE 278**
Baroque consoles, along the lines of the Louis XV style.

*Municipal Museum, Madrid*

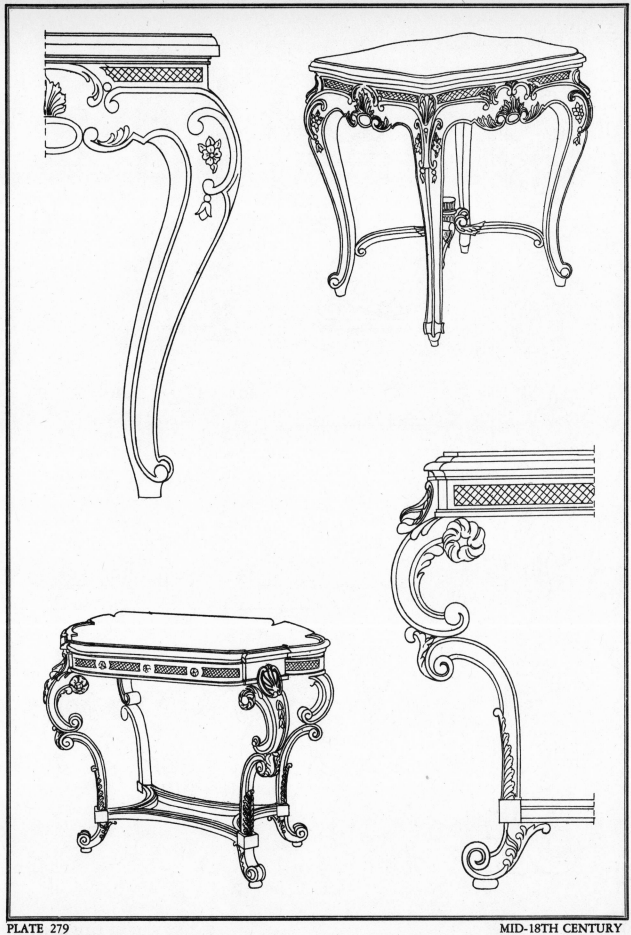

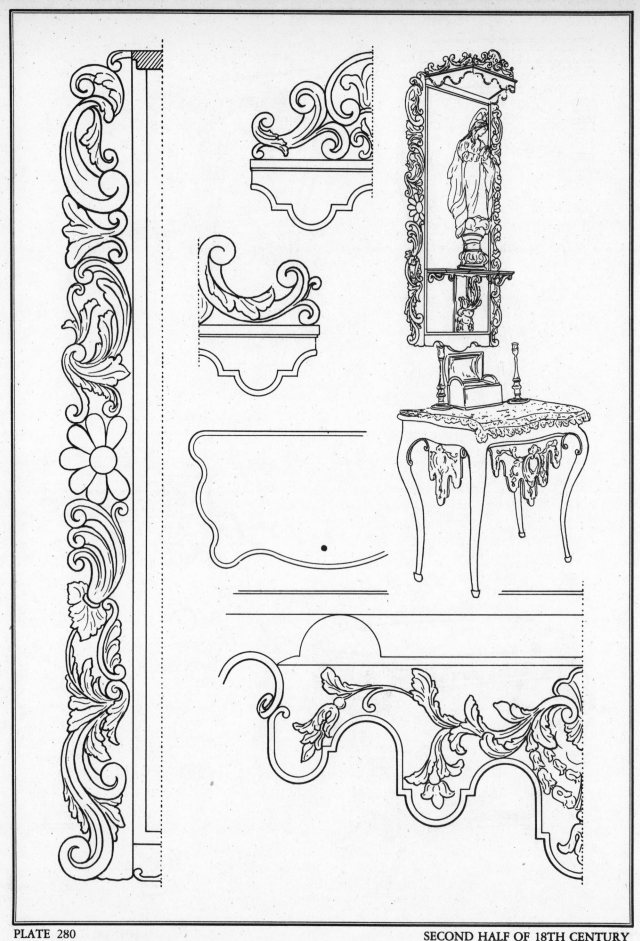

PLATE 280
Small console, shelf and canopy decorated with baroque carvings.

SECOND HALF OF 18TH CENTURY

PLATE 281
Small console and mirror decorated with baroque carvings.

**PLATE 282**
Mirror framed with Central European style of baroque carvings.

FIRST HALF OF 18TH CENTURY

*Museum of Painting, Seville*

**PLATE 283**
Frame decorated with Central European style of baroque carvings.

FIRST HALF OF 18TH CENTURY

*Museum of Decorative Arts, Madrid*

PLATE 284
Frame decorated with Central European style of baroque carvings.

FIRST HALF OF 18TH CENTURY

*Museum of Decorative Arts, Madrid*

**PLATE 285**
Frame decorated with baroque carvings.

**PLATE 286**
Sconces with mirrors decorated with baroque carvings, inspired by the French "rococo."

**MID-18TH CENTURY**

*Museum of Decorative Arts, Madrid*

PLATE 287
Spanish sconce with mirror inspired by French "rococo."

*Museum of Decorative Arts, Madrid*

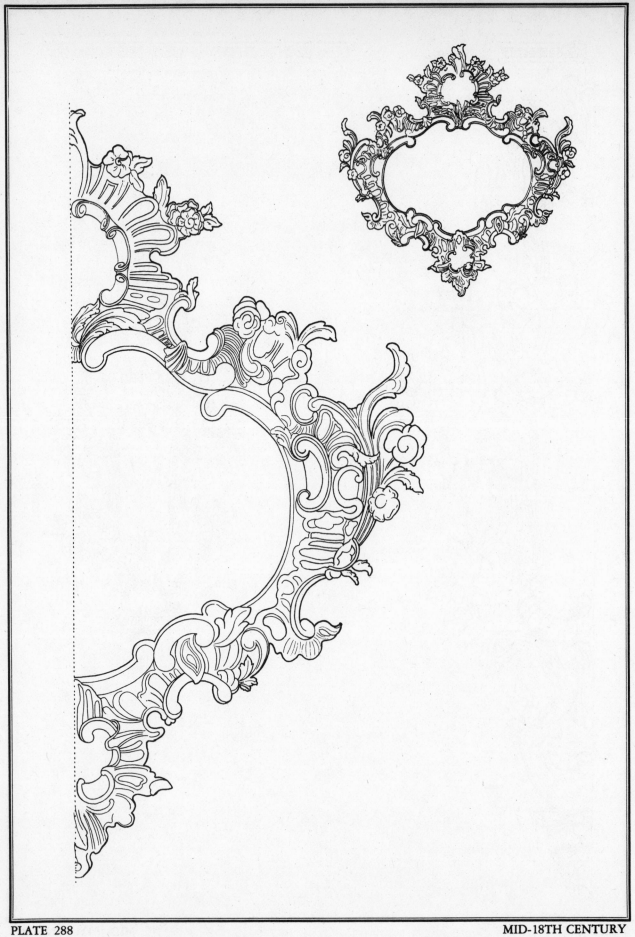

PLATE 289
Wardrobe decorated with baroque motifs.

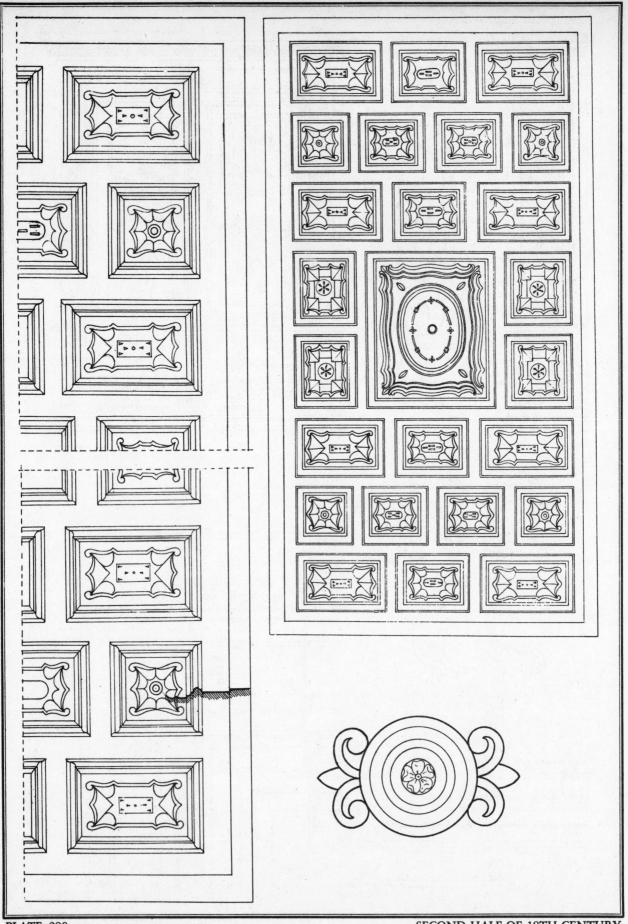

**PLATE 290**
Panelled door decorated with baroque motifs of Chinese origin.

SECOND HALF OF 18TH CENTURY

*Private collection*

PLATE 291
Door decorated with "rococo" carvings.

*Museum of Decorative Arts, Madrid*

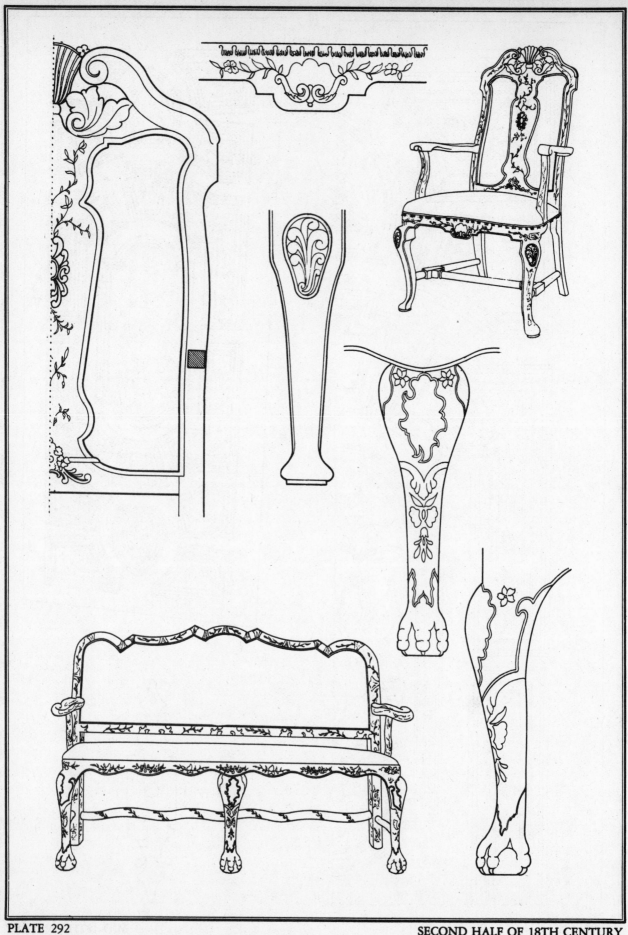

PLATE 292

SECOND HALF OF 18TH CENTURY

Spanish armchair and sofa; inspired by the Queen Anne style.

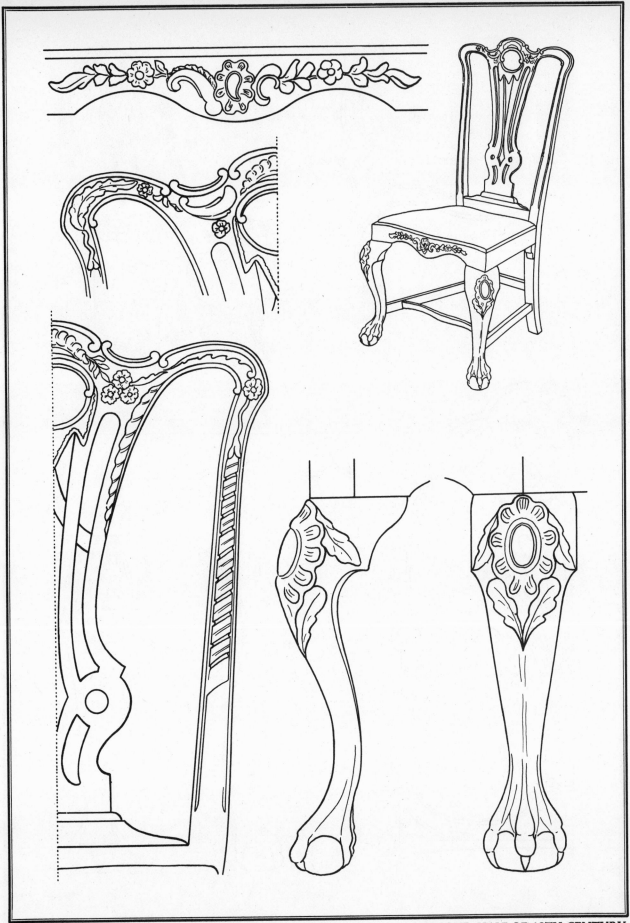

**PLATE 293**

SECOND HALF OF 18TH CENTURY

Spanish chair inspired by the Queen Anne style.

PLATE 294
Spanish Queen Anne chair.

**PLATE 295**
Chair decorated with baroque carvings, Spanish adaption of Queen Anne style.

*National Archeological Museum, Madrid*

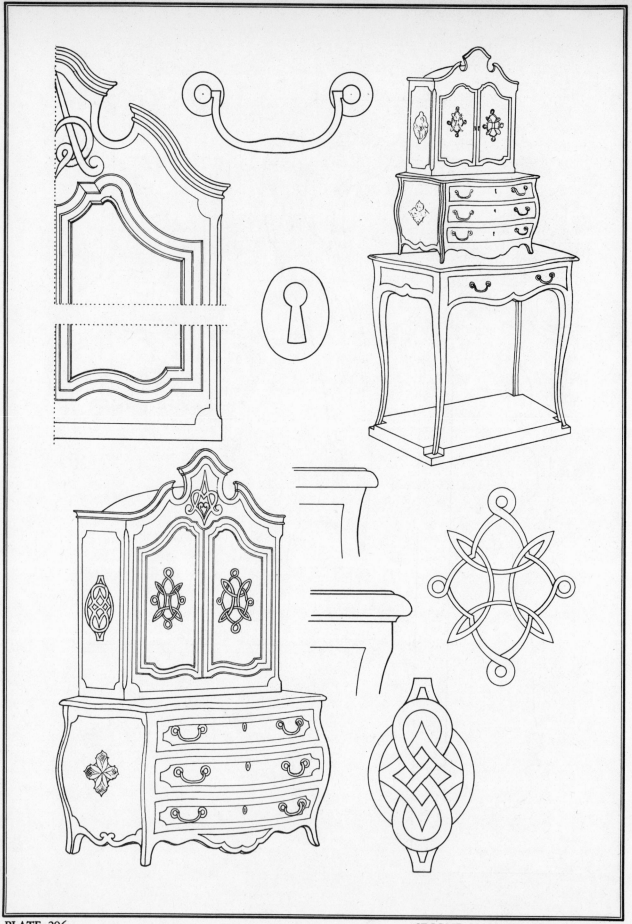

**PLATE 296**
Console table supporting a miniature English-style commode-wardrobe.

SECOND HALF OF 18TH CENTURY

*Valencia Don Juan Institute, Madrid*

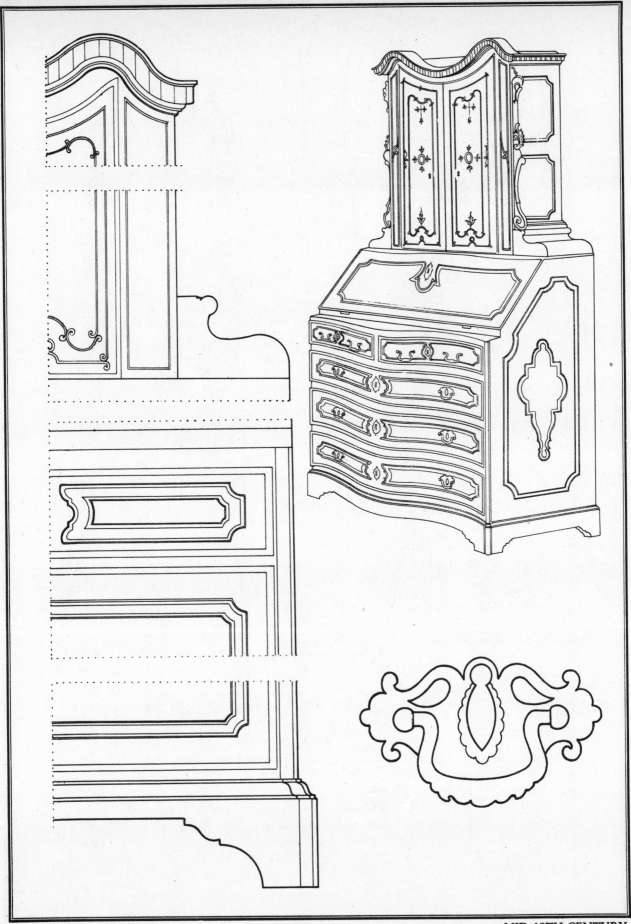

**PLATE 297**
English-style commode-wardrobe.

*Municipal Museum, Madrid*

PLATE 298
Small English-style console table. Mirror framed with baroque carving.

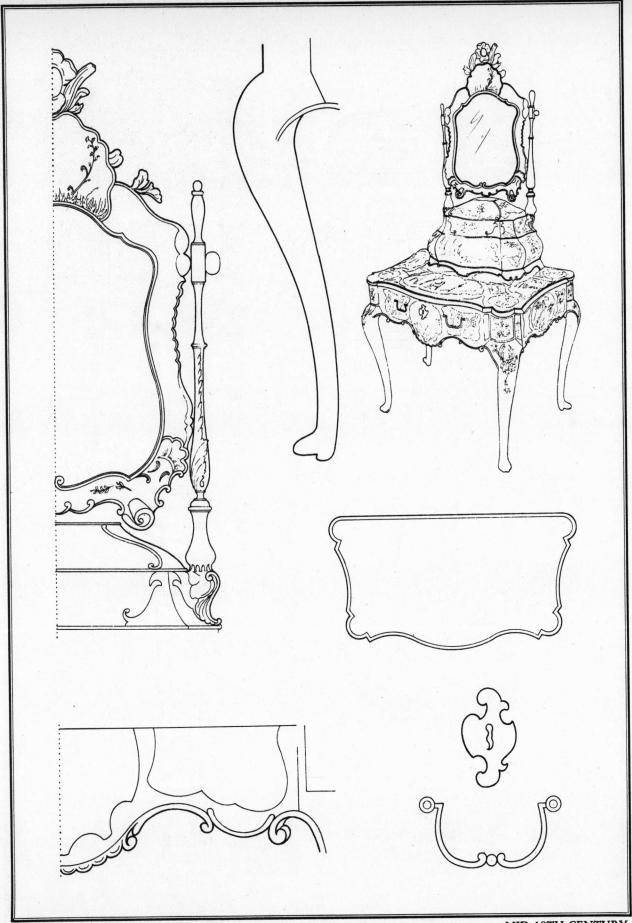

PLATE 299
Dressing table inspired by Queen Anne style.

MID-18TH CENTURY

*Conde del Valle de Marles collection, Barcelona*

303

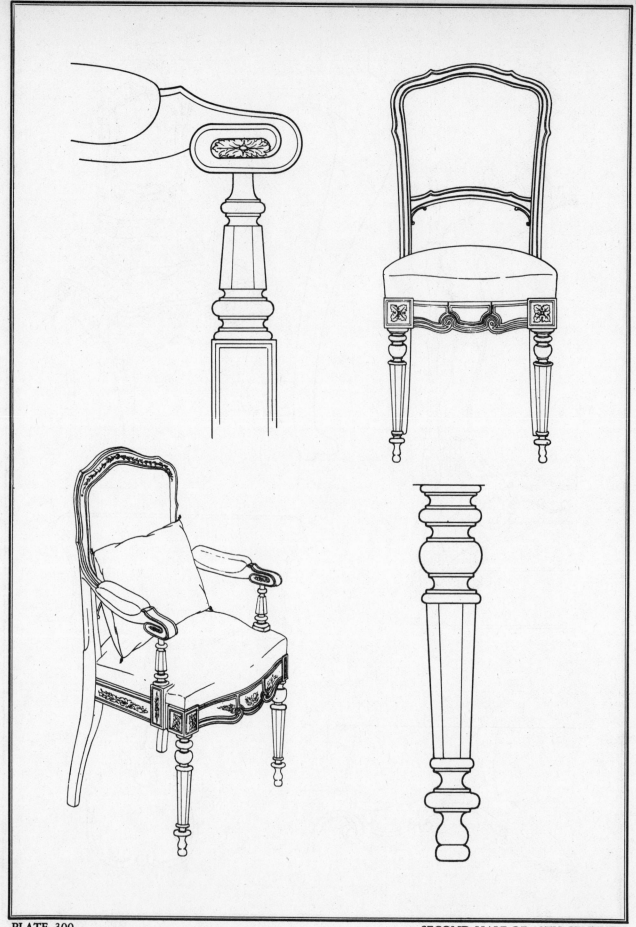

**PLATE 300**
Spanish chair and armchair inspired by Louis XVI style.

SECOND HALF OF 18TH CENTURY

*Palace of El Infante Don Alonso de Orleans, Sanlucar de Barrameda*

304

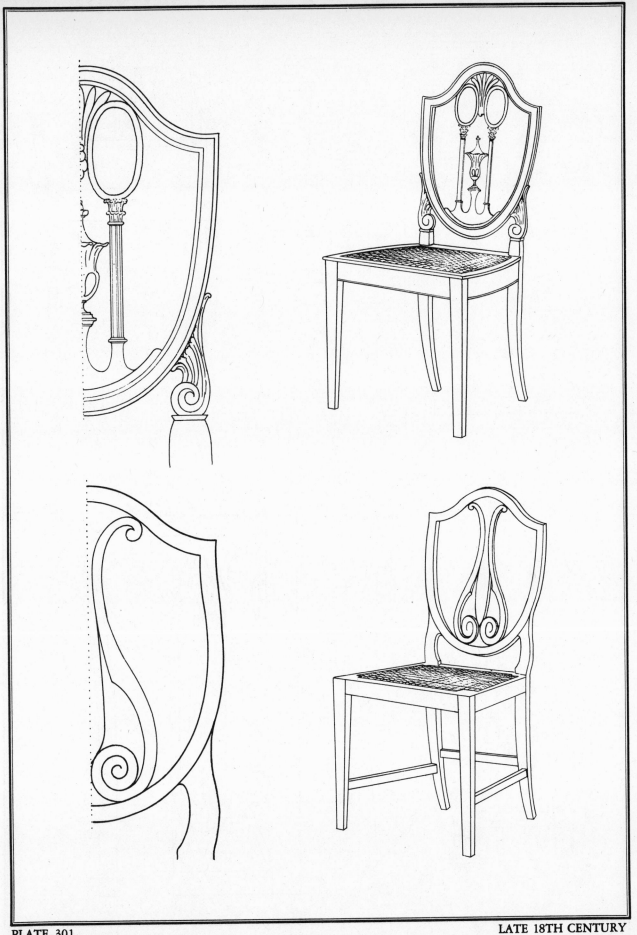

PLATE 301
Charles IV cane chairs.

LATE 18TH CENTURY

*Pontevedra Museum and Casa Cabanyes, Argentona*

PLATE 302
Charles IV armchairs.

*Museum of Decorative Arts and Municipal Museum, Madrid*

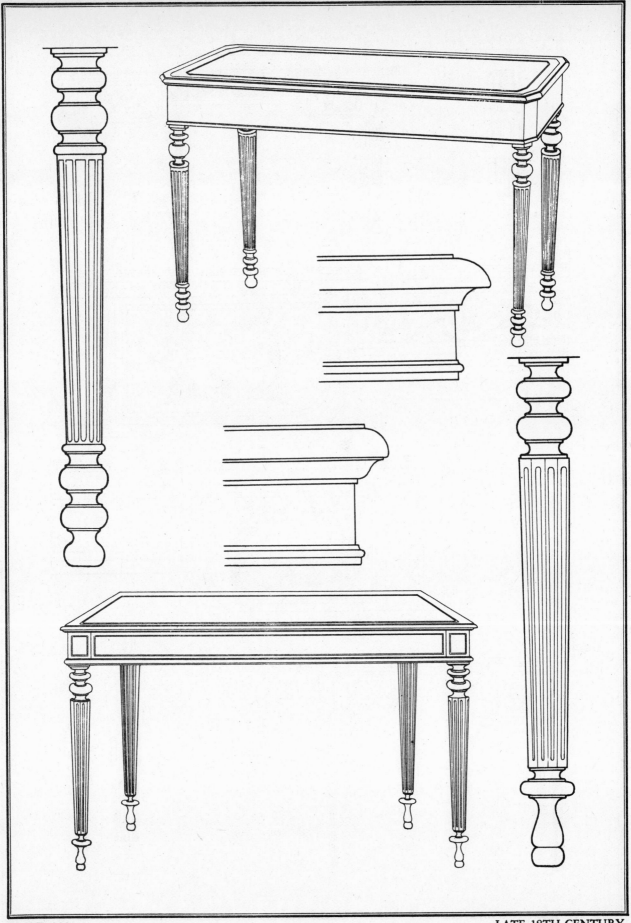

PLATE 304
Louis XVI writing tables, decorated with marquetry.

LATE 18TH CENTURY

*Museum of Decorative Arts, Madrid*

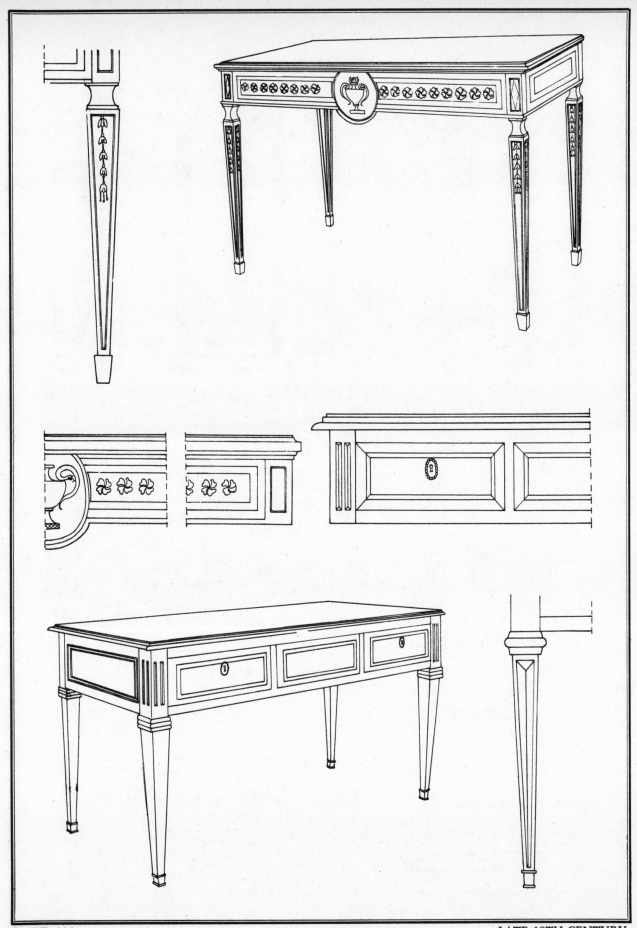

PLATE 305
Louis XVI tables with carved decorations.

LATE 18TH CENTURY

*Municipal Museum, Madrid*

PLATE 306
Charles IV secretary inspired by the English Sheraton style.

**PLATE 307**

SECOND HALF OF 18TH CENTURY

Catalonian bed, reminiscent of rococo and Louis XVI styles.

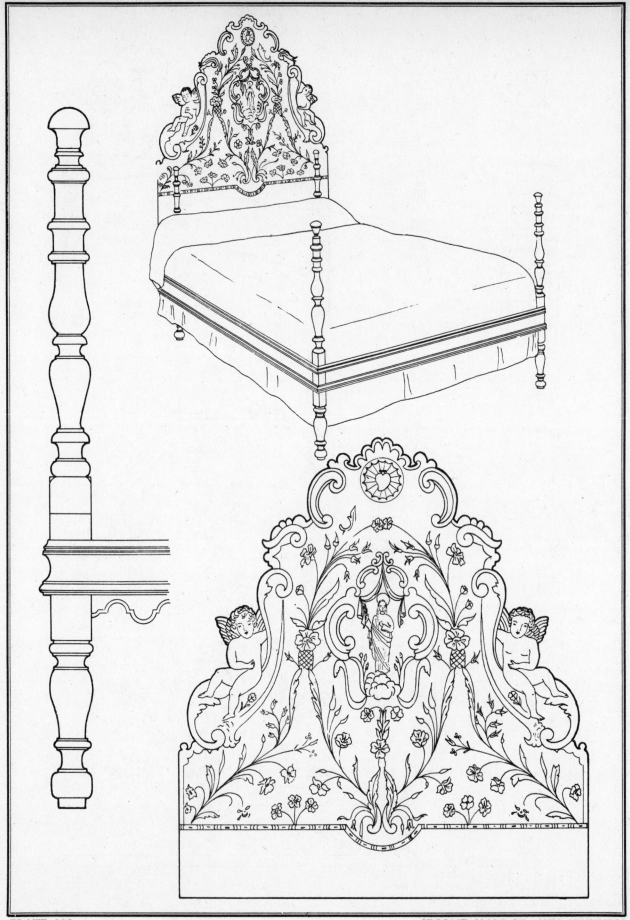

PLATE 308
Catalonian bed, reminiscent of rococo and Louis XVI styles.

SECOND HALF OF 18TH CENTURY

*Cunill collection*

**PLATE 309**
Catalonian bed, reminiscent of rococo and Louis XVI styles.

*Gallifa collection*

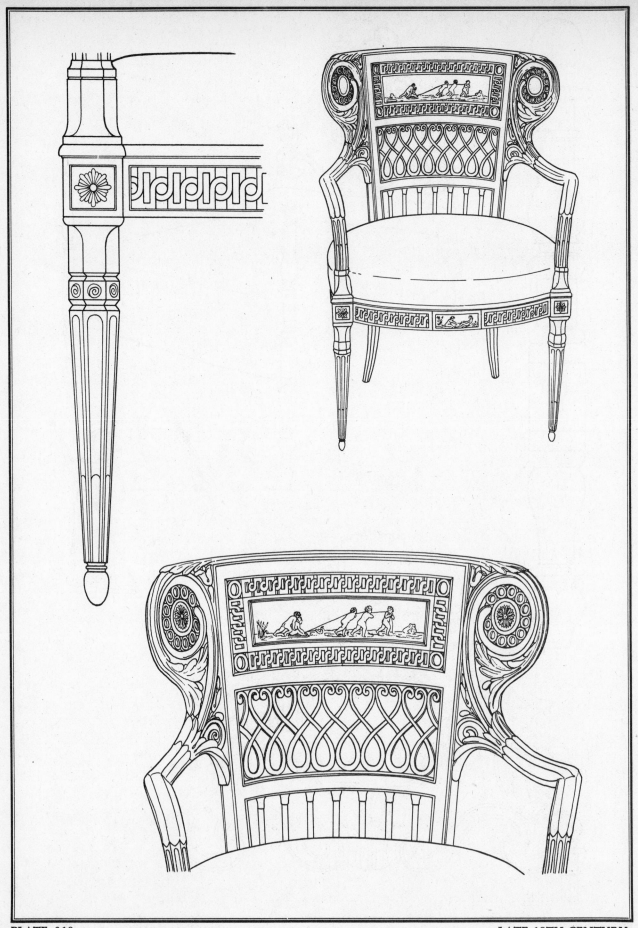

PLATE 310
Charles IV armchair decorated with wood marquetry.

LATE 18TH CENTURY

*Royal Palace, Madrid*

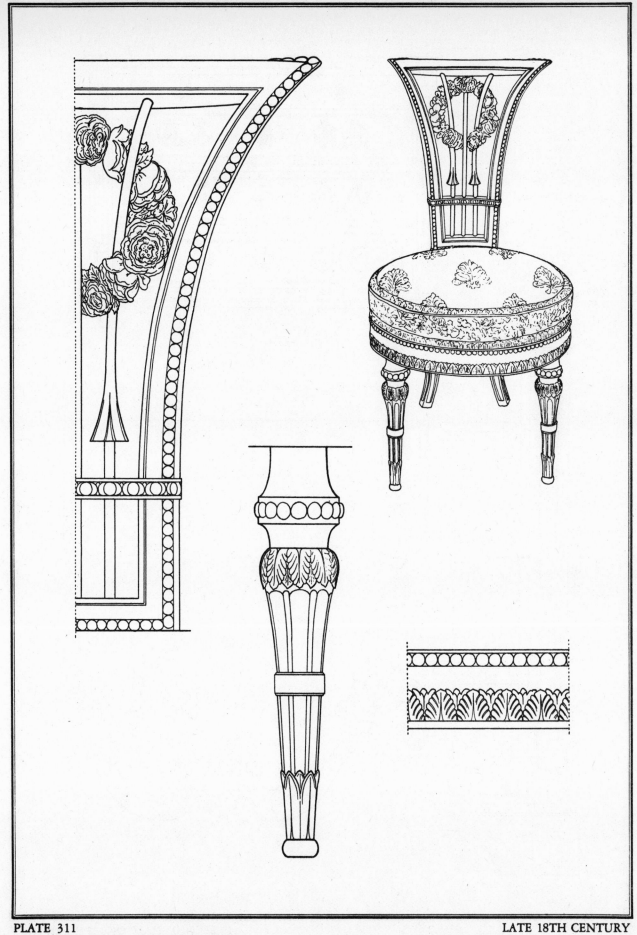

**PLATE 311**
Charles IV chair trimmed with brushed silk.

*Royal Palace, Madrid*

**PLATE 312**
Commode with classical lines, decorated with rococo drawer pulls.

SECOND HALF OF 18TH CENTURY

*Gallifa Saborit collection*

**PLATE 313**
Charles IV bed.

LATE 18TH CENTURY

*Gallifa Saborit collection*

PLATE 314
Louis XV–Louis XVI mirror frame.

*Gallifa Saborit collection*

**PLATE 315**
Louis XVI mirror frames.

*Romantic Museum and Museum of Decorative Arts, Madrid*

PLATE 316
Catalonian bed, reminiscent of rococo and Louis XVI styles.

SECOND HALF OF 18TH CENTURY

*Anglada Coll collection*

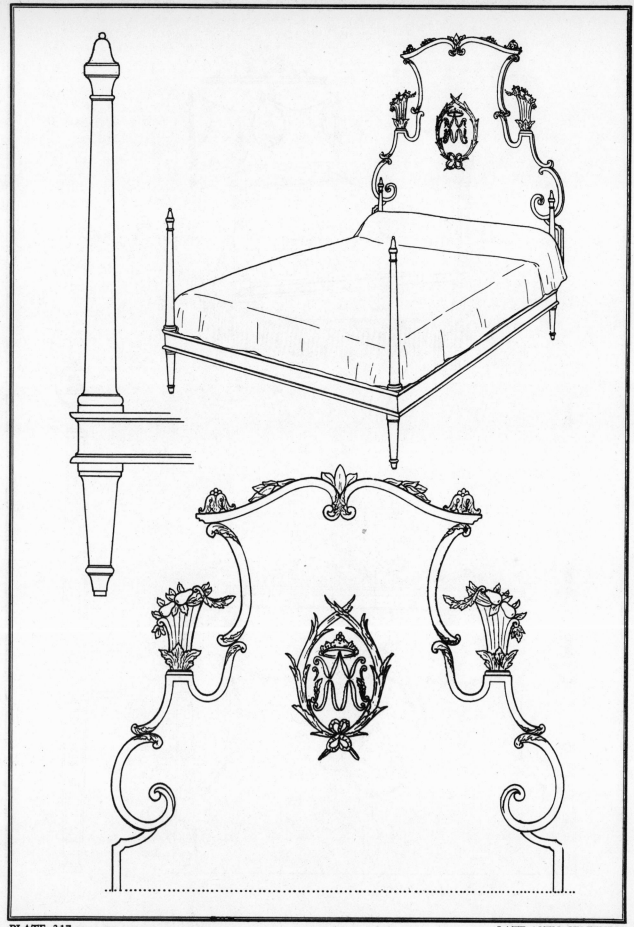

**PLATE 317**
Catalonian bed, inspired by Louis XVI style.

*Babra Arroyos collection*

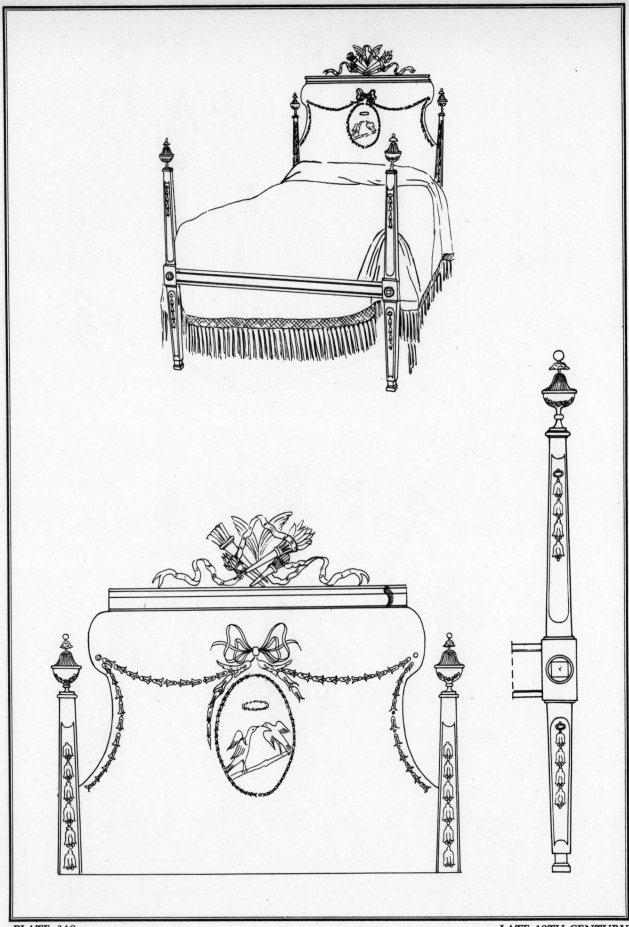

PLATE 318
Charles IV bed.

LATE 18TH CENTURY

*Romantic Museum, Madrid*

**PLATE 319**
Charles IV bed.

*Gallifa collection*

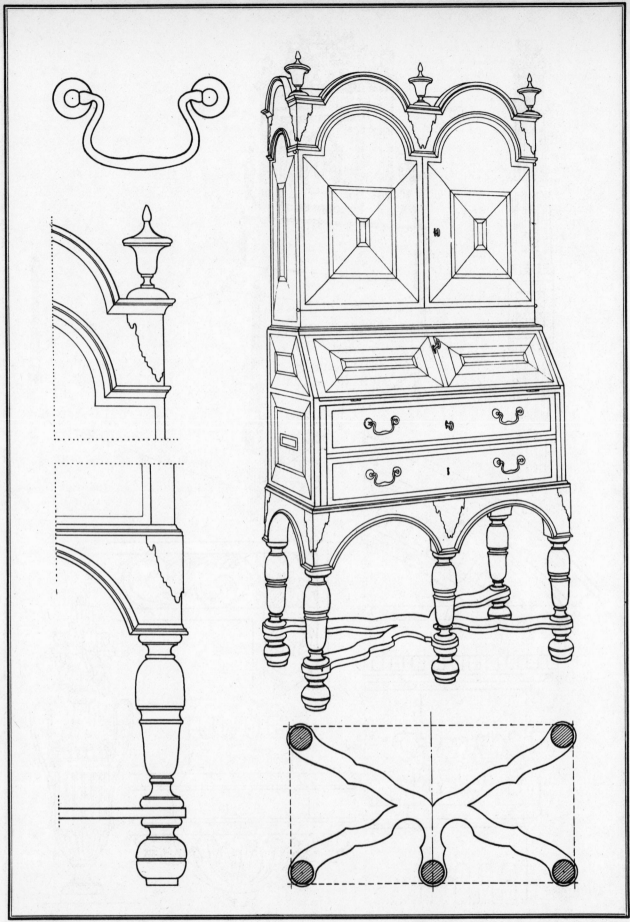

**PLATE 320**
Spanish desk, reminiscent of Louis XVI style.

LATE 18TH OR EARLY 19TH CENTURY

**PLATE 321**
Charles IV chair and small cane sofa.

LATE 18TH OR EARLY 19TH CENTURY

*Patrimonio Nacional*

**PLATE 323**
Charles IV commode-dressing table.

*Vda. Gallifa collection*

**PLATE 324**
Charles IV cradle with turned balusters.

LATE 18TH OR EARLY 19TH CENTURY

*Mrs. Anton Matheus collection*

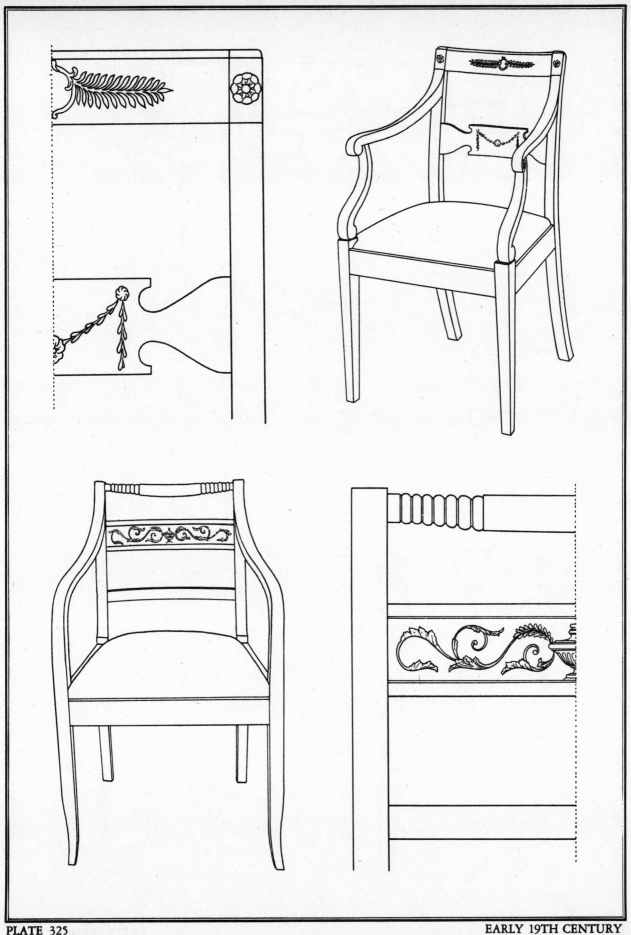

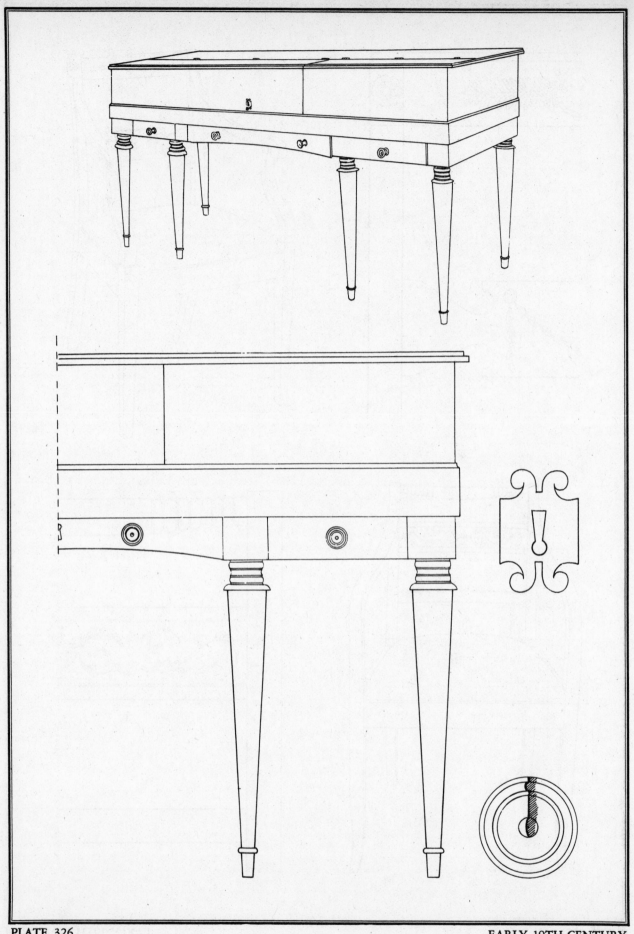

**PLATE 326**
Louis XVI pianoforte.

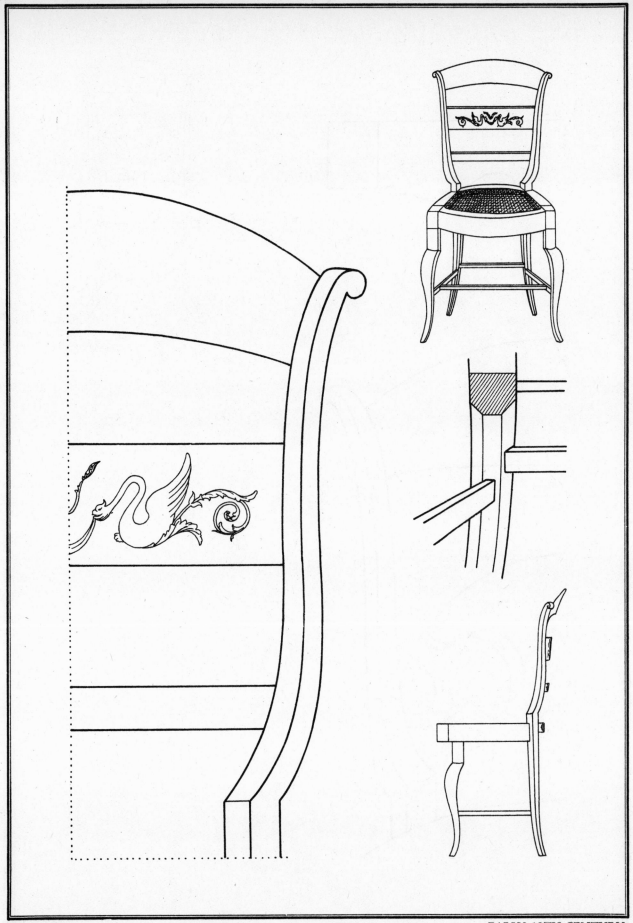

**PLATE 327**
Spanish cane chair with Empire-style decorative motifs.

EARLY 19TH CENTURY

*Antonio Moragas Gallisa collection*

331

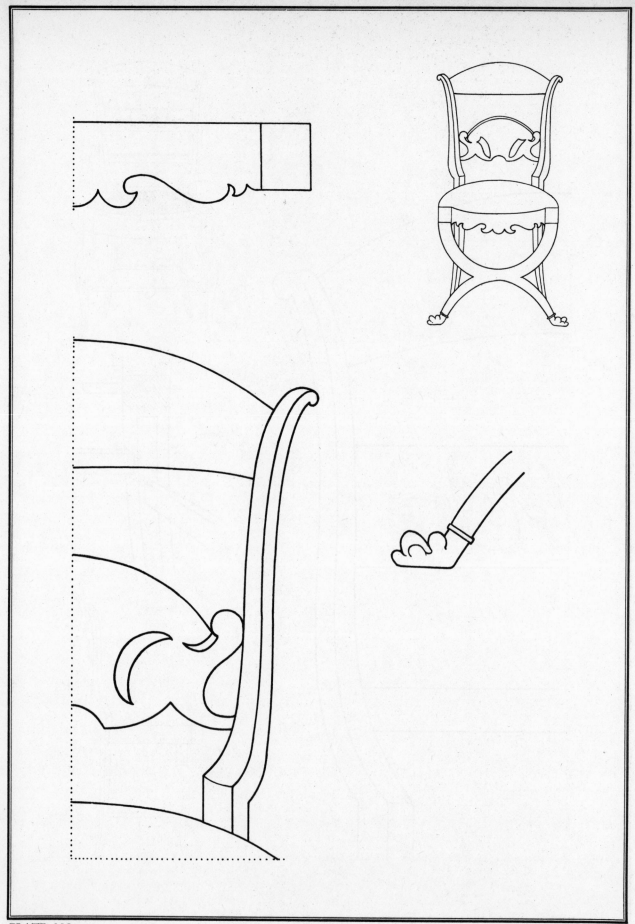

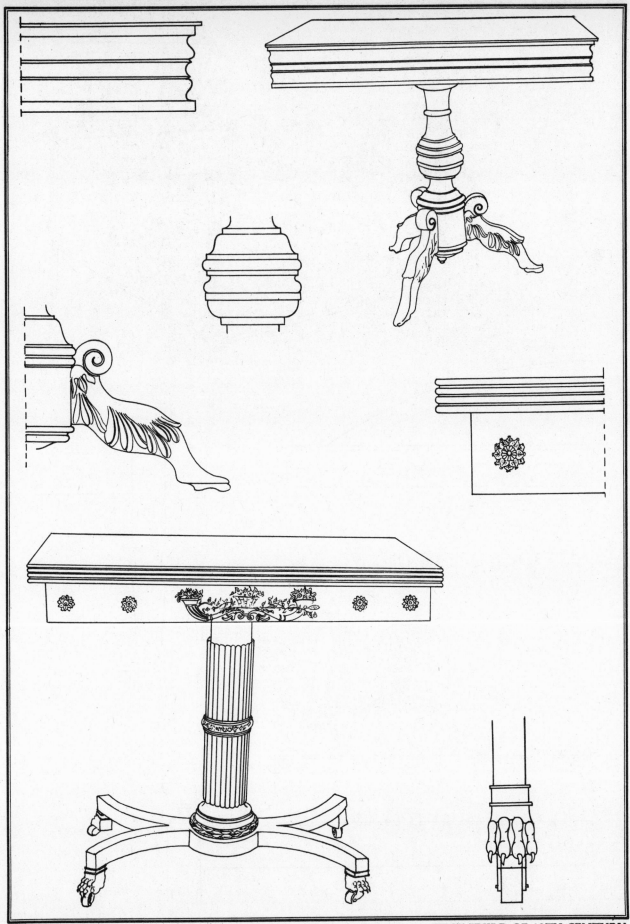

PLATE 329
FIRST THIRD OF 19TH CENTURY

Pedestal tables. The upper one is Louis Philippe style. The lower one is Empire style.

*Romantic Museum and Museum of Decorative Arts, Madrid*

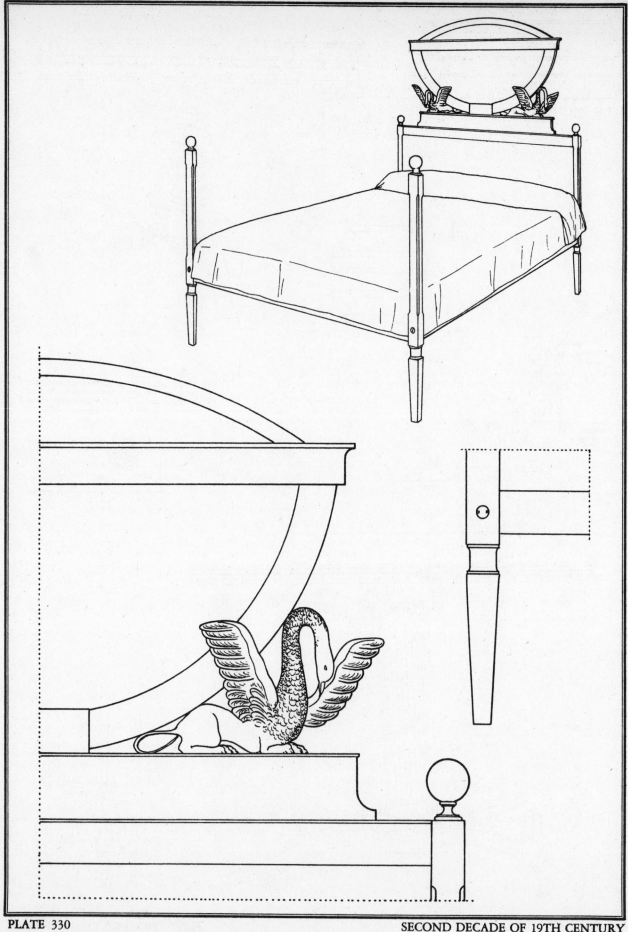

**PLATE 330**
Catalonian bed with decorative motifs inspired by Empire style.

SECOND DECADE OF 19TH CENTURY

*Antonio Moragas Gallisa collection*

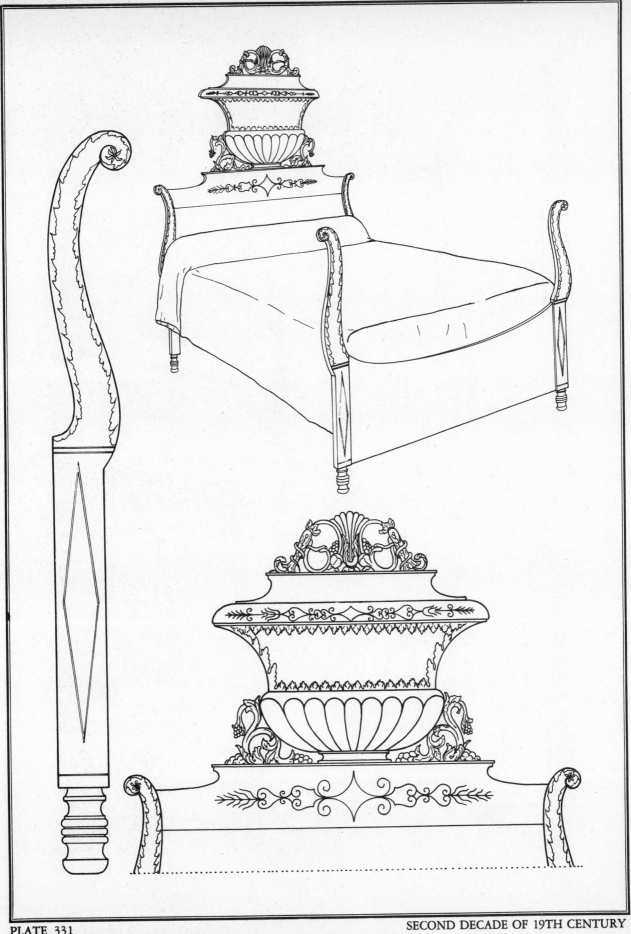

PLATE 331
Catalonian bed with decorative elements taken from Empire style.

SECOND DECADE OF 19TH CENTURY

*Antonio Moragas Gallisa collection*

**PLATE 332**
Catalonian bed with decorative marquetry inspired by Empire style.

*Louis Armengou Torra collection*

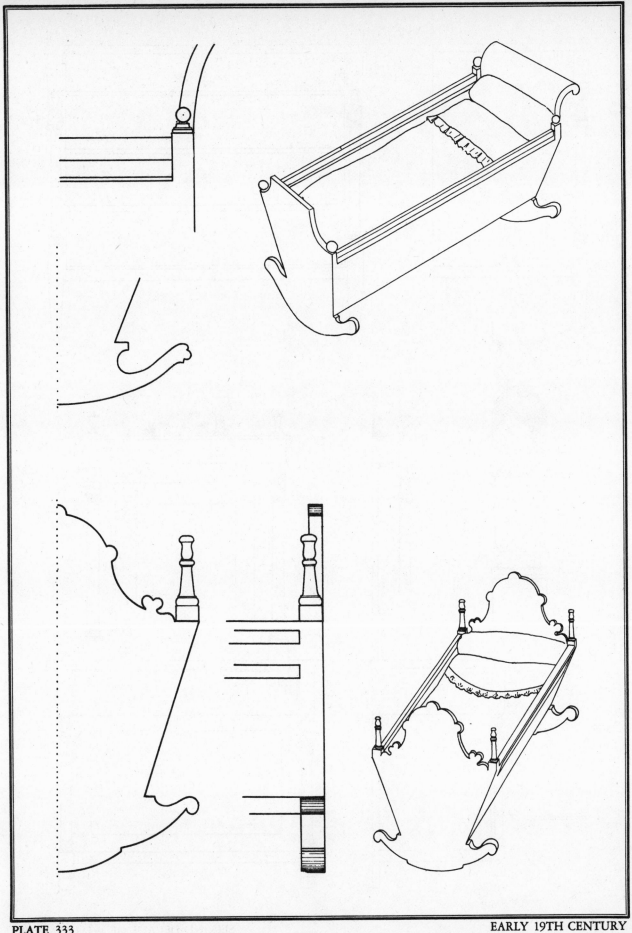

PLATE 333
Catalonian cradles.

EARLY 19TH CENTURY

*Manuel Gallifa Greuzner collection*

**PLATE 334**

Mahogany Empire-style commode and dressing table with gilt carved decorations.

*Antonio Moragas Gallisa collection*

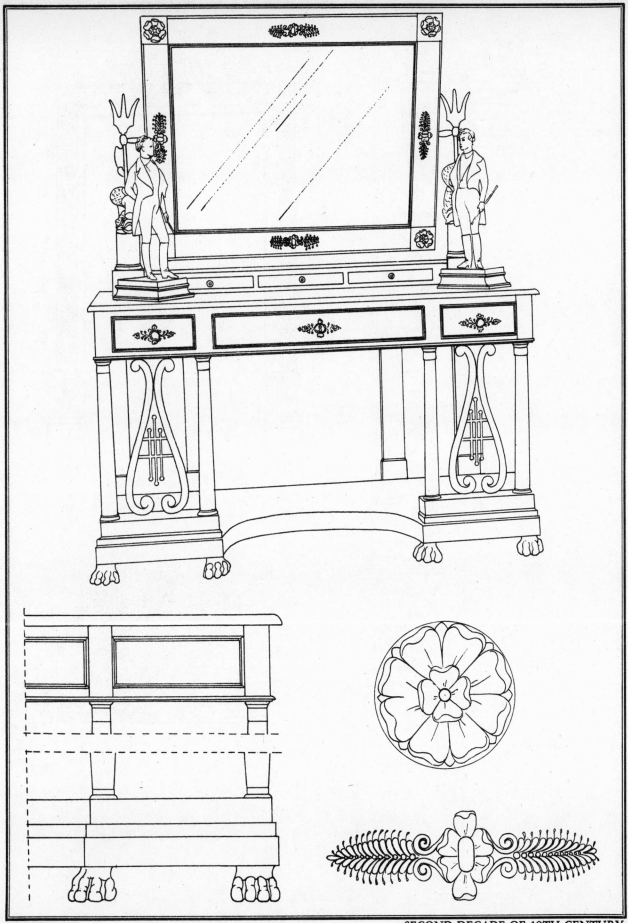

PLATE 335

Mahogany Empire-style dressing table with gilt metal decorations.

SECOND DECADE OF 19TH CENTURY

*Romantic Museum, Madrid*

PLATE 336
Door trimming with decorative motifs inspired by Empire style.

**EARLY 19TH CENTURY**

*Museum of Decorative Arts, Madrid*

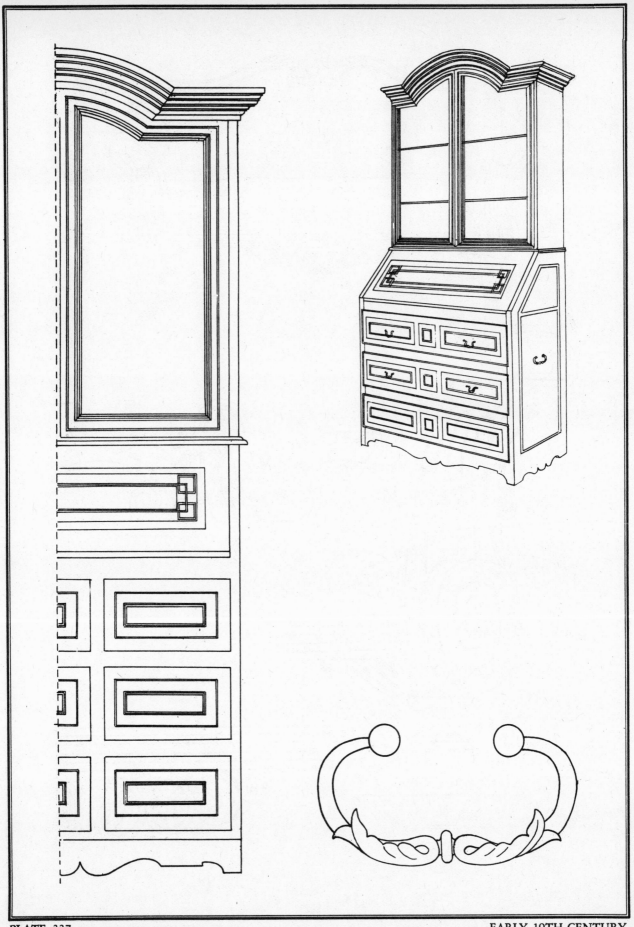

PLATE 337
English-style commode-bookcase.

*Romantic Museum, Madrid*

PLATE 338
Restoration-style (Ferdinand VII) sofa.

*Romantic Museum, Madrid*

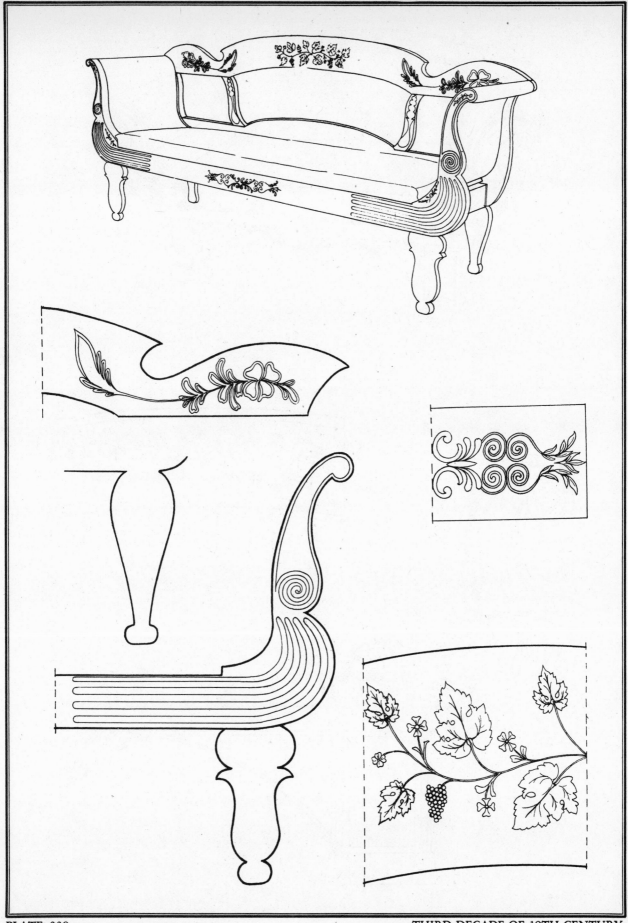

PLATE 339
Ferdinand VII sofa with decorative marquetry.

**THIRD DECADE OF 19TH CENTURY**

*Romantic Museum, Madrid*

PLATE 340
Ferdinand VII sofa with decorative carving and marquetry.

**THIRD DECADE OF 19TH CENTURY**

*Museum of Decorative Arts, Madrid*

**PLATE 341**
Ferdinand VII dressing table with decorative marquetry.

*Museum of Decorative Arts, Madrid*

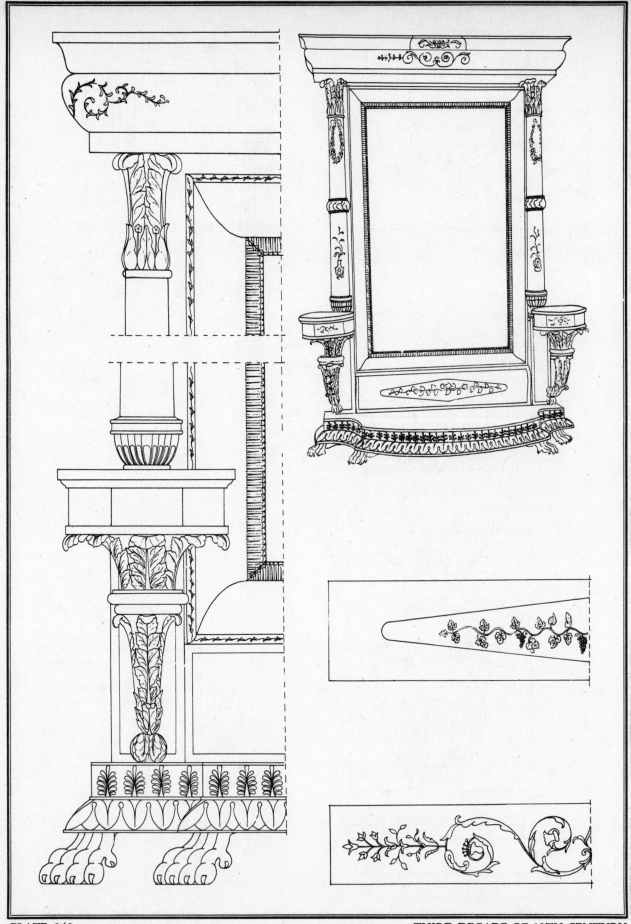

PLATE 342
THIRD DECADE OF 19TH CENTURY

Ferdinand VII dressing-table mirror, decorated with gilt carvings and marquetry.

*Museum of Decorative Arts, Madrid*

**PLATE 343**
Louis Philippe console table with turned decorations.

FOURTH DECADE OF 19TH CENTURY

*Romantic Museum, Madrid*

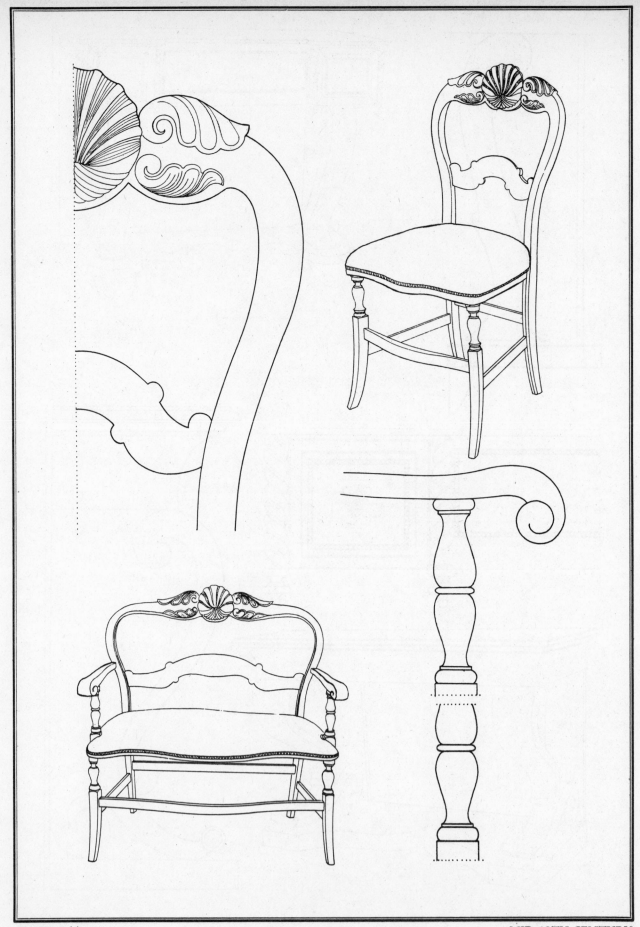

PLATE 344
Chair and sofa, Isabella style, reminiscent of Louis XV style.

MID-19TH CENTURY

*Romantic Museum, Madrid*

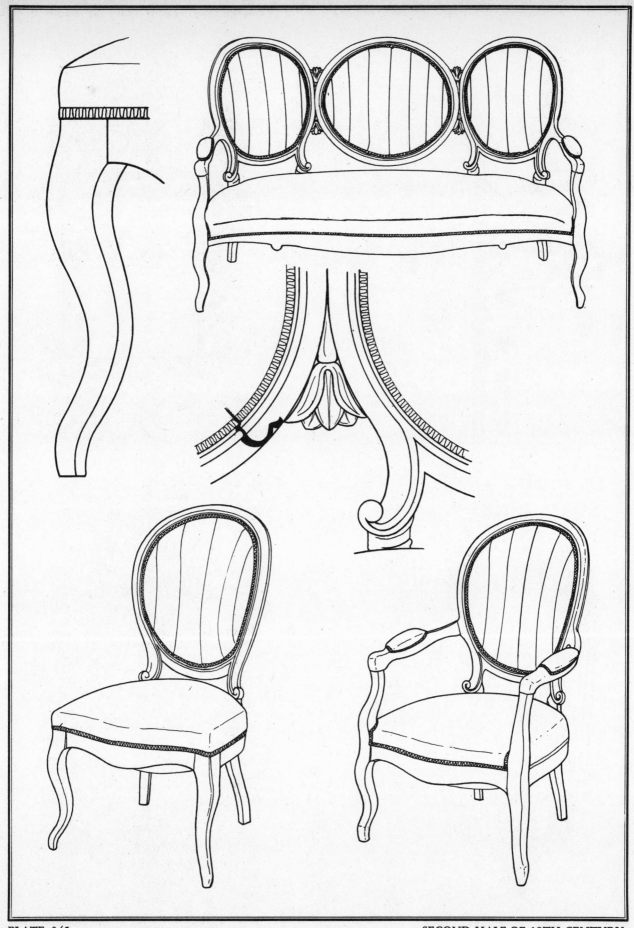

**PLATE 345**
Sofa, chair and armchair, Isabella style, reminiscent of Louis XVI style.

SECOND HALF OF 19TH CENTURY

*Romantic Museum, Madrid*

PLATE 346
Gilt carved frames inspired by 18th-century motifs.

*Museum of Decorative Arts, Madrid*

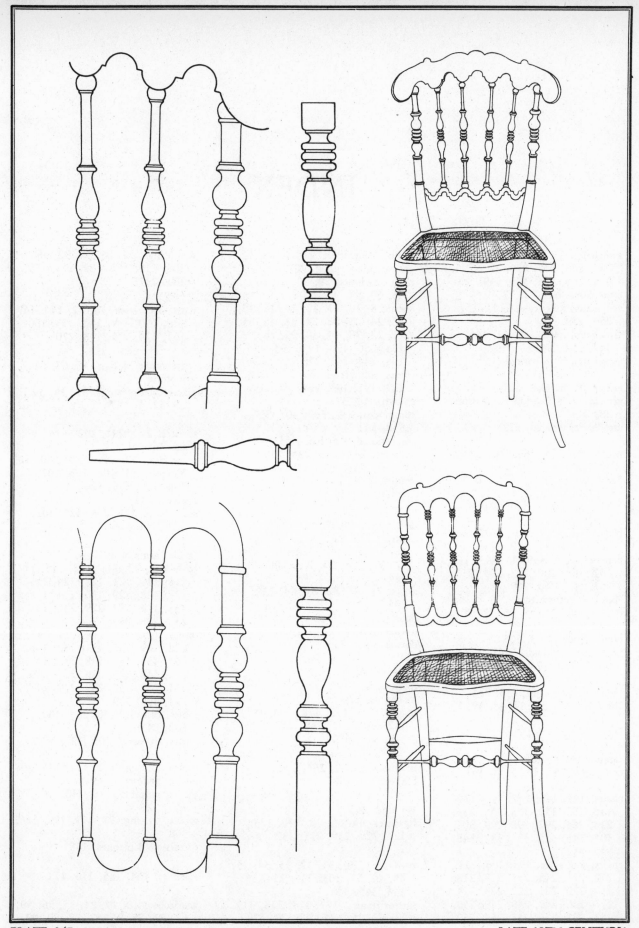

**PLATE 347**
Chairs from the time of Alfonso XII, inspired by French designs.

LATE 19TH CENTURY

*Palace of El Infante Don Alfonse de Orleans, Sanlucar de Barrameda*

# INDEX

# Volume Three
# Encyclopedia of English Period Furniture Designs

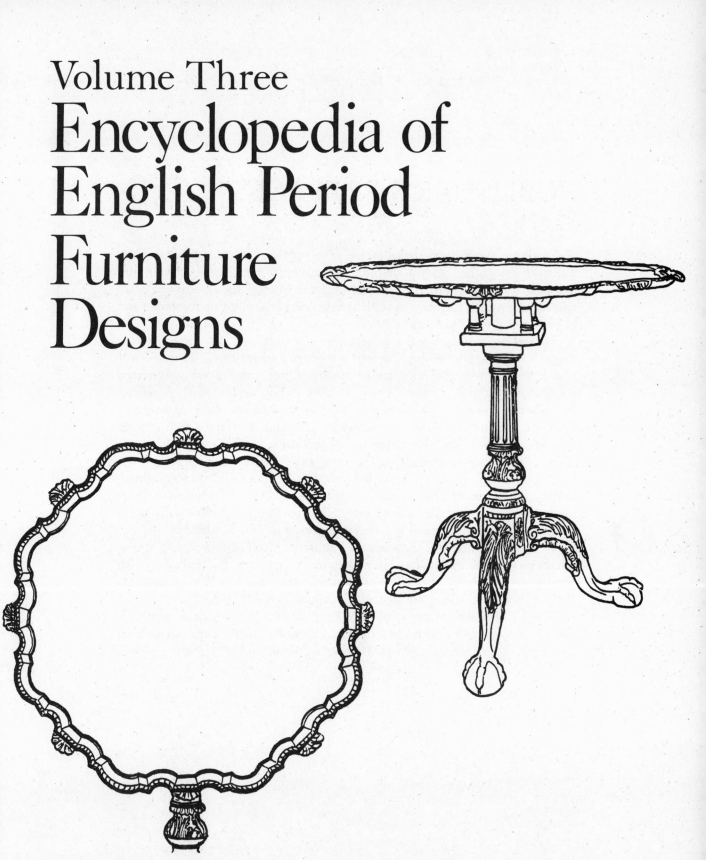

# PUBLISHER'S PREFACE

Given the extent of the British Empire, it was perhaps inevitable that English furniture design had such a far-reaching influence. But even if the Empire had never extended beyond the shores of Great Britain, the beauty and practicality of English furniture would have assured it a place in museums and homes throughout the world.

Historians, furniture makers, restorers, decorators, set designers and students—all those who wish to identify a piece or authenticate a design—will find in the following pages a pictorial history of English furniture design from the Tudors to the Victorians. There is also a section dealing with American Colonial and—a rarity in books published in the English-speaking world—a section on English Minorcan furniture. Although England's control over Minorca was brief and intermittent, its influence in the area of furniture design was as extensive and long-lasting as in North America.

English furniture design "travelled well" largely because of its extraordinary adaptability—frequently to environments totally different from those for which it was originally intended. The furniture is as comfortable to live with in the warm climate of Minorca as it is in the rigors of a New England winter.

It is a furniture that also adapts readily to quite different life styles. Although some of the very large pieces require large rooms, the bulk of English furnishings will fit as gracefully into a small urban apartment as it does into the stately homes of England for which it was originally intended.

There is another unique quality to English furniture which is perhaps a part of its adaptability. It is the only furniture to be found in museums which it is possible to envision children clambering about and living with.

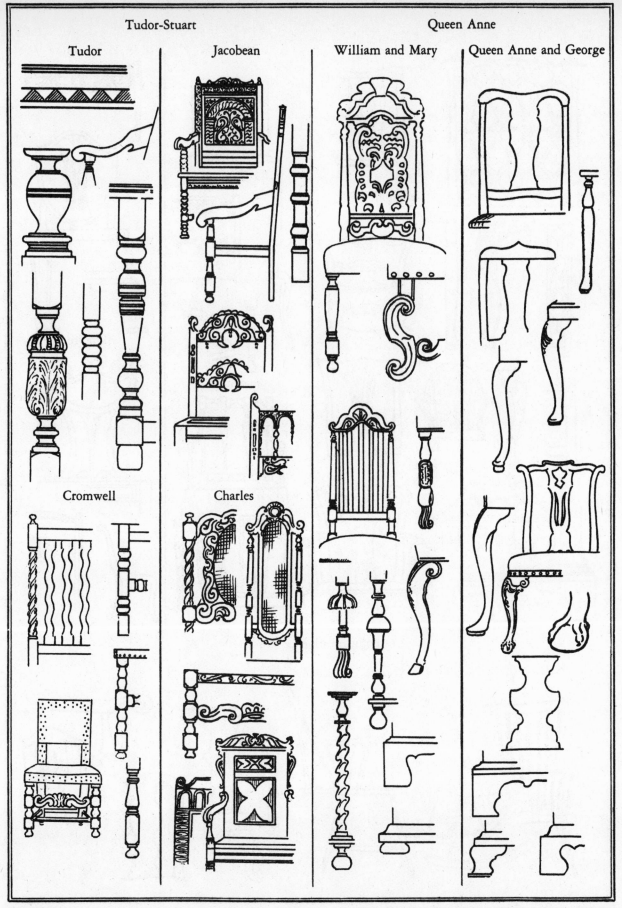

Tudor-Stuart

Queen Anne

Tudor

Jacobean

William and Mary

Queen Anne and George

Cromwell

Charles

PLATE 1.

TUDOR-STUART AND QUEEN ANNE STYLE.

5

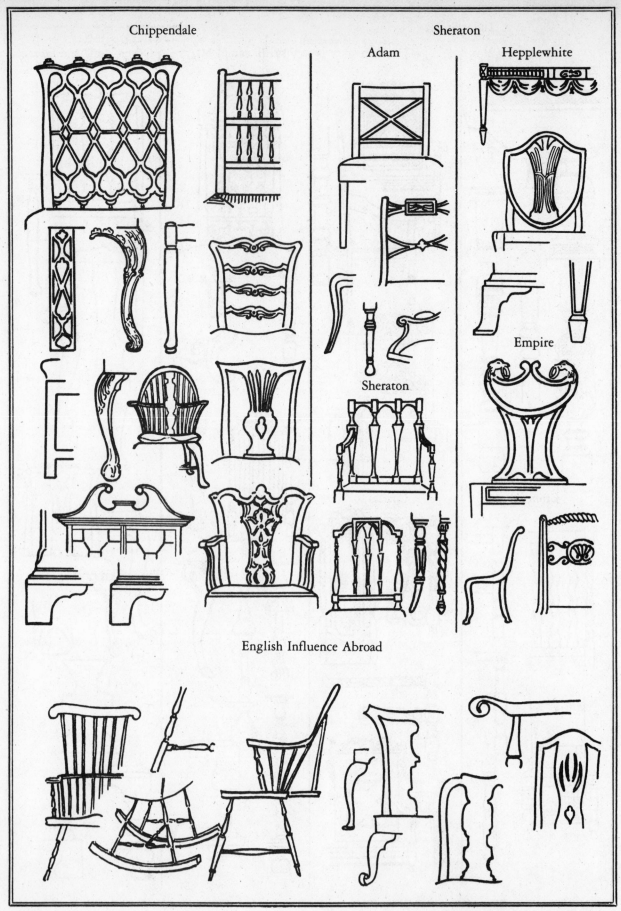

Chippendale

Sheraton

Adam

Hepplewhite

Empire

Sheraton

English Influence Abroad

PLATE 2.                                                    ENGLISH FURNITURE STYLES.

6

**PLATE 3.**                                                            TUDOR-STUART STYLE (architectural features).

1 and 2. Oak panels, period of Henry VIII. Layer Marney Hall, Essex.    3. Oak Panel, 1535. Costessey Hall, Norfolk.    4. Receiving room with oak panels, Manor House, Upton Grey, Hampshire.    5. Ceiling section with simple mouldings. Layer Marney Hall, Essex.    6. Ceiling section with delicate bas-relief. Chastleton House, Oxfordshire.

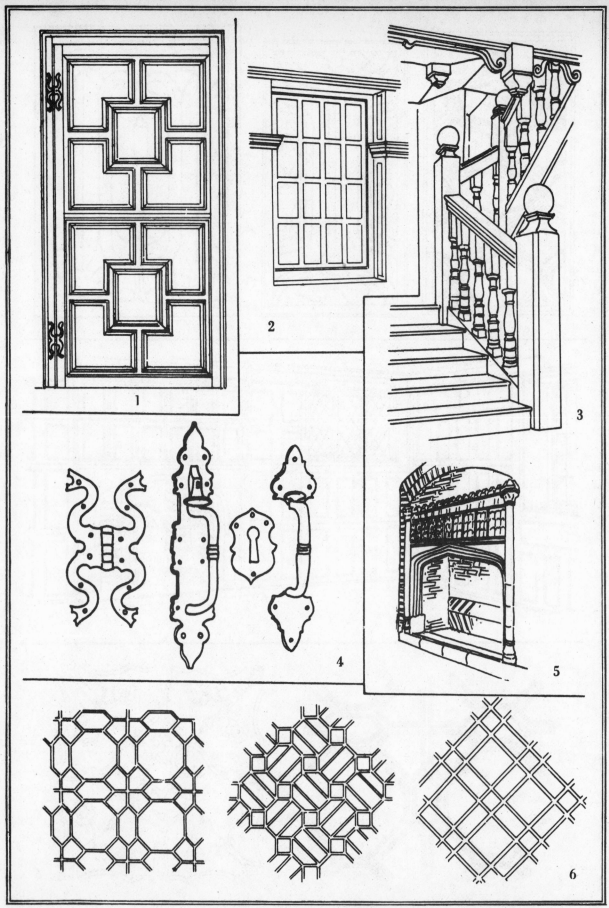

PLATE 4.                                        TUDOR-STUART STYLE (architectural features).

1. Door with panels from the period of James I. Lynsted, Kent.   2. Window from reigns of Elizabeth I and James I. Powis Castle.   3. Stairway section from reigns of Elizabeth I and James I. Mance House, Upton Grey, Hampshire.   4. Hinge, escutcheon plate and door pulls from the period.   5. Fireplace, second floor of Tattershall Castle, Lincoln County.   6. Three geometric forms used for window panes in Elizabethan period.

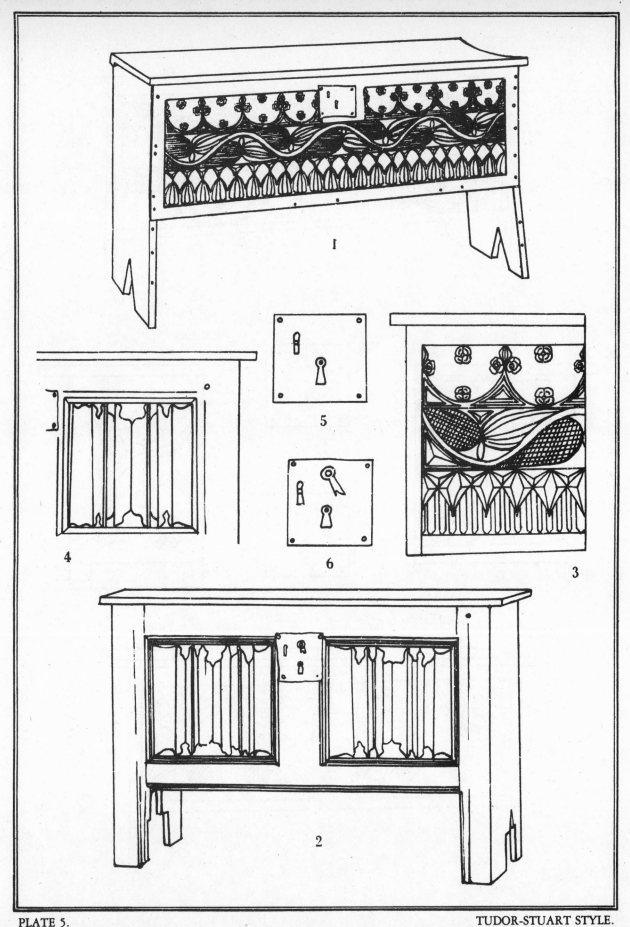

PLATE 5.                                                    TUDOR-STUART STYLE.

1 and 2. Simple chests from the 17th century.    3 and 4. Decorations on their respective panels.    5 and 6. Escutcheon plates.

*Victoria and Albert Museum.*

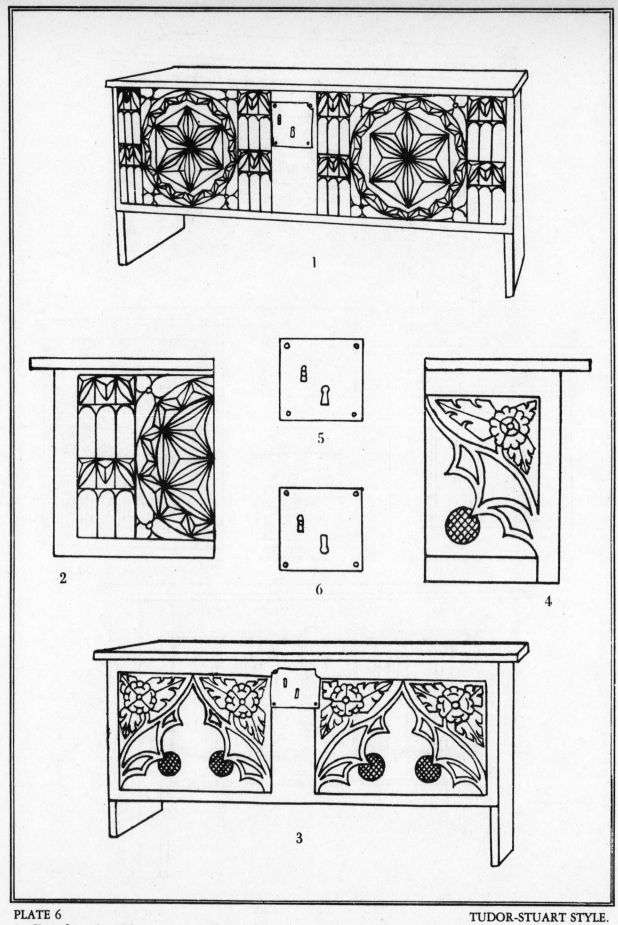

PLATE 6                                                          TUDOR-STUART STYLE.

1. Chest from the 15th century.   2. Detail of same.   3. Chest from the early 16th century.   4. Detail of same.
5 and 6. Escutcheon plates.

*Victoria and Albert Museum.*

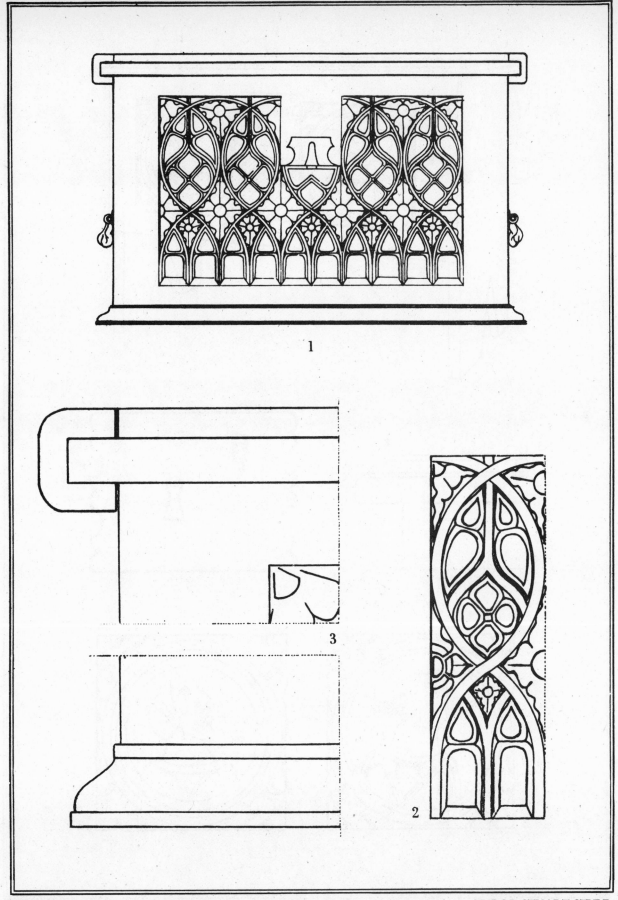

**1**

**3**

**2**

PLATE 7.                                                TUDOR-STUART STYLE.

1. Gothic chest from the 16th century, with decorative motifs from the end of the 14th century.   2. Detail of decoration.   3. Upper and lower mouldings.

*Private collection.*

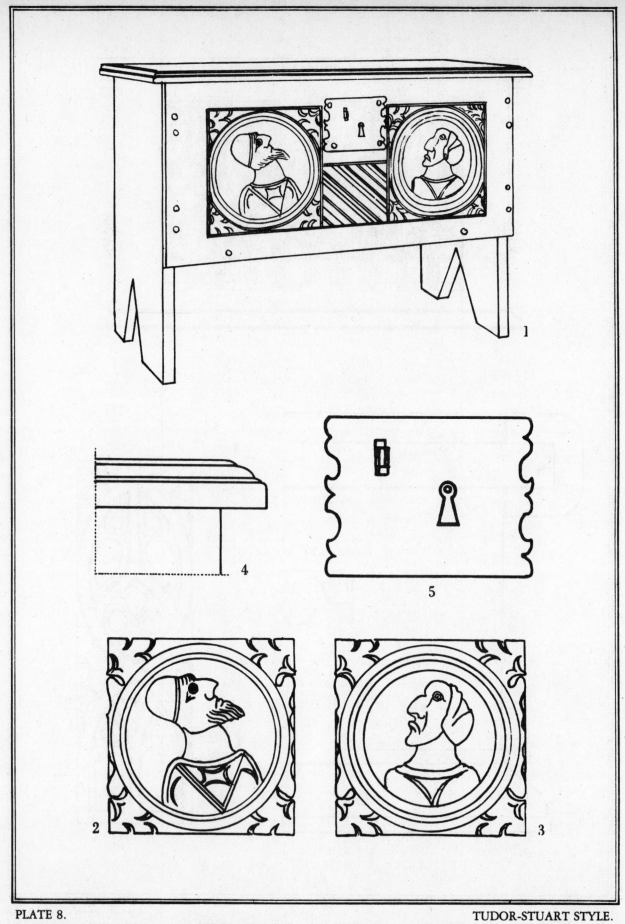

**PLATE 8.**                                                          TUDOR-STUART STYLE.

1. Chest with type of decoration called Romayne work.   2 and 3. Detail of decorative panels.   4. Moulding on the lid.   5. Escutcheon plate.

*Metropolitan Museum of Art.*

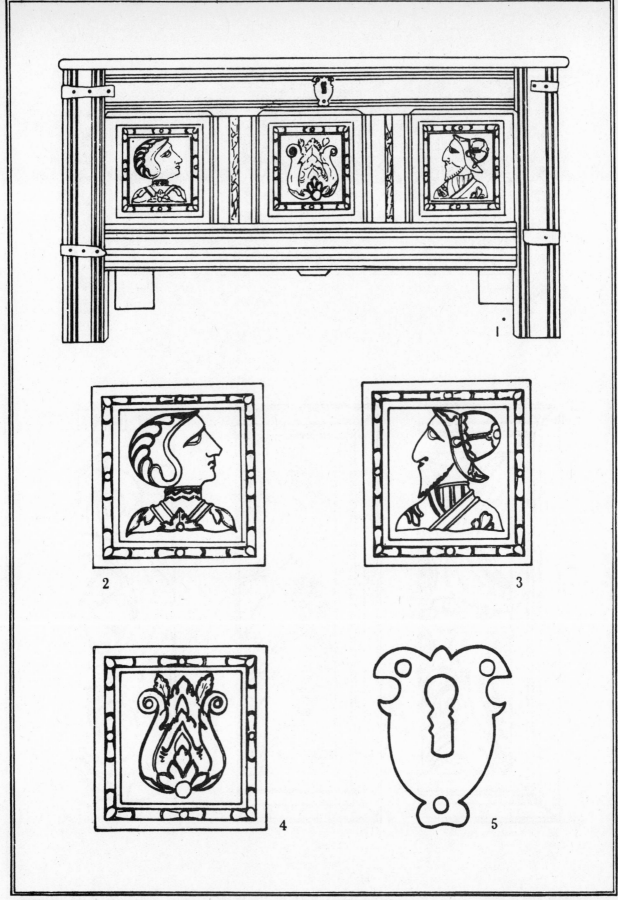

**PLATE 9**                                                    TUDOR-STUART STYLE.

1. Chest with Romayne work, from the 16th century.   2, 3 and 4. Details of panels.   5. Escutcheon plate.

*Victoria and Albert Museum.*

13

PLATE 10.                                                    TUDOR-STUART STYLE.
1. Chest from the first half of the 17th century.   2. Detail of the side panels.   3. Detail of the central panels.   4. Decoration on the uprights.

*Victoria and Albert Museum.*

**PLATE 11.**
1. Chest from the 17th century.    2 and 3. Decorative details.

TUDOR-STUART STYLE.

*Victoria and Albert Museum.*

PLATE 12.                                                          TUDOR-STUART STYLE.
1. Chest from the 17th century.  2. Decoration on upright.  3. Decoration on socle.  4. Detail of panel.  5. Detail
of upper frieze.  6. Rosette.

*Victoria and Albert Museum.*

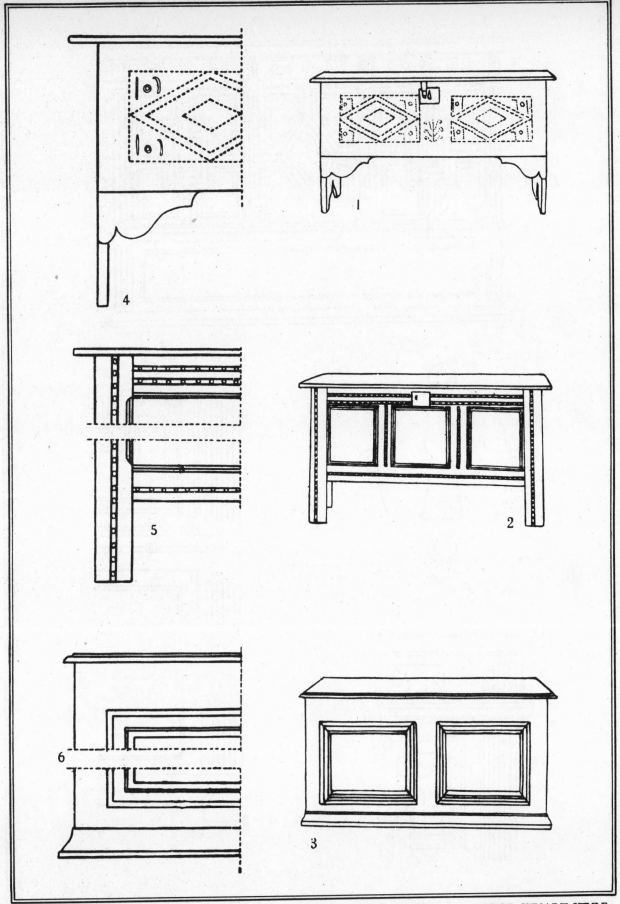

PLATE 13.

TUDOR-STUART STYLE.

1, 2 and 3. Simple chests from the 17th century.   4, 5 and 6. Details of same.

*Private collection.*

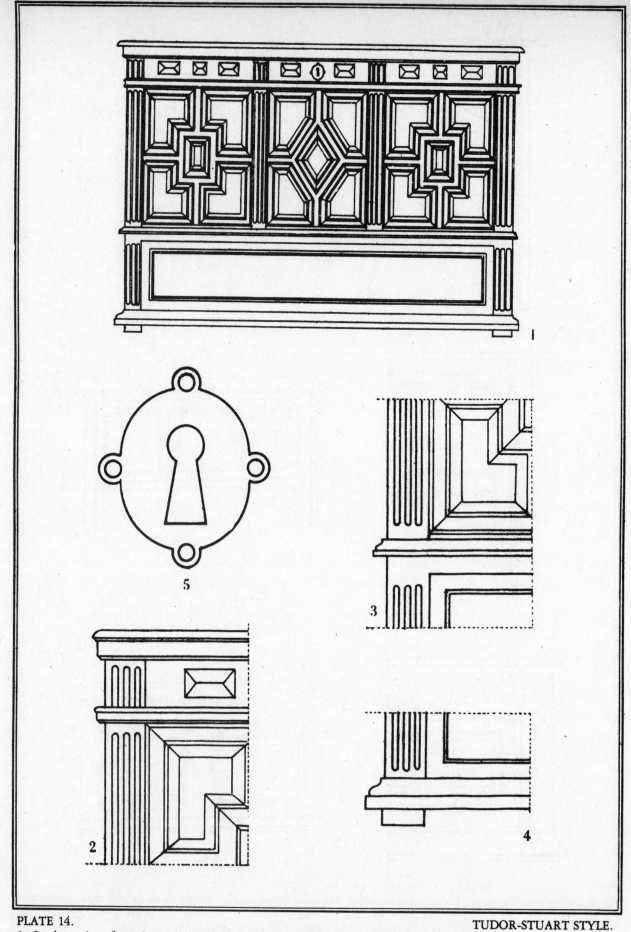

PLATE 14.                                                          TUDOR-STUART STYLE.

1. Jacobean chest from the 17th century.    2, 3 and 4. Decorative details.    5. Escutcheon plate.

*Private collection.*

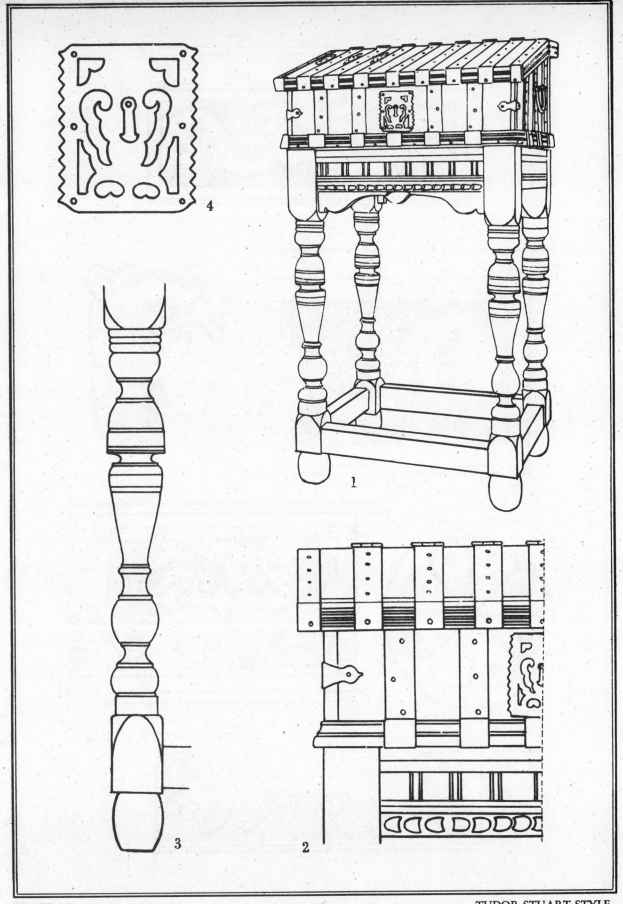

**PLATE 15.**                                    TUDOR-STUART STYLE.

1. Box for the Bible, with pedestal table.   2. Detail of box.   3. Leg.   4. Escutcheon plate.

*Victoria and Albert Museum.*

PLATE 16.

1 and 2. Boxes for the Bible, 17th century.   3, 4, 5 and 6. Decorations on same.

TUDOR-STUART STYLE.

*Victoria and Albert Museum.*

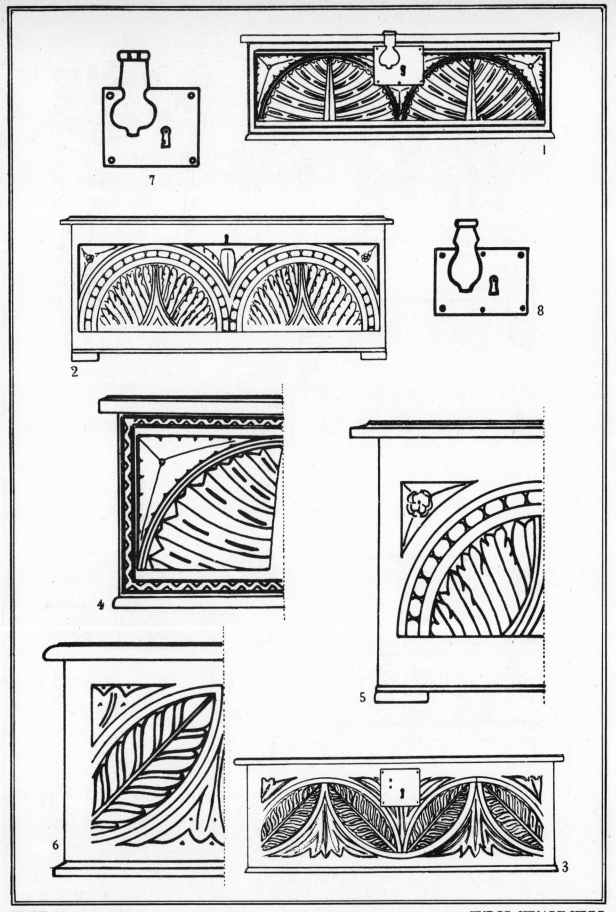

PLATE 17.                                                    TUDOR-STUART STYLE.

1, 2 and 3. Bible boxes, end of 17th century.    4, 5 and 6. Decorations on same. 7 and 8. Iron hardware.

*Private collection.*

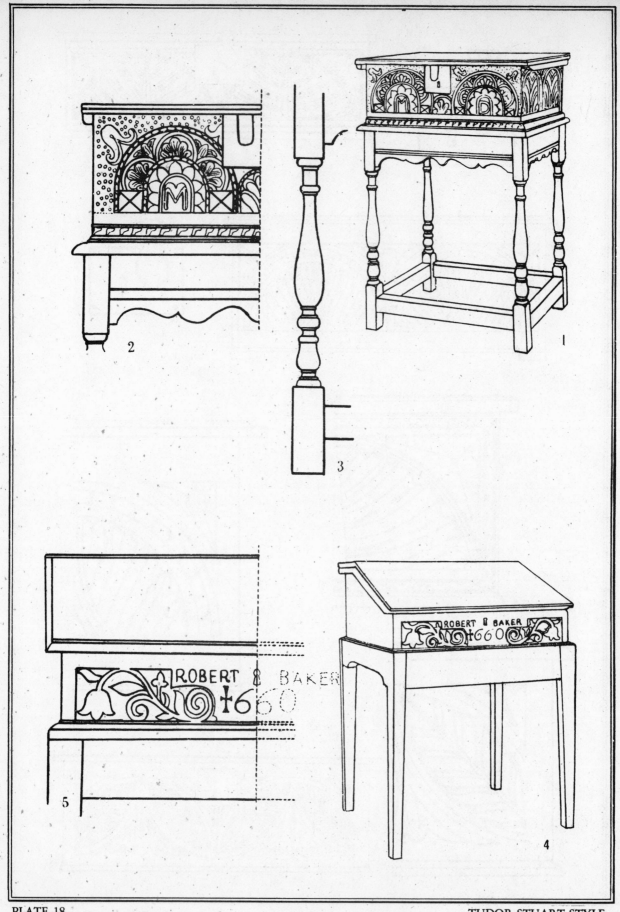

PLATE 18.                                                    TUDOR-STUART STYLE.

1. Bible box, with pedestal table.   2 and 3. Decorative detail and leg of same.   4. Box for Bible with owner's name.   5. Decorative detail.

*Private collection.*

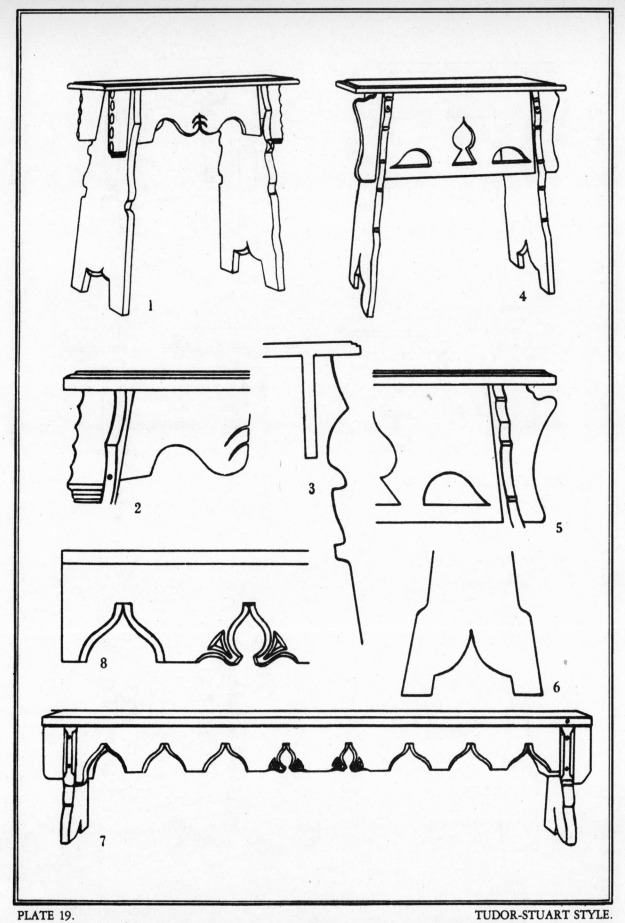

PLATE 19.                                                          TUDOR-STUART STYLE.
1. Stool from the end of the 15th century.   2 and 3. Details of same.   4. Stool from beginning of 16th century.
5 and 6. Details of same.   7. Bench from 16th century.   8. Decoration on bench.

*Victoria and Albert Museum.*

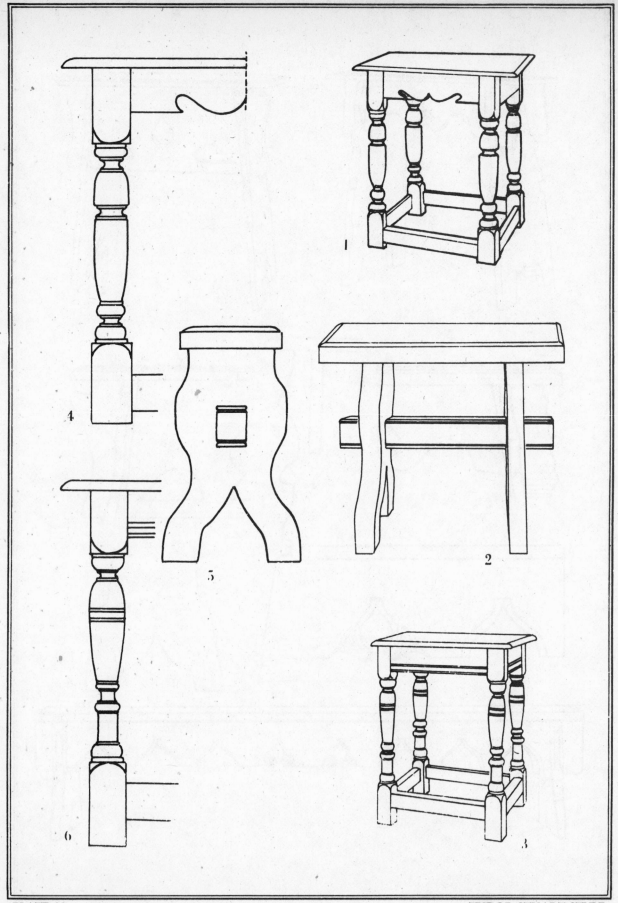

PLATE 20.                                                    TUDOR-STUART STYLE.

1, 2 and 3. Stools from 17th century.   4, 5 and 6.   Details of numbers 1, 2 and 3, respectively.

*Charterhouse School, London.*

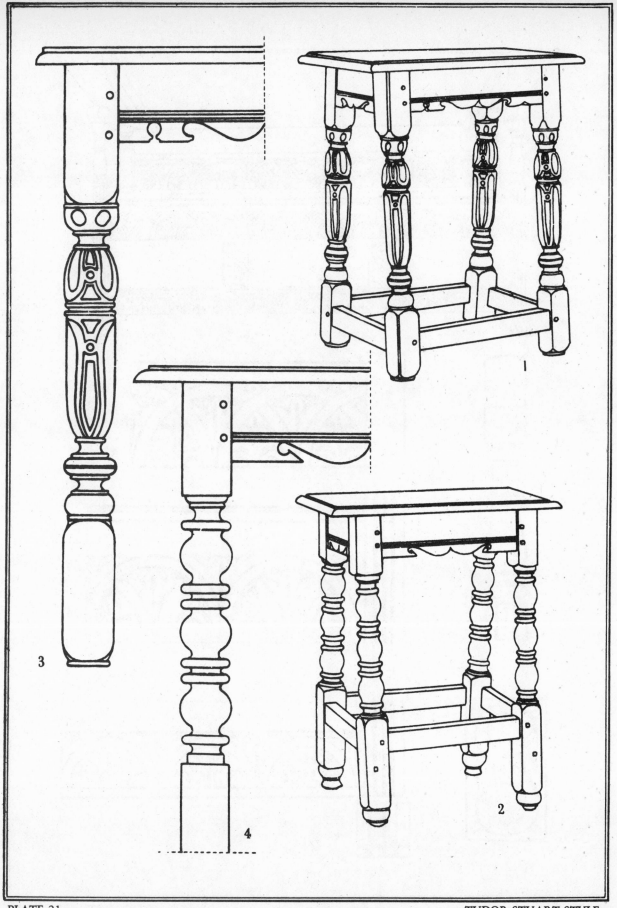

PLATE 21.

1 and 2. Stools from the 17th century.   3 and 4. Detail of legs and profile of numbers 1 and 2, respectively.

TUDOR-STUART STYLE.

*Victoria and Albert Museum.*

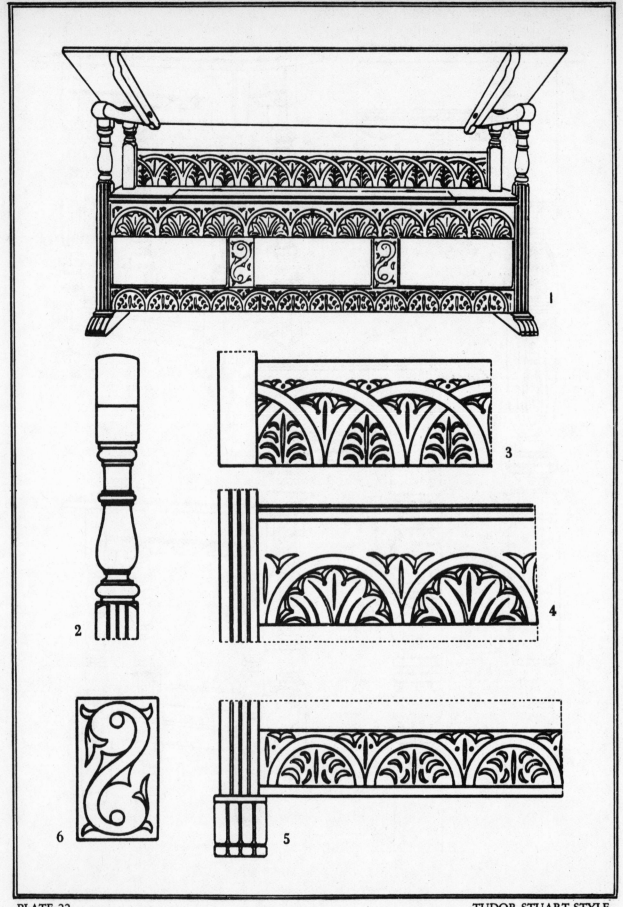

PLATE 22.                                                    TUDOR-STUART STYLE.

1. Table bench from the 17th century.   2. Detail of upright.   3. Detail of frieze on back.   4. Detail of upper crosspiece.   5. Detail of lower crosspiece.   6. Decoration on rail.

*Victoria and Albert Museum.*

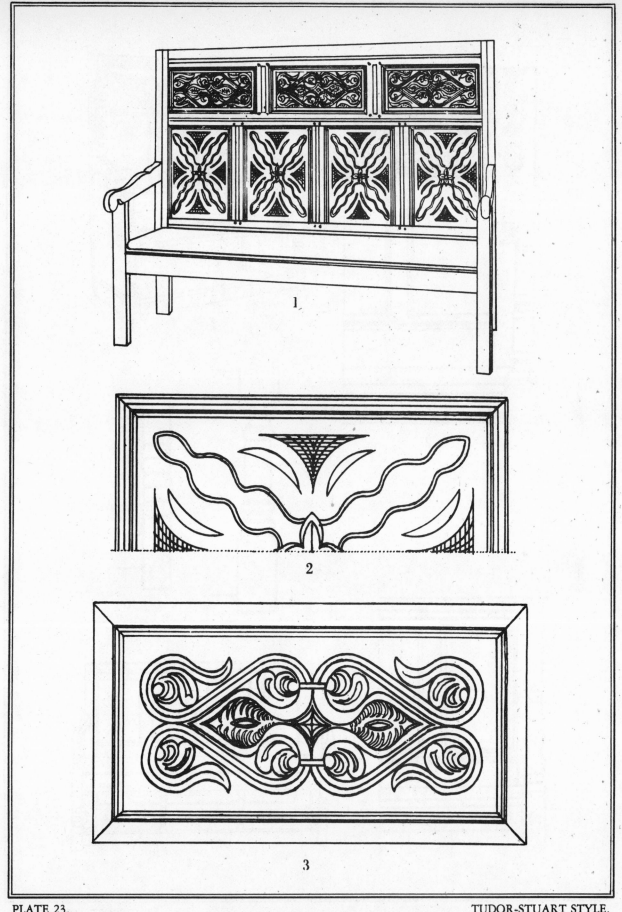

**PLATE 23.**                                                    TUDOR-STUART STYLE.

1. Bench from early 17th century.   2. Detail of lower back panels.   3. Detail of upper back panels.

*Private collection.*

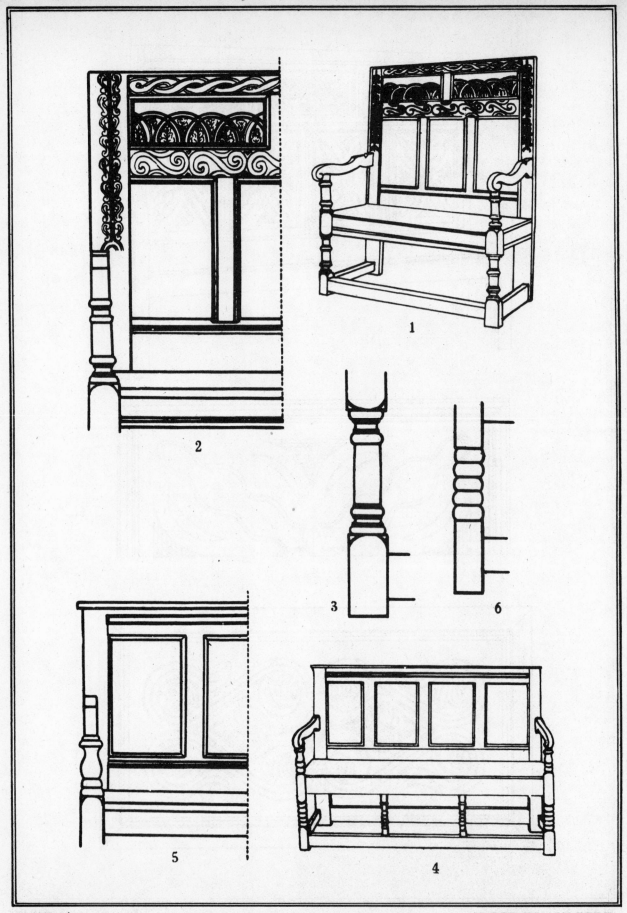

PLATE 24.                                                                TUDOR-STUART STYLE.

1. Bench with "S" decorations from the 17th century.   2. Decorative detail of same.   3. Detail of front legs.   4. Simple bench from 17th century.   5. Detail of back.   6. Detail of front legs.

*Private collection.*

PLATE 25.                                                                    TUDOR-STUART STYLE.

1. Armchair with Romayne motifs; 16th century.   2, 3 and 4. Decorative details.   5. Turned chair; 16th century.   6. Detail of its structure.

*Private colleciton.*

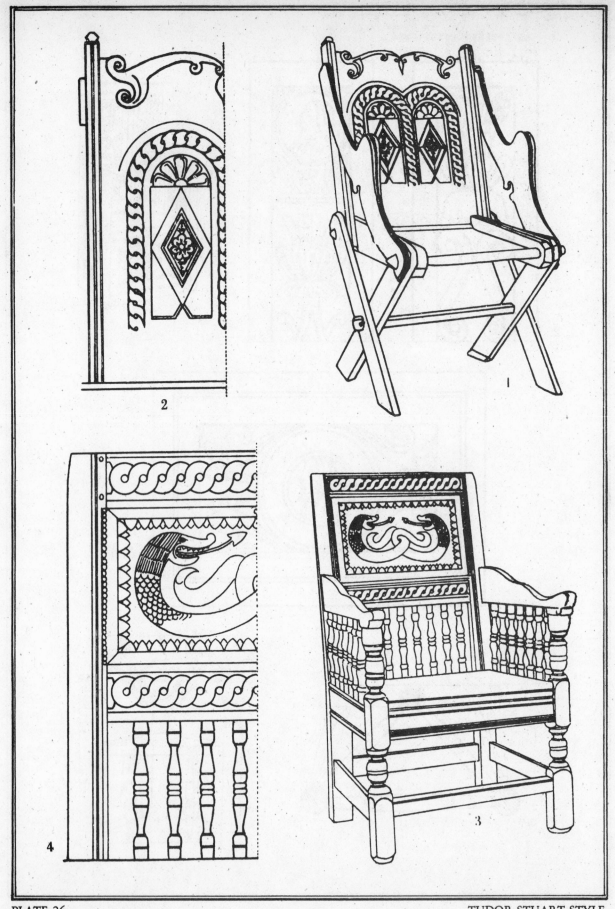

PLATE 26.

TUDOR-STUART STYLE.

1. Armchair from the 16th century; with "guilloche" design on back.  2. Decorative detail.  3. Armchair from 16th century.  4. Detail of back.

*Victoria and Albert Museum.*

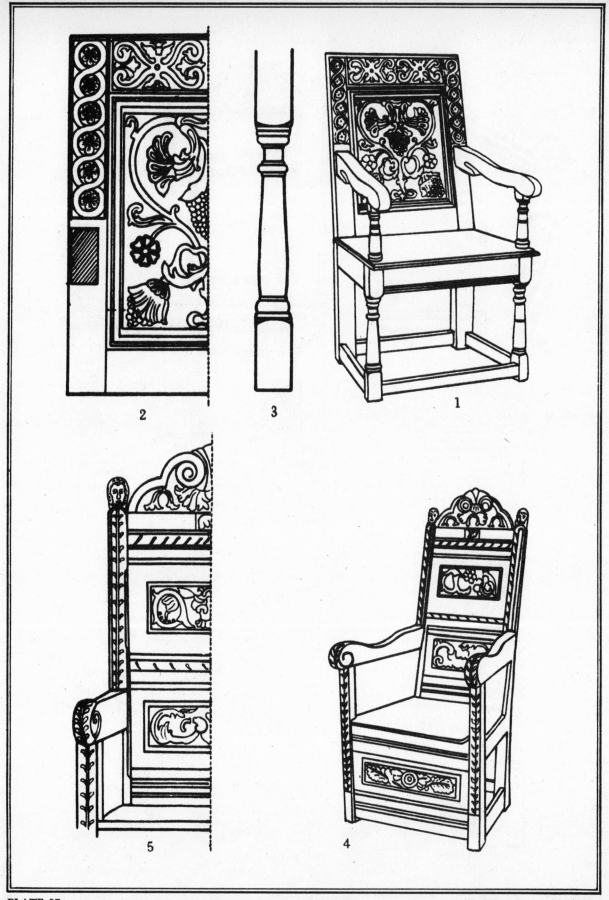

PLATE 27.

TUDOR-STUART STYLE.

1. Jacobean armchair.   2. Decoration on back.   3. Front leg.   4. Jacobean armchair.   5. Decorative detail of same.

*Private collection.*

31

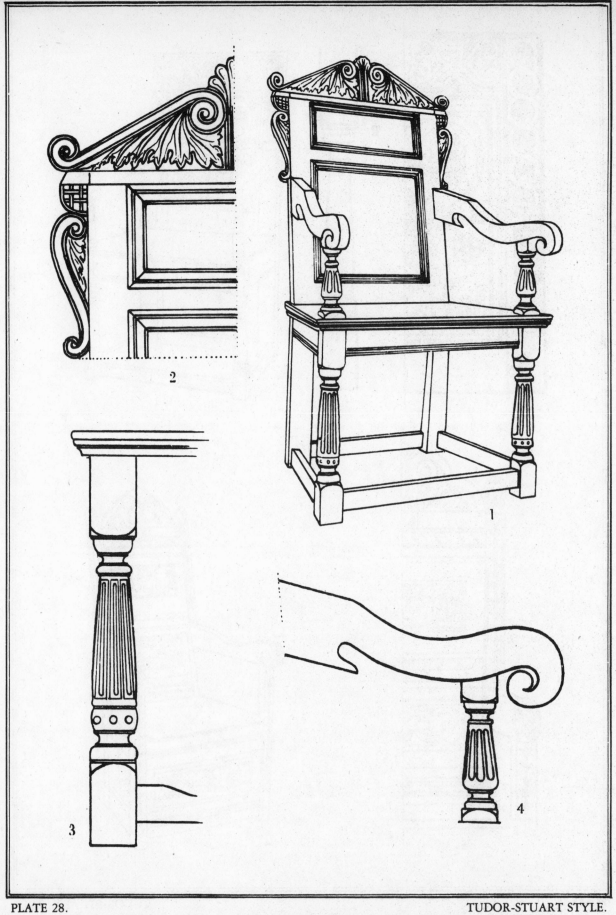

PLATE 28.                                                                TUDOR-STUART STYLE.
1. Armchair from 17th century.   2. Decoration on crest.   3. Front leg.   4. Arm and support column.

*Victoria and Albert Museum.*

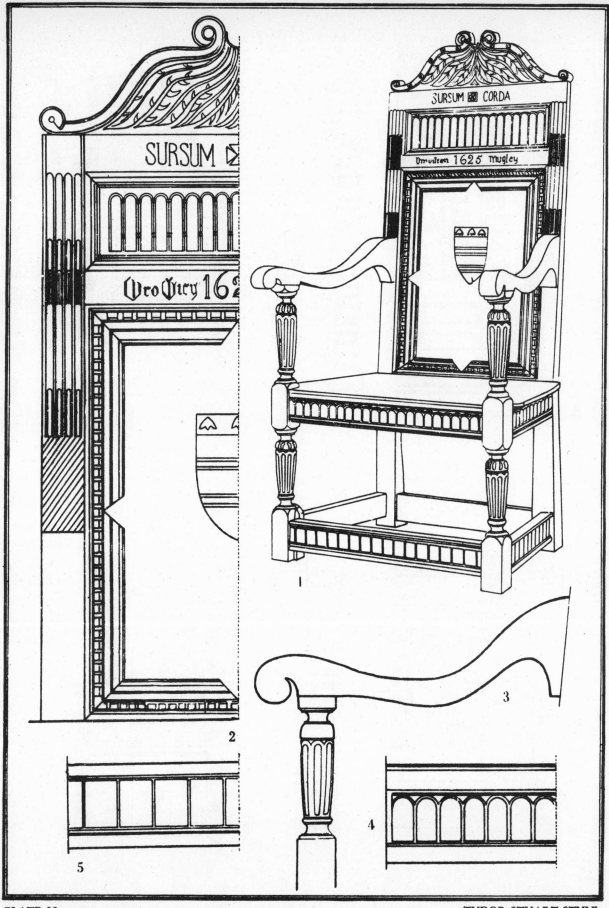

SURSUM ☒

Cro Cicy 162

SURSUM ☒ CORDA

Omultron 1625 mugley

**PLATE 29.**                                        TUDOR-STUART STYLE.

1. Armchair from 17th century.   2. Decoration on back.   3. Arm and support column.   4. Detail of upper cross-piece.   5. Detail of lower crosspiece.

*Victoria and Albert Museum.*

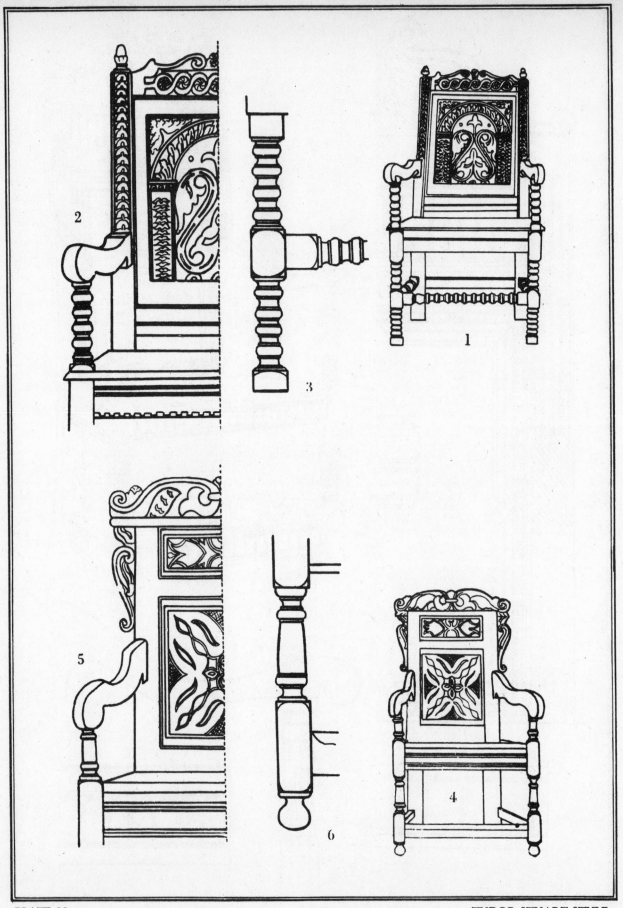

PLATE 30.

TUDOR-STUART STYLE.

1. Armchair from early 17th century. 2. Decoration on same. 3. Detail of turned legs and cross-pieces. 4. Armchair from early 17th century. 5. Detail of back. 6. Turned front legs.

*Private collection.*

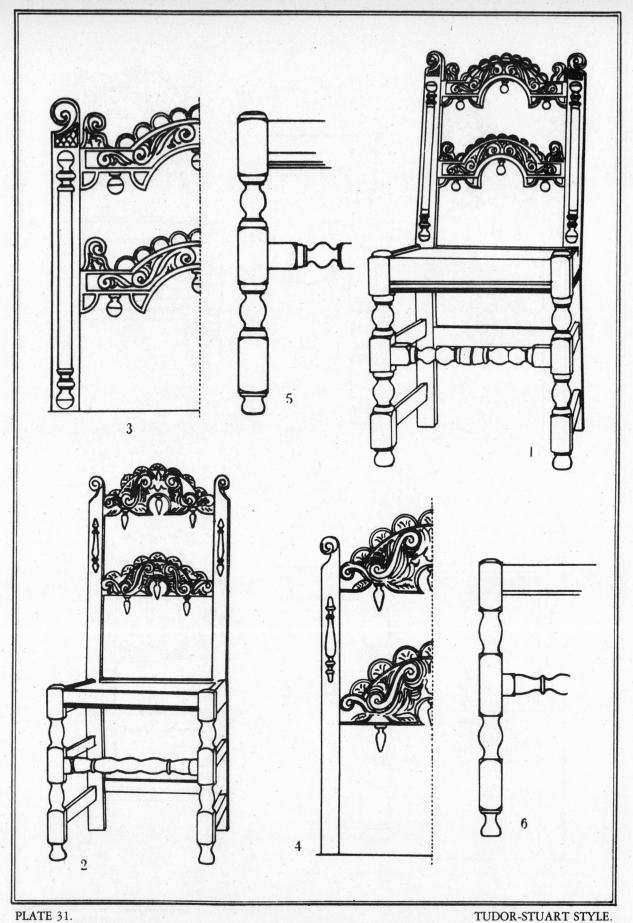

PLATE 31.                                                                TUDOR-STUART STYLE.
1 and 2. Yorkshire and Derbyshire armchairs, 17th century.   3. Back detail of first armchair.   4. Detail of back of
second armchair.   5. Turned legs and crosspieces of first armchair.   6. Turned legs and crosspieces of second armchair.
*Victoria and Albert Museum.*

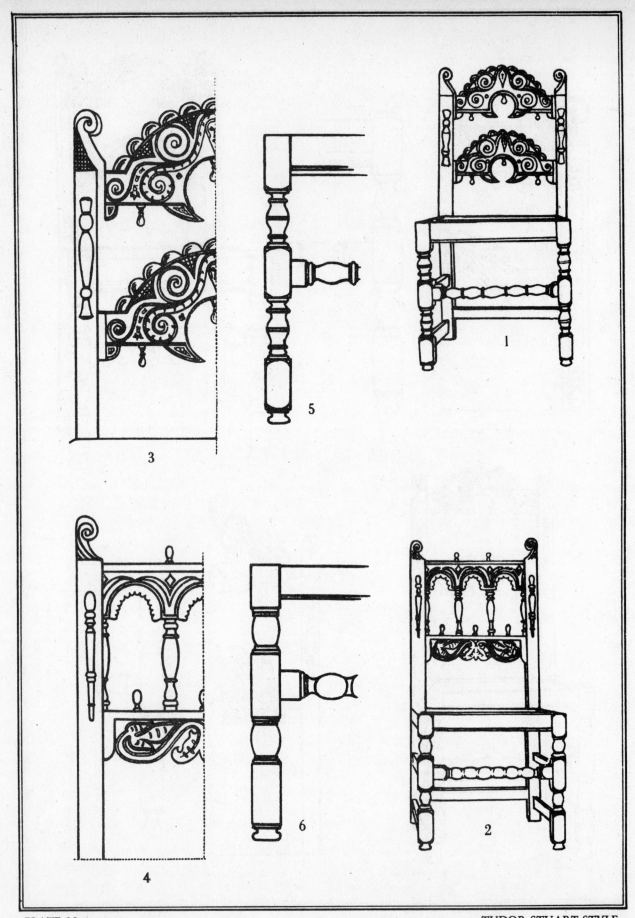

PLATE 32.                                                TUDOR-STUART STYLE.

1 and 2. Yorkshire and Derbyshire armchairs, 17th century.   3. Detail of back of first armchair.   4. Detail of back of second armchair.   5. Turned legs and crosspiece of first armchair.   6. Turned legs and crosspiece of second armchair.

*Victoria and Albert Museum.*

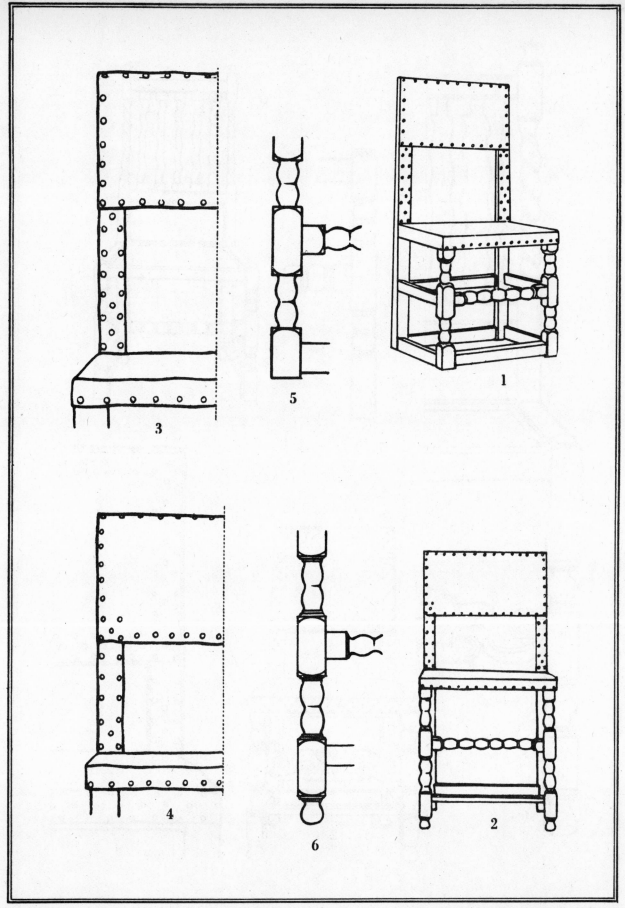

PLATE 33.                                                        TUDOR-STUART STYLE.

1 and 2. Cromwell chairs.    3 and 4. Details of backs.    5 and 6. Turned legs and crosspieces.

*Private collection.*

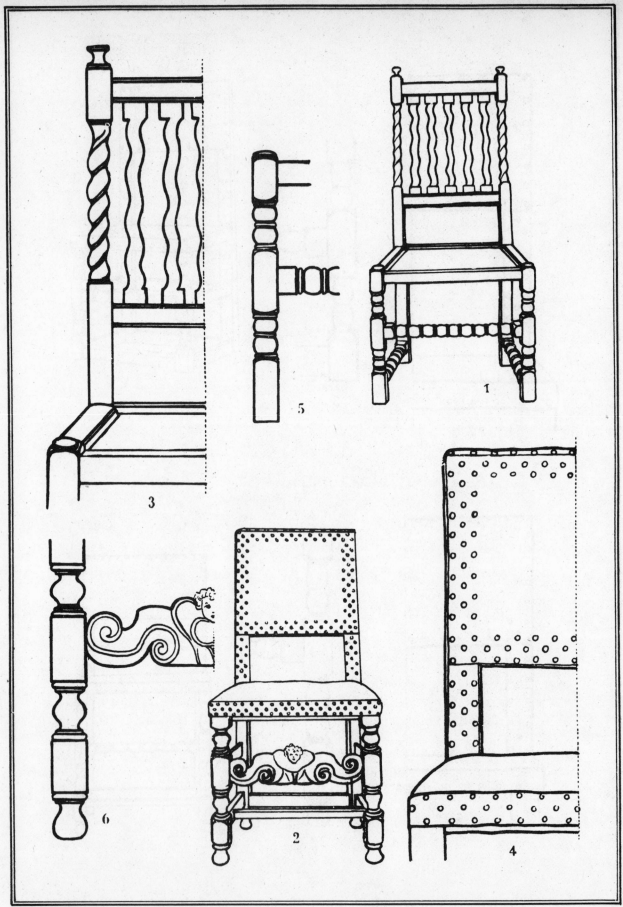

PLATE 34.                                                                TUDOR-STUART STYLE.
1 and 2. Chairs from the end of the Cromwellian period, with decorative motifs from the next period.   3 and 4. Details
of backs.   5. Turned legs and crosspiece of first chair.   6. Turned legs and crosspiece of second chair.
*Private collection and Victoria and Albert Museum.*

**PLATE 35.**                                          TUDOR-STUART STYLE.

1. Armchair from 17th century.   2. Back decoration.   3. Turned leg and decoration on back.   4. Armchair from the 17th century.   5. Back decoration.   6. Upper crosspiece.   7. Lower crosspiece.   8. Turned leg.

*Private collection.*

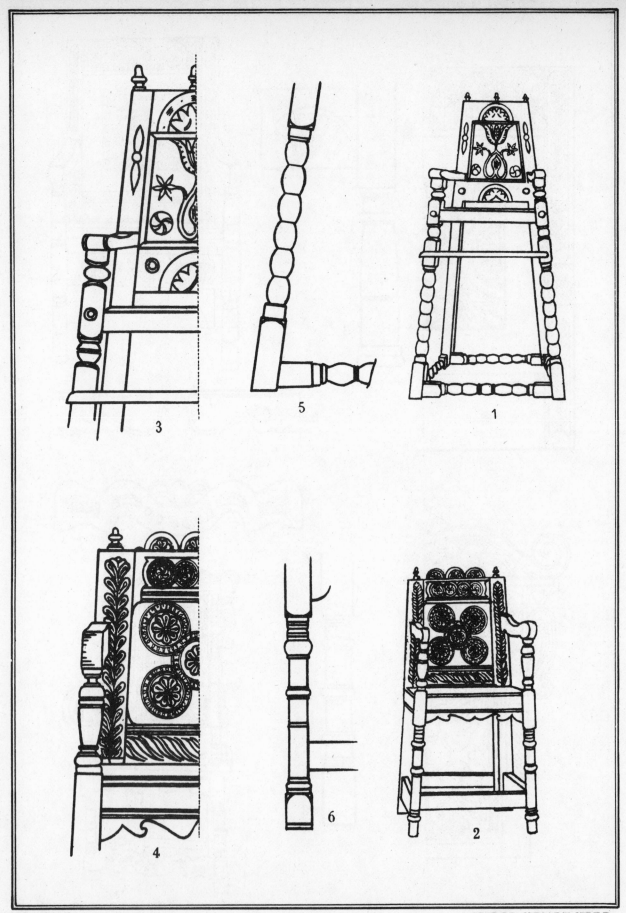

PLATE 36.                                                        TUDOR-STUART STYLE.
1 and 2. Children's chairs; 17th century.   3 and 4. Decorations on back.   5 and 6. Turned legs and crosspieces.
*Victoria and Albert Museum.*

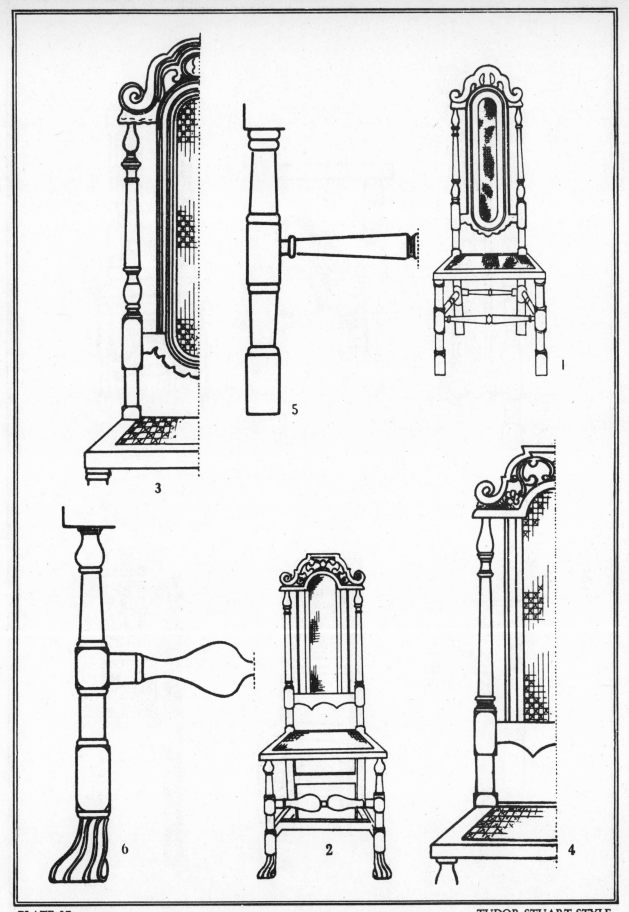

**PLATE 37.**

1 and 2. Stuart chairs from the 17th century.    3 and 4. Turned uprights and crest on backs.    5 and 6. Turned legs and crosspieces.

TUDOR-STUART STYLE.

*Private collection.*

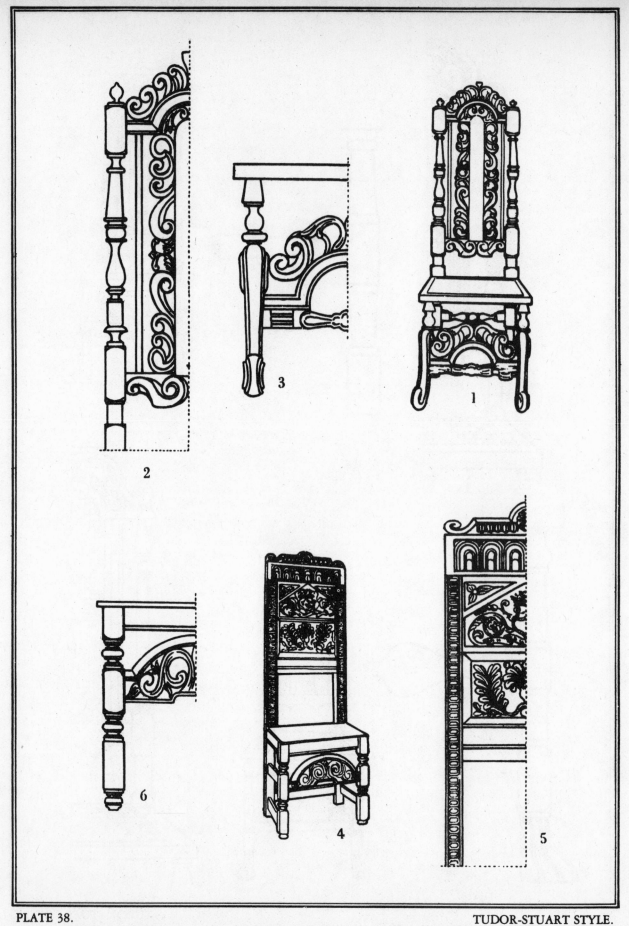

PLATE 38.                                                                                    TUDOR-STUART STYLE.
1. Stuart chair.    2. Detail of turned upright and back decoration.    3. Detail of legs and front crosspiece.    4. Caroline
chair.    5. Back decoration.    6. Turned front legs and crosspiece.

*Private collection and Victoria and Albert Museum*

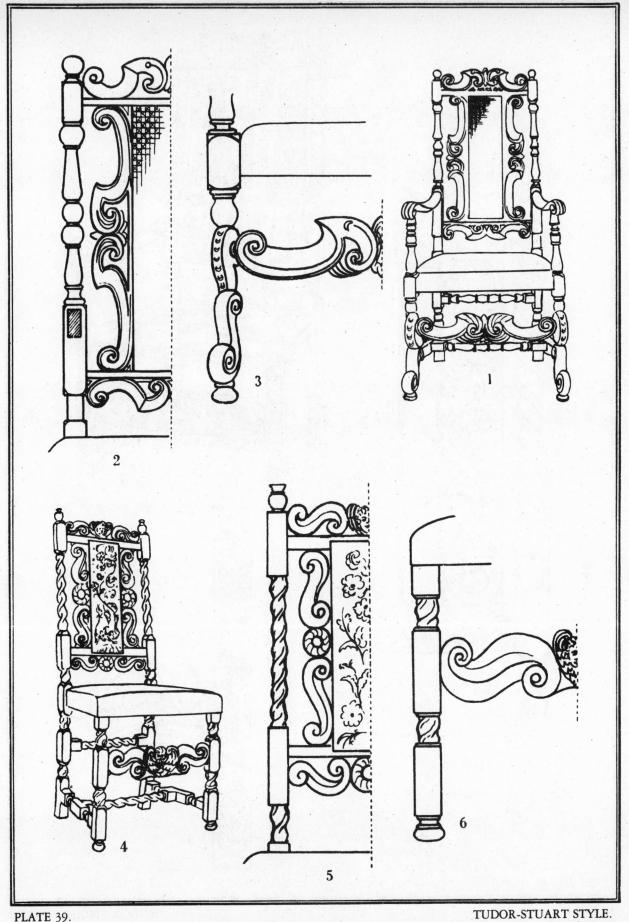

PLATE 39.                                                                     TUDOR-STUART STYLE.
1. Stuart armchair.  2. Detail of back.  3. Detail of leg and crosspiece.  4. Stuart chair.  5. Detail of
back.  6. Detail of leg and crosspiece.

*Private collection.*

43

PLATE 40.

1. Stuart armchair.   2. Detail of back.   3. Decoration on leg and crosspiece.

TUDOR-STUART STYLE.

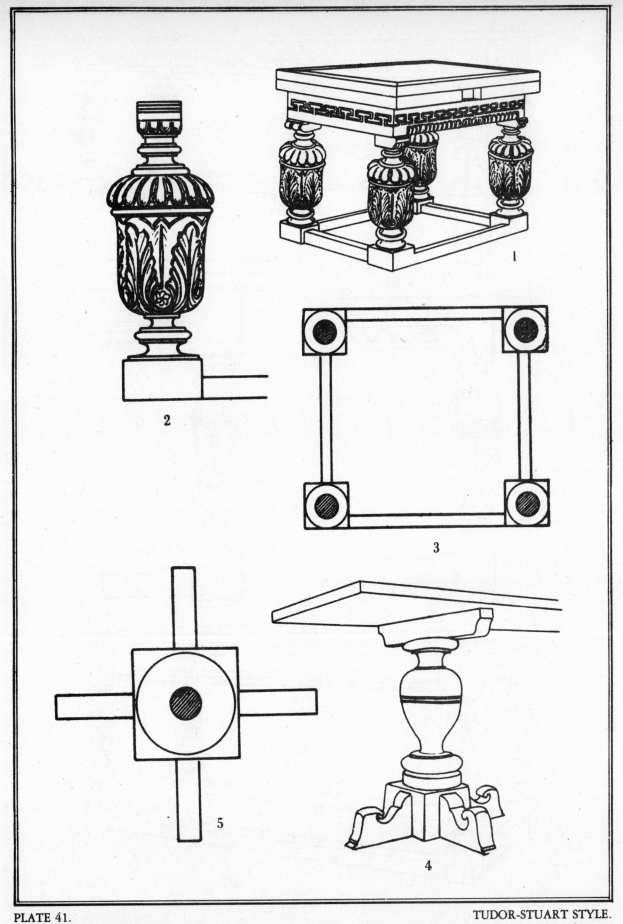

PLATE 41.                                                                    TUDOR-STUART STYLE.

1. Table from the Elizabethan period.    2. Decoration on leg.    3. Base of the table.    4. Table from the 16th century.    5. Base of same.

PLATE 42.                                                        TUDOR-STUART STYLE.
1. Table from end of 16th century.   2. Decoration.   3. Table from early 17th century.   4. Decoration.
*Private collection.*

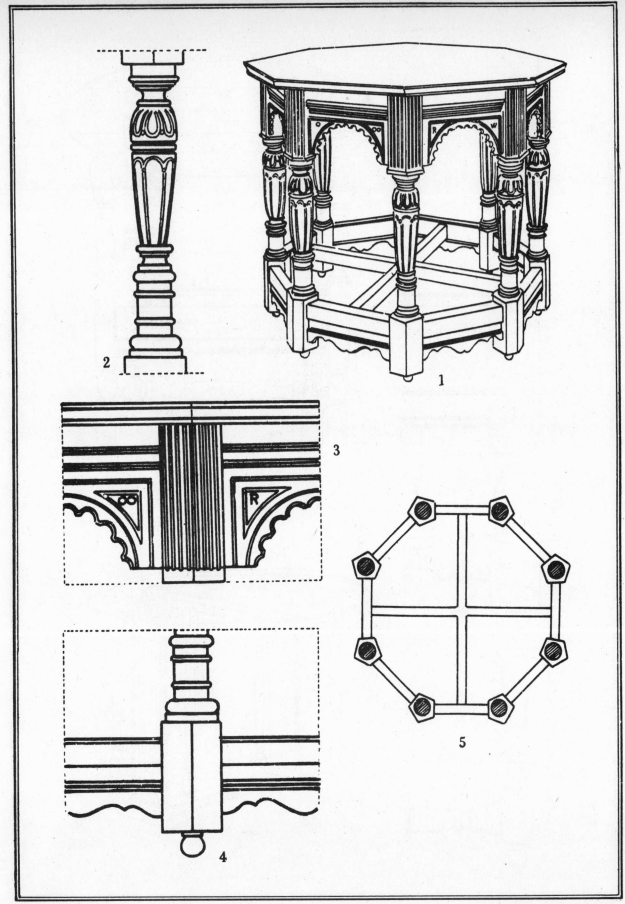

PLATE 43.                                                    TUDOR-STUART STYLE.
1. Typical table from the end of the Elizabethan period, early 17th century.   2. Decoration on legs.   3 and
4. Decorations.   5. Base.

*Private collection.*

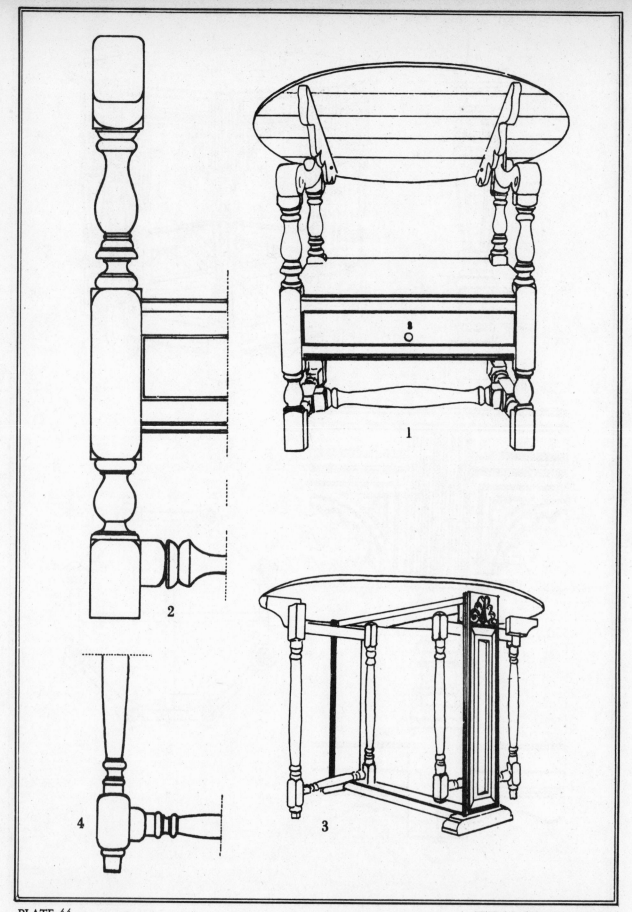

**PLATE 44.**                                                    **TUDOR-STUART STYLE.**

1. Bench table from 17th century.  2. Details of legs and box seat.  3. Folding (gate-leg) table from the 17th century.  4. Turned legs and crosspiece.

*Victoria and Albert Museum.*

**PLATE 45.**

1, 2, 3 and 4. Folding (gate-leg) tables from the 17th century.   5, 6, 7 and 8.  Turned legs of each table, respectively.

*Private collection and Guild Hall Museum, London (3).*

TUDOR-STUART STYLE.

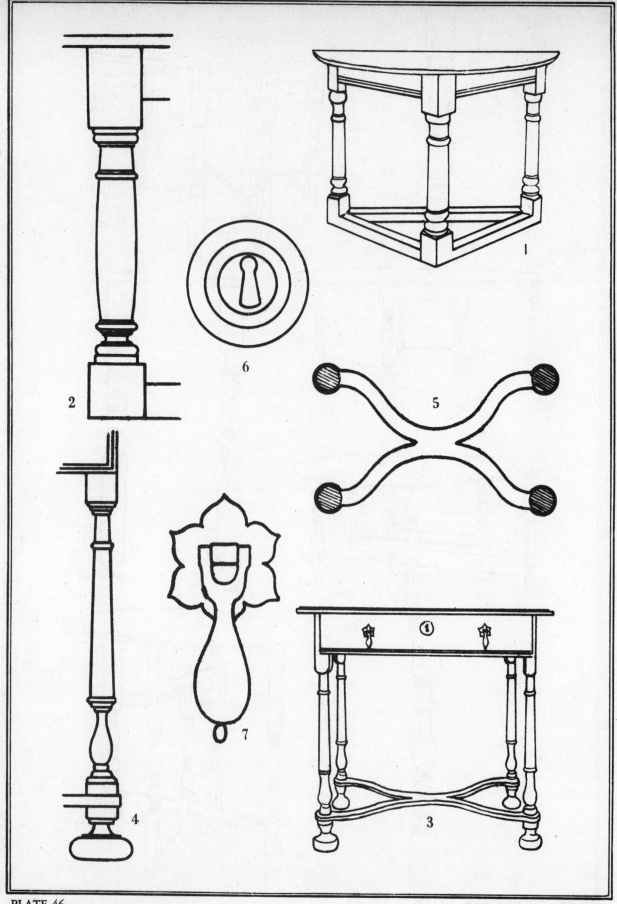

PLATE 46.                                    TUDOR-STUART STYLE.
1. Cromwell table.   2. Turned leg.   3. Stuart table.   4. Turned leg.   5. Base of crosspiece.   6. Escutcheon
plate.   7. Drawer pull.

PLATE 47.                                                                              TUDOR-STUART STYLE.

1. Cupboard, beginning of 16th century.   2. Decoration on side panels.   3 and 4. Decorations on middle panel.
5 and 6. Hinges.   7. Cupboard; 16th century.   8. Escutcheon plate.

*Victoria and Albert Museum.*

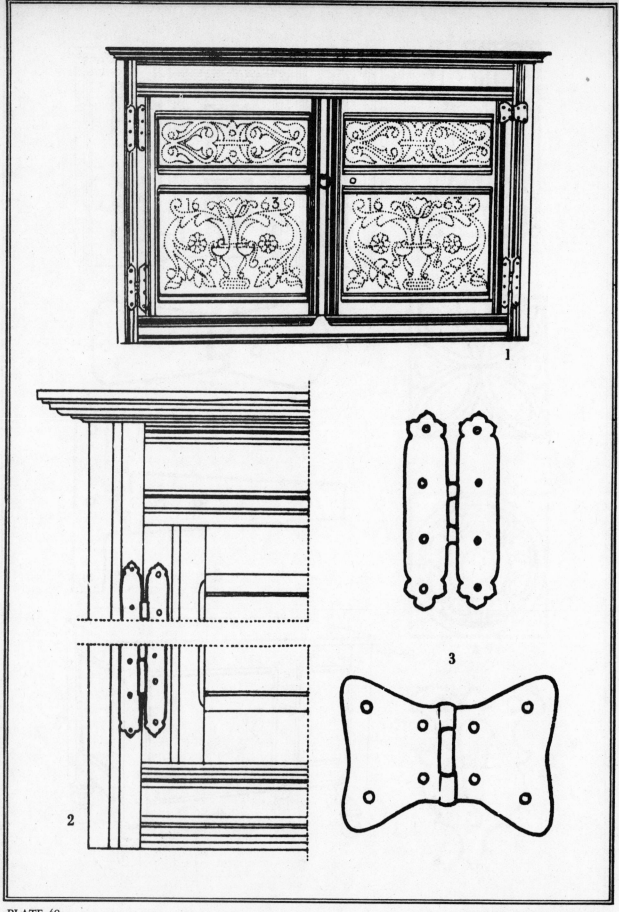

PLATE 48.
1. Cupboard, 17th century.   2. Detail.   3. Hinges.

TUDOR-STUART STYLE.

*Victoria and Albert Museum.*

PLATE 49.                                                                           TUDOR-STUART STYLE.

1. Dresser from the 17th century.    2. Detail of side.    3. Decoration on upper portion.

*Victoria and Albert Museum.*

53

PLATE 50.                                                    TUDOR-STUART STYLE.

1. Elizabethan dresser, 17th century.  2. Decorations on legs and posts.  3. Middle panel on upper portion.  4. Decoration on side panels.

*Metropolitan Museum of Art.*

PLATE 51.                                                                    TUDOR-STUART STYLE.

1. Dresser from Elizabethan period, second half of 17th century.   2. Detail of upper side posts.   3. Detail of friezes.   4. Door panels.   5. Decoration on uprights.

*Private collection.*

55

PLATE 52.                                                    TUDOR-STUART STYLE.
1. Dresser from 17th century with "guilloche" design on arches decorating doors.    2. Decoration on side panels.    3. Detail
of upper and lower friezes and uprights.    4. Escutcheon plate.    5. Hinge.

*Victoria and Albert Museum.*

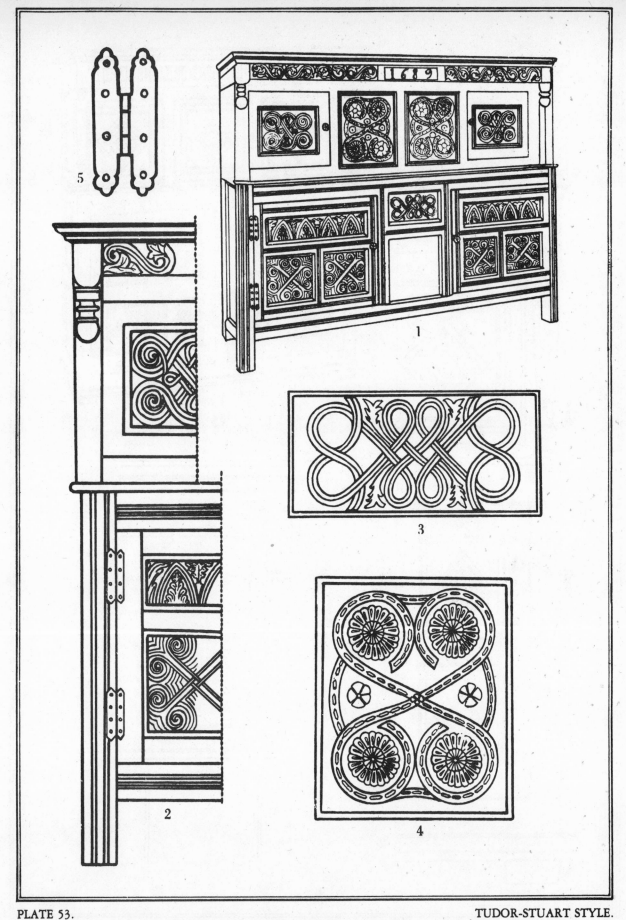

PLATE 53. TUDOR-STUART STYLE.

1. Dresser from 17th century.    2. Details of uprights, panels and side friezes.    3. Lower middle panel.    4. Upper middle panel.    5. Hinge.

*Private collection.*

PLATE 54.

TUDOR-STUART STYLE.

1. Dresser from beginning of the Jacobean period, 17th century.   2. Details of posts and decorative panels.   3. Detail of side.   4. Hinge.

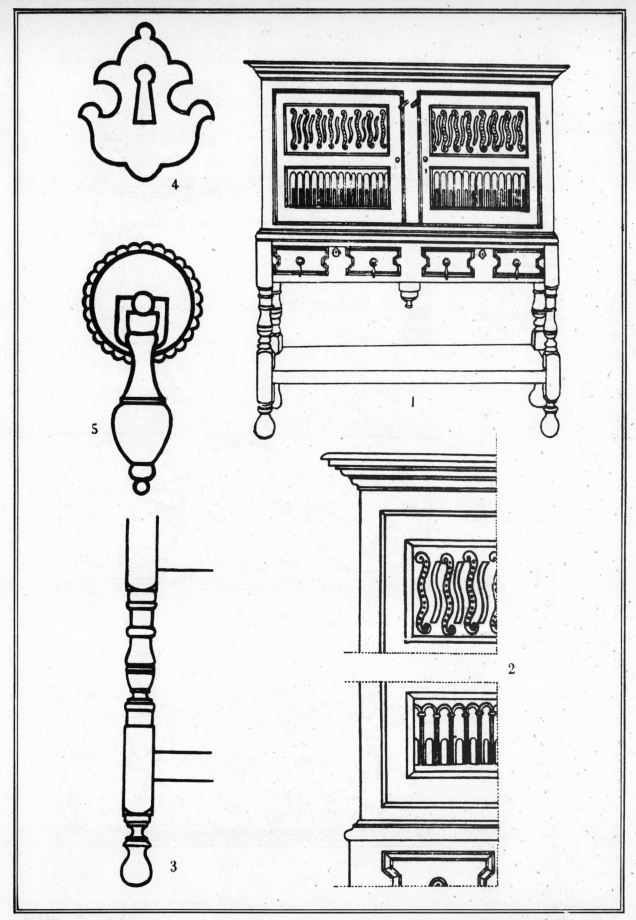

**PLATE 55.** TUDOR-STUART STYLE.

1. Dresser on stand from 17th century. 2. Detail of mouldings and decorative panels. 3. Turned legs. 4. Escutcheon plate. 5. Drawer pull.

*Private collection.*

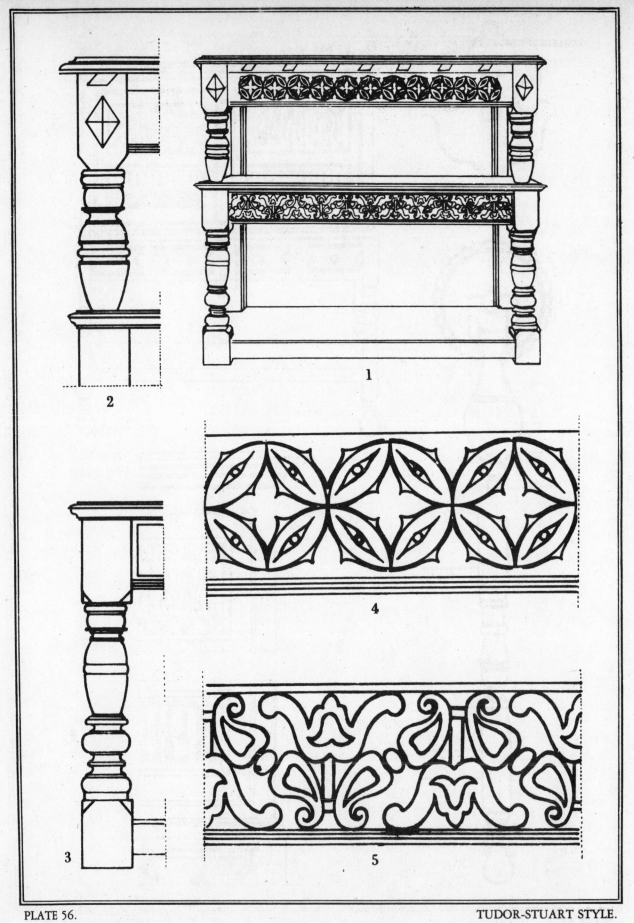

PLATE 56.                                                                TUDOR-STUART STYLE.
1. Sideboard from middle of 17th century.   2. Turned posts.   3. Turned legs.   4. Upper frieze.   5. Central frieze.
*Victoria and Albert Museum.*

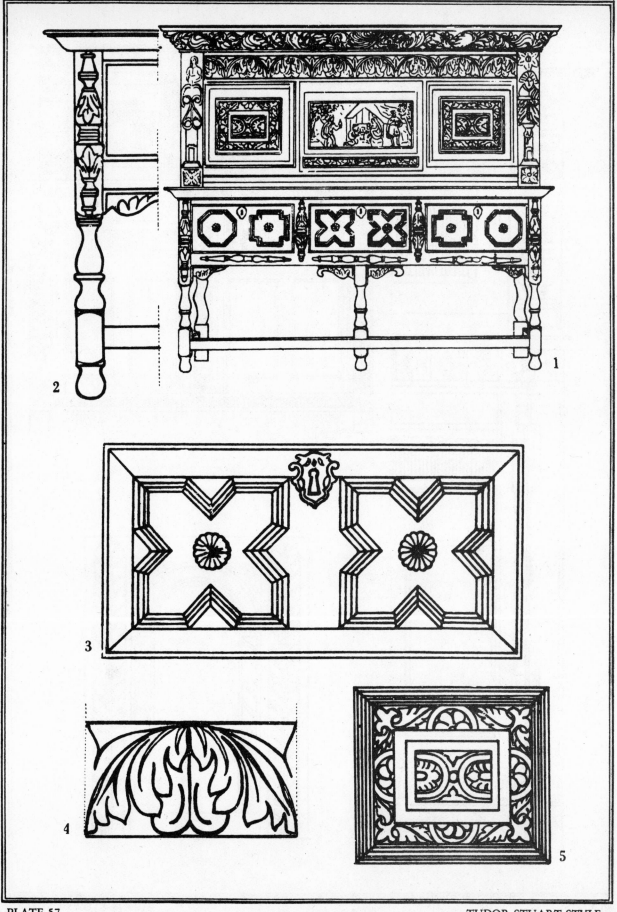

PLATE 57.                                                        TUDOR-STUART STYLE.

1. Dresser from 17th century.  2. Detail of uprights.  3. Middle drawer panel.  4. Detail of upper frieze.  5. Upper side panel.

*Victoria and Albert Museum.*

PLATE 58.

1. Dresser, upper section has supports.  2. Detail.  3. Upper middle panel.

TUDOR-STUART STYLE.

*Private collection.*

**PLATE 59.**                                                    TUDOR-STUART STYLE.

1. Cabinet with ornately carved crosspieces.   2. Detail of front legs.   3. Decoration on crosspiece.   4. Escutcheon plate.

*J. S. Sykes collection.*

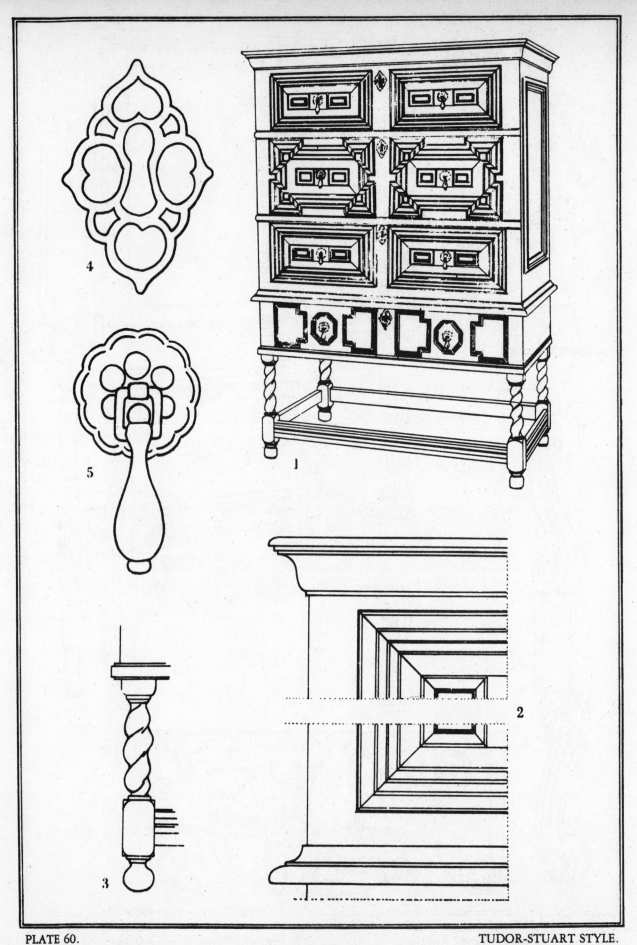

PLATE 60.                                             TUDOR-STUART STYLE.

1. Commode with turned legs, end of 17th century.   2. Detail of cornice and panels.   3. Turned legs.   4. Escutcheon
plate.   5. Drawer pull.

*Victoria and Albert Museum.*

64

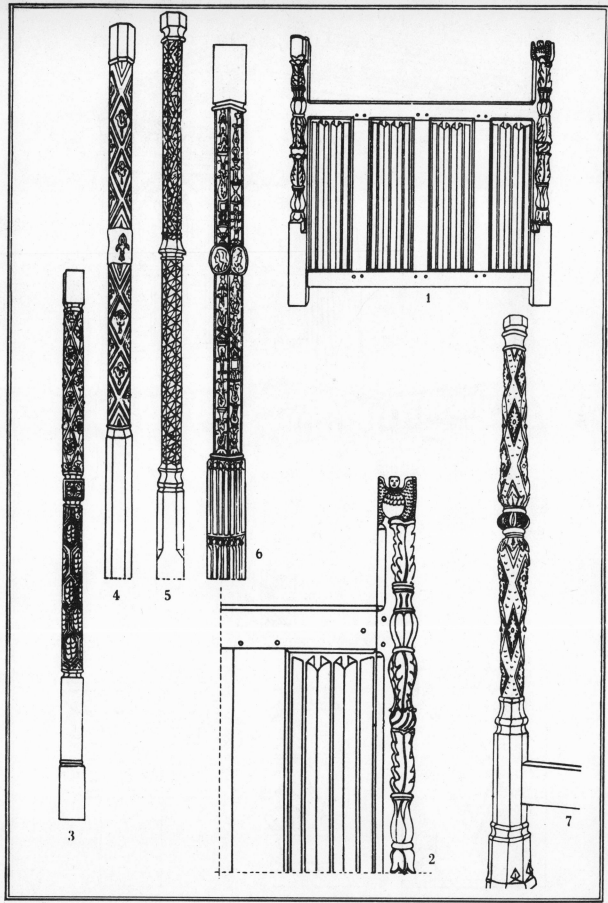

PLATE 61.

TUDOR-STUART STYLE.

1. Bed with panels imitating pleated cloth (Gothic influence), 16th century.   2. Details of post and decorative panels.
3, 4, 5, 6 and 7. Posts from other beds from the early 16th century.

*Victoria and Albert Museum.*

PLATE 62.                                                                                    TUDOR-STUART STYLE.
1. Canopy bed with bulbous posts.    2. Detail of footboard panels.    3. Detail of posts.    4. Detail of canopy frieze.
*Victoria and Albert Museum.*

PLATE 63.

TUDOR-STUART STYLE.

1. Canopy bed, end of 16th century.   2. Headboard decoration.   3. Mouldings on pilasters at foot.   4. Decoration on canopy mouldings.   5. Post.

*Victoria and Albert Museum.*

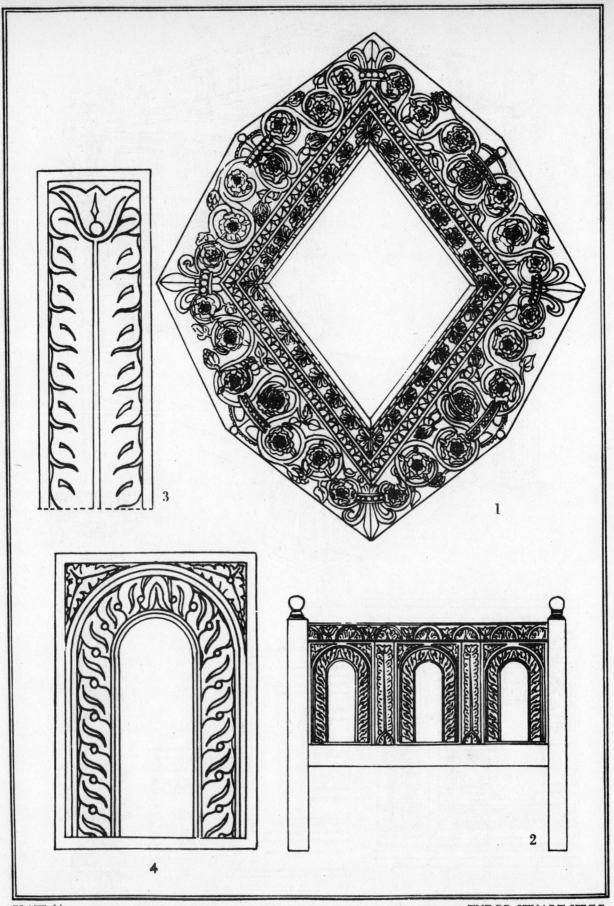

PLATE 64.                                                    TUDOR-STUART STYLE.

1. Headboard section from 16th-century bed.   2. Bed with arches in "guilloche" design, 16th century.   3. Millet decoration.   4. Panel decorations.

*Victoria and Albert Museum.*

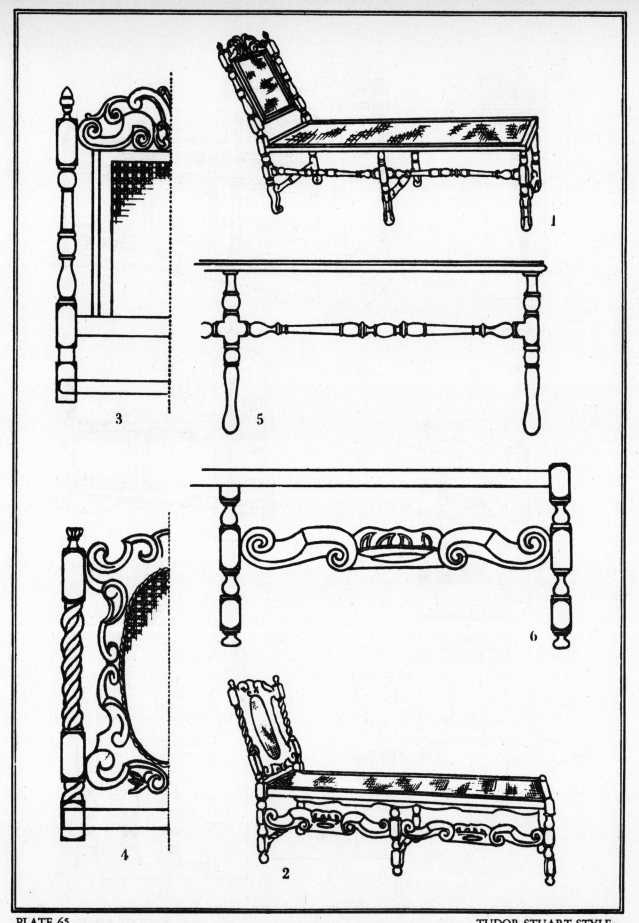

**PLATE 65.**                                                                          **TUDOR-STUART STYLE.**

1 and 2. Sofas from period of Charles II, 17th century.    3 and 4. Details of their respective headboards.    5 and
6. Details of legs and crosspieces.

*Private collection.*

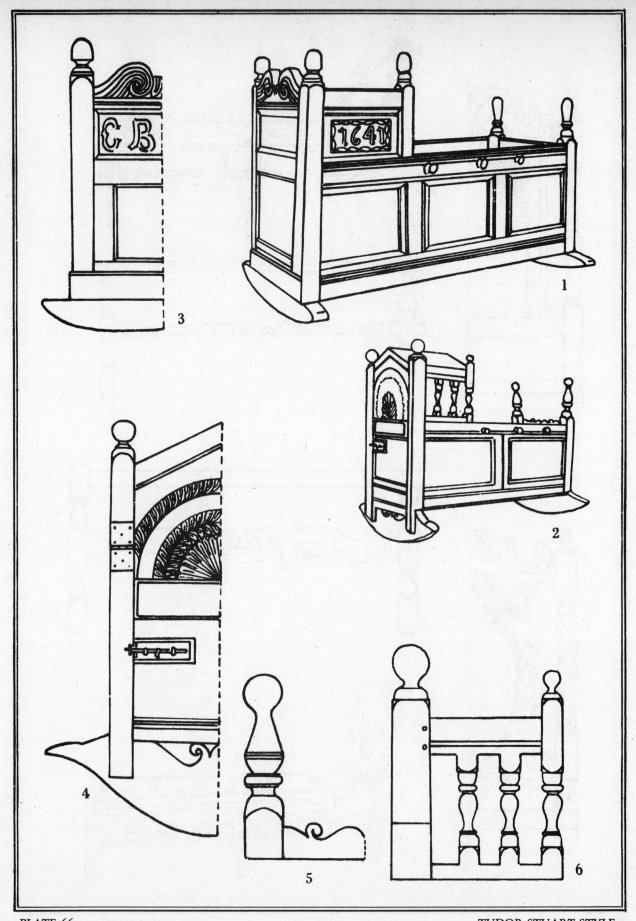

PLATE 66.

TUDOR-STUART STYLE.

1 and 2. Cradles from the 17th century.   3 and 4. Details of their respective headboards.   5. Post at foot of second cradle.   6. Detail of upper post on second cradle.

*Victoria and Albert Museum.*

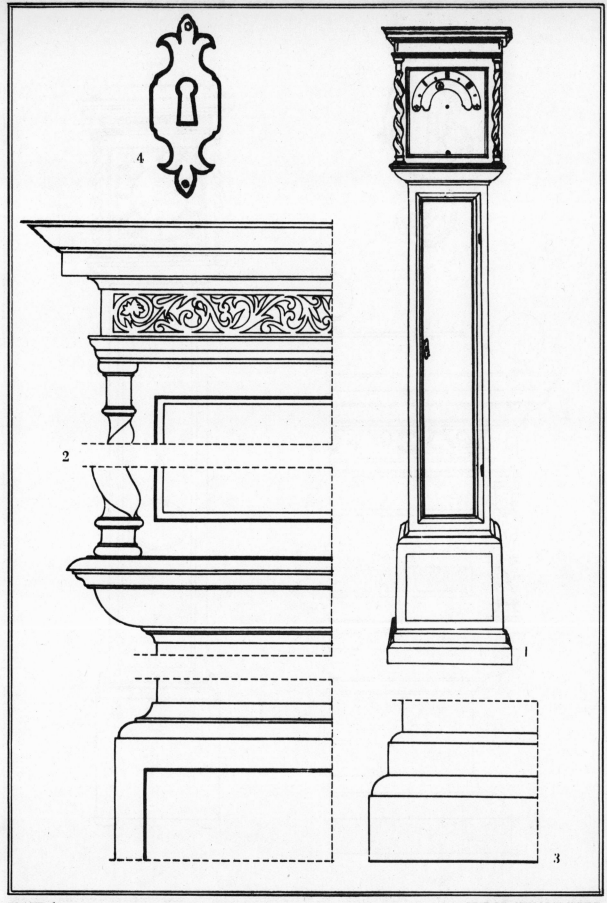

**PLATE 67.**  TUDOR-STUART STYLE.

1. Clock case from period of Charles II.  2. Details of mouldings and upper frieze.  3. Detail of socle.  4. Escutcheon plate.

*J. S. Sykes collection.*

PLATE 68.

TUDOR-STUART STYLE.

1. Clock case from period of Charles II.   2. Details of mouldings, finials and frieze.   3. Escutcheon plate.

*Property of J. M. Botibol.*

PLATE 69.
1. Clock case from the period of Charles II.   2. Detail of mouldings, turned post and frieze.   3. Escutcheon plate.

*Sir John Prestige Sr. collection.*

TUDOR-STUART STYLE.

**PLATE 70.**

1. Clock case from the 17th century.   2. Twenty-four-hour clockface.   3. Detail of mouldings and crest.

**TUDOR-STUART STYLE.**

*S. E. Prestige collection.*

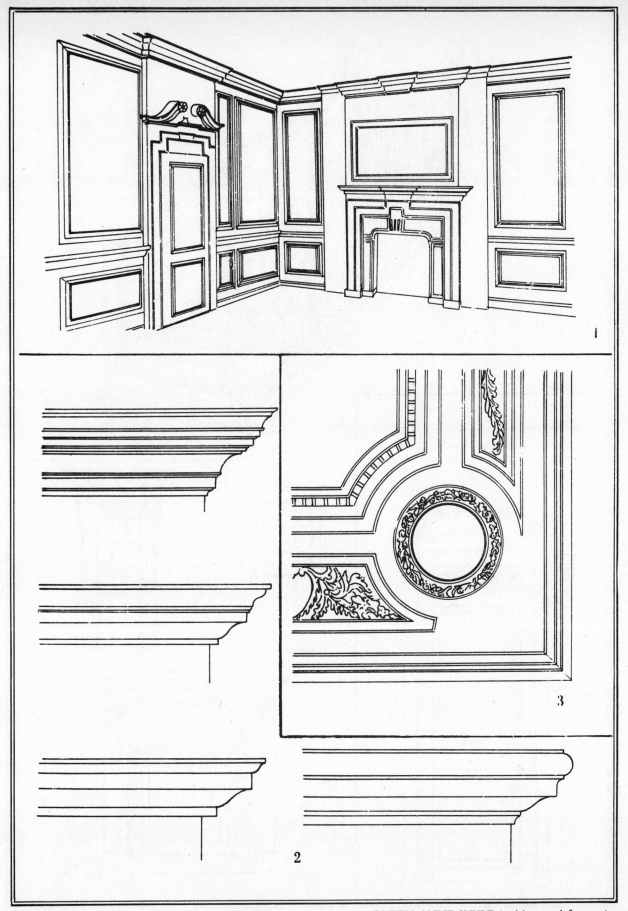

PLATE 71.                                                                QUEEN ANNE STYLE (architectural features).
1. Room with oak wall panels, 1686–88. Clifford's Inn, London.   2. Several kinds of mouldings used during Queen
Anne's reign.   3. Ceiling section, 1689. Dining room of the Belton House, Grantham, Lincoln County.

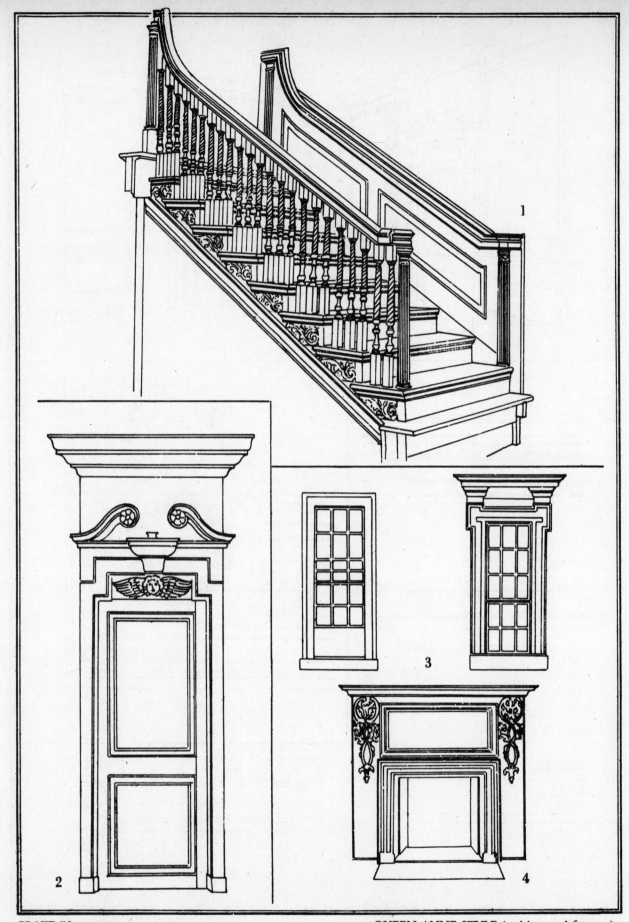

**PLATE 72.**    QUEEN ANNE STYLE (architectural features).

1. Section of carved pine stairway, end of 17th century. Castlenau house, Chortlake. 2. Door. Clifford's Inn, London. 3. Georgian windows. The first is from Swan House, Chichester; the second from Raynham Hall, Norfolk. 4. Fireplace by Grinling Gibbon, Hampton Court.

**PLATE 73.**                                                                 QUEEN ANNE STYLE (William and Mary period).

1. Chair from William and Mary period.   2. Back detail.   3. Front leg.   4. William and Mary chair.   5. Back detail.   6. Turned leg.

*Metropolitan Museum of Art and Kunstgewerbe Museum, Budapest.*

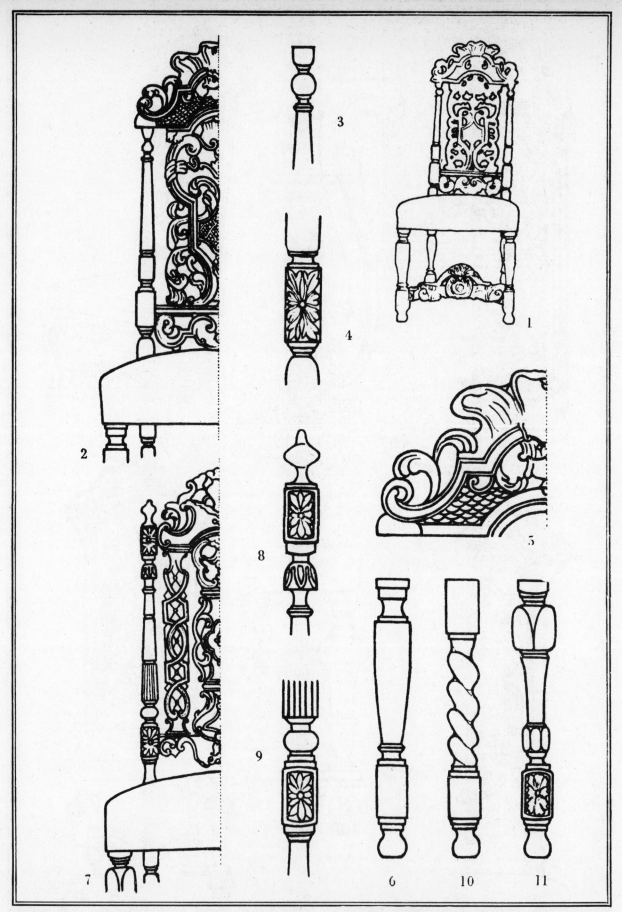

**PLATE 74.**                                    QUEEN ANNE STYLE (William and Mary period).

1. Chair from William and Mary period.    2. Back detail.    3 and 4. Detail of turned section and back-post decoration.    5. Decoration on crest.    6. Turned leg.    7. Back detail of another William and Mary chair.    8 and 9. Detail of turned section and decorations on posts at sides of back.    10 and 11. Turned legs in this style.

*From the old Richmond Palace.*

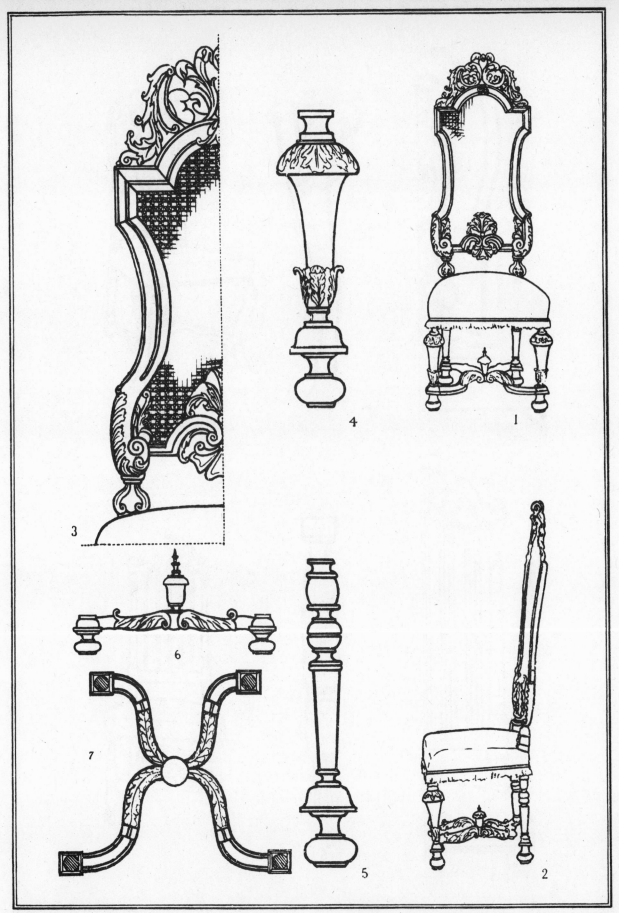

PLATE 75.                                                QUEEN ANNE STYLE (William and Mary period).
1 and 2.  William and Mary chair with cane back.    3.  Back detail.    4.  Front leg.    5.  Back leg.    6 and 7.  Decoration on x-shaped crosspieces.

*Metropolitan Museum of Art.*

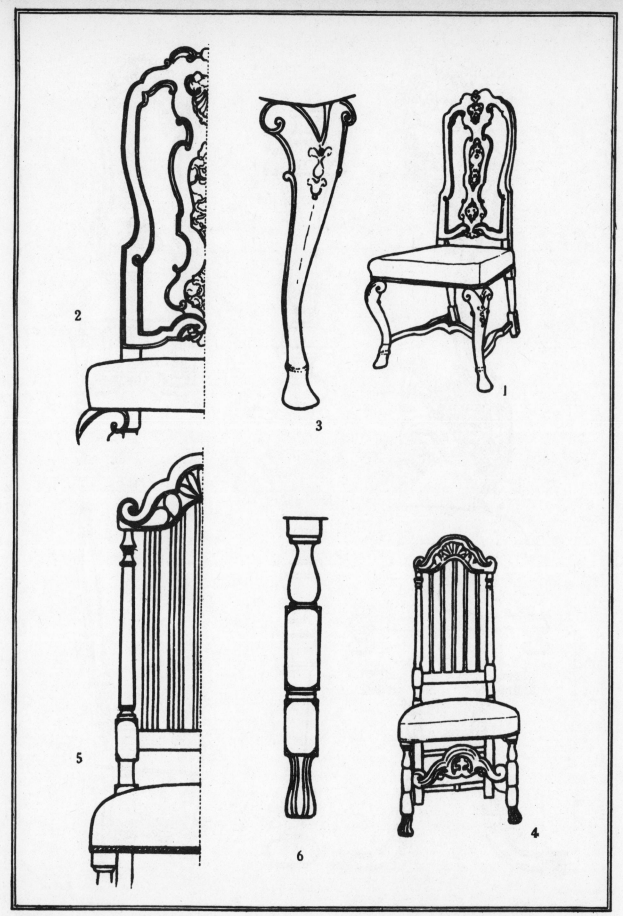

PLATE 76.                                      QUEEN ANNE STYLE (William and Mary period).
1. William and Mary chair.  2. Detail of back.  3. Front leg.  4. William and Mary chair.  5. Back detail.  6. Front leg.

*Victoria and Albert Museum and private collection.*

PLATE 77.                                    QUEEN ANNE STYLE (William and Mary period).
1. William and Mary sofa.  2. Detail of front leg.  3. William and Mary stool.  4. Bottom of the cross-pieces.  5. Detail of leg.

*Private collection.*

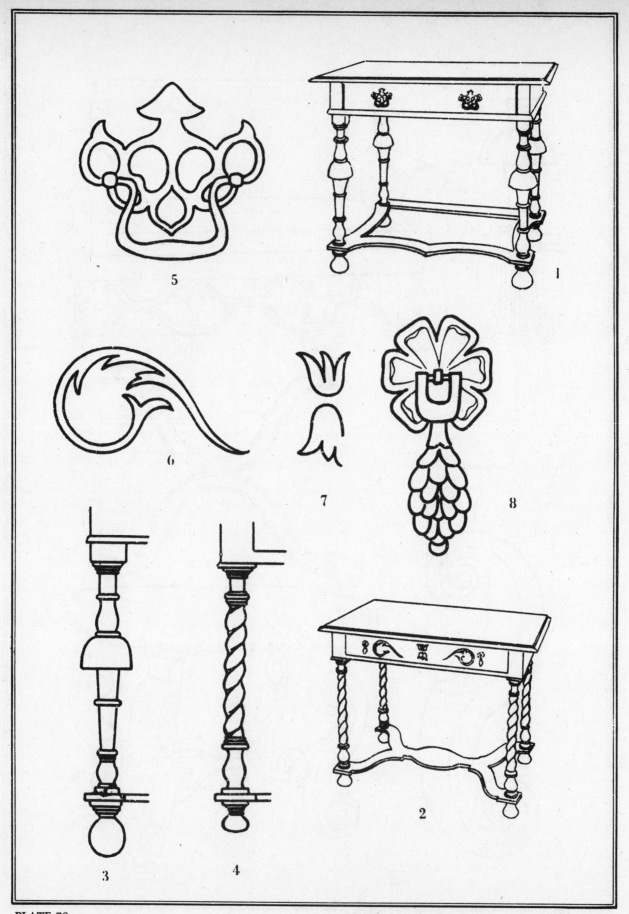

**PLATE 78.** QUEEN ANNE STYLE (William and Mary period).
1 and 2. William and Mary tables with turned legs. 3 and 4. Turned legs of first and second tables, respectively. 5. Drawer pull of first table. 6 and 7. Marquetry decorations on drawer front of second table. 8. Drawer pull of second table.

*Private collection.*

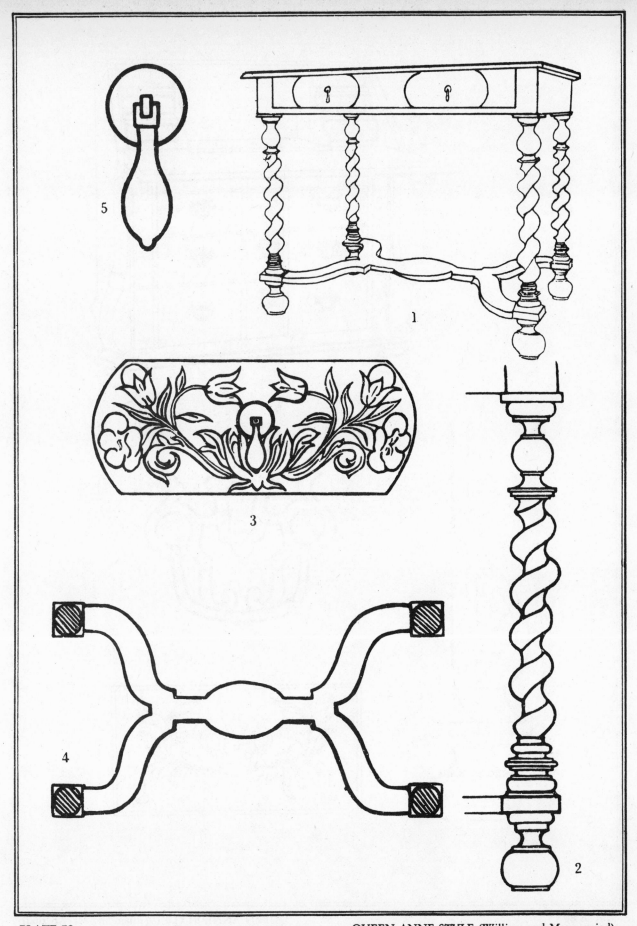

PLATE 79.                              QUEEN ANNE STYLE (William and Mary period).
1. William and Mary table with marquetry decorations.   2. Turned leg.   3. Drawer front panel decorated with marquetry.   4. Base of crosspiece.   5. Drawer pull.

*Victoria and Albert Museum.*

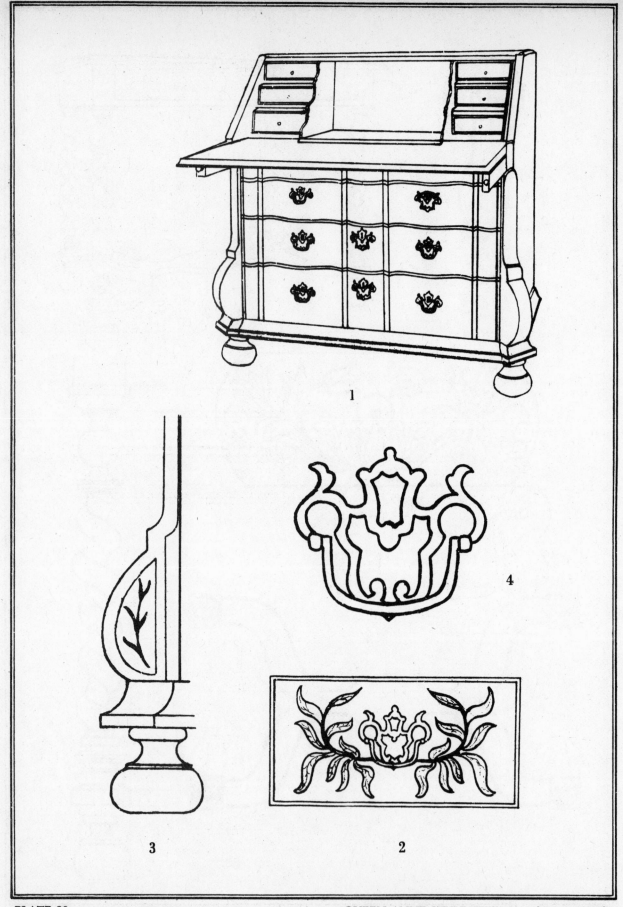

PLATE 80.                                                QUEEN ANNE STYLE (William and Mary period).
1. William and Mary desk, beginning of 18th century.   2. Decoration on drawer panel.   3. Detail of upright and foot.   4. Drawer pull.

*Private collection.*

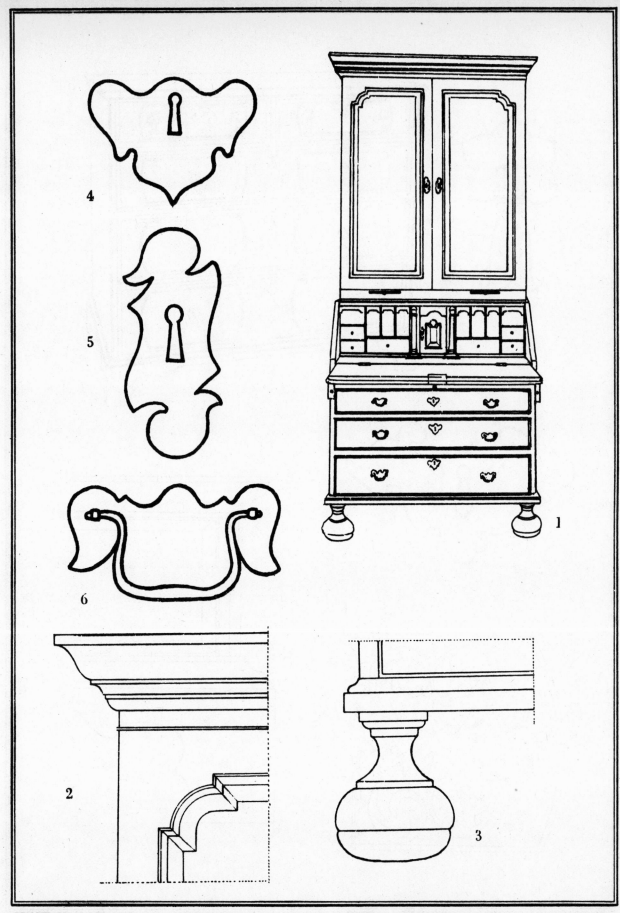

**PLATE 81.** QUEEN ANNE STYLE (William and Mary period).
1. William and Mary desk, beginning of 18th century. 2. Detail of moulding and upper section. 3. Socle and foot. 4 and 5. Escutcheon plates. 6. Drawer pull.

*Private collection.*

PLATE 82.

QUEEN ANNE STYLE (William and Mary period).

1. Richly adorned commode from period of William and Mary. 2. Upper moulding, socle and foot. 3. Decorative drawer panels. 4. Drawer pull. 5. Escutcheon plate.

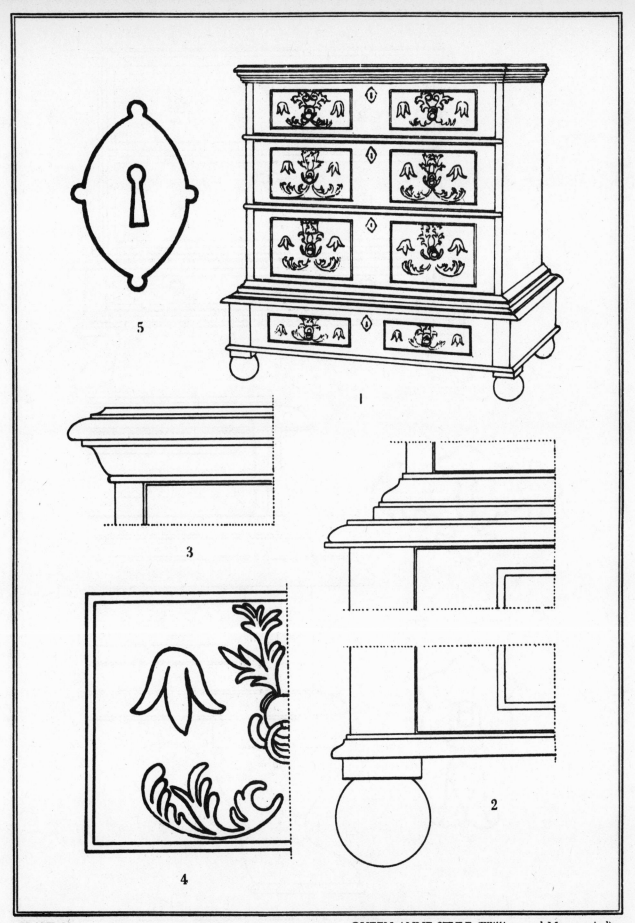

PLATE 83.                                    QUEEN ANNE STYLE (William and Mary period).

1. William and Mary commode with marquetry decoration. 2. Moulding of socle and foot. 3. Upper cornice. 4. Drawer panels with marquetry decoration. 5. Escutcheon plate.

*Private collection.*

**PLATE 84.**                           QUEEN ANNE STYLE (William and Mary period).
1. William and Mary commode.   2. Moulding on cornice, socles and foot.   3. Escutcheon plate.   4. Drawer pull.
*Victoria and Albert Museum.*

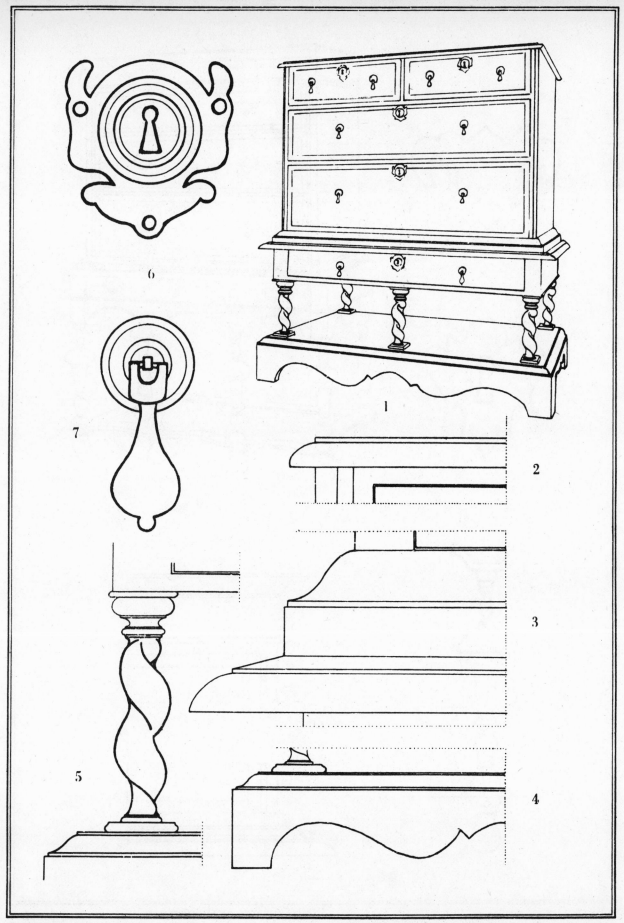

**PLATE 85.** QUEEN ANNE STYLE (William and Mary period).

1. Commode on turned legs from the period of William and Mary.   2. Cornice.   3. Socle.   4. Foot.   5. Turned leg.   6. Escutcheon plate.   7. Drawer pull.

*Victoria and Albert Museum.*

**PLATE 86.**                                   QUEEN ANNE STYLE (William and Mary period).

1. Commode on stand from period of William and Mary.  2. Cornice mouldings.  3. Moulding on socle.
4. Leg.  5. Drawer pull.  6. Escutcheon plate.

*Private collection.*

**PLATE 87.**                                                 QUEEN ANNE STYLE (William and Mary period).

1. William and Mary commode on stand.   2. Cornice.   3. Socle of upper section.   4. Leg.   5. Escutcheon
plate.   6. Drawer pull.

*Private collection.*

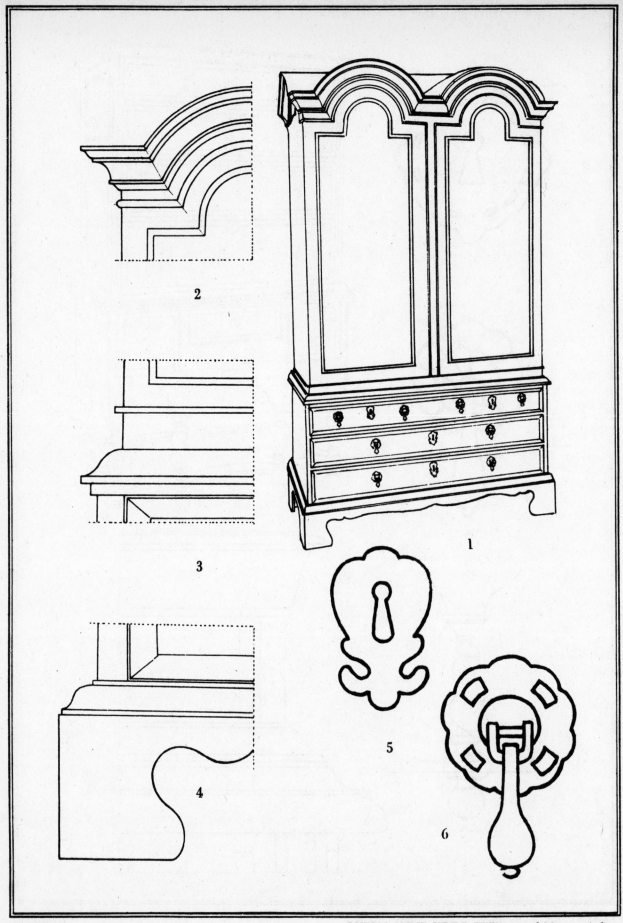

**PLATE 88.**                              QUEEN ANNE STYLE (William and Mary period).

1. William and Mary wardrobe, end of 17th century.  2. Cornice.  3. Socle of upper section.  4. Foot.
5. Escutcheon plate.  6. Drawer pull.

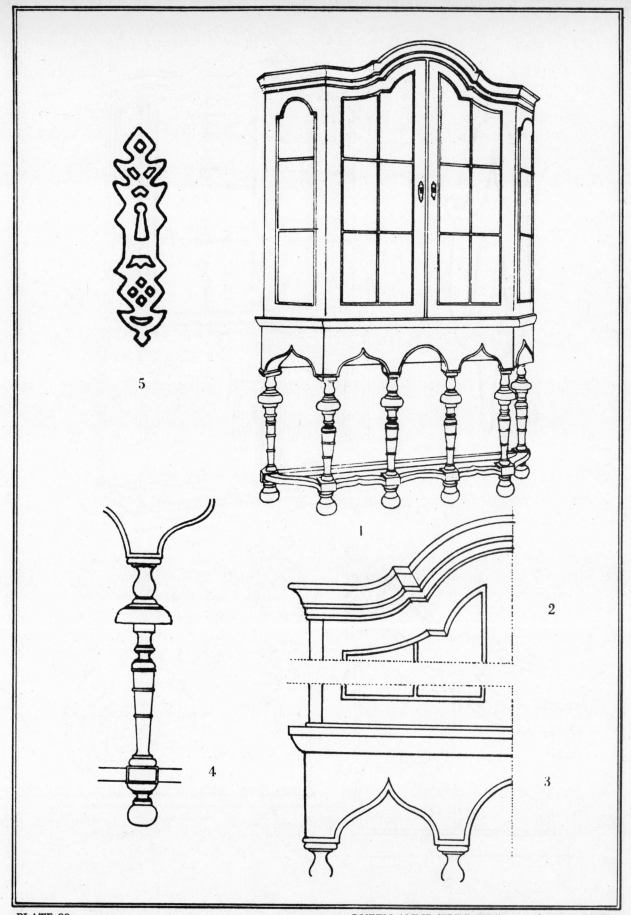

**PLATE 89.**                                                QUEEN ANNE STYLE (William and Mary period).

1. William and Mary display cabinet.    2. Cornice.    3. Top of base.    4. Leg.    5. Escutcheon plate.

*Property of M. M. Story et Triggs, Ltd., London.*

**PLATE 90.**  QUEEN ANNE STYLE (William and Mary period).

1. Display cabinet from end of 17th century.  2. Details of upper section.  3. Details of lower section.  4. Escutcheon plate.

*Private collection.*

PLATE 91.                                    QUEEN ANNE STYLE (William and Mary period).
1. Clock from 17th century.   2 and 3. Details.   4. Handle.   5. Hands.

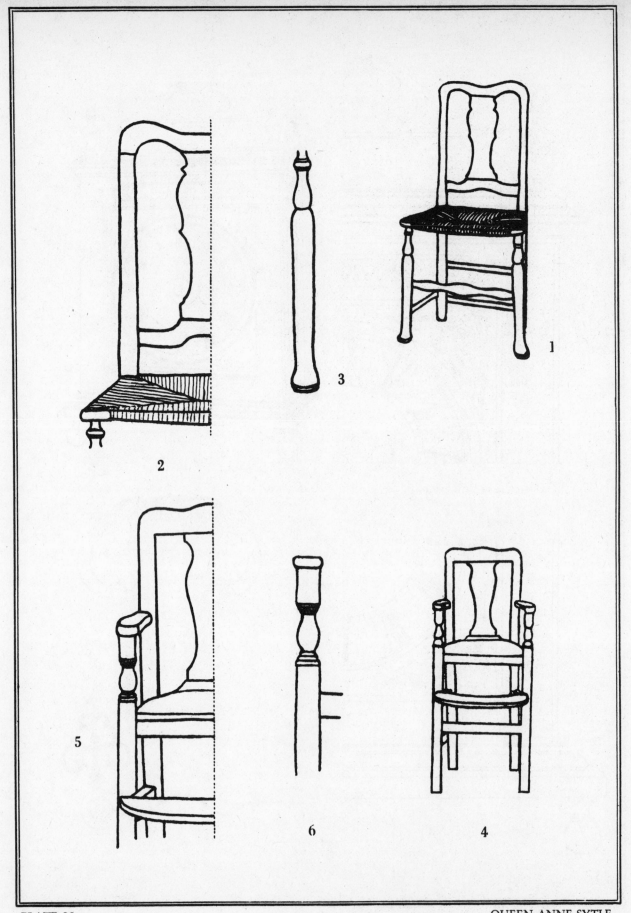

**PLATE 92.** QUEEN ANNE SYTLE.

1. Country chair from Queen Anne period.   2. Back detail.   3. Turned front leg.   4. Country child's chair of the same period.   5. Detail.   6. Turned post.

*Private collection.*

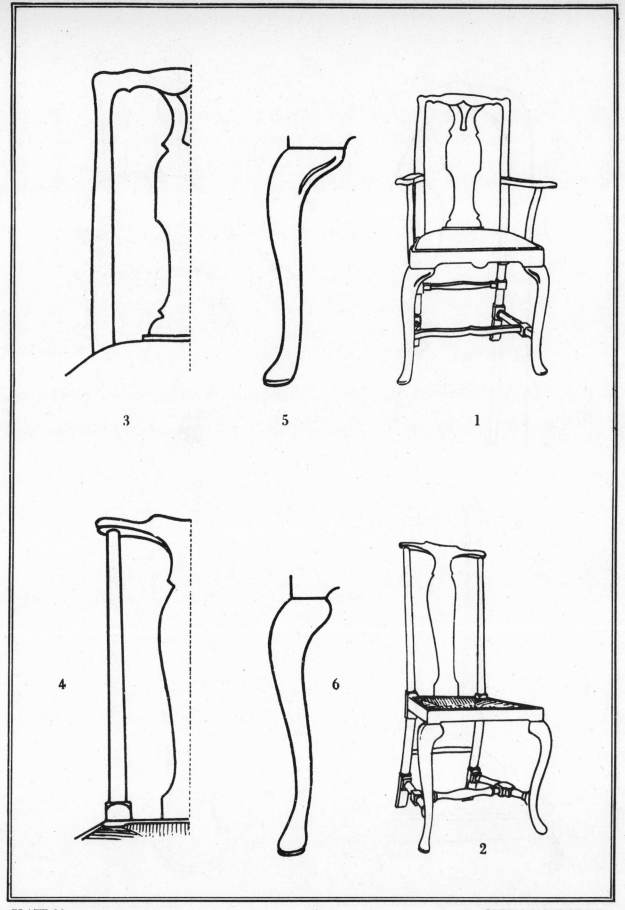

PLATE 93.                                                                    QUEEN ANNE STYLE.
1 and 2. Armchair and chair with connected legs from the Queen Anne period.   3 and 4. Details of backs.   5 and
6. Legs of armchair and chair, respectively.

*Private collection.*

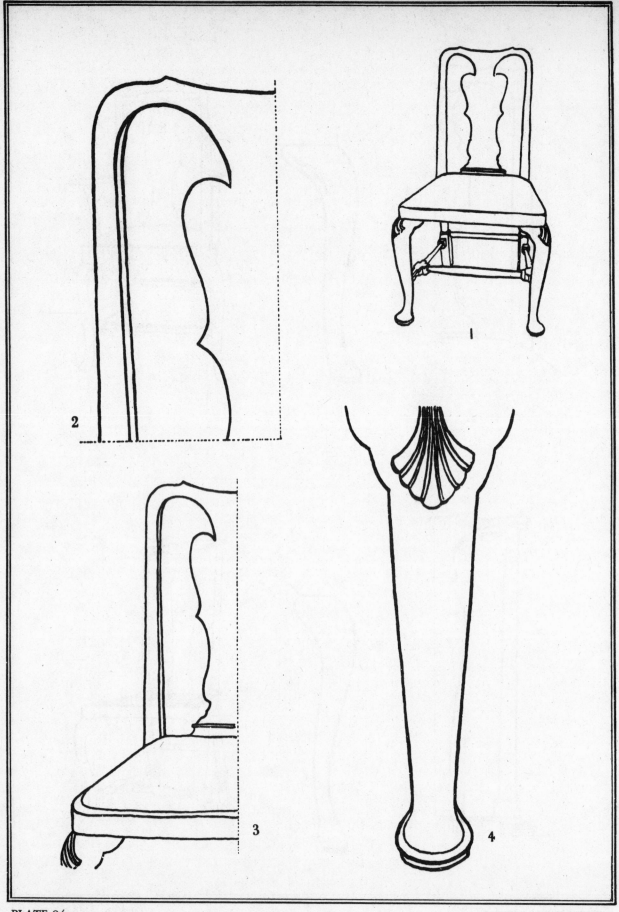

PLATE 94.

1. Simple but reinforced Queen Anne chair.   2 and 3. Details.   4. Front leg.

QUEEN ANNE STYLE.

*Private collection.*

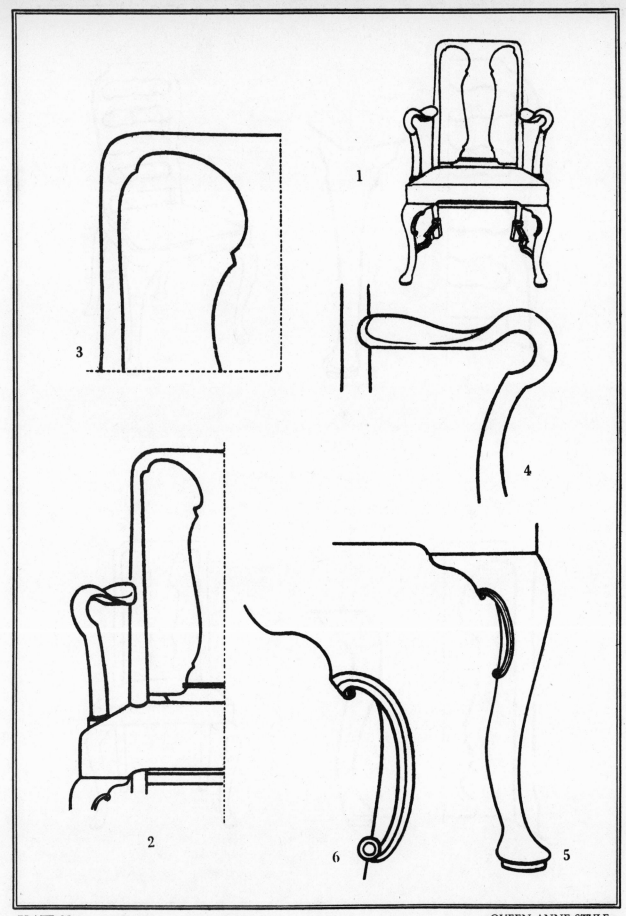

PLATE 95.                                                    QUEEN ANNE STYLE.
1. Queen Anne armchair.   2. Detail.   3. Upper corner of back.   4. Detail of arm.   5. Front leg.   6. Leg decoration.

*Victoria and Albert Museum.*

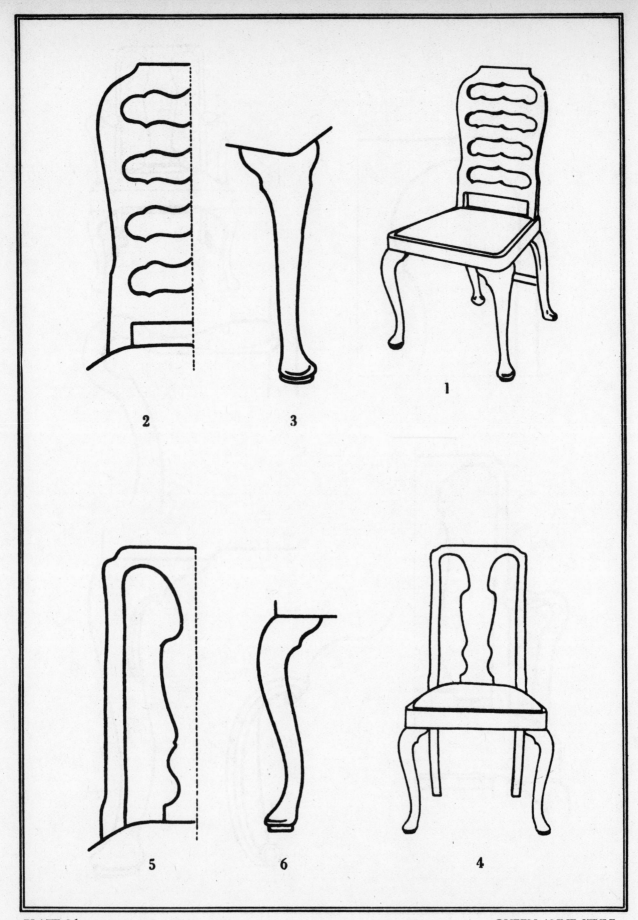

PLATE 96.                                                        QUEEN ANNE STYLE.
1. Delicate chair from end of Queen Anne period.   2. Detail of back.   3. Front leg.   4. Delicate chair from same
period.   5. Detail of back.   6. Front leg.

*Private collection.*

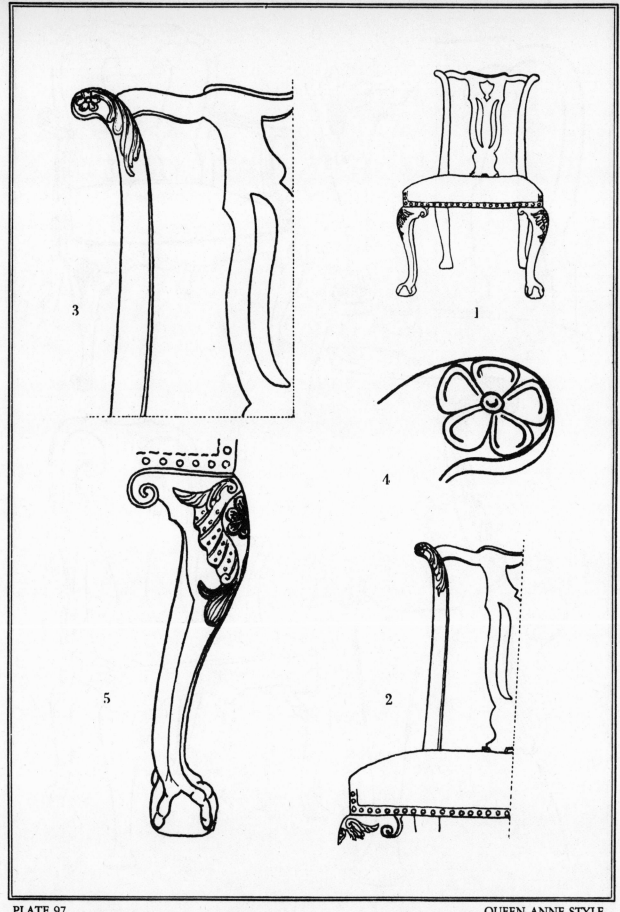

PLATE 97. QUEEN ANNE STYLE.

1. Ornate chair from end of Queen Anne period. 2. Detail. 3. Back. 4. Decoration on end of back support. 5. Decoration on front leg.

*Victoria and Albert Museum.*

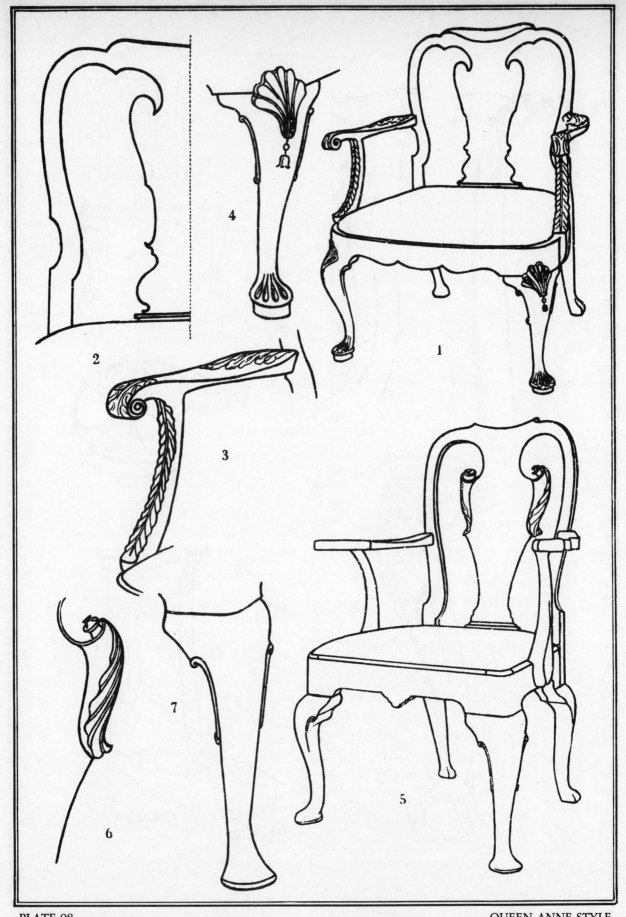

PLATE 98.                                                    QUEEN ANNE STYLE.
1. Queen Anne armchair.   2, 3 and 4. Decorations: back, arms and front leg.   5. Armchair from same period.
6 and 7. Decorations: carving on back and front leg.

*Metropolitan Museum of Art and private collection.*

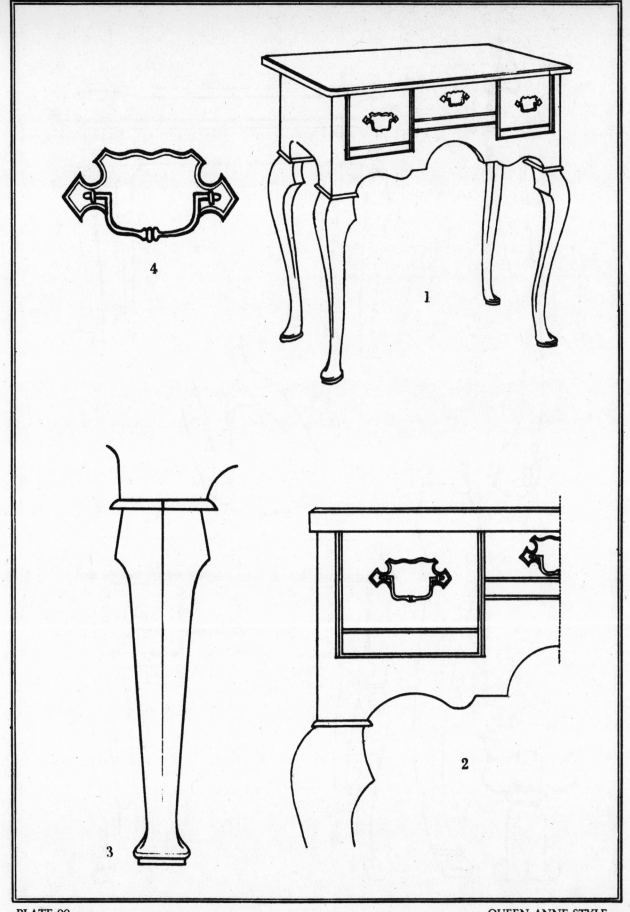

**PLATE 99.**
1. Cabriole table. 2. Detail. 3. Leg. 4. Drawer pull.

QUEEN ANNE STYLE.

*Private collection.*

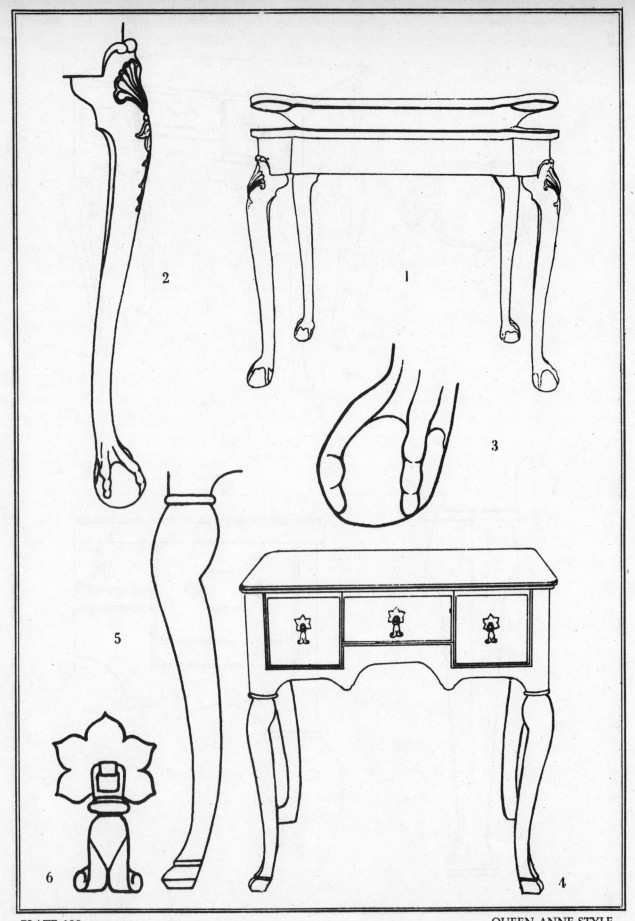

PLATE 100.                                                                                    QUEEN ANNE STYLE.
1. Queen Anne table.    2. Leg.    3. Base of leg.    4. Table from same period.    5. Leg.    6. Drawer pull.
*Victoria and Albert Museum and private collection.*

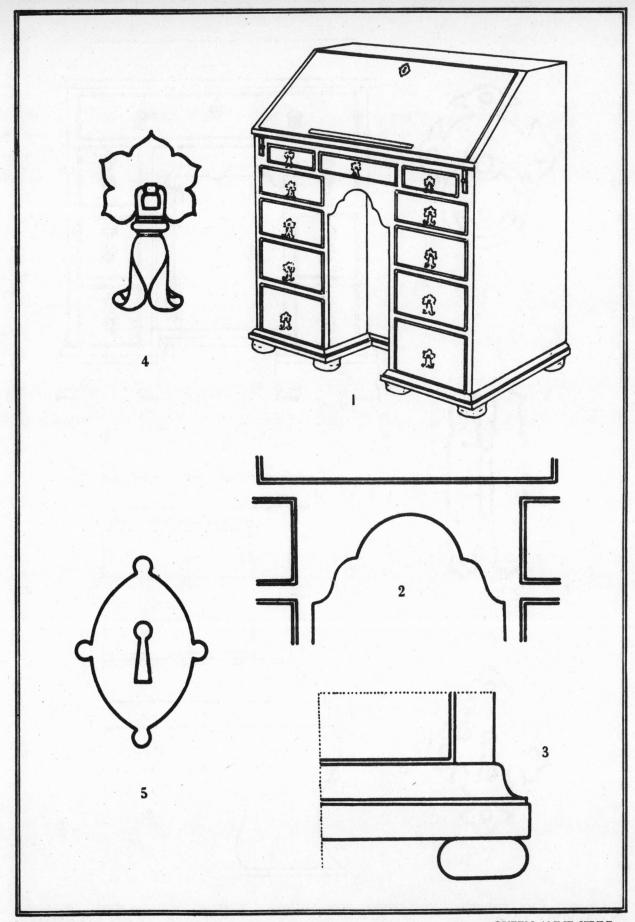

PLATE 101.                                                          QUEEN ANNE STYLE.
1. Queen Anne desk.   2. Central detail.   3. Socle and foot.   4. Drawer pull.   5. Escutcheon plate.

*Private collection.*

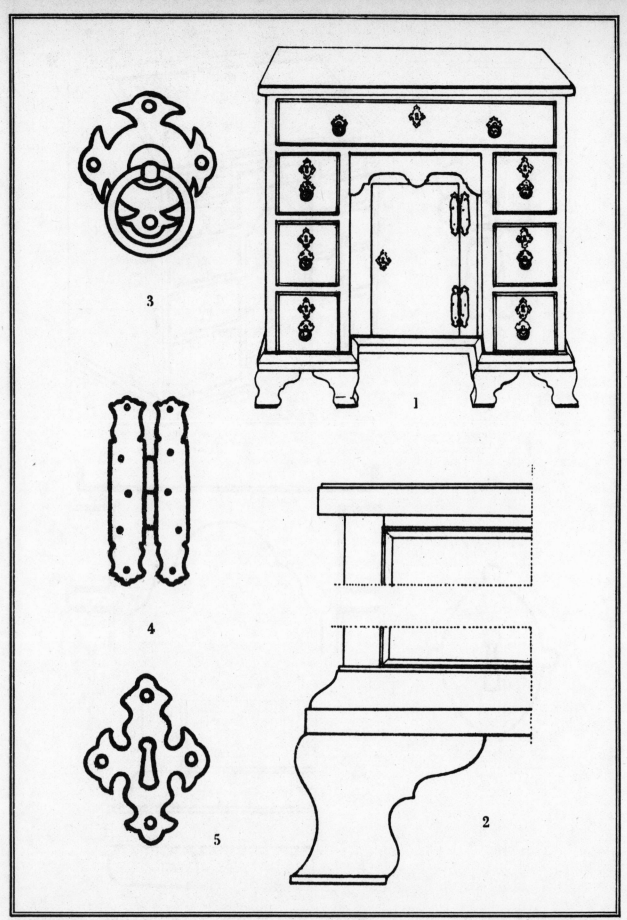

**PLATE 102.**  QUEEN ANNE STYLE.

1. Queen Anne desk.  2. Mouldings, socle and leg.  3. Drawer pull.  4. Hinge.  5. Escutcheon plate.

*Private collection.*

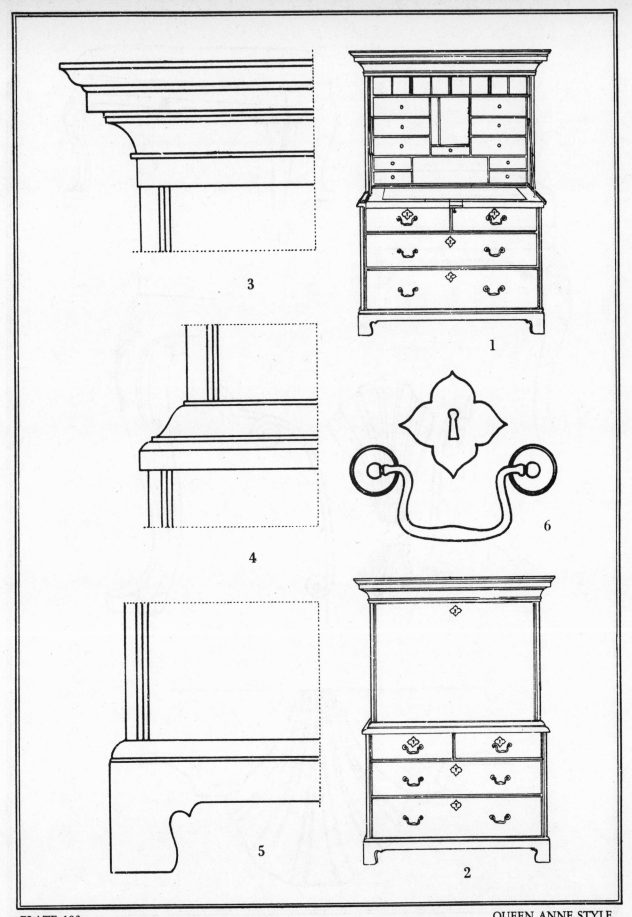

**PLATE 103.**                                                    QUEEN ANNE STYLE.

1. Opened chest-on-chest from Queen Anne period.   2. Same chest-on-chest, closed.   3. Upper cornice.   4. Socle of upper chest.   5. Socle and foot of lower chest.   6. Escutcheon plate and drawer pull.

*Private collection.*

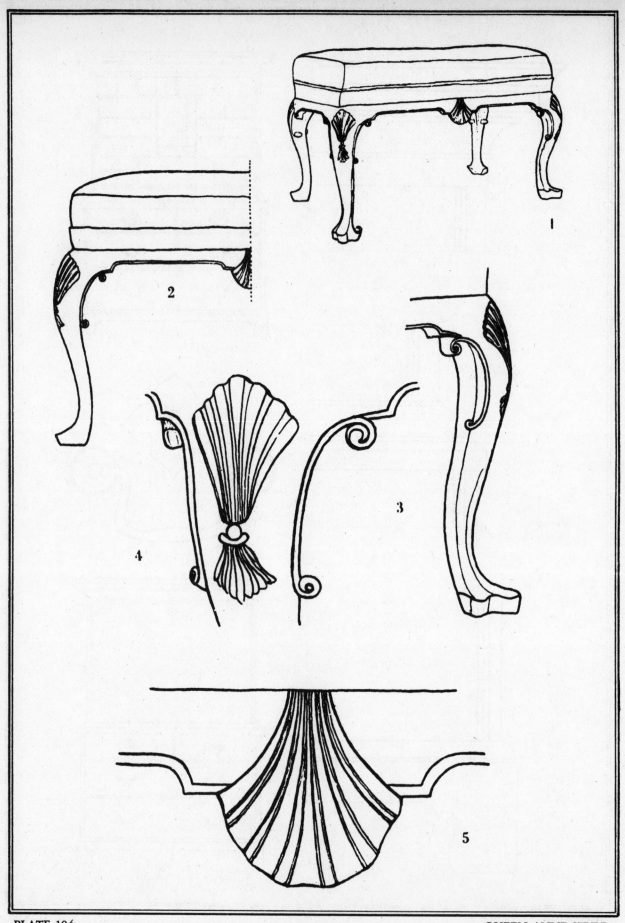

PLATE 104.                                                                                QUEEN ANNE STYLE.
1. Queen Anne stool.   2. Detail.   3. Leg.   4. Decoration on angle of leg.   5. Central decoration on crosspiece.
*Victoria and Albert Museum.*

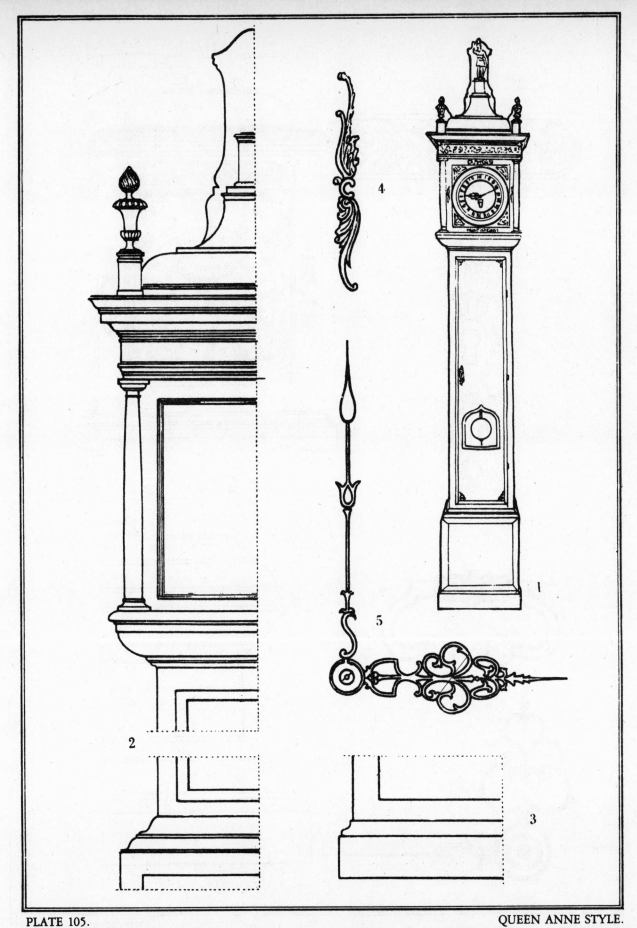

PLATE 105.                                                          QUEEN ANNE STYLE.

1. Elegant clock case from beginning of 18th century.  2. Details of crest and moulding.  3. Detail of socle.  4. Hardware.  5. Hands.

*S. E. Prestige collection.*

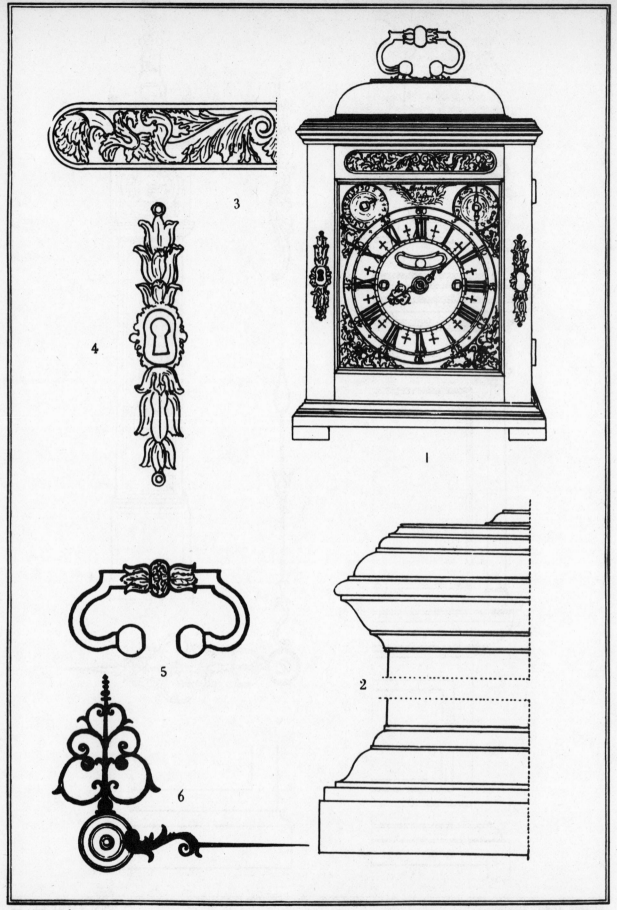

PLATE 106.                                                                        QUEEN ANNE STYLE.
1. Queen Anne desk clock.    2. Detail of moulding.    3. Frieze.    4. Escutcheon plate.    5. Handle.    6. Hands.

*S. E. Prestige collection.*

PLATE 107.

QUEEN ANNE STYLE.

1. Queen Anne clock case (by Thomas Tompion).   2. Detail of crest.   3. Decoration on lower part and foot.   4. Hands.

*Private collection.*

PLATE 108.

1. Clock case from early 18th century.   2. Details.

QUEEN ANNE STYLE.

*Victoria and Albert Museum.*

PLATE 109.
1. Clock case from early 18th century.   2. Detail of moulding.

2

1

QUEEN ANNE STYLE.

*Victoria and Albert Museum.*

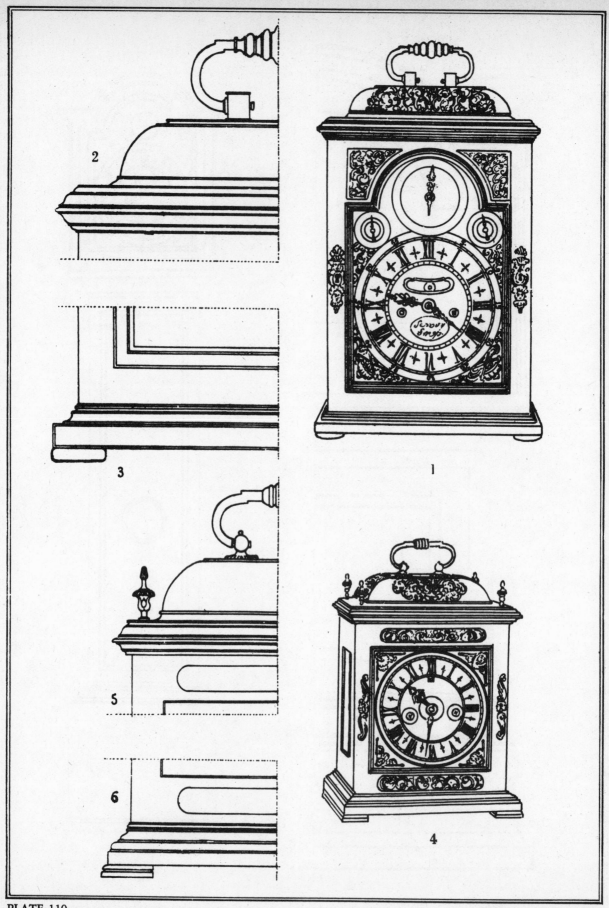

**PLATE 110.**                                                              QUEEN ANNE STYLE.

1. Desk clock from early 18th century.    2 and 3.  Details.    4.  Desk clock from end of 17th century.    5 and 6.  Details.

*S. E. Prestige and J. S. Sykes collections.*

PLATE 111.                                                  QUEEN ANNE STYLE.
1. Wall clock by Anthony Marsh (between 1720 and 1730).   2. Detail of cornice and upper moulding.   3. Detail of bottom of clock.   4. Face.

*Private collection.*

PLATE 112.

QUEEN ANNE STYLE.

1. Clock case decorated with marquetry, late 17th century. 2. Details of moulding. 3. Decoration on central panel. 4. Decoration on socle panel.

*Victoria and Albert Museum.*

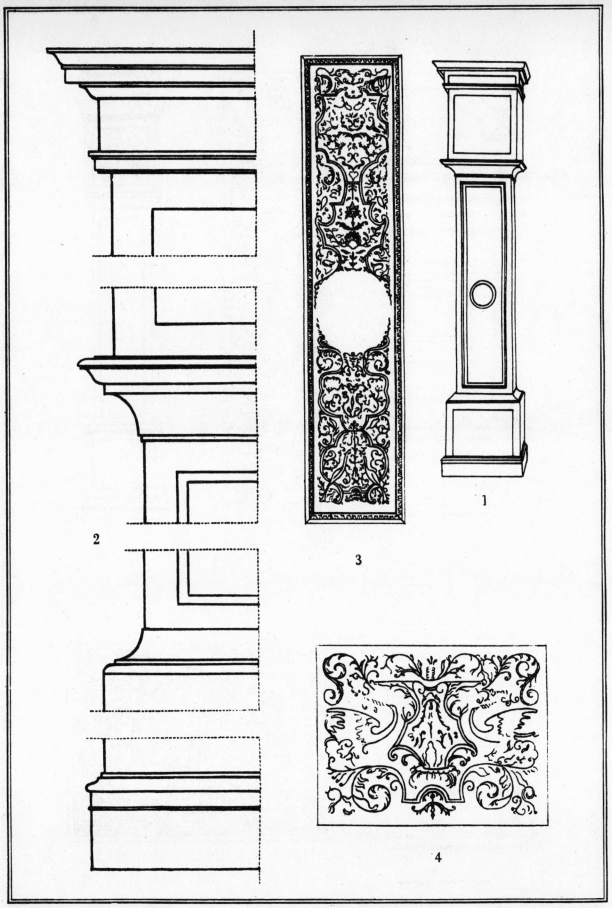

**PLATE 113.**  QUEEN ANNE STYLE.

1. Clock decorated with marquetry, early 18th century.  2. Details of moulding.  3. Central panel.  4. Panel on socle.

*Victoria and Albert Museum.*

PLATE 114.                                          QUEEN ANNE STYLE.

1. Clock case decorated with marquetry, early 18th century.  2. Details of crest and moulding.  3. Central panel.  4. Lower panel.

*Victoria and Albert Museum.*

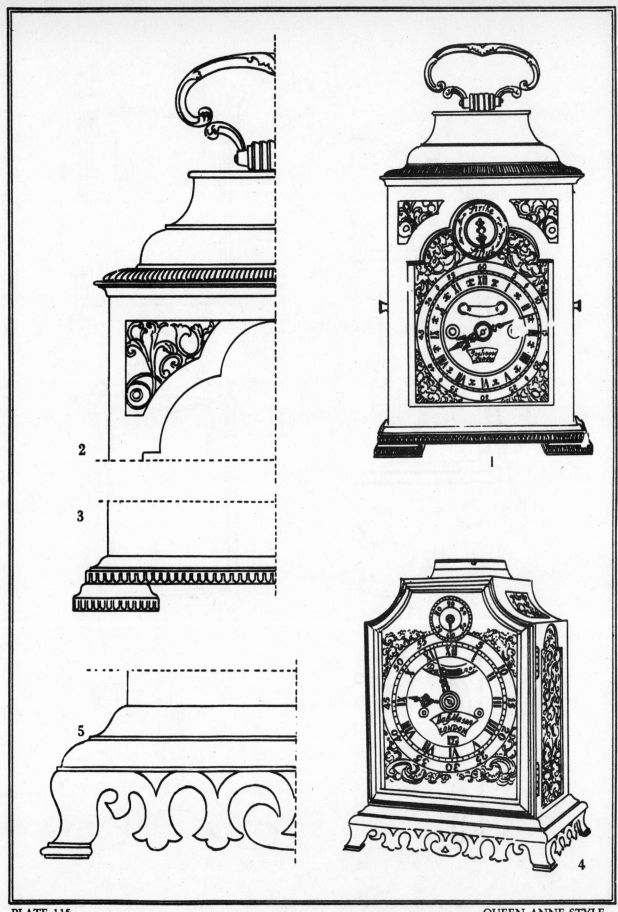

**PLATE 115.**                                                                    QUEEN ANNE STYLE.

1. Desk clock from mid-18th century.   2 and 3. Details.   4. Desk clock from mid-18th century.   5. Decoration on foot.

*S. E. Prestige and Malcolm Webster collections.*

PLATE 116.                                                                QUEEN ÀNNE STYLE.
1 and 2. Simple Queen Anne mirrors.   3, 4 and 5. Decorations on same.   6. Foot of second mirror.

*Private collection.*

PLATE 117.                                                   QUEEN ANNE STYLE.

1. Queen Anne mirror.    2. Detail of moulding.    3. Profile of moulding.    4. Queen Anne mirror.    5. Detail of moulding and upper frame.    6. Detail of lower frame.    7. Profile of moulding.

*Private collection.*

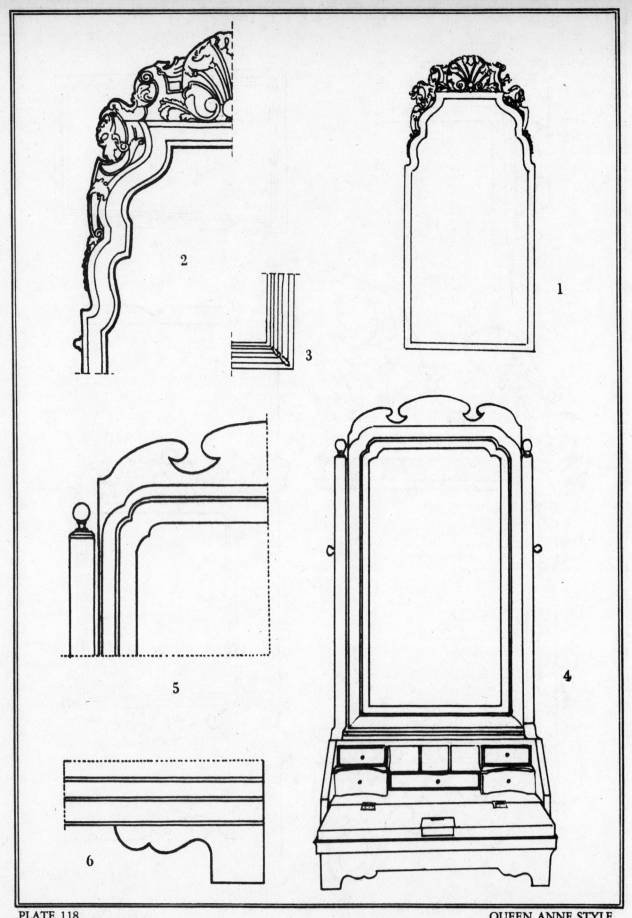

**PLATE 118.**                                                                                     QUEEN ANNE STYLE.

1. Queen Anne mirror.   2. Frame decoration.   3. Detail of moulding.   4. Dressing-table mirror.   5. Detail of frame and support.   6. Detail of foot.

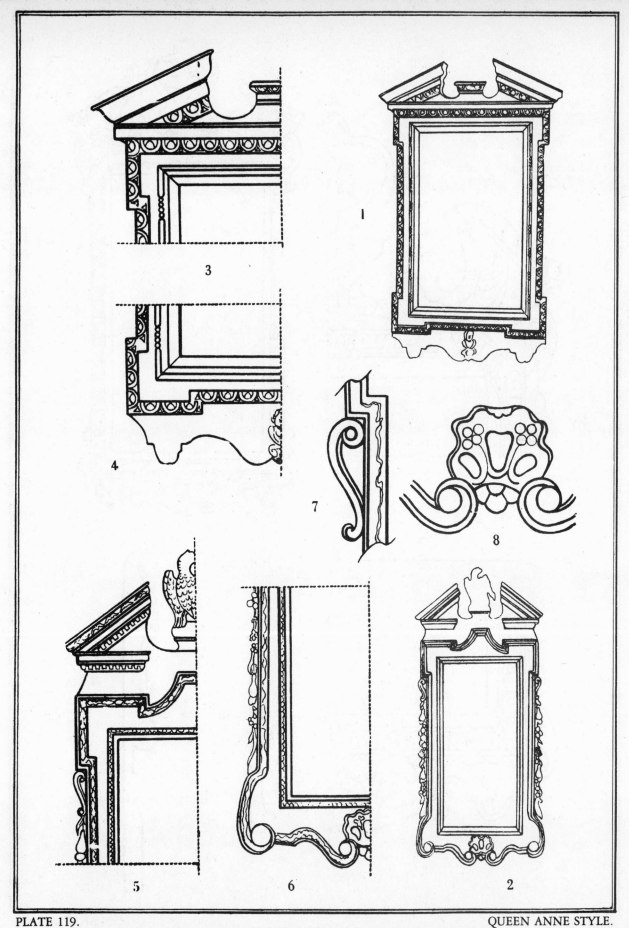

**PLATE 119.** QUEEN ANNE STYLE.

1 and 2. Mirrors with architectonic elements.   3 and 4. Details of mouldings and top and bottom of frame of first mirror.   5 and 6. Details of top and bottom of second frame.   7 and 8. Decorations on second frame.

*Private collection.*

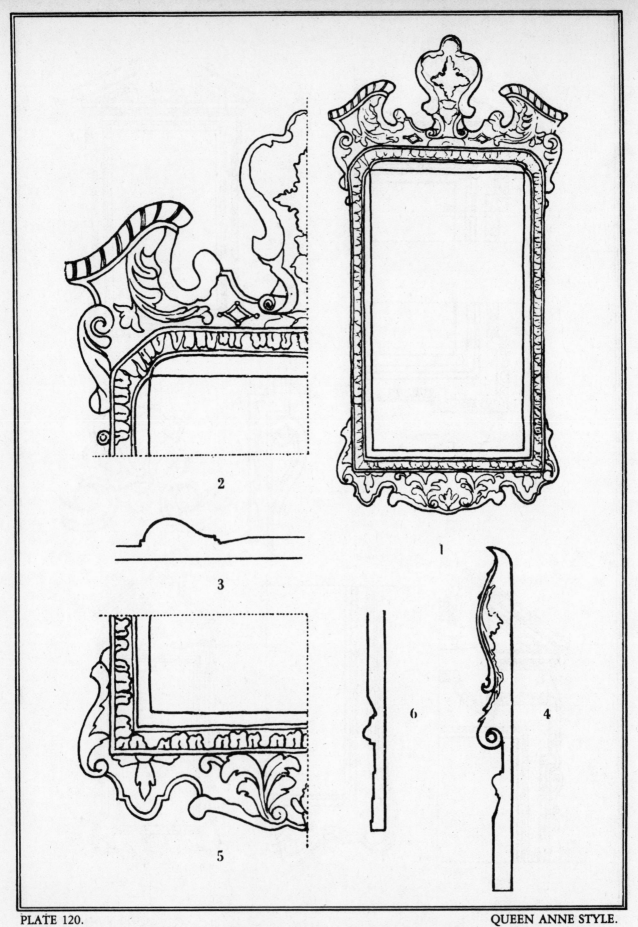

PLATE 120.                                                                QUEEN ANNE STYLE.

1. Ornate Queen Anne mirror.    2. Detail of top of frame.    3. Profile of side moulding.    4. Profile of central part
of frame and upper moulding.    5. Detail of bottom of frame.    6. Profile of moulding and bottom of frame.

*Victoria and Albert Museum.*

124

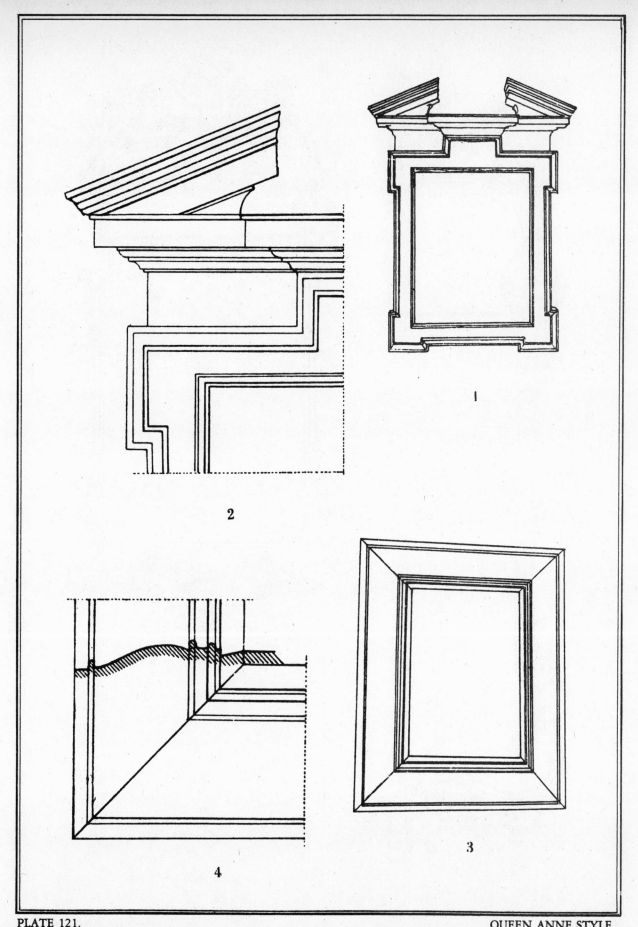

PLATE 121.

QUEEN ANNE STYLE.

1. Mirror from early 18th century.   2. Details of mouldings and upper frame.   3. Mirror from early 18th century.   4. Detail of corner showing profile of moulding.

*Private collection.*

**PLATE 122.**

1. Ornately decorated Queen Anne mirror.   2. Detail of upper frame.   3. Detail of lower frame.

*Collection of Lord Plender G.B.E.*

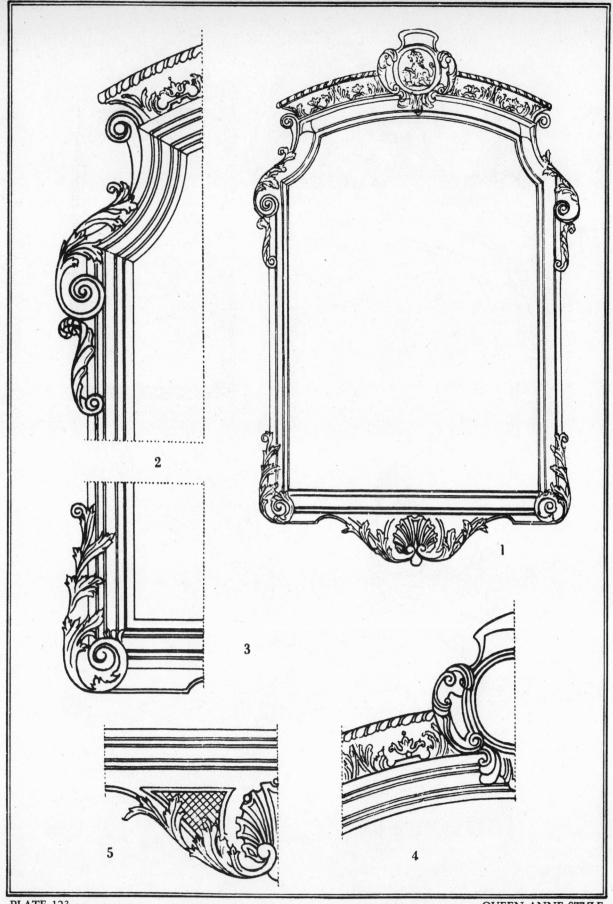

PLATE 123.                                                                                    QUEEN ANNE STYLE.

1. Queen Anne mirror.    2 and 3. Details of frame side.    4. Detail of upper frame.    5. Detail of lower frame.

*Private collection.*

PLATE 124.                                                                    QUEEN ANNE STYLE.

1 and 2. Queen Anne mirrors.    3. Detail of top of frame of first mirror.    4 and 5. Detail of top and bottom of second frame.

*J. S. Sykes collection.*

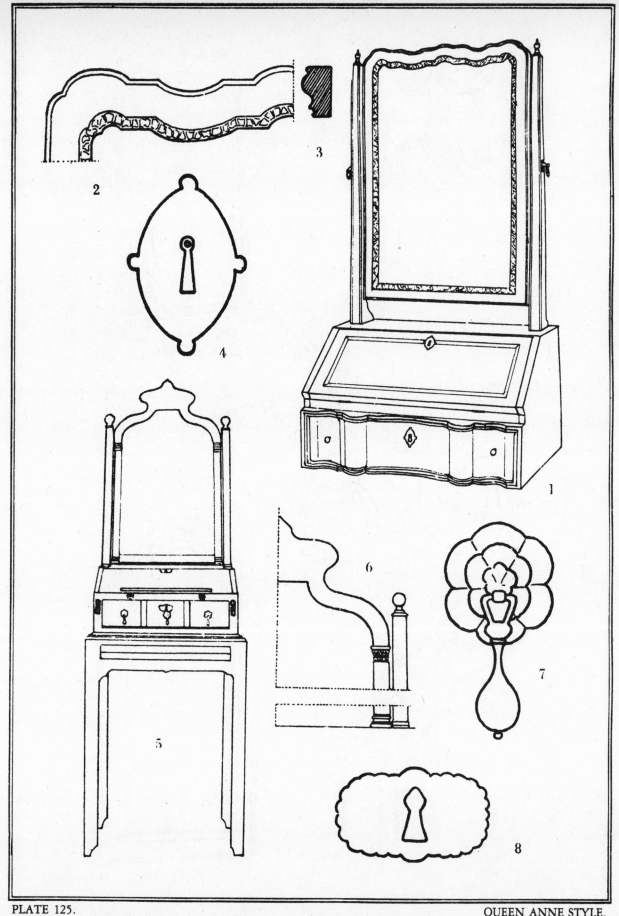

PLATE 125.                                                    QUEEN ANNE STYLE.
1. Queen Anne dressing-table mirror.   2. Detail of top.   3. Profile of moulding.   4. Escutcheon plate. Private
collection.   5. Queen Anne dressing-table mirror.   6. Details of frame top, uprights and supports.   7. Drawer pull.
8. Escutcheon plate.

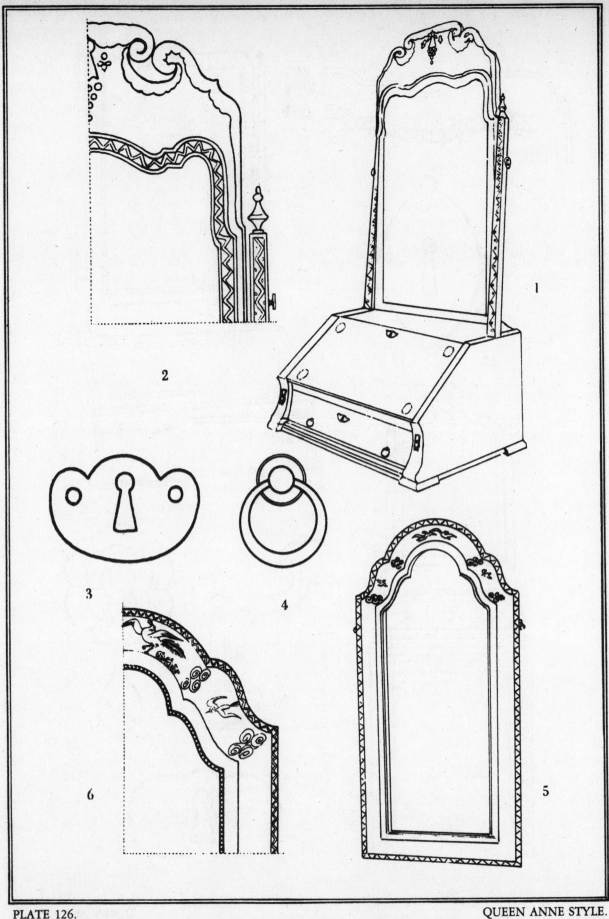

PLATE 126.                                                QUEEN ANNE STYLE.
1. Dressing-table mirror.   2. Detail of top of frame and support.   3. Escutcheon plate.   4. Drawer pull.   5. Mirror
showing Dutch influence.   6. Detail of frame.

*Victoria and Albert Museum.*

PLATE 127.                                                    QUEEN ANNE STYLE.

1. Cabinet from early 18th century.   2. Detail of corner of upper section.   3. Leg.   4. Escutcheon plate.

*Geoffrey Hart collection.*

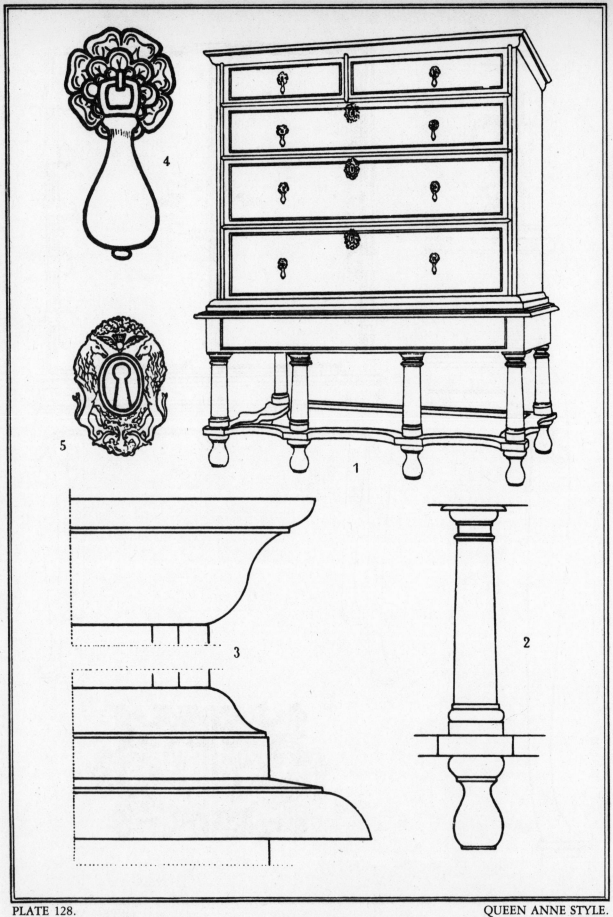

**PLATE 128.**                                                      QUEEN ANNE STYLE.

1. Queen Anne commode on stand.   2. Leg.   3. Mouldings of cornice and socle.   4. Drawer pull.   5. Escutcheon plate.

*Victoria and Albert Museum.*

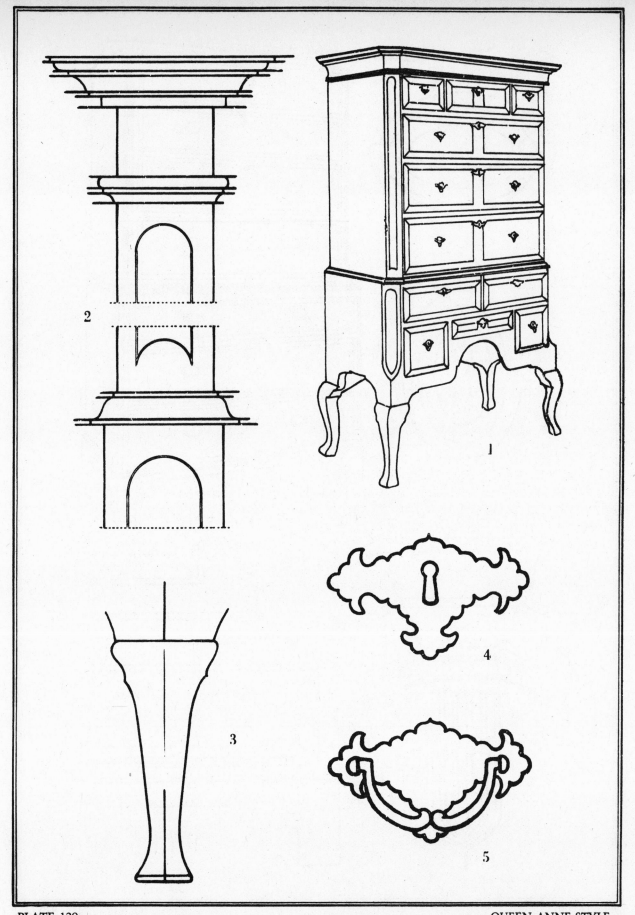

**PLATE 129.**

QUEEN ANNE STYLE.

1. Type of commode called a Tallboy, from the middle of the Queen Anne period.　2. Detail of mouldings and beveled upright.　3. Leg.　4. Escutcheon plate.　5. Drawer pull.

*Private collection.*

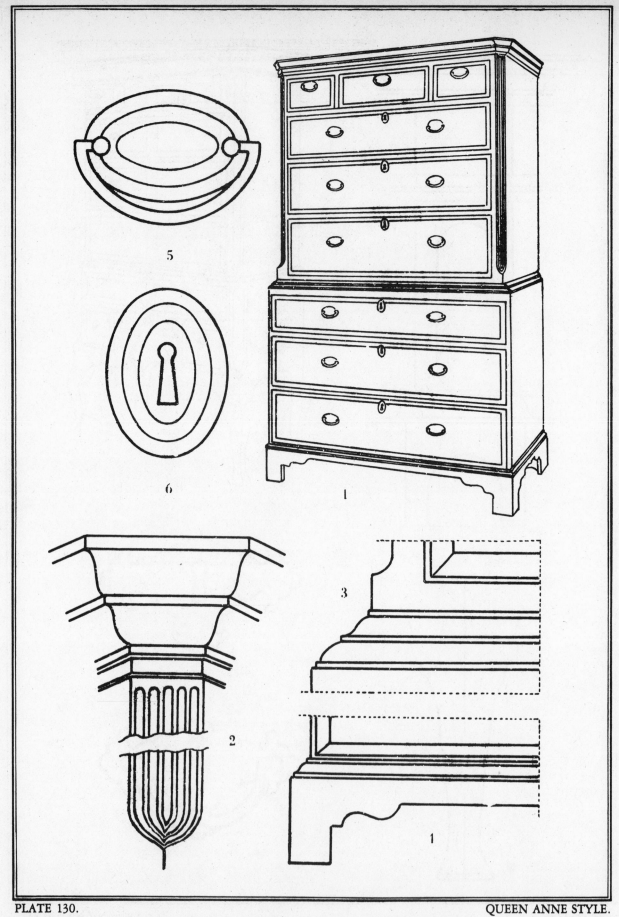

**PLATE 130.**                                          QUEEN ANNE STYLE.

1. Tallboy from the end of the Queen Anne period.    2. Cornice and carving on upright.    3. Socle of upper section.    4. Foot.    5. Drawer pull.    6. Escutcheon plate.

*Private collection.*

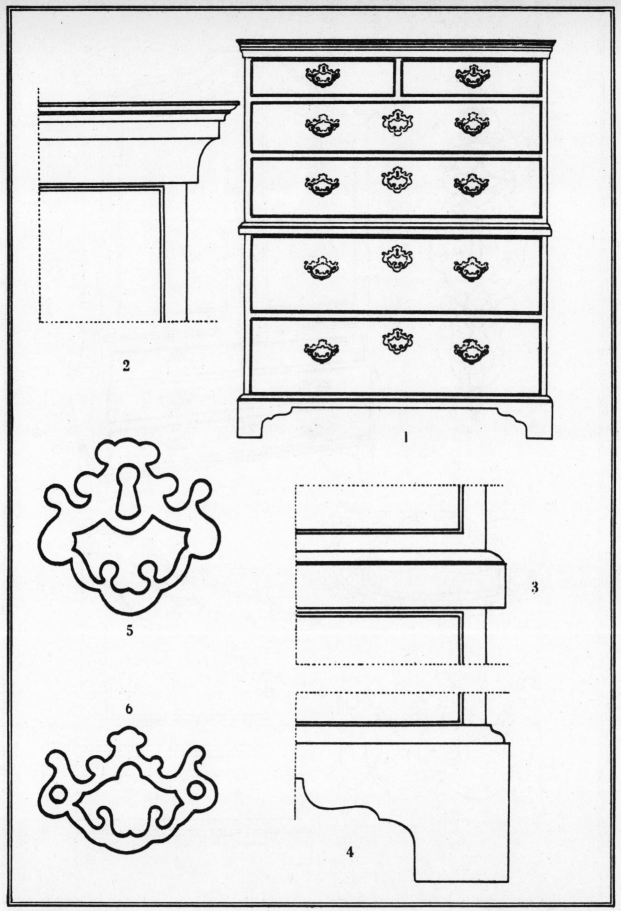

PLATE 131.                                                              QUEEN ANNE STYLE.
1. Tallboy from early 18th century.  2. Upper corner.  3. Socle of upper section.  4. Foot.  5. Escutcheon plate.  6. Drawer pull.

*Property of M.J.H. Springett, Rochester.*

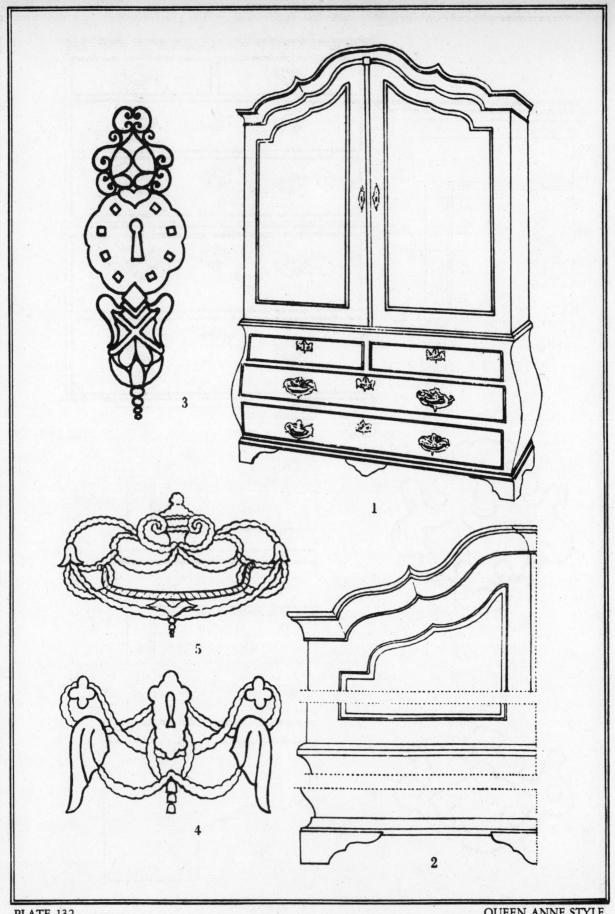

PLATE 132.                                                    QUEEN ANNE STYLE.

1. Wardrobe showing Dutch influence. 2. Detail of cornice, mouldings and foot. 3 and 4. Escutcheon plates. 5. Drawer pull.

*Private collection.*

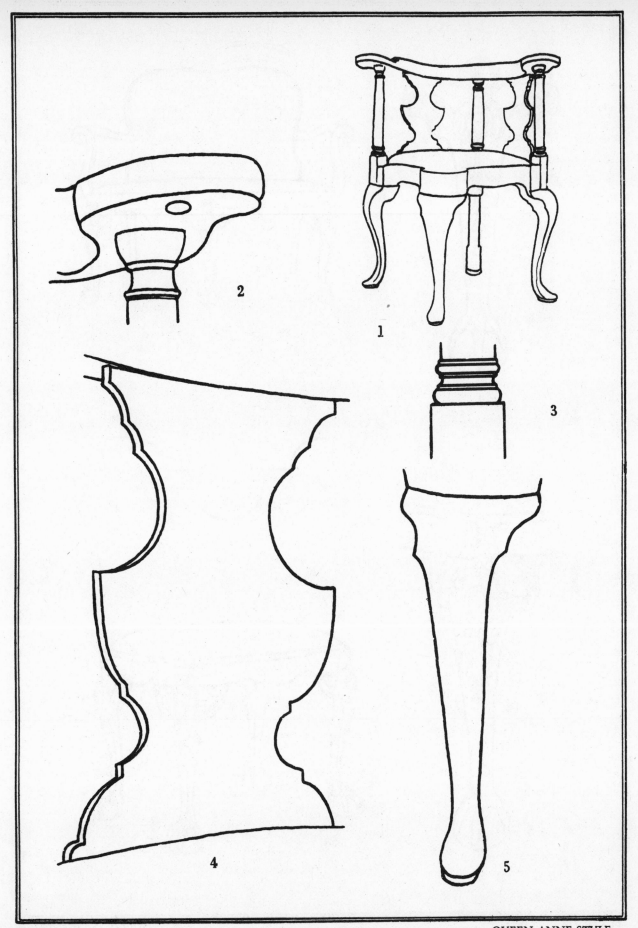

PLATE 133.                                                    QUEEN ANNE STYLE.
1. Corner armchair from end of Queen Anne period.   2. Detail of arm support.   3. Base of support.   4. Detail of back.   5. Leg.

*Victoria and Albert Museum.*

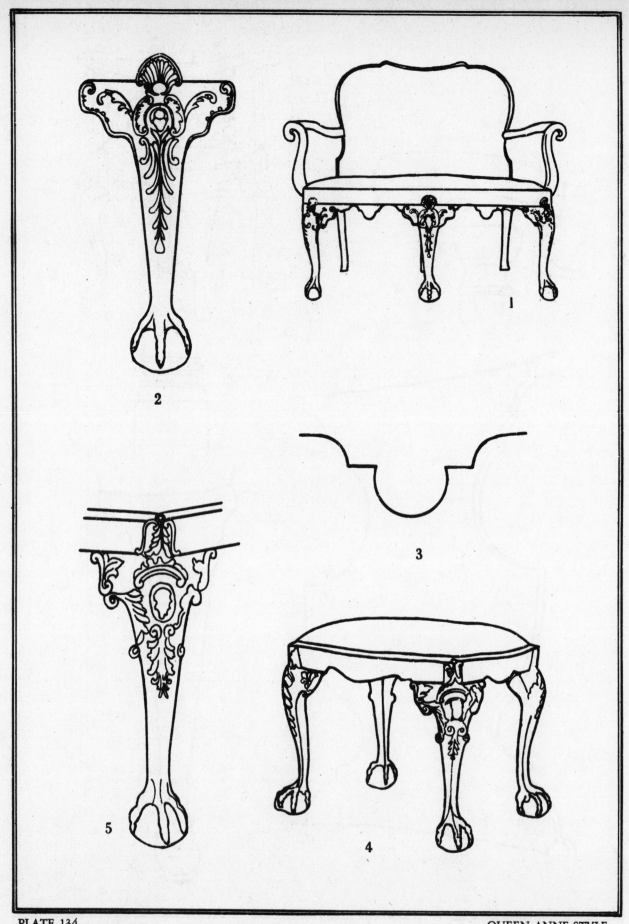

PLATE 134.                                                    QUEEN ANNE STYLE.
1. Sofa from end of Queen Anne period.    2. Front leg.    3. Festoon on crosspiece.    4. Stool from end of Queen Anne period.    5. Leg.

*Private collections.*

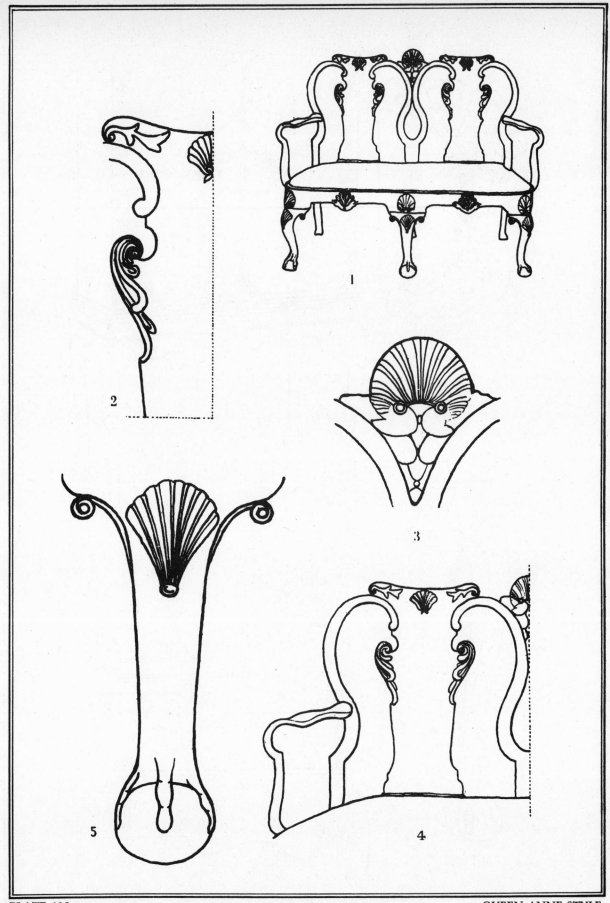

PLATE 135.                                                              QUEEN ANNE STYLE.

1. Sofa from end of Queen Anne period.   2, 3 and 4.  Details of back.   5.  Leg.

*Victoria and Albert Museum.*

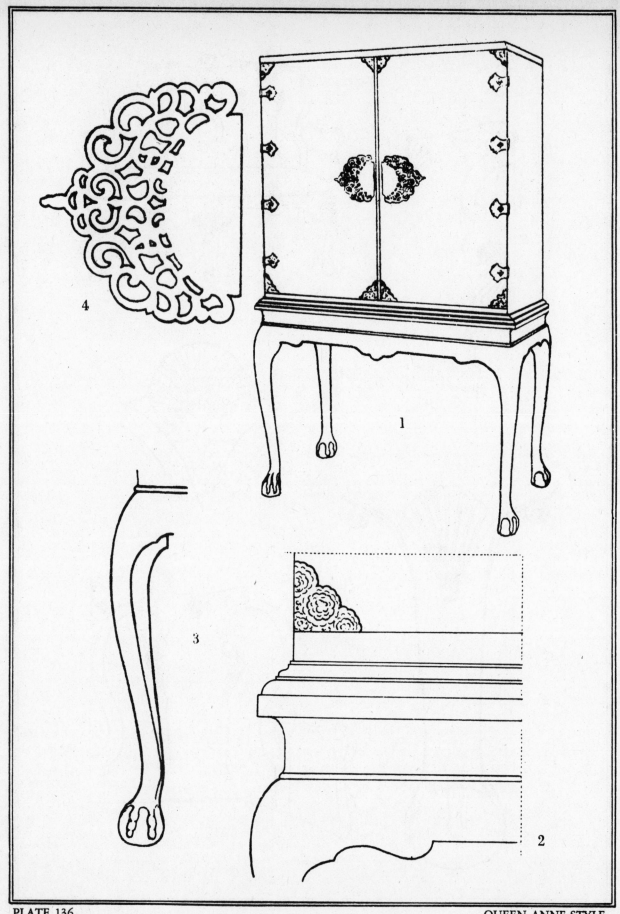

PLATE 136.                                                           QUEEN ANNE STYLE.
1. Queen Anne cabinet.   2. Corner and socle of upper section and spring of leg arch.   3. Leg.   4. Escutcheon plate.
*Private collection.*

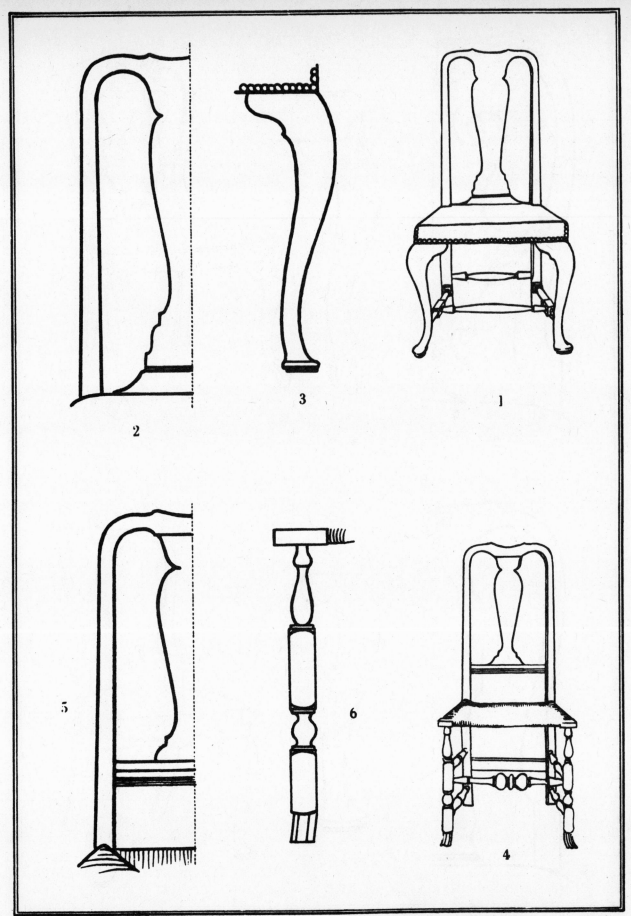

PLATE 137.                              QUEEN ANNE STYLE (Georgian period).
1. Simple Georgian chair.  2. Detail of back.  3. Front leg.  4. Simple Georgian chair.  5. Detail of back.  6. Turned leg.

*Private collection.*

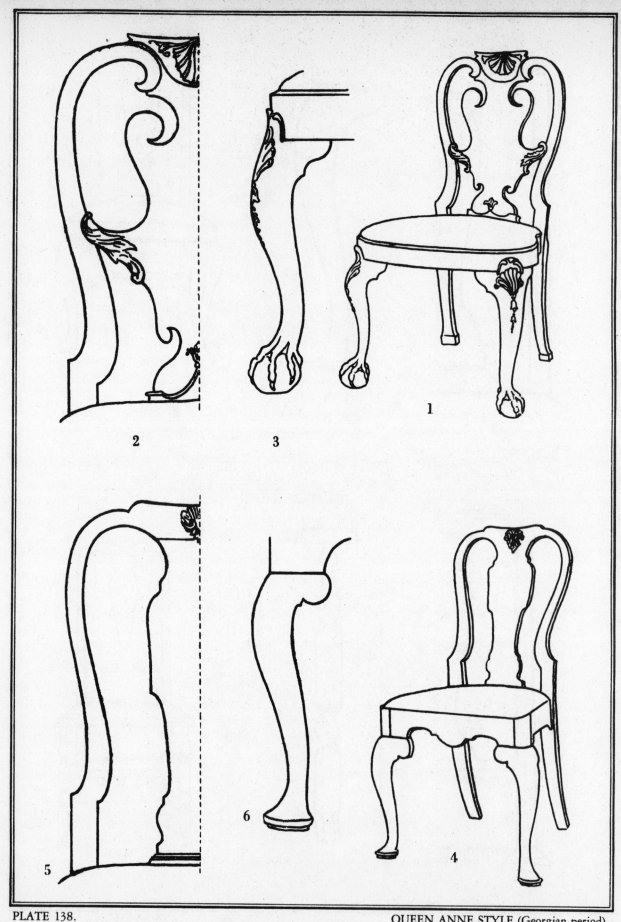

PLATE 138.                                                                                    QUEEN ANNE STYLE (Georgian period).
1. Chair from period of George I.   2. Detail of back.   3. Front leg.   4. Chair from period of George I.   5. Back detail.   6. Front leg.

*Geoffrey Hart and Lord Plender collections.*

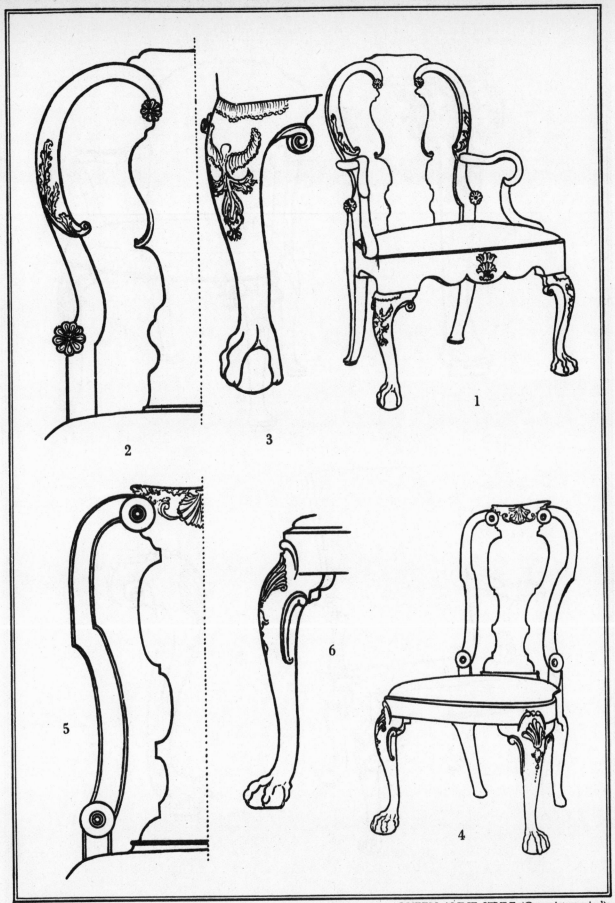

PLATE 139.                                                          QUEEN ANNE STYLE (Georgian period).
1. Armchair from period of George I.   2. Back detail.   3. Front leg.   4. Chair from George I period.   5. Back
detail.   6. Front leg.

*J. S. Sykes and Guy N. Charrington collections.*

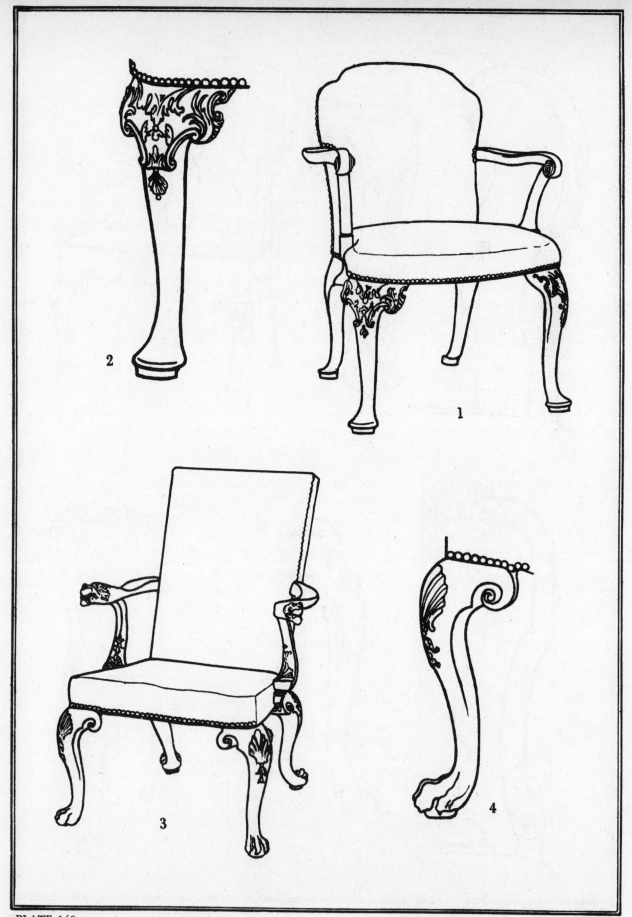

PLATE 140.                                        QUEEN ANNE STYLE. (Georgian period).
1. Armchair from reign of George I.    2. Detail of front leg.    3. Armchair from reign of George II.    4. Front leg.

*J. S. Sykes collection.*

144

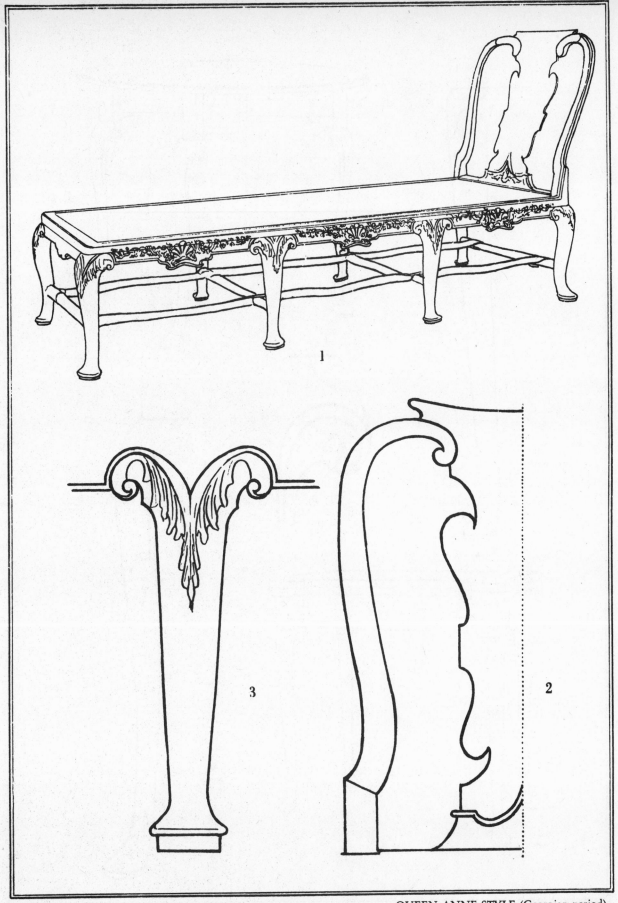

PLATE 141.

QUEEN ANNE STYLE (Georgian period).

1. Sofa from reign of George I.   2. Detail of back.   3. Leg.

*Private collection.*

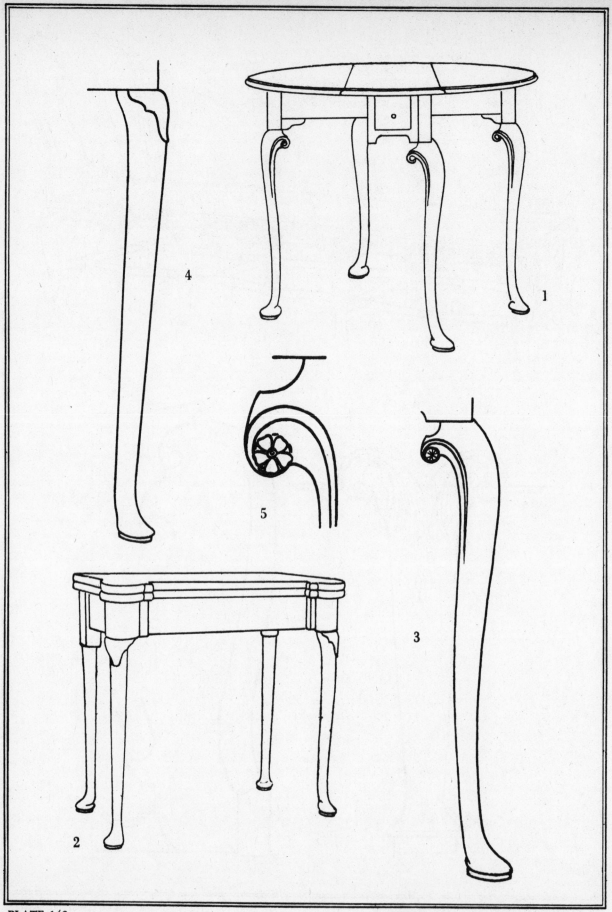

**PLATE 142.**
1 and 2. Graceful Georgian tables.   3 and 4. Legs.   5. Decoration on first table.

QUEEN ANNE STYLE (Georgian period).

*Private collections.*

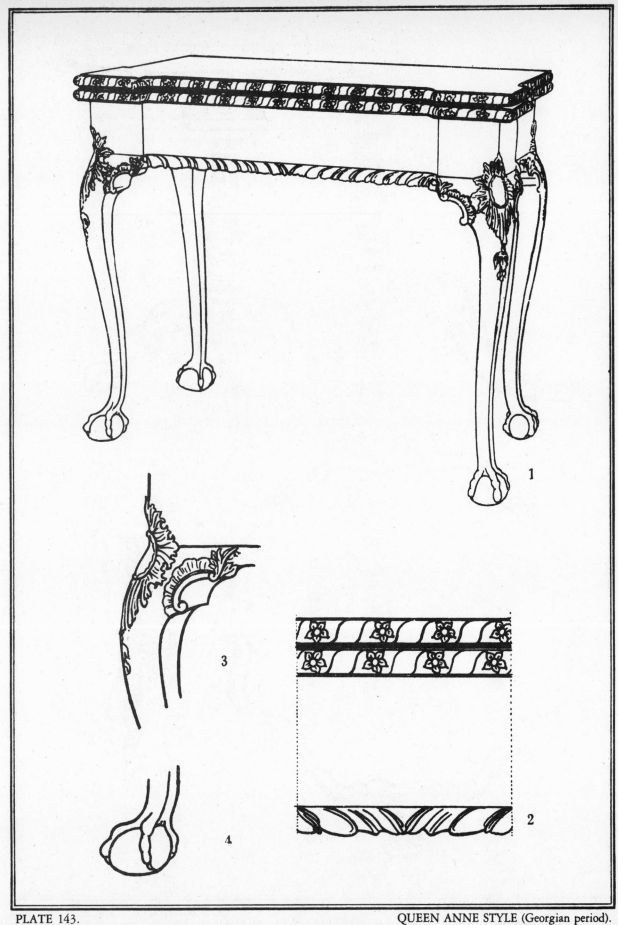

PLATE 143.                                          QUEEN ANNE STYLE (Georgian period).
1. Mahogany table from the mid-18th century.   2. Detail of friezes.   3 and 4. Decorations on legs.

*J. S. Sykes Collection.*

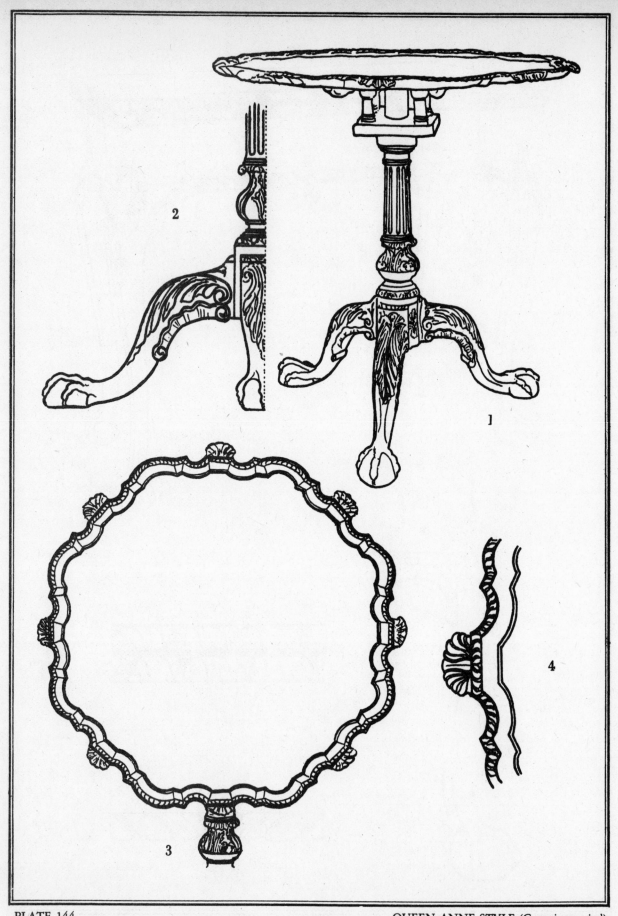

PLATE 144.

QUEEN ANNE STYLE (Georgian period).

1. Mahogany table from the mid-18th century.   2. Decoration on legs.   3. Tabletop.   4. Detail of moulding and frieze on tabletop.

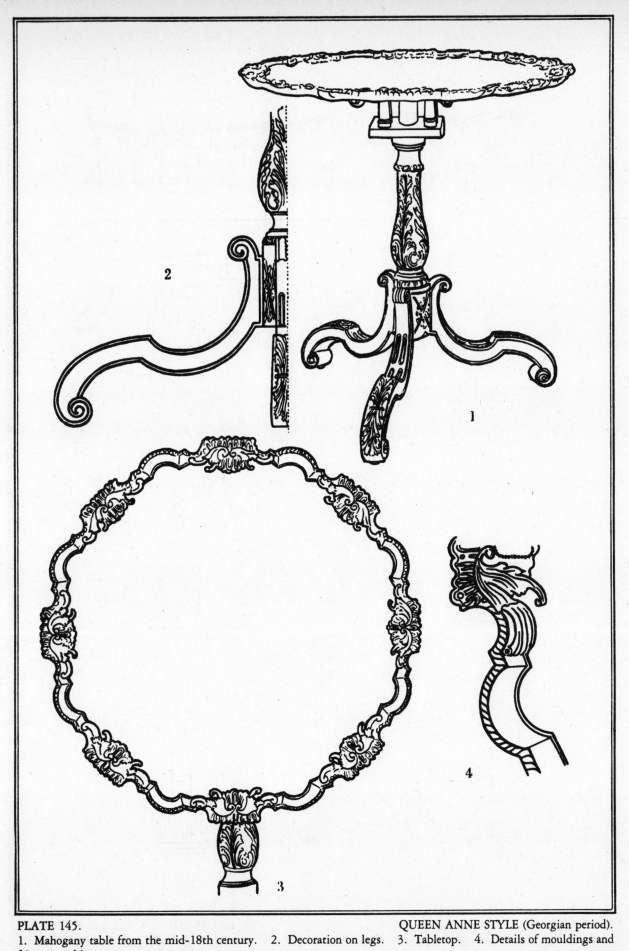

**PLATE 145.**
1. Mahogany table from the mid-18th century.   2. Decoration on legs.   3. Tabletop.   4. Details of mouldings and frieze on tabletops.

QUEEN ANNE STYLE (Georgian period).

*J. S. Sykes collection.*

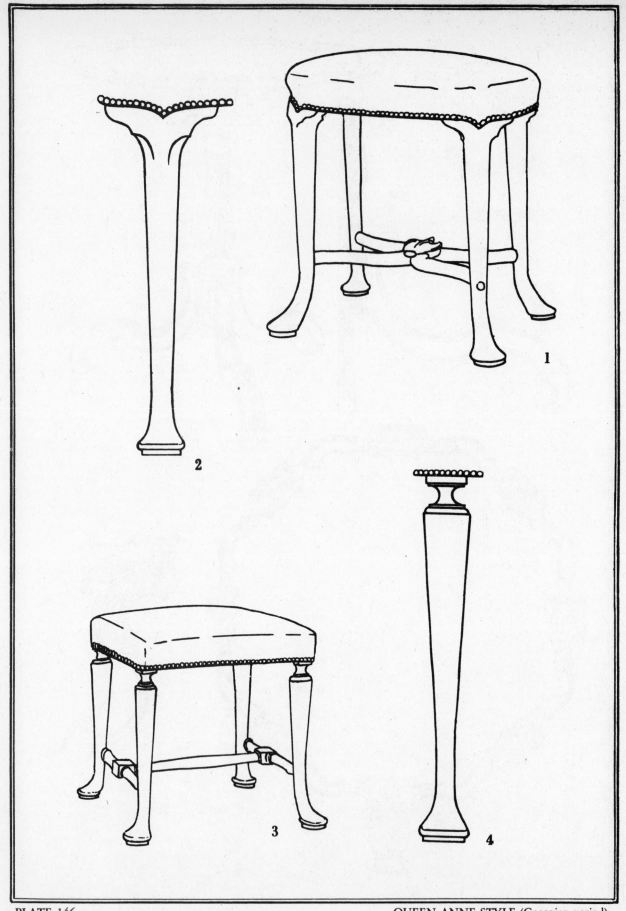

PLATE 146.                                          QUEEN ANNE STYLE (Georgian period).
1. Stool from period of George I.   2. Leg.   3. Stool from period of George I.   4. Leg.

*Private and J. S. Sykes collections.*

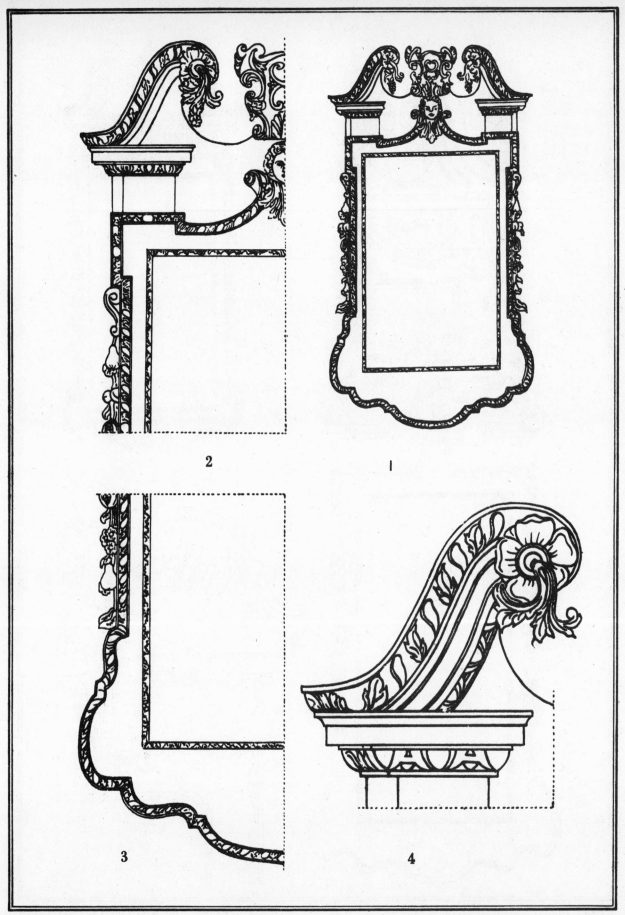

**PLATE 147.**

QUEEN ANNE STYLE (Georgian period).

1. Mirror from reign of George I.   2. Detail of top of frame.   3. Detail of frame bottom.   4. Decoration.

*Collection of Lord Plender G. B. E.*

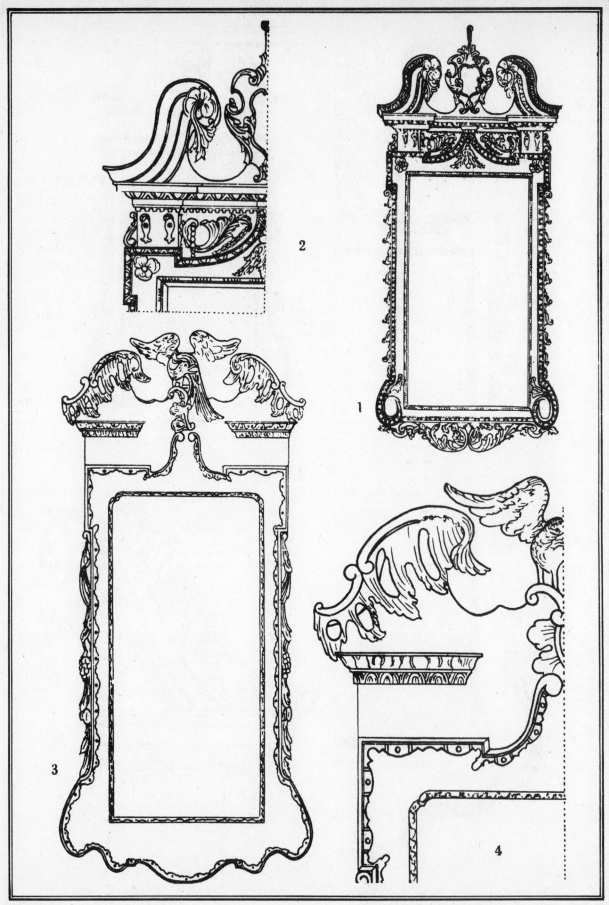

PLATE 148.                                                    QUEEN ANNE STYLE (Georgian period).

1. Mirror from reign of George II.   2. Decoration on frame.   3. Mirror from reign of George II.   4. Frame decoration.

*Private and J. S. Sykes collections.*

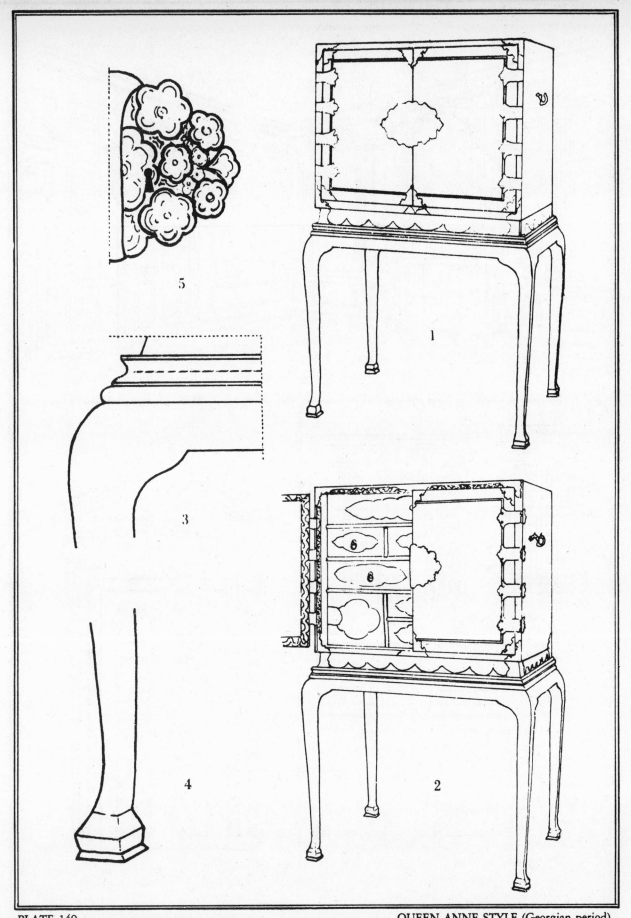

PLATE 149.                                  QUEEN ANNE STYLE (Georgian period).
1. Cabinet from reign of George II, closed.    2. Same, opened.    3. Mouldings and spring of leg arch.    4. Base of leg.    5. Escutcheon plate.

**PLATE 150.**  CHIPPENDALE STYLE (architectural features).

1. Room with pine wall panels, 1730.  2. Windows from Georgian homes; the second one with sash was more common than the first.  3. Type of moulding used during Chippendale period. 4. Doorway of room.

*Hatton Garden, London.*

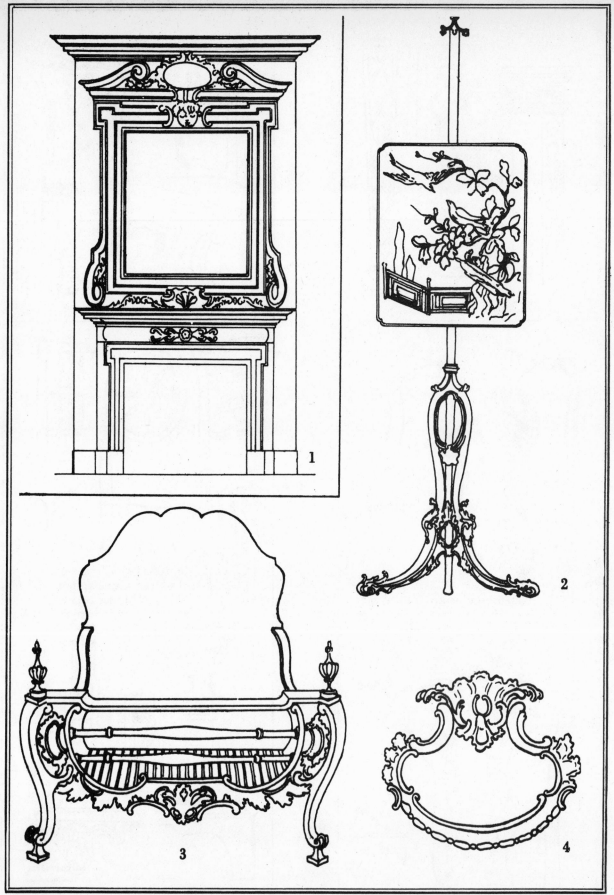

**PLATE 151.**                                         CHIPPENDALE STYLE (architectural features).
1. Fireplace designed by Gibbs.    2. Fireplace screen designed by Chippendale.    3. Iron fireplace basket designed by Chippendale.    4. Drawer pull designed by Chippendale.

*The Gentleman and Cabinet Maker's Director*, T. Chippendale.

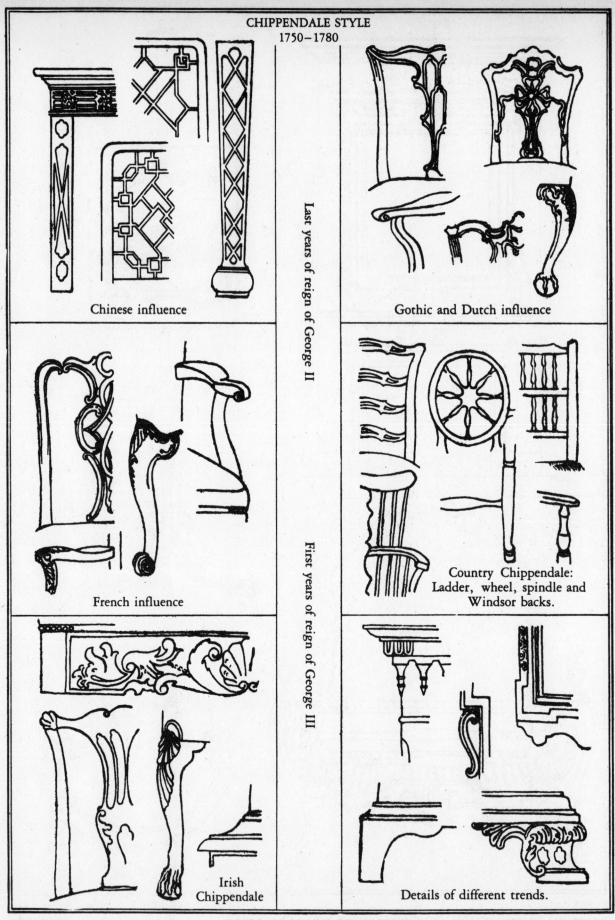

Chinese influence

Last years of reign of George II

Gothic and Dutch influence

French influence

First years of reign of George III

Country Chippendale:
Ladder, wheel, spindle and
Windsor backs.

Irish
Chippendale

Details of different trends.

PLATE 152.                    DIAGRAM OF THE DEVELOPMENT OF THE CHIPPENDALE STYLE.

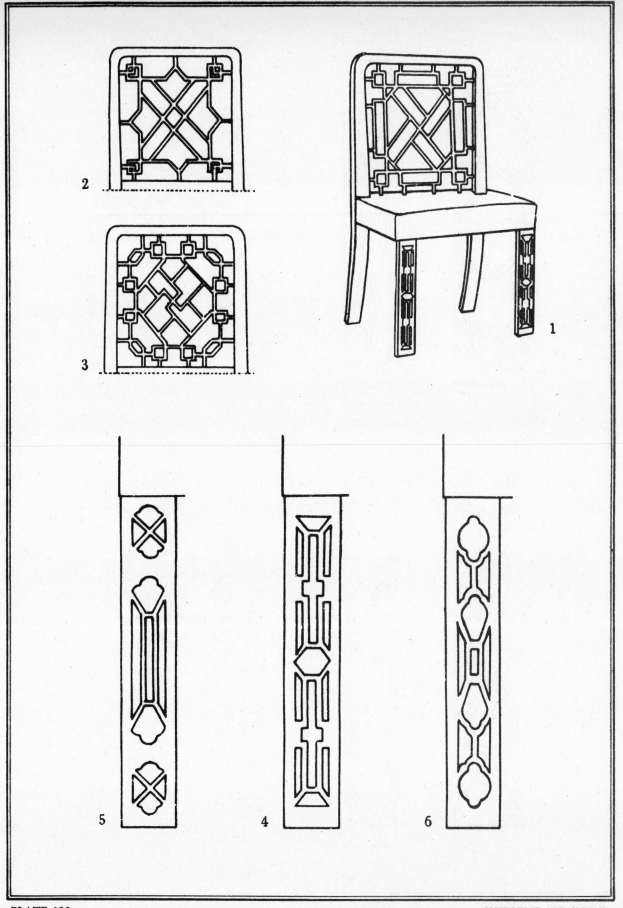

PLATE 153.                                                                    CHIPPENDALE STYLE.

1. Chippendale chair in the style called "Chinese."   2 and 3. Backs of other chairs in the same style.   4. Leg of first chair.   5 and 6. Legs in same style.

*The Gentleman and Cabinet Maker's Director.* T. Chippendale.

157

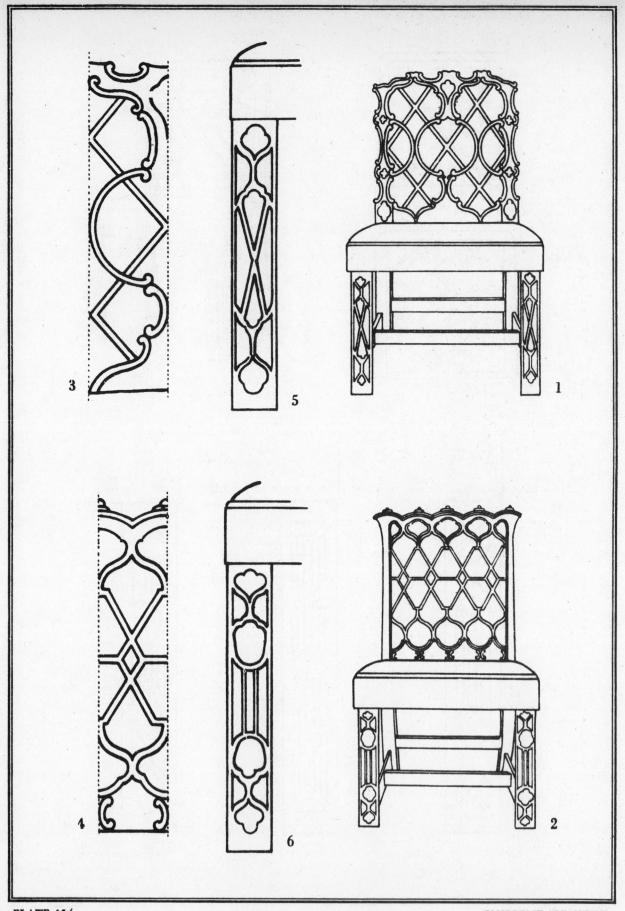

**PLATE 154.**

1 and 2. Chippendale chairs showing Gothic influence. 3 and 4. Details of backs. 5 and 6. Legs of first and second chair, respectively.

CHIPPENDALE STYLE.

*The Gentleman and Cabinet Maker's Director.* T. Chippendale.

158

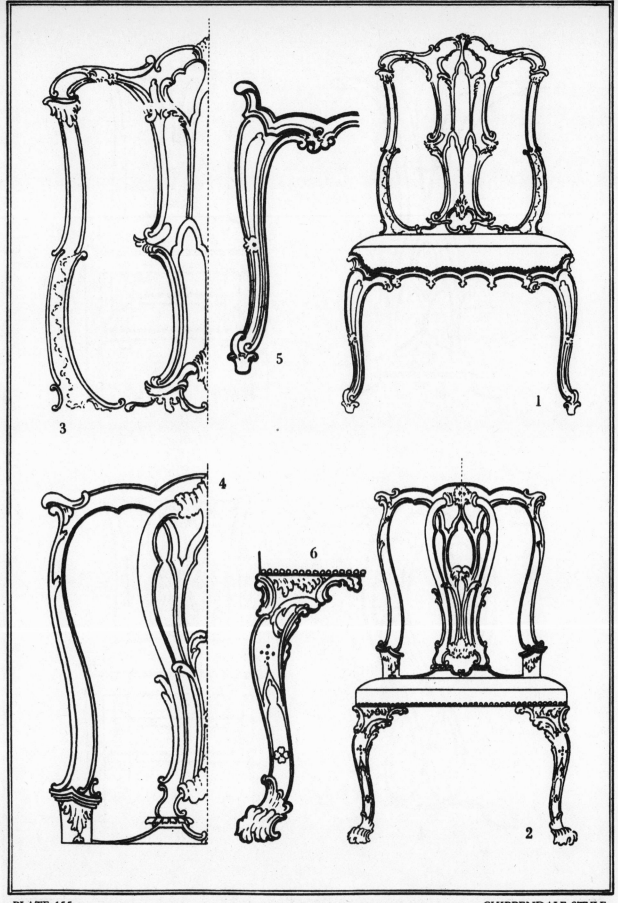

PLATE 155.

CHIPPENDALE STYLE.

1 and 2. Gothic Chippendale chairs.    3 and 4. Details of backs.    5 and 6. Legs.

*The Gentleman and Cabinet Maker's Director.* T. Chippendale.

PLATE 156.
1 and 2. Chippendale chairs with Gothic backs.   3 and 4. Detail of backs.
*The Gentleman and Cabinet Maker's Director.* T. Chippendale.

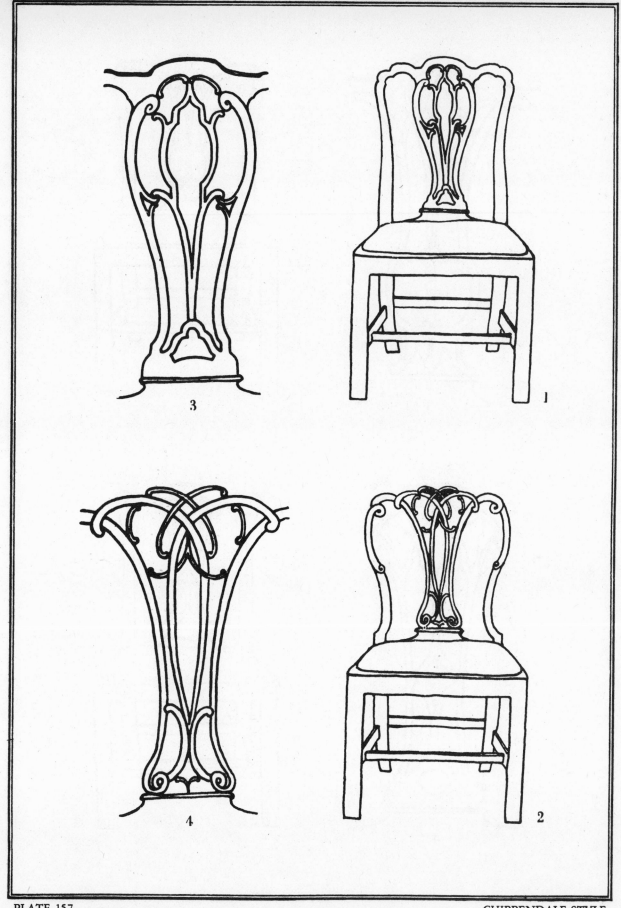

PLATE 157.

1 and 2. Chippendale chairs with Gothic backs.   3 and 4. Details of backs.

*The Gentleman and Cabinet Maker's Director.* T. Chippendale.

CHIPPENDALE STYLE.

PLATE 158.

CHIPPENDALE STYLE.

1 and 2. Chippendale chairs with Gothic backs.   3 and 4. Detail of backs.

*The Gentleman and Cabinet Maker's Director.* T. Chippendale.

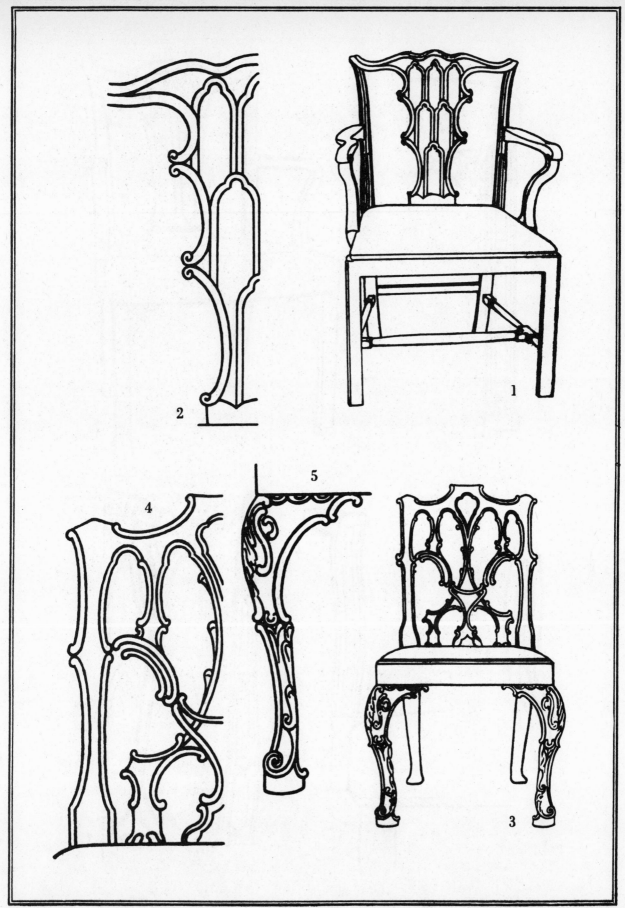

PLATE 159.                                                                CHIPPENDALE STYLE.
1. Armchair with Gothic back.    2. Detail of back.    3. Gothic Chippendale chair.    4. Back detail.    5. Leg.
*The Gentleman and Cabinet Maker's Director*. T. Chippendale.

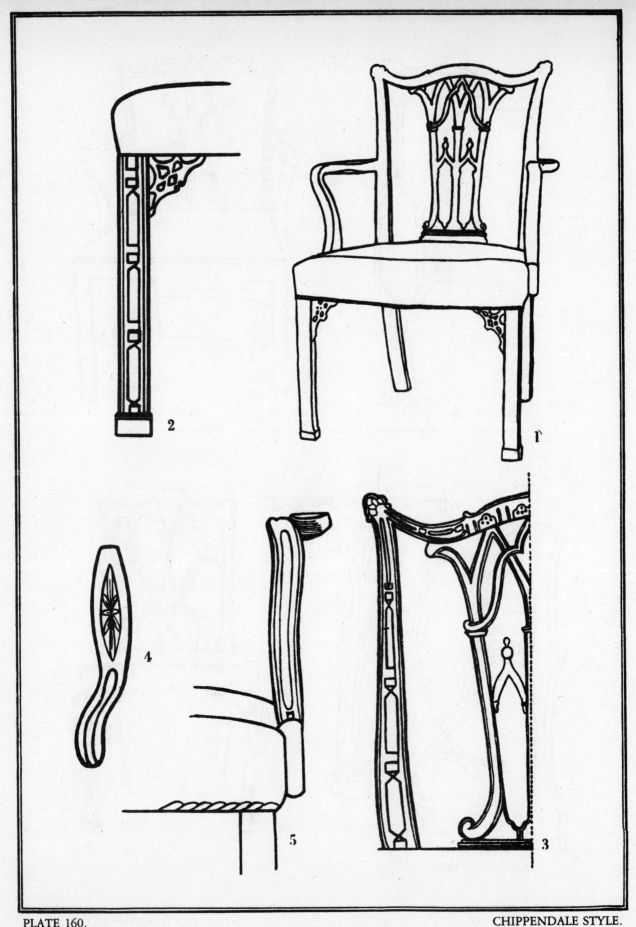

PLATE 160.                                                    CHIPPENDALE STYLE.
1. Gothic armchair.   2. Detail of leg.   3. Detail of back.   4. Decoration on arm.   5. Arm.
*Metropolitan Museum of Art.*

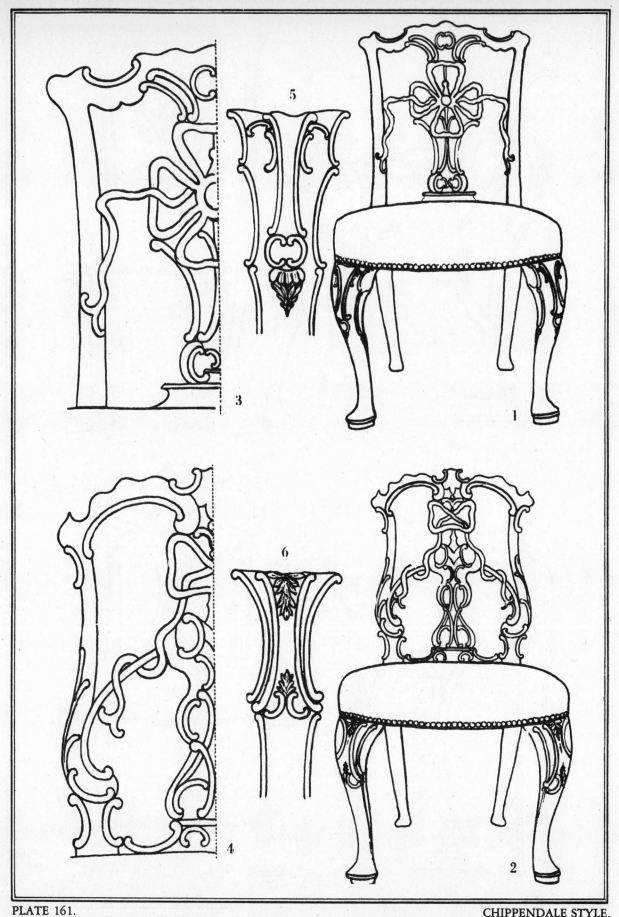

PLATE 161.

CHIPPENDALE STYLE.

1 and 2. Chippendale chairs with backs of intertwining ribbons.   3 and 4. Detail of respective backs.   5 and 6. Decoration on legs.

*The Gentleman and Cabinet Maker's Director.* T. Chippendale.

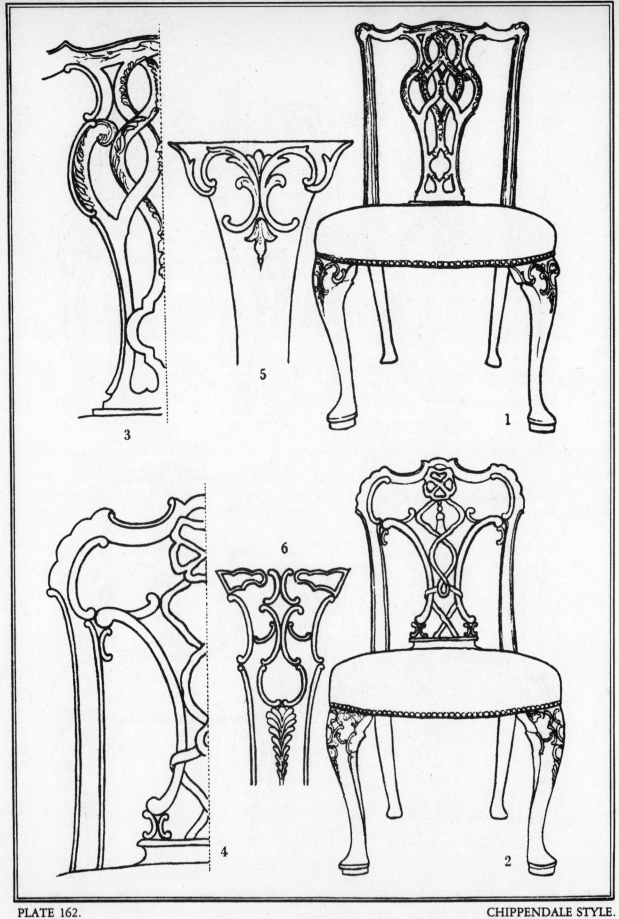

PLATE 162. CHIPPENDALE STYLE.
1 and 2. Chippendale chairs with backs of intertwining ribbons.   3 and 4. Details of backs.   5 and 6. Decoration on legs.

*Private collection.*

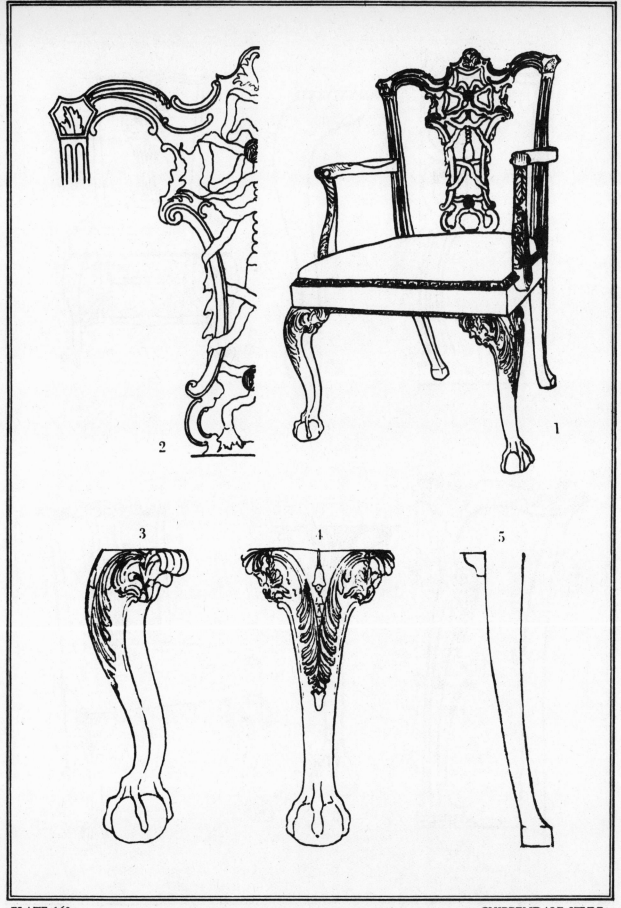

**PLATE 163.**  CHIPPENDALE STYLE.

1. Chippendale armchair with intertwining ribbon back of French influence and Dutch style legs.  2. Detail of back.
3 and 4. Details of decorations on front legs.  5. Back leg.

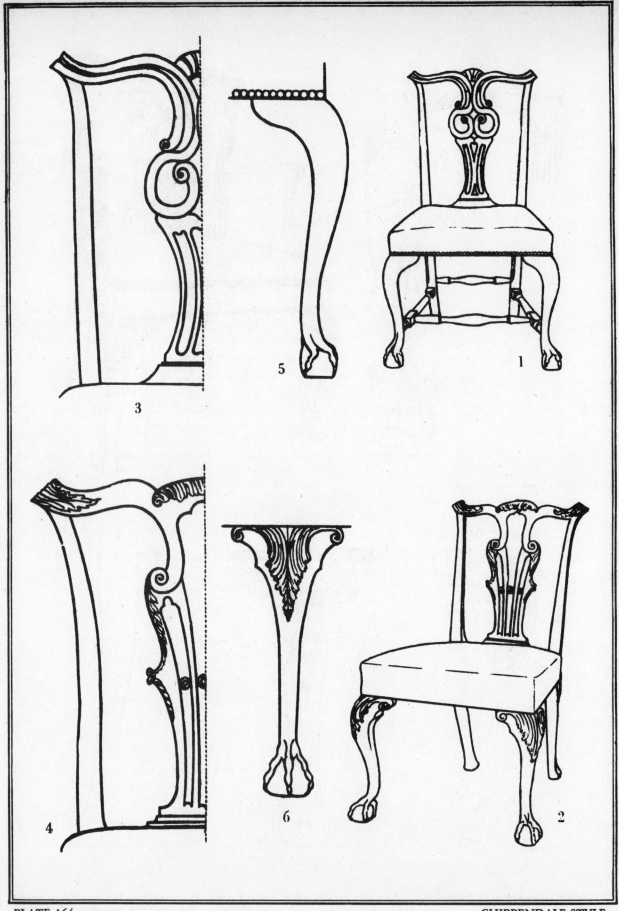

PLATE 164.

CHIPPENDALE STYLE.

1 and 2. Elegant straight-backed Chippendale chairs. 3 and 4. Detail of backs. 5 and 6. Legs.

*Private collection.*

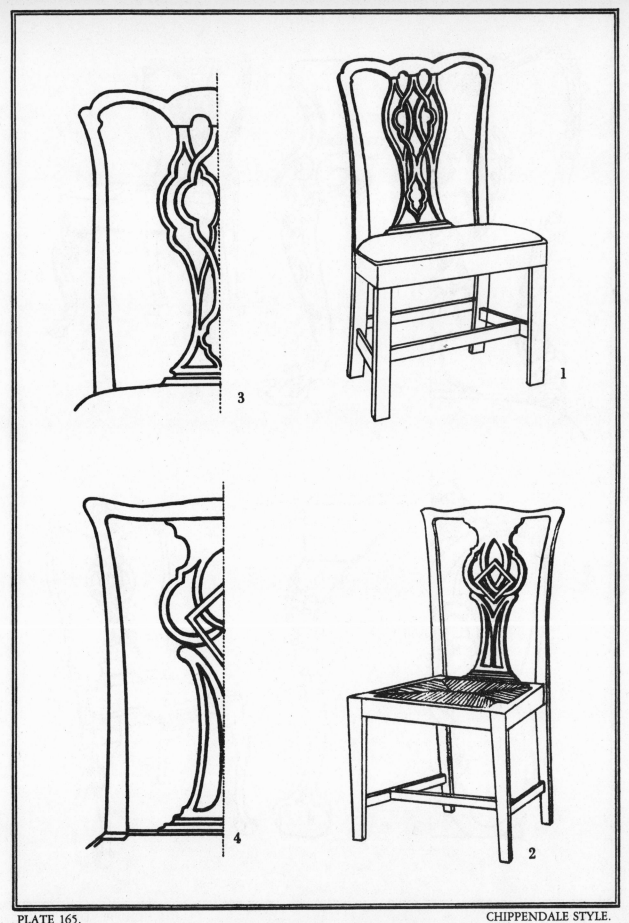

**PLATE 165.**
1 and 2. Simple straight-backed Chippendale chairs. 3 and 4. Detail of backs.

*Sketches of photographs in "Revista Oro" and "The Studio," respectively.*

CHIPPENDALE STYLE.

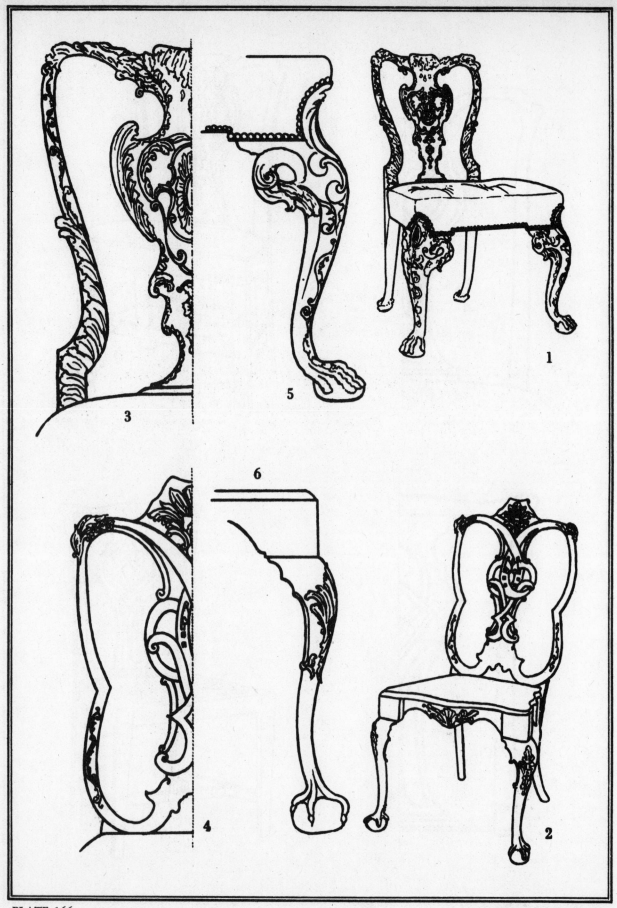

PLATE 166.                                                         CHIPPENDALE STYLE.
1 and 2.  Extremely ornate Chippendale chairs.   3 and 4.  Detail of backs.   5 and 6.  Detail of legs.

*Private collections.*

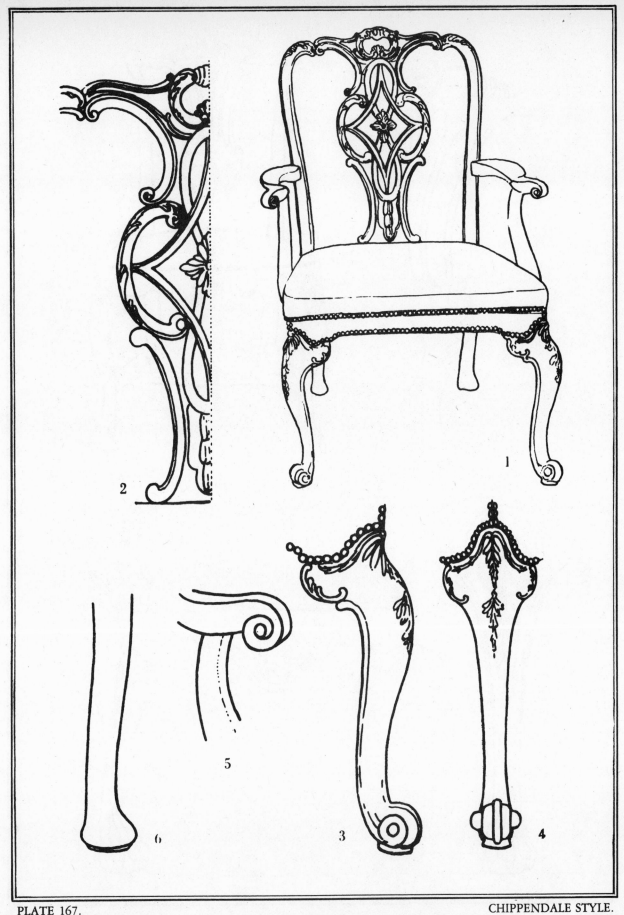

PLATE 167.                                                              CHIPPENDALE STYLE.

1. Chippendale armchair showing French influence.    2. Detail of back.    3 and 4. Decoration on front legs.    5. Detail of arm end.    6. Back leg.

*Saint Pierre Hospital, Bristol.*

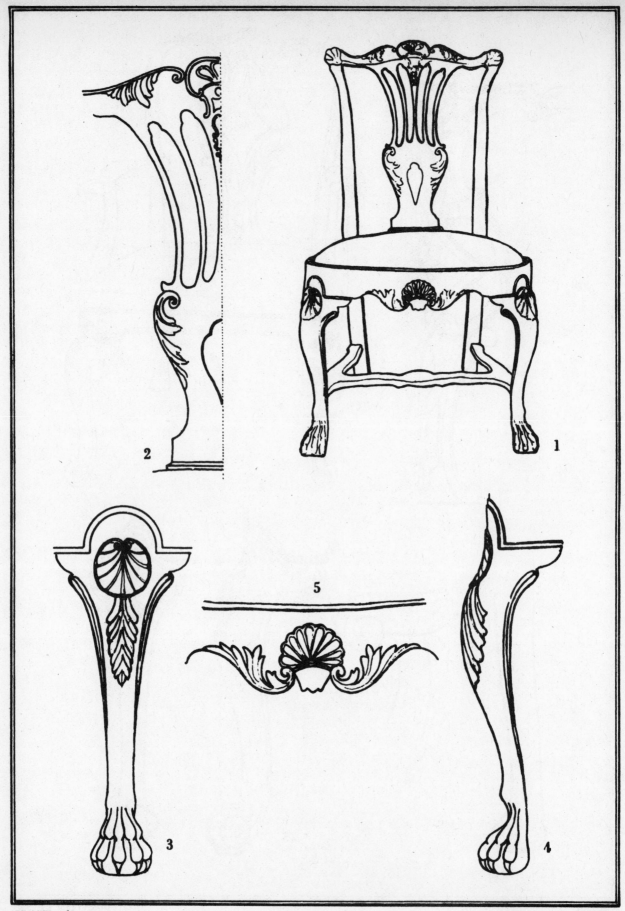

**PLATE 168.** CHIPPENDALE STYLE.

1. Irish Chippendale chair.  2. Detail of back.  3 and 4. Decoration on front legs.  5. Decoration on front edge of seat.

*Private collection.*

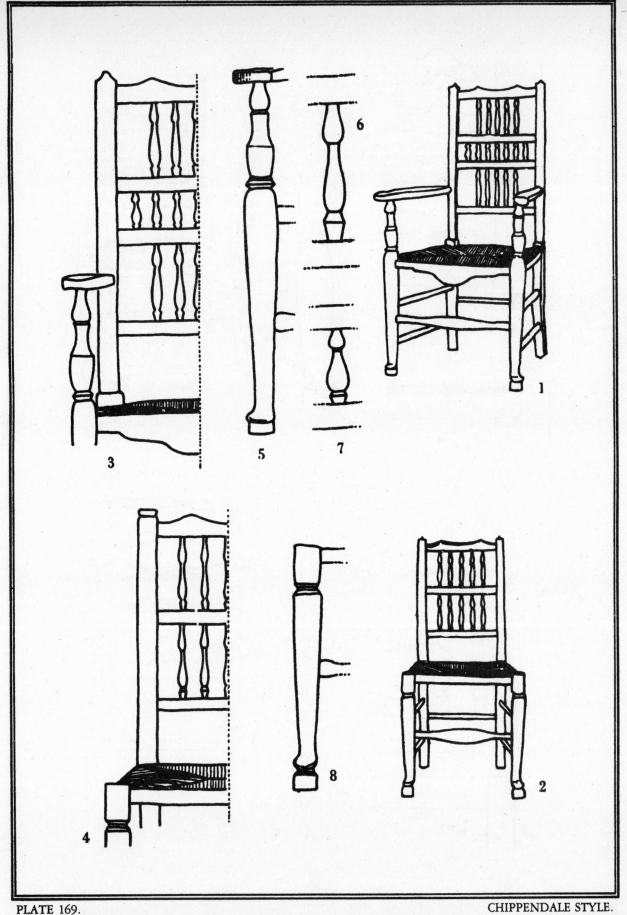

PLATE 169.                                                        CHIPPENDALE STYLE.

1 and 2. Chippendale armchair and chair with spindle backs.    3 and 4. Details of backs.    5. Front leg of armchair.    6
and 7. Details of back spindles.    8. Front leg of chair.

*Private collection.*

173

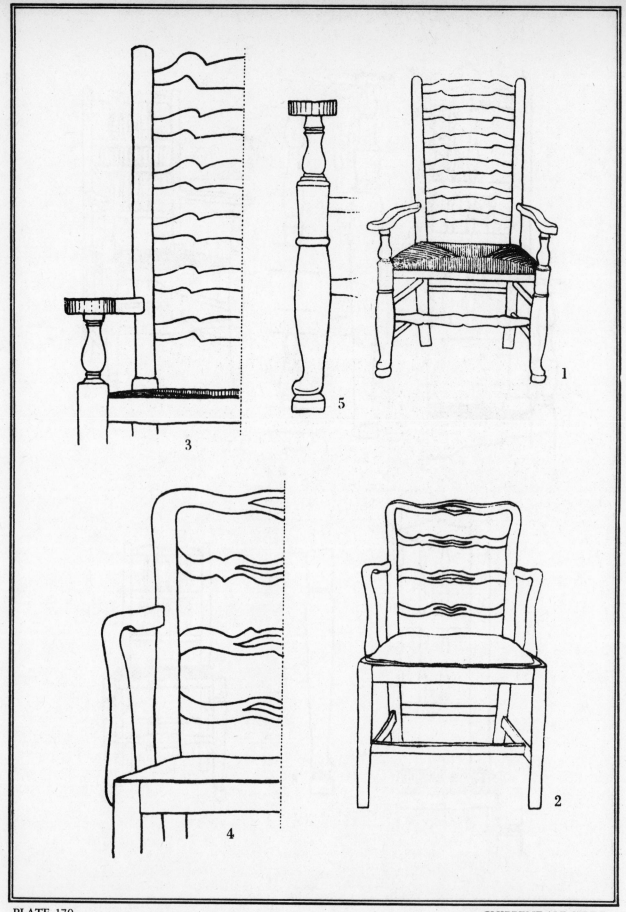

PLATE 170.                                                                    CHIPPENDALE STYLE.
1 and 2. Chippendale armchairs with ladder backs.   3 and 4. Detail of backs.   5. Front leg of first armchair.

*Private collection.*

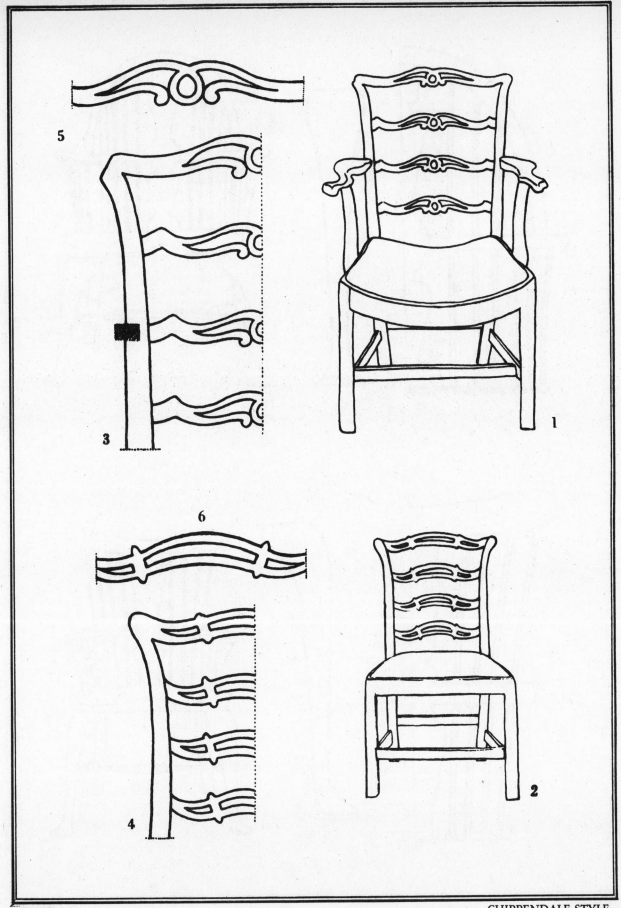

PLATE 171.
1 and 2. Chippendale armchair and chair with ladder backs.   3 and 4. Detail of backs.   5 and 6. Detail of back crosspieces.

*Private collection.*

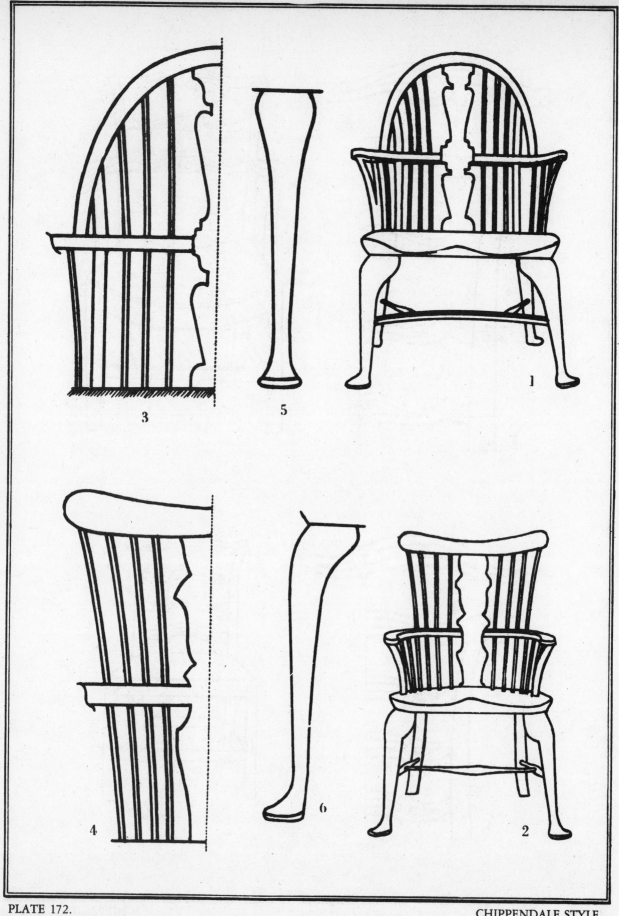

PLATE 172.
1 and 2. Windsor chairs.   3 and 4. Detail of backs.   5 and 6. Legs.

CHIPPENDALE STYLE.

*Private collection.*

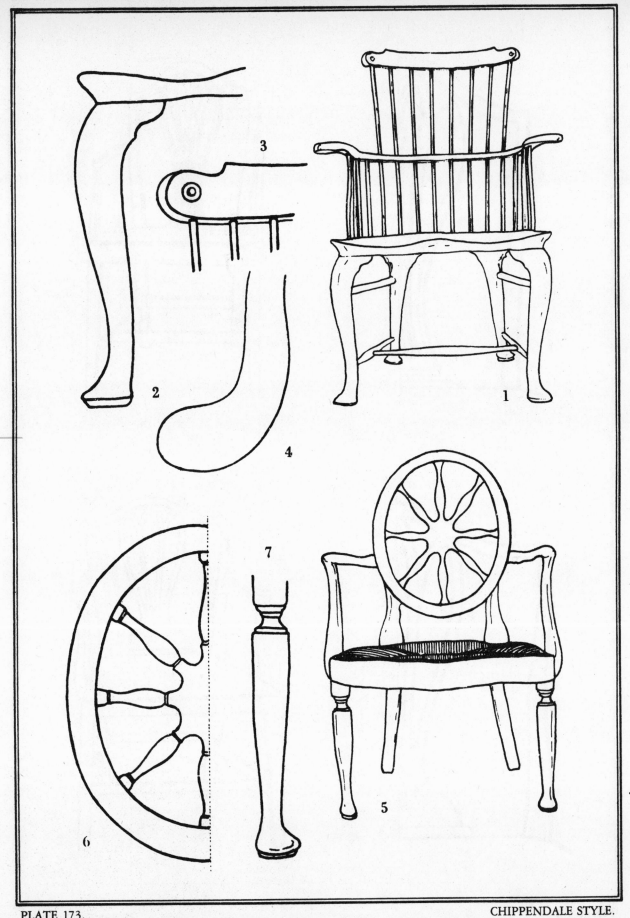

PLATE 173.

1. Windsor armchair.  2. Front leg.  3. Detail of top of back.  4. Blade of arm.  5. Armchair with wheel back.  6. Detail of back.  7. Leg.

*Private collection.*

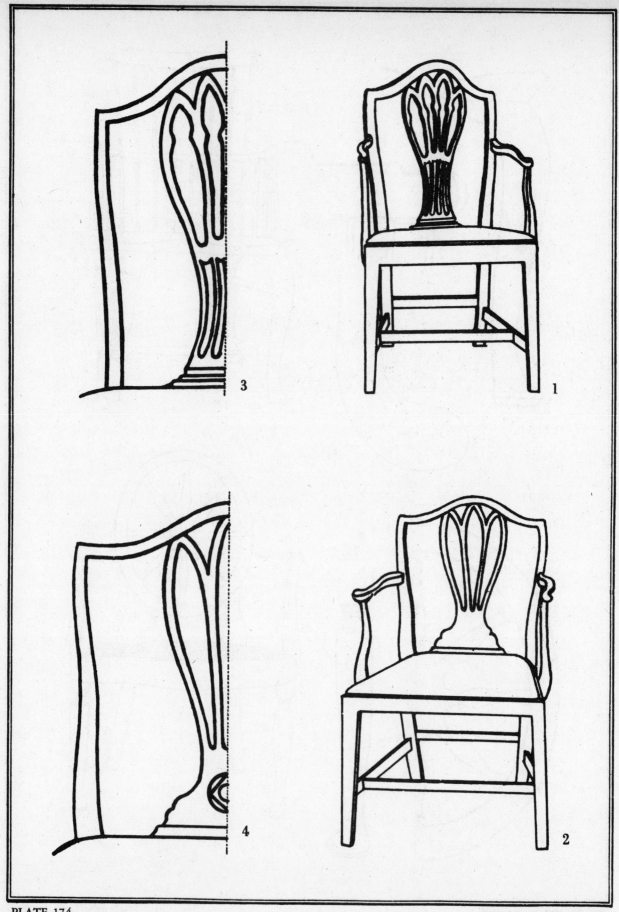

PLATE 174.

CHIPPENDALE STYLE.

1 and 2. Straight-backed Chippendale armchairs with Hepplewhite frame (almost Colonial style). 3 and 4. Detail of backs.

*Private collection.*

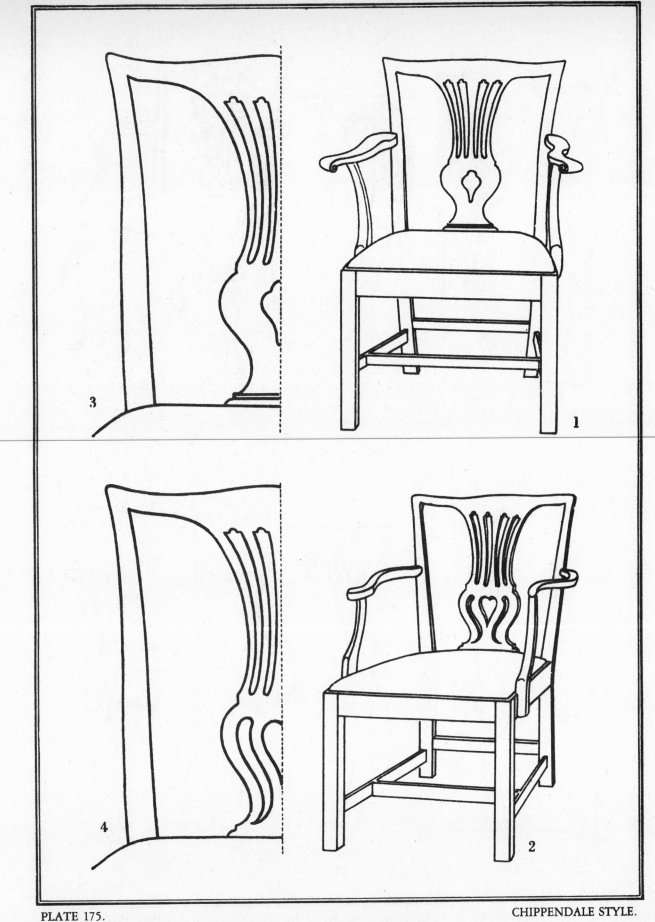

PLATE 175.

CHIPPENDALE STYLE.

1 and 2. Straight-backed Chippendale armchairs.    3 and 4. Detail of backs.

*Private collection.*

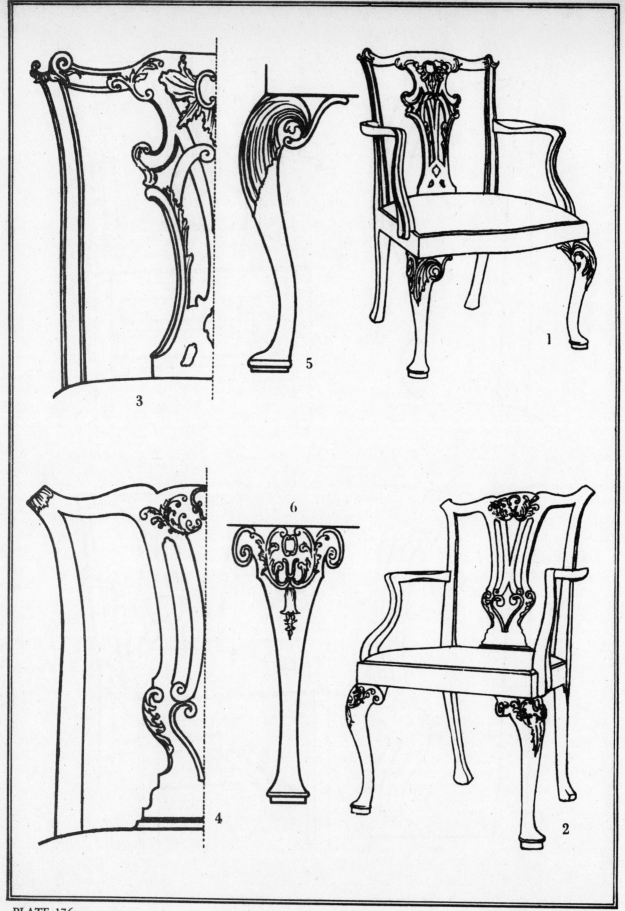

PLATE 176.

1 and 2. Elegant straight-backed Chippendale armchairs. 3 and 4. Detail of backs. 5 and 6. Details of front legs.

*Private collection.*

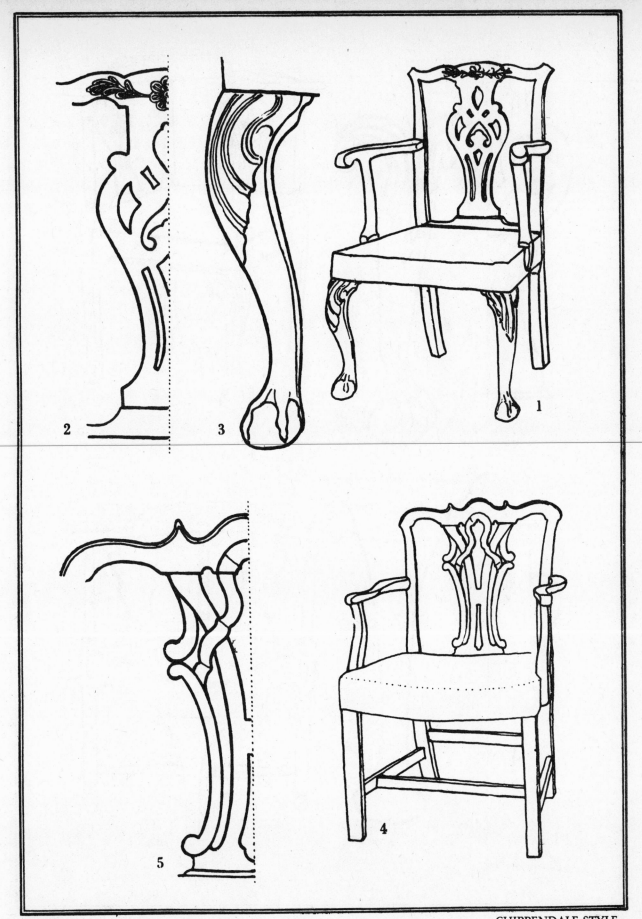

PLATE 177.                                                                    CHIPPENDALE STYLE.

1. Straight-backed Chippendale armchair. 2. Detail of back. 3. Leg. 4. Chippendale armchair with ribbon back. 5. Detail of back.

*Private collection.*

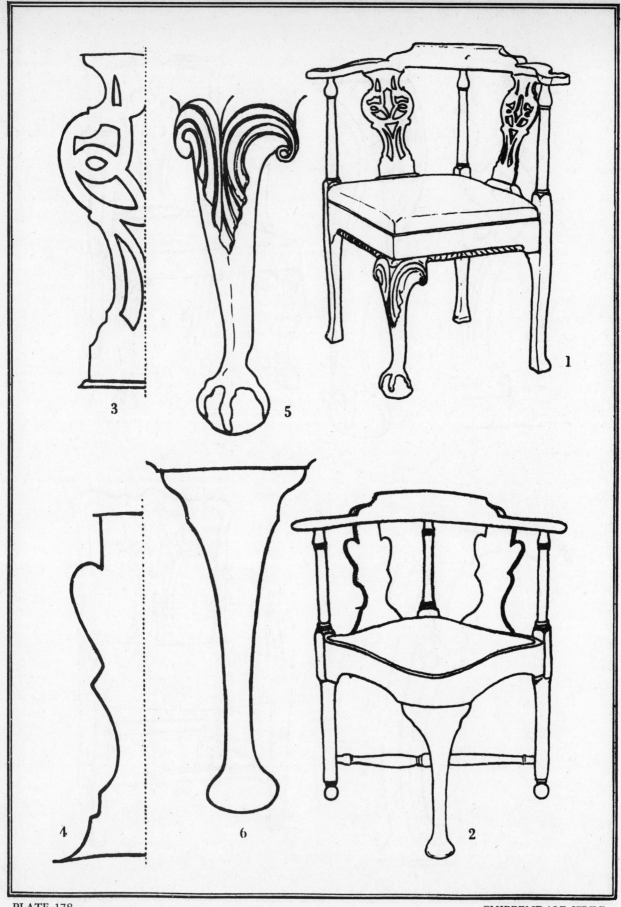

PLATE 178.

1 and 2. Chippendale corner armchairs.    3 and 4. Detail of backs.    5 and 6. Legs.

CHIPPENDALE STYLE.

*Private collection.*

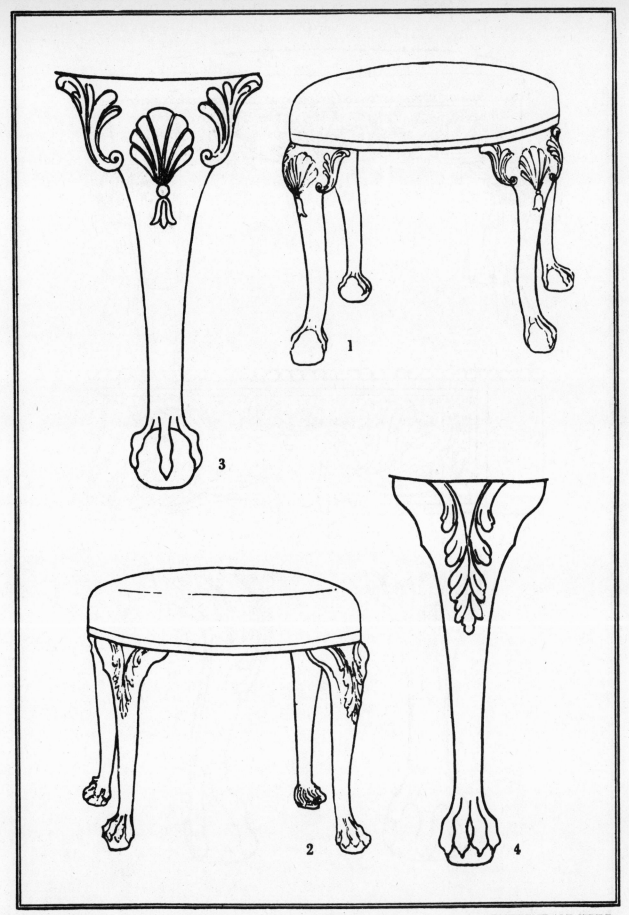

PLATE 179.
1 and 2. Chippendale stools with elegant legs.   3 and 4. Decorations on legs.

CHIPPENDALE STYLE.

*Victoria and Albert Museum and private collection.*

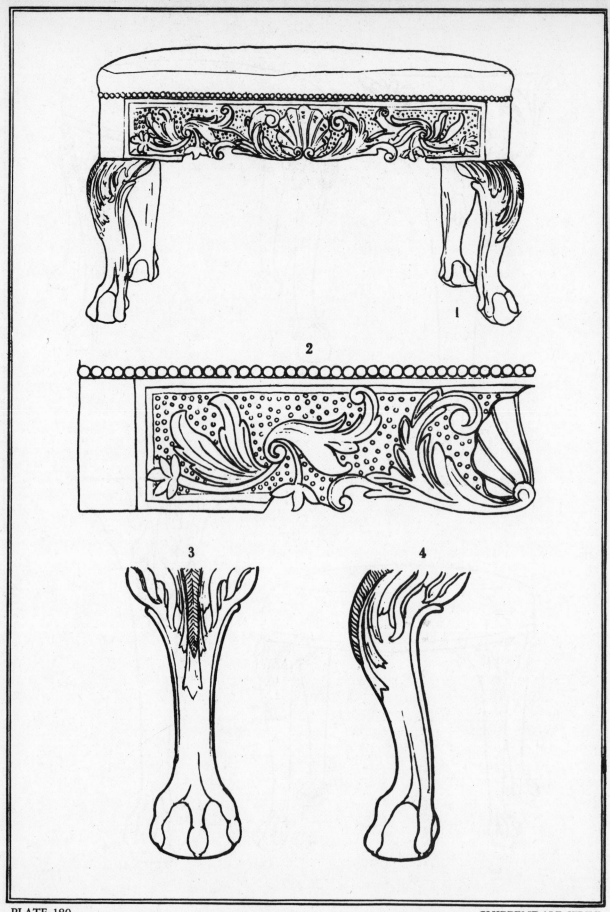

PLATE 180.                                                    CHIPPENDALE STYLE.
1. Irish Chippendale stool.   2. Decoration on edge of seat.   3 and 4. Decorations on legs.

PLATE 181.                                                    CHIPPENDALE STYLE.
1. Sofa from the first Chippendale period.    2. Detail of back.    3. Leg.    4. Simple Chippendale sofa.    5. Detail of back.

*Private collection.*

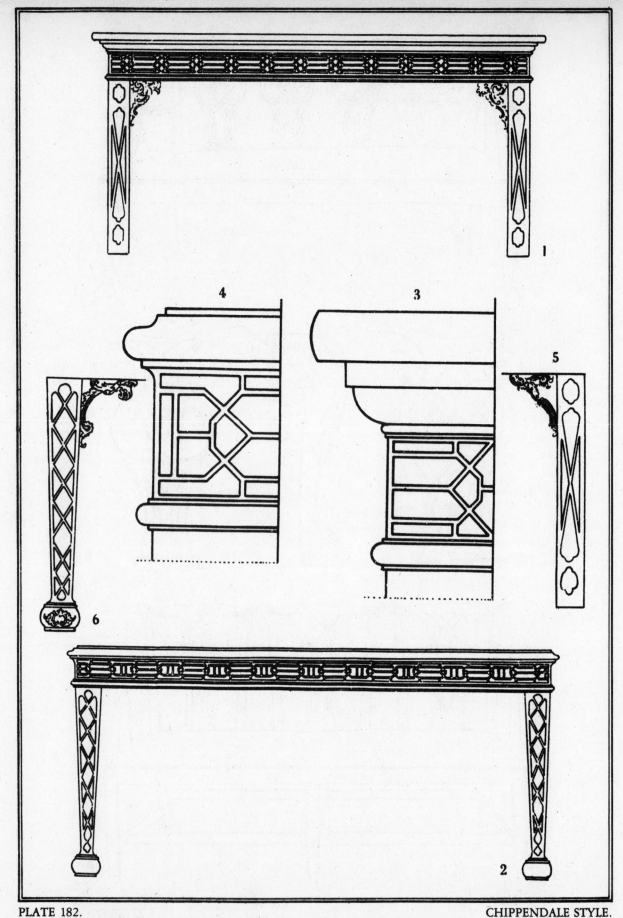

PLATE 182.
CHIPPENDALE STYLE.

1 and 2. Chippendale tables with Chinese motifs.   3. Moulding and frieze of first table.   4. Moulding and frieze of second table.   5 and 6. Details of their respective legs.

*The Gentleman and Cabinet Maker's Director.* T. Chippendale.

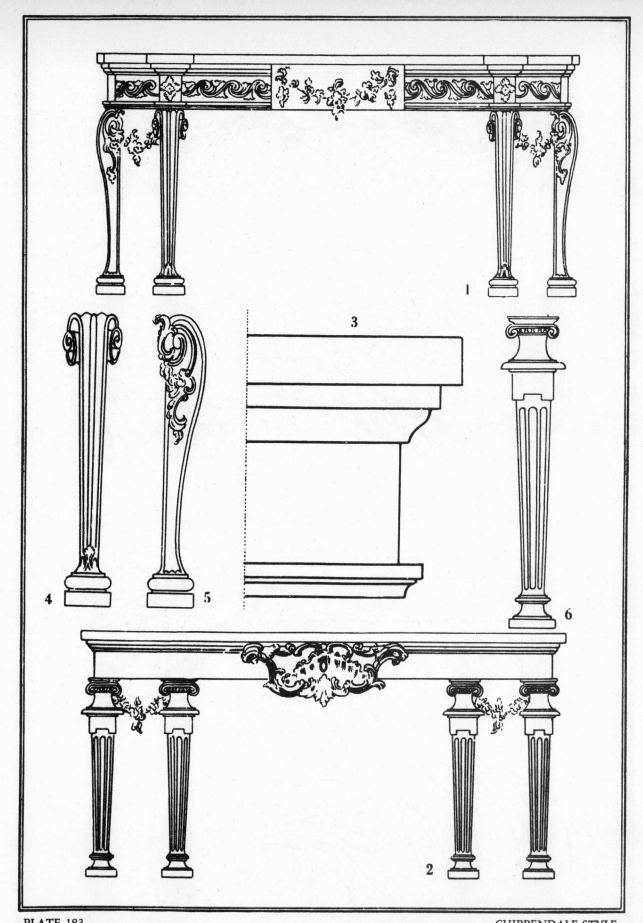

**PLATE 183.**

1 and 2. Elegant Chippendale tables.   3. Detail of first table's mouldings.   4 and 5. Decorations on legs of first table.   6. Same, second table.

*The Gentleman and Cabinet Maker's Director.* T. Chippendale.

PLATE 184.                                                    CHIPPENDALE STYLE.
1. Irish Chippendale table.    2. Decoration on crosspiece.    3. Mouldings and top of leg.    4. Decoration on legs.
*Private collection.*

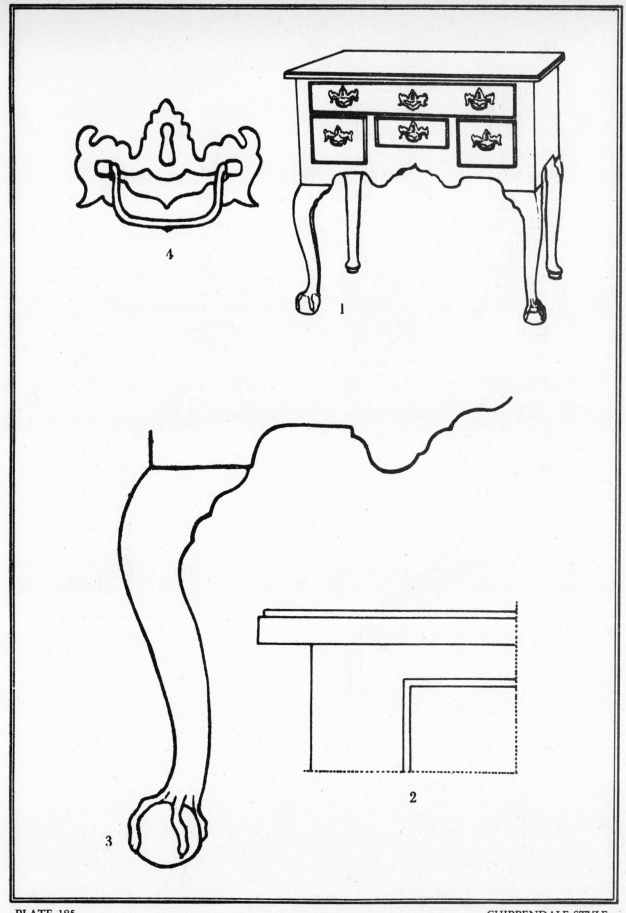

PLATE 185.                                                        CHIPPENDALE STYLE.
1. Early Chippendale dressing table.   2. Detail of moulding.   3. Detail of leg and festoon on crosspiece.   4. Drawer
pull.

*Private collection.*

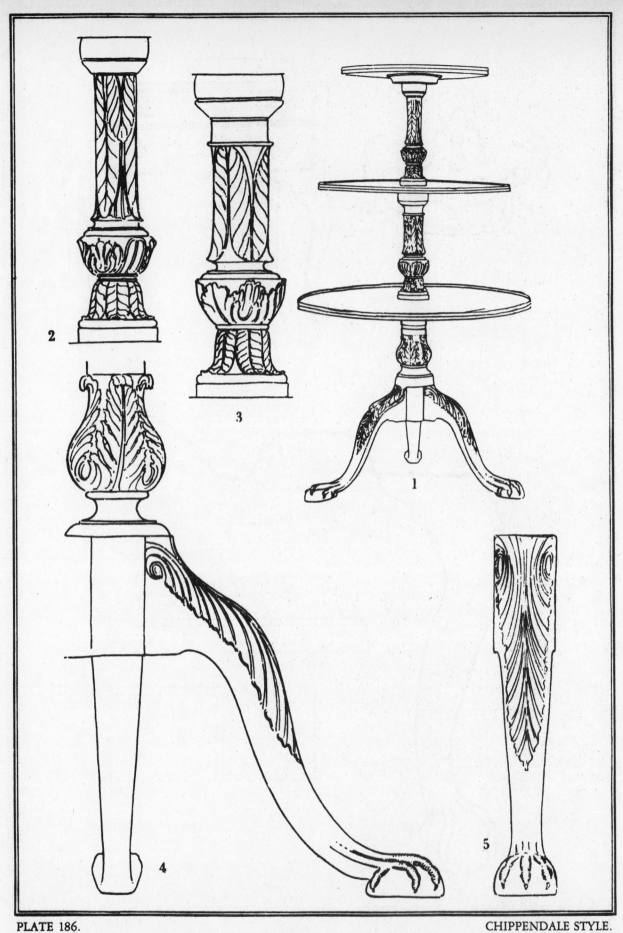

**PLATE 186.**                                                    CHIPPENDALE STYLE.

1. Practical piece of furniture sometimes called a "silent butler."   2. Upper column.   3. Middle column.   4. Detail of base.   5. Decoration on leg.

*Private collection.*

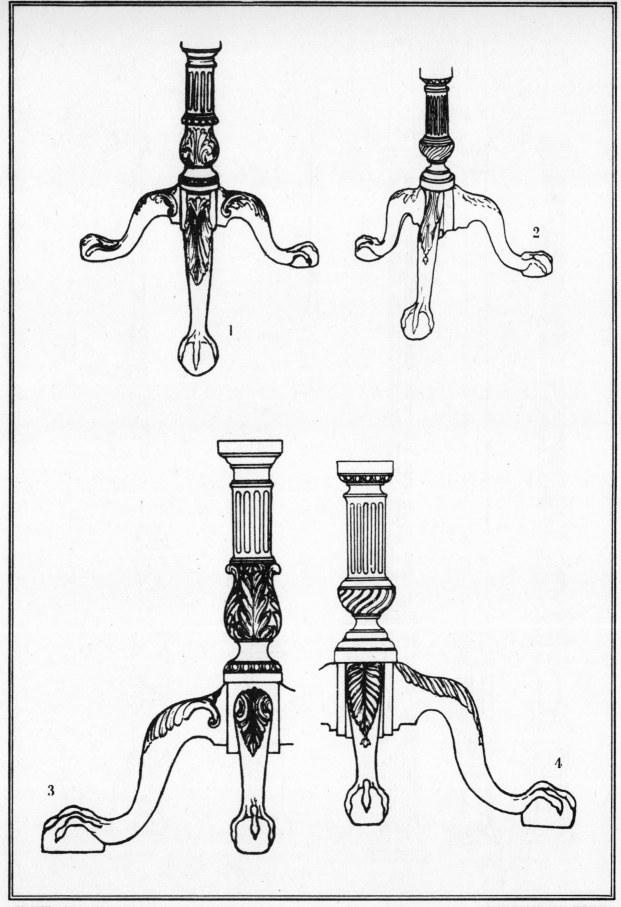

PLATE 187.                                                        CHIPPENDALE STYLE.
1 and 2. Legs of pedestal tables.   3 and 4. Decorations on same.

*Victoria and Albert Museum and private collection.*

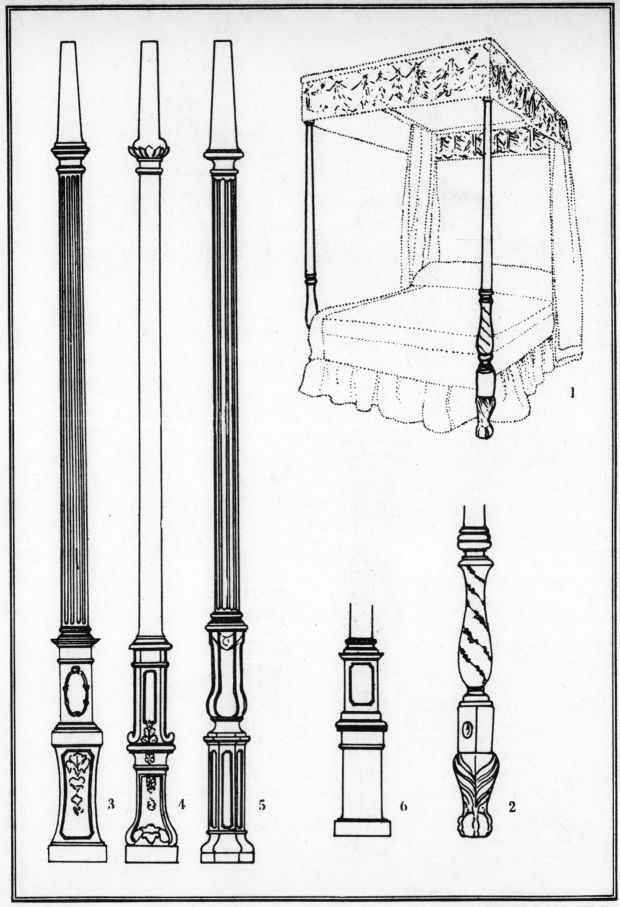

PLATE 188.

CHIPPENDALE STYLE.

1. Canopy bed.   2. Detail of post.   3, 4, 5 and 6. Posts of other beds in the same style.

*The Gentleman and Cabinet Maker's Director.* T. Chippendale.

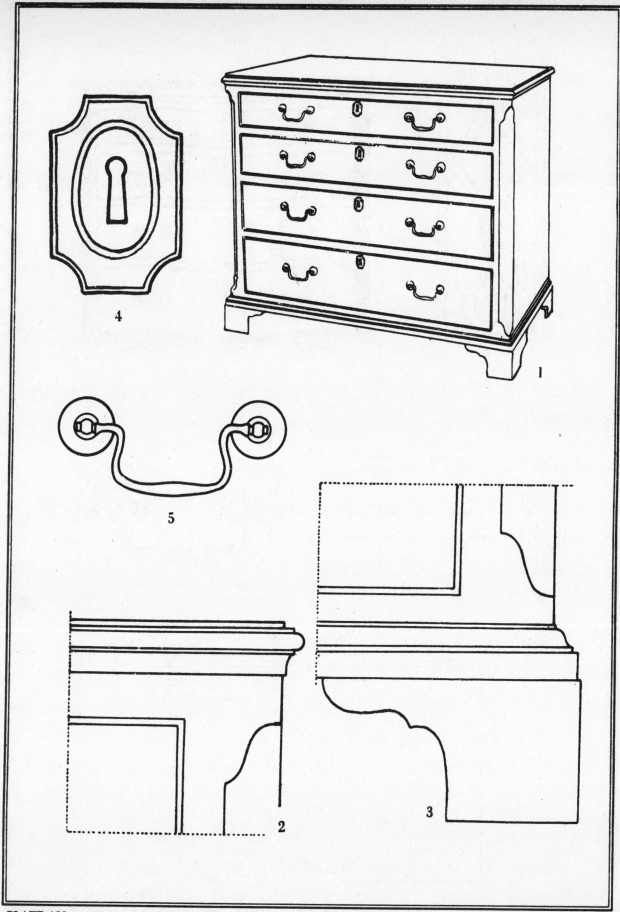

PLATE 189.                                                    CHIPPENDALE STYLE.
1. Simple commode with straight lines.   2. Detail of upper corner.   3. Detail of lower moulding and foot.
4. Escutcheon plate.   5. Drawer pull.

*Private collection.*

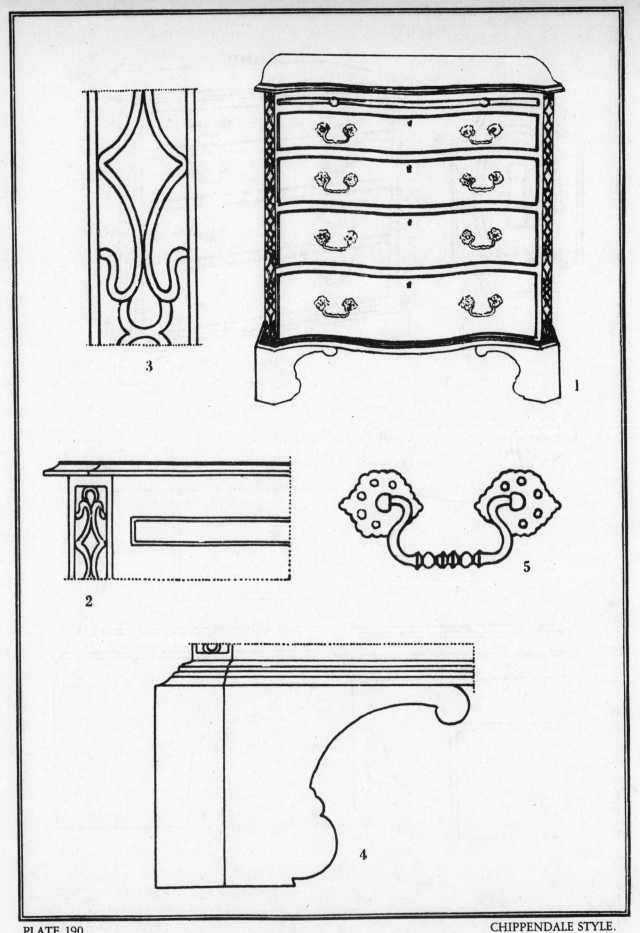

**PLATE 190.** CHIPPENDALE STYLE.

1. Simple commode with curved lines. 2. Detail of upper corner. 3. Frieze decoration on upright. 4. Lower moulding and foot. 5. Drawer pull.

PLATE 191.                                                                                                                    CHIPPENDALE STYLE.

1. Tall commode with severe lines.   2. Cornice decoration.   3. Moulding at base of upper section.   4. Lower moulding and foot.   5. Drawer pull.

PLATE 192.

CHIPPENDALE STYLE.

1 and 2. Desks designed by Chippendale.   3. Upper moulding of first desk.   4. Decoration on foot.   5. Detail of mouldings on second desk.   6 and 7. Drawer pulls on second desk.

*The Gentleman and Cabinet Maker's Director.* T. Chippendale.

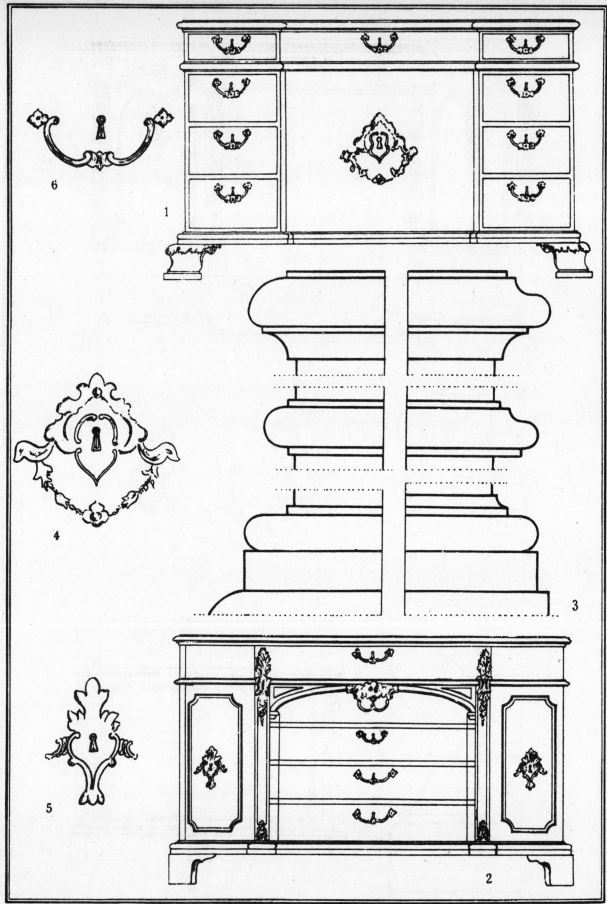

PLATE 193.                                                    CHIPPENDALE STYLE.
1 and 2. Desks designed by Chippendale.    3. Comparison of mouldings on the two desks.    4. Middle escutcheon
plate of first desk.    5. Side escutcheon plate of second desk.    6. Drawer pull.

*The Gentleman and Cabinet Maker's Director.* T. Chippendale.

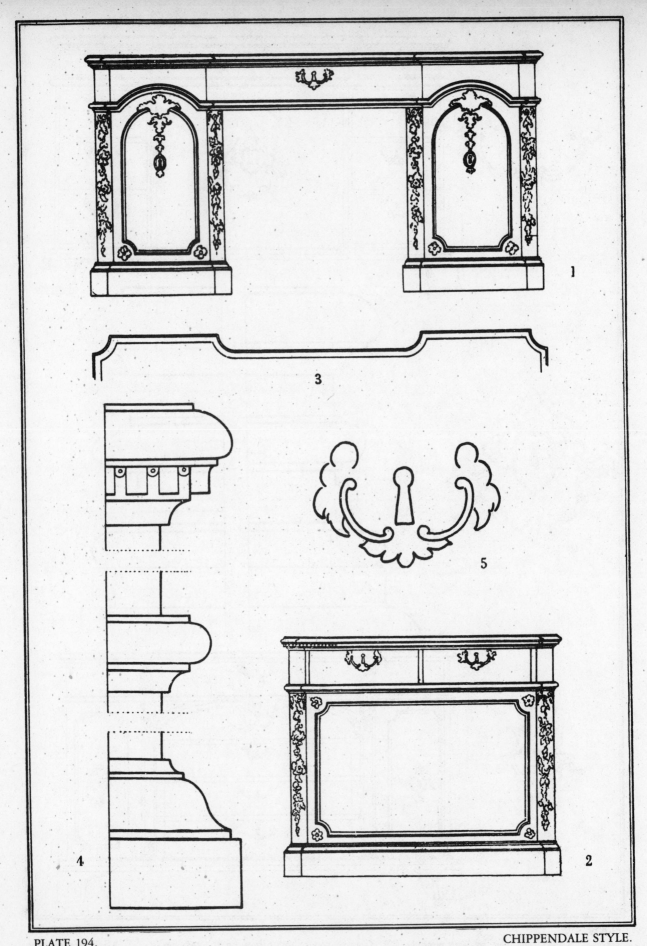

PLATE 194.

1. Desk designed by Chippendale.   2. Side.   3. Silhouette of top.   4. Detail of cornice, mouldings and base.
5. Drawer pull.

*The Gentleman and Cabinet Maker's Director*. T. Chippendale.

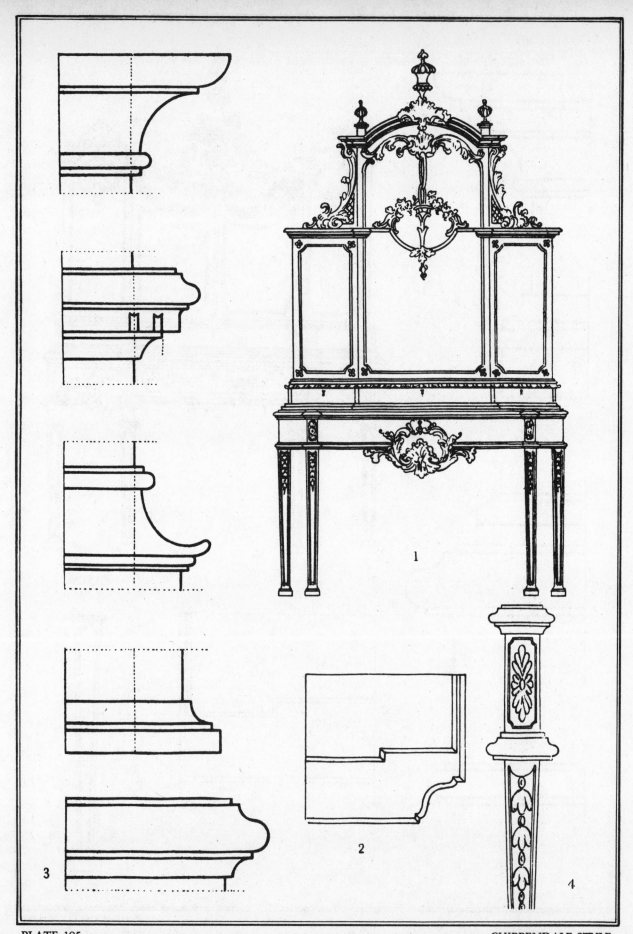

PLATE 195. CHIPPENDALE STYLE.

1. Lady's desk designed by Chippendale.   2. Bottom of the table top and upper section.   3. Detail of cornices and mouldings.   4. Decoration on legs.

*The Gentleman and Cabinet Maker's Director.* T. Chippendale.

**PLATE 196.**

1. Lady's secretary designed by Chippendale.   2. Bottom of tabletop and upper section.   3. Detail of cornices and mouldings.   4. Leg.

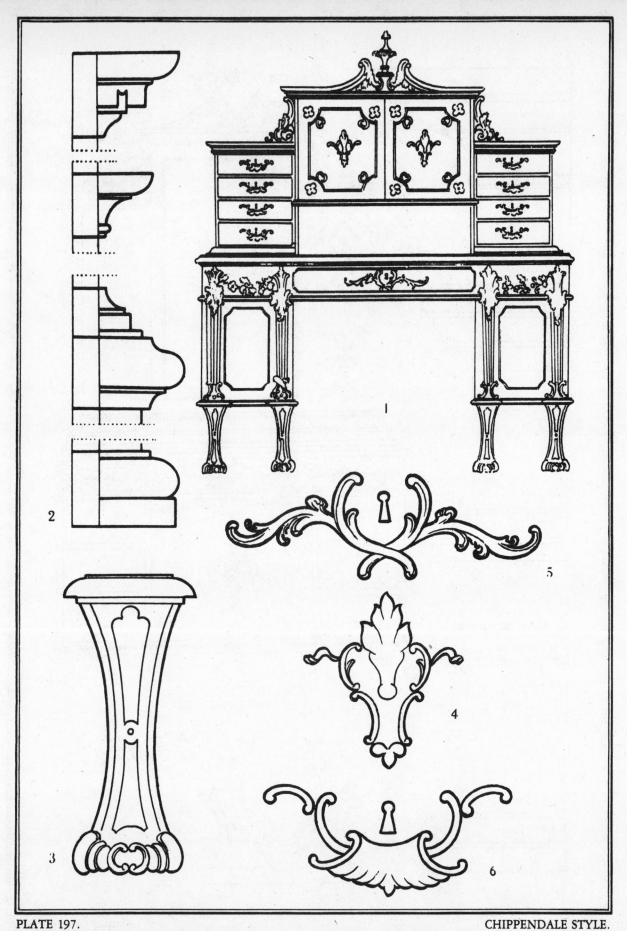

PLATE 197.                                                      CHIPPENDALE STYLE.
1. Secretary designed by Chippendale.   2. Detail of cornices and mouldings.   3. Leg.   4. Central decoration on upper panels.   5 and 6. Escutcheon plates.

*The Gentleman and Cabinet Maker's Director.* T. Chippendale.
201

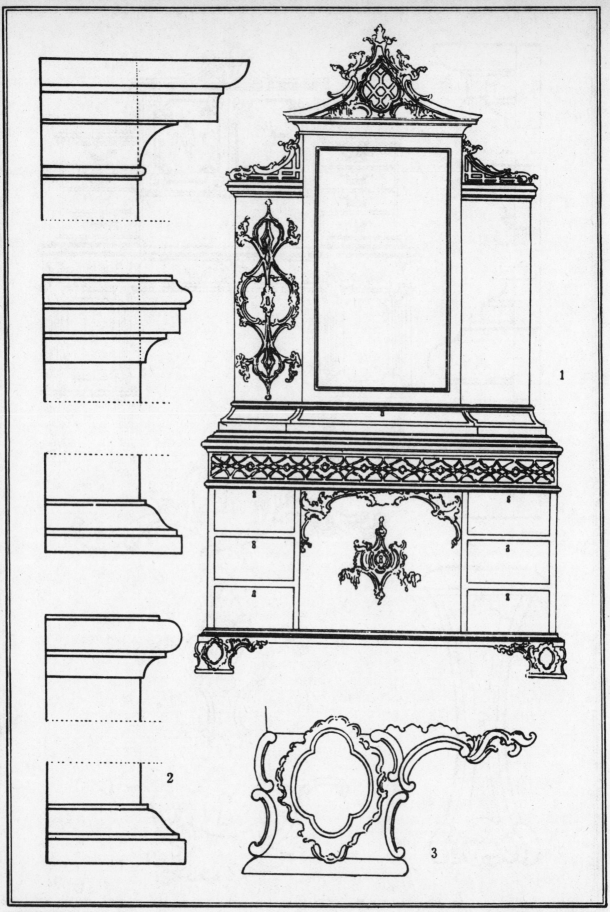

PLATE 198.                                        CHIPPENDALE STYLE.
1. Secretary designed by Chippendale.    2. Detail of cornices and mouldings.    3. Decoration on foot.
*The Gentleman and Cabinet Maker's Director.* T. Chippendale.

**PLATE 199.**

1. Secretary designed by Chippendale.   2. Detail of cornices and mouldings.   3. Detail of middle section, covered when secretary is closed.

CHIPPENDALE STYLE.

*The Gentleman and Cabinet Maker's Director.* T. Chippendale.

203

PLATE 200.                                                                                    CHIPPENDALE STYLE.

1. Secretary with architectonic frame designed by Chippendale.   2. Detail of cornice, mouldings and foot decoration.   3. Detail of middle section, covered when secretary is closed.   4. Drawer pull.

*The Gentleman and Cabinet Maker's Director.* T. Chippendale.

204

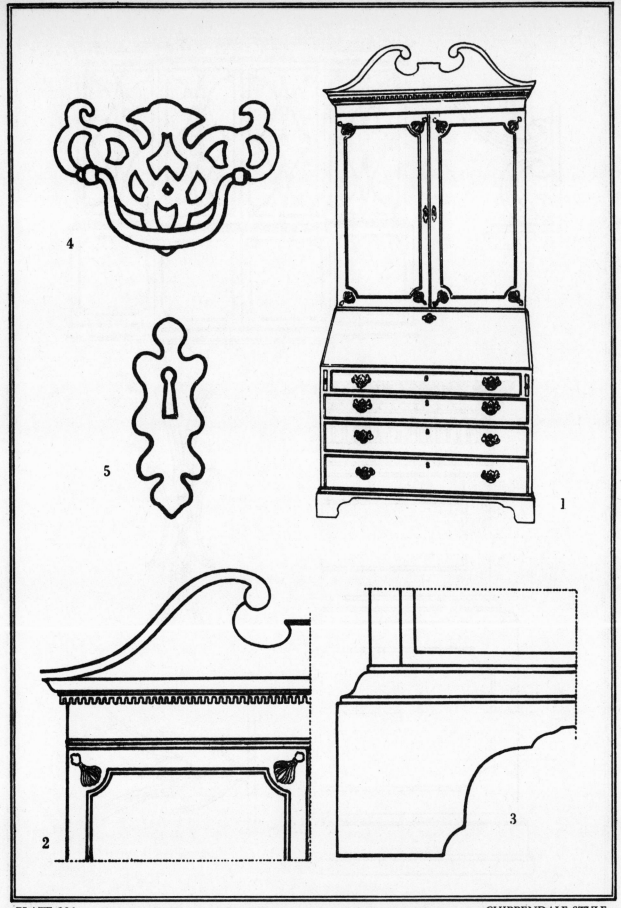

PLATE 201.                                                    CHIPPENDALE STYLE.
1. Secretary.   2. Detail of crest and decoration.   3. Detail of foot.   4. Drawer pull.   5. Escutcheon plate.

*Private collection.*

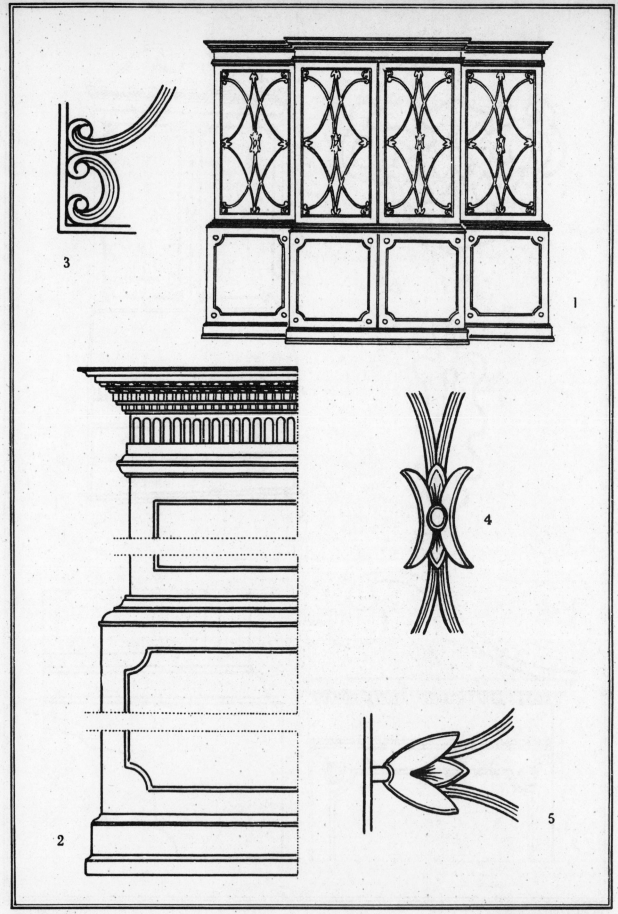

PLATE 202.                                                    CHIPPENDALE STYLE.
1. Beautiful four-piece bookcase.   2. Detail of cornice, mouldings and socle.   3, 4 and 5. Decorations on glass doors.
*Property of the Life Insurance Company, Norwich Union.*

**PLATE 203.** CHIPPENDALE STYLE.
1. Bookcase designed by Chippendale.  2. Cornice.  3. Crest.  4. Base and lower moulding of upper section.  5. Mouldings of lower section.

*The Gentleman and Cabinet Maker's Director*. T. Chippendale.

PLATE 204.
1. Simple wardrobe.  2. Cornice.  3. Detail of foot and lower profile.  4. Door knob.

CHIPPENDALE STYLE.

*Private collection.*

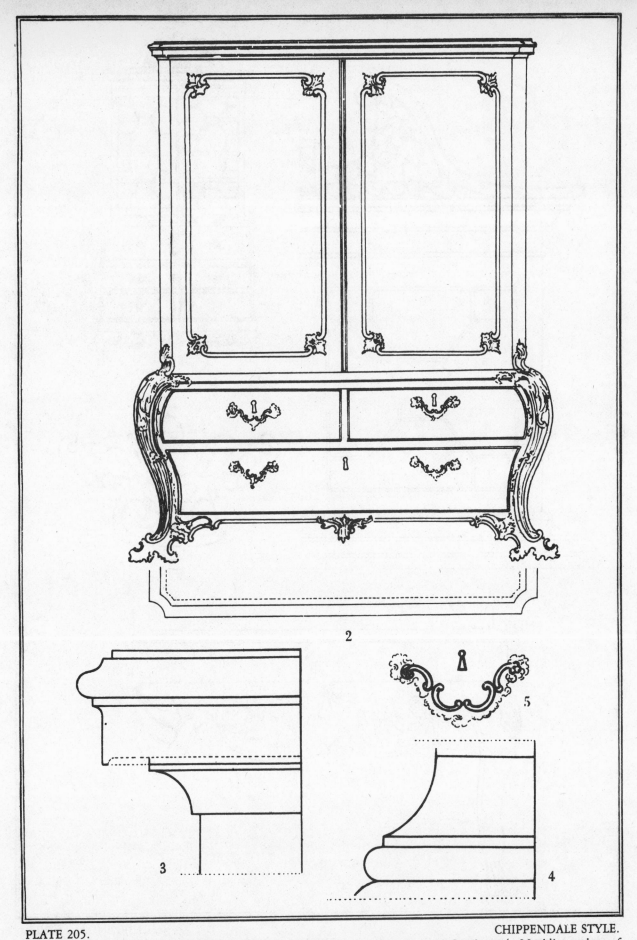

PLATE 205.

1. Wardrobe commode designed by Chippendale.   2. Base of lower section.   3. Cornice.   4. Moulding at base of upper section.   5. Drawer pull.

*The Gentleman and Cabinet Maker's Director.* T. Chippendale.

**PLATE 206.**

1. Irish Chippendale showcase.   2. Decoration of crest, mouldings and glass panes.   3. Decoration on foot and lower crosspiece.   4. Drawer pull.

CHIPPENDALE STYLE.

*Private collection.*

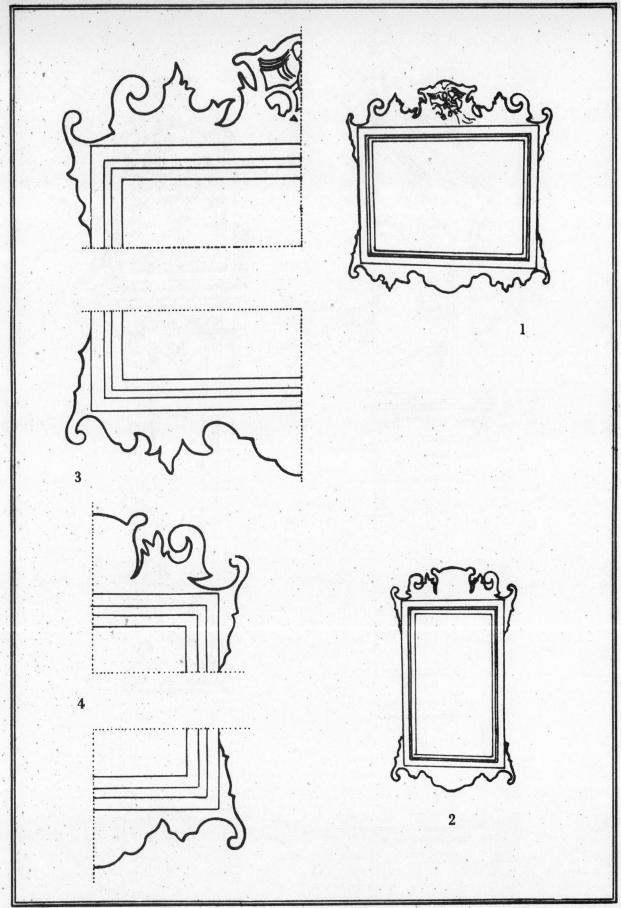

PLATE 207.

1 and 2. Mirrors with sprung frames.   3 and 4. Details of same.

CHIPPENDALE STYLE.

*Private collection.*

PLATE 208.

1. Ornately decorated clock case.    2. Details of crest, face and mouldings.

CHIPPENDALE STYLE.

*Pennsylvania Museum, Philadelphia.*

PLATE 209.
1. Irish Chippendale clock case.    2. Decoration of crest and mouldings.    3. Socle.

CHIPPENDALE STYLE.

*Private collection.*

PLATE 210.                                                    CHIPPENDALE STYLE.

1. Clock case with Chippendale traits.   2. Decorations, columns and mouldings.   3. Socle.

*Private collection.*

214

2

1

PLATE 211.                                                              CHIPPENDALE STYLE.
1. Clock case with Chinese motifs, designed by Chippendale.    2. Decorations: crest, column, mouldings and socle.
*The Gentleman and Cabinet Maker's Director*. T. Chippendale.

PLATE 212.

CHIPPENDALE STYLE.

1. Clock case designed by Chippendale.    2. Decorations: crest, frieze, pilaster, mouldings and foot.

*The Gentleman and Cabinet Maker's Director.* T. Chippendale.

PLATE 213.

1. Case for desk clock designed by Chippendale.   2. Decorations.   3. Base of upper cornice.   4. Lower base.

*The Gentleman and Cabinet Maker's Director.* T. Chippendale.

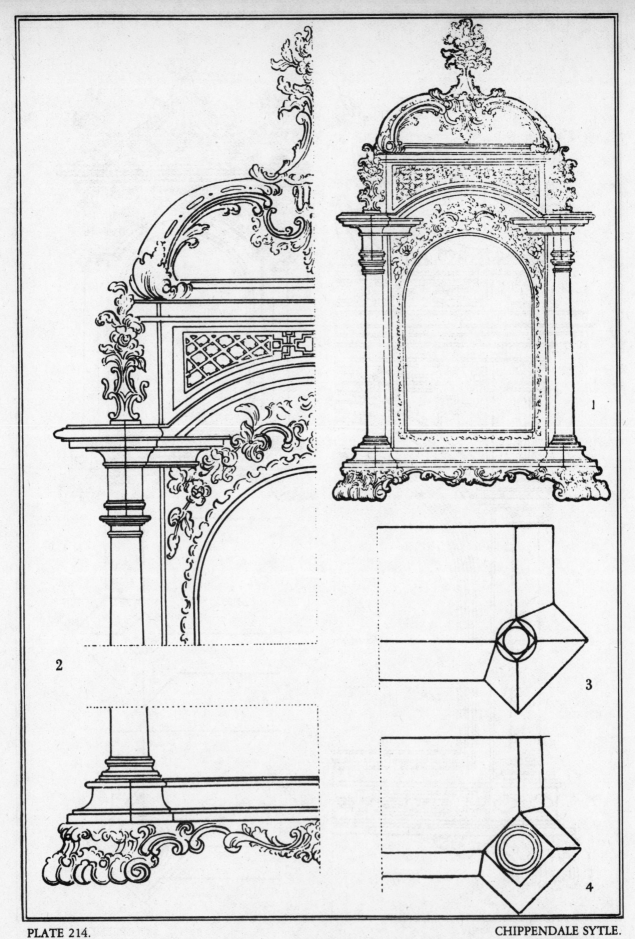

PLATE 214.                                                                  CHIPPENDALE SYTLE.

1. Case for desk clock designed by Chippendale.   2. Decorations.   3. Base of upper cornice.   4. Lower base.

*The Gentleman and Cabinet Maker's Director*. T. Chippendale.

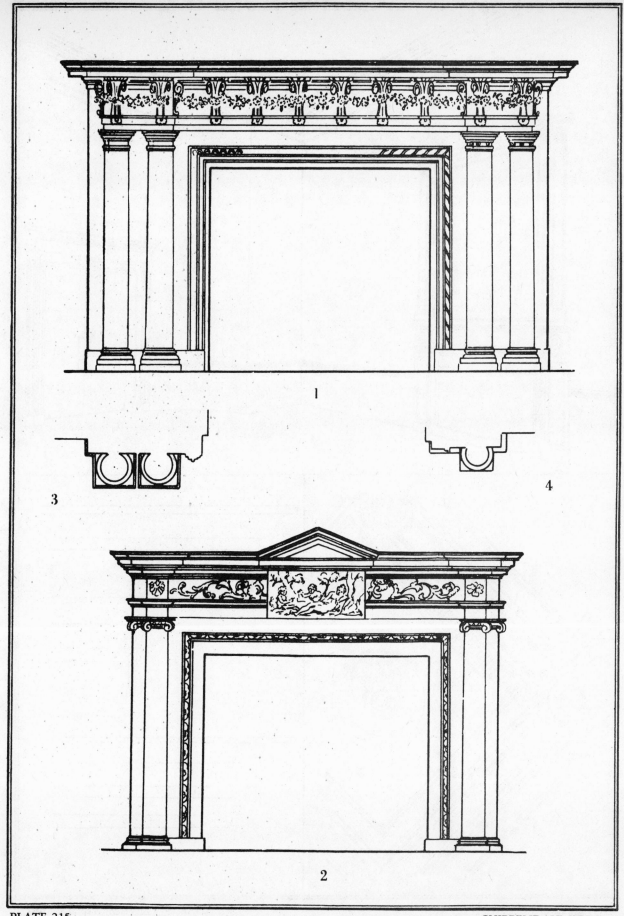

PLATE 215.                                                                    CHIPPENDALE STYLE.

1 and 2. Fireplaces designed by Chippendale.    3. Base of first fireplace.    4. Base of second fireplace.

*The Gentleman and Cabinet Maker's Director.* T. Chippendale.

219

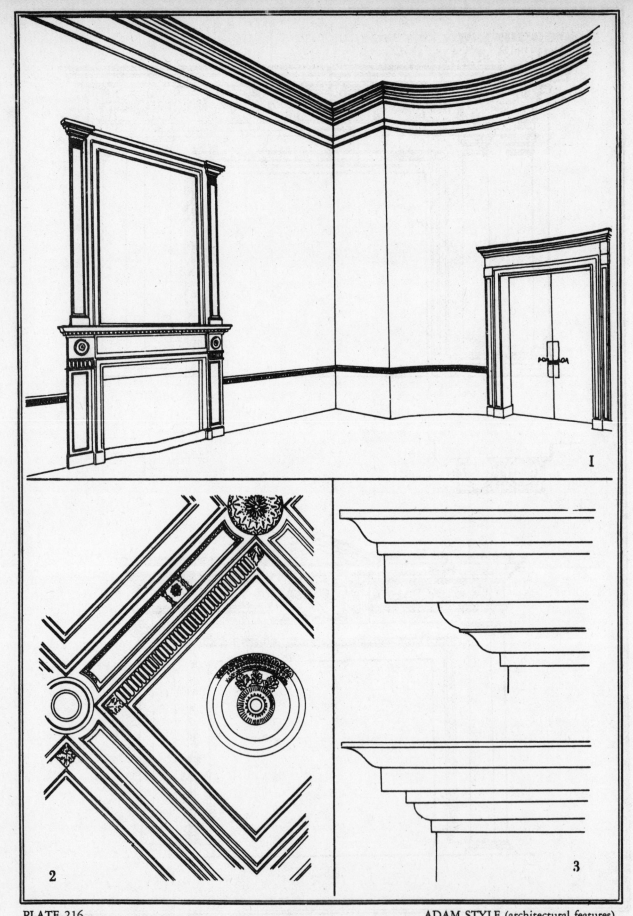

PLATE 216.                                                                    ADAM STYLE (architectural features).
1. Room designed by Adam, 20 St. James Square, London.  2. Ceiling section designed by Adam, foyer of Syon
House.  3. Types of moulding used during period.

**PLATE 217.**                                                                                    ADAM STYLE (architectural features).

1. Room designed by Adam, foyer of Kedleston.    2. Sketches by Robert Adam for door decorations.    3. Door, dining room at 20 St. James Square, London.    4. Type of Venetian window often used by Adam.    5. Window, pavilion of Hopeton House.

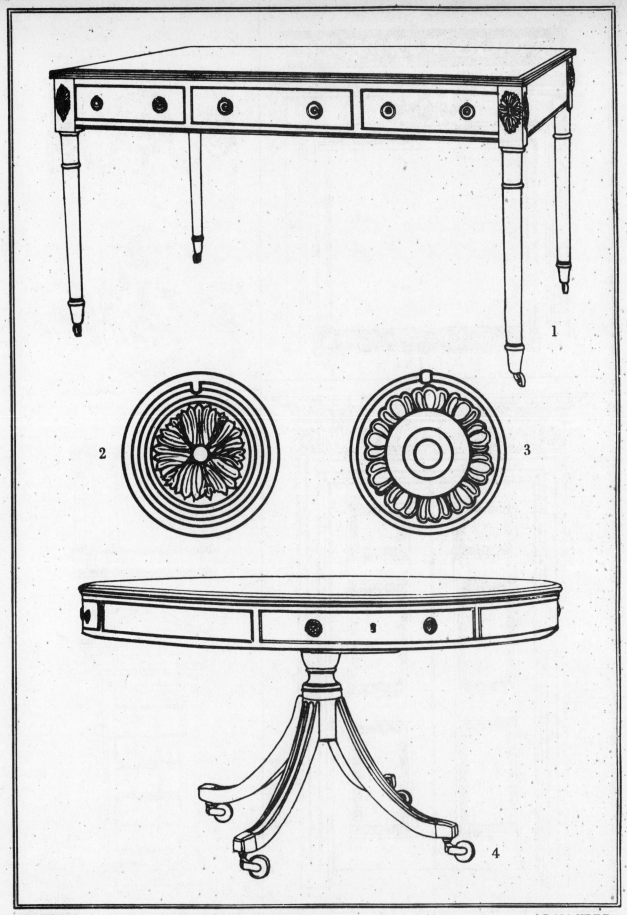

**PLATE 218.**
1 and 4. Adam tables.   2 and 3. Drawer pulls.

ADAM STYLE.

*Private collections.*

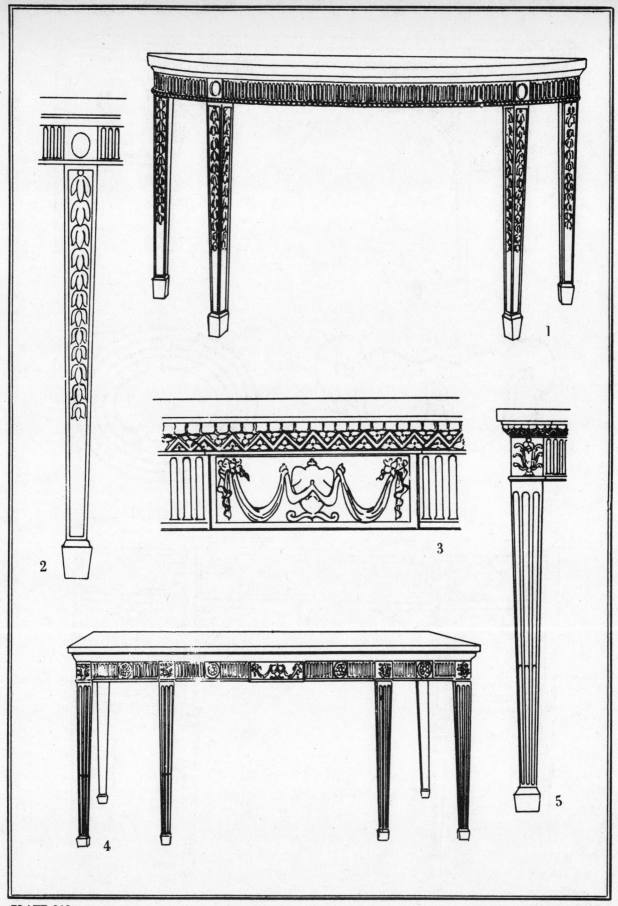

PLATE 219.

ADAM STYLE.

1 and 4.   Adam console tables.   2 and 5.  Decorations on their respective legs.   3. Central detail of frieze on second table.

*Property of C. J. Charles.*

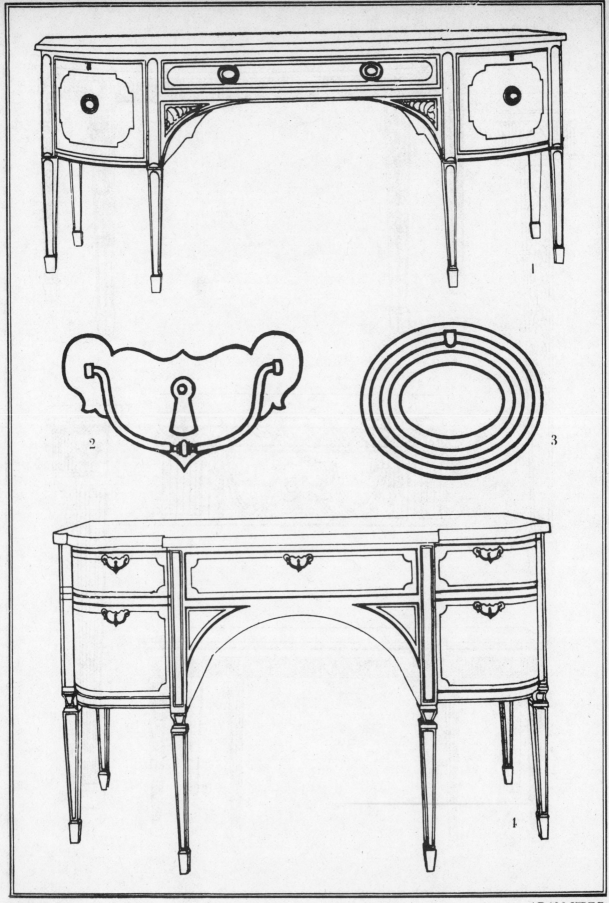

PLATE 220.
1 and 4. Adam credenzas.   2 and 3. Drawer pulls.

ADAM STYLE.

*Private collection.*

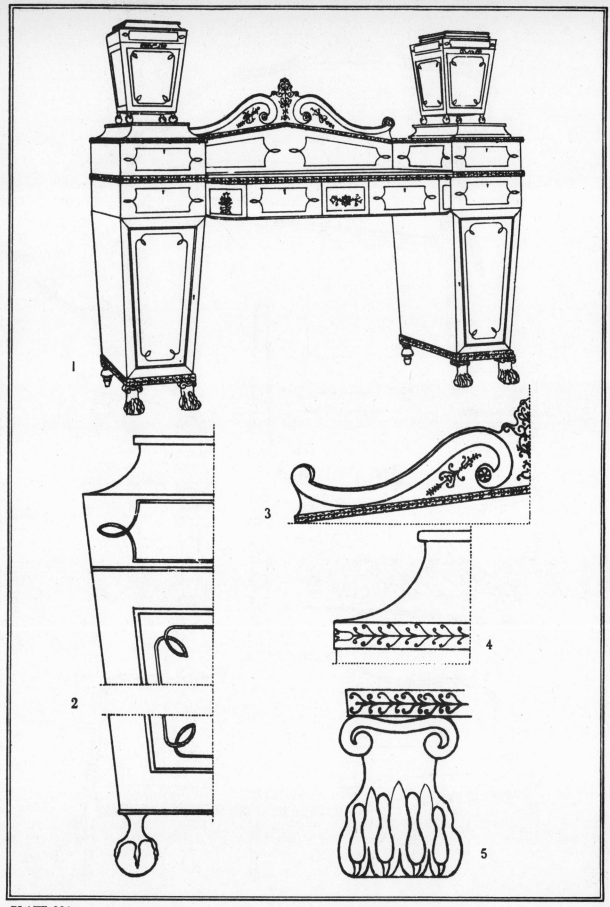

PLATE 221                                                          ADAM STYLE.
1. Adam desk.    2. Detail of urns.    3. Detail of crest.    4. Detail of base for urns.    5. Leg.

*Victoria and Albert Museum.*

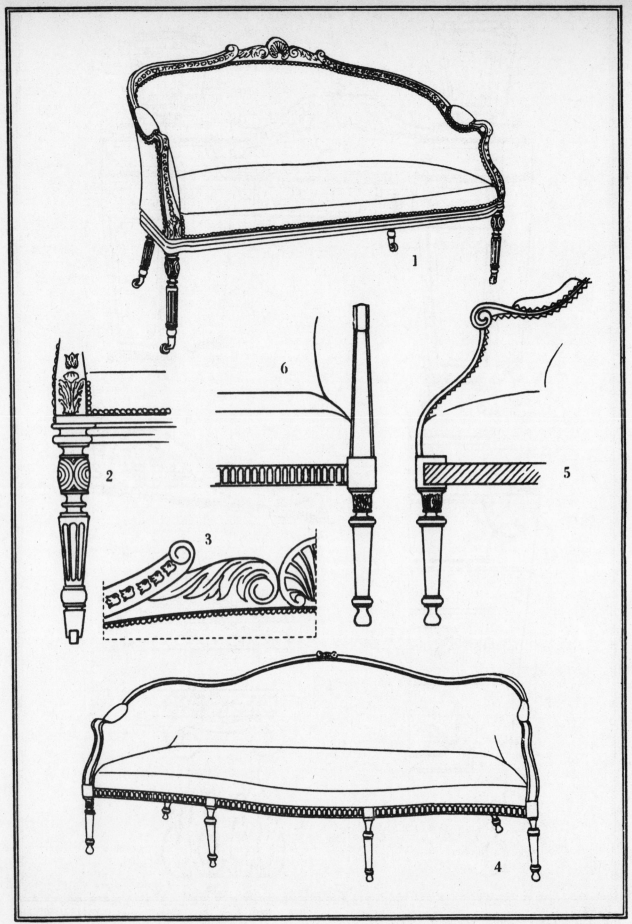

PLATE 222.
1 and 4. Adam sofas.    2 and 3. Decorations on first sofa—leg and crest.    5 and 6. Decorations on second sofa—leg and arm.

ADAM STYLE.

*Property of F. W. Phillips.*

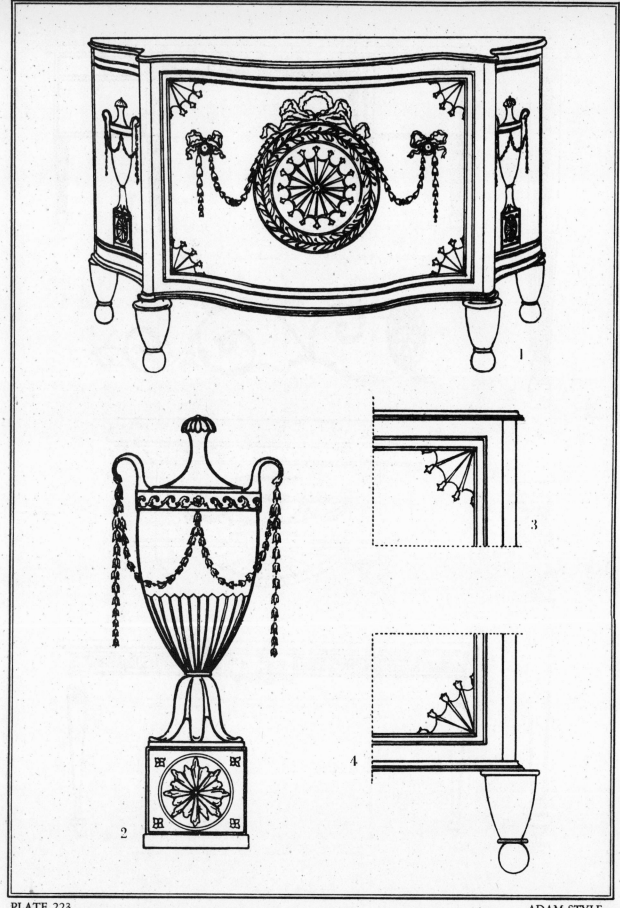

PLATE 223.                                                                                      ADAM STYLE.

1. Adam commode.    2. Decoration on side panels.    3 and 4. Decorations on corners and leg.

*Victoria and Albert Museum.*

PLATE 224.                                                           HEPPLEWHITE STYLE.
1 and 4. Hepplewhite console tables.   2 and 5. Decorations on legs.   3. Central detail of frieze on first table.   6. Central detail of frieze on second table.

*The Cabinet-Maker and Upholsterer's Guide.* G. Hepplewhite.

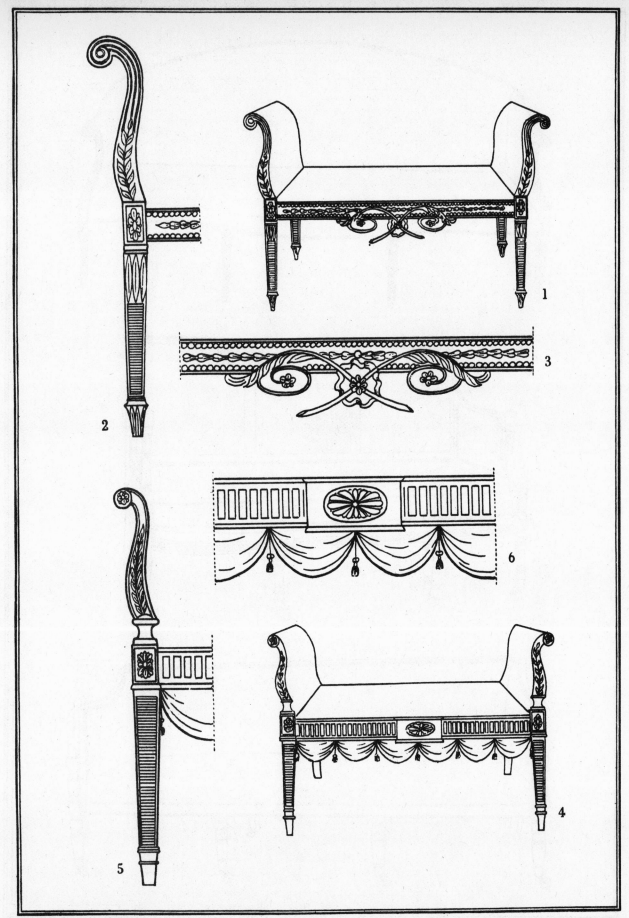

1 and 4. Hepplewhite benches.  2 and 3. Decorations on first one — leg, arm and crosspiece.  5 and 6. Decorations on second one — leg, arm and crosspiece.

*The Cabinet-Maker and Upholsterer's Guide.* G. Hepplewhite.

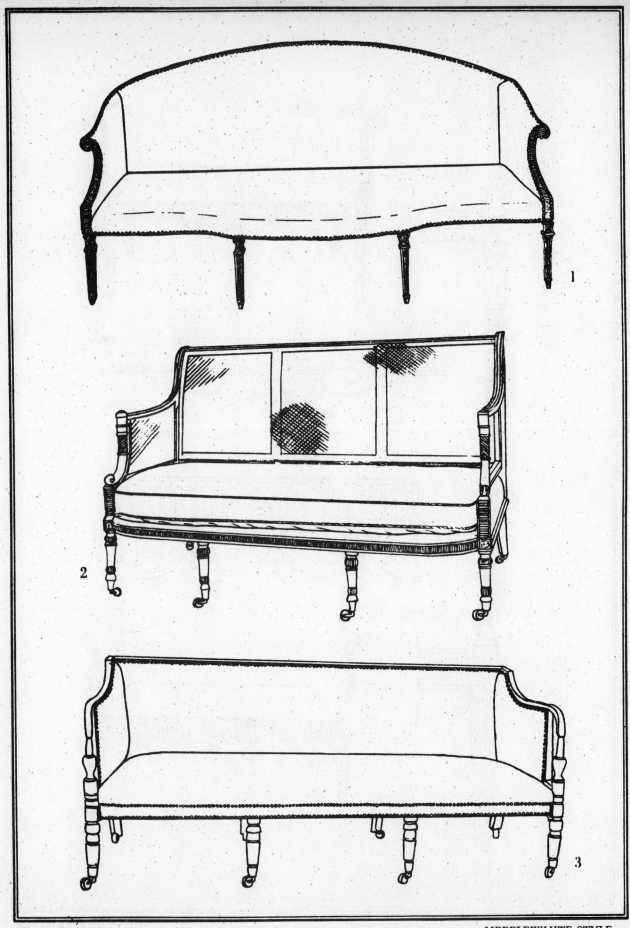

PLATE 226.                                    HEPPLEWHITE STYLE.

Hepplewhite sofas:   1. From *The Cabinet-Maker and Upholsterer's Guide.*   2. Property of F. W. Phillips.   3. Private collection.

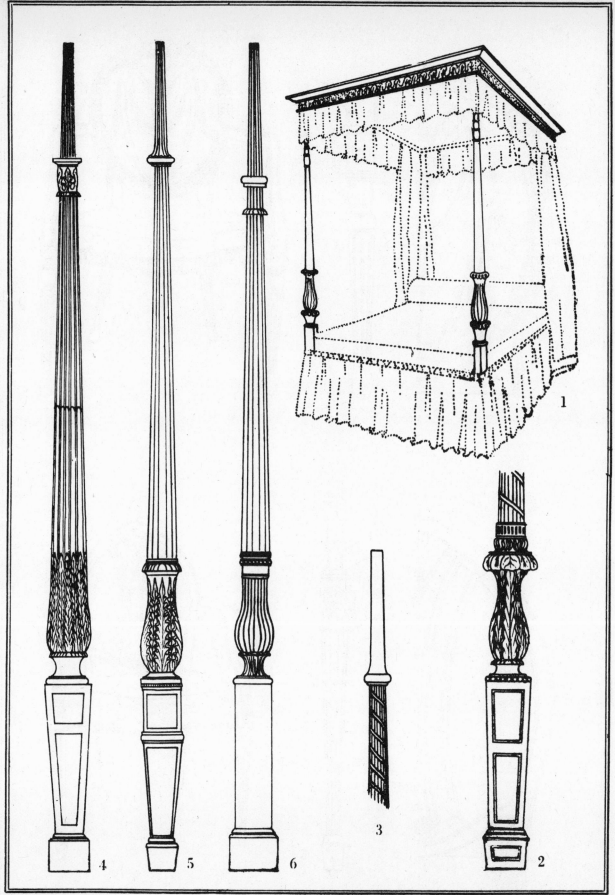

PLATE 227.                                                                HEPPLEWHITE STYLE.

1. Hepplewhite canopy bed.    2 and 3. Details of post.    4, 5 and 6. Other posts in the same style.

*The Cabinet-Maker and Upholsterer's Guide.* G. Hepplewhite.

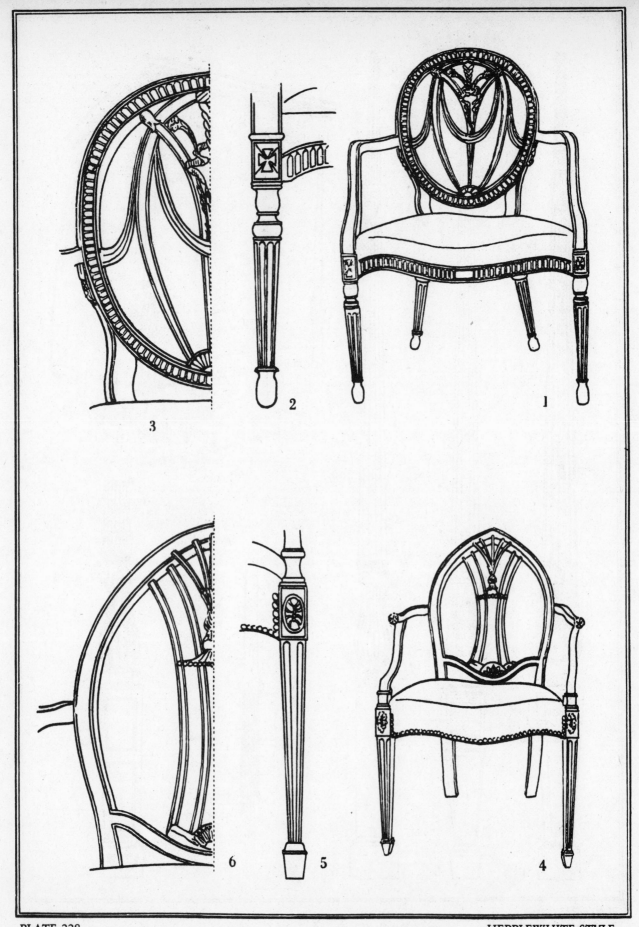

PLATE 228.                                                 HEPPLEWHITE STYLE.
1. Hepplewhite armchair.   2. Detail of leg.   3. Detail of back.   4. Hepplewhite armchair.   5. Detail of leg.
6. Detail of back.

*Victoria and Albert Museum and property of F. W. Phillips.*

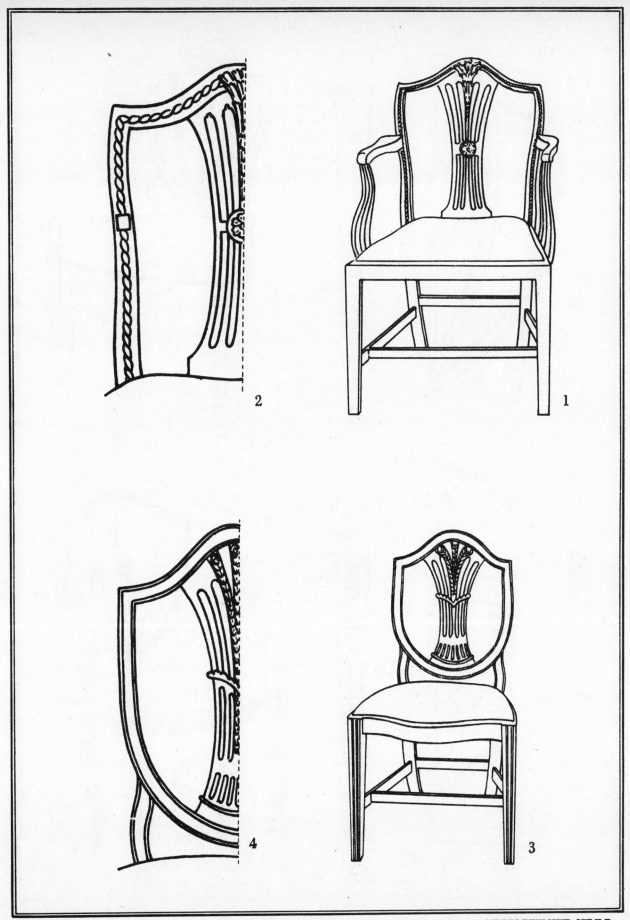

**PLATE 229.**

1. Hepplewhite armchair.   2. Detail of back.   3. Hepplewhite chair.   4. Detail of back.

HEPPLEWHITE STYLE.

*Private collection and property of F. W. Phillips.*

233

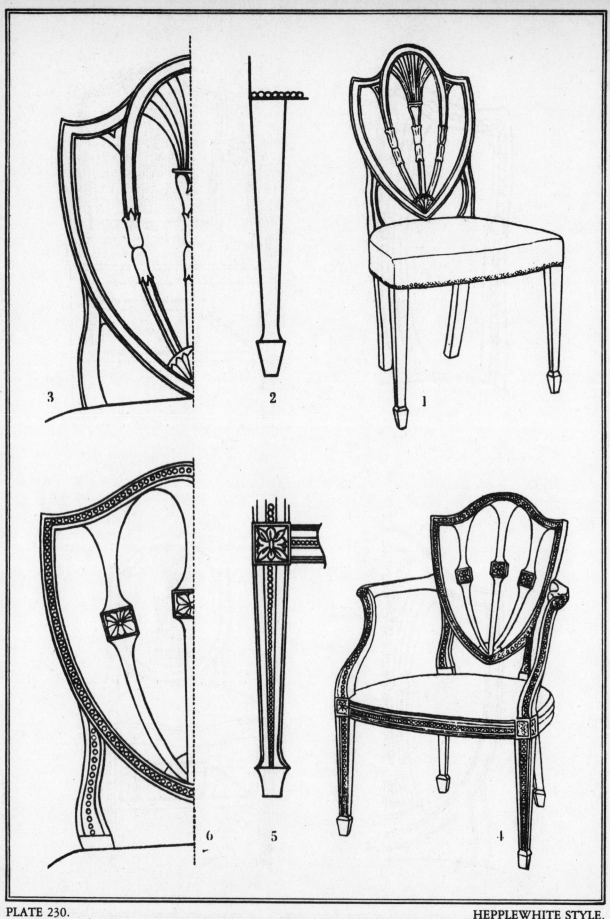

PLATE 230.                                                                                    HEPPLEWHITE STYLE.
1. Hepplewhite armchair with shield-shaped back.   2. Front leg.   3. Detail of back.   4. Hepplewhite armchair with shield back.   5. Front leg.   6. Detail of back.

*Metropolitan Museum of Art.*

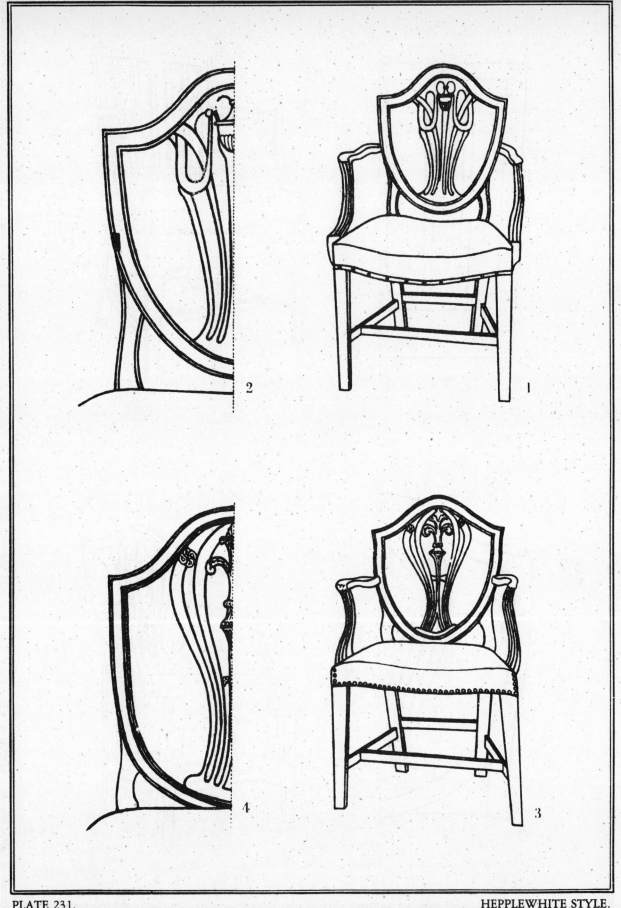

PLATE 231.                                                                                                                          HEPPLEWHITE STYLE.
1. Hepplewhite armchair with shield back.   2. Detail of back.   3. Hepplewhite armchair with shield back.   4. Detail
of back.

*Private collection and Victoria and Albert Museum.*

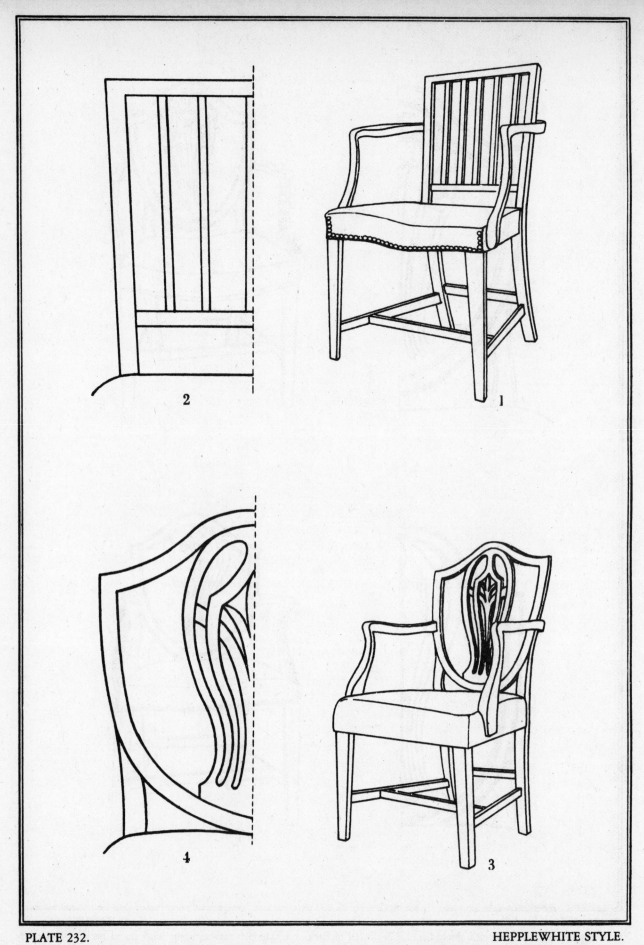

PLATE 232.                                                    HEPPLEWHITE STYLE.
1. Hepplewhite armchair.   2. Detail of back.   3. Hepplewhite armchair with shield back.   4. Detail of back.
*Private collection and North Ockenden Hall, Essex.*

236

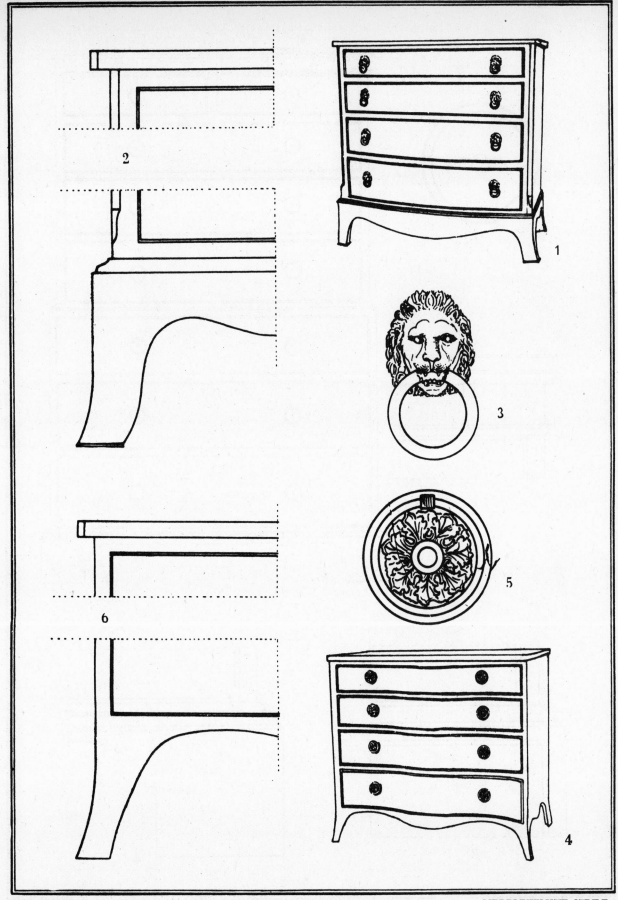

**PLATE 233.** HEPPLEWHITE STYLE.
1 and 4. Hepplewhite commodes. 2 and 3. Details of first commode; moulding, foot and drawer pull. 5 and 6. Details of second commode: drawer pull and foot.

*Private collection.*

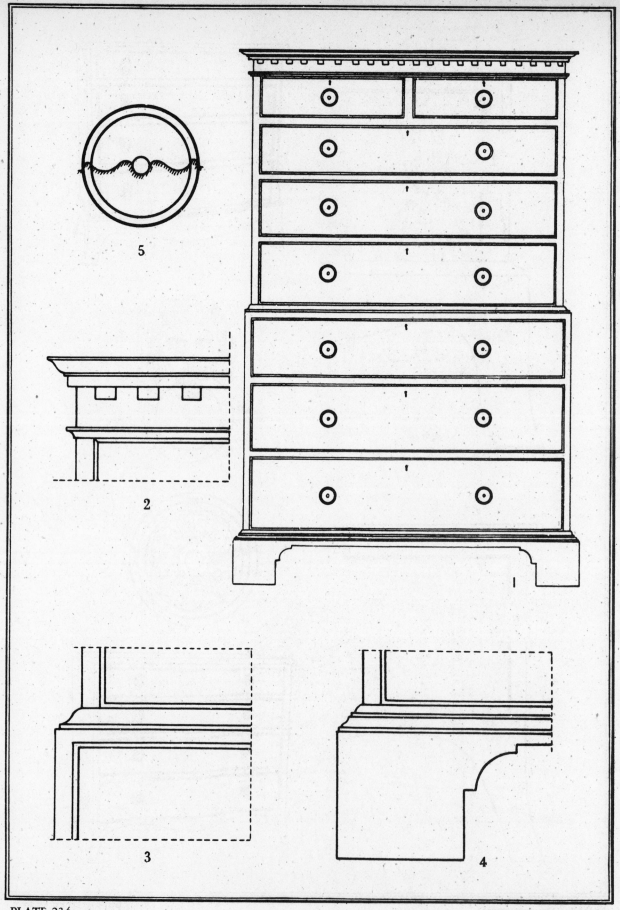

PLATE 234.                                    HEPPLEWHITE STYLE.
1. Tall Hepplewhite commode.    2. Cornice.    3. Base of upper section.    4. Mouldings at base of lower section and
foot.    5. Drawer pull.

*The Cabinet-Maker and Upholsterer's Guide.* G. Hepplewhite.

**PLATE 235.**                                                          HEPPLEWHITE STYLE.

1. Hepplewhite secretary.   2. Detail of middle section of secretary, covered when closed.   3. Crest, cornice and glass decoration.   4. Base of lower section and foot.   5. Drawer pull.

*The Cabinet-Maker and Upholsterer's Guide.* G. Hepplewhite.

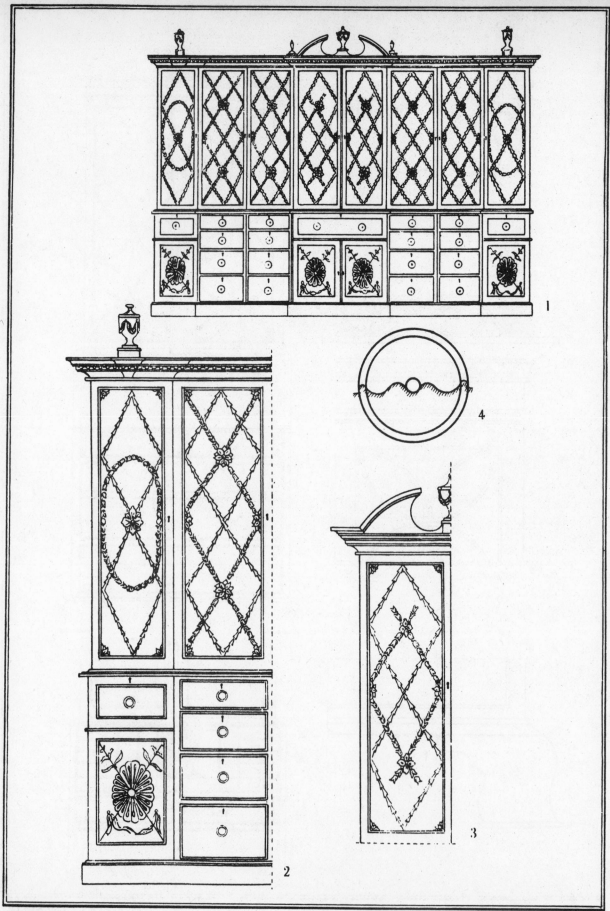

PLATE 236.                                                                HEPPLEWHITE STYLE.
1. Hepplewhite bookcase.   2. Detail of side sections.   3. Detail of glass pane central finial.   4. Drawer pull.
*The Cabinet-Maker and Upholsterer's Guide*. G. Hepplewhite.

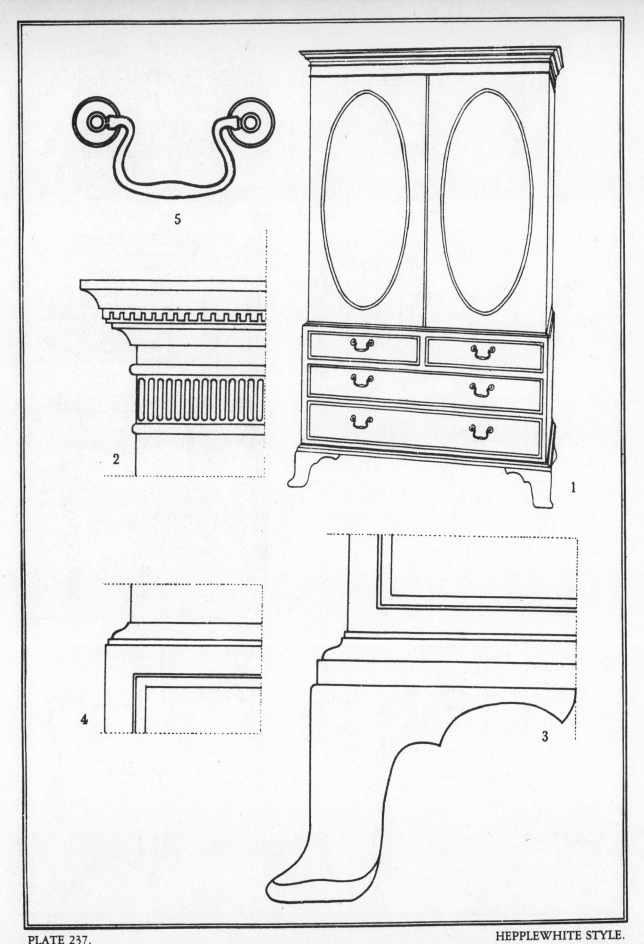

PLATE 237.

1. Hepplewhite wardrobe commode.    2, 3 and 4. Decorations: cornice, frieze, mouldings and leg.    5. Drawer pull.

HEPPLEWHITE STYLE.

*Property of F. W. Phillips.*

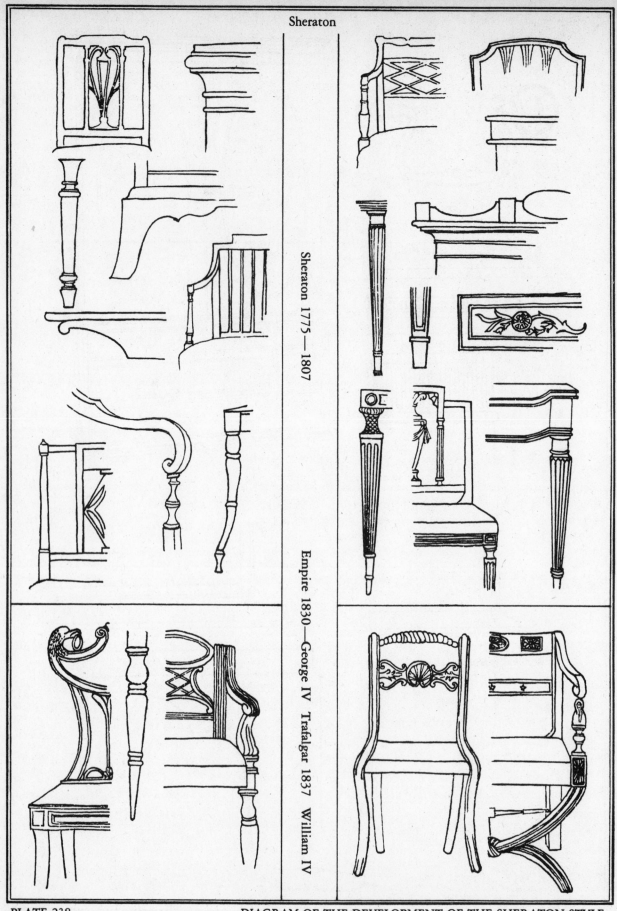

Sheraton 1775 — 1807

Empire 1830 — George IV Trafalgar 1837 William IV

**PLATE 238.**  DIAGRAM OF THE DEVELOPMENT OF THE SHERATON STYLE.

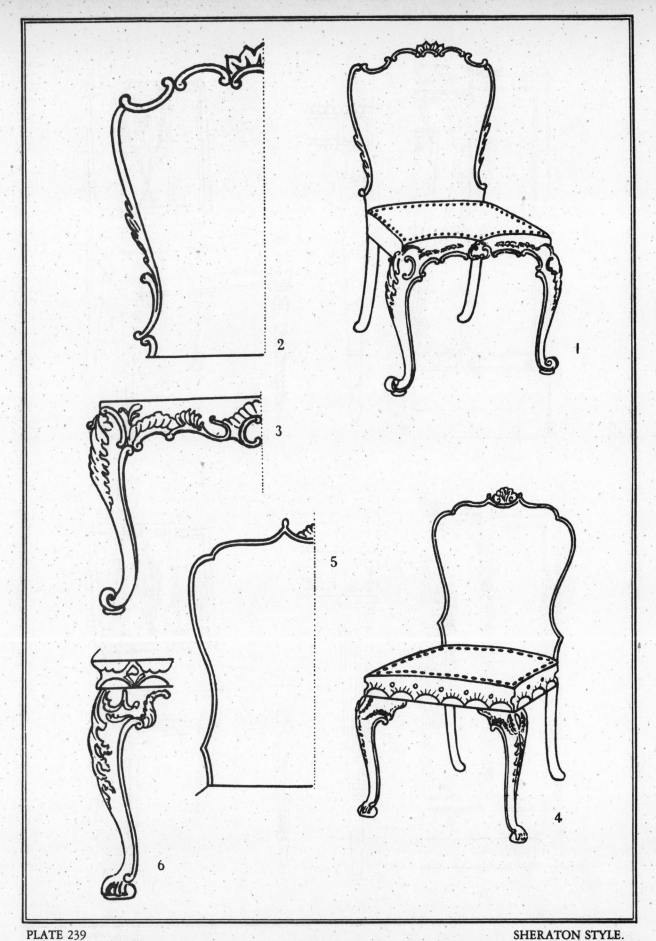

PLATE 239                                                                    SHERATON STYLE.

1 and 4. Chairs with upholstered backs and seats.    2 and 5. Detail of their respective backs.    3. Decoration on leg
and edge of seat of first chair.    6. Decoration on leg of second chair.

*Universal Systems of Household Furniture 1762*, Ince and Mayhew.

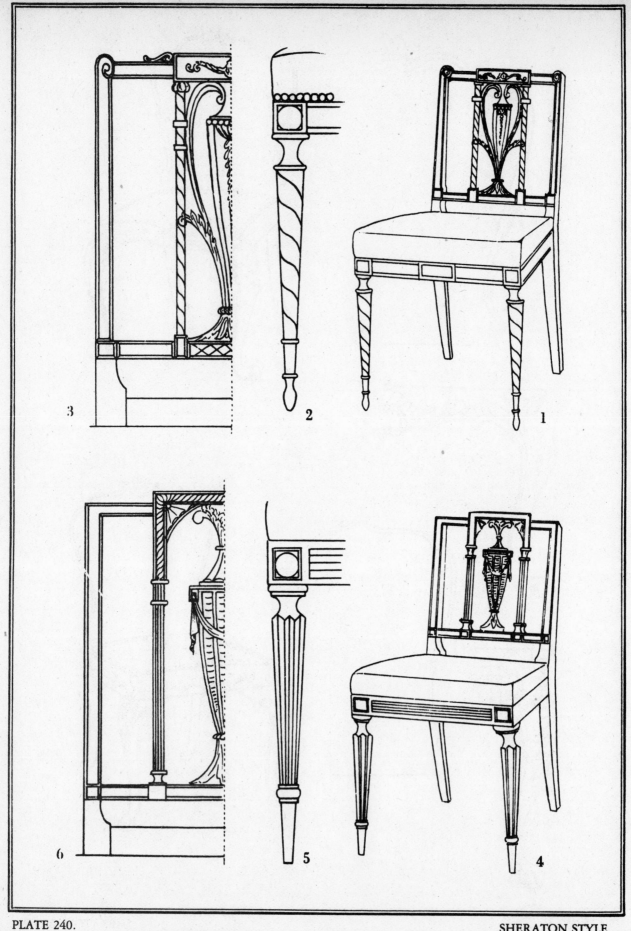

**PLATE 240.**

1 and 4. Sheraton chairs with urn design on backs.   2 and 5. Details of front legs.   3 and 6. Details of backs.

SHERATON STYLE.

*Album of designs by Sheraton.*

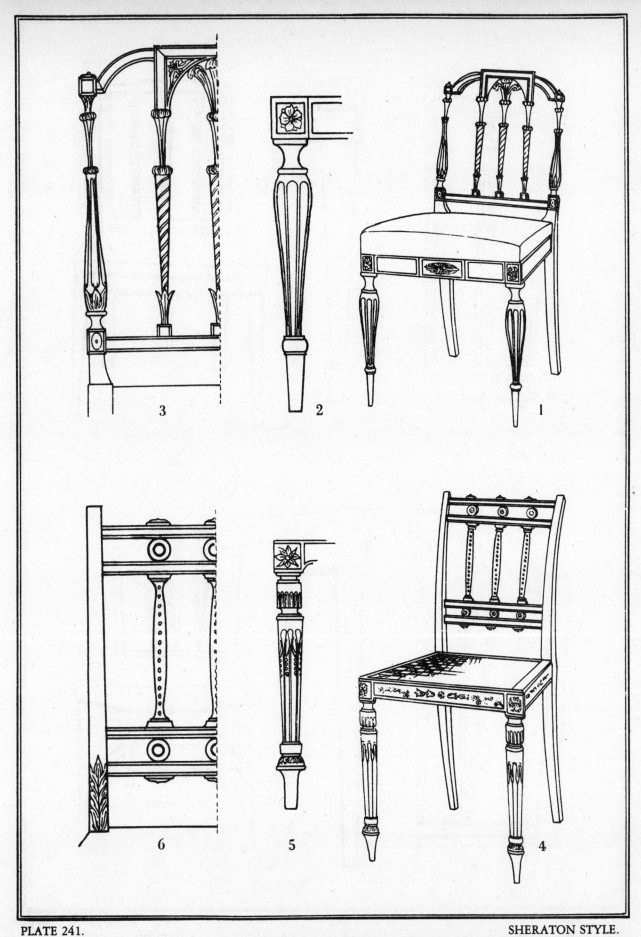

PLATE 241.                                                    SHERATON STYLE.

1. Sheraton chair.   2. Front leg.   3. Detail of back.   4. Sheraton chair.   5. Front leg.   6. Detail of back.

*Album of designs by Sheraton and collection of George Stoner, West Wickham, Kent.*

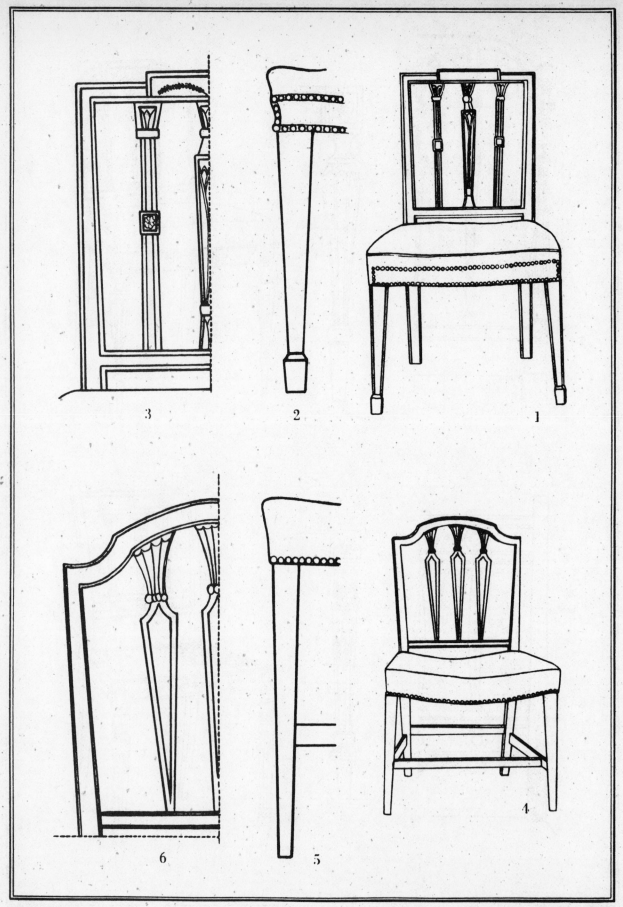

PLATE 242.

SHERATON STYLE.

1 and 4. Sheraton chairs showing Hepplewhite influence.  2 and 5. Front legs.  3 and 6. Details of backs.

*Private collection.*

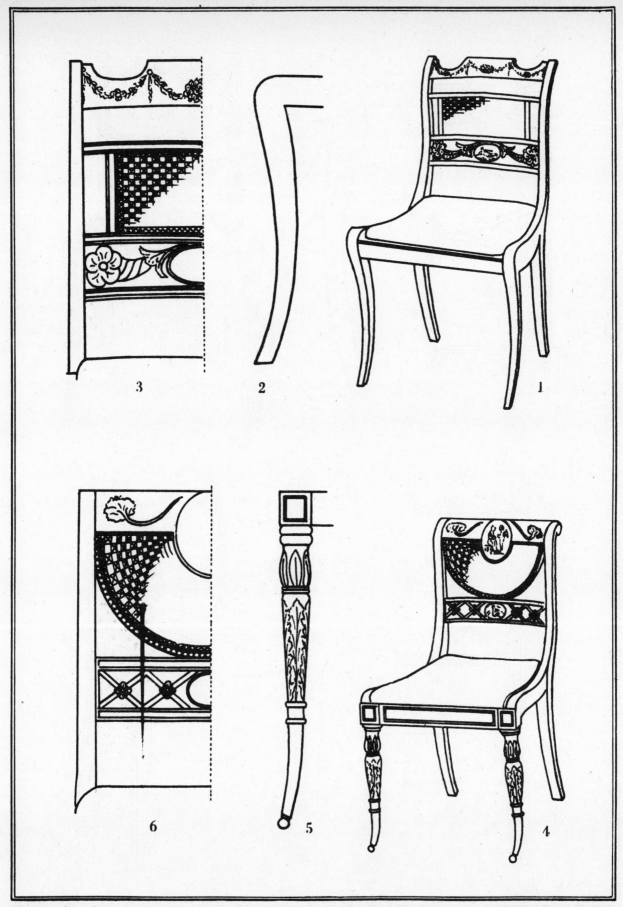

PLATE 243.

SHERATON STYLE.

1 and 4. Sheraton chairs.    2 and 5. Front legs.    3 and 6. Details of backs.

*Collection of George Stoner, West Wickham, Kent.*

247

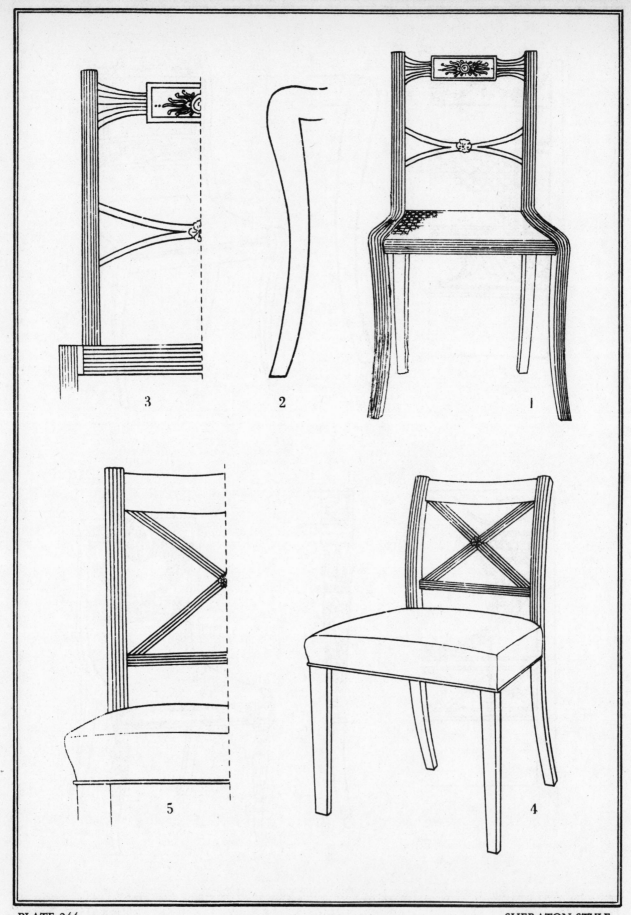

PLATE 244.                                                                      SHERATON STYLE.
1. Sheraton chair showing influence of Adam.   2. Front leg.   3. Detail of back.   4. Sheraton chair showing influence of Adam.   5. Detail of back.

*Property of Sir Spencer Ponsonby-Fane and a private collection.*

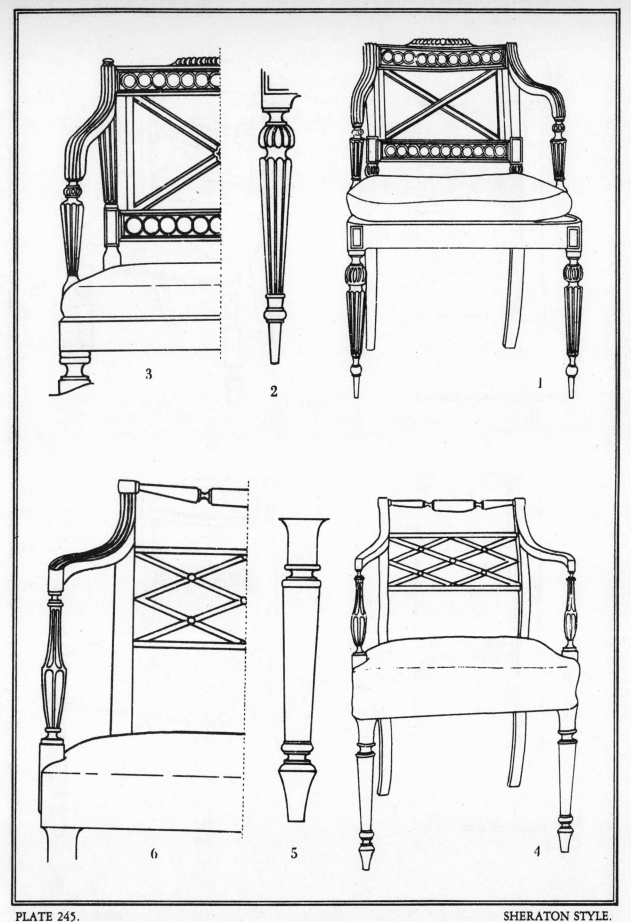

**PLATE 245.**                                                                    SHERATON STYLE.

1. Sheraton armchair showing Adam influence.   2. Front leg.   3. Details of back and arm.   4. Sheraton armchair.   5. Front leg.   6. Details of back and arm.

*Victoria and Albert Museum (private property) and a private collection.*

249

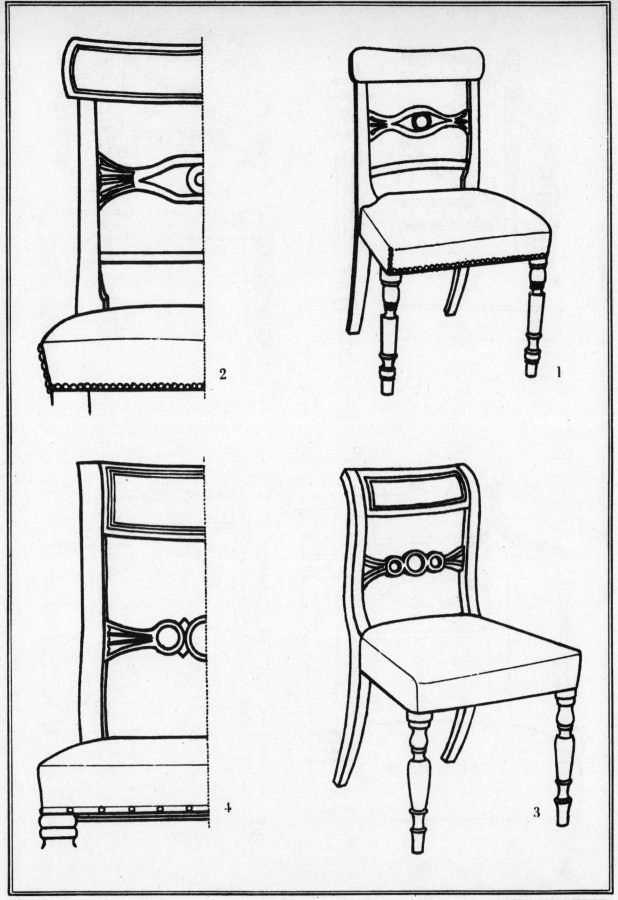

PLATE 246.

SHERATON STYLE.

1 and 3. Chairs from the last Sheraton period, early 19th century.   2 and 4. Detail of backs.

*Victoria and Albert Museum.*

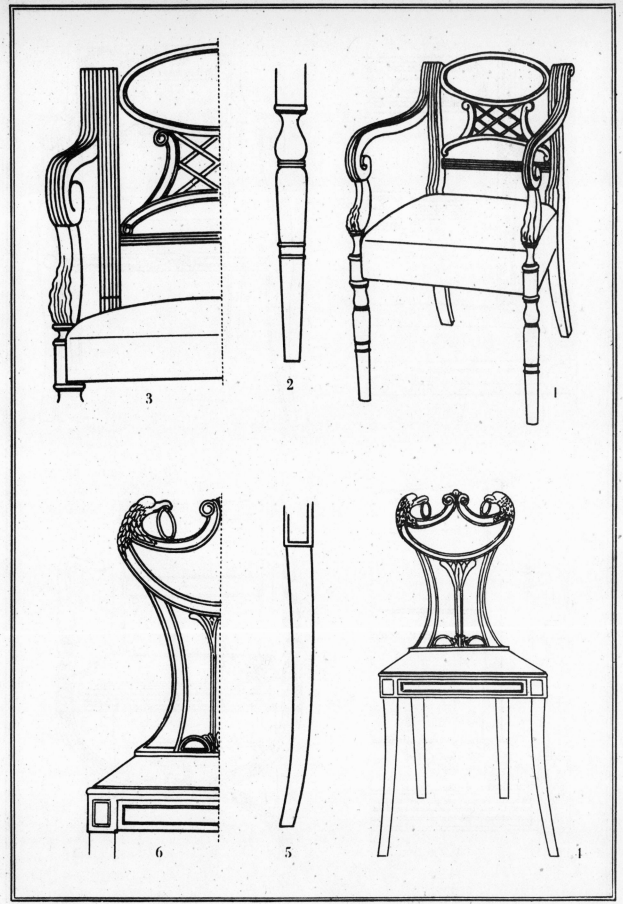

PLATE 247.                                                         SHERATON STYLE.
1. Armchair in English Empire style.   2. Front leg.   3. Detail of back and arm.   4. Chair in English Empire
style.   5. Front leg.   6. Detail of back.

*Private collection and Victoria and Albert Museum.*

251

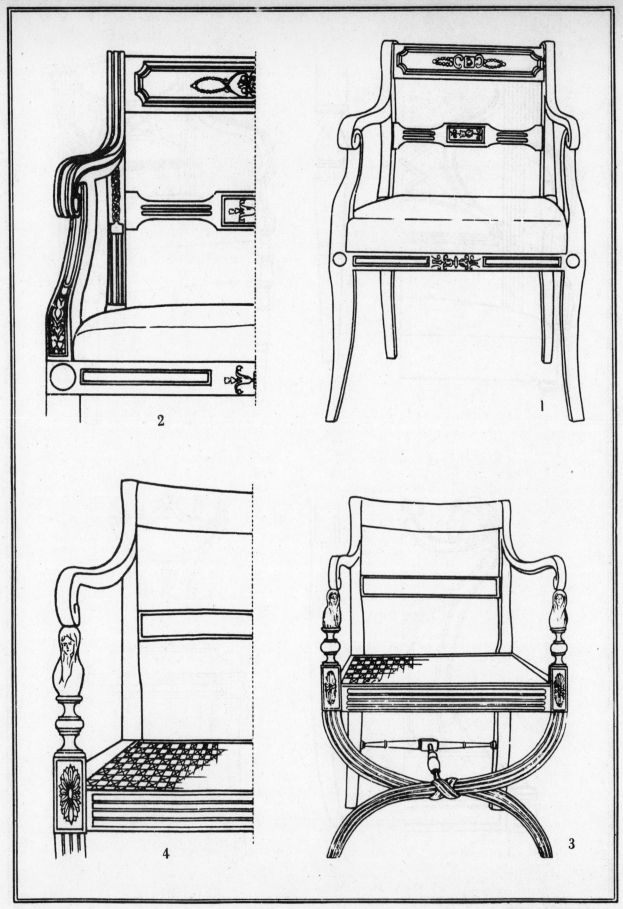

PLATE 248.

SHERATON STYLE.

1 and 3. Sheraton armchairs showing Adam and Trafalgar influence.  2 and 4. Details of backs and arms.

*Property of Sir Spencer Ponsonby-Fane.*

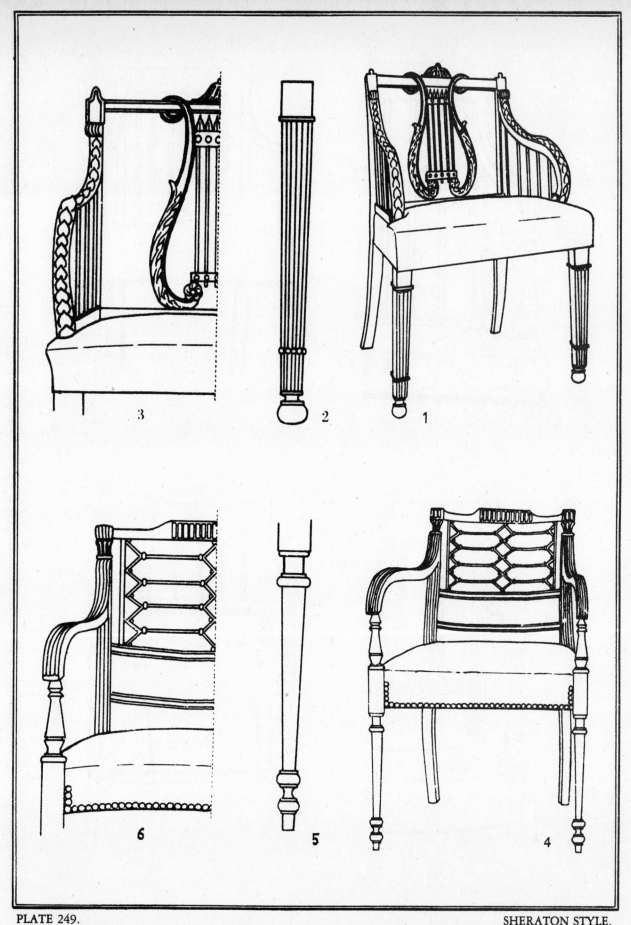

PLATE 249.                                                                                      SHERATON STYLE.

1. Sheraton armchair.    2. Front leg.    3. Details of back and arm.    4. Sheraton armchair.    5. Front leg.    6. Details of back and arm.

*Victoria and Albert Museum and property of Henry Willet of Brighton.*

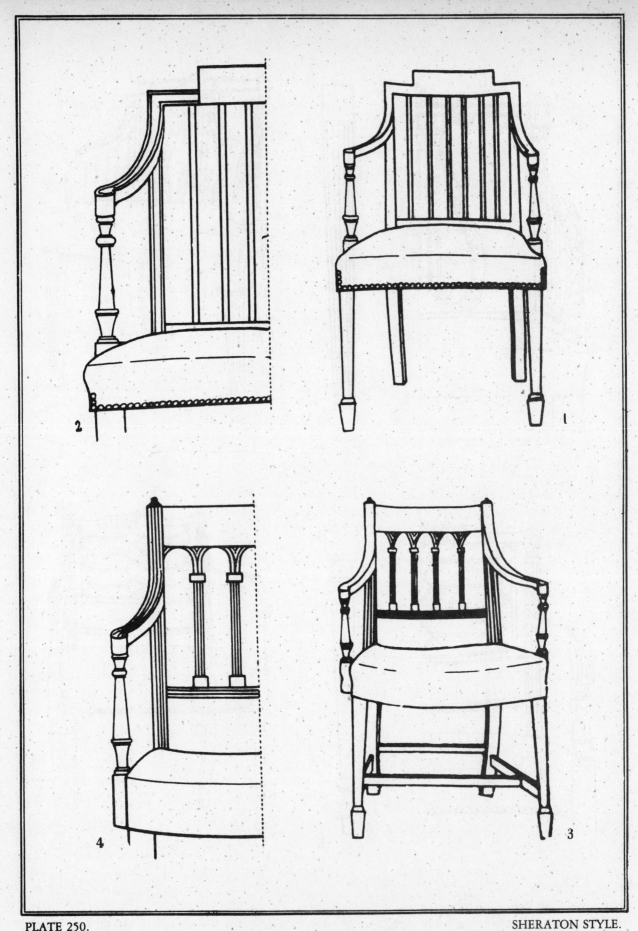

PLATE 250.                                                        SHERATON STYLE.

1. Sheraton armchair.    2. Details of back and arm.    3. Sheraton armchair.    4. Details of back and arm.

*Property of E. Hugh Spottiswoode and Victoria and Albert Museum.*

254

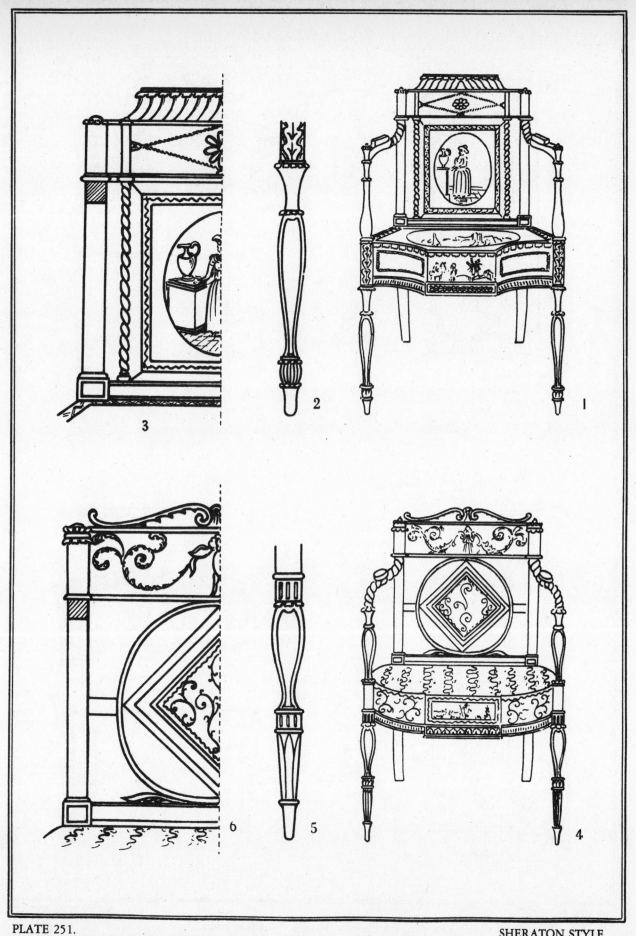

PLATE 251.

SHERATON STYLE.

1 and 4. Sheraton armchairs.   2 and 5. Front legs.   3 and 6. Detail of backs.

*Album of designs by Sheraton.*

PLATE 252.

SHERATON STYLE

1 and 4. Sheraton armchairs.  2 and 5. Front legs.  3 and 6. Details of backs.

*Victoria and Albert Museum.*

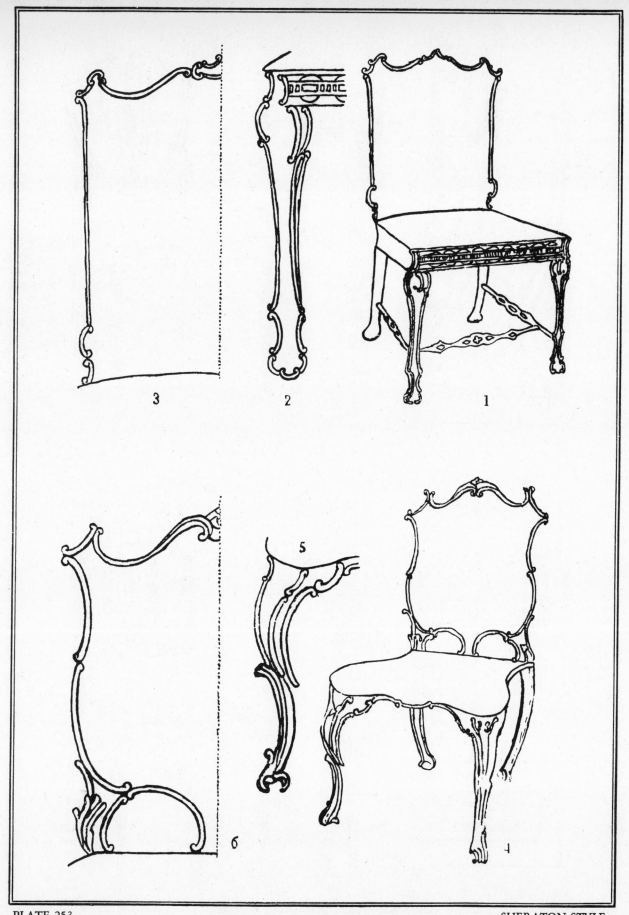

PLATE 253.                                                        SHERATON STYLE.
1 and 4. Sketches of chairs.   2 and 5. Details of legs.   3 and 6. Details of backs.
*The Universal System of Household Furniture 1762.* Ince and Mayhew.

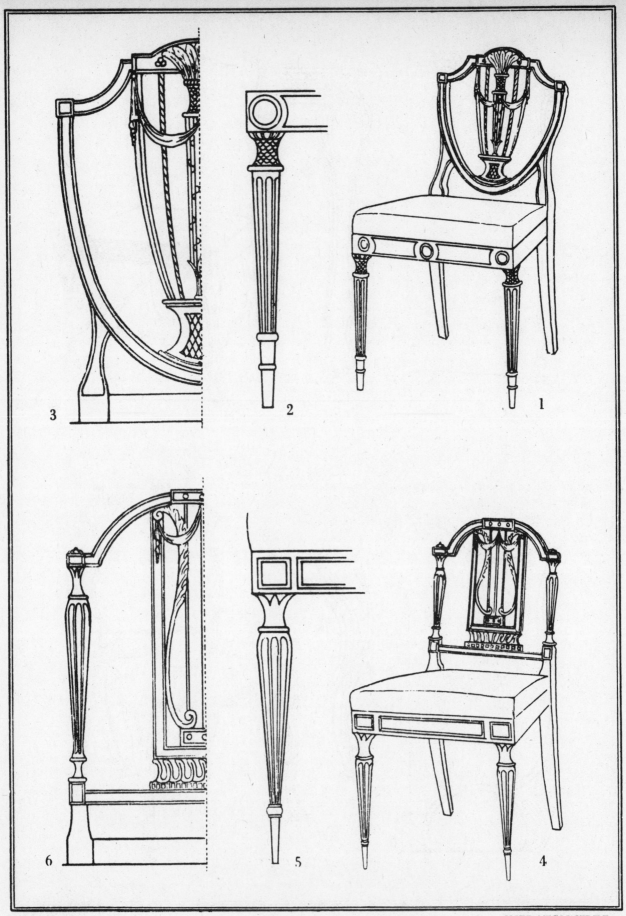

PLATE 254.

SHERATON STYLE.

1 and 4. Sheraton chairs.  2 and 5. Detail of front legs.  3 and 6. Detail of backs.

*Album of designs by Sheraton.*

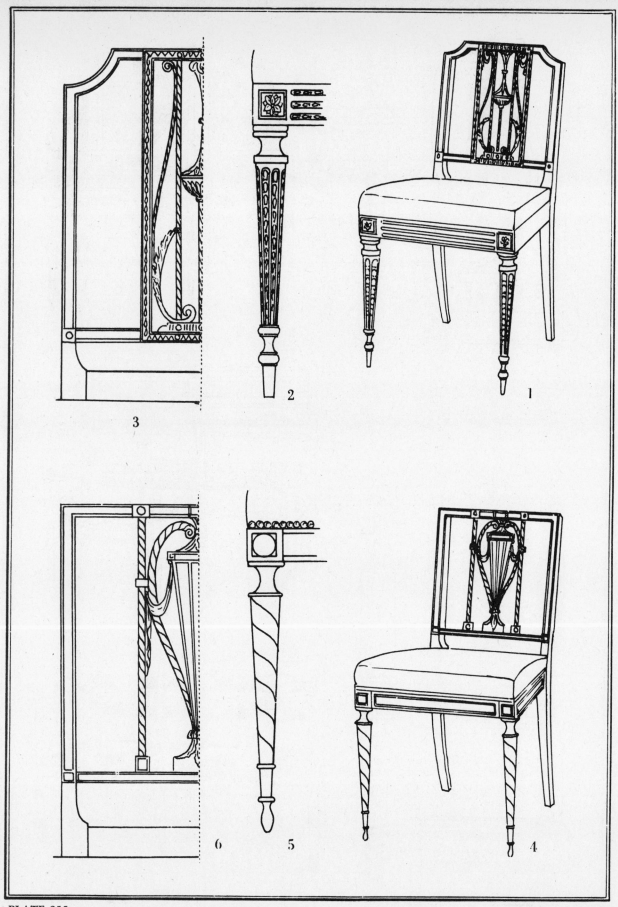

PLATE 255.
1 and 4. Sheraton chairs.    2 and 5. Detail of front legs.    3 and 6. Detail of backs.

SHERATON STYLE.

*Album of designs by Sheraton.*

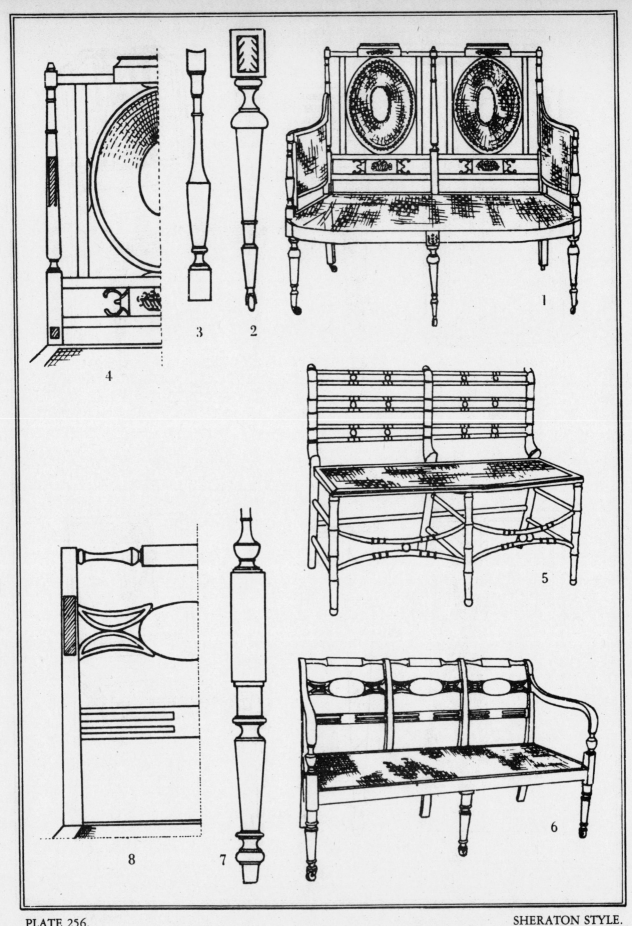

PLATE 256.                                                                          SHERATON STYLE.
1. Sheraton sofa.    2. Leg.    3. Arm support.    4. Detail of back.    5. Sheraton sofa.    6. Sheraton sofa.    7. Leg.
8. Detail of back.

*Property of Mr. Edward; a private collection and property of F. W. Phillips.*

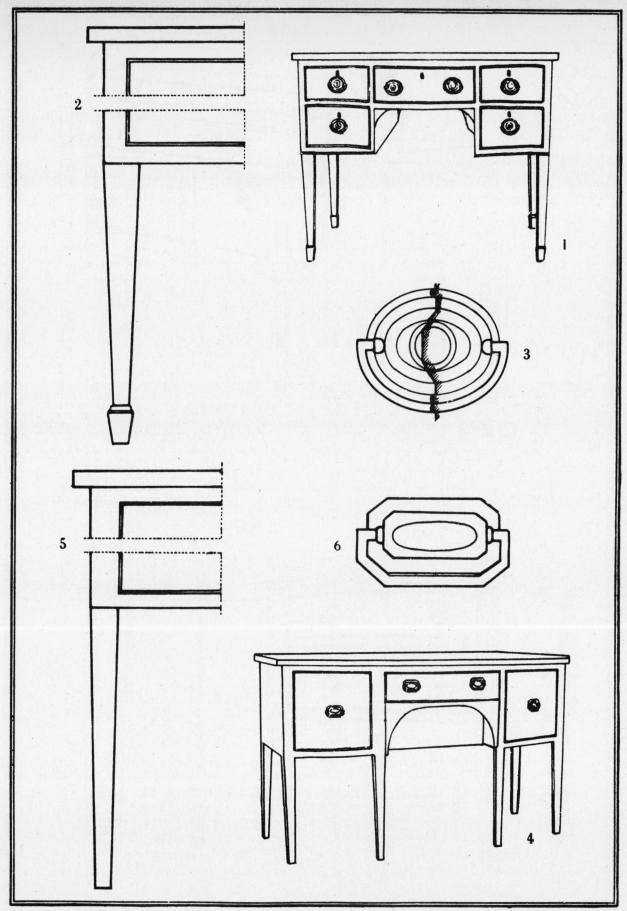

PLATE 257.                                                        SHERATON STYLE.
1. Sheraton desk.   2. Detail.   3. Drawer pull.   4. Sheraton desk.   5. Detail.   6. Drawer pull.
*Property of F. W. Phillips, Hitchin and J. H. Springett, Rochester.*

261

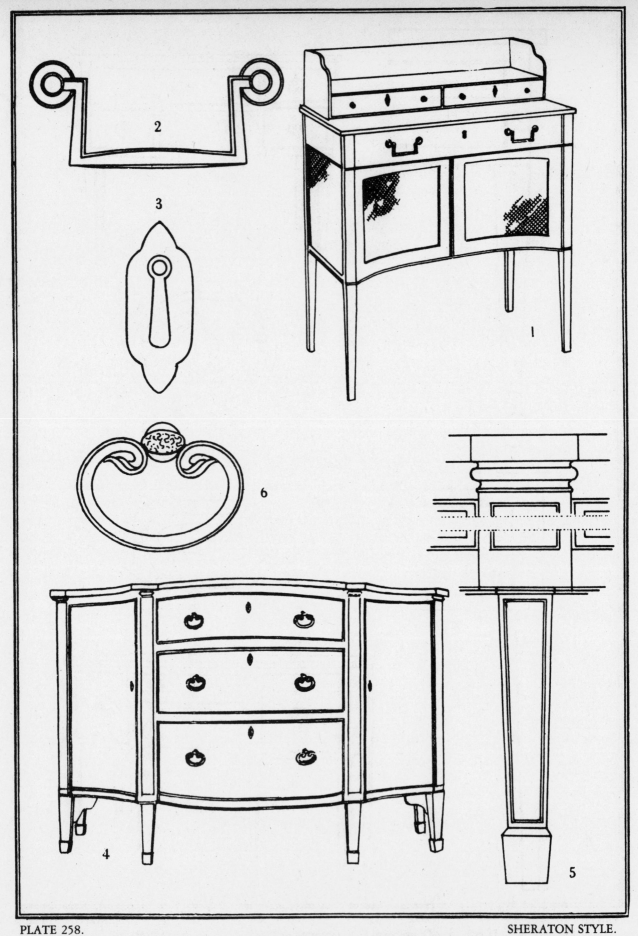

**PLATE 258.**                                                                SHERATON STYLE.

1. Sheraton cabinet.  2. Drawer pull.  3. Escutcheon plate.  4. Sheraton cabinet.  5. Details of leg and upright.  6. Drawer pull.

*Property of George Stoner, West Wickham, Kent and Victoria and Albert Museum.*

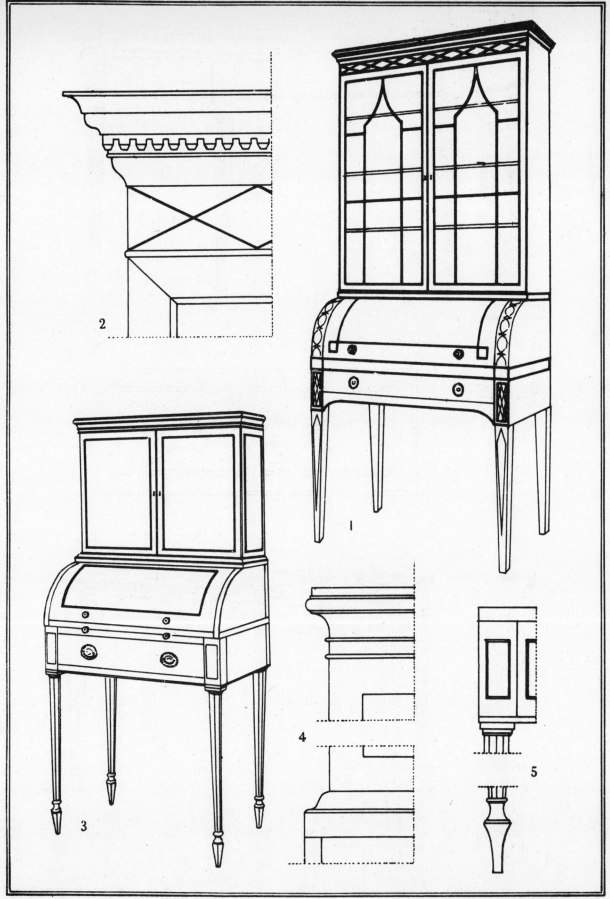

**PLATE 259.**                                                          **SHERATON STYLE.**

1. Sheraton desk.   2. Details of cornice and upper corner.   3. Sheraton desk.   4. Moulding on upper section.
5. Detail of leg.

*Victoria and Albert Museum and property of George Stoner, West Wickham, Kent.*

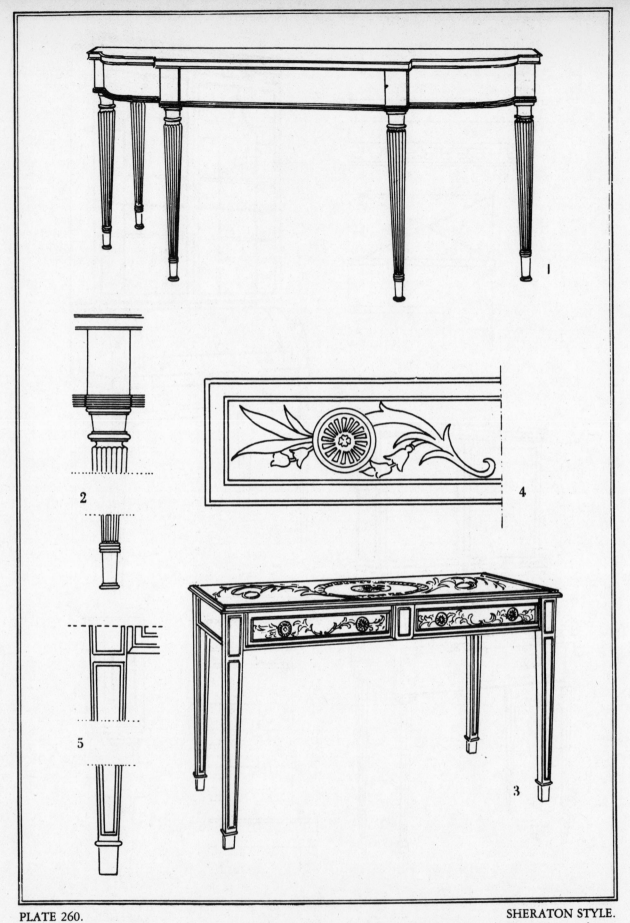

PLATE 260.                                                                    SHERATON STYLE.
1. Sheraton console table.    2. Detail of mouldings and leg.    3. Sheraton console table.    4. Decoration on drawer panels.    5. Leg.

*Victoria and Albert Museum and property of C. J. Charles.*

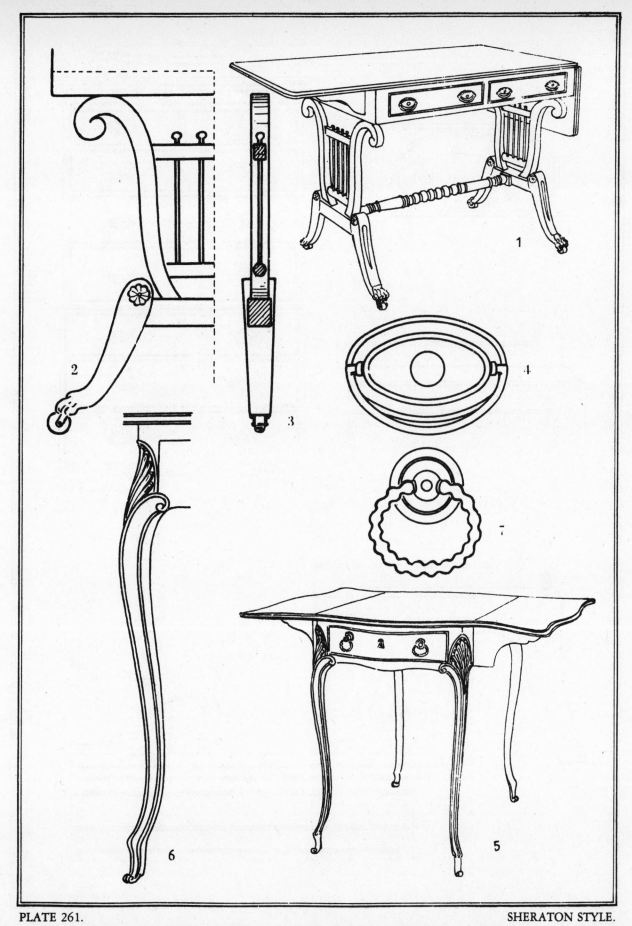

PLATE 261.                                                    SHERATON STYLE.

1. Sheraton table.   2. Decoration on support.   3. Detail of support construction.   4. Drawer pull.   5. Sheraton table.   6. Leg.   7. Drawer pull.

*Property of Frederick Poke and Leonard Knight.*

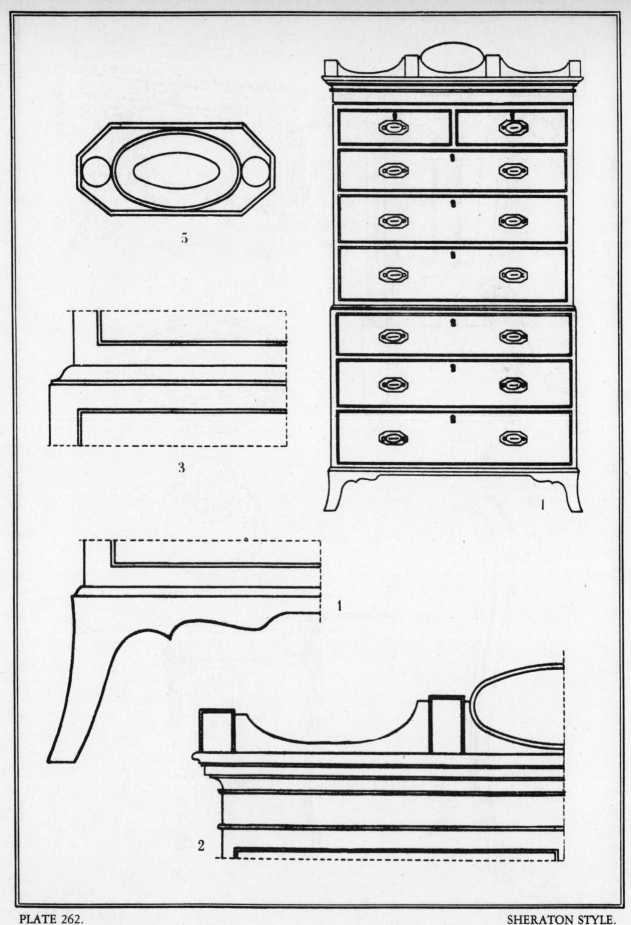

PLATE 262.                                                    SHERATON STYLE.
1. Tall Sheraton commode.   2. Cornice and crest.   3. Base of upper section.   4. Foot.   5. Drawer pull.
*Property of J. H. Springett of Rochester.*

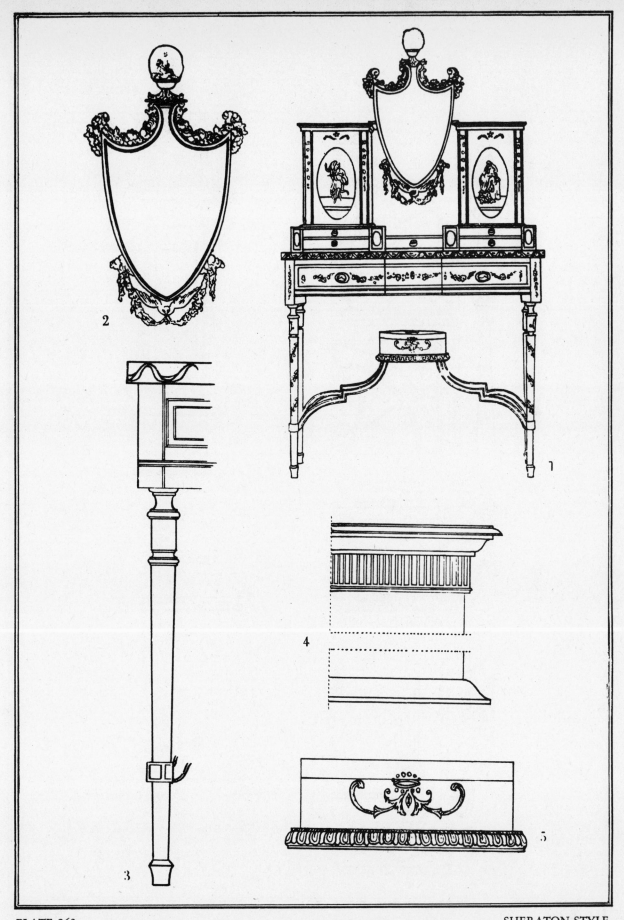

PLATE 263.                                    SHERATON STYLE.

1. Sheraton dressing table with delicate paintings by Angelica Kauffman.   2. Detail of mirror.   3. Details of leg and corner of table.   4. Mouldings and frieze.   5. Small box supported by crosspieces.

*Victoria and Albert Museum.*

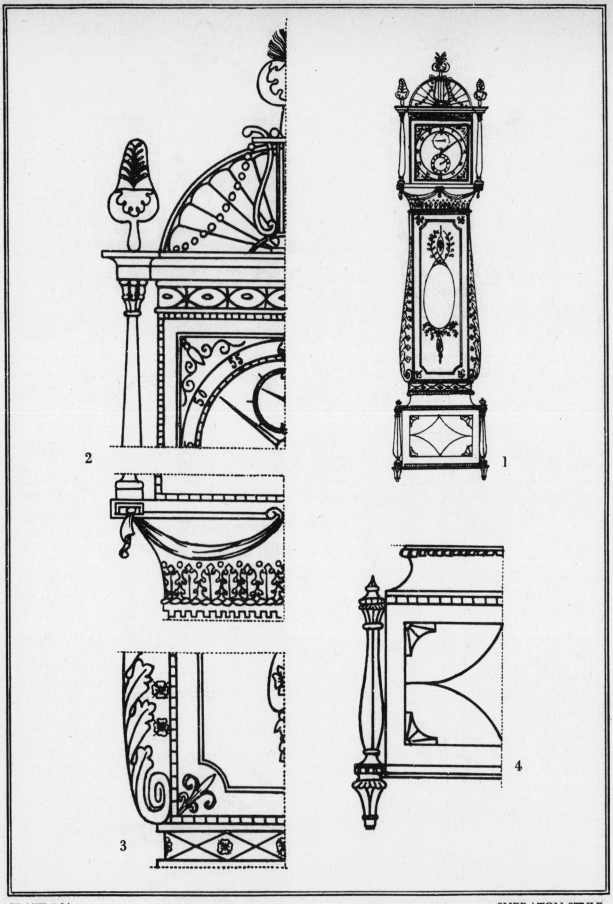

PLATE 264.                                                    SHERATON STYLE.

1. Intricately designed Sheraton clock case.   2. Details of crest, face and upper section.   3. Decoration at bottom of middle section.   4. Detail of lower section.

*Album of designs by Sheraton.*

268

PLATE 265.                                                                    SHERATON STYLE.

1.  Sheraton clock case.    2.  Crest and face.    3.  Detail of top of middle section.    4.  Side column.    5.  Detail of lower
section.    6.  Decorative motif at bottom of middle section.

*Album of designs by Sheraton.*

PLATE 266.                                                                SHERATON STYLE.
1 and 5. Shearer desks.    2. Decoration on first desk: mouldings at top and base, and upright.    3. Drawer pull of
second desk.    4. Drawer pull of first desk.    6. Detail of base of leg, second desk.

*From Shearer catalogue.*

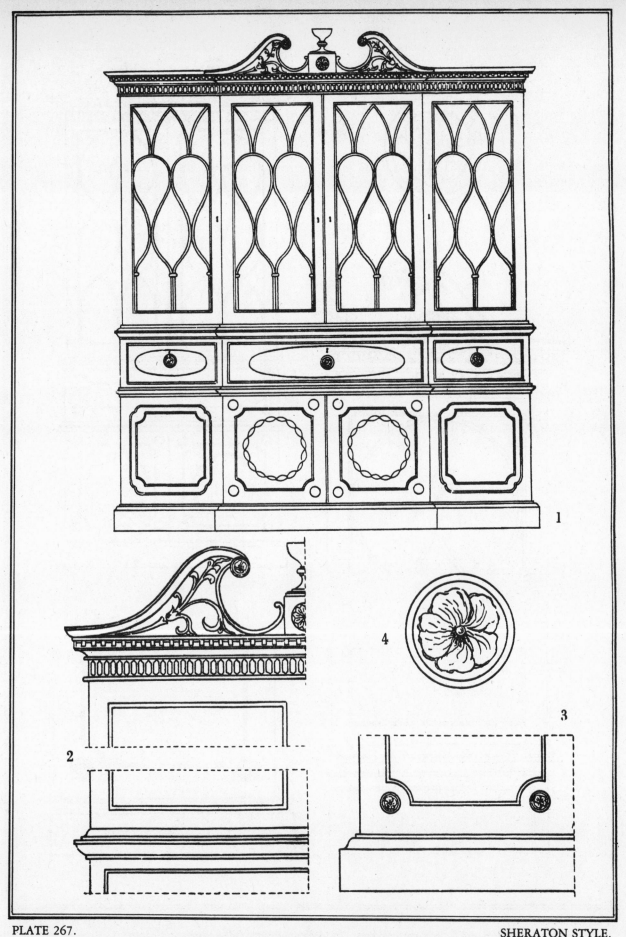

PLATE 267.                                                    SHERATON STYLE.
1. Shearer bookcase.   2 and 3. Decoration: crest, cornices, mouldings and base.   4. Drawer pull.

*From Shearer catalogue.*

PLATE 268.                                                    SHERATON STYLE.
1. Shearer bookcase, 2, 3 and 4. Decorations: crest, cornice, mouldings, glass panes and base.   5. Rosette.

*Shearer catalogue.*

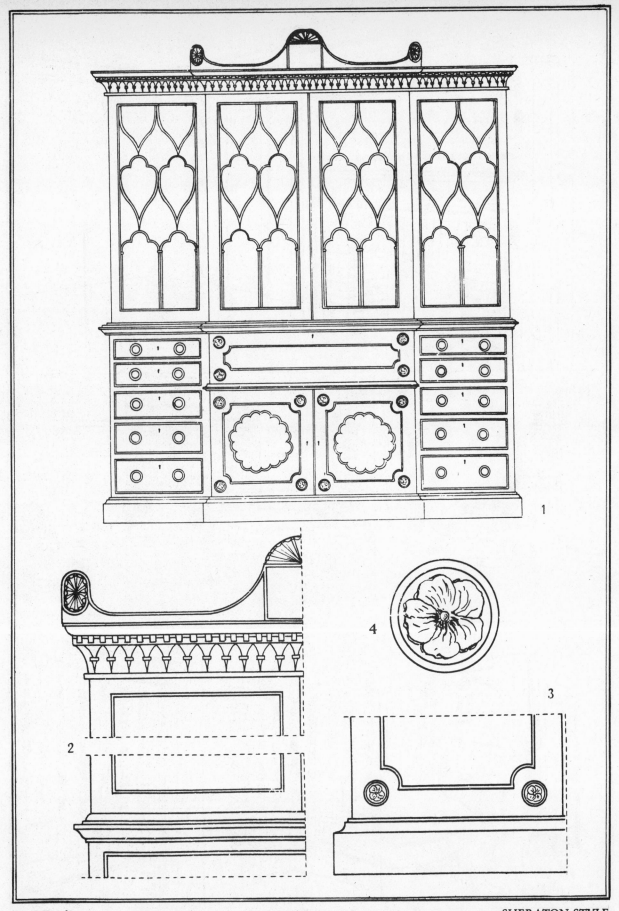

PLATE 269.                                                      SHERATON STYLE.

1. Shearer bookcase with two sections. 2 and 3.   Decoration: crests, cornice, mouldings and base.   4. Rosette.

*Shearer catalogue.*

PLATE 270.

COLONIAL STYLE (architectural features).

1. Living room of a Colonial house.   2. Typical Colonial foyer.   3. Simple Colonial dining room.   4. Another dining room with typical decorations.   5 and 6. Stairway balustrades.

274

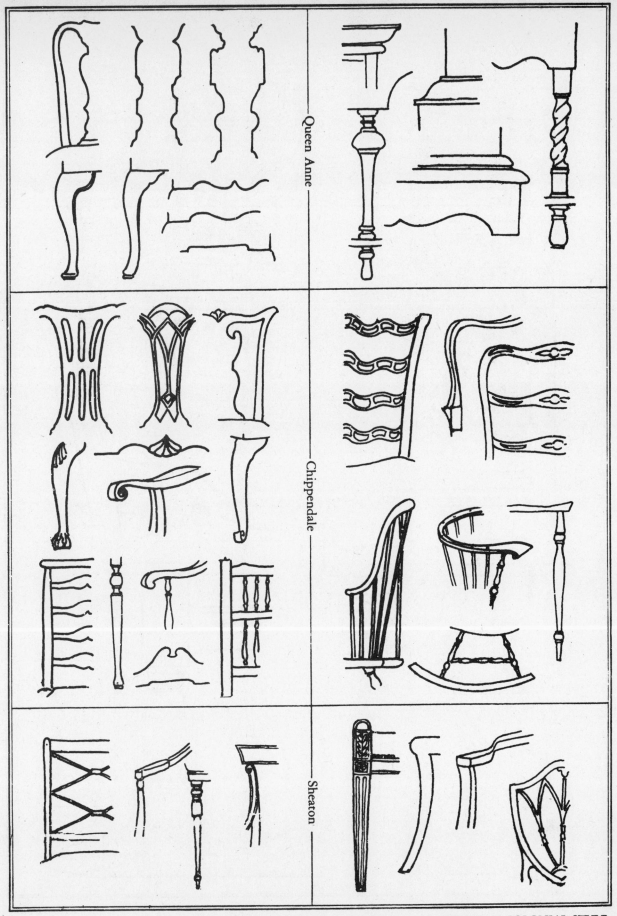

Queen Anne

Chippendale

Sheaton

PLATE 271.  DIAGRAM OF THE DEVELOPMENT OF AMERICAN COLONIAL STYLE.

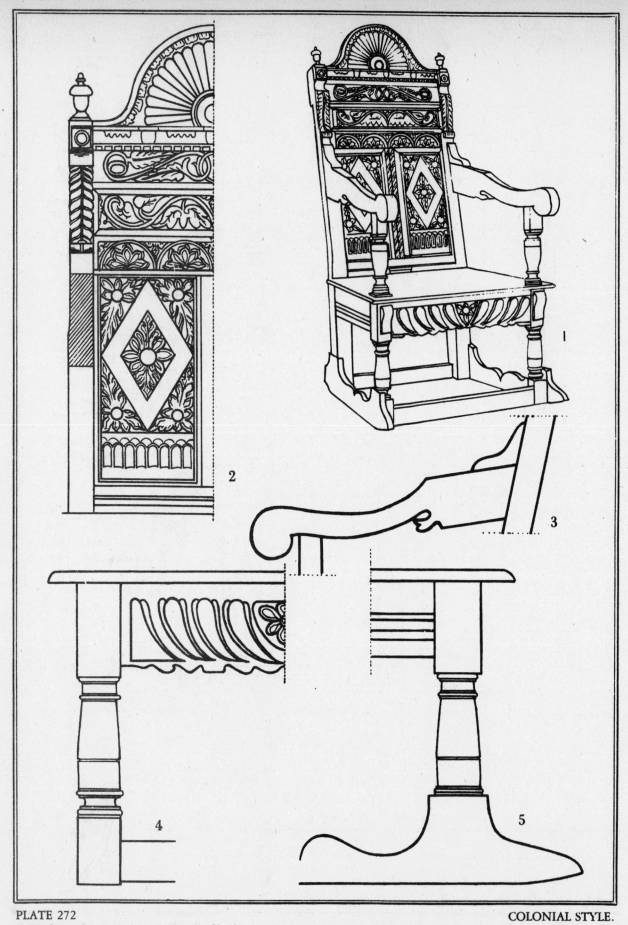

PLATE 272                                                    COLONIAL STYLE.
1. Tudor-style armchair.   2. Detail of back.   3. Detail of arm.   4. Front view of leg and crosspiece.   5. Side view
of leg and rocker.

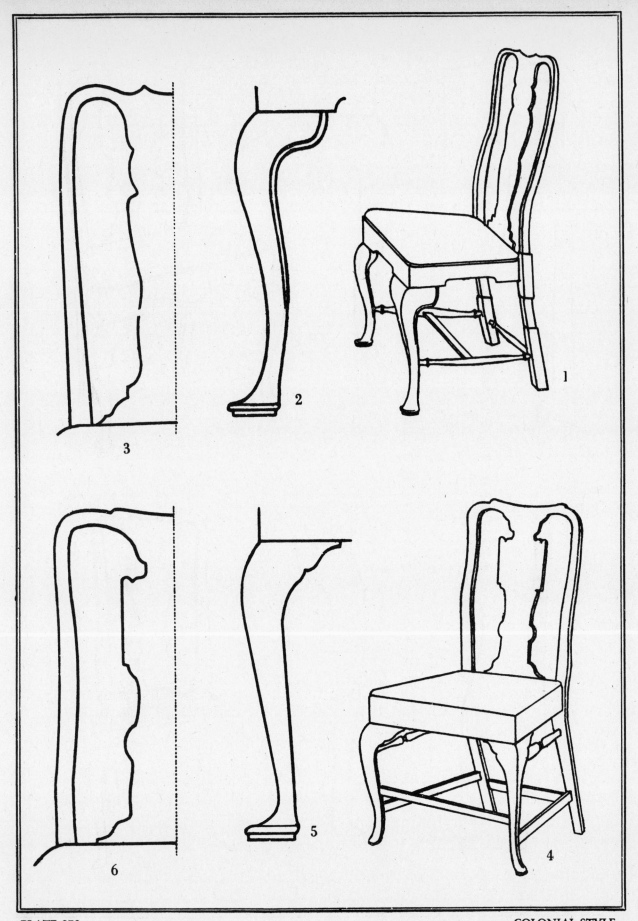

PLATE 273.                                                           COLONIAL STYLE.
1. Queen Anne style chair.   2. Leg.   3. Detail of back.   4. Queen Anne style chair.   5. Leg.   6. Detail of back.
*Private collection and the residence of Lady Jowitt.*

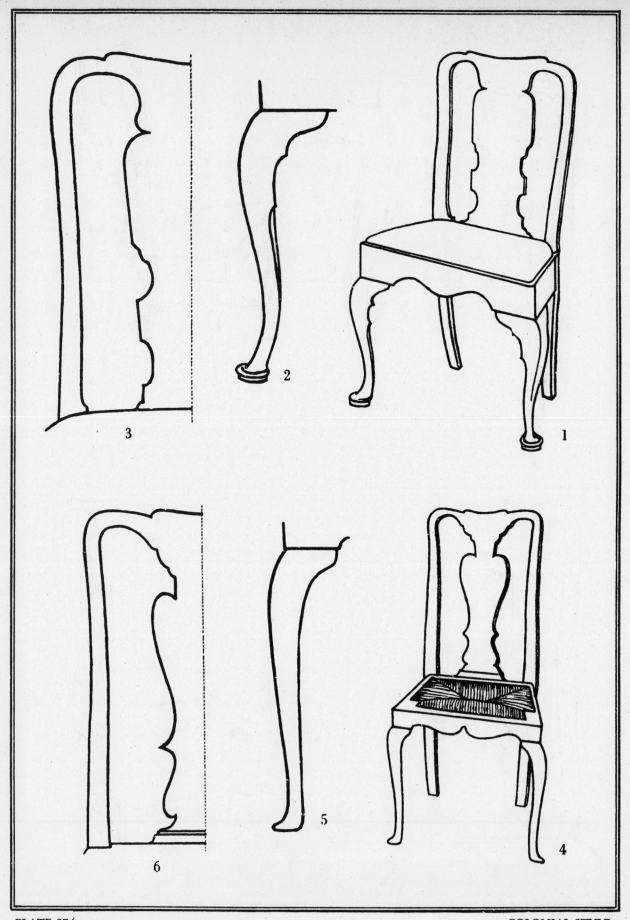

PLATE 274.

1 and 4. Chairs with Queen Anne traits.    2 and 5. Legs.    3 and 6. Details of backs.

COLONIAL STYLE.

*Private collection.*

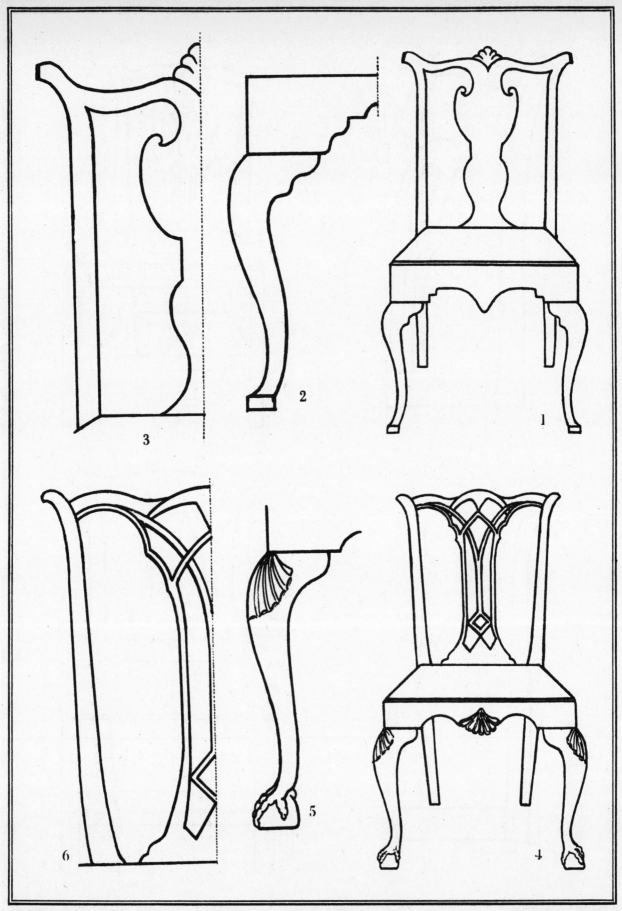

PLATE 275.                                                    COLONIAL STYLE.
1 and 4. Chippendale style chairs.    2 and 5. Legs.    3 and 6. Details of backs.

*Private collections.*

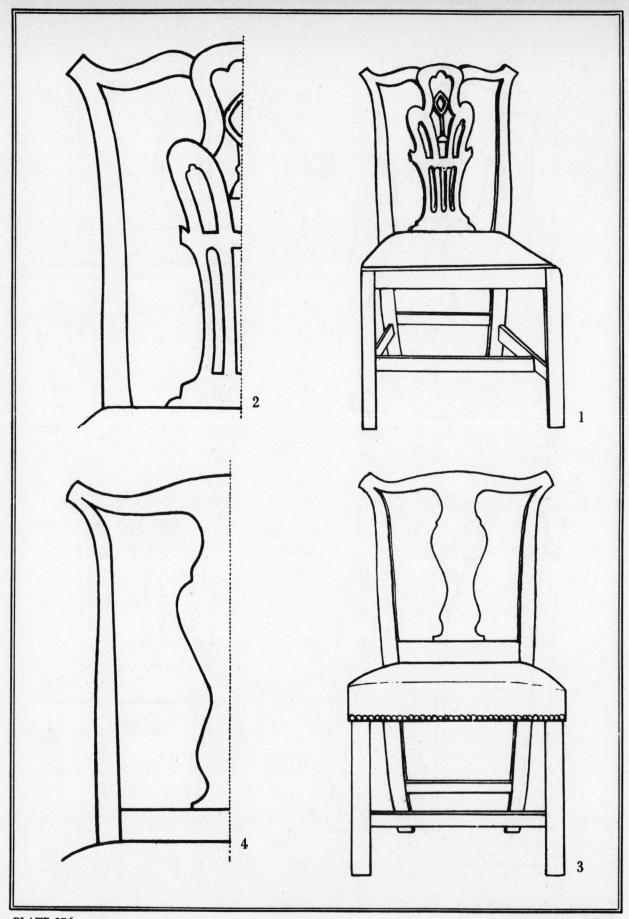

PLATE 276.
1 and 3. Chippendale style chairs.   2 and 4. Detail of backs.

*Private collections.*

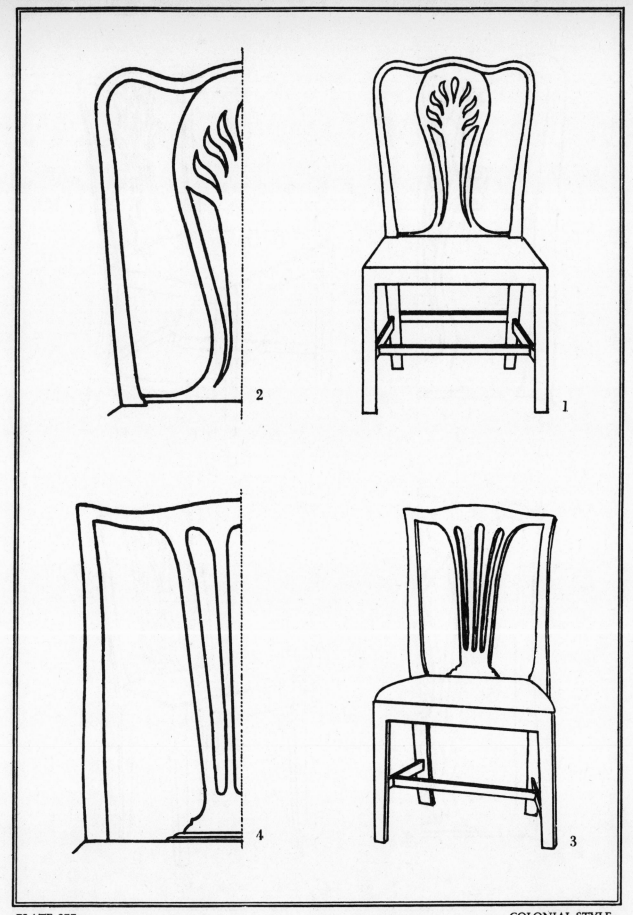

PLATE 277.

COLONIAL STYLE.

1 and 3. Chippendale style chairs with straight backs.  2 and 4. Detail of backs.

*Private collectinos.*

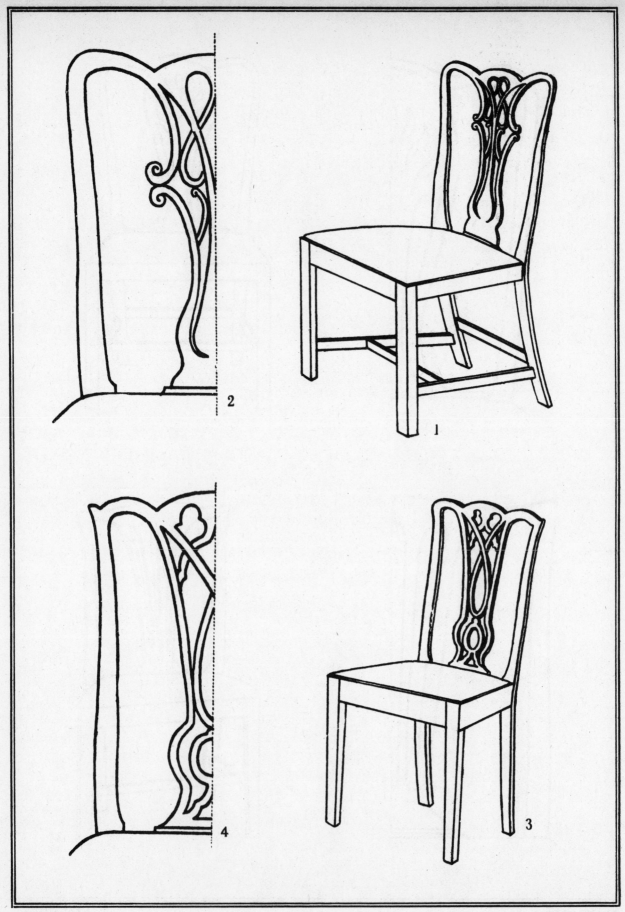

PLATE 278.                                                              COLONIAL STYLE.
1. Chippendale style chair.   2. Detail of back.   3. Chippendale style chair.   4. Detail of back.

*Private collection and the residence of James P. Magill.*

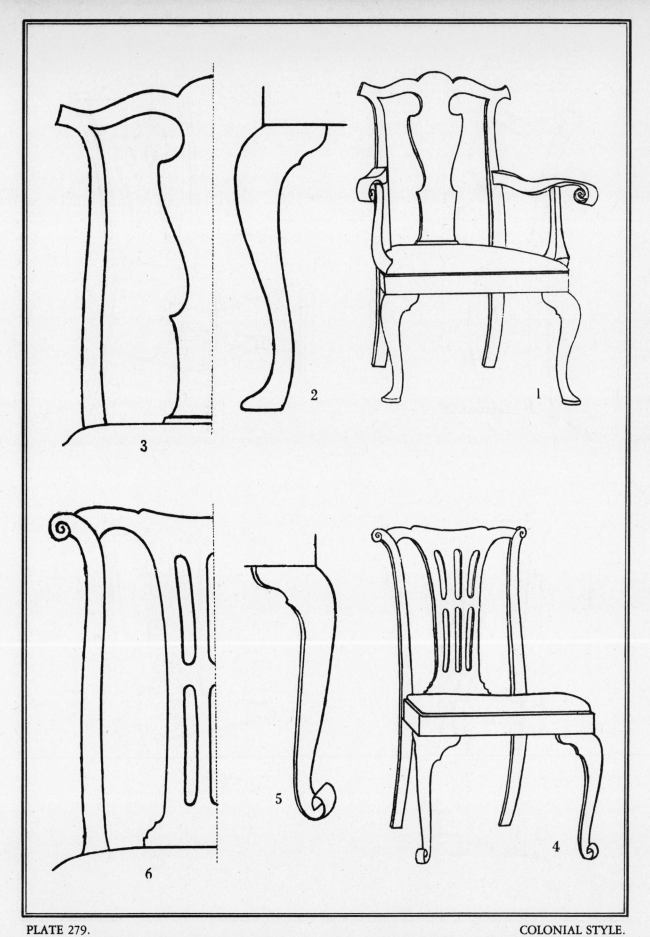

PLATE 279.                                                                          COLONIAL STYLE.

1. Free interpretation of Chippendale style armchair.   2. Leg.   3. Detail of back.   4. Free interpretation of Chippendale style chair.   5. Leg.   6. Detail of back.

*From the residence of Bruce MacLeish and a private collection.*

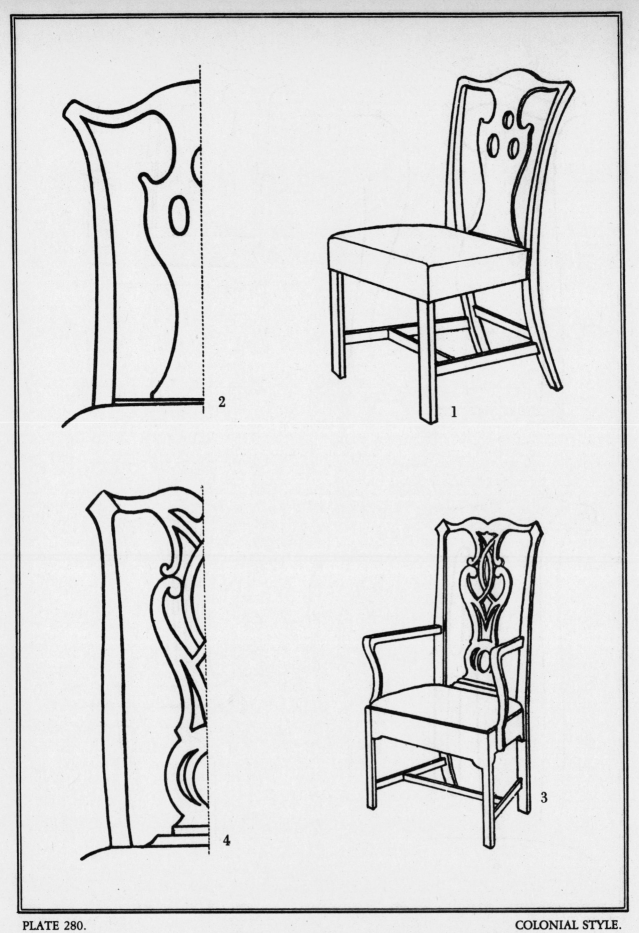

PLATE 280.                                                    COLONIAL STYLE.
1. Chippendale style chair.   2. Detail of back.   3. Chippendale style armchair.   4. Detail of back.

*Private collections.*

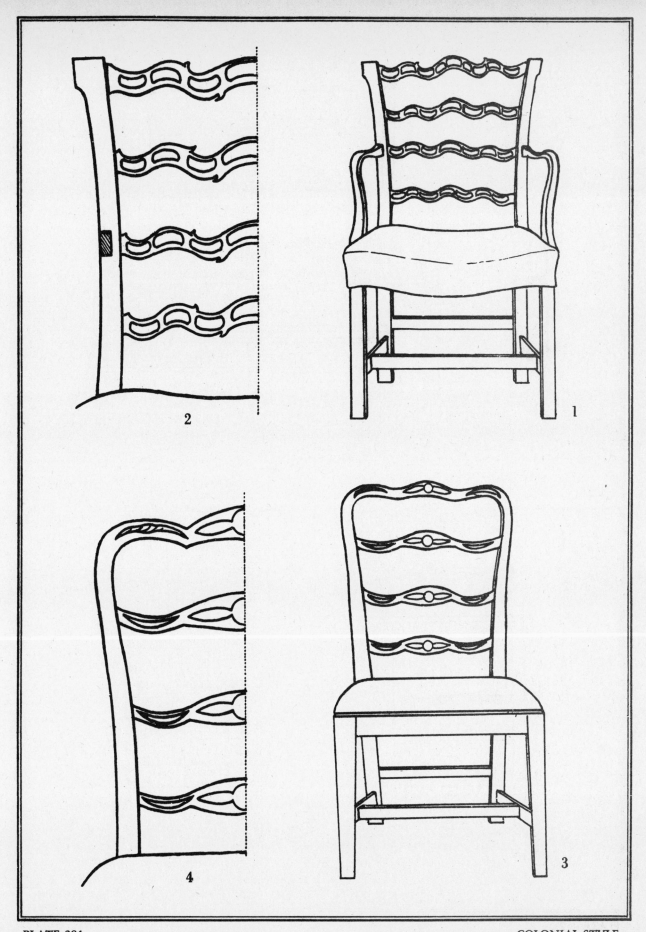

PLATE 281.                                                     COLONIAL STYLE.
1. Chippendale style armchair with horizontal ladder back.   2. Detail of back.   3. Chippendale style chair with horizontal ladder back.   4. Detail of back.

*Private collections.*

285

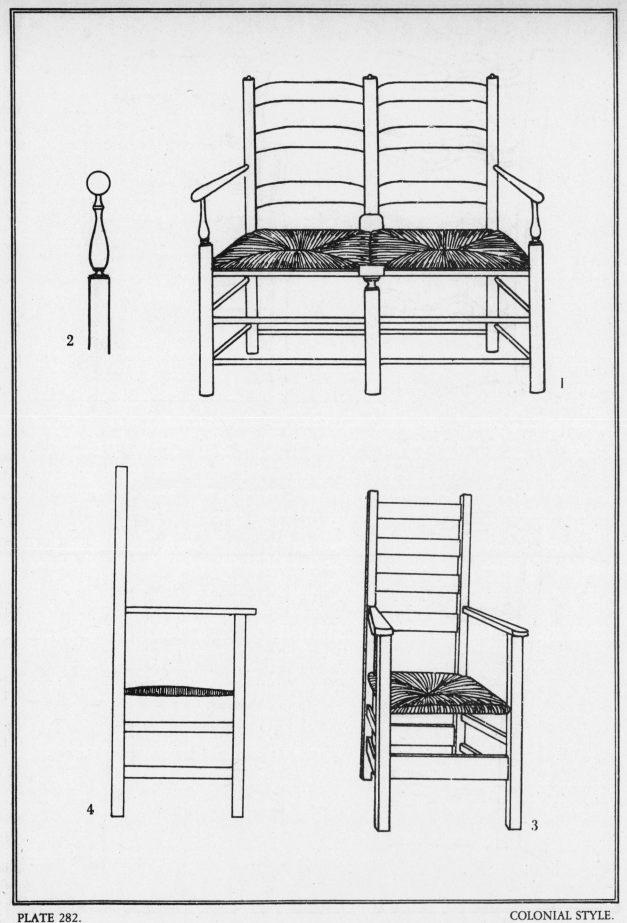

**PLATE 282.** COLONIAL STYLE.
1. Sofa in rustic Chippendale style. 2. Detail of arm support. 3. Armchair in rustic Chippendale style. 4. Detail of structure.

*Private collections.*

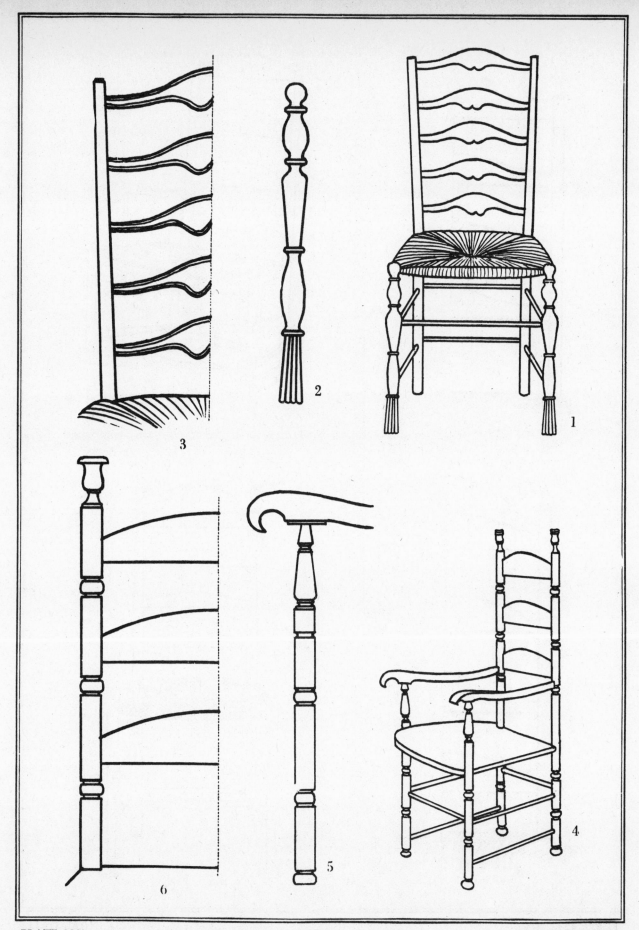

PLATE 283.                                                    COLONIAL STYLE.
1. Chippendale style chair with turned legs and horizontal back.   2. Turned leg.   3. Detail of back.   4. Chippendale style armchair with turned posts and horizontal back.   5. Turned leg.   6. Detail of back and turned upright.

*Private collections.*

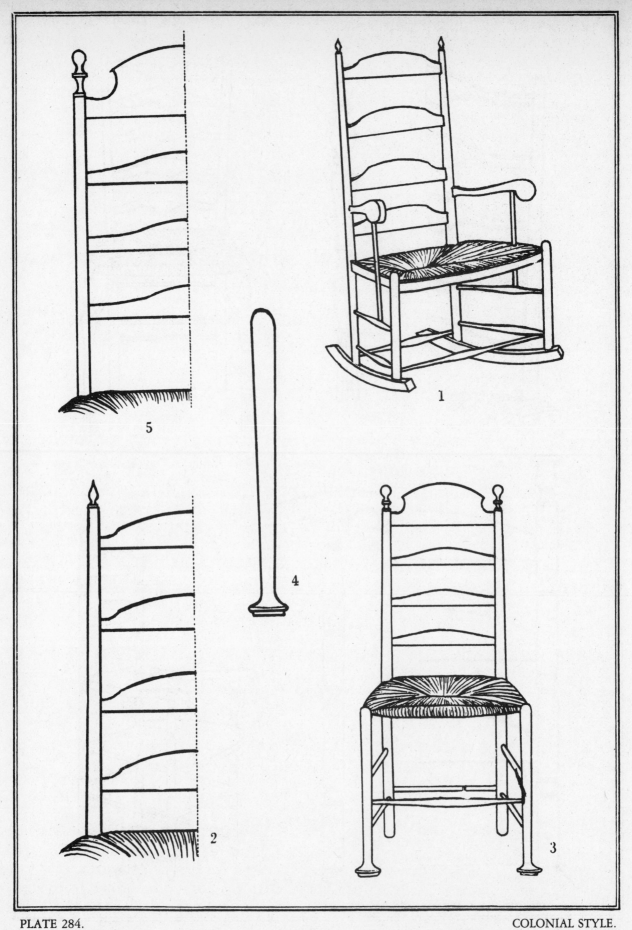

**PLATE 284.**

COLONIAL STYLE.

1. Simple rocking chair.   2. Detail of back.   3. Simple chair.   4. Front leg.   5. Detail of back.

*Private collections.*

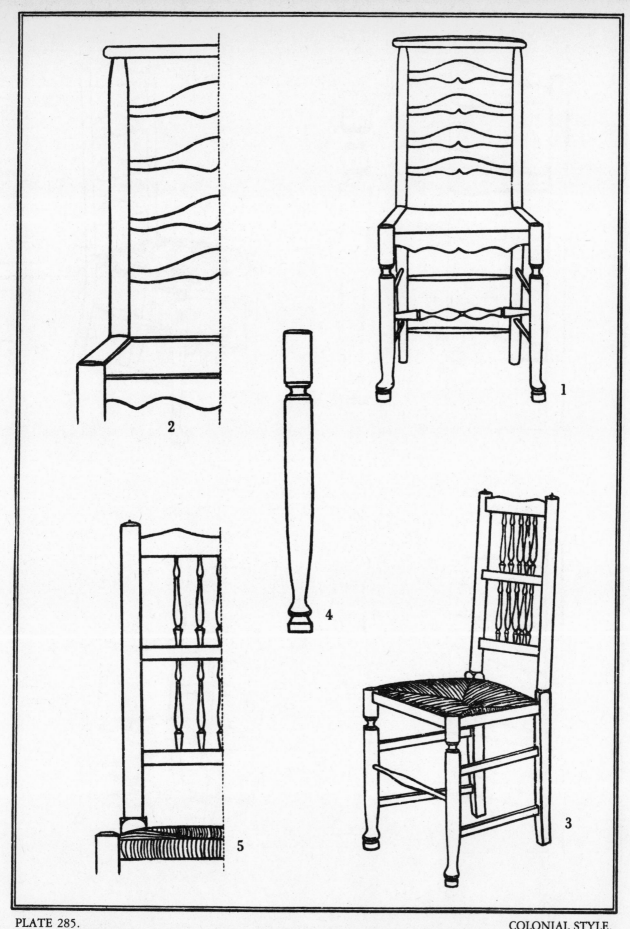

PLATE 285.                                                    COLONIAL STYLE.

1. Chair with horizontal back.  2. Detail of back.  3. Chair with horizontal back and spindles.  4. Turned leg.  5. Detail of back.

*Private collections.*

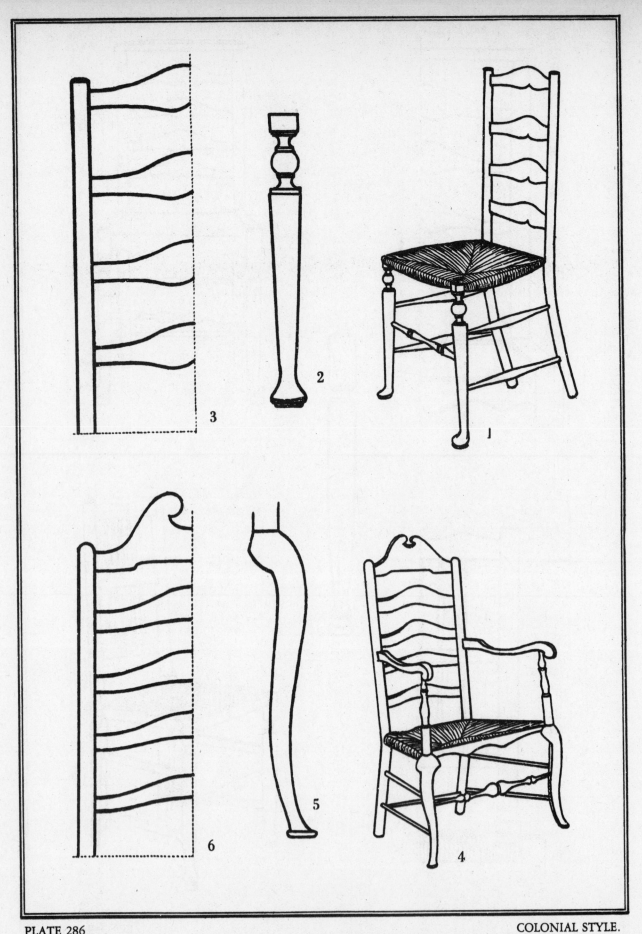

PLATE 286                                                    COLONIAL STYLE.

1. Chair with horizontal back.   2. Turned leg.   3. Detail of back.   4. Armchair with horizontal back.   5. Front
leg.   6. Detail of back.

*Private collections.*

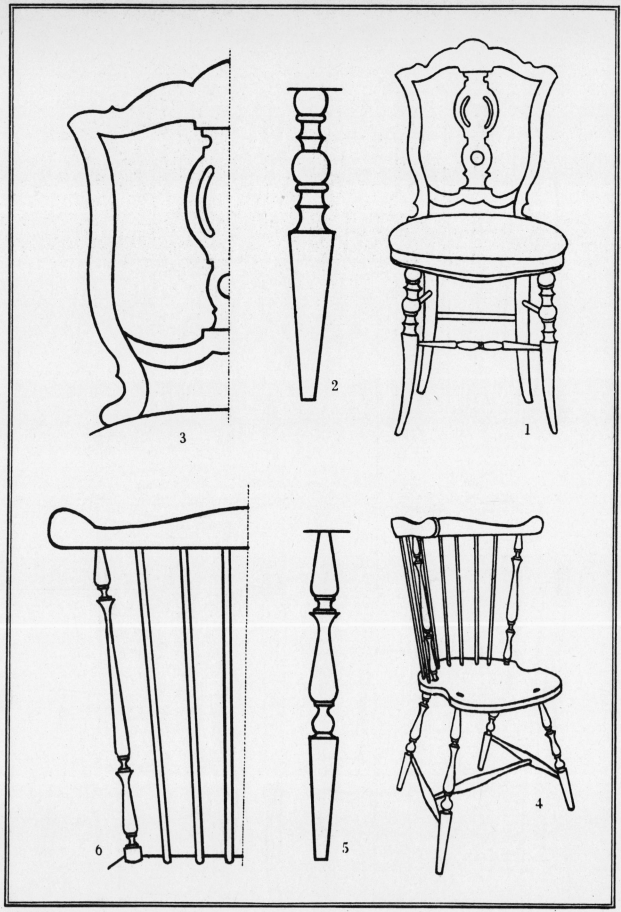

PLATE 287.

COLONIAL STYLE.

1. Chair with whimsical lines.   2. Turned leg.   3. Detail of back.   4. Typical colonial chair.   5. Turned leg.
6. Detail of back.

*Private collections.*

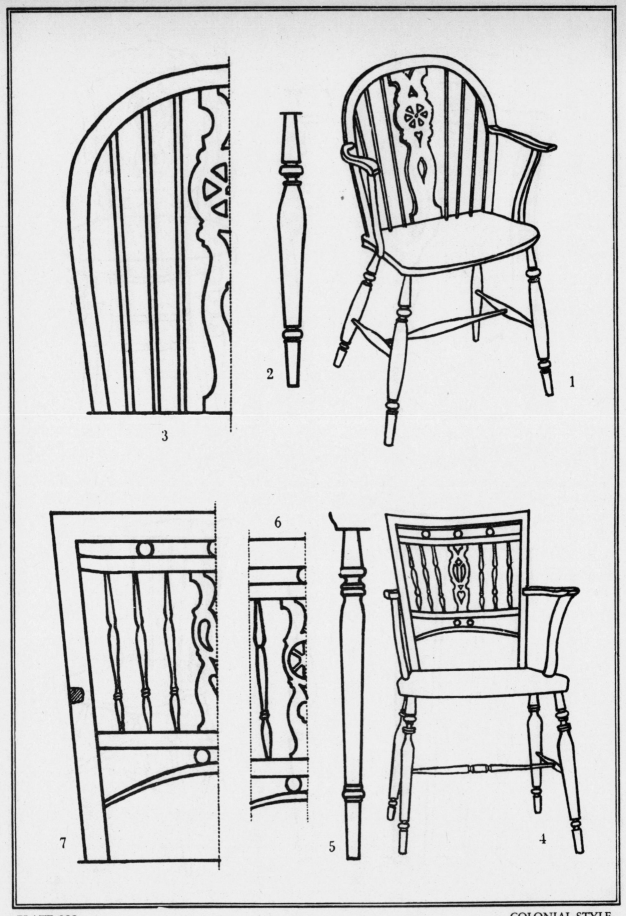

PLATE 288.                                                                                    COLONIAL STYLE.

1. Colonial chair.   2. Turned leg.   3. Detail of back.   4. Chair of distinctly Sheraton style.   5. Turned leg.
6 and 7.  Details of back.

*Private collections.*

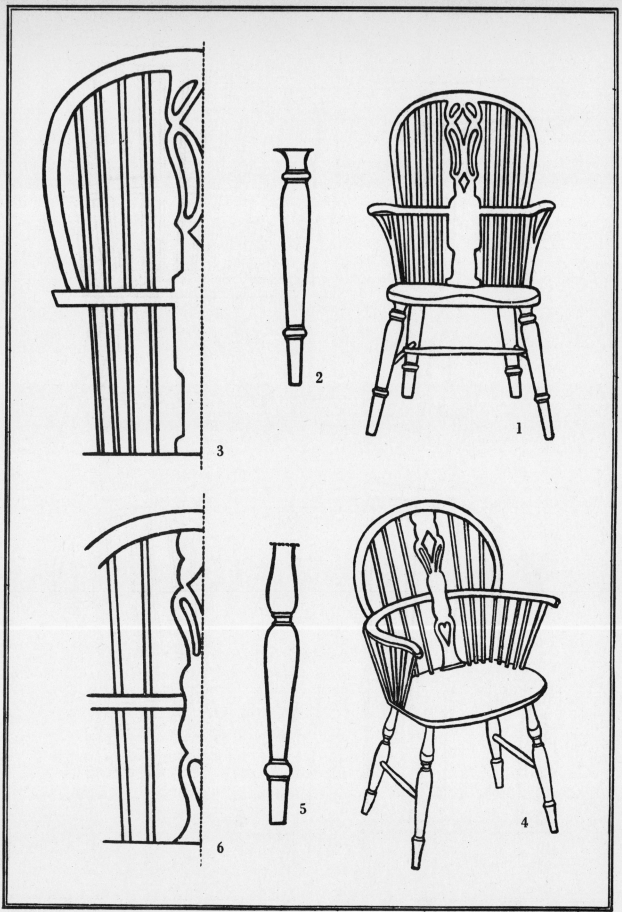

PLATE 289                                                    COLONIAL STYLE.

1 and 4. Typical Colonial chairs.   2 and 5. Respective turned legs.   3 and 6. Detail of backs.

*Private collections.*

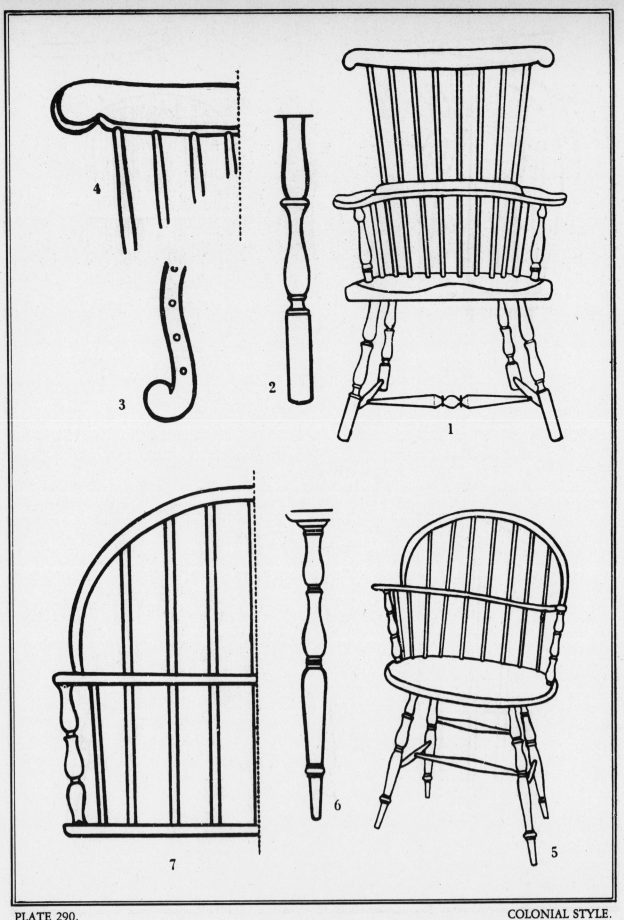

PLATE 290.                                                     COLONIAL STYLE.
1. Windsor chair.   2. Turned leg.   3. Arm.   4. Detail of back.   5. Windsor chair.   6. Turned leg.   7. Detail
of back.

*From the residences of Thomas Evans and Paul Pulliani.*

PLATE 291.

COLONIAL STYLE.

1. Simple chair.   2. Detail of back.   3. Simple chair.   4. Turned leg.   5. Detail of back.

*Private collections.*

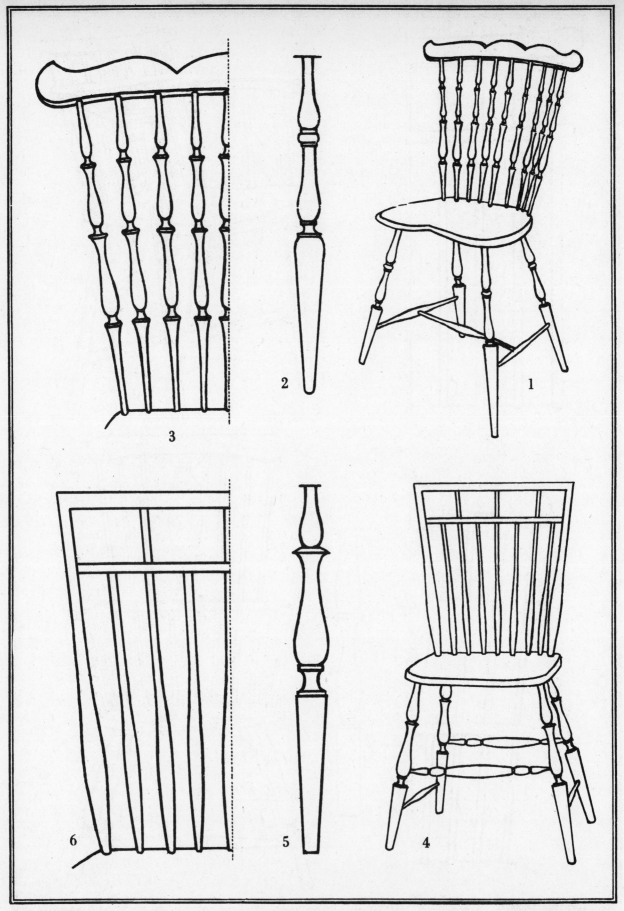

PLATE 292.                                                                                        COLONIAL STYLE.
1 and 4. Chairs with turned posts.    2 and 5. Turned legs.    3 and 6. Detail of backs.

*Private collections.*

PLATE 293.

COLONIAL STYLE.

1. Typical Colonial chair.   2. Detail of back.   3. Turned spindle.   4. Typical Colonial chair.   5. Detail of end of arm.   6 and 7. Turned legs.   8. Detail of back structure.

*Private collections.*

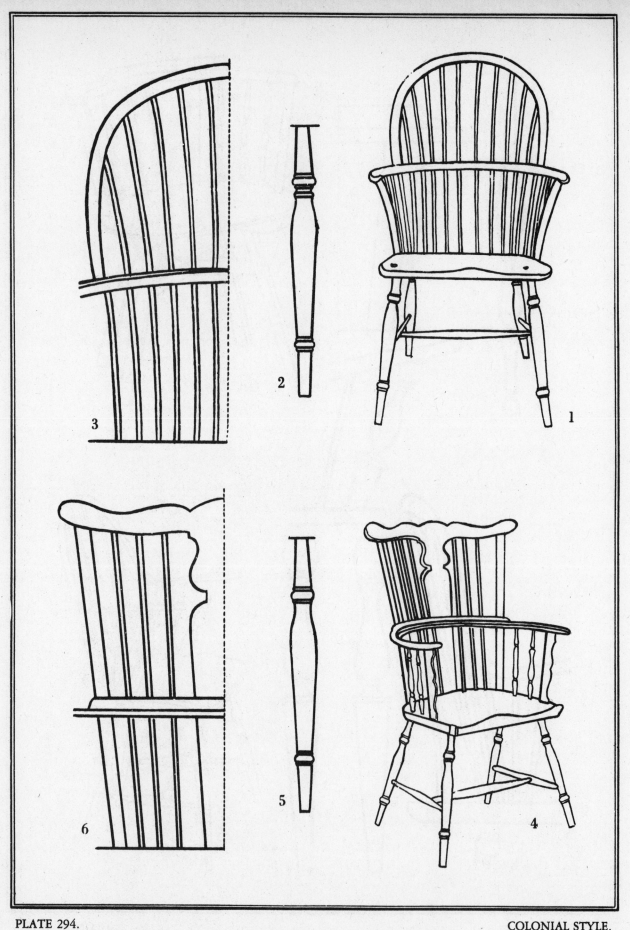

PLATE 294.                                                COLONIAL STYLE.
1 and 4. High backed chairs.    2 and 5. Turned legs.    3 and 6. Details of backs.

*Private collections.*

298

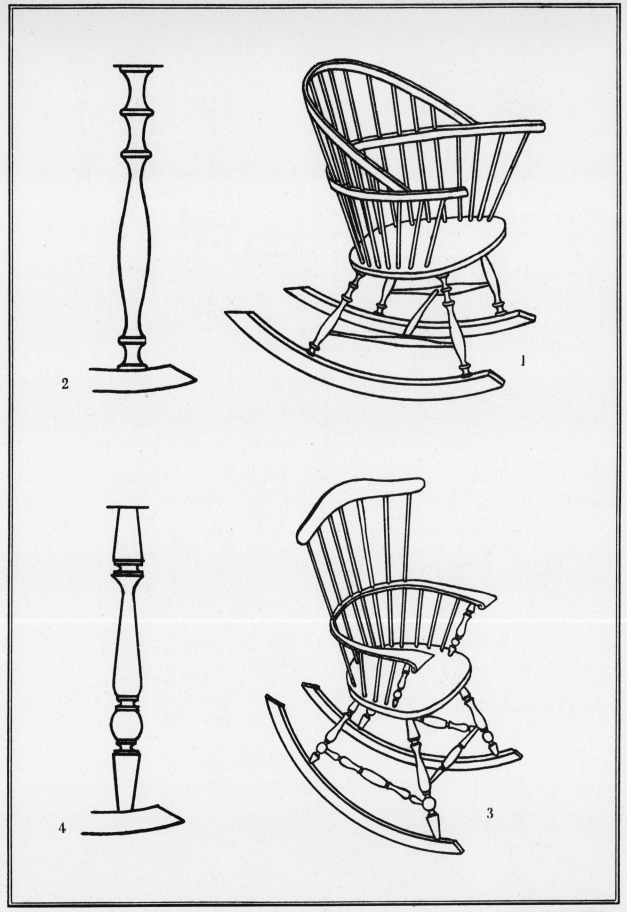

PLATE 295.
1 and 3. Rocking chairs with graceful lines.   2 and 4. Turned legs.

COLONIAL STYLE.

*Private collections.*

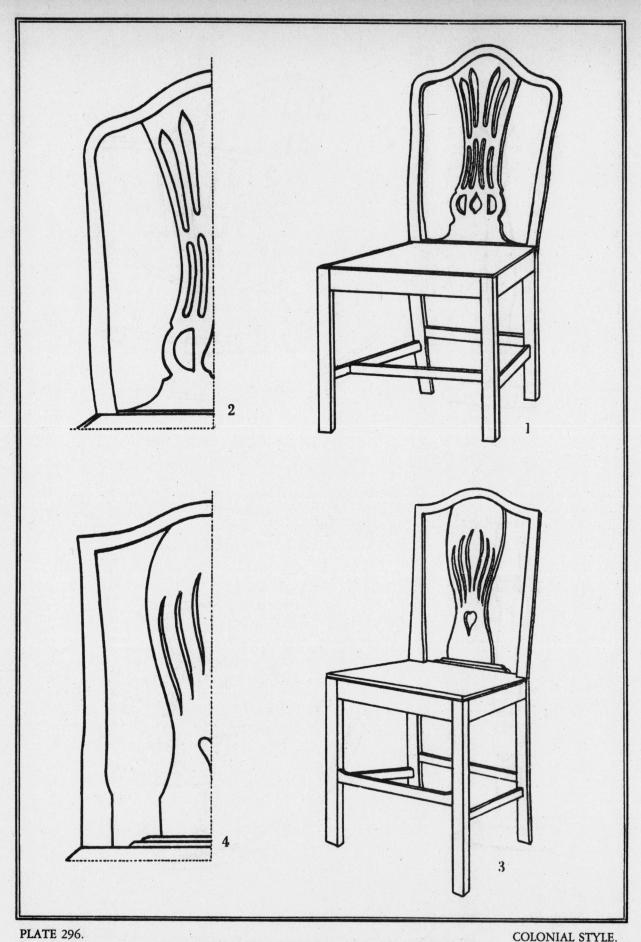

PLATE 296.

COLONIAL STYLE.

1 and 3. Chairs which are suggestive of the Hepplewhite style.   2 and 4. Detail of backs.

*Private collections.*

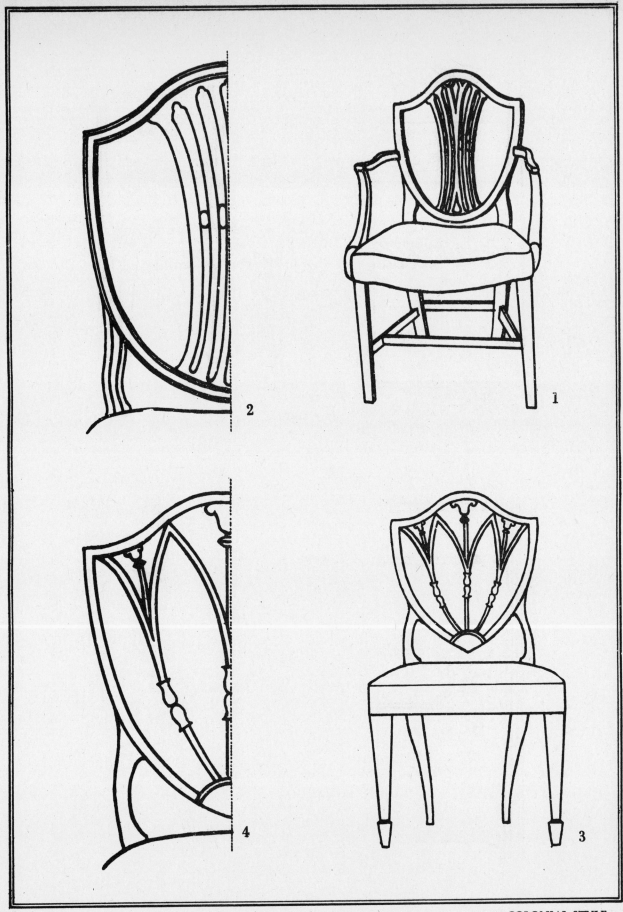

PLATE 297.
1. Hepplewhite style armchair.    2. Detail of back.    3. Hepplewhite style chair.

COLONIAL STYLE.

*Private collections.*

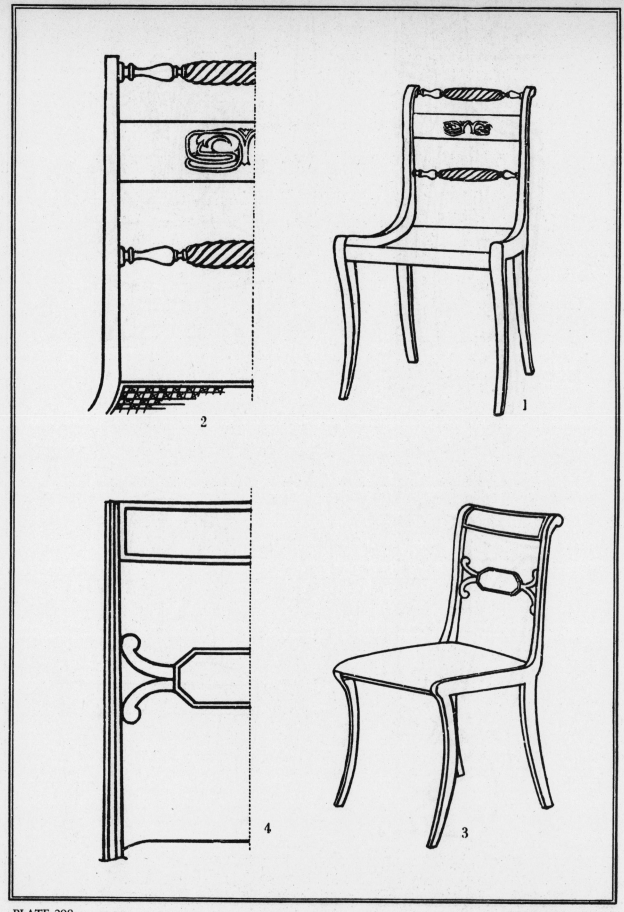

PLATE 298.

COLONIAL STYLE.

1 and 3. Chairs of Sheraton and Adam (Duncan Phyfe) style.    2 and 4. Detail of backs.

*Private collections.*

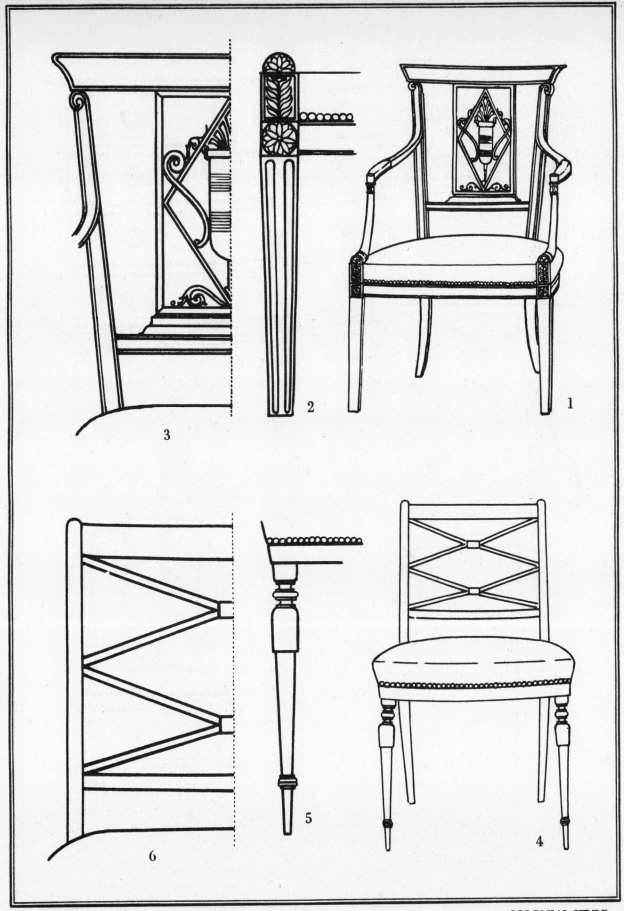

**PLATE 299.**                                     COLONIAL STYLE.

1. Armchair of Sheraton and Adam (Duncan Phyfe) style.  2. Leg decoration.  3. Detail of back.  4. Chair of Sheraton and Adam (Duncan Phyfe) style.  5. Turned leg.  6. Detail of back.

*Private collections.*

303

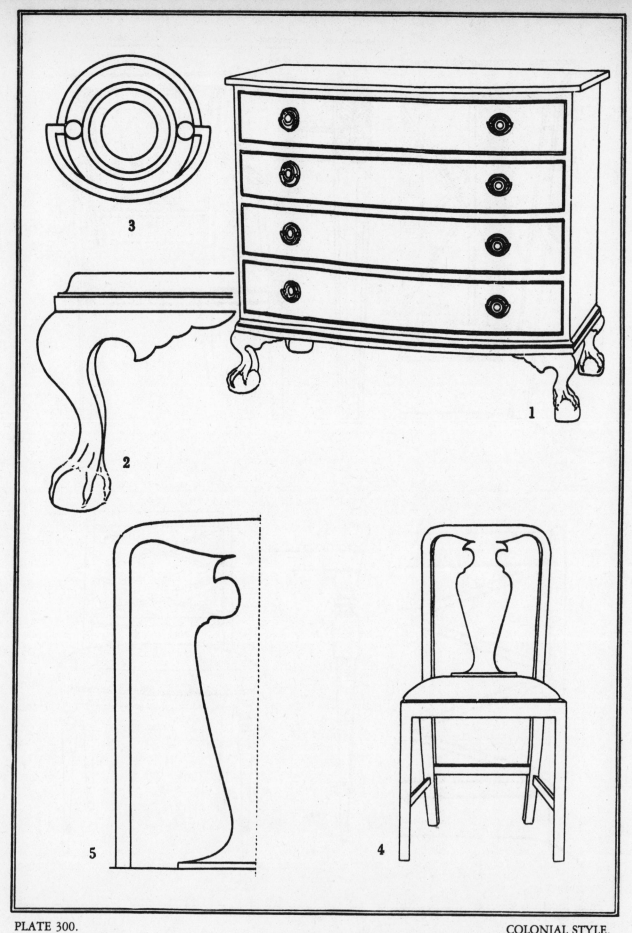

PLATE 300.

1. Colonial commode.    2. Detail of leg.    3. Drawer pull.    4. Colonial chair.    5. Detail of back.

*Metropolitan Museum of Art and a private collection.*

PLATE 301.

COLONIAL STYLE.

1. William and Mary style highboy.   2. Drawer pull.   3. Detail of moulding.   4. Turned leg.

*Private collection.*

305

PLATE 302.

COLONIAL STYLE.

1. William and Mary style highboy.  2. Drawer pull.  3. Turned leg.  4. Decoration: cornice, moulding and profile of crosspiece.

PLATE 303.                                                           COLONIAL STYLE.

1. William and Mary style highboy.   2. Detail of moulding.   3. Turned leg.   4. Drawer pull.

*Private collection.*

307

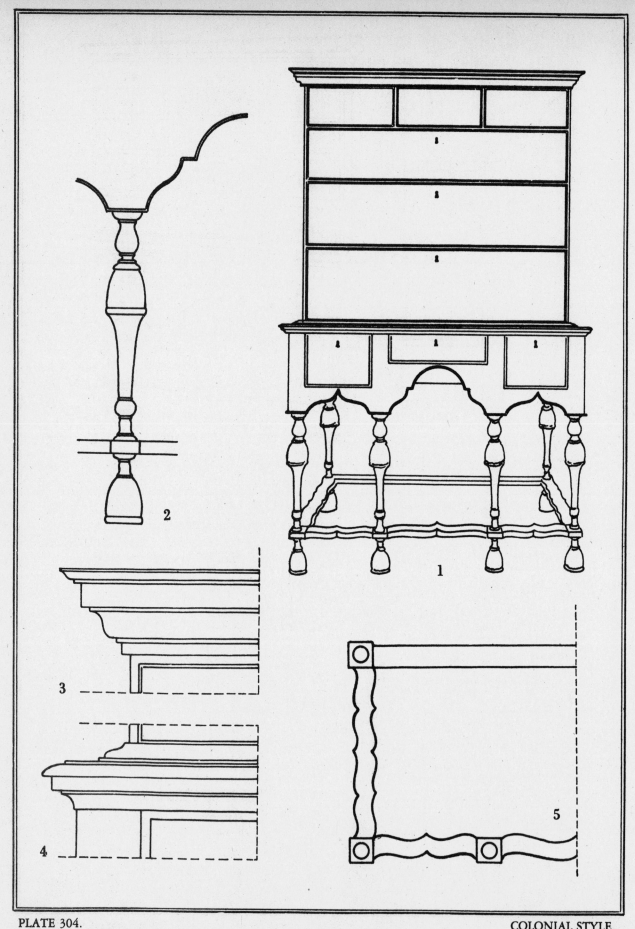

PLATE 304.                                                    COLONIAL STYLE.
1. William and Mary style highboy.   2. Turned leg and front profile of support.   3 and 4. Details of moulding.   5. Profile of crosspieces.

*Private collection.*

**PLATE 305.**                    ENGLISH MINORCAN STYLE (architectural features).

1. Foyer of a Minorcan manor.  2. Ceiling with whitewashed exposed beams.  3. Living room of Minorcan house.  4. Typical Minorcan sashed window.  5. Balcony showing neoclassical influence.  6. Type of iron stairway, which was very popular in Minorca.

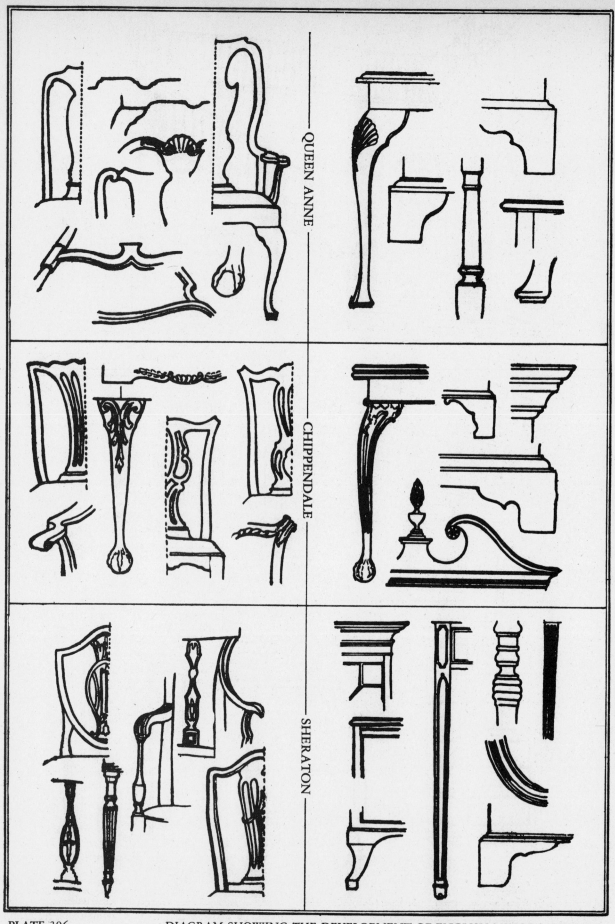

QUEEN ANNE

CHIPPENDALE

SHERATON

PLATE 306.     DIAGRAM SHOWING THE DEVELOPMENT OF ENGLISH MINORCAN STYLE.

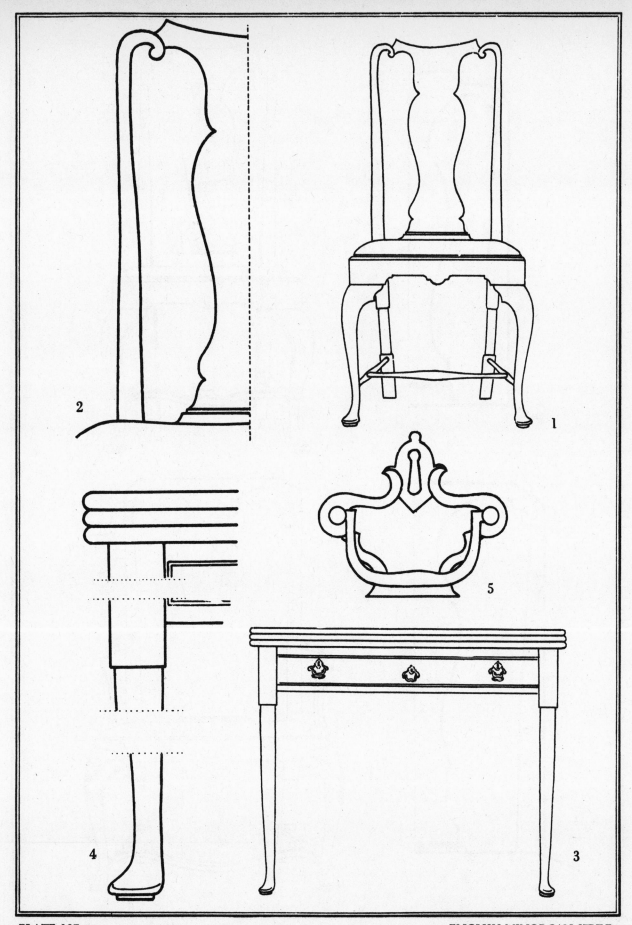

**PLATE 307.**

ENGLISH MINORCAN STYLE.

1. Queen Anne style chair. 2. Detail of back. 3. Queen Anne style table. 4. Details of moulding and legs. 5. Drawer pull.

*From the residence of Cosme Trebol Pons. Alayor.*

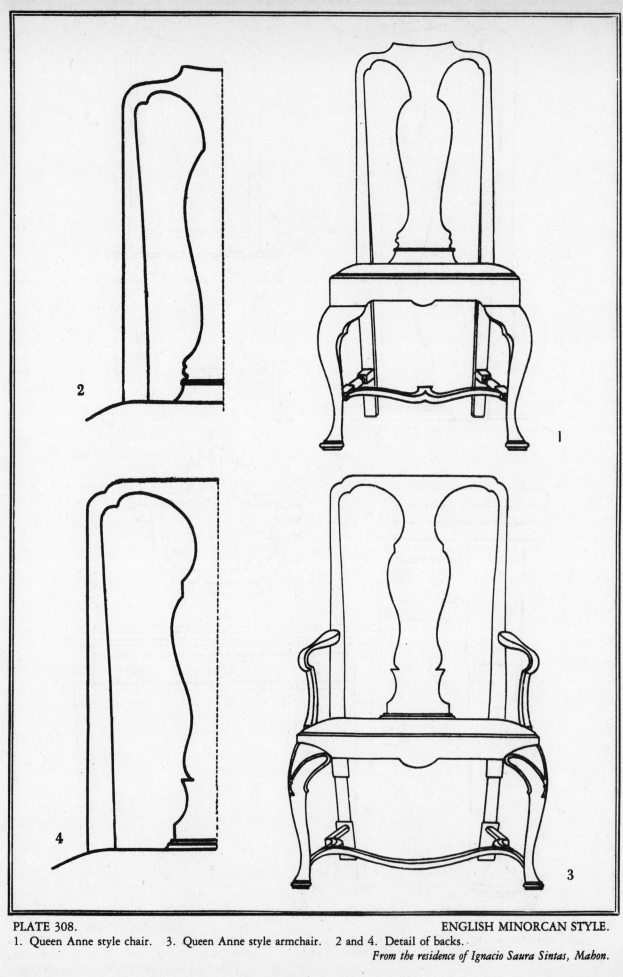

PLATE 308.                                                                                    ENGLISH MINORCAN STYLE.

1. Queen Anne style chair.    3. Queen Anne style armchair.    2 and 4. Detail of backs.

*From the residence of Ignacio Saura Sintas, Mahon.*

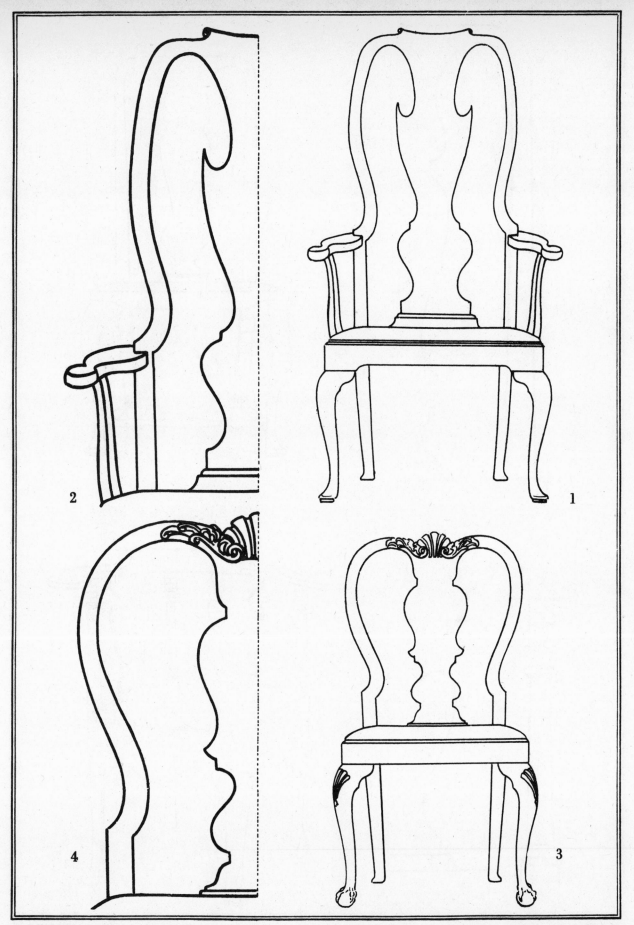

PLATE 309.                                                        ENGLISH MINORCAN STYLE.
1.  Queen Anne style armchair.    3.  Queen Anne style chair.    2 and 4.  Details of backs.
*From the residence of Simon Vidal Sintas, Mahon.*

313

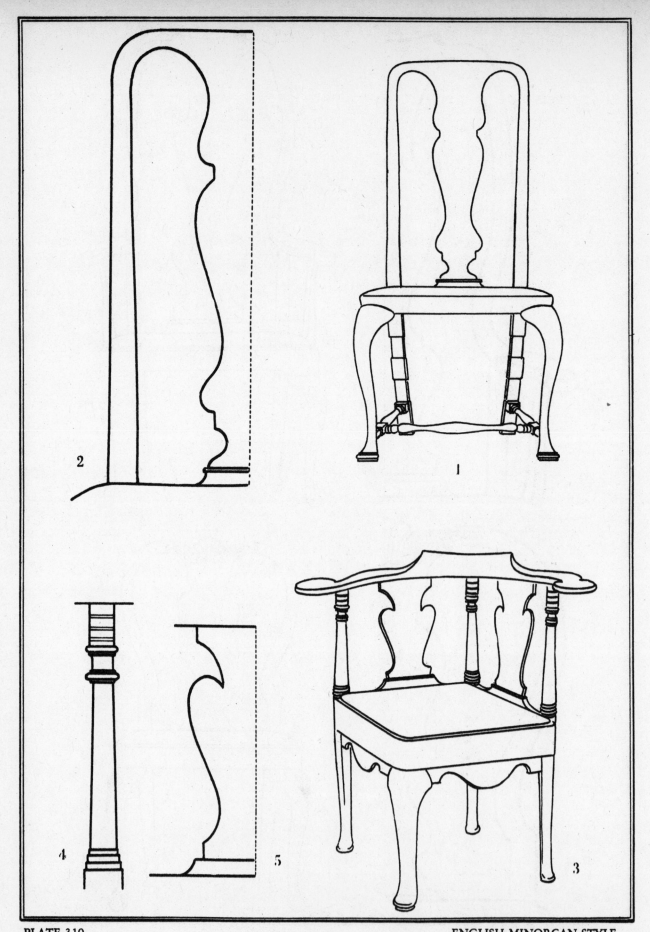

PLATE 310.                                    ENGLISH MINORCAN STYLE.
1. Queen Anne style chair.   2. Detail of back.   3. Corner armchair.   4 and 5. Details of back.
*From "Sa Cudia Cremada," the residence of Francisca Martorell.*

314

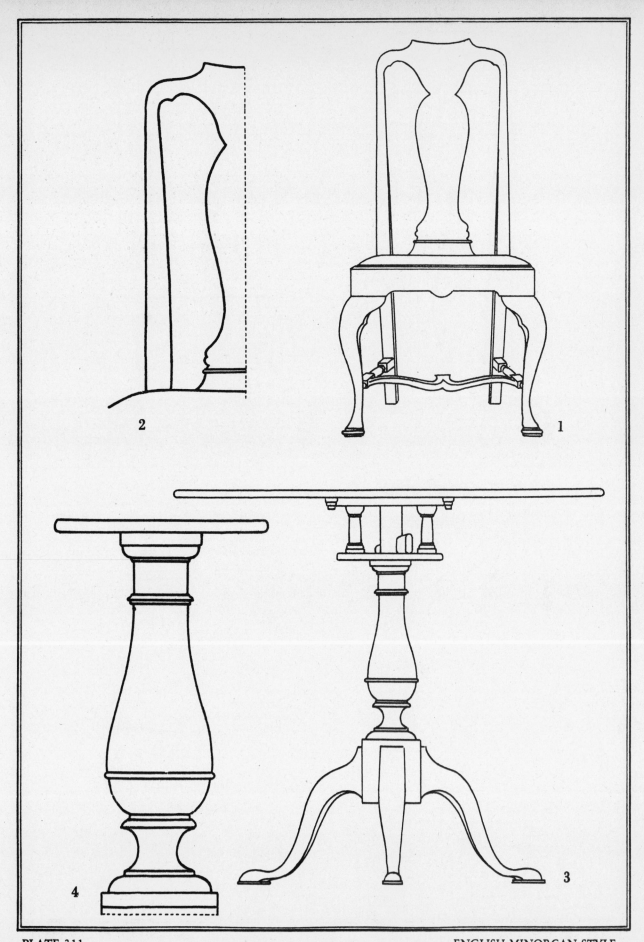

**PLATE 311.**                                                        ENGLISH MINORCAN STYLE.

1. Queen Anne style chair.    2. Detail of back.    3. Queen Anne style table.    4. Turned central column.
*From the residence of Simon de Oliver Canet, Baron of Leuriach, Ciudadela.*

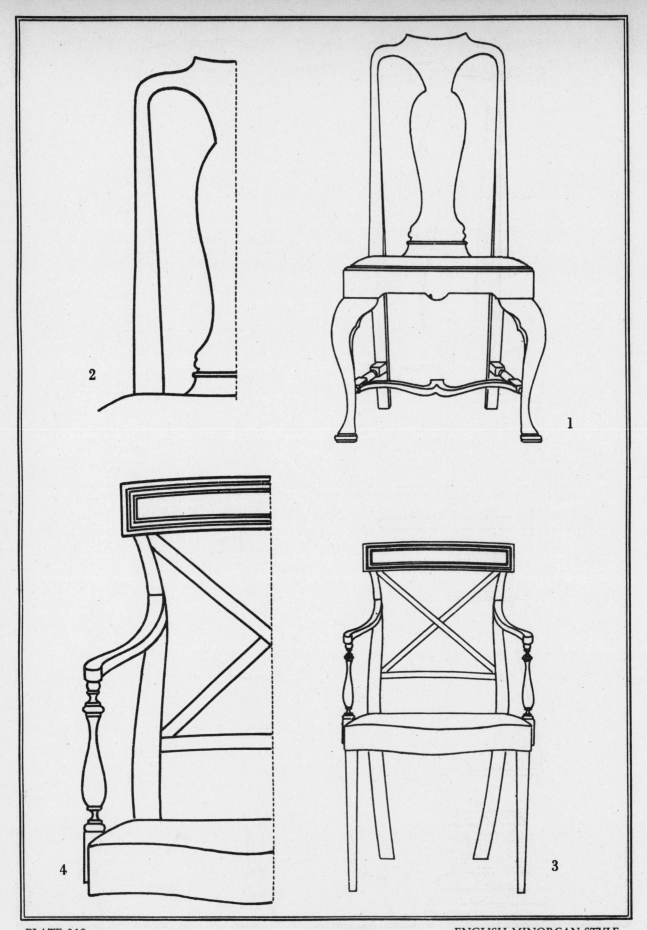

PLATE 312.                                                    ENGLISH MINORCAN STYLE.
1.  Queen Anne style chair.    2.  Detail of back.    3.  Sheraton style armchair.    4.  Detail of back and arm.
*From the residence of Carlos de Olivar de Olives. Ciudadela.*

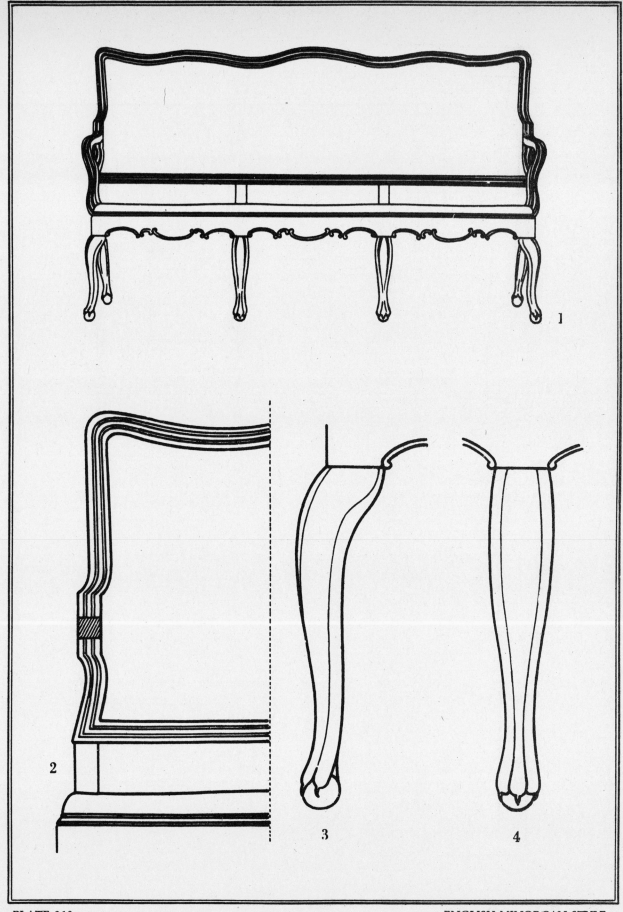

PLATE 313.

1. Sofa.    2. Detail of back.    3. End leg.    4. Middle leg.

ENGLISH MINORCAN STYLE.

*From the residence of Francisco Terres Coll. Mahon*

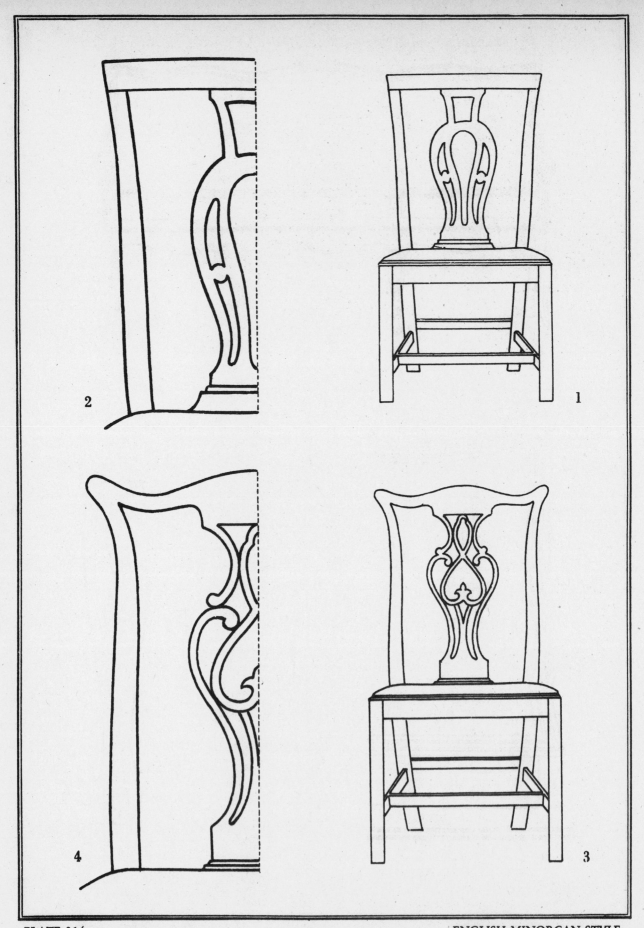

PLATE 314.                                                    ENGLISH MINORCAN STYLE.

1. Chippendale style chair.    2. Detail of back.    3. Chippendale style chair.    4. Detail of back.

*From the residences of Juana Pons Guinart de Salort, Alayor and Lorenzo de Salort de Martorell, Ciudadela.*

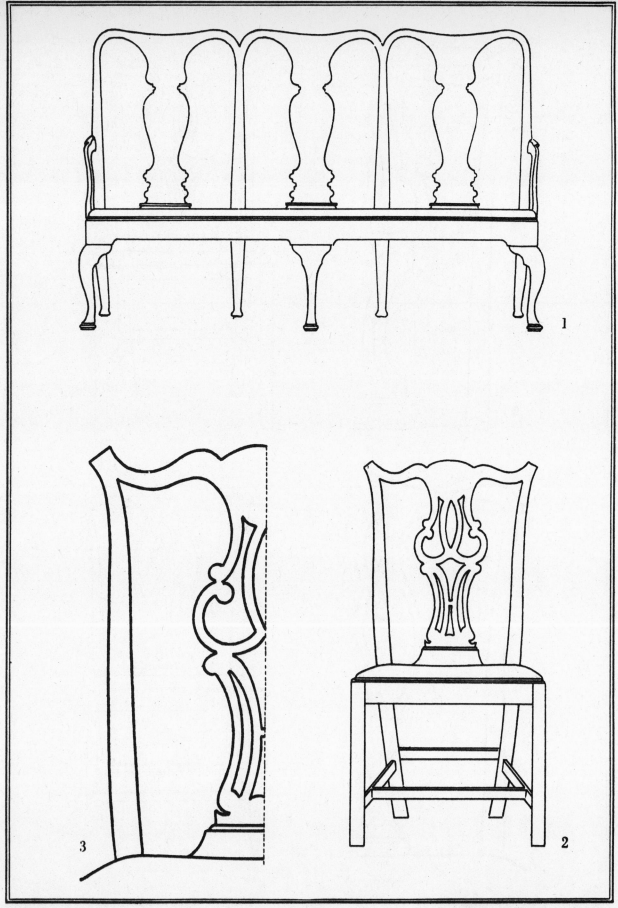

PLATE 315.                                          ENGLISH MINORCAN STYLE.
1. Queen Anne sofa.   2. Chippendale style chair.   3. Detail of chair back.

*From the residence of Ignacio Saura de Sintas, Ciudadela.*

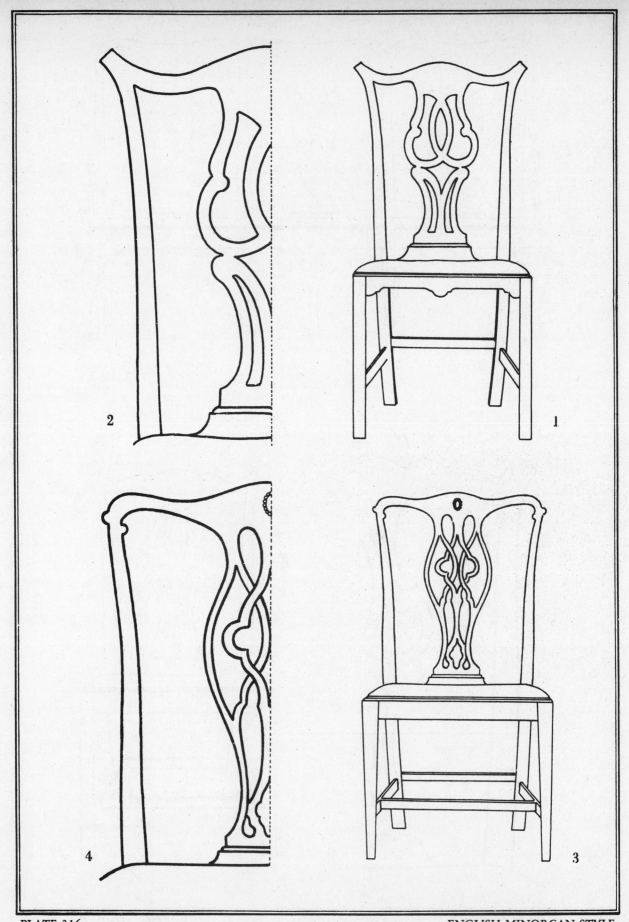

PLATE 316.                                                    ENGLISH MINORCAN STYLE.
1. Chippendale style chair.   2. Detail of back.   3. Chippendale style chair.   4. Detail of back.
*From the residences of Cosme Trebol Pons, Alayor and Juan de Salort de Salort, Alayor.*

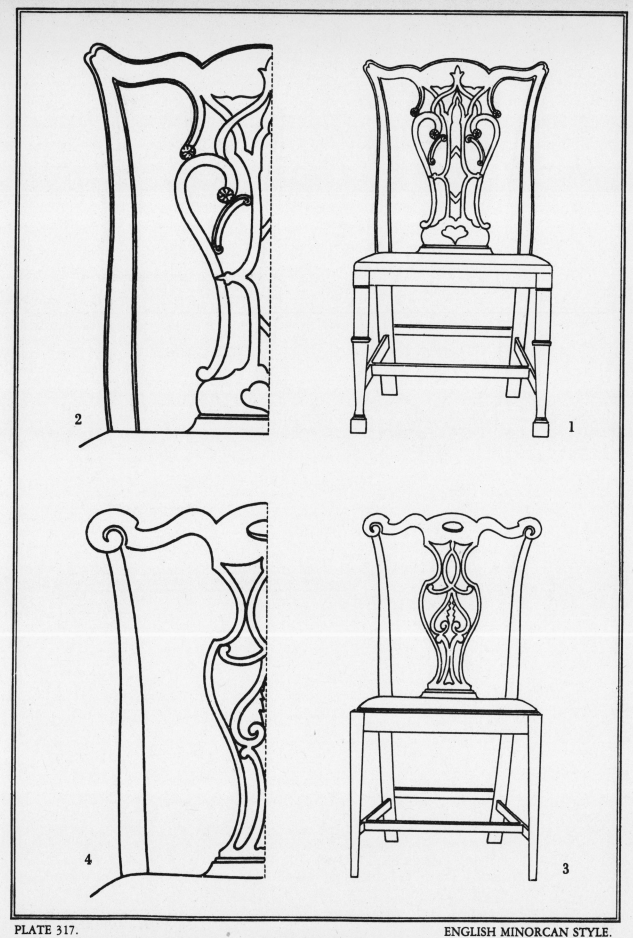

**PLATE 317.**
1 and 3.  Chairs with Chippendale backs.    2 and 4.  Details of backs.

*From "Sa Cudia Cremada," the residence of Francisca Martorell, Mahon.*

ENGLISH MINORCAN STYLE.

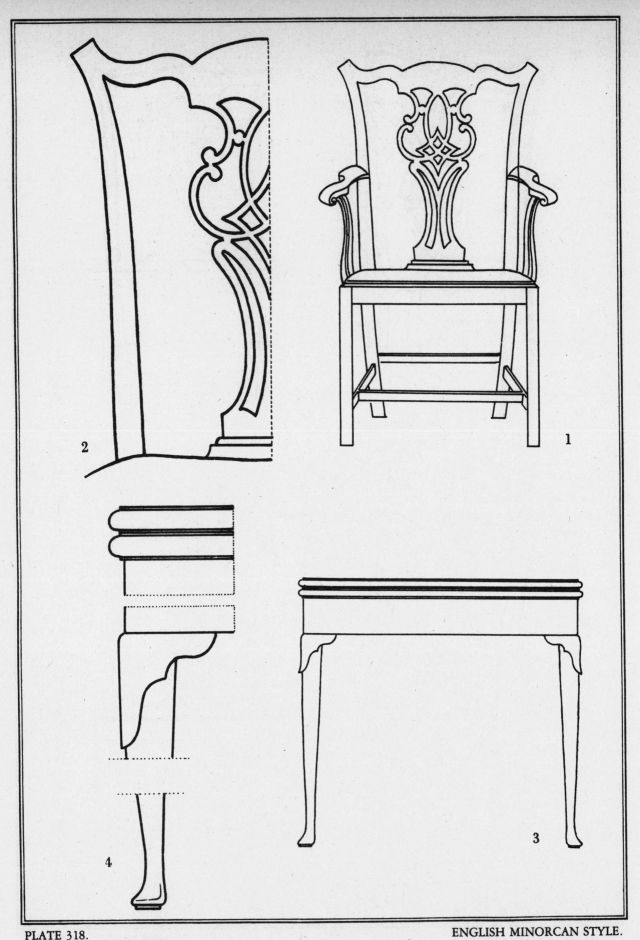

PLATE 318.                                                                 ENGLISH MINORCAN STYLE.
1. Chippendale style armchair.    2. Detail of back.    3. Queen Anne style table.    4. Detail of moulding and leg.
*From the residence of Francisco Mercadal Montanari, Mahon.*

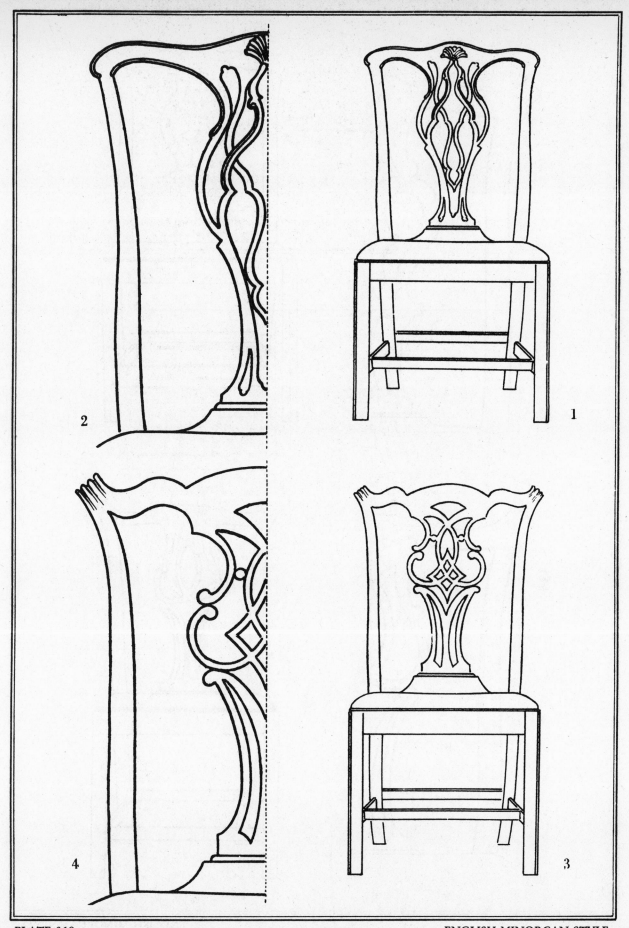

PLATE 319.

ENGLISH MINORCAN STYLE.

1 and 3. Chairs with Chippendale backs. 2 and 4. Detail of backs.

*From the residence of Clotilde de Olivar, Vda, de Corral. Mahon.*

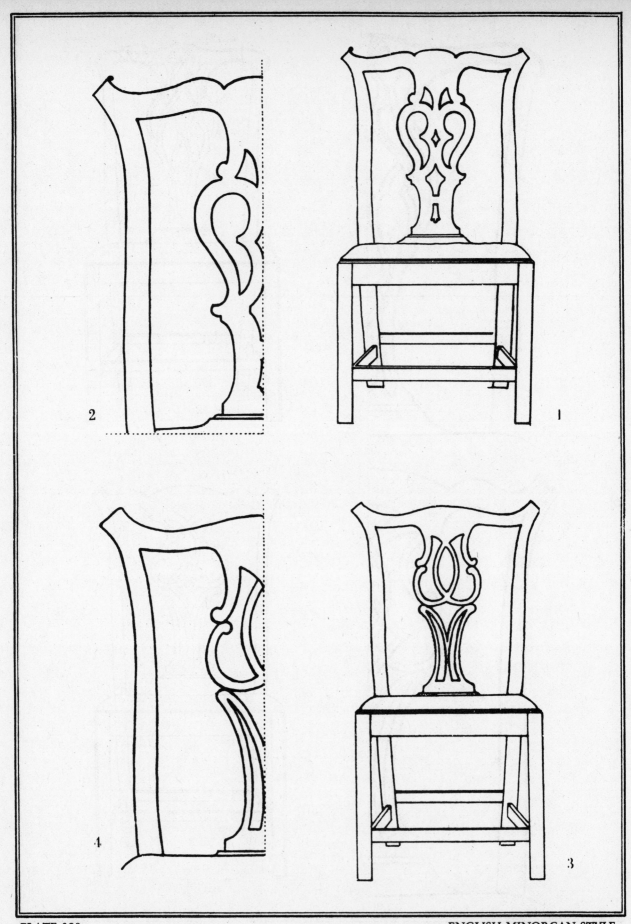

PLATE 320.

ENGLISH MINORCAN STYLE.

1 and 3. Chairs with Chippendale backs.    2 and 4. Details of backs.

*From the residence of Francisco Vidal Sintas, Mahon.*

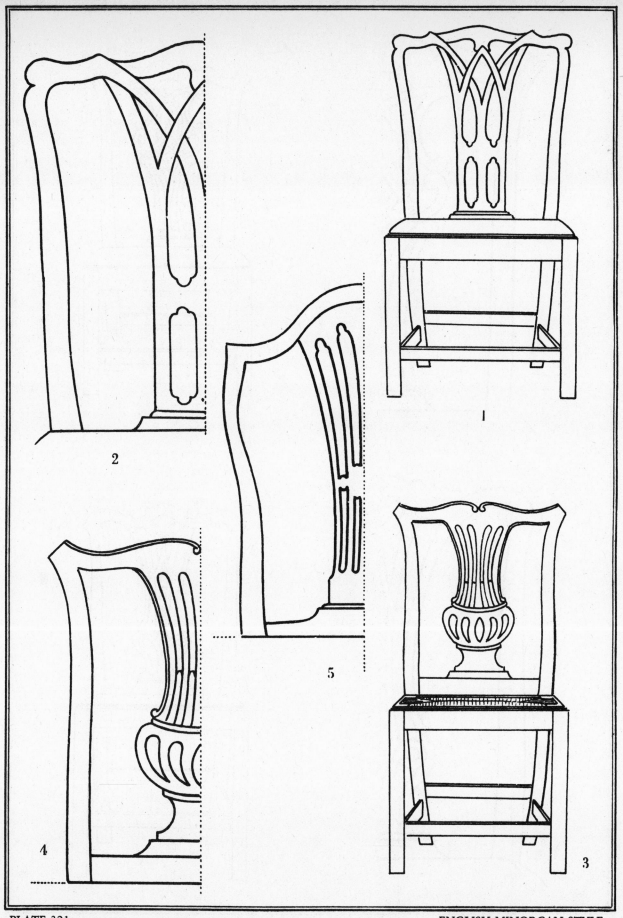

PLATE 321.                                              ENGLISH MINORCAN STYLE.
1 and 3.  Chairs with Chippendale backs.    2 and 4.  Details of backs.    5.  Another Chippendale back.
*From the residence of Francisco Vidal Sintas, Mahon.*

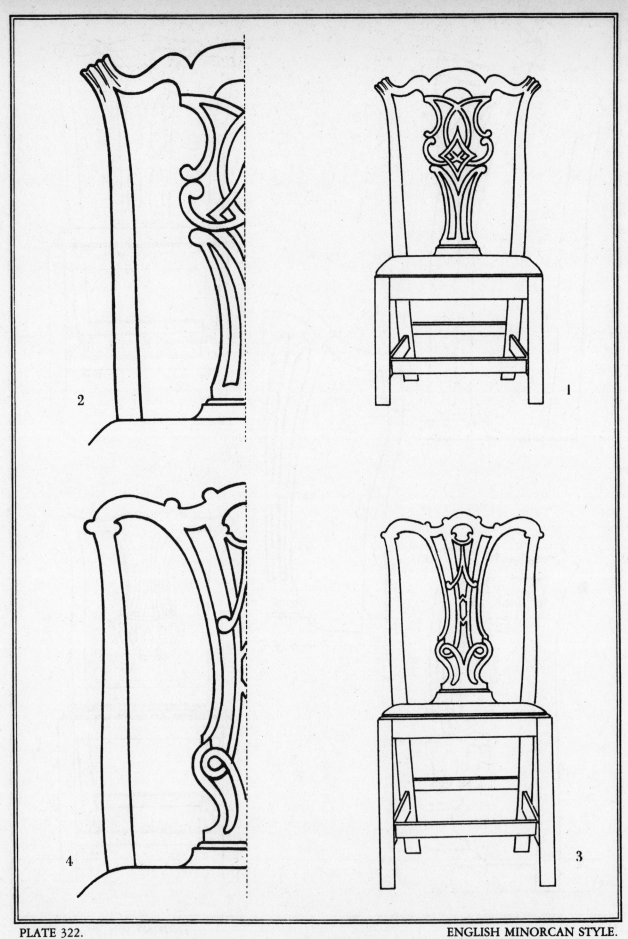

PLATE 322.

ENGLISH MINORCAN STYLE.

1 and 3. Chairs with Chippendale backs. 2 and 4. Details of backs.

*From the residence of Juan Francisco and Jose Maria Andreu, Mahon.*

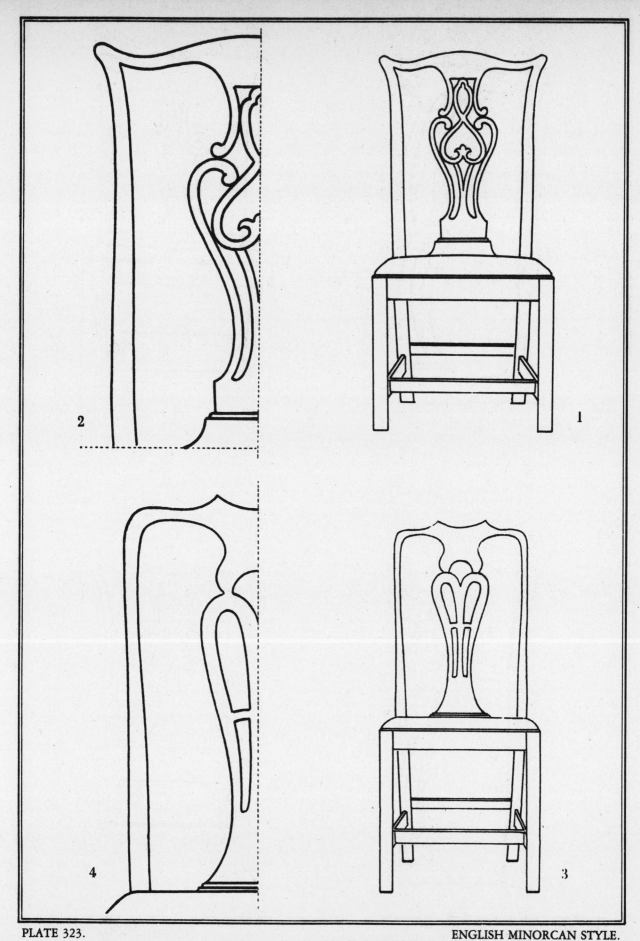

PLATE 323.                                                    ENGLISH MINORCAN STYLE.
1. Chair with Chippendale back.    2. Detail of back.    3. Chair with whimsical back.    4. Detail of back.
*From the residence of Antonia del Amo, Vda. de Alberti, Mahon.*

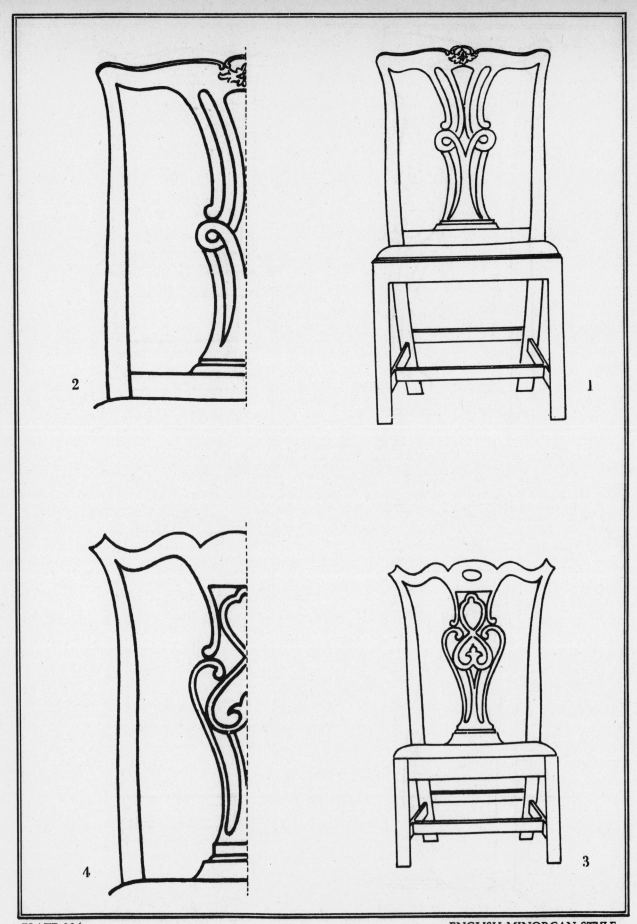

PLATE 324.

1 and 3. Chairs with Chippendale backs.    2 and 4. Details of backs.

ENGLISH MINORCAN STYLE.

*From the residence of Luis Victory Manella, Mahon.*

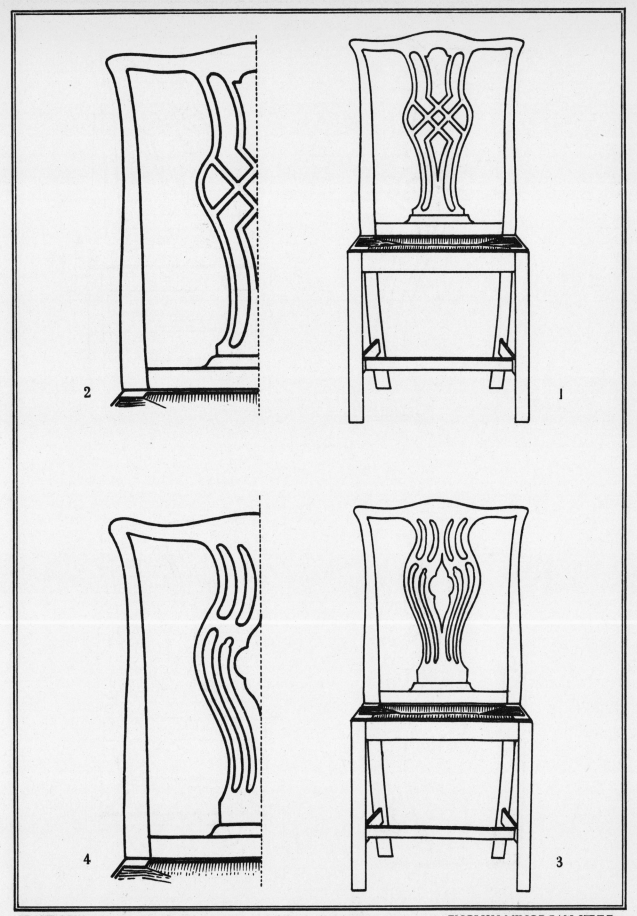

PLATE 325.
1 and 3. Chairs with vertical Chippendale backs.   2 and 4. Details of backs.

ENGLISH MINORCAN STYLE.

*From the residence of Juan Campo, Mahon.*

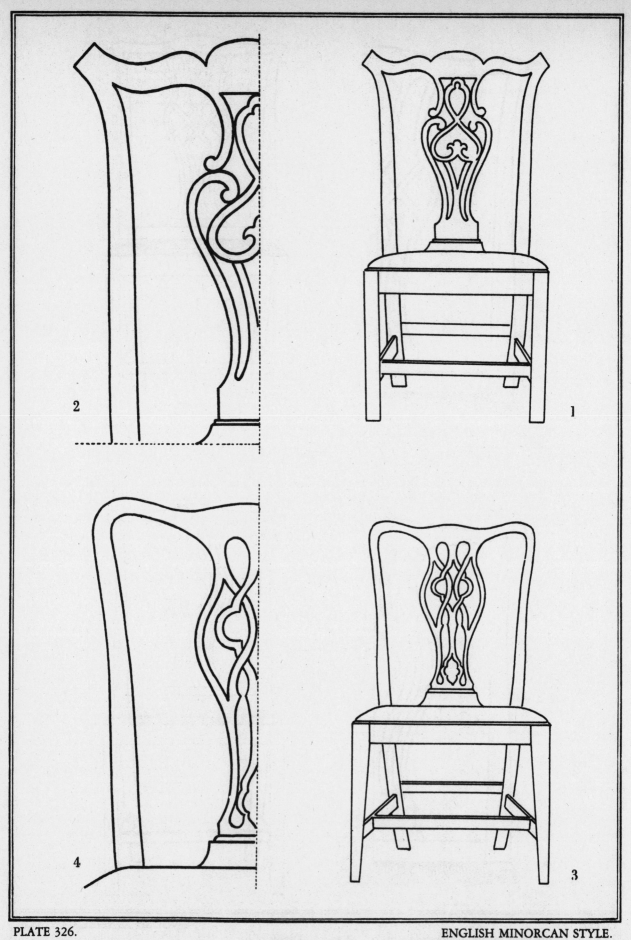

PLATE 326.

ENGLISH MINORCAN STYLE.

1 and 3. Chairs with Chippendale backs.    2 and 4. Detail of backs.

*From the residence of Juan de Salort de Salort, Alayor.*

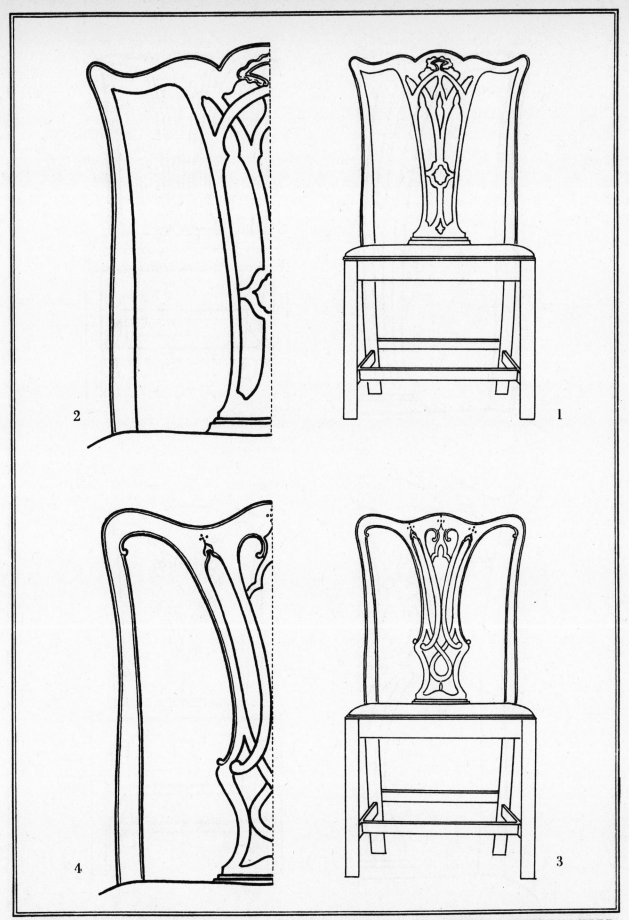

PLATE 327.

1 and 3.  Chairs with Chippendale backs.    2 and 4.  Detail of backs.

ENGLISH MINORCAN STYLE.

*From the residence of Juan de Salort de Salort, Alayor.*

331

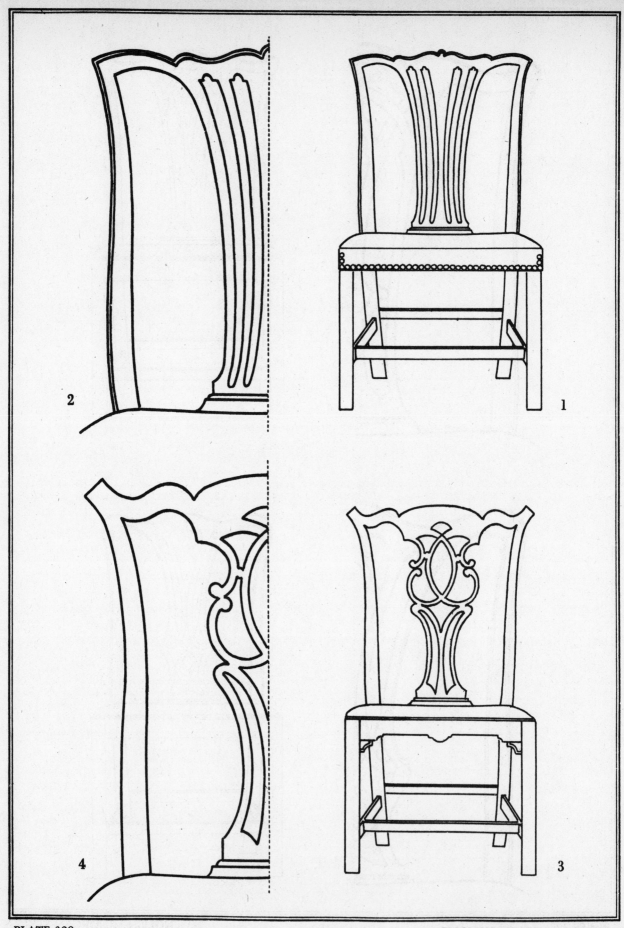

**PLATE 328.**
1 and 3. Chairs with Chippendale backs.    2 and 4. Details of backs.

ENGLISH MINORCAN STYLE.

*From the residence of Dolores Vives, Vda. de Batione, Mahon.*

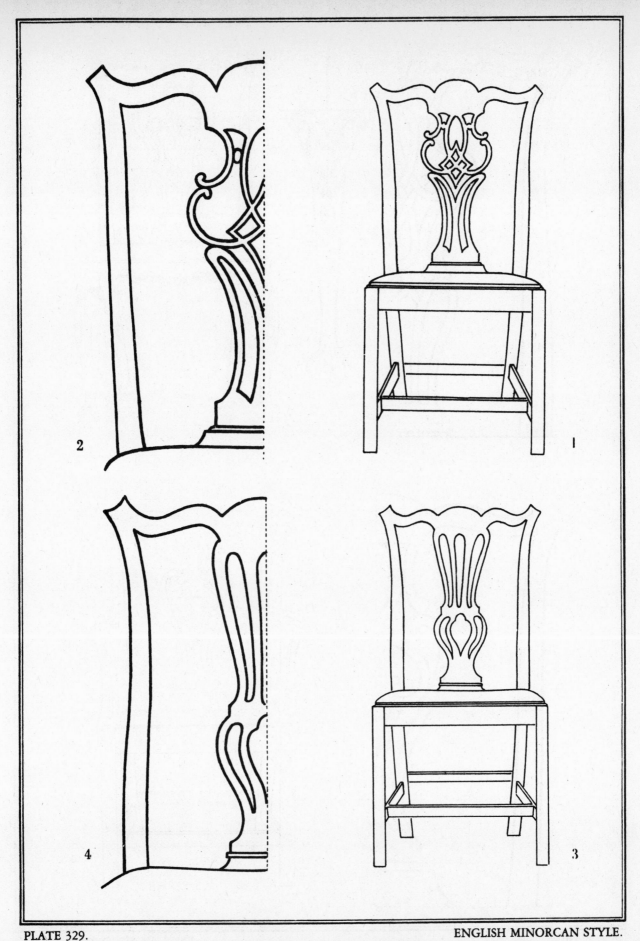

PLATE 329.                                                                ENGLISH MINORCAN STYLE.
1. Chair with Chippendale back.    2. Detail of back.    3. Chair with Chippendale back.    4. Detail of back.
*From the residences of Juan Vives Llull, Mahon and Simon Vidal Sintas. Mahon.*

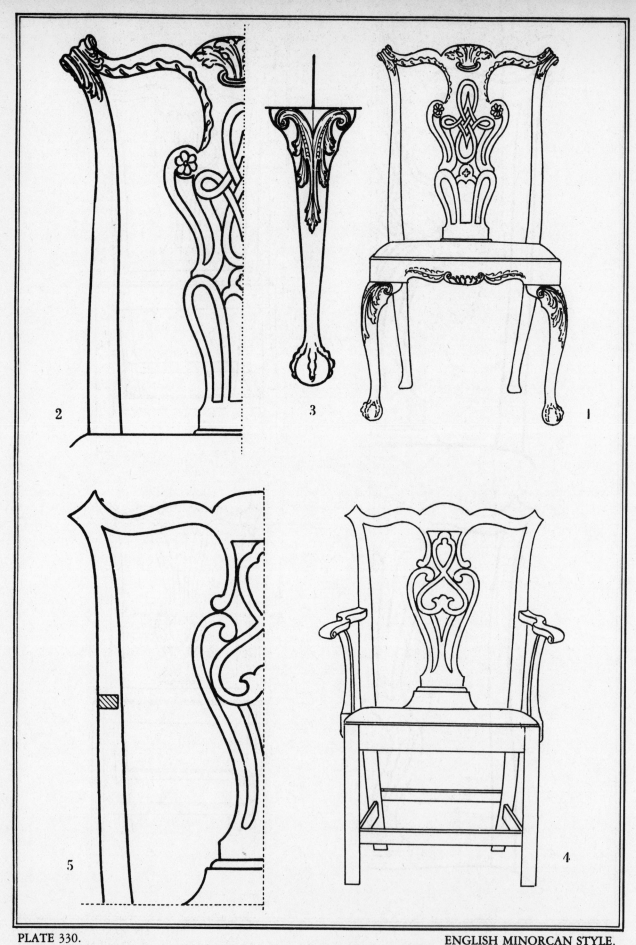

PLATE 330.                                                    ENGLISH MINORCAN STYLE.
1. Chippendale style chair.    2. Detail of back.    3. Leg decoration.    4. Armchair with Chippendale back.    5. Detail of back.

*From the residence of Francisco Segui Poli Moncada, Mahon.*

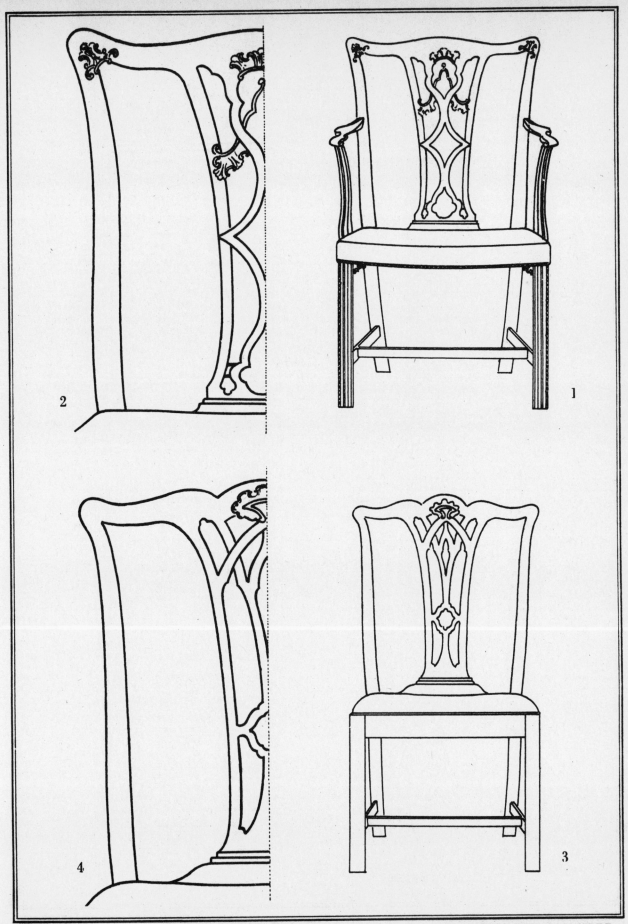

PLATE 331.                                                    ENGLISH MINORCAN STYLE.
Armchair with Chippendale back.    3. Chair with Chippendale back.    2 and 4. Details of backs.
*From the residence of Francisco Terres Coll, Mahon.*

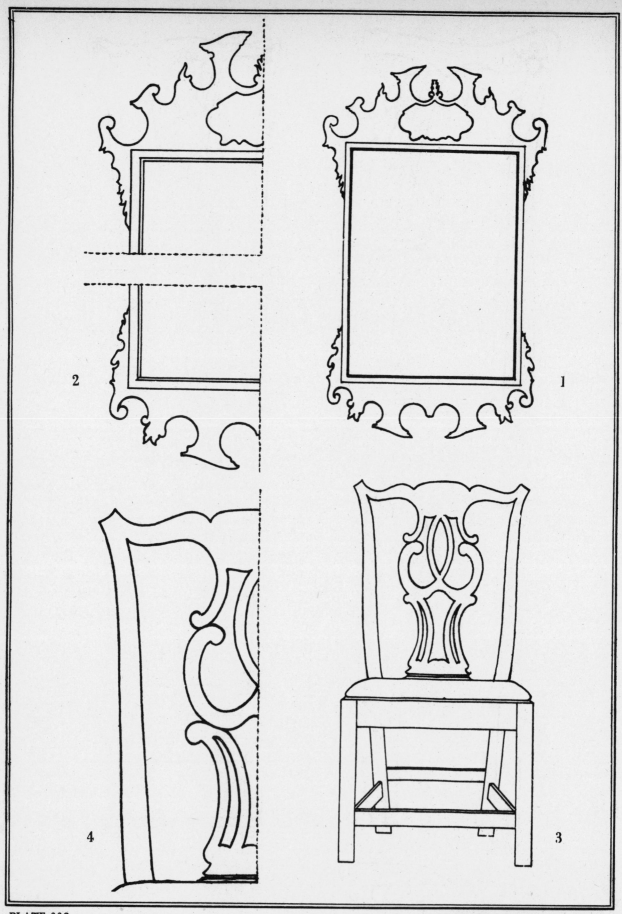

**PLATE 332,**                                                              ENGLISH MINORCAN STYLE.

1. Mirror.    2. Detail of upper and lower frame.    3. Chair with Chippendale back.    4. Detail of back.

*From the residence of Juan Victory Manella, Mahon.*

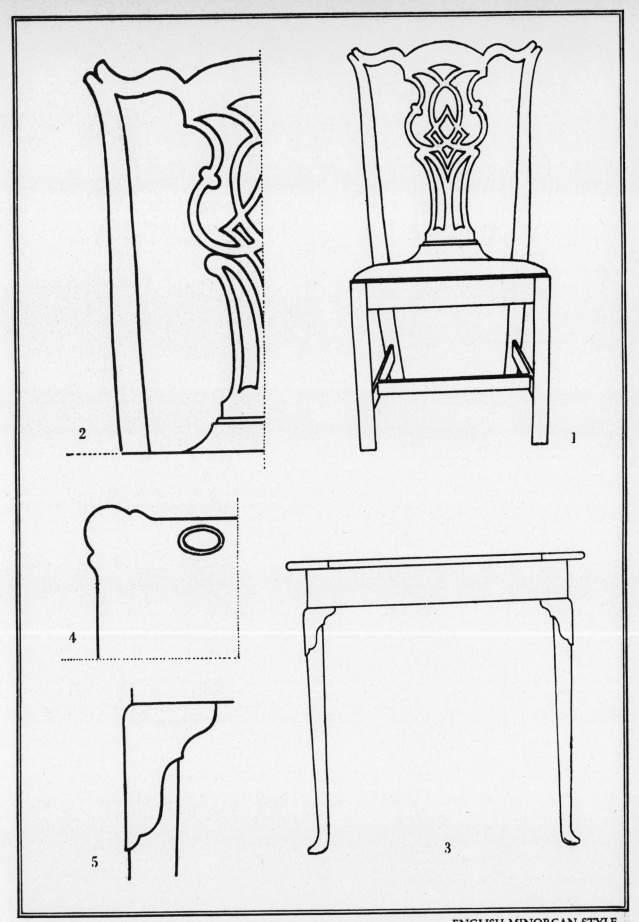

PLATE 333.
1. Chair with Chippendale back.    2. Detail of back. 3. Queen Anne style table.    4. Profile of table top.    5. Decoration at base of leg.

ENGLISH MINORCAN STYLE.

*From the residence of Francisco Orfila Alberti, Mahon.*

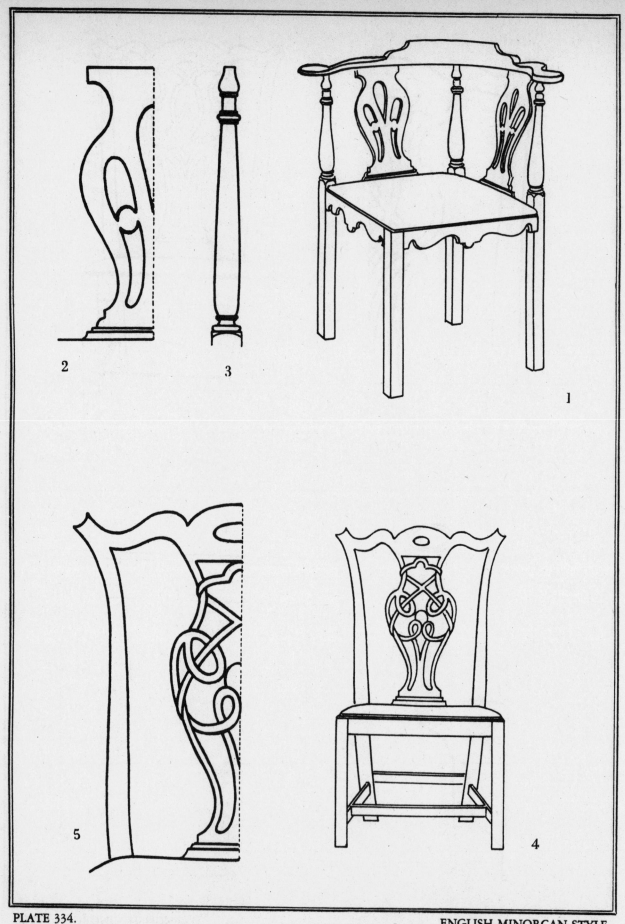

**PLATE 334.** ENGLISH MINORCAN STYLE.
1. Corner armchair.   2 and 3. Details of back.   4. Chair with Chippendale back.   5. Detail of back.

*From the residence of Juan de Salort de Salort, Alayor.*

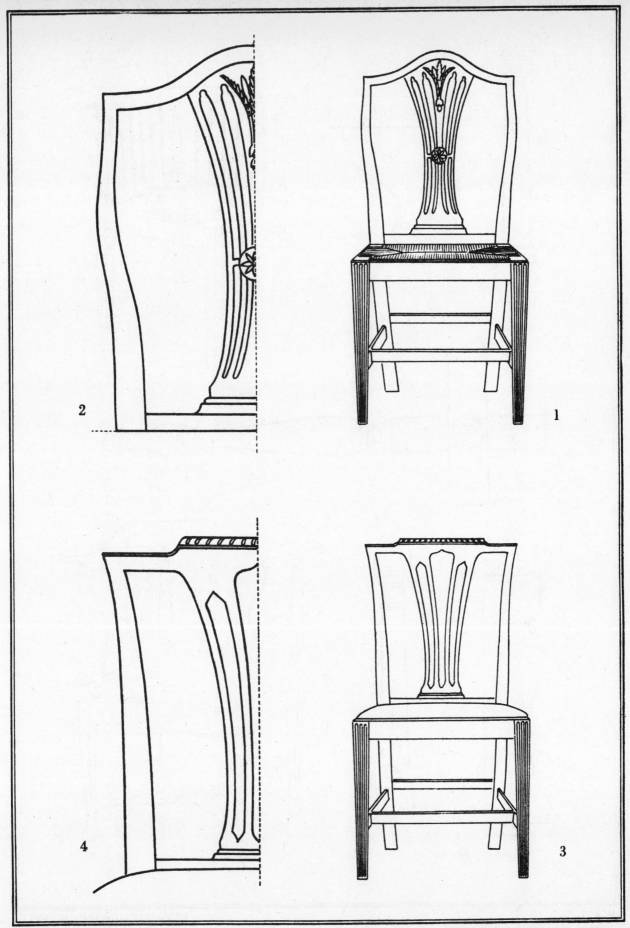

PLATE 335.

ENGLISH MINORCAN STYLE.

1. Chair with Hepplewhite back.   2. Detail of back.   3. Chair with Sheraton back.   4. Detail of back.

*From the residence of D. Arnaldo Socias, Mahon.*

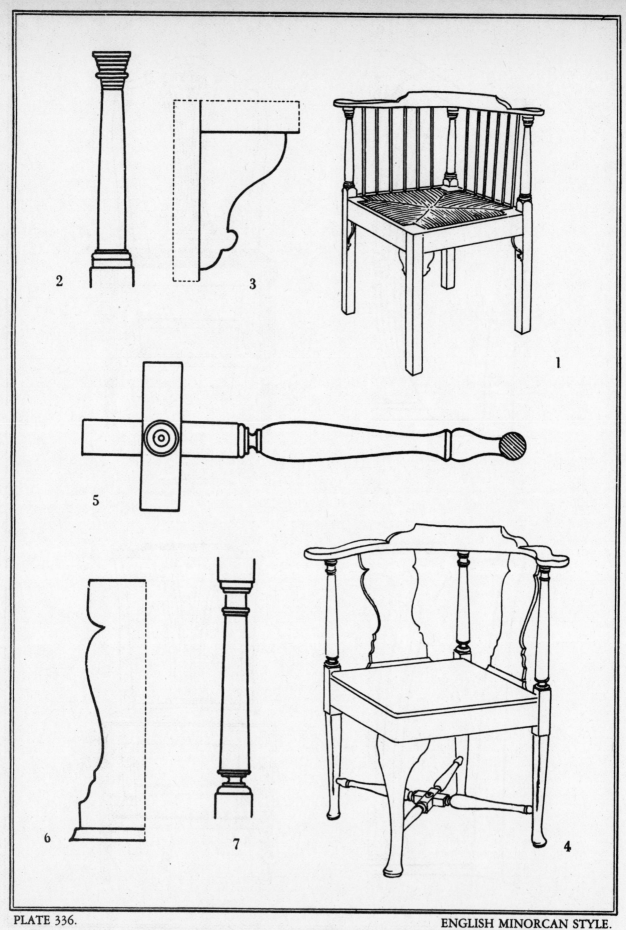

PLATE 336.                                                      ENGLISH MINORCAN STYLE.
1. Corner armchair.   2. Small support column in back.   3. Bracket.   4. Corner armchair.   5. Detail of x-shaped crosspiece.   6 and 7. Details of back.

*From the residence of Carlos de Olivar de Olives, Ciudadela.*

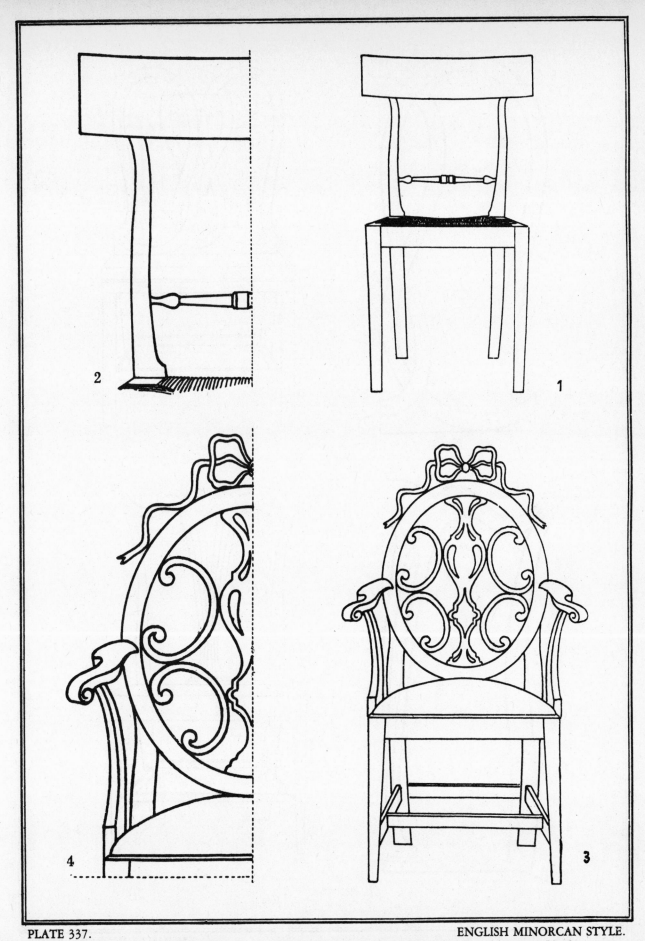

PLATE 337.                                                    ENGLISH MINORCAN STYLE.

1. Very narrow chair.    2. Detail of back.    3. Armchair with original interlaced back.    4. Detail of back.

*From the residences of Francisco Mercadal Montanari, Mahon and Mrs. Guillermo de Olives, Mahon.*

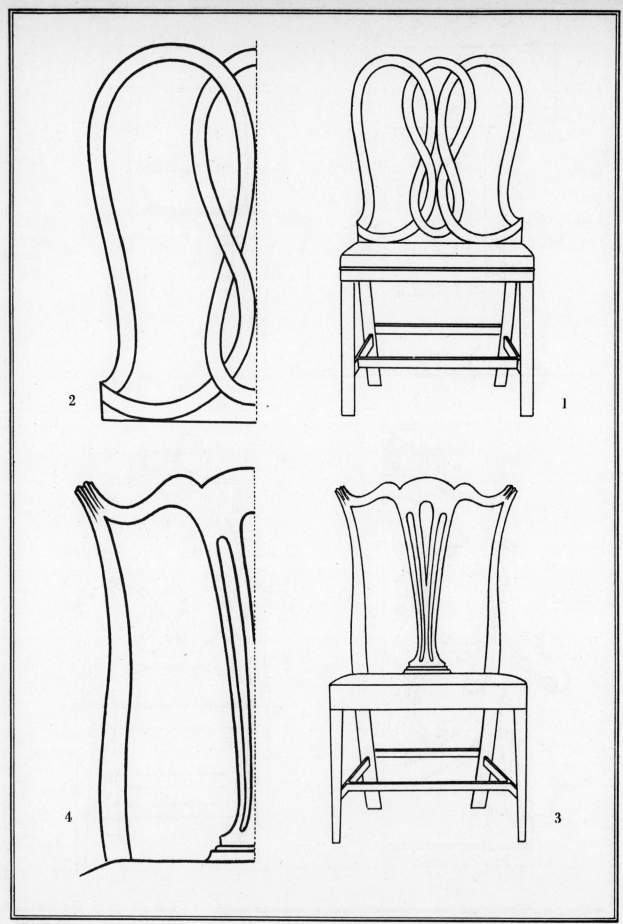

PLATE 338.                                          ENGLISH MINORCAN STYLE.
1. Chair showing French influence.   2. Detail of back.   3. Chair showing Dutch influence.   4. Detail of back.
*From the residences of Antonia del Amo, Vda. de Alberti, Mahon and Juana Villalonga, Vda. de Alberti, Mahon.*

PLATE 339.                                                         ENGLISH MINORCAN STYLE.
1. Mirror.   2. Decoration on upper and lower frame.   3. Sheraton style chair.   4. Detail of back.
*From "Sa Cudia Cremada," the residence of Francisca Martorell, Mahon.*

PLATE 340

ENGLISH MINORCAN STYLE.

1. Mirror.  2. Decoration on upper and lower frame.  3. Corner armchair.  4. Small support column in back.
5. Detail of leg and bracket.

*From the residence of Lorenzo de Salort y de Martorell, Ciudadela.*

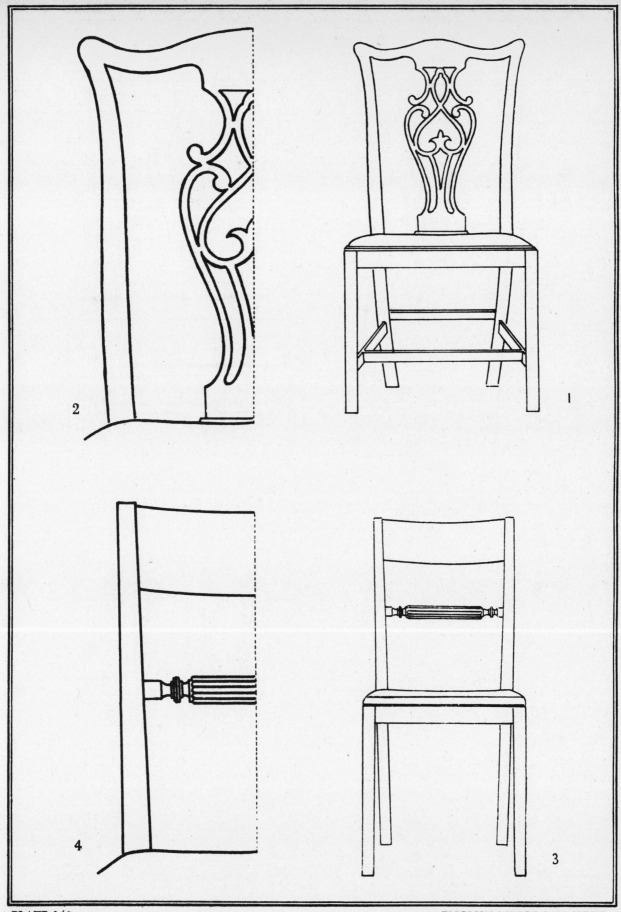

PLATE 341.
1 and 3.  Chairs.    2 and 4.  Detail of backs.

ENGLISH MINORCAN STYLE.

*From residence of Juan Mir Llambias, Mahon.*

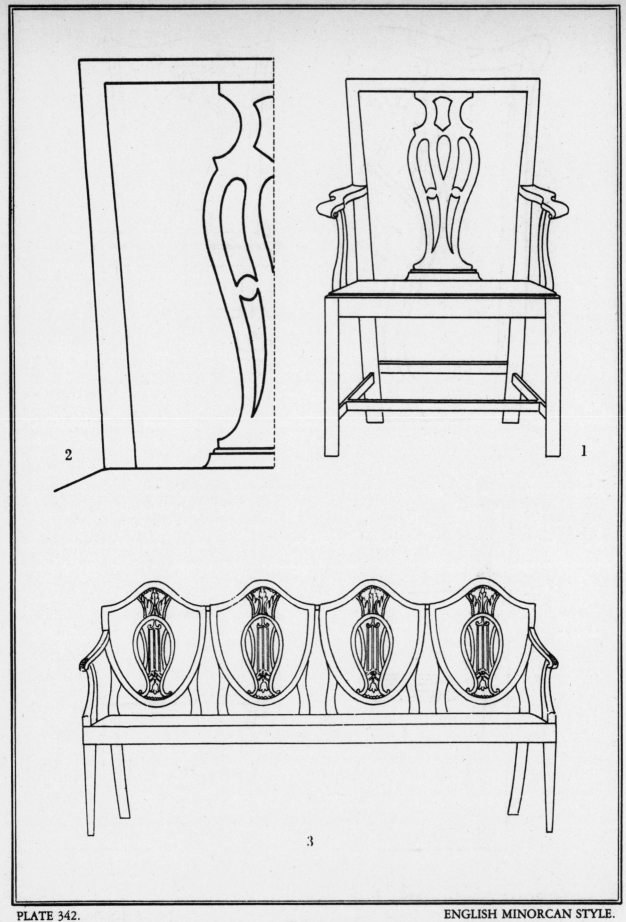

PLATE 342.                                                    ENGLISH MINORCAN STYLE.
1. Armchair.   2. Detail of back.   3. Sofa with shield-shaped sections, characteristic of Hepplewhite style.
*From the residence of Simon de Olivar Canet, Baron de Lluriach, Ciudadela.*

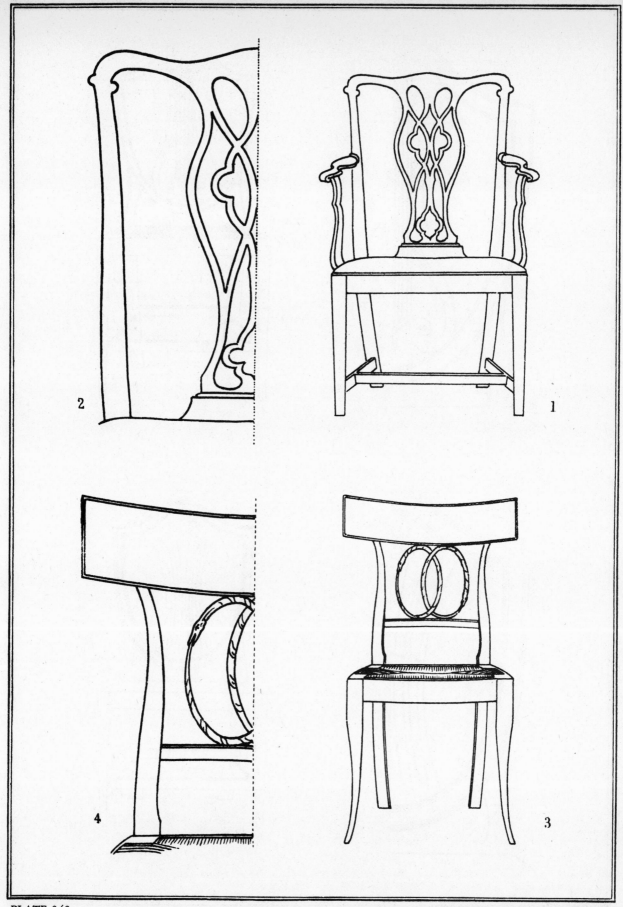

PLATE 343.                                                    ENGLISH MINORCAN STYLE.

1. Armchair.    2. Detail of back.    3. Chair showing French influence.    4. Detail of back.

*From the residence of Juan Campo, Mahon.*

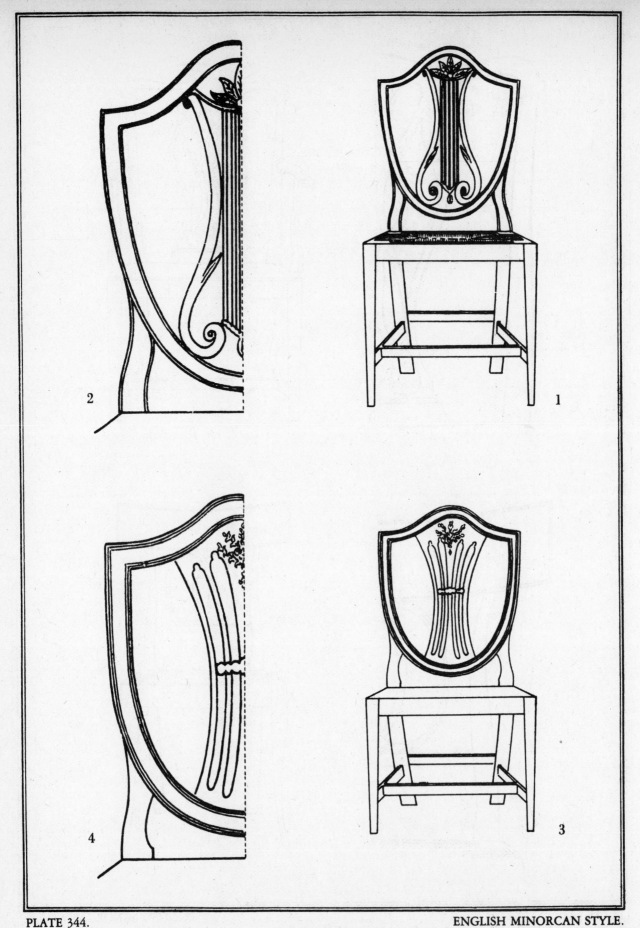

PLATE 344.

1 and 3. Chairs with Hepplewhite backs.　2 and 4. Details of backs.

ENGLISH MINORCAN STYLE.

*From "Sa Cudia Cremada," the residence of Francisca Martorell, Mahon.*

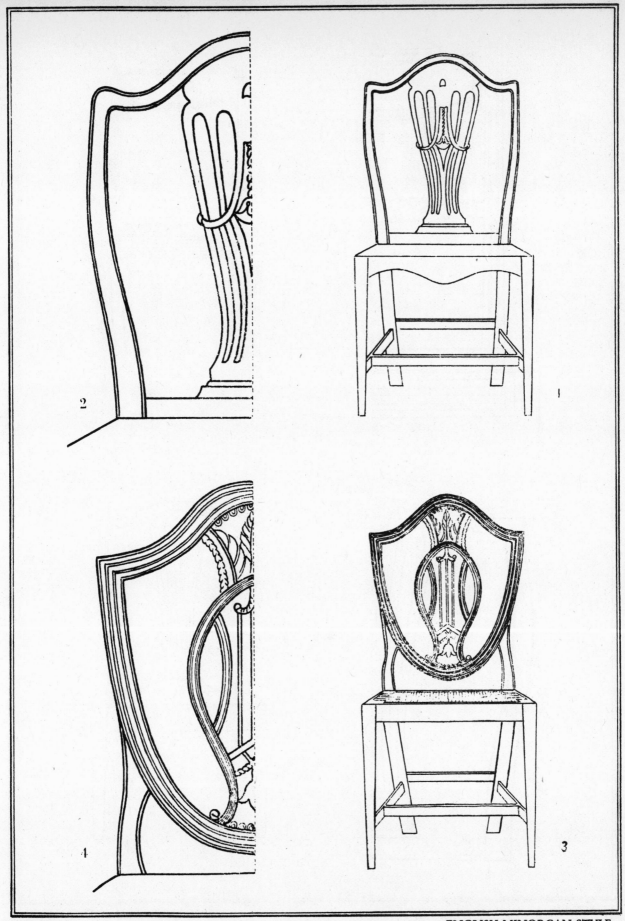

**PLATE 345.**

1 and 3.  Hepplewhite style chairs.    2 and 4.  Details of backs.

*From the residence of Simon de Olivar Canet, Baron of Lluriach, Ciudadela.*

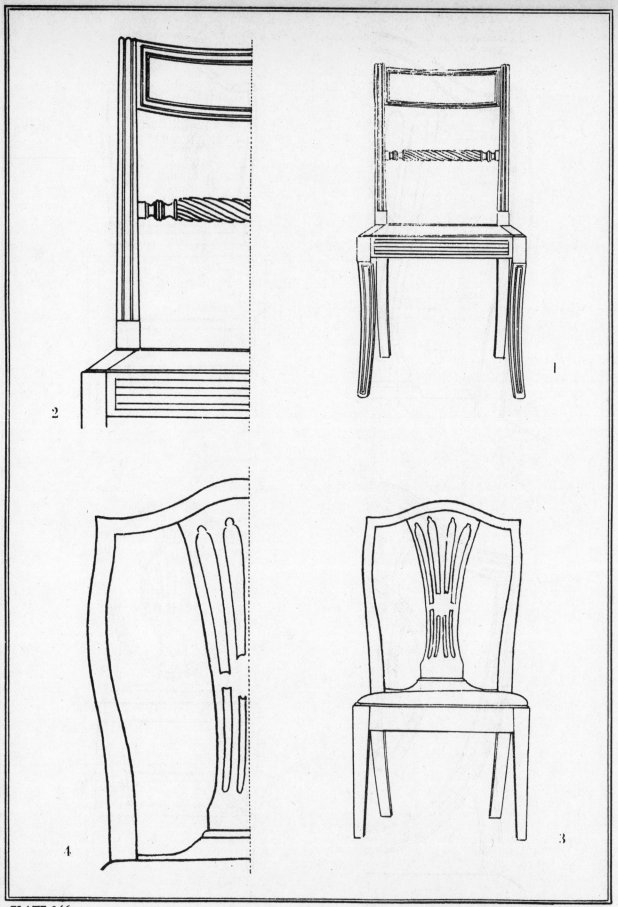

PLATE 346.
1 and 3. Chairs.    2 and 4. Details of backs.

ENGLISH MINORCAN STYLE.

*From the residence of Juan Victory Manella, Mahon.*

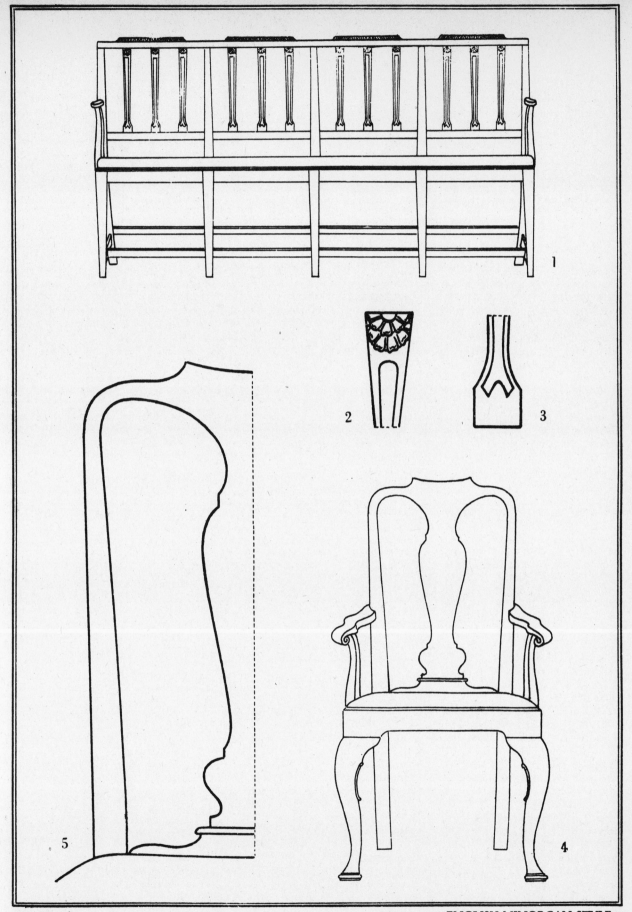

PLATE 347.                                                    ENGLISH MINORCAN STYLE.

1. Sheraton style sofa.    2 and 3. Decorations on listels.    4. Queen Anne style armchair.    5. Detail of back.
*From the residence of Alfonso Vivo Salort, Ciudadela.*

# INDEX